NISSAN
SENTRA
1982-1985 GAS & DIESEL
SHOP MANUAL

ALAN AHLSTRAND
Editor

CLYMER PUBLICATIONS

World's largest publisher of books
devoted exclusively to automobiles and motorcycles

A division of INTERTEC PUBLISHING CORPORATION
P.O. Box 12901, Overland Park, Kansas 66212

Copyright © 1985 Intertec Publishing Corporation

FIRST EDITION
First Printing July, 1984

SECOND EDITION
Updated by Alan Ahlstrand to include 1984-1985 models
First Printing June, 1985
Second Printing April, 1987
Third Printing December, 1987
Fourth Printing September, 1988

Printed in U.S.A.

ISBN: 0-89287-368-8

Production Coordinators, Linda Glover and Paul Purkhiser

COVER: Photographed by Michael Brown Photographic Productions, Los Angeles, California. Assisted by Bill Masho. Car courtesy of Dick Barbour Performance Datsun, San Diego, California.

CONTENTS

QUICK REFERENCE DATA

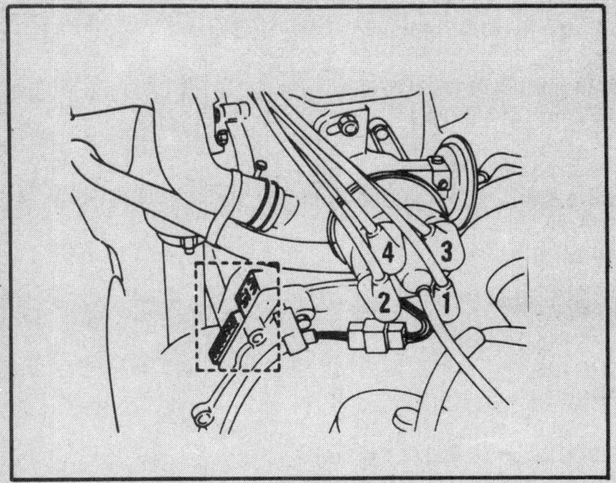

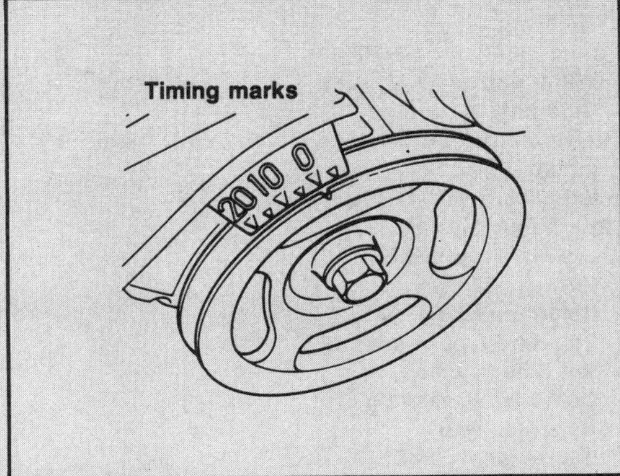

TUNE-UP SPECIFICATIONS (1982-1983)

Engine compression (gasoline)	
Standard	12.7 kg/cm² (181 psi)
Minimum	10 kg/cm² (142 psi)
Valve clearance (gasoline)	
Warm engine	0.28 mm (0.011 in.)
Cold engine	0.22 mm (0.009 in.)
Valve clearance (diesel)	
Intake	0.2-0.3 mm (0.008-0.012 in.)
Exhaust	0.4-0.5 mm (0.016-0.020 in.)
Spark plug type (NGK brand)	
U.S.	
Standard type	BPR5ES-11
Hot type	BPR4ES-11
Cold type	BPR6ES-11
Canada	
Standard type	BPR5ES
Hot type	BPR4ES
Cold type	BPR6ES
Spark plug gap	
U.S.	1.0-1.1 mm (0.039-0.043 in.)
Canada	0.8-0.9 mm (0.031-0.035 in.)
Firing order	1-3-4-2 counterclockwise
Ignition timing (at idle speed)	
1982	
U.S. manual	2 ±2° ATDC
Canadian manual (non-MPG)	4 ±2° ATDC
Canadian manual (MPG)	2 ±2° ATDC
Automatic	6 ±2° ATDC
1983	
Non-MPG	5 ±2° ATDC*
MPG	2 ±2° ATDC*
Idle speed	
Manual (except MPG)	750 ±50 rpm
Automatic	
(except 1982 Canada)	650 ±50 rpm
(1982 Canada)	600 ±50 rpm
MPG	700 ±50 rpm
Idle mixture (Canadian non-MPG only)	2 ±1 per cent

*On U.S. models and Canadian MPG models, disconnect and plug the distributor vacuum line.

TUNE-UP SPECIFICATIONS (1984-ON)

Engine compression	
Standard	12.7 kg/cm² (181 psi)
Minimum	10 kg/cm² (142 psi)
Valve clearance (gasoline)	
Warm engine	0.28 mm (0.011 in.)
Cold engine	0.22 mm (0.009 in.)
Valve clearance (diesel)	
Intake	0.2-0.3 mm (0.008-0.012 in.)
Exhaust	0.4-0.5 mm (0.016-0.020 in.)
Spark plug type (NGK)*	
Standard type (U.S.)	BPR5ES-11
Hot type (U.S.)	BPR4ES-11
Cold type (U.S.)	BPR6ES-11
Standard type (Canada)	BPR5ES
Hot type (Canada)	BPR4ES
Cold type (Canada)	BPR6ES
Spark plug gap	
U.S. (except BP4ES)	1.0-1.1 mm (0.039-0.043 in.)
U.S. (BP4ES)	0.8-0.9 mm (0.031-0.035 in.)
Canada	0.8-0.9 mm (0.031-0.035 in.)
Firing order	1-3-4-2 counterclockwise
Ignition timing (at idle speed)**	
California	5 ±2° ATDC
49-state manual	15 ±2° BTDC
49-state automatic	8 ±2° BTDC
Canada	5 ±2° ATDC
Idle speed (rpm)	
California manual	750 ±50
California automatic	650 ±50 (in DRIVE)
49-state manual	800 ±100
49-state automatic	650 ±100 (in DRIVE)
Canada manual	750 ±50
Canada automatic	650 ±50 (in DRIVE)
Idle mixture (Canada only)	2 ±1 per cent

* Some 1984 models were equipped with BP4ES spark plugs after the car was initially sold. These are indicated by a sticker on the air cleaner. On these models, use only the plug specified on the sticker.
** On California and Canadian models, disconnect and plug the distributor vacuum line.

APPROXIMATE REFILL CAPACITIES (1982-1983)

	Liters	Quarts
Cooling system (gasoline)		
Manual transmission	4.7	5
Automatic transmission	5.3	5 5/8
Cooling system (diesel)	7	7 3/8
Cooling system reservoir tank	0.7	3/4
Engine oil (gasoline)		
With filter change	3.9	4 1/8
Without filter change	3.4	3 5/8
Engine oil (diesel)		
With filter change	4.1	4 3/8
Without filter change	3.5	3 3/4
Transaxle		
4-speed manual	2.3	4 7/8 pt.
5-speed manual	2.7	5 3/4 pt.
Automatic	6	6 3/8
Windshield washer tank	1.5	1 5/8
Power steering system	1	1 1/8
Fuel tank	50	13 1/4 gal.

APPROXIMATE REFILL CAPACITIES (1984-ON)

	Liters	Quarts
Cooling system (gasoline)		
Manual transmission	4.7	5
Automatic transmission	5.3	5 5/8
Cooling system (diesel)	7	7 3/8
Cooling system reservoir tank	0.7	3/4
Engine oil (gasoline)		
With filter change		
1984	3.7	3 7/8
1985	3.3	3 1/2
Without filter change		
1984	3.3	3 1/2
1985	2.9	3 1/8
Engine oil (diesel)		
With filter change	4.1	4 3/8
Without filter change	3.5	3 3/4
Transaxle		
4-speed manual	2.3	4 7/8 pt.
5-speed manual	2.7	5 3/4 pt.
Automatic	6	6 3/8
Windshield washer tank	1.5	1 5/8
Power steering system		
1984	1	1 1/8
1985	0.9	1
Fuel tank		
All except MPG diesel	50	13 1/4 gal.
MPG diesel	40	10 5/8 gal.

LUBRICANT VISCOSITIES

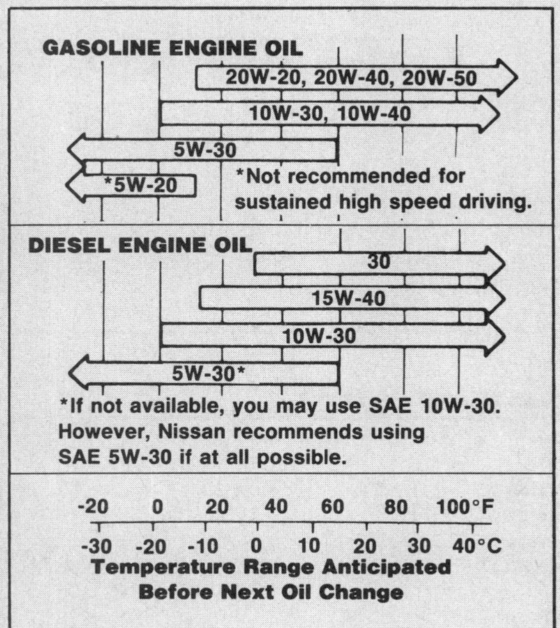

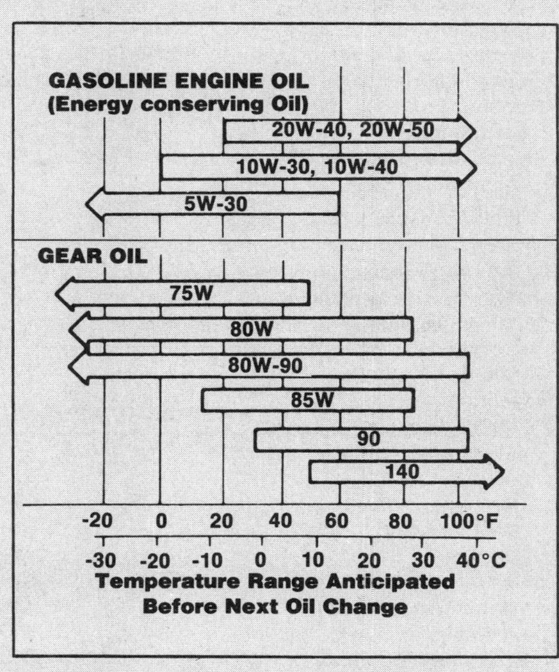

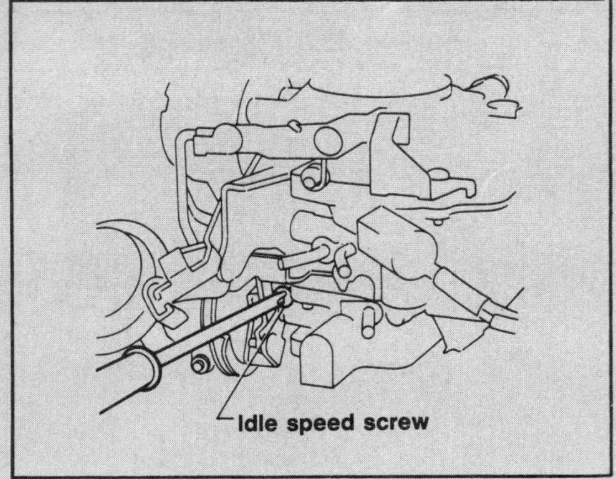

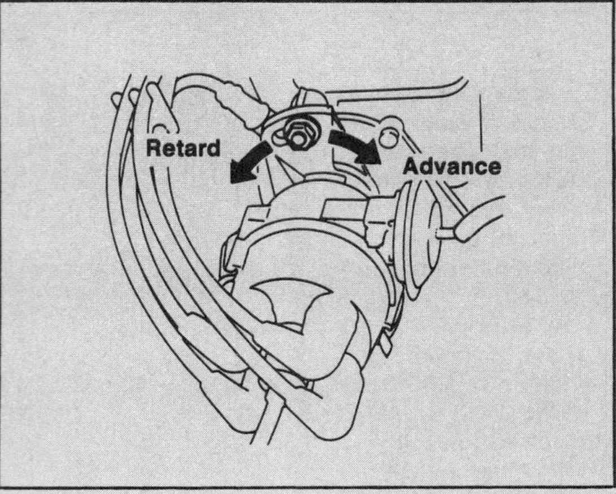

TIRE PRESSURES

1982	
155-13/6.15-13, front and rear	24 psi
155SR-13, 175/70SR-13, front and rear	26 psi
1983	
155SR-13 front	
With E15 and diesel engine	28 psi
With E16 engine	26 psi
155SR-13 rear	26 psi
175/70SR-13 front and rear	26 psi
P155/80D-13 spare	35 psi
1984-on	See placard in glove compartment

DRIVE BELT DEFLECTION

	New belt, mm (in.)	Used belt, mm (in.)
Gasoline engines		
Alternator belt[1]	10-14 (0.39-0.55)	13-17 (0.51-0.67)
Air conditioner belt[2]	7-9 (0.28-0.35)	9-11 (0.35-0.43)
Power steering belt[3]	6.5-8.5 (0.25-0.33)	7-9 (0.28-0.35)
Diesel engines		
Alternator belt	9-11 (0.35-0.43)	11-13 (0.43-0.51)
Air conditioner belt	11-13 (0.43-0.51)	12-14 (0.47-0.55)
Maximum deflection, all diesel belts	16 (0.63)	16 (0.63)

1. Maximum deflection on 1985 models: 19 mm (0.75 in.)
2. Maximum deflection on 1985 models: 12.5 mm (0.5 in.)
3. Maximum deflection on 1985 models: 10.5 mm (0.41 in.)

RECOMMENDED LUBRICANTS AND FLUIDS

Engine oil	
Gasoline	
Non-MPG models	API Service SF
MPG models	API Service SF or SE
Diesel	API Service SE/CC, SF/CC, SE/CD, SF/CD or CD
Manual transaxle oil	API GL-4
Automatic transaxle fluid	DEXRON type ATF
Power steering fluid	DEXRON type ATF

NISSAN
SENTRA
1982-1985 GAS & DIESEL
SHOP MANUAL

INTRODUCTION

This detailed, comprehensive manual covers 1982-1985 Nissan Sentras. The expert text gives complete information on maintenance, repair and overhaul. Hundreds of photos and drawings guide you through every step. The book includes all you need to know to keep your Sentra running right.

Chapters One-Twelve contain basic service information on all Sentras and specific information on 1982-1983 models. The Supplement at the end of the book contains specific information on 1984 and later models which differ from previous years.

Where repairs are practical for the owner/ mechanic, complete procedures are given. Equally important, difficult jobs are pointed out. Such operations are usually more economically performed by a dealer or independent garage.

A shop manual is a reference. You want to be able to find information fast. As in all Clymer books, this one is designed with such use in mind. All chapters are thumb tabbed. Important items are indexed at the rear of the book. All of the most frequently used specifications and capacities are summarized on the *Quick Reference Data* pages at the front of the book.

Keep the book handy. Carry it in your glove box. It will help you to better understand your Sentra, lower repair and maintenance costs and generally improve your satisfaction with your vehicle.

CHAPTER ONE

GENERAL INFORMATION

The troubleshooting, tune-up, maintenance, and step-by-step repair procedures in this book are written for the owner and home mechanic. The text is accompanied by useful photos and diagrams to make the job as clear and correct as possible.

Troubleshooting, tune-up, maintenance, and repair are not difficult if you know what tools and equipment to use and what to do. Anyone not afraid to get their hands dirty, of average intelligence, and with some mechanical ability can perform most of the procedures in this book.

In some cases, a repair job may require tools or skills not reasonably expected of the home mechanic. These procedures are noted in each chapter and it is recommended that you take the job to your dealer, a competent mechanic, or machine shop.

MANUAL ORGANIZATION

This chapter provides general information and safety and service hints. Also included are lists of recommended shop and emergency tools as well as a brief description of troubleshooting and tune-up equipment.

Chapter Two provides methods and suggestions for quick and accurate diagnosis and repair of problems. Troubleshooting procedures discuss typical symptoms and logical methods to pinpoint the trouble.

Chapter Three explains all periodic lubrication and routine maintenance necessary to keep your vehicle running well. Chapter Three also includes recommended tune-up procedures, eliminating the need to constantly consult chapters on the various subassemblies.

Subsequent chapters cover specific systems such as the engine, transmission, and electrical systems. Each of these chapters provides disassembly, repair, and assembly procedures in a simple step-by-step format. If a repair requires special skills or tools, or is otherwise impractical for the home mechanic, it is so indicated. In these cases it is usually faster and less expensive to have the repairs made by a dealer or competent repair shop. Necessary specifications concerning a particular system are included at the end of the appropriate chapter.

When special tools are required to perform a procedure included in this manual, the tool is illustrated either in actual use or alone. It may be possible to rent or borrow these tools. The inventive mechanic may also be able to find a suitable substitute in his tool box, or to fabricate one.

The terms NOTE, CAUTION, and WARNING have specific meanings in this manual. A NOTE provides additional or explanatory information. A CAUTION is used to emphasize areas where equipment damage could result if proper precautions are not taken. A WARNING is used to stress those areas where personal injury or death could result from negligence, in addition to possible mechanical damage.

SERVICE HINTS

Observing the following practices will save time, effort, and frustration, as well as prevent possible injury.

Throughout this manual keep in mind two conventions. "Front" refers to the front of the vehicle. The front of any component, such as the transmission, is that end which faces toward the front of the vehicle. The "left" and "right" sides of the vehicle refer to the orientation of a person sitting in the vehicle facing forward. For example, the steering wheel is on the left side. These rules are simple, but even experienced mechanics occasionally become disoriented.

Most of the service procedures covered are straightforward and can be performed by anyone reasonably handy with tools. It is suggested, however, that you consider your own capabilities carefully before attempting any operation involving major disassembly of the engine.

Some operations, for example, require the use of a press. It would be wiser to have these performed by a shop equipped for such work, rather than to try to do the job yourself with makeshift equipment. Other procedures require precision measurements. Unless you have the skills and equipment required, it would be better to have a qualified repair shop make the measurements for you.

Repairs go much faster and easier if the parts that will be worked on are clean before you begin. There are special cleaners for washing the engine and related parts. Brush or spray on the cleaning solution, let it stand, then rinse it away with a garden hose. Clean all oily or greasy parts with cleaning solvent as you remove them.

WARNING
Never use gasoline as a cleaning agent. It presents an extreme fire hazard. Be sure to work in a well-ventilated area when using cleaning solvent. Keep a fire extinguisher, rated for gasoline fires, handy in any case.

Much of the labor charge for repairs made by dealers is for the removal and disassembly of other parts to reach the defective unit. It is frequently possible to perform the preliminary operations yourself and then take the defective unit in to the dealer for repair, at considerable savings.

Once you have decided to tackle the job yourself, make sure you locate the appropriate section in this manual, and read it entirely. Study the illustrations and text until you have a good idea of what is involved in completing the job satisfactorily. If special tools are required, make arrangements to get them before you start. Also, purchase any known defective parts prior to starting on the procedure. It is frustrating and time-consuming to get partially into a job and then be unable to complete it.

Simple wiring checks can be easily made at home, but knowledge of electronics is almost a necessity for performing tests with complicated electronic testing gear.

During disassembly of parts keep a few general cautions in mind. Force is rarely needed to get things apart. If parts are a tight fit, like a bearing in a case, there is usually a tool designed to separate them. Never use a screwdriver to pry apart parts with machined surfaces such as cylinder head and valve cover. You will mar the surfaces and end up with leaks.

Make diagrams wherever similar-appearing parts are found. You may think you can remember where everything came from — but mistakes are costly. There is also the possibility you may get sidetracked and not return to work for days or even weeks — in which interval, carefully laid out parts may have become disturbed.

Tag all similar internal parts for location, and mark all mating parts for position. Record number and thickness of any shims as they are removed. Small parts such as bolts can be identified by placing them in plastic sandwich bags that are sealed and labeled with masking tape.

Wiring should be tagged with masking tape and marked as each wire is removed. Again, do not rely on memory alone.

When working under the vehicle, do not trust a hydraulic or mechanical jack to hold the vehicle up by itself. Always use jackstands. See **Figure 1**.

Disconnect battery ground cable before working near electrical connections and before disconnecting wires. Never run the engine with the battery disconnected; the alternator could be seriously damaged.

Protect finished surfaces from physical damage or corrosion. Keep gasoline and brake fluid off painted surfaces.

Frozen or very tight bolts and screws can often be loosened by soaking with penetrating oil like Liquid Wrench or WD-40, then sharply striking the bolt head a few times with a hammer and punch (or screwdriver for screws). Avoid heat unless absolutely necessary, since it may melt, warp, or remove the temper from many parts.

Avoid flames or sparks when working near a charging battery or flammable liquids, such as brake fluid or gasoline.

No parts, except those assembled with a press fit, require unusual force during assembly. If a part is hard to remove or install, find out why before proceeding.

Cover all openings after removing parts to keep dirt, small tools, etc., from falling in.

When assembling two parts, start all fasteners, then tighten evenly.

The clutch plate, wiring connections, brake shoes, drums, pads, and discs should be kept clean and free of grease and oil.

When assembling parts, be sure all shims and washers are replaced exactly as they came out.

Whenever a rotating part butts against a stationary part, look for a shim or washer. Use new gaskets if there is any doubt about the condition of old ones. Generally, you should apply gasket cement to one mating surface only, so the parts may be easily disassembled in the future. A thin coat of oil on gaskets helps them seal effectively.

Heavy grease can be used to hold small parts in place if they tend to fall out during assembly. However, keep grease and oil away from electrical, clutch, and brake components.

High spots may be sanded off a piston with sandpaper, but emery cloth and oil do a much more professional job.

Carburetors are best cleaned by disassembling them and soaking the parts in a commercial carburetor cleaner. Never soak gaskets and rubber parts in these cleaners. Never use wire to clean out jets and air passages; they are easily damaged. Use compressed air to blow out the carburetor, but only if the float has been removed first.

Take your time and do the job right. Do not forget that a newly rebuilt engine must be broken in the same as a new one. Refer to your owner's manual for the proper break-in procedures.

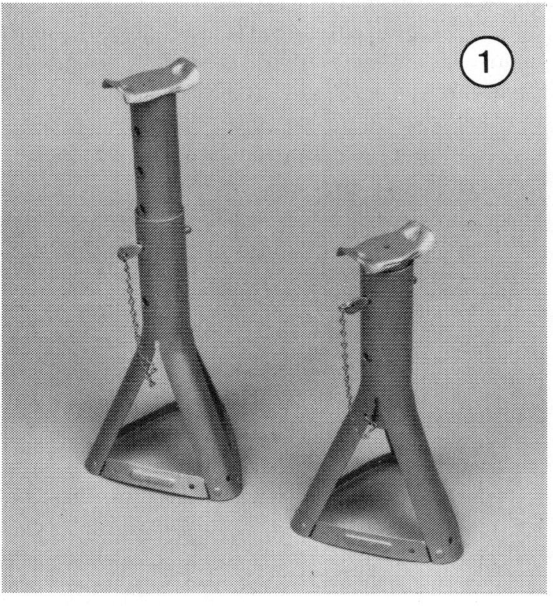

SAFETY FIRST

Professional mechanics can work for years and never sustain a serious injury. If you observe a few rules of common sense and safety, you can enjoy many safe hours servicing your vehicle. You could hurt yourself or damage the vehicle if you ignore these rules.

1. Never use gasoline as a cleaning solvent.

2. Never smoke or use a torch in the vicinity of flammable liquids such as cleaning solvent in open containers.

3. Never smoke or use a torch in an area where batteries are being charged. Highly explosive hydrogen gas is formed during the charging process.

4. Use the proper sized wrenches to avoid damage to nuts and injury to yourself.

5. When loosening a tight or stuck nut, be guided by what would happen if the wrench should slip. Protect yourself accordingly.

6. Keep your work area clean and uncluttered.

7. Wear safety goggles during all operations involving drilling, grinding, or use of a cold chisel.

8. Never use worn tools.

9. Keep a fire extinguisher handy and be sure it is rated for gasoline (Class B) and electrical (Class C) fires.

EXPENDABLE SUPPLIES

Certain expendable supplies are necessary. These include grease, oil, gasket cement, wiping rags, cleaning solvent, and distilled water.

Also, special locking compounds, silicone lubricants, and engine cleaners may be useful. Cleaning solvent is available at most service stations and distilled water for the battery is available at most supermarkets.

SHOP TOOLS

For proper servicing, you will need an assortment of ordinary hand tools (**Figure 2**).

As a minimum, these include:

a. Combination wrenches
b. Sockets
c. Plastic mallet
d. Small hammer
e. Snap ring pliers
f. Gas pliers
g. Phillips screwdrivers
h. Slot (common) screwdrivers
i. Feeler gauges
j. Spark plug gauge
k. Spark plug wrench

Special tools necessary are shown in the chapters covering the particular repair in which they are used.

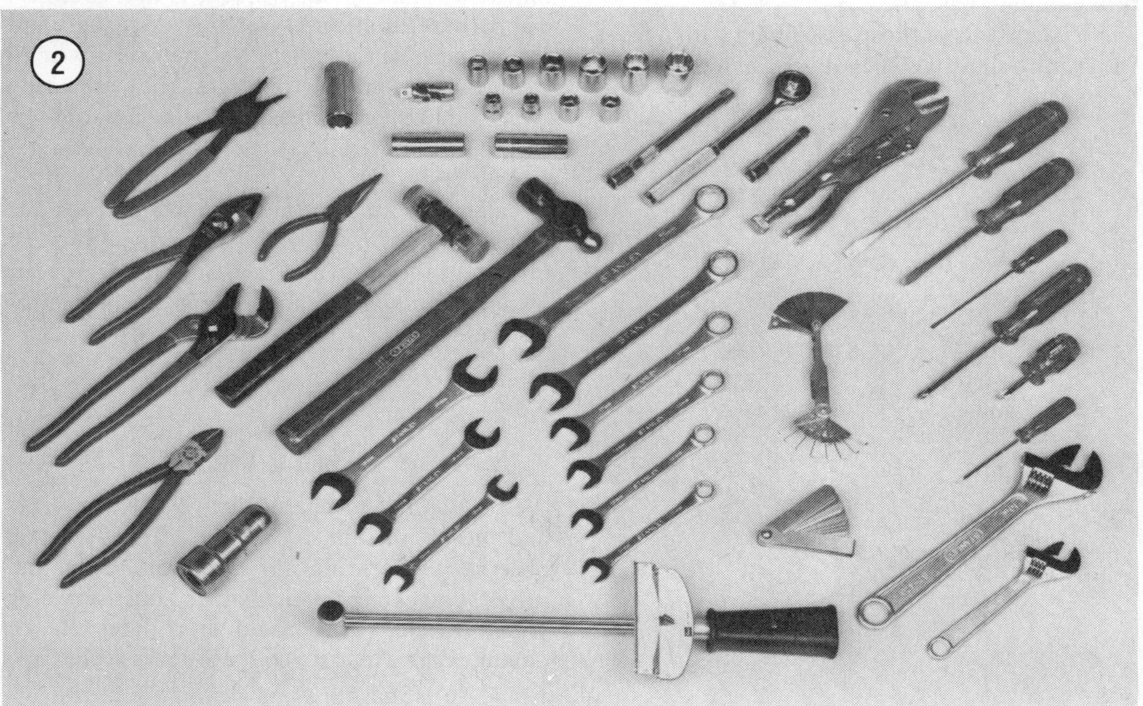

Engine tune-up and troubleshooting procedures require other special tools and equipment. These are described in detail in the following sections.

EMERGENCY TOOL KIT

A small emergency tool kit kept in the trunk is handy for road emergencies which otherwise could leave you stranded. The tools listed below and shown in **Figure 3** will let you handle most roadside repairs.

a. Combination wrenches

b. Crescent (adjustable) wrench

c. Screwdrivers — common and Phillips

d. Pliers — conventional (gas) and needle nose

e. Vise Grips

f. Hammer — plastic and metal

g. Small container of waterless hand cleaner

h. Rags for clean up

i. Silver waterproof sealing tape (duct tape)

j. Flashlight

k. Emergency road flares — at least four

l. Spare drive belts (water pump, alternator, etc.)

TROUBLESHOOTING AND TUNE-UP EQUIPMENT

Voltmeter, Ohmmeter, and Ammeter

For testing the ignition or electrical system, a good voltmeter is required. For automotive use, an instrument covering 0-20 volts is satisfac-

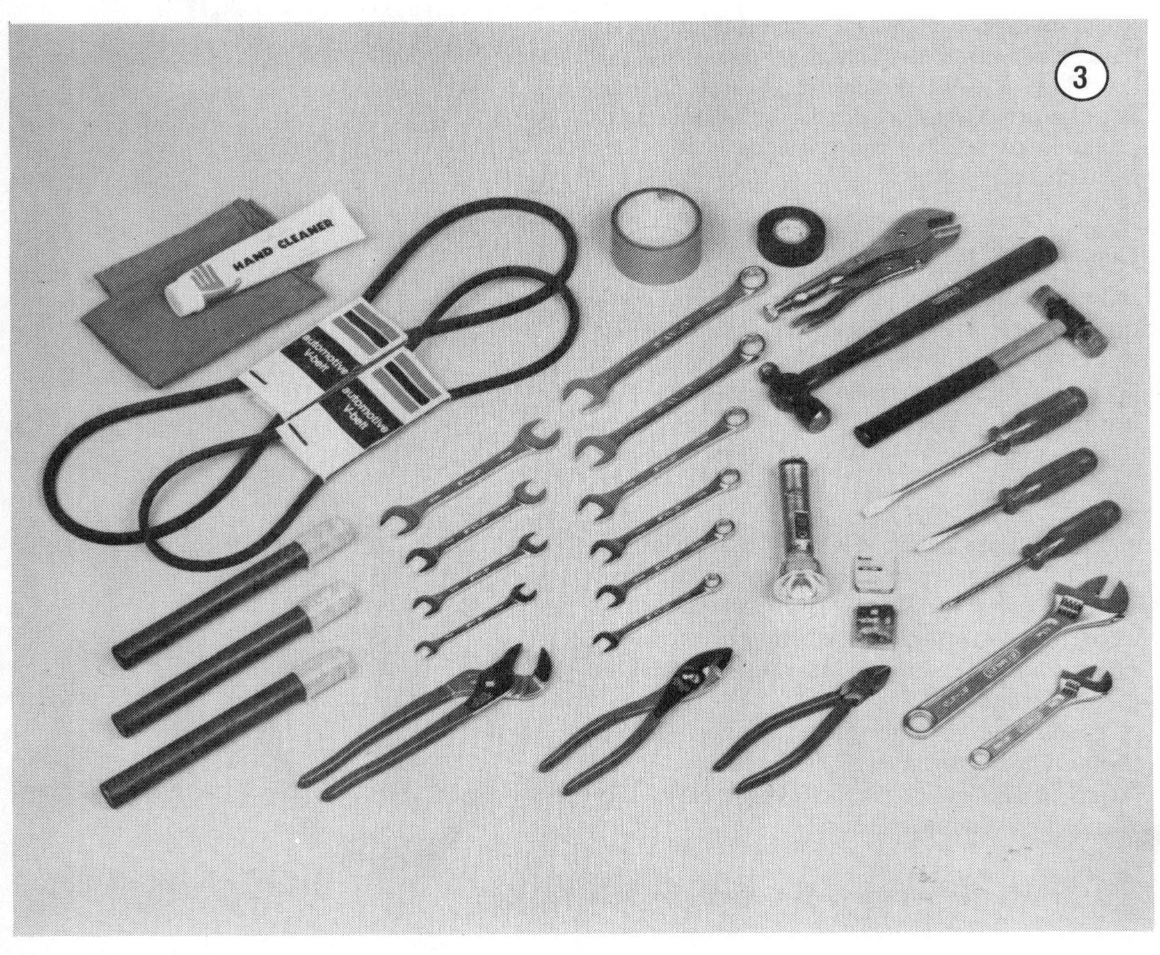

tory. One which also has a 0-2 volt scale is necessary for testing relays, points, or individual contacts where voltage drops are much smaller. Accuracy should be ± ½ volt.

An ohmmeter measures electrical resistance. This instrument is useful for checking continuity (open and short circuits), and testing fuses and lights.

The ammeter measures electrical current. Ammeters for automotive use should cover 0-50 amperes and 0-250 amperes. These are useful for checking battery charging and starting current.

Several inexpensive VOM's (volt-ohm-milliammeter) combine all three instruments into one which fits easily in any tool box. See **Figure 4**. However, the ammeter ranges are usually too small for automotive work.

Hydrometer

The hydrometer gives a useful indication of battery condition and charge by measuring the specific gravity of the electrolyte in each cell. See **Figure 5**. Complete details on use and interpretation of readings are provided in the electrical chapter.

Compression Tester

The compression tester measures the compression pressure built up in each cylinder. The results, when properly interpreted, can indicate general cylinder and valve condition. See **Figure 6**.

Vacuum Gauge

The vacuum gauge (**Figure 7**) is one of the easiest instruments to use, but one of the most difficult for the inexperienced mechanic to interpret. The results, when interpreted with other findings, can provide valuable clues to possible trouble.

To use the vacuum gauge, connect it to a vacuum hose that goes to the intake manifold. Attach it either directly to the hose or to a T-fitting installed into the hose.

> NOTE: *Subtract one inch from the reading for every 1,000 ft. elevation.*

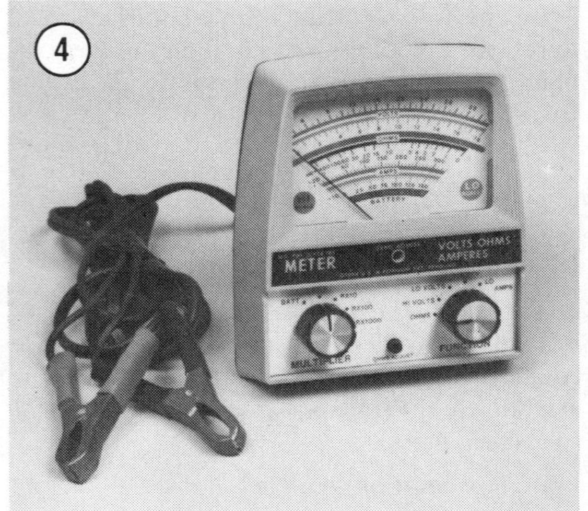

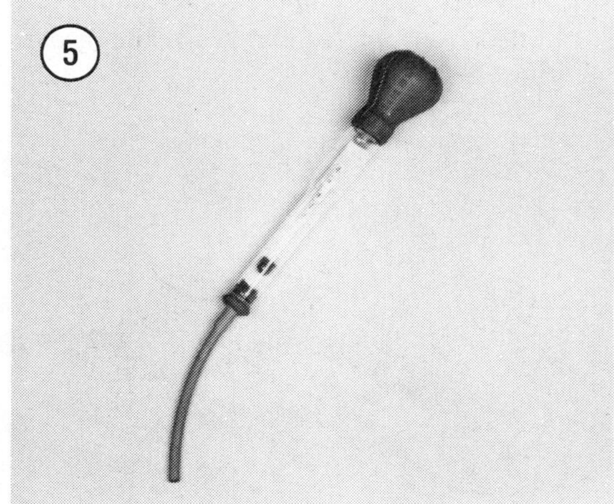

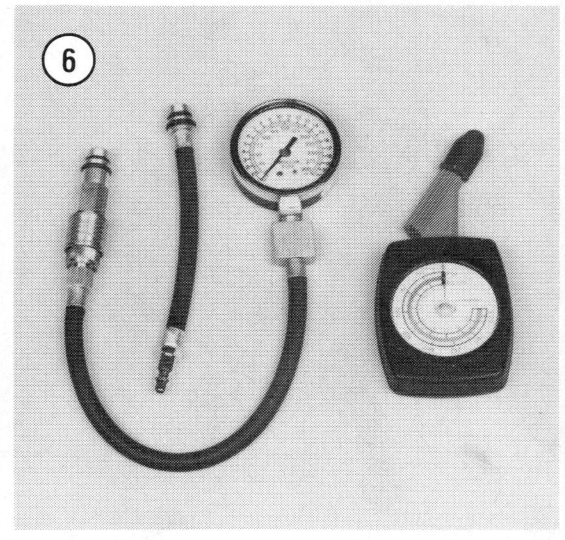

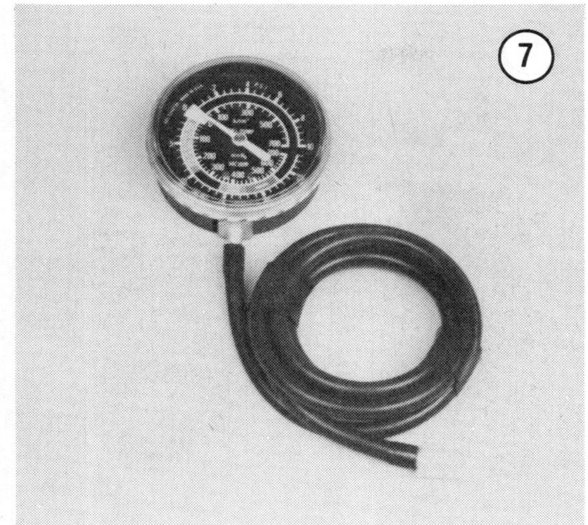

Fuel Pressure Gauge

This instrument is invaluable for evaluating fuel pump performance. Fuel system troubleshooting procedures in this manual use a fuel pressure gauge. Usually a vacuum gauge and fuel pressure gauge are combined.

Dwell Meter (Contact Breaker Point Ignition Only)

A dwell meter measures the distance in degrees of cam rotation that the breaker points remain closed while the engine is running. Since this angle is determined by breaker point gap, dwell angle is an accurate indication of breaker point gap.

Many tachometers intended for tuning and testing incorporate a dwell meter as well. See **Figure 8**. Follow the manufacturer's instructions to measure dwell.

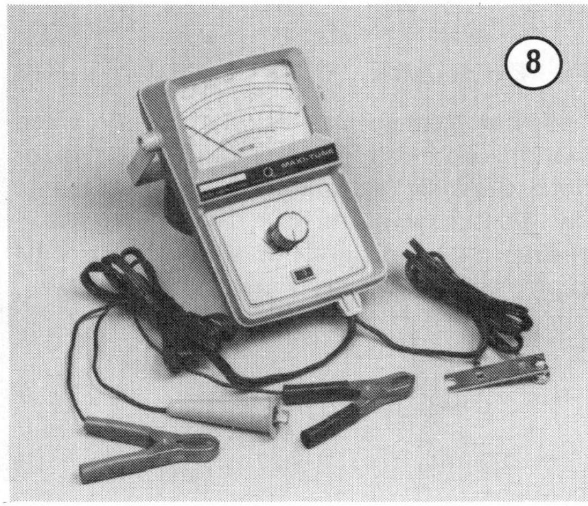

Tachometer

A tachometer is necessary for tuning. See **Figure 8**. Ignition timing and carburetor adjustments must be performed at the specified idle speed. The best instrument for this purpose is one with a low range of 0-1,000 or 0-2,000 rpm for setting idle, and a high range of 0-4,000 or more for setting ignition timing at 3,000 rpm. Extended range (0-6,000 or 0-8,000 rpm) instruments lack accuracy at lower speeds. The instrument should be capable of detecting changes of 25 rpm on the low range.

Strobe Timing Light

This instrument is necessary for tuning, as it permits very accurate ignition timing. The light flashes at precisely the same instant that No. 1 cylinder fires, at which time the timing marks on the engine should align. Refer to Chapter Three for exact location of the timing marks for your engine.

Suitable lights range from inexpensive neon bulb types ($2-3) to powerful xenon strobe lights ($20-40). See **Figure 9**. Neon timing lights are difficult to see and must be used in dimly lit areas. Xenon strobe timing lights can be used outside in bright sunlight. Both types work on this vehicle; use according to the manufacturer's instructions.

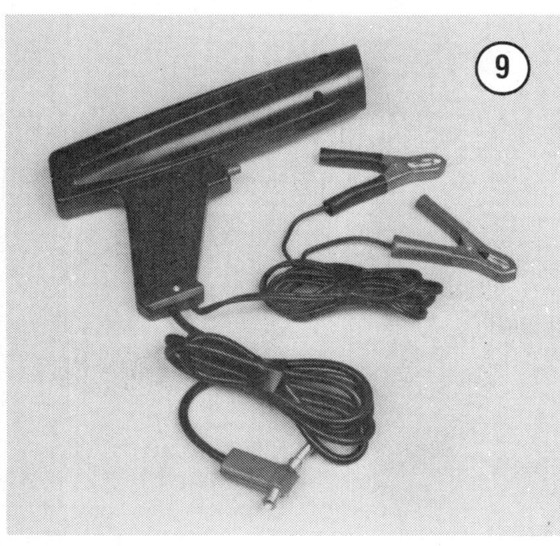

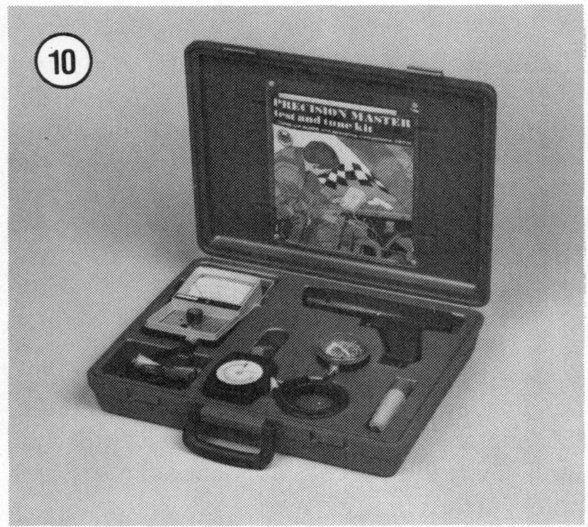

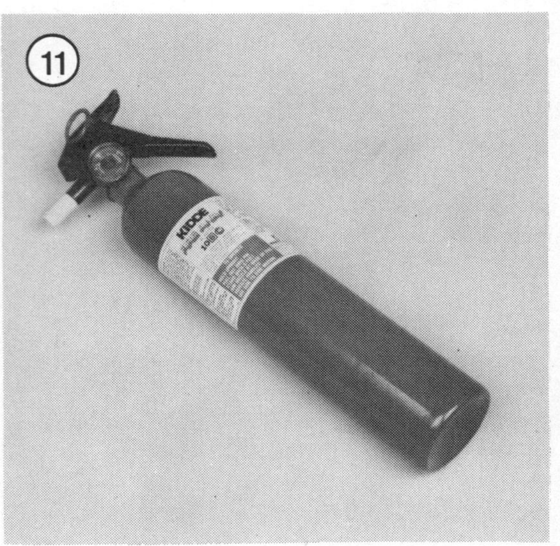

Tune-up Kits

Many manufacturer's offer kits that combine several useful instruments. Some come in a convenient carry case and are usally less expensive than purchasing one instrument at a time. **Figure 10** shows one of the kits that is available. The prices vary with the number of instruments included in the kit.

Fire Extinguisher

A fire extinguisher is a necessity when working on a vehicle. It should be rated for both *Class B* (flammable liquids—gasoline, oil, paint, etc.) and *Class C* (electrical—wiring, etc.) type fires. It should always be kept within reach. See **Figure 11**.

CHAPTER TWO

TROUBLESHOOTING

Troubleshooting can be a relatively simple matter if it is done logically. The first step in any troubleshooting procedure must be defining the symptoms as closely as possible. Subsequent steps involve testing and analyzing areas which could cause the symptoms. A haphazard approach may eventually find the trouble, but in terms of wasted time and unnecessary parts replacement, it can be very costly.

The troubleshooting procedures in this chapter analyze typical symptoms and show logical methods of isolation. These are not the only methods. There may be several approaches to a problem, but all methods must have one thing in common — a logical, systematic approach.

STARTING SYSTEM

The starting system consists of the starter motor and the starter solenoid. The ignition key controls the starter solenoid, which mechanically engages the starter with the engine flywheel, and supplies electrical current to turn the starter motor.

Starting system troubles are relatively easy to find. In most cases, the trouble is a loose or dirty electrical connection. **Figures 1 and 2** provide routines for finding the trouble.

CHARGING SYSTEM

The charging system consists of the alternator (or generator on older vehicles), voltage regulator, and battery. A drive belt driven by the engine crankshaft turns the alternator which produces electrical energy to charge the battery. As engine speed varies, the voltage from the alternator varies. A voltage regulator controls the charging current to the battery and maintains the voltage to the vehicle's electrical system at safe levels. A warning light or gauge on the instrument panel signals the driver when charging is not taking place. Refer to **Figure 3** for a typical charging system.

Complete troubleshooting of the charging system requires test equipment and skills which the average home mechanic does not possess. However, there are a few tests which can be done to pinpoint most troubles.

Charging system trouble may stem from a defective alternator (or generator), voltage regulator, battery, or drive belt. It may also be caused by something as simple as incorrect drive belt tension. The following are symptoms of typical problems you may encounter.

1. ***Battery dies frequently, even though the warning lamp indicates no discharge*** — This can be caused by a drive belt that is slightly too

STARTER PROBLEMS
STARTER DOES NOT TURN
BATTERY CONDITION TEST
Turn on headlights.*
Operate the starter.
LIGHTS DIM
• Battery needs charging.
• Check all related electrical connections.
• Check alternator drive belt tension.
• Starter may be shorted, remove and test it.
* On some models, the headlights are automatically turned off when the starter is operated.
STARTER DOES NOT TURN
ELECTRICAL CONNECTIONS
• Check, clean, and tighten battery cable connections.
• Check electrical wires for breaks, shorts, and dirty and/or loose connections.
NEUTRAL SAFETY SWITCH
Disconnect wiring at switch, place a jumper wire between terminals on wiring connector.
STARTER TURNS
Replace switch.
STARTER SOLENOID
Short the two large terminals together (not to ground).
STARTER TURNS
Replace solenoid.
1

STARTER PROBLEMS
STARTER TURNS
DOES NOT ENGAGE WITH ENGINE
Check pinion or solenoid shifting fork and teeth on flywheel gear.
ENGAGES WITH ENGINE — WILL NOT RELEASE
Check for sticking solenoid or jammed pinion onto flywheel.
LOUD GRINDING NOISE
Check flywheel to pinion alignment. The overrunning clutch may be broken.
Remove the starter and examine the gear teeth; replace if necessary.
2

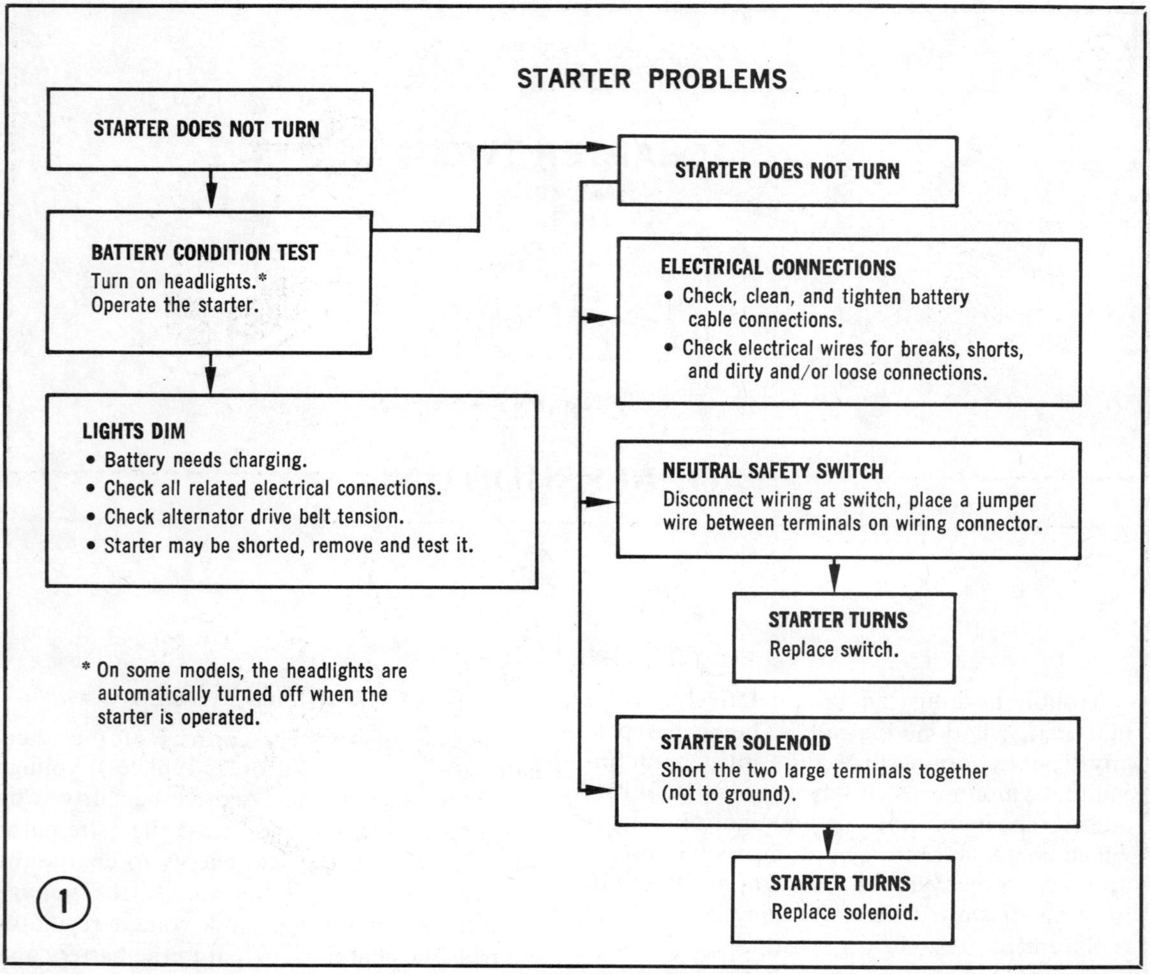

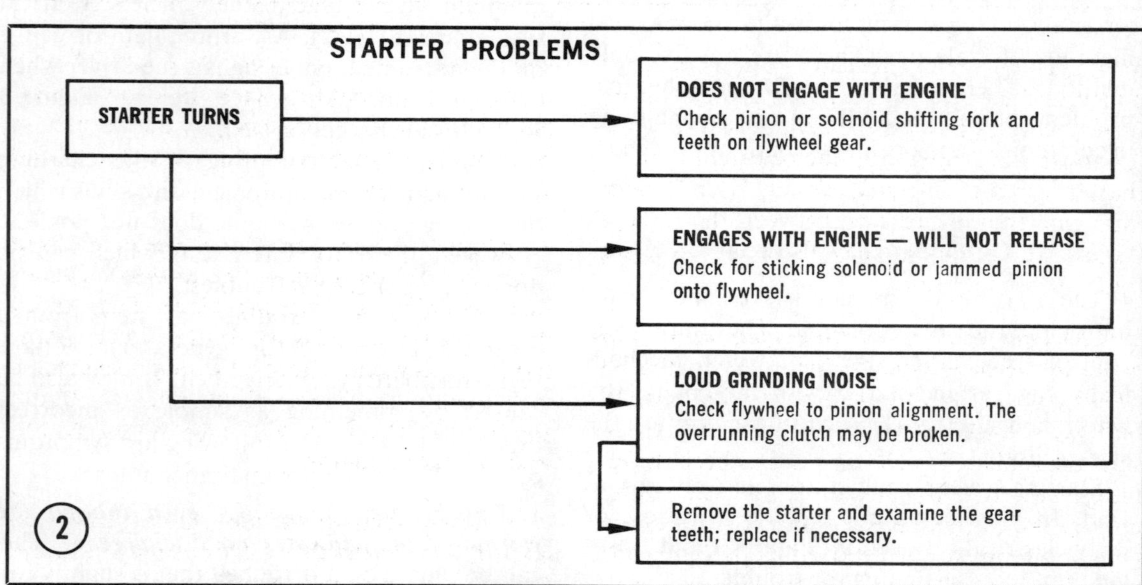

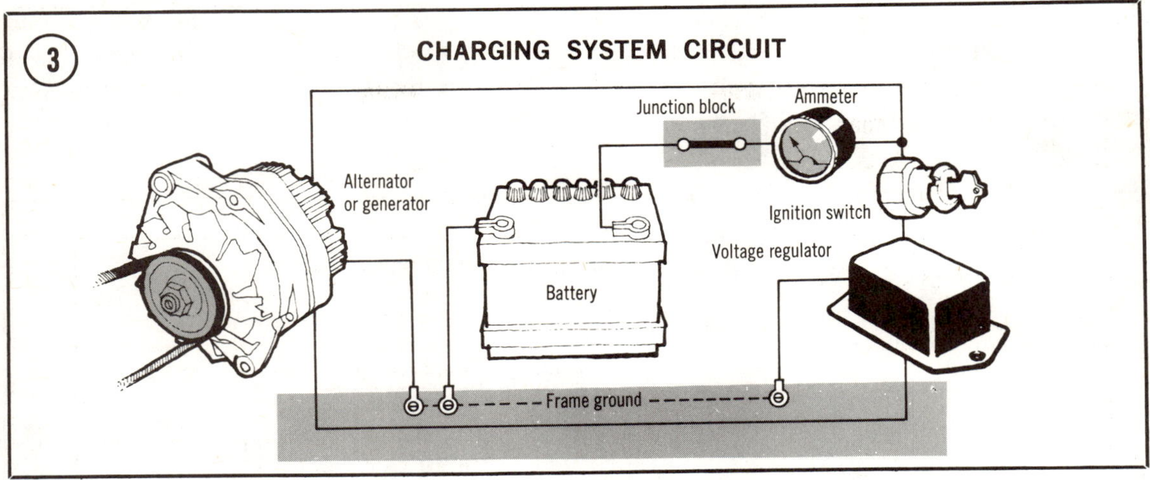

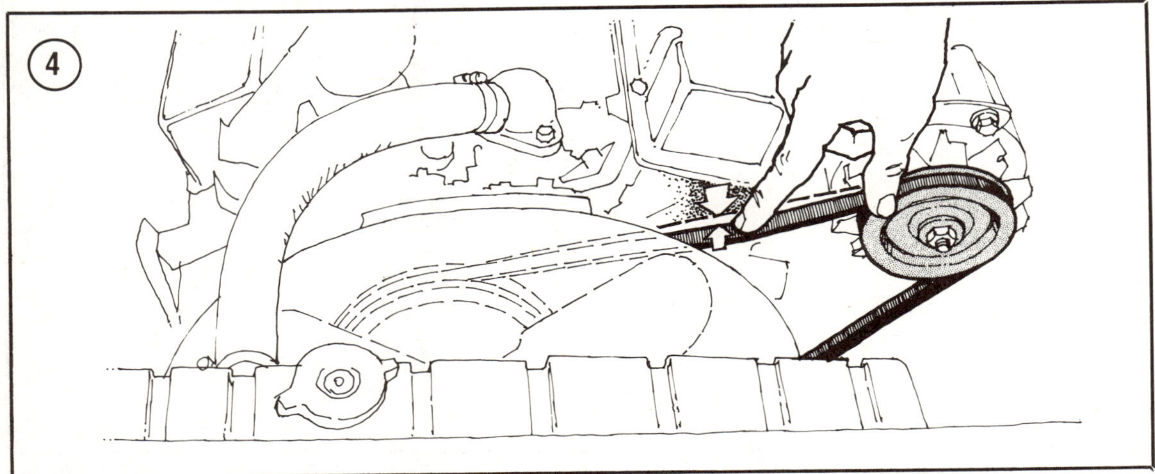

loose. Grasp the alternator (or generator) pulley and try to turn it. If the pulley can be turned without moving the belt, the drive belt is too loose. As a rule, keep the belt tight enough that it can be deflected about ½ in. under moderate thumb pressure between the pulleys (**Figure 4**). The battery may also be at fault; test the battery condition.

2. ***Charging system warning lamp does not come on when ignition switch is turned on —*** This may indicate a defective ignition switch, battery, voltage regulator, or lamp. First try to start the vehicle. If it doesn't start, check the ignition switch and battery. If the car starts, remove the warning lamp; test it for continuity with an ohmmeter or substitute a new lamp. If the lamp is good, locate the voltage regulator and make sure it is properly grounded (try tightening the mounting screws). Also the alternator (or generator) brushes may not be making contact. Test the alternator (or generator) and voltage regulator.

3. ***Alternator (or generator) warning lamp comes on and stays on —*** This usually indicates that no charging is taking place. First check drive belt tension (**Figure 4**). Then check battery condition, and check all wiring connections in the charging system. If this does not locate the trouble, check the alternator (or generator) and voltage regulator.

4. ***Charging system warning lamp flashes on and off intermittently —*** This usually indicates the charging system is working intermittently.

Check the drive belt tension **(Figure 4)**, and check all electrical connections in the charging system. Check the alternator (or generator). *On generators only*, check the condition of the commutator.

5. *Battery requires frequent additions of water, or lamps require frequent replacement* — The alternator (or generator) is probably overcharging the battery. The voltage regulator is probably at fault.

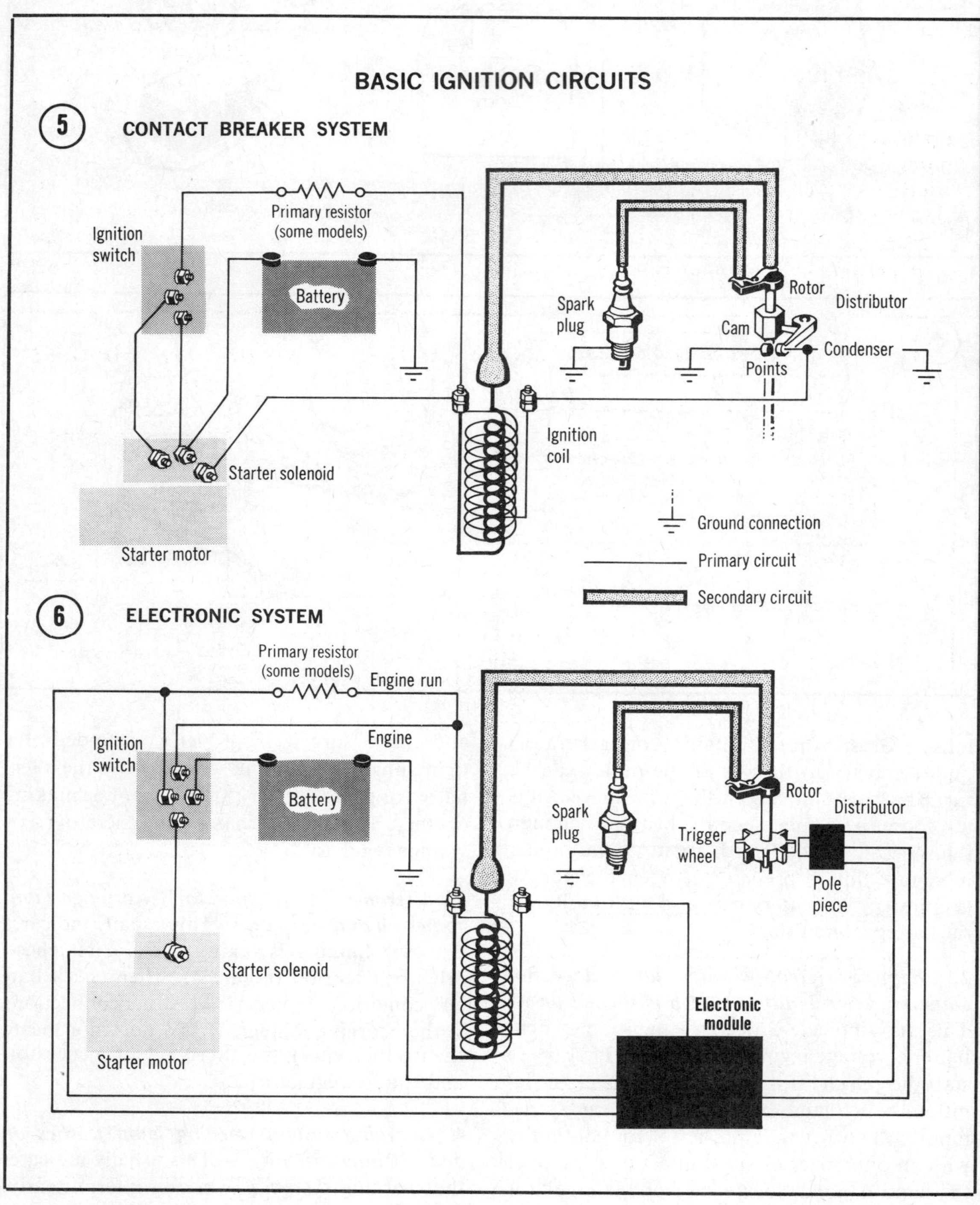

6. *Excessive noise from the alternator (or generator)* — Check for loose mounting brackets and bolts. The problem may also be worn bearings or the need of lubrication in some cases. If an alternator whines, a shorted diode may be indicated.

IGNITION SYSTEM

The ignition system may be either a conventional contact breaker type or an electronic ignition. See electrical chapter to determine which type you have. **Figures 5 and 6** show simplified diagrams of each type.

Most problems involving failure to start, poor performance, or rough running stem from trouble in the ignition system, particularly in contact breaker systems. Many novice troubleshooters get into trouble when they assume that these symptoms point to the fuel system instead of the ignition system.

Ignition system troubles may be roughly divided between those affecting only one cylinder and those affecting all cylinders. If the trouble affects only one cylinder, it can only be in the spark plug, spark plug wire, or portion of the distributor associated with that cylinder. If the trouble affects all cylinders (weak spark or no spark), then the trouble is in the ignition coil, rotor, distributor, or associated wiring.

The troubleshooting procedures outlined in **Figure 7** (breaker point ignition) or **Figure 8**

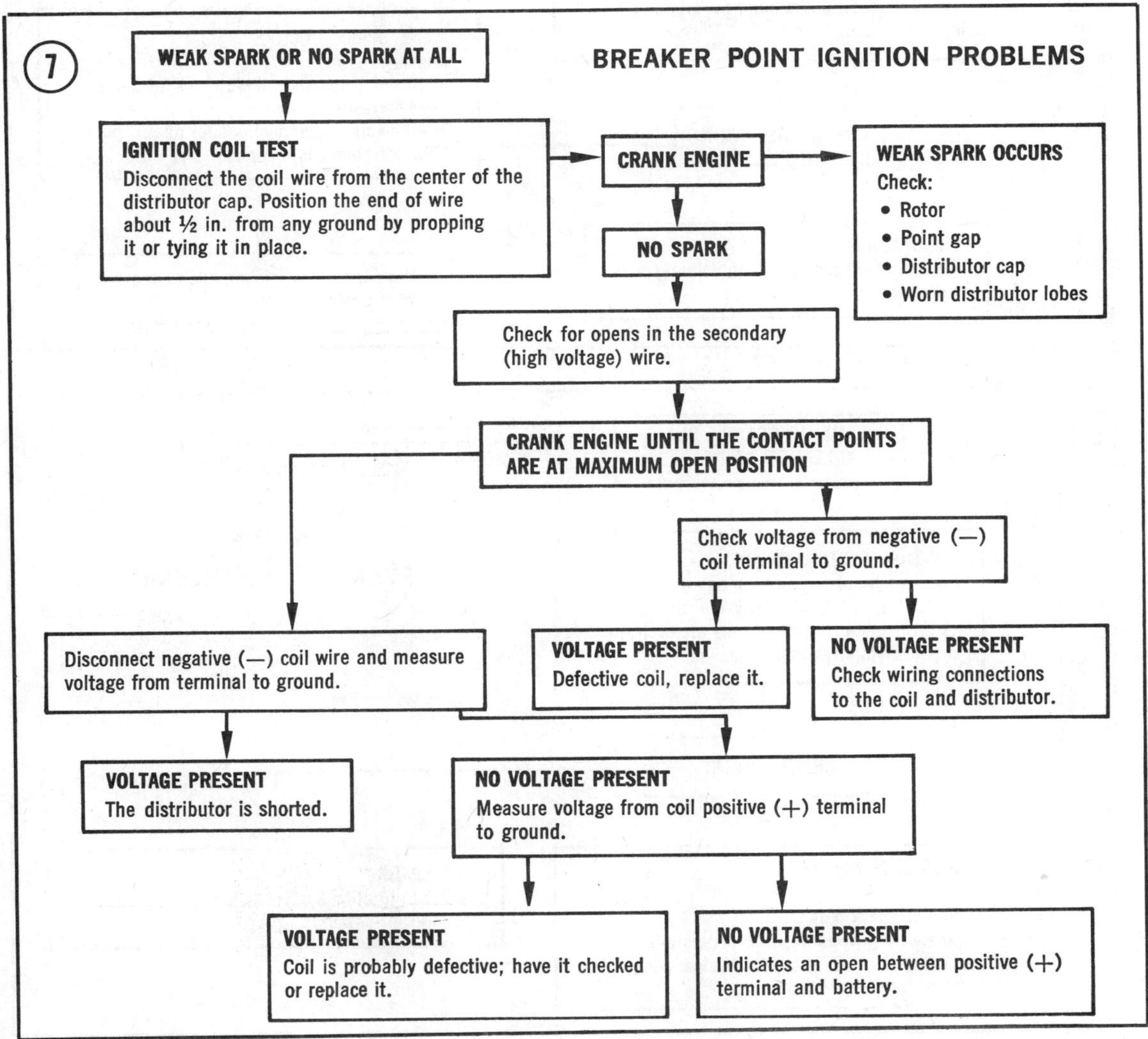

(electronic ignition) will help you isolate ignition problems fast. Of course, they assume that the battery is in good enough condition to crank the engine over at its normal rate.

ENGINE PERFORMANCE

A number of factors can make the engine difficult or impossible to start, or cause rough running, poor performance and so on. The majority of novice troubleshooters immediately suspect the carburetor or fuel injection system. In the majority of cases, though, the trouble exists in the ignition system.

The troubleshooting procedures outlined in **Figures 9 through 14** will help you solve the majority of engine starting troubles in a systematic manner.

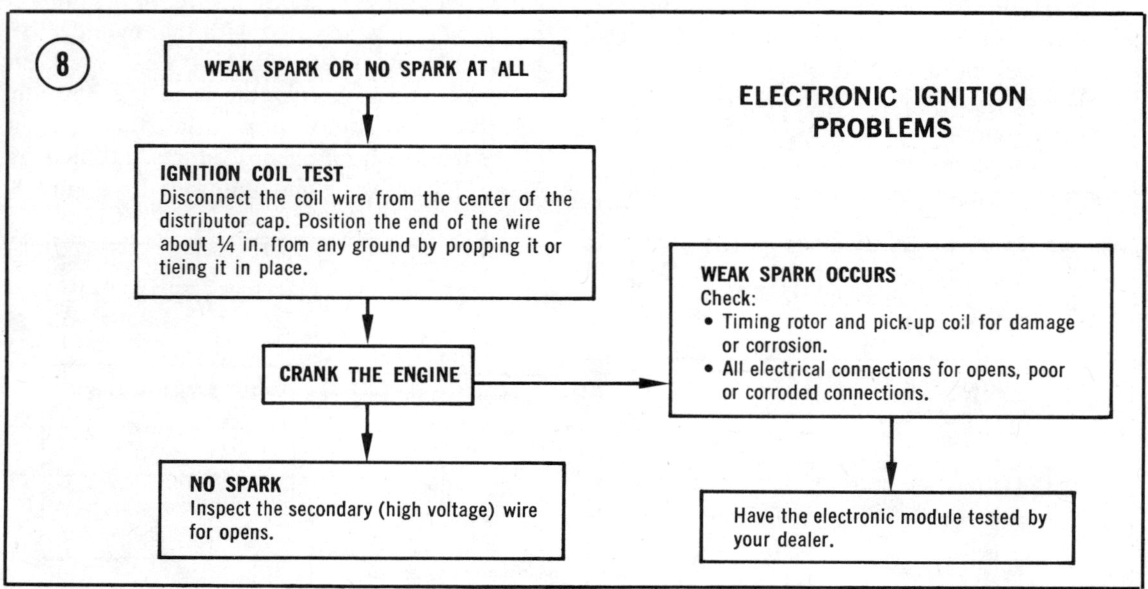

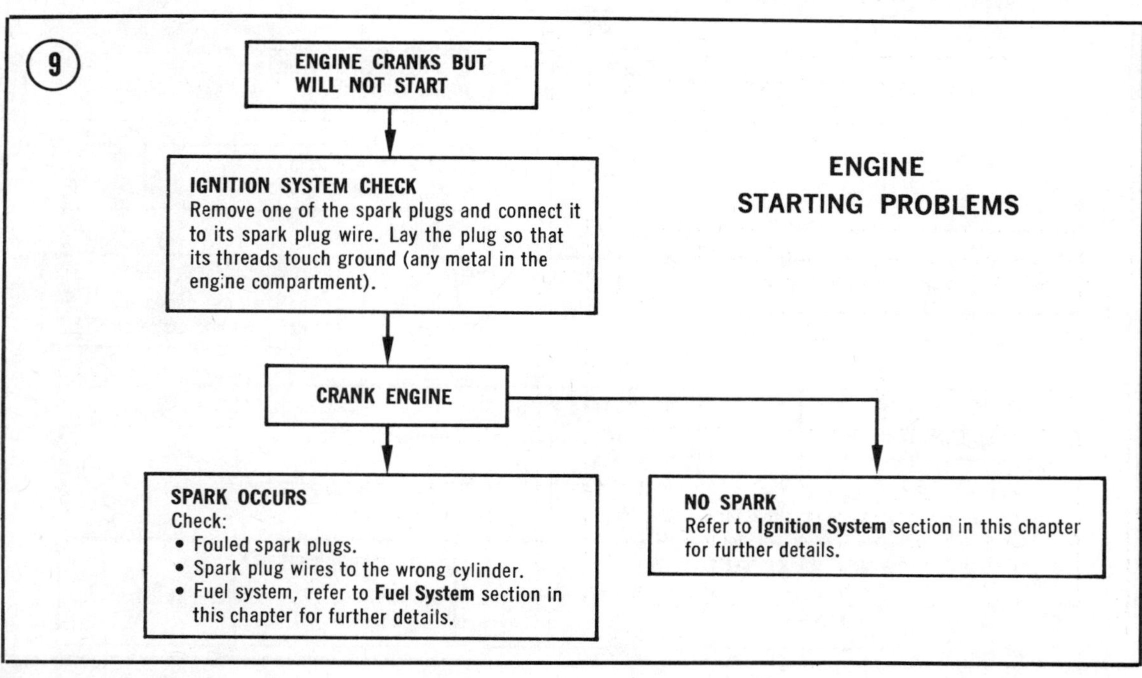

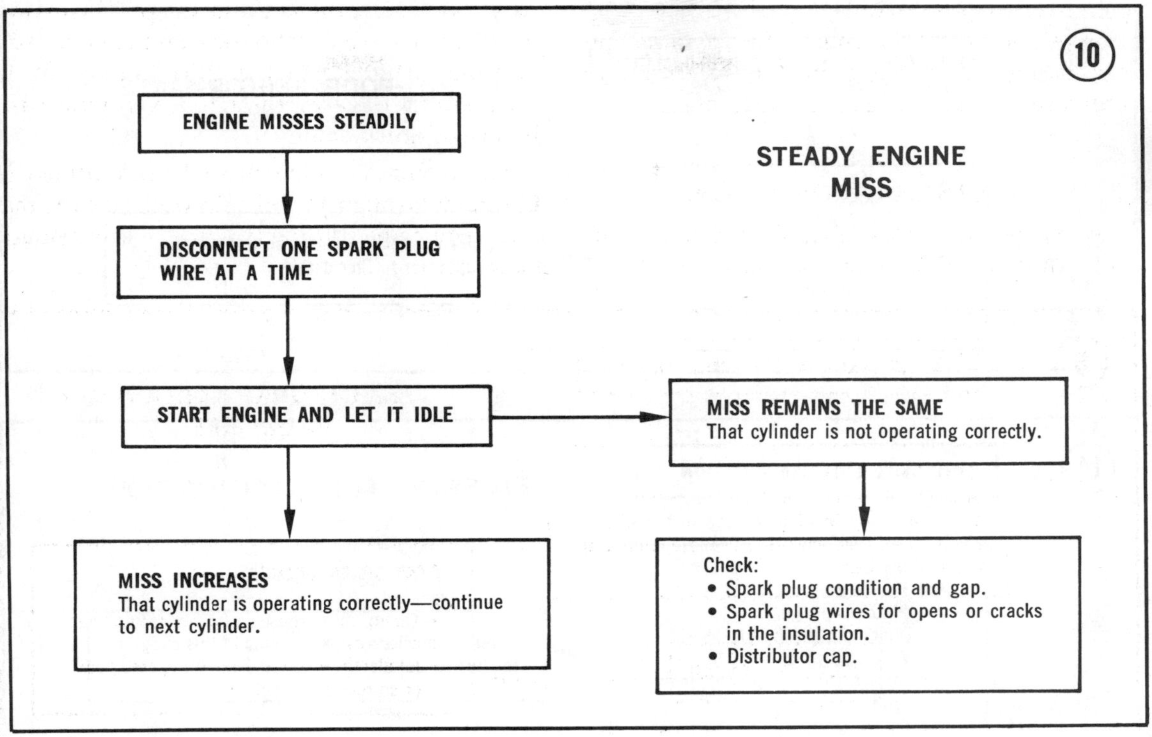

2

(10)

ENGINE MISSES STEADILY

STEADY ENGINE
MISS

DISCONNECT ONE SPARK PLUG
WIRE AT A TIME

START ENGINE AND LET IT IDLE → MISS REMAINS THE SAME
That cylinder is not operating correctly.

MISS INCREASES
That cylinder is operating correctly—continue
to next cylinder.

Check:
- Spark plug condition and gap.
- Spark plug wires for opens or cracks
  in the insulation.
- Distributor cap.

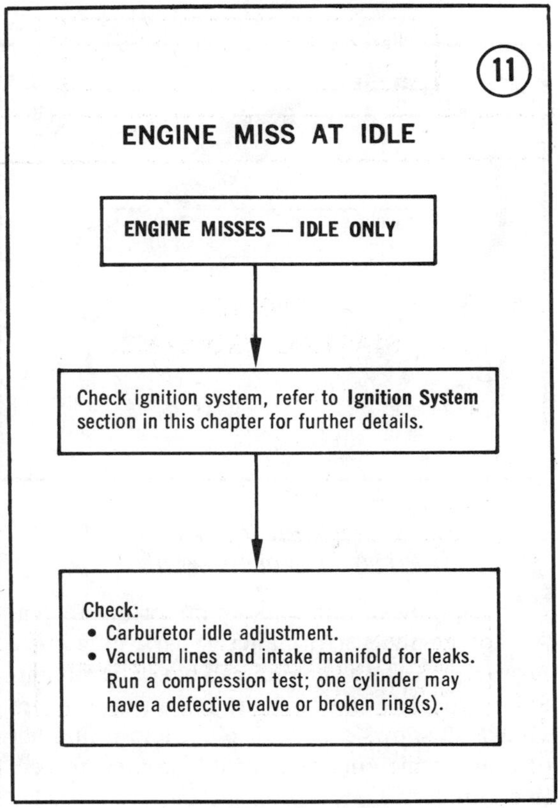

(11)

ENGINE MISS AT IDLE

ENGINE MISSES — IDLE ONLY

Check ignition system, refer to **Ignition System**
section in this chapter for further details.

Check:
- Carburetor idle adjustment.
- Vacuum lines and intake manifold for leaks.
  Run a compression test; one cylinder may
  have a defective valve or broken ring(s).

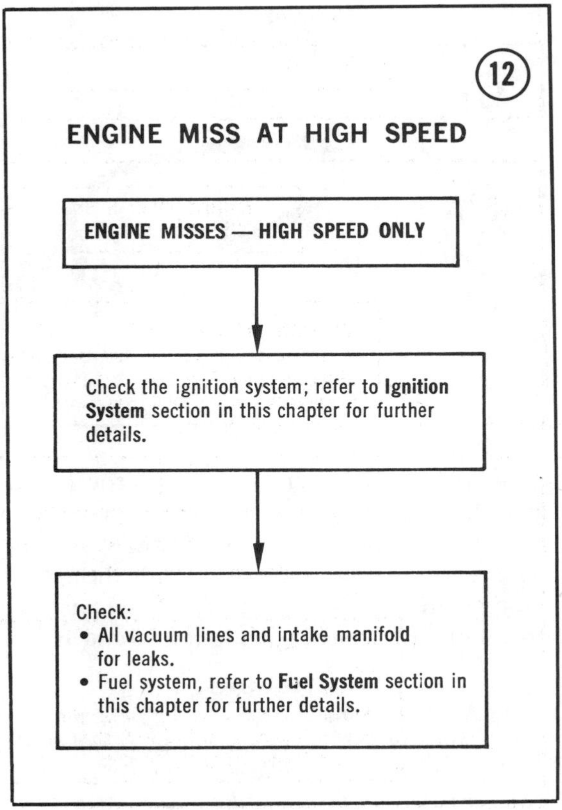

(12)

ENGINE MISS AT HIGH SPEED

ENGINE MISSES — HIGH SPEED ONLY

Check the ignition system; refer to **Ignition
System** section in this chapter for further
details.

Check:
- All vacuum lines and intake manifold
  for leaks.
- Fuel system, refer to **Fuel System** section in
  this chapter for further details.

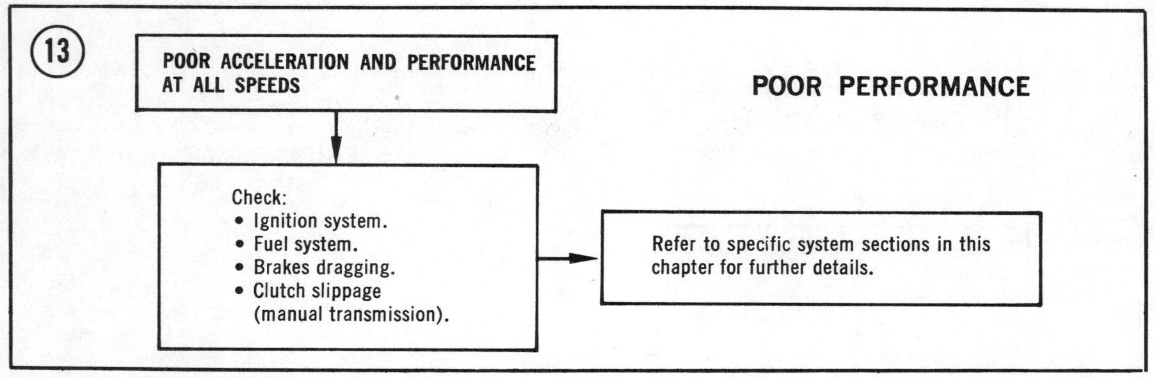

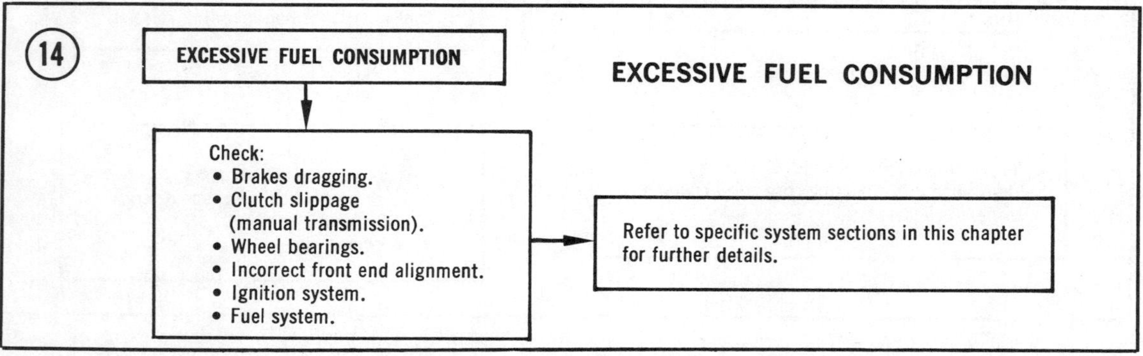

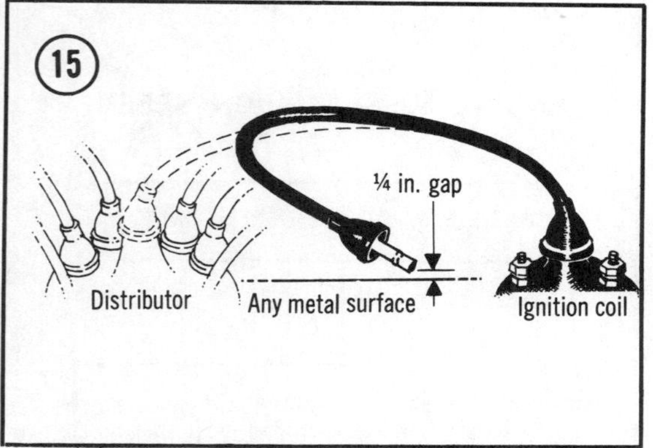

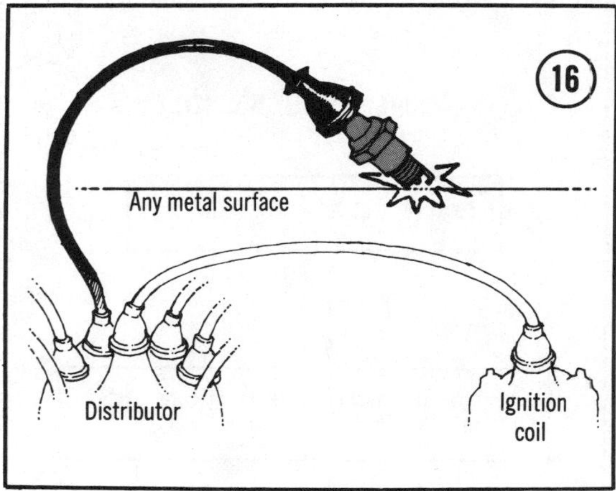

Some tests of the ignition system require running the engine with a spark plug or ignition coil wire disconnected. The safest way to do this is to disconnect the wire with the engine stopped, then prop the end of the wire next to a metal surface as shown in **Figures 15 and 16**.

WARNING
Never disconnect a spark plug or ignition coil wire while the engine is running. The high voltage in an ignition system, particularly the newer high-energy electronic ignition systems could cause serious injury or even death.

Spark plug condition is an important indication of engine performance. Spark plugs in a properly operating engine will have slightly pitted electrodes, and a light tan insulator tip. **Figure 17** shows a normal plug, and a number of others which indicate trouble in their respective cylinders.

- Appearance—Firing tip has deposits of light gray to light tan.
- Can be cleaned, regapped and reused.

- Appearance—Glazed yellow deposits with a slight brownish tint on the insulator tip and ground electrode.
- Replace with new plugs.

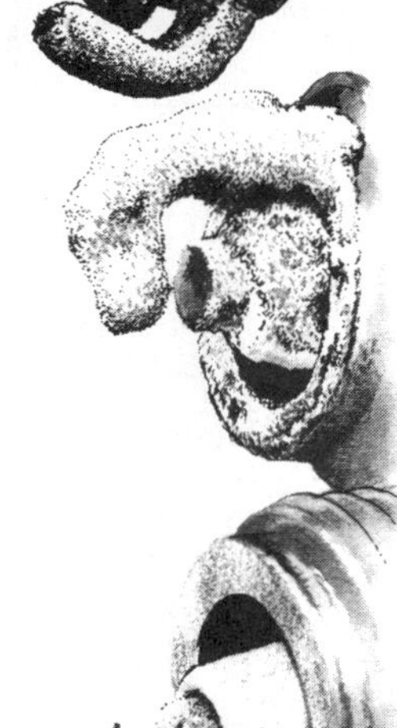

- Appearance — Brown colored hardened ash deposits on the insulator tip and ground electrode.
- Caused by—Fuel and/or oil additives.
- Replace with new plugs.

- Appearance—Dull, dry black with fluffy carbon deposits on the insulator tip, electrode and exposed shell.
- Caused by—Fuel/air mixture too rich, plug heat range too cold, weak ignition system, dirty air cleaner, faulty automatic choke or excessive idling.
- Can be cleaned, regapped and reused.

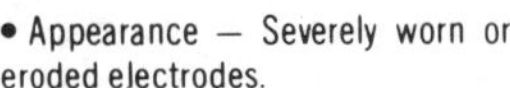

- Appearance — Severely worn or eroded electrodes.
- Caused by—Normal wear or unusual oil and/or fuel additives.
- Replace with new plugs.

- Appearance—Wet black deposits on insulator and exposed shell.
- Caused by—Excessive oil entering the combustion chamber through worn rings, pistons, valve guides or bearings.
- Replace with new plugs (use a hotter plug if engine is not repaired).

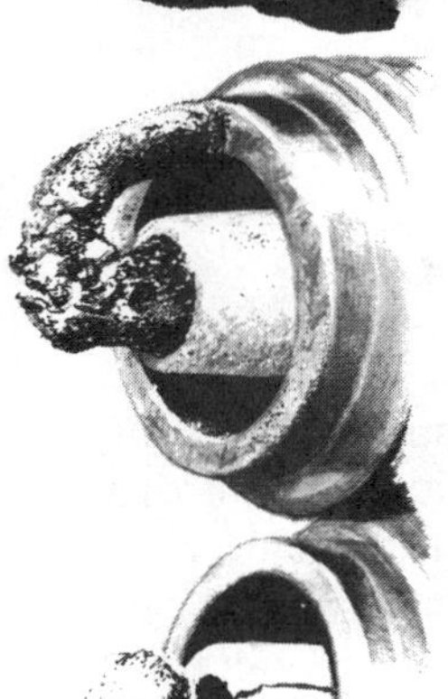

- Appearance — Melted ground electrode.
- Caused by—Overadvanced ignition timing, inoperative ignition advance mechanism, too low of a fuel octane rating, lean fuel/air mixture or carbon deposits in combustion chamber.

- Appearance — Yellow insulator deposits (may sometimes be dark gray, black or tan in color) on the insulator tip.
- Caused by—Highly leaded gasoline.
- Replace with new plugs.

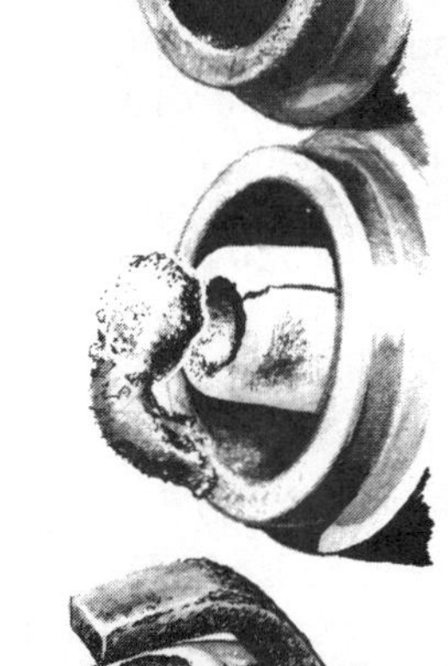

- Appearance—Melted center electrode.
- Caused by—Abnormal combustion due to overadvanced ignition timing or incorrect advance, too low of a fuel octane rating, lean fuel/air mixture, or carbon deposits in combustion chamber.
- Correct engine problem and replace with new plugs.

- Appearance—Yellow glazed deposits indicating melted lead deposits due to hard acceleration.
- Caused by—Highly leaded gasoline.
- Replace with new plugs.

- Appearance—Melted center electrode and white blistered insulator tip.
- Caused by—Incorrect plug heat range selection.
- Replace with new plugs.

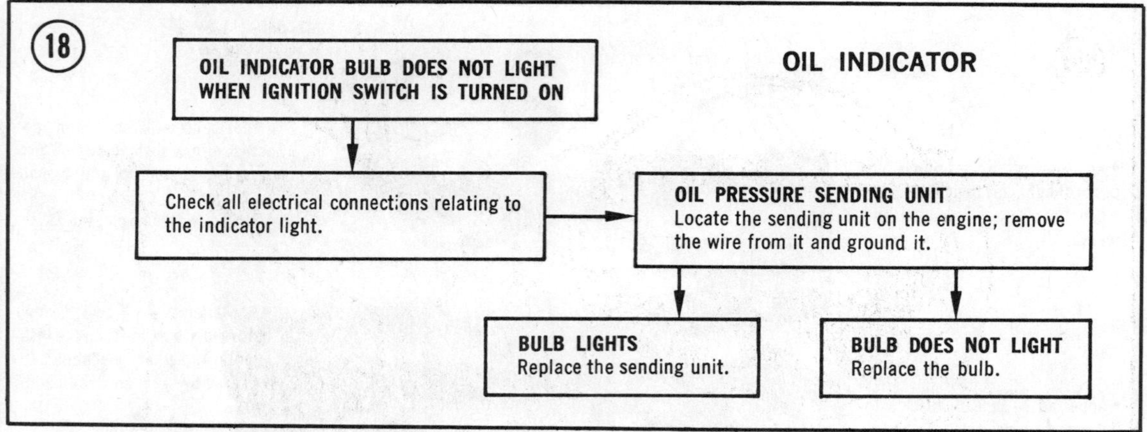

ENGINE OIL PRESSURE LIGHT

Proper oil pressure to the engine is vital. If oil pressure is insufficient, the engine can destroy itself in a comparatively short time.

The oil pressure warning circuit monitors oil pressure constantly. If pressure drops below a predetermined level, the light comes on.

Obviously, it is vital for the warning circuit to be working to signal low oil pressure. Each time you turn on the ignition, but before you start the car, the warning light should come on. If it doesn't, there is trouble in the warning circuit, not the oil pressure system. See **Figure 18** to troubleshoot the warning circuit.

Once the engine is running, the warning light should stay off. If the warning light comes on or acts erratically while the engine is running there is trouble with the engine oil pressure system. *Stop the engine immediately*. Refer to **Figure 19** for possible causes of the problem.

FUEL SYSTEM (CARBURETTED)

Fuel system problems must be isolated to the fuel pump (mechanical or electric), fuel lines, fuel filter, or carburetor. These procedures assume the ignition system is working properly and is correctly adjusted.

1. *Engine will not start* — First make sure that fuel is being delivered to the carburetor. Remove the air cleaner, look into the carburetor throat, and operate the accelerator

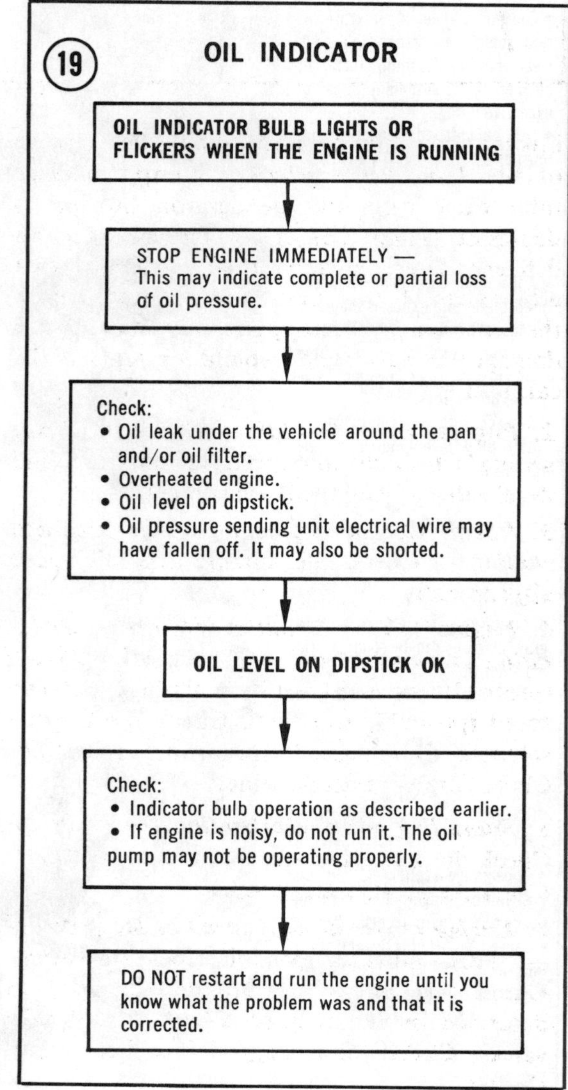

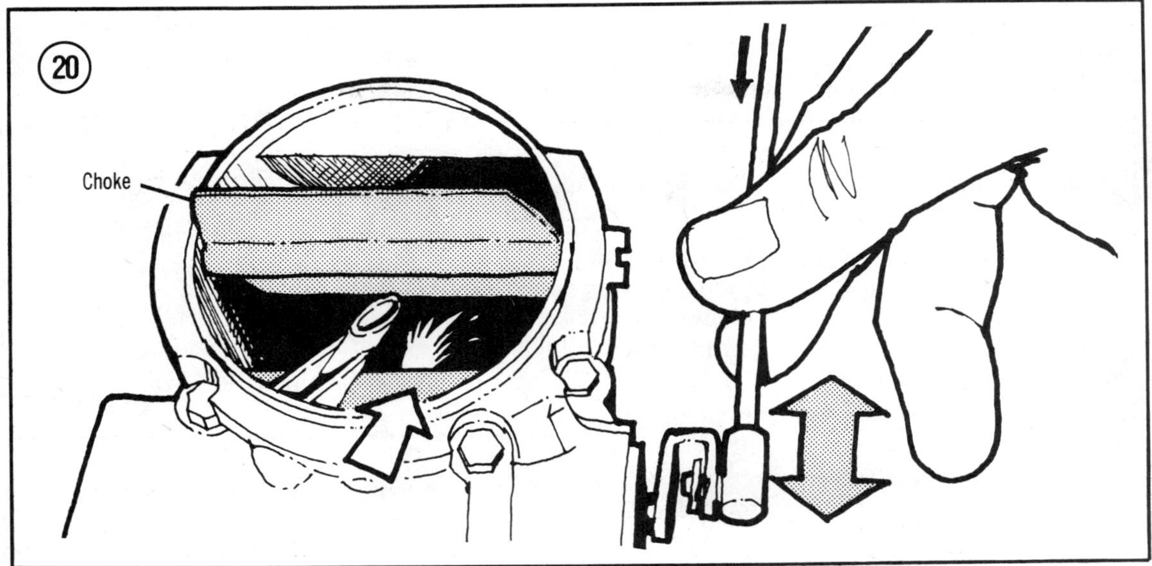

linkage several times. There should be a stream of fuel from the accelerator pump discharge tube each time the accelerator linkage is depressed (**Figure 20**). If not, check fuel pump delivery (described later), float valve, and float adjustment. If the engine will not start, check the automatic choke parts for sticking or damage. If necessary, rebuild or replace the carburetor.

2. *Engine runs at fast idle* — Check the choke setting. Check the idle speed, idle mixture, and decel valve (if equipped) adjustment.

3. *Rough idle or engine miss with frequent stalling* — Check idle mixture and idle speed adjustments.

4. *Engine "diesels" (continues to run) when ignition is switched off* — Check idle mixture (probably too rich), ignition timing, and idle speed (probably too fast). Check the throttle solenoid (if equipped) for proper operation. Check for overheated engine.

5. *Stumbling when accelerating from idle* — Check the idle speed and mixture adjustments. Check the accelerator pump.

6. *Engine misses at high speed or lacks power* — This indicates possible fuel starvation. Check fuel pump pressure and capacity as described in this chapter. Check float needle valves. Check for a clogged fuel filter or air cleaner.

7. *Black exhaust smoke* — This indicates a badly overrich mixture. Check idle mixture and idle speed adjustment. Check choke setting. Check for excessive fuel pump pressure, leaky floats, or worn needle valves.

8. *Excessive fuel consumption* — Check for overrich mixture. Make sure choke mechanism works properly. Check idle mixture and idle speed. Check for excessive fuel pump pressure, leaky floats, or worn float needle valves.

FUEL SYSTEM (FUEL INJECTED)

Troubleshooting a fuel injection system requires more thought, experience, and know-how than any other part of the vehicle. A logical approach and proper test equipment are essential in order to successfully find and fix these troubles.

It is best to leave fuel injection troubles to your dealer. In order to isolate a problem to the injection system make sure that the fuel pump is operating properly. Check its performance as described later in this section. Also make sure that fuel filter and air cleaner are not clogged.

FUEL PUMP TEST (MECHANICAL AND ELECTRIC)

1. Disconnect the fuel inlet line where it enters the carburetor or fuel injection system.

2. Fit a rubber hose over the fuel line so fuel can be directed into a graduated container with about one quart capacity. See **Figure 21**.

3. To avoid accidental starting of the engine, disconnect the secondary coil wire from the coil or disconnect and insulate the coil primary wire.

4. Crank the engine for about 30 seconds.

5. If the fuel pump supplies the specified amount (refer to the fuel chapter later in this book), the trouble may be in the carburetor or fuel injection system. The fuel injection system should be tested by your dealer.

6. If there is no fuel present or the pump cannot supply the specified amount, either the fuel pump is defective or there is an obstruction in the fuel line. Replace the fuel pump and/or inspect the fuel lines for air leaks or obstructions.

7. Also pressure test the fuel pump by installing a T-fitting in the fuel line between the fuel pump and the carburetor. Connect a fuel pressure gauge to the fitting with a short tube **(Figure 22)**.

8. Reconnect the coil wire, start the engine, and record the pressure. Refer to the fuel chapter later in this book for the correct pressure. If the pressure varies from that specified, the pump should be replaced.

9. Stop the engine. The pressure should drop off very slowly. If it drops off rapidly, the outlet valve in the pump is leaking and the pump should be replaced.

EMISSION CONTROL SYSTEMS

Major emission control systems used on nearly all U.S. models include the following:

a. Positive crankcase ventilation (PCV)

b. Thermostatic air cleaner

c. Air injection reaction (AIR)

d. Fuel evaporation control

e. Exhaust gas recirculation (EGR)

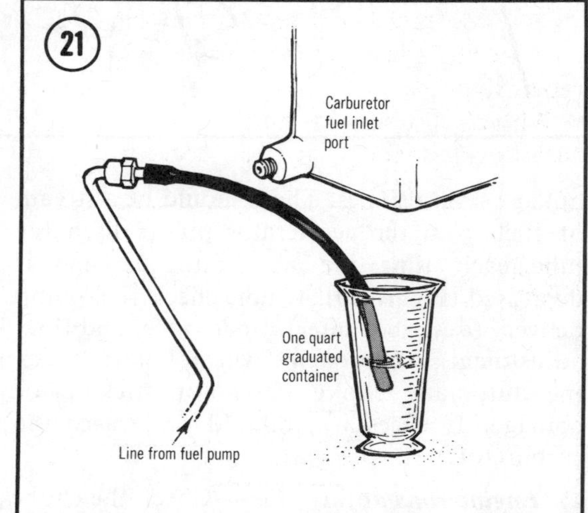

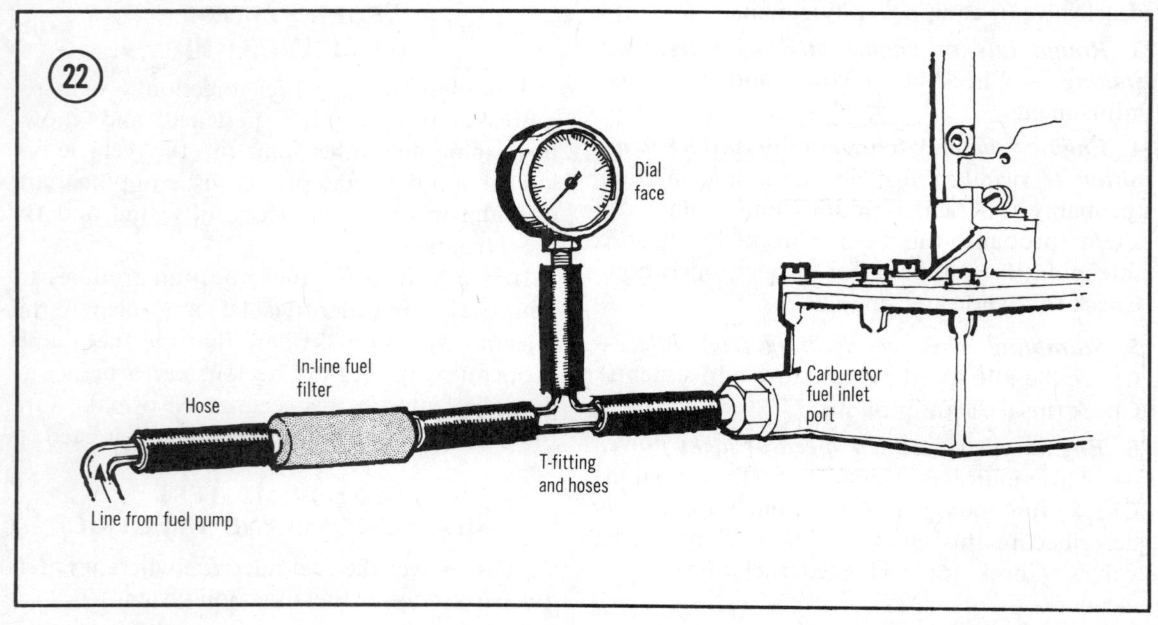

Emission control systems vary considerably from model to model. Individual models contain variations of the four systems described here. In addition, they may include other special systems. Use the index to find specific emission control components in other chapters.

Many of the systems and components are factory set and sealed. Without special expensive test equipment, it is impossible to adjust the systems to meet state and federal requirements.

Troubleshooting can also be difficult without special equipment. The procedures described below will help you find emission control parts which have failed, but repairs may have to be entrusted to a dealer or other properly equipped repair shop.

With the proper equipment, you can test the carbon monoxide and hydrocarbon levels.

Figure 23 provides some sources of trouble if the readings are not correct.

Positive Crankcase Ventilation

Fresh air drawn from the air cleaner housing scavenges emissions (e.g., piston blow-by) from the crankcase, then the intake manifold vacuum draws emissions into the intake manifold. They can then be reburned in the normal combustion process. **Figure 24** shows a typical system. **Figure 25** provides a testing procedure.

Thermostatic Air Cleaner

The thermostatically controlled air cleaner maintains incoming air to the engine at a predetermined level, usually about 100°F or higher. It mixes cold air with heated air from the exhaust manifold region. The air cleaner in-

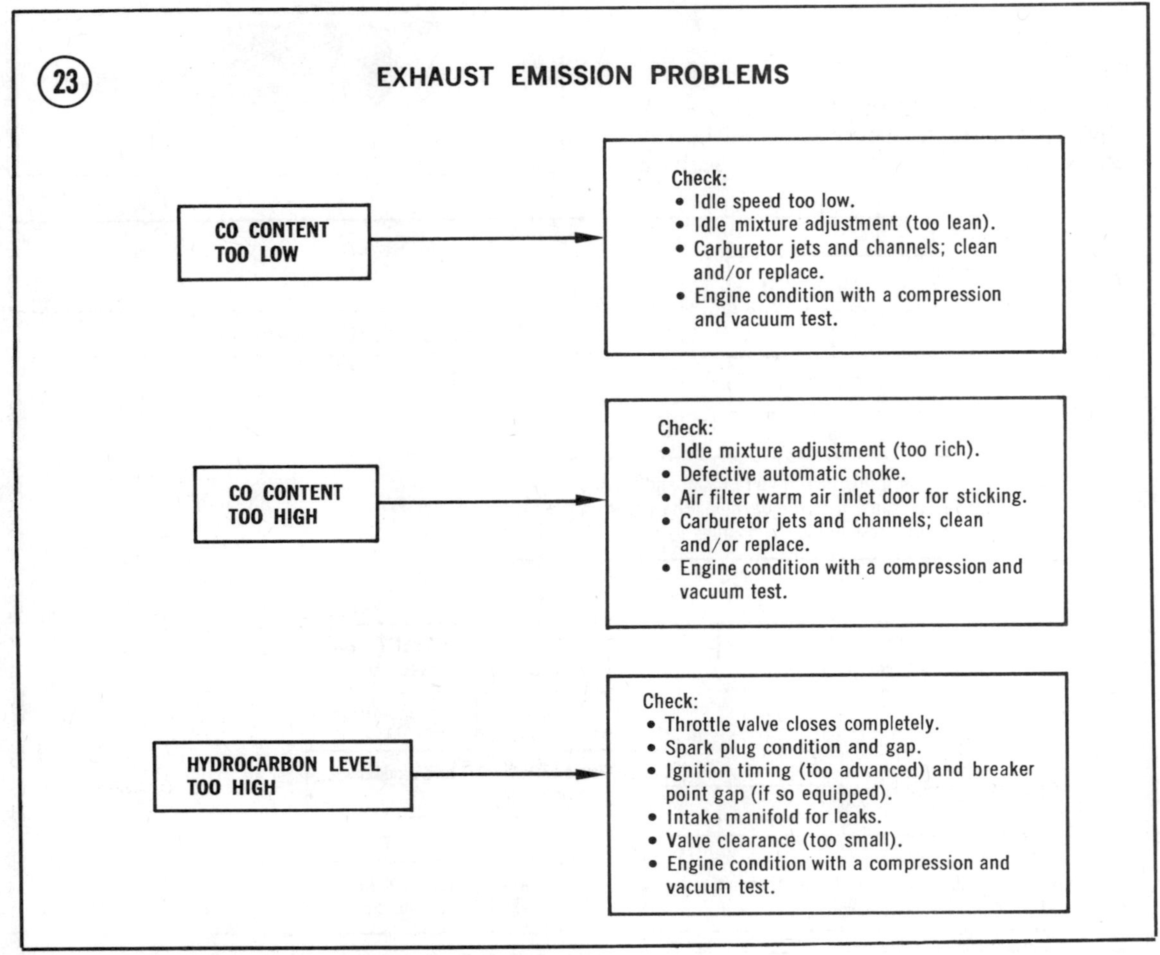

cludes a temperature sensor, vacuum motor, and a hinged door. See **Figure 26**.

The system is comparatively easy to test. See **Figure 27** for the procedure.

Air Injection Reaction System

The air injection reaction system reduces air pollution by oxidizing hydrocarbons and carbon monoxide as they leave the combustion chamber. See **Figure 28**.

The air injection pump, driven by the engine, compresses filtered air and injects it at the exhaust port of each cylinder. The fresh air mixes with the unburned gases in the exhaust and promotes further burning. A check valve prevents exhaust gases from entering and damaging the air pump if the pump becomes inoperative, e.g., from a fan belt failure.

Figure 29 explains the testing procedure for this system.

Fuel Evaporation Control

Fuel vapor from the fuel tank passes through the liquid/vapor separator to the carbon canister. See **Figure 30**. The carbon absorbs and

(24)

(25)

POSITIVE CRANKCASE VENTILATION

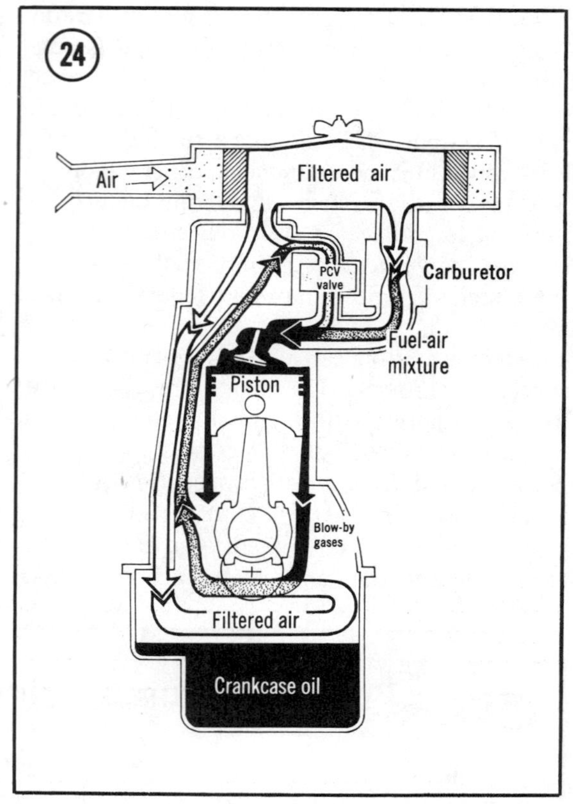

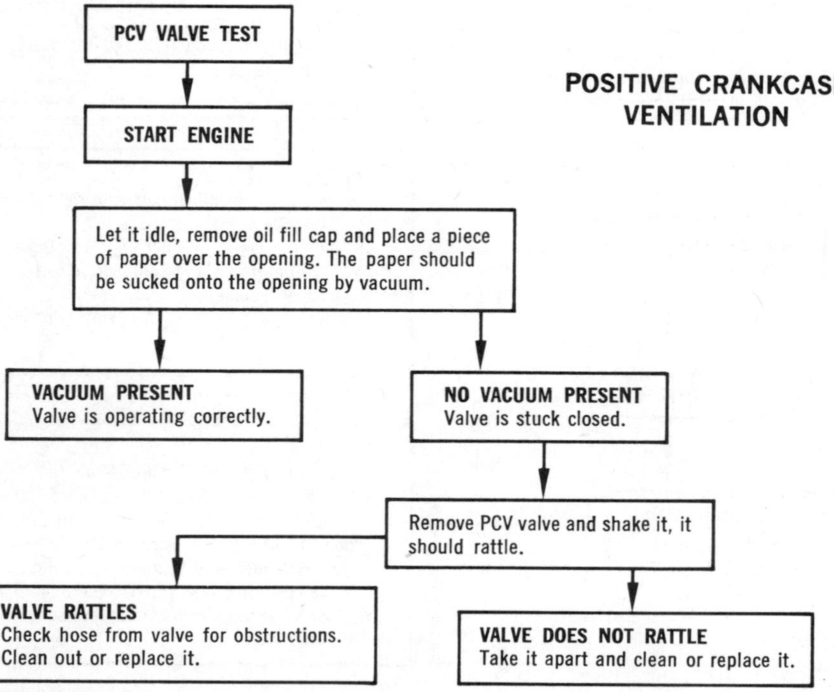

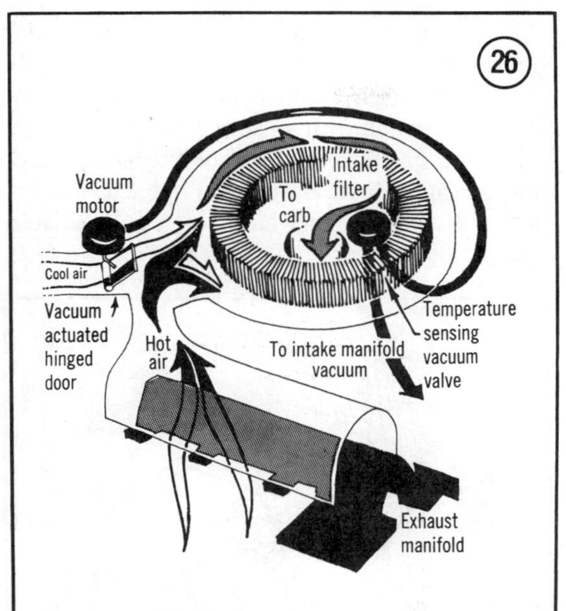
26
Vacuum motor
Intake filter
To carb
Cool air
Vacuum actuated hinged door
Hot air
Temperature sensing vacuum valve
To intake manifold vacuum
Exhaust manifold

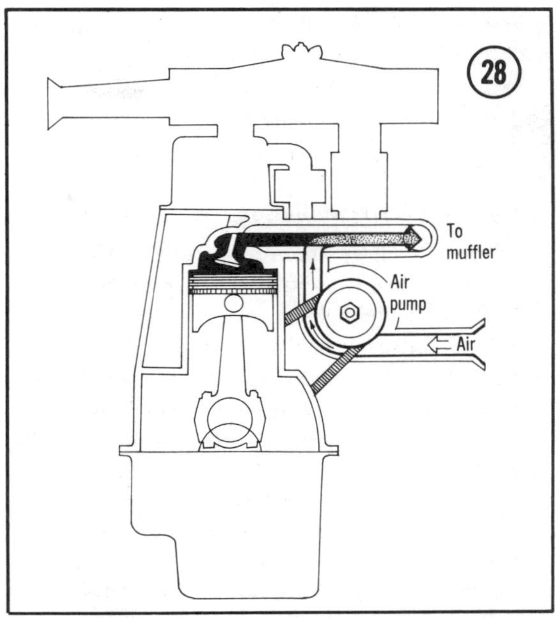
28
To muffler
Air pump
Air

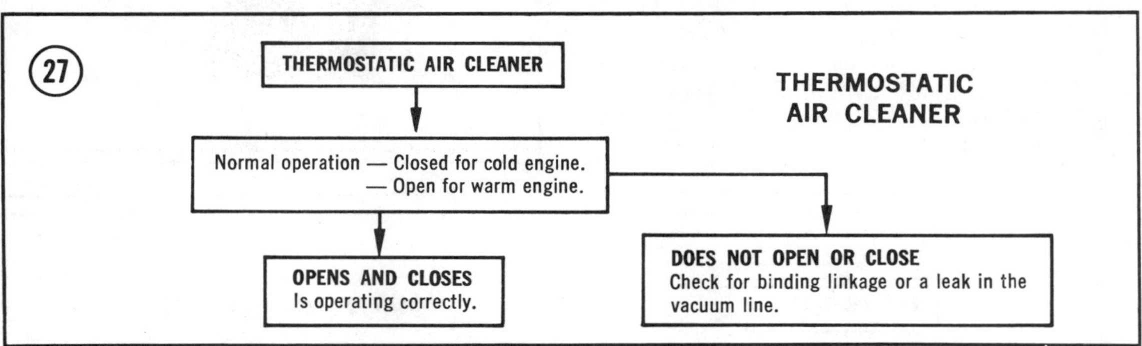
27
THERMOSTATIC AIR CLEANER
THERMOSTATIC AIR CLEANER
Normal operation — Closed for cold engine.
— Open for warm engine.
OPENS AND CLOSES
Is operating correctly.
DOES NOT OPEN OR CLOSE
Check for binding linkage or a leak in the vacuum line.

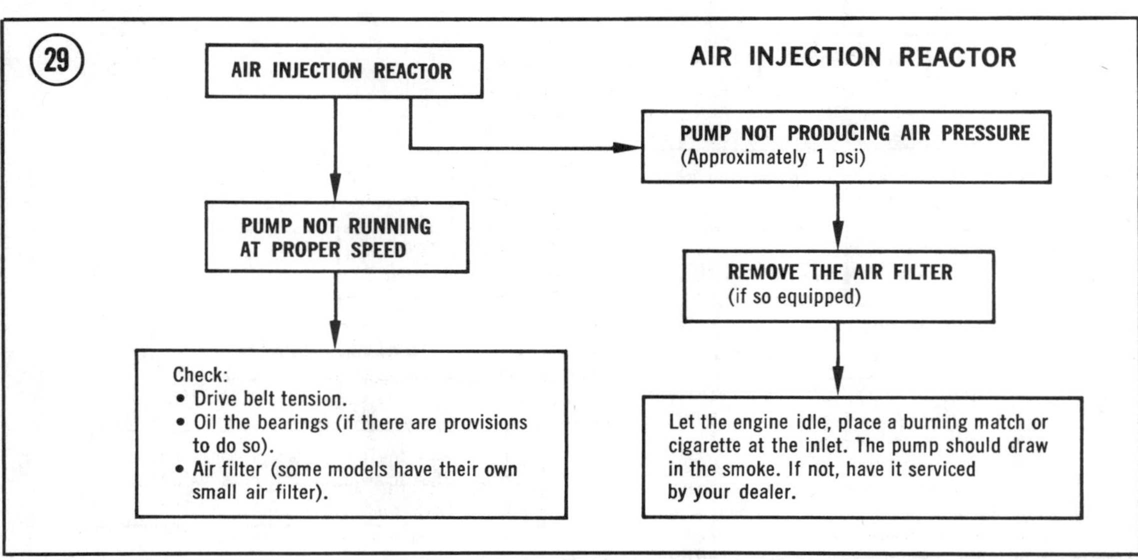
29
AIR INJECTION REACTOR
AIR INJECTION REACTOR
PUMP NOT PRODUCING AIR PRESSURE
(Approximately 1 psi)
PUMP NOT RUNNING AT PROPER SPEED
REMOVE THE AIR FILTER
(if so equipped)
Check:
• Drive belt tension.
• Oil the bearings (if there are provisions to do so).
• Air filter (some models have their own small air filter).
Let the engine idle, place a burning match or cigarette at the inlet. The pump should draw in the smoke. If not, have it serviced by your dealer.

stores the vapor when the engine is stopped. When the engine runs, manifold vacuum draws the vapor from the canister. Instead of being released into the atmosphere, the fuel vapor takes part in the normal combustion process.

Exhaust Gas Recirculation

The exhaust gas recirculation (EGR) system is used to reduce the emission of nitrogen oxides (NOx). Relatively inert exhaust gases are introduced into the combustion process to slightly reduce peak temperatures. This reduction in temperature reduces the formation of NOx.

Figure 31 provides a simple test of this system.

ENGINE NOISES

Often the first evidence of an internal engine trouble is a strange noise. That knocking, clicking, or tapping which you never heard before may be warning you of impending trouble.

While engine noises can indicate problems, they are sometimes difficult to interpret correctly; inexperienced mechanics can be seriously misled by them.

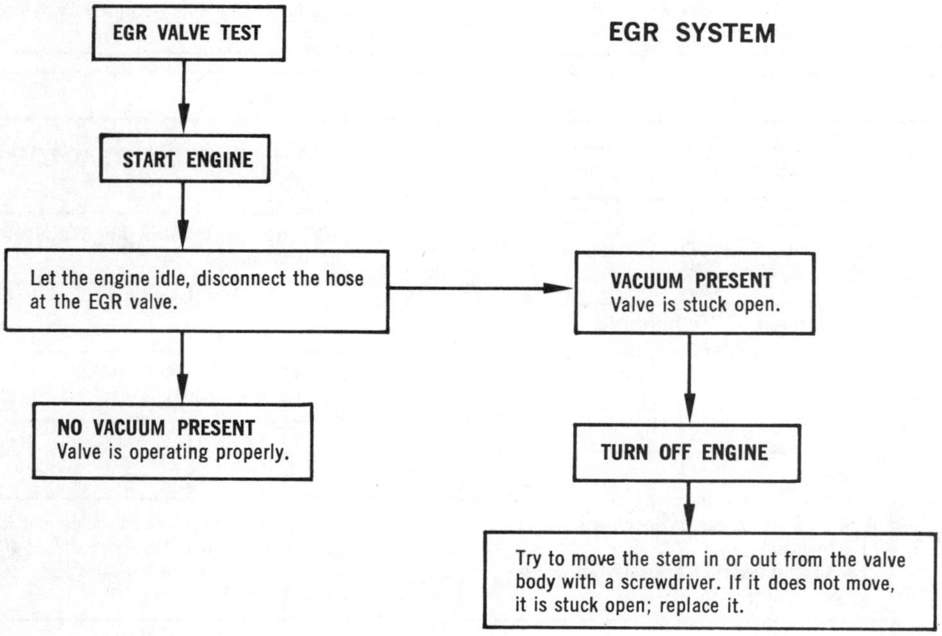

Professional mechanics often use a special stethoscope which looks similar to a doctor's stethoscope for isolating engine noises. You can do nearly as well with a "sounding stick" which can be an ordinary piece of doweling or a section of small hose. By placing one end in contact with the area to which you want to listen and the other end near your ear, you can hear

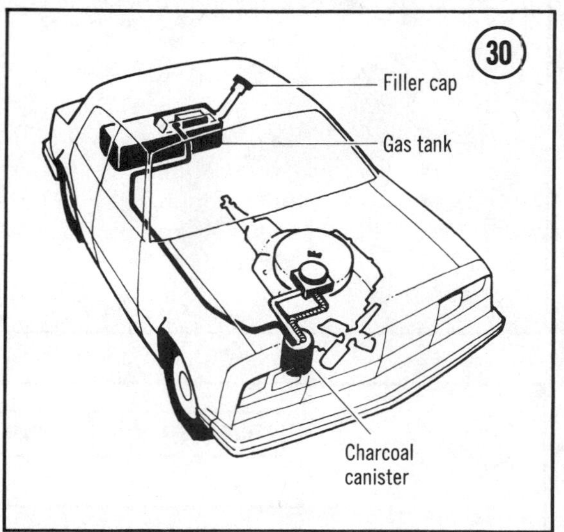

sounds emanating from that area. The first time you do this, you may be horrified at the strange noises coming from even a normal engine. If you can, have an experienced friend or mechanic help you sort the noises out.

Clicking or Tapping Noises

Clicking or tapping noises usually come from the valve train, and indicate excessive valve clearance.

If your vehicle has adjustable valves, the procedure for adjusting the valve clearance is explained in Chapter Three. If your vehicle has hydraulic lifters, the clearance may not be adjustable. The noise may be coming from a collapsed lifter. These may be cleaned or replaced as described in the engine chapter.

A sticking valve may also sound like a valve with excessive clearance. In addition, excessive wear in valve train components can cause similar engine noises.

Knocking Noises

A heavy, dull knocking is usually caused by a worn main bearing. The noise is loudest when the engine is working hard, i.e., accelerating hard at low speed. You may be able to isolate the trouble to a single bearing by disconnecting

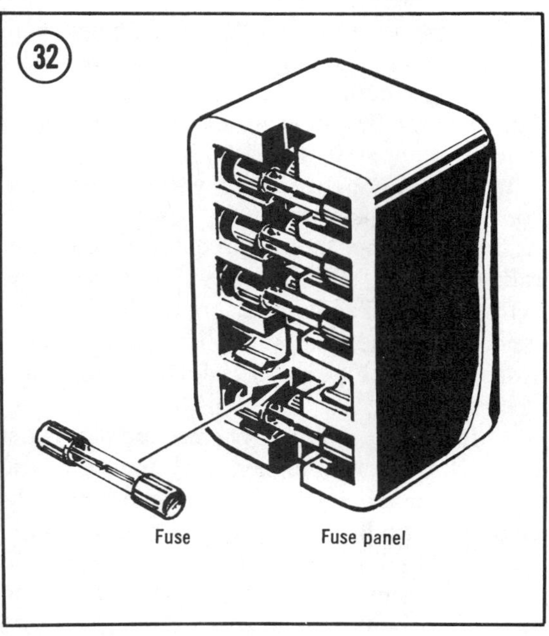

the spark plugs one at a time. When you reach the spark plug nearest the bearing, the knock will be reduced or disappear.

Worn connecting rod bearings may also produce a knock, but the sound is usually more "metallic." As with a main bearing, the noise is worse when accelerating. It may even increase further just as you go from accelerating to coasting. Disconnecting spark plugs will help isolate this knock as well.

A double knock or clicking usually indicates a worn piston pin. Disconnecting spark plugs will isolate this to a particular piston, however, the noise will *increase* when you reach the affected piston.

A loose flywheel and excessive crankshaft end play also produce knocking noises. While similar to main bearing noises, these are usually intermittent, not constant, and they do not change when spark plugs are disconnected.

Some mechanics confuse piston pin noise with piston slap. The double knock will distinguish the piston pin noise. Piston slap is identified by the fact that it is always louder when the engine is cold.

ELECTRICAL ACCESSORIES

Lights and Switches (Interior and Exterior)

1. *Bulb does not light* — Remove the bulb and check for a broken element. Also check the inside of the socket; make sure the contacts are clean and free of corrosion. If the bulb and socket are OK, check to see if a fuse has blown or a circuit breaker has tripped. The fuse panel **(Figure 32)** is usually located under the instrument panel. Replace the blown fuse or reset the circuit breaker. If the fuse blows or the breaker trips again, there is a short in that circuit. Check that circuit all the way to the battery. Look for worn wire insulation or burned wires.

If all the above are all right, check the switch controlling the bulb for continuity with an ohmmeter at the switch terminals. Check the switch contact terminals for loose or dirty electrical connections.

2. *Headlights work but will not switch from either high or low beam* — Check the beam selector switch for continuity with an ohmmeter

at the switch terminals. Check the switch contact terminals for loose or dirty electrical connections.

3. *Brake light switch inoperative* — On mechanically operated switches, usually mounted near the brake pedal arm, adjust the switch to achieve correct mechanical operation. Check the switch for continuity with an ohmmeter at the switch terminals. Check the switch contact terminals for loose or dirty electrical connections.

4. *Back-up lights do not operate* — Check light bulb as described earlier. Locate the switch, normally located near the shift lever. Adjust switch to achieve correct mechanical operation. Check the switch for continuity with an ohmmeter at the switch terminals. Bypass the switch with a jumper wire; if the lights work, replace the switch.

Directional Signals

1. *Directional signals do not operate* — If the indicator light on the instrument panel burns steadily instead of flashing, this usually indicates that one of the exterior lights is burned out. Check all lamps that normally flash. If all are all right, the flasher unit may be defective. Replace it with a good one.

2. *Directional signal indicator light on instrument panel does not light up* — Check the light bulbs as described earlier. Check all electrical connections and check the flasher unit.

3. *Directional signals will not self-cancel* — Check the self-cancelling mechanism located inside the steering column.

4. *Directional signals flash slowly* — Check the condition of the battery and the alternator (or generator) drive belt tension (**Figure 4**). Check the flasher unit and all related electrical connections.

Windshield Wipers

1. *Wipers do not operate* — Check for a blown fuse or circuit breaker that has tripped; replace or reset. Check all related terminals for loose or dirty electrical connections. Check continuity of the control switch with an ohmmeter at the switch terminals. Check the linkage and arms

for loose, broken, or binding parts. Straighten out or replace where necessary.

2. *Wiper motor hums but will not operate* — The motor may be shorted out internally; check and/or replace the motor. Also check for broken or binding linkage and arms.

3. *Wiper arms will not return to the stowed position when turned off* — The motor has a special internal switch for this purpose. Have it inspected by your dealer. Do not attempt this yourself.

Interior Heater

1. *Heater fan does not operate* — Check for a blown fuse or circuit breaker that has tripped. Check the switch for continuity with an ohmmeter at the switch terminals. Check the switch contact terminals for loose or dirty electrical connections.

2. *Heat output is insufficient* — Check the heater hose/engine coolant control valve usually located in the engine compartment; make sure it is in the open position. Ensure that the heater door(s) and cable(s) are operating correctly and are in the open position. Inspect the heat ducts; make sure that they are not crimped or blocked.

COOLING SYSTEM

The temperature gauge or warning light usually signals cooling system troubles before there is any damage. As long as you stop the vehicle at the first indication of trouble, serious damage is unlikely.

In most cases, the trouble will be obvious as soon as you open the hood. If there is coolant or steam leaking, look for a defective radiator, radiator hose, or heater hose. If there is no evidence of leakage, make sure that the fan belt is in good condition. If the trouble is not obvious, refer to **Figures 33 and 34** to help isolate the trouble.

Automotive cooling systems operate under pressure to permit higher operating temperatures without boil-over. The system should be checked periodically to make sure it can withstand normal pressure. **Figure 35** shows the equipment which nearly any service station has for testing the system pressure.

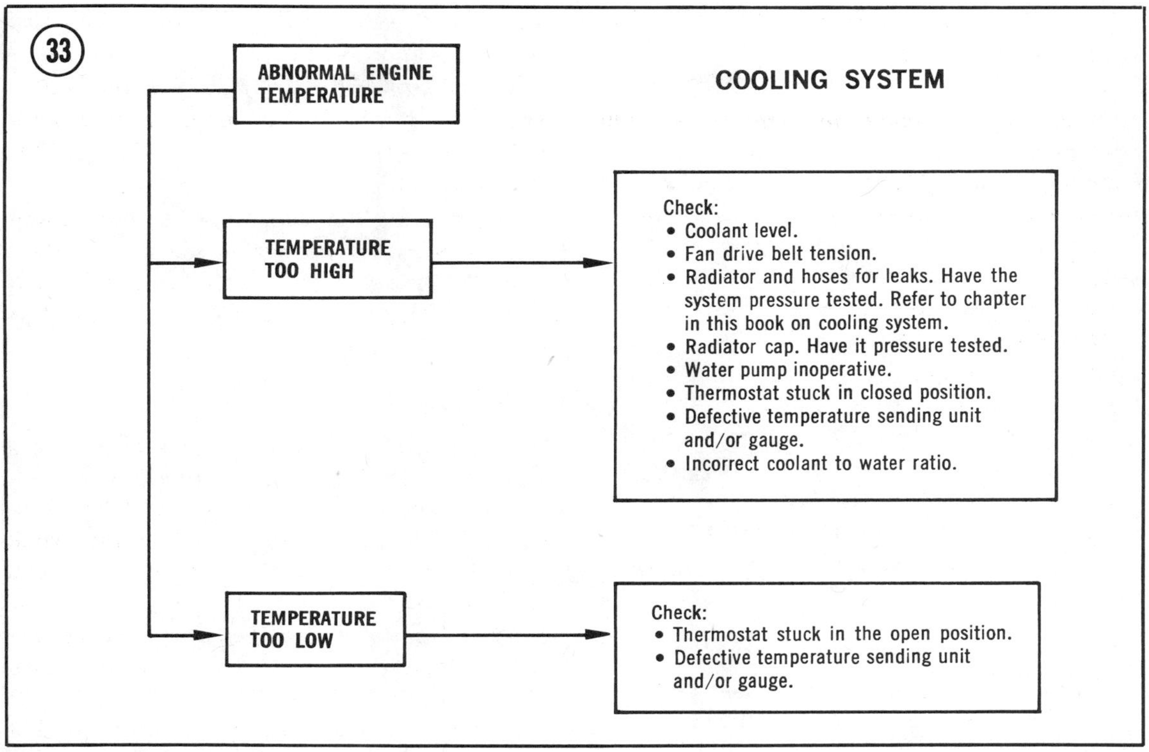

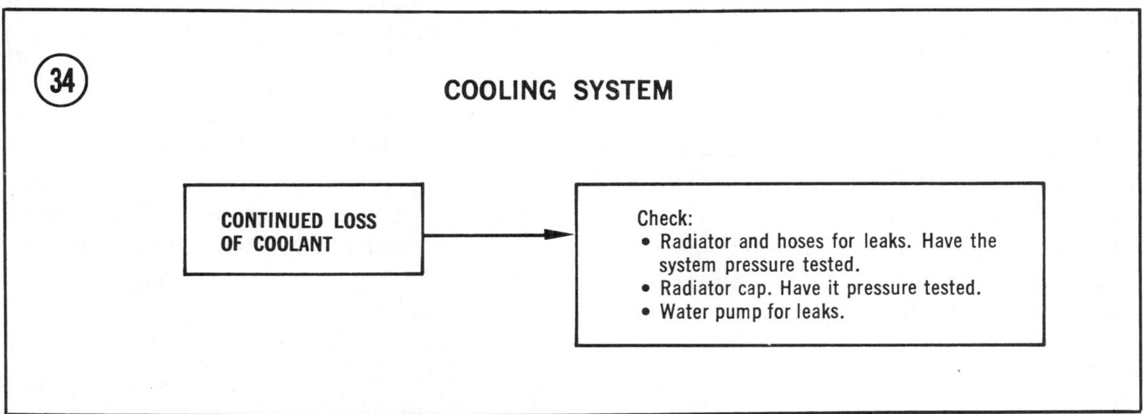

CLUTCH

All clutch troubles except adjustments require transmission removal to identify and cure the problem.

1. *Slippage* — This is most noticeable when accelerating in a high gear at relatively low speed. To check slippage, park the vehicle on a level surface with the handbrake set. Shift to 2nd gear and release the clutch as if driving off. If the clutch is good, the engine will slow and stall. If the clutch slips, continued engine speed will give it away.

Slippage results from insufficient clutch pedal free play, oil or grease on the clutch disc, worn pressure plate, or weak springs.

2. *Drag or failure to release* — This trouble usually causes difficult shifting and gear clash, especially when downshifting. The cause may be excessive clutch pedal free play, warped or bent pressure plate or clutch disc, broken or

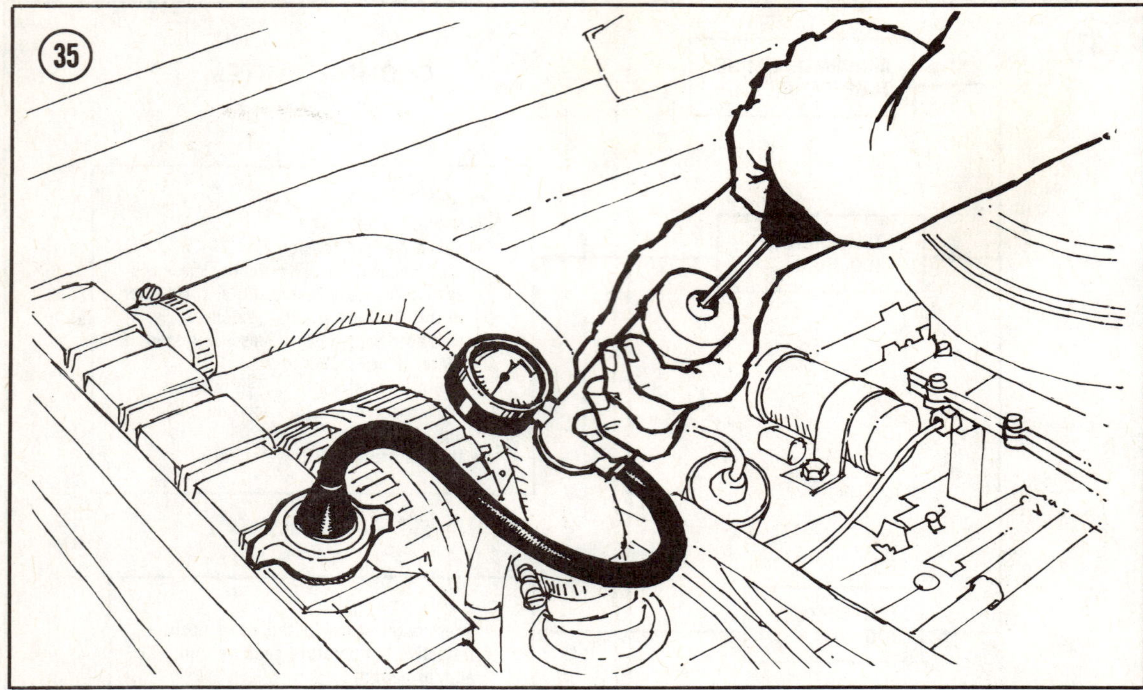

loose linings, or lack of lubrication in pilot bearing. Also check condition of transmission main shaft splines.

3. *Chatter or grabbing* — A number of things can cause this trouble. Check tightness of engine mounts and engine-to-transmission mounting bolts. Check for worn or misaligned pressure plate and misaligned release plate.

4. *Other noises* — Noise usually indicates a dry or defective release or pilot bearing. Check the bearings and replace if necessary. Also check all parts for misalignment and uneven wear.

MANUAL TRANSMISSION/TRANSAXLE

Transmission and transaxle troubles are evident when one or more of the following symptoms appear:

  a. Difficulty changing gears

  b. Gears clash when downshifting

  c. Slipping out of gear

  d. Excessive noise in NEUTRAL

  e. Excessive noise in gear

  f. Oil leaks

Transmission and transaxle repairs are not recommended unless the many special tools required are available.

Transmission and transaxle troubles are sometimes difficult to distinguish from clutch troubles. Eliminate the clutch as a source of trouble before installing a new or rebuilt transmission or transaxle.

AUTOMATIC TRANSMISSION

Most automatic transmission repairs require considerable specialized knowledge and tools. It is impractical for the home mechanic to invest in the tools, since they cost more than a properly rebuilt transmission.

Check fluid level and condition frequently to help prevent future problems. If the fluid is orange or black in color or smells like varnish, it is an indication of some type of damage or failure within the transmission. Have the transmission serviced by your dealer or competent automatic transmission service facility.

BRAKES

Good brakes are vital to the safe operation of the vehicle. Performing the maintenance speci-

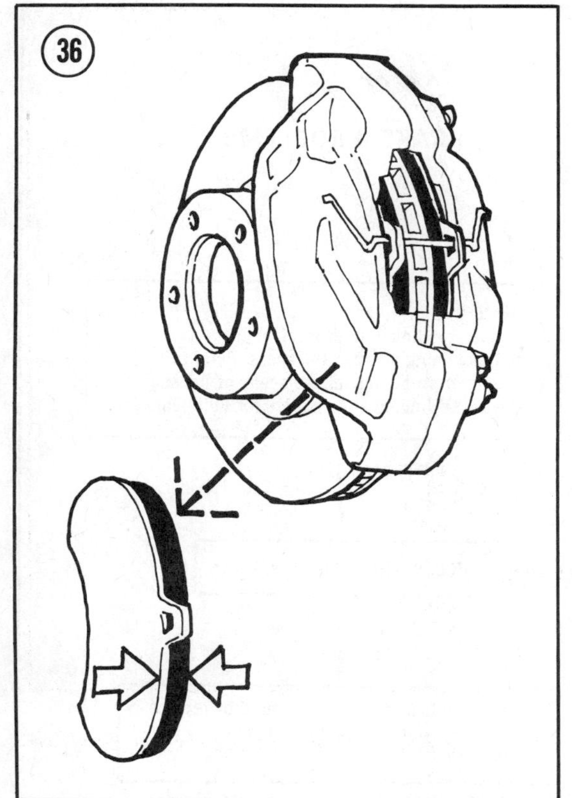

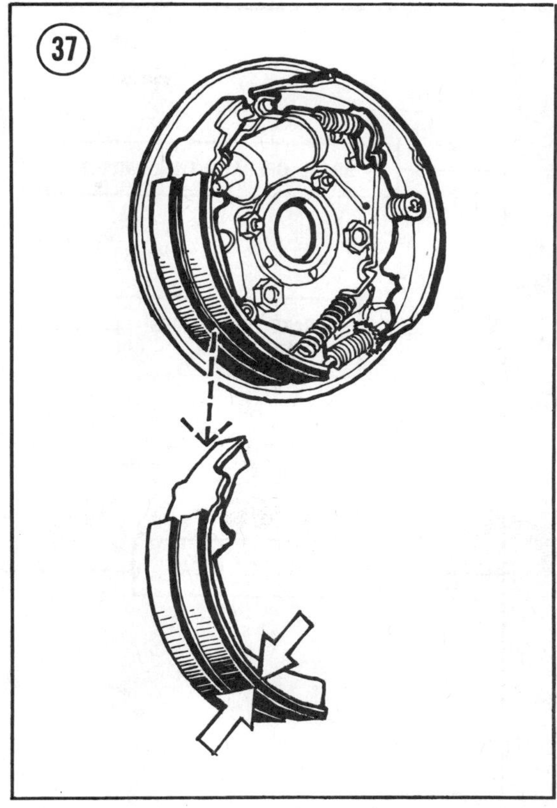

fied in Chapter Three will minimize problems with the brakes. Most importantly, check and maintain the level of fluid in the master cylinder, and check the thickness of the linings on the disc brake pads (**Figure 36**) or drum brake shoes (**Figure 37**).

If trouble develops, **Figures 38 through 40** will help you locate the problem. Refer to the brake chapter for actual repair procedures.

STEERING AND SUSPENSION

Trouble in the suspension or steering is evident when the following occur:

   a. Steering is hard

   b. Car pulls to one side

   c. Car wanders or front wheels wobble

   d. Steering has excessive play

   e. Tire wear is abnormal

Unusual steering, pulling, or wandering is usually caused by bent or otherwise misaligned suspension parts. This is difficult to check without proper alignment equipment. Refer to the suspension chapter in this book for repairs that you can perform and those that must be left to a dealer or suspension specialist.

If your trouble seems to be excessive play, check wheel bearing adjustment first. This is the most frequent cause. Then check ball-joints (refer to Suspension chapter). Finally, check tie rod end ball-joints by shaking each tie rod. Also check steering gear, or rack-and-pinion assembly to see that it is securely bolted down.

TIRE WEAR ANALYSIS

Abnormal tire wear should be analyzed to determine its causes. The most common causes are the following:

   a. Incorrect tire pressure

   b. Improper driving

   c. Overloading

   d. Bad road surfaces

   e. Incorrect wheel alignment

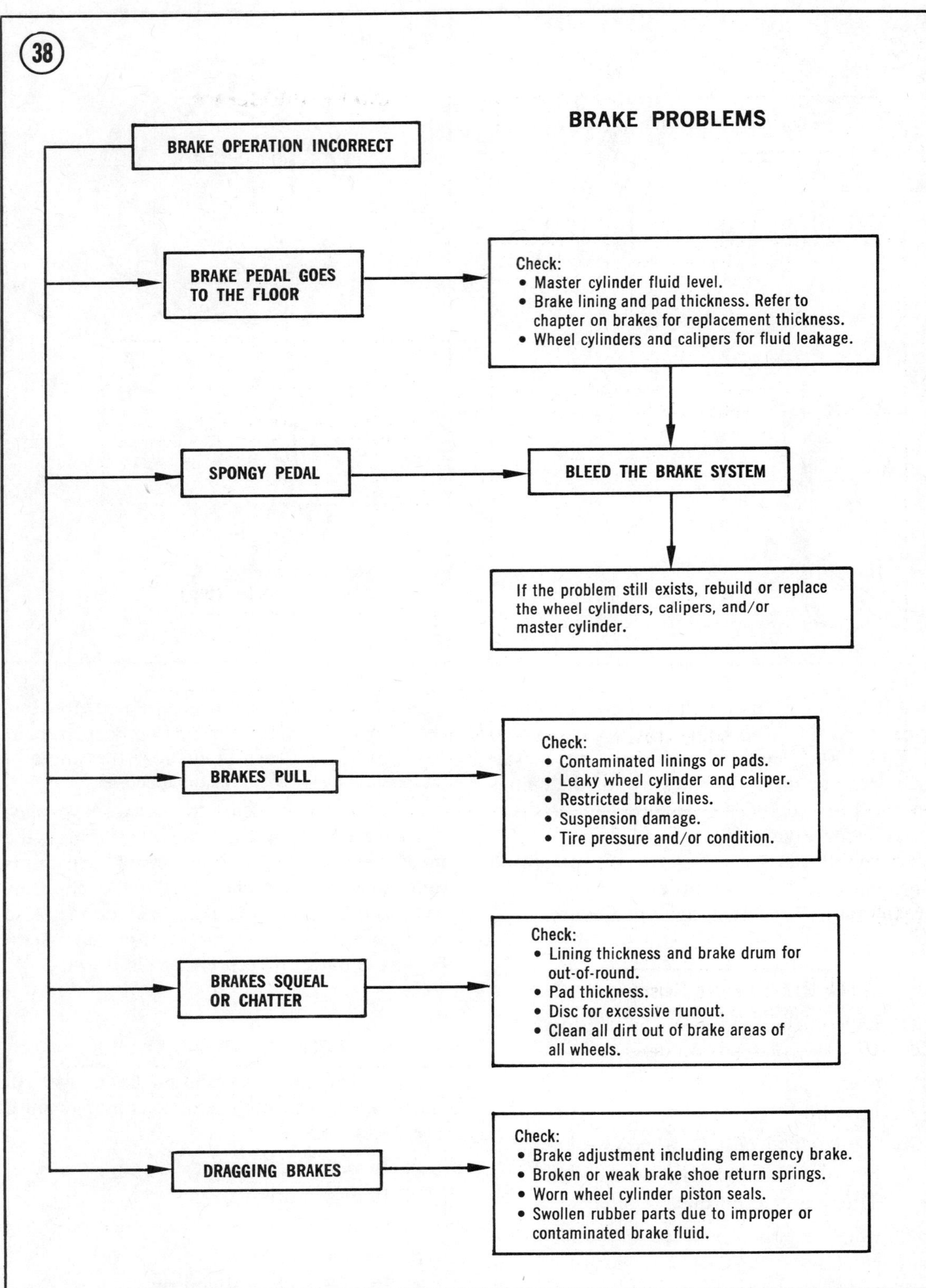
38
BRAKE PROBLEMS
BRAKE OPERATION INCORRECT
BRAKE PEDAL GOES TO THE FLOOR
Check:
• Master cylinder fluid level.
• Brake lining and pad thickness. Refer to chapter on brakes for replacement thickness.
• Wheel cylinders and calipers for fluid leakage.
SPONGY PEDAL
BLEED THE BRAKE SYSTEM
If the problem still exists, rebuild or replace the wheel cylinders, calipers, and/or master cylinder.
BRAKES PULL
Check:
• Contaminated linings or pads.
• Leaky wheel cylinder and caliper.
• Restricted brake lines.
• Suspension damage.
• Tire pressure and/or condition.
BRAKES SQUEAL OR CHATTER
Check:
• Lining thickness and brake drum for out-of-round.
• Pad thickness.
• Disc for excessive runout.
• Clean all dirt out of brake areas of all wheels.
DRAGGING BRAKES
Check:
• Brake adjustment including emergency brake.
• Broken or weak brake shoe return springs.
• Worn wheel cylinder piston seals.
• Swollen rubber parts due to improper or contaminated brake fluid.

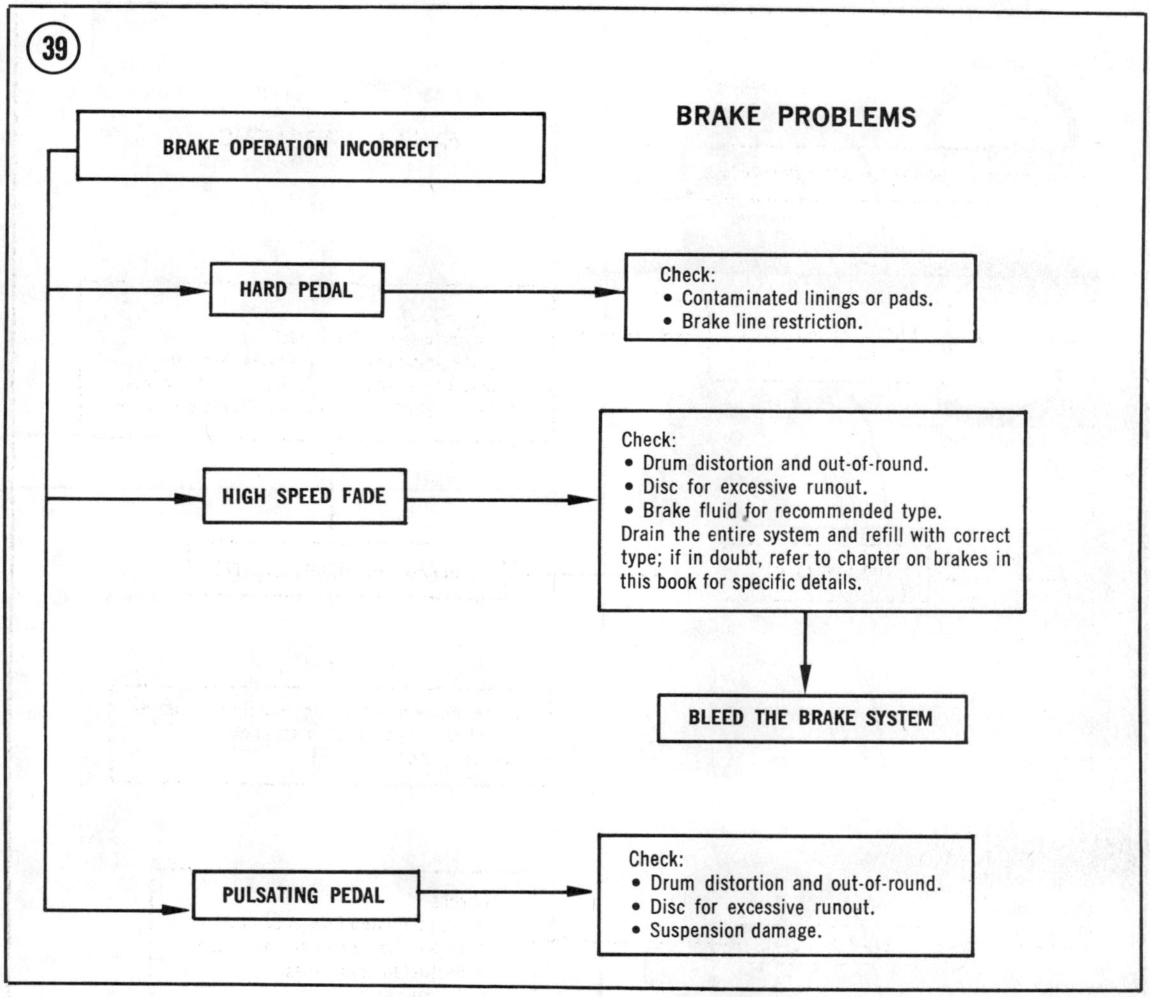

39

BRAKE PROBLEMS

2

BRAKE OPERATION INCORRECT

HARD PEDAL → Check:
- Contaminated linings or pads.
- Brake line restriction.

HIGH SPEED FADE → Check:
- Drum distortion and out-of-round.
- Disc for excessive runout.
- Brake fluid for recommended type.

Drain the entire system and refill with correct type; if in doubt, refer to chapter on brakes in this book for specific details.

↓

BLEED THE BRAKE SYSTEM

PULSATING PEDAL → Check:
- Drum distortion and out-of-round.
- Disc for excessive runout.
- Suspension damage.

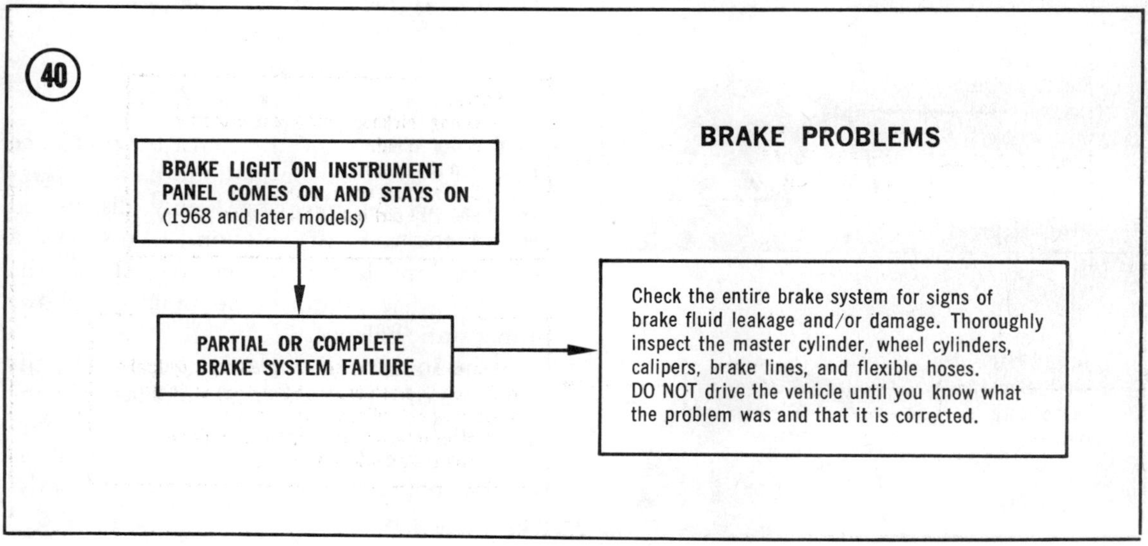

40

BRAKE PROBLEMS

BRAKE LIGHT ON INSTRUMENT PANEL COMES ON AND STAYS ON
(1968 and later models)

↓

PARTIAL OR COMPLETE BRAKE SYSTEM FAILURE → Check the entire brake system for signs of brake fluid leakage and/or damage. Thoroughly inspect the master cylinder, wheel cylinders, calipers, brake lines, and flexible hoses.
DO NOT drive the vehicle until you know what the problem was and that it is corrected.

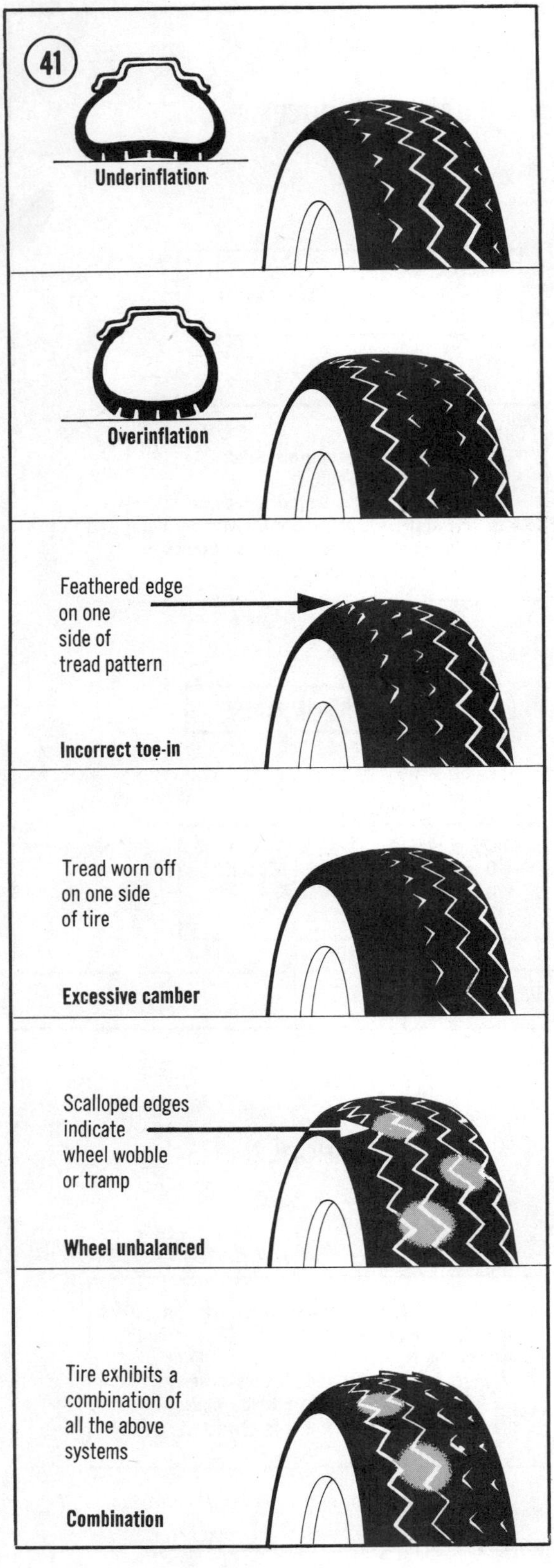

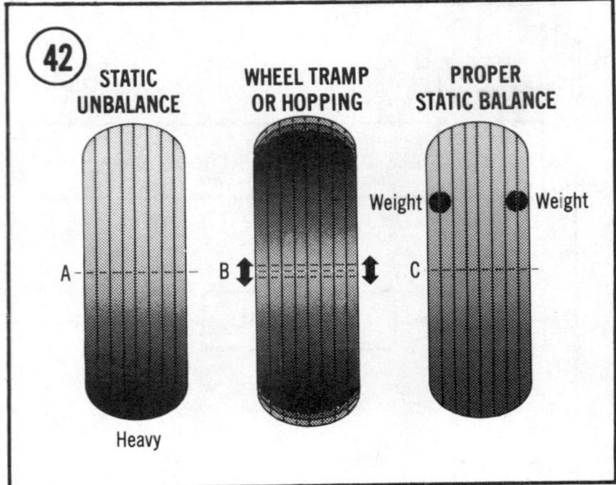

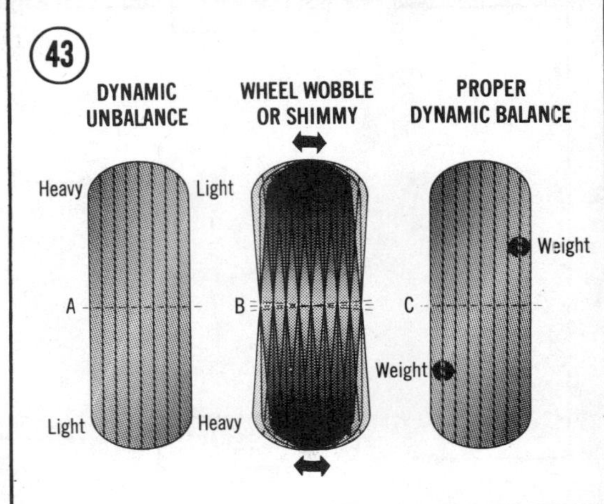

Figure 41 identifies wear patterns and indicates the most probable causes.

WHEEL BALANCING

All four wheels and tires must be in balance along two axes. To be in static balance (**Figure 42**), weight must be evenly distributed around the axis of rotation. (A) shows a statically unbalanced wheel; (B) shows the result — wheel tramp or hopping; (C) shows proper static balance.

To be in dynamic balance (**Figure 43**), the centerline of the weight must coincide with the centerline of the wheel. (A) shows a dynamically unbalanced wheel; (B) shows the result — wheel wobble or shimmy; (C) shows proper dynamic balance.

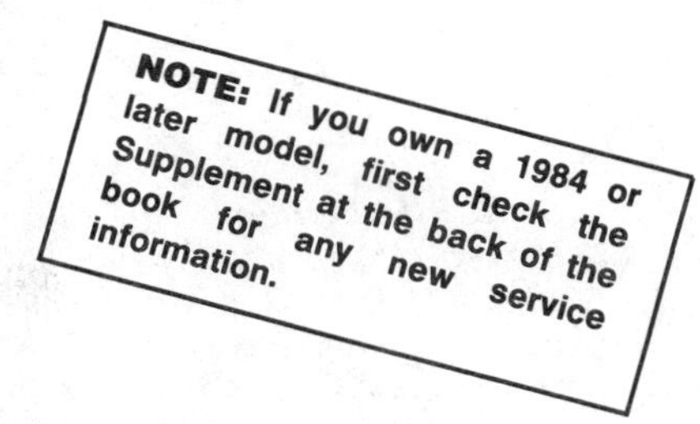

CHAPTER THREE

3

LUBRICATION, MAINTENANCE AND TUNE-UP

This chapter deals with the maintenance necessary to keep your car running properly. **Table 1** lists checks which should be done at each fuel stop. **Table 2** lists gasoline engine maintenance intervals as well as chassis and body maintenance intervals for all models. **Table 3** lists diesel engine maintenance intervals. Some procedures are done at fuel stops, while others are done at specified intervals of miles or time.

The service schedules are intended for cars given normal use. More frequent service is required under the following conditions:
   a. Stop-and-go driving.
   b. Constant high-speed driving.
   c. Severe dust.
   d. Rough or salted roads.
   e. Very hot, very cold or rainy weather.
Maintenance intervals for severe service conditions are listed in **Table 4**.

General maintenance items are those for which the manufacturer does not recommend specific intervals of miles or time but which should be done periodically, such as when washing the car or before a trip. These are listed in **Table 5**.

Some maintenance procedures are included under *Tune-Up* in this chapter and detailed instructions will be found there. Other steps are described in various chapters. Chapter references are included with these steps.

Tables 1-11 are at the end of the chapter.

FUEL STOP CHECKS

1. With the engine off, pull out the dipstick. See **Figure 1** (gasoline) or **Figure 2** (diesel). Wipe it with a clean rag, insert it and pull it out again. Check oil level and top up to the "H" mark on the dipstick if necessary, using a grade recommended in **Table 6** and **Table 7**. Add oil through the hole in the rocker arm cover. See **Figure 3** (gasoline) or **Figure 4** (diesel).
2. Check coolant level in the reservoir tank (**Figure 5**). It should be between the "MAX" and "MIN" marks. Top up if necessary.

> *NOTE*
> *If the cooling system requires frequent topping up, there is a leak. If you can't find it with a visual inspection, have the system pressure tested by a service station or radiator shop.*

> *WARNING*
> *The engine should be cold for the next step. The radiator cap should not be removed when the engine is warm or*

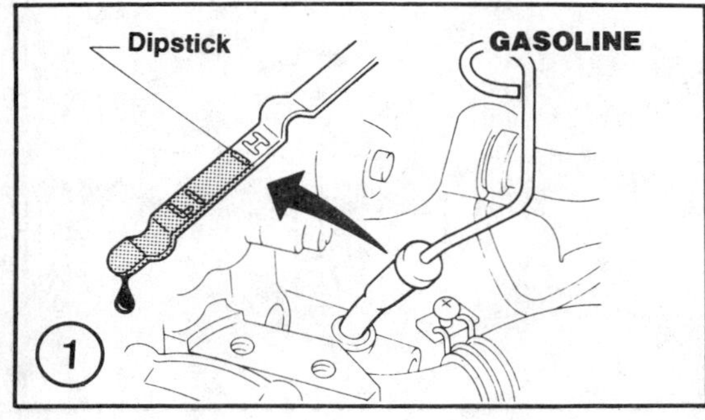

*hot. If this is unavoidable, cover the cap with a thick rag. Turn it slowly counterclockwise against the first stop (about 1/4 turn). Let **all** pressure (hot water and steam) escape. Then press the cap down and turn counter-clockwise to remove. If the cap is removed too soon, a fountain of scalding coolant may shoot out of the radiator, bounce off the hood and spray all over you.*

3. If the reservoir tank is completely empty, remove the radiator cap. See **Figure 6** (gasoline) or **Figure 7** (diesel). Fill the radiator to the top with a 50/50 mixture of ethylene glycol-based antifreeze and water.

WARNING
During the next step, keep all heat sources (such as lighted cigarettes) away from the battery. Batteries give off explosive hydrogen gas. If this ignites, the battery may explode and spray acid.

4. Check battery condition:
   a. Most models are equipped with maintenance-free batteries. To check this type, look at the indicator (**Figure 8**). If it is blue, the battery is okay. If it is transparent, the battery needs to be recharged.
   b. Some MPG models use an unsealed battery. To check this type, remove the battery filler

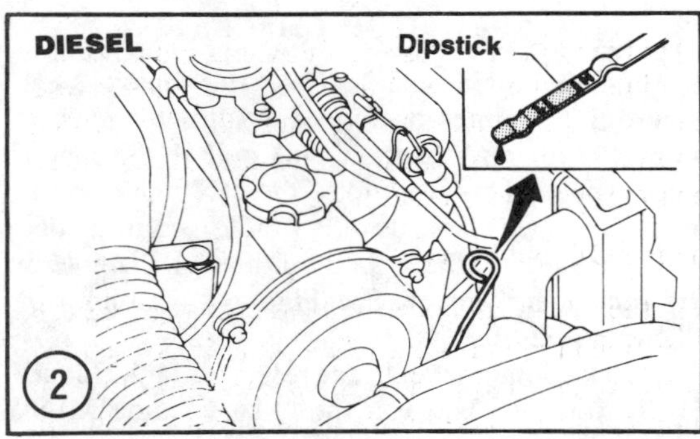

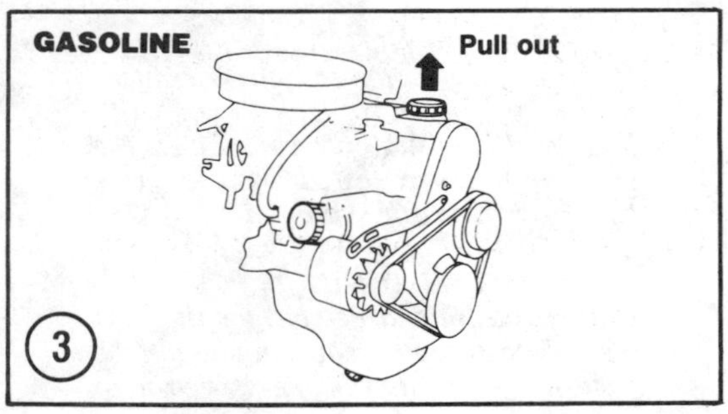

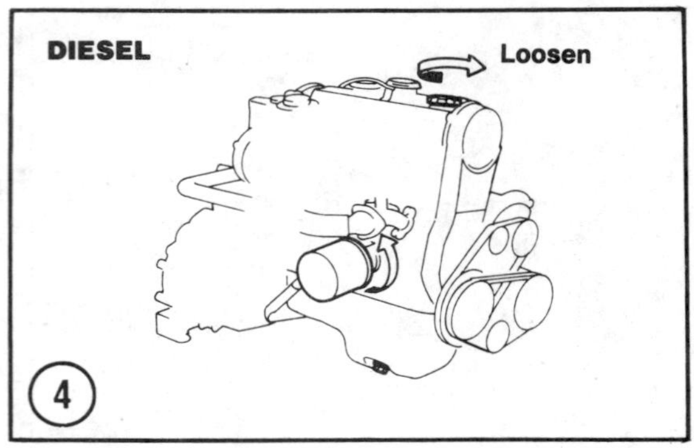

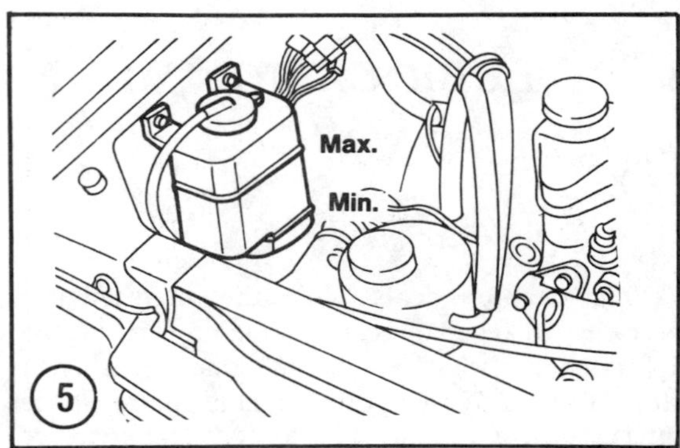

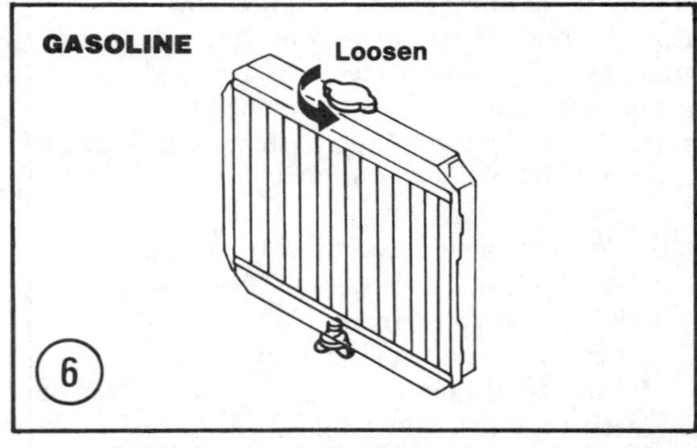

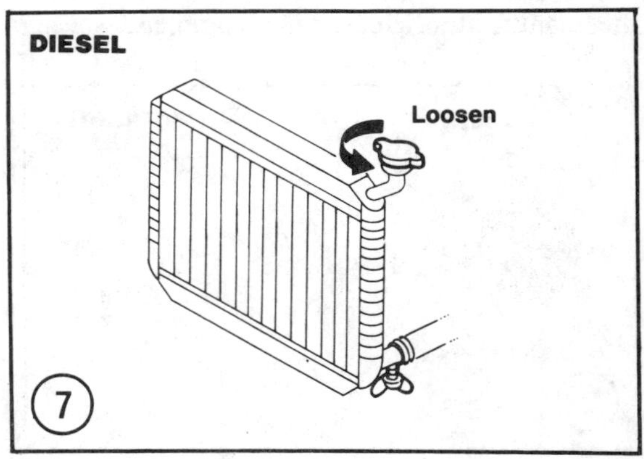

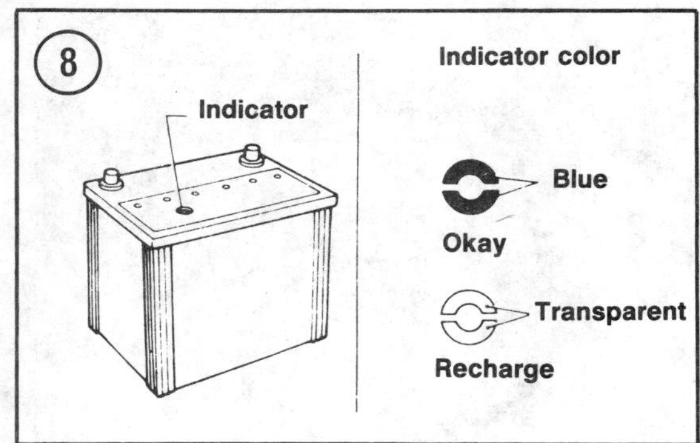

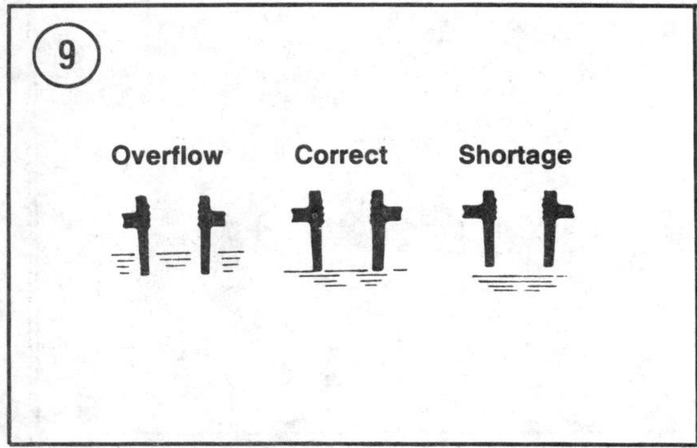

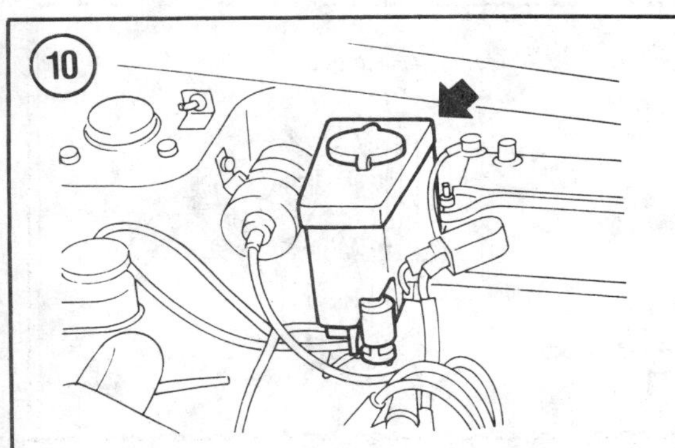

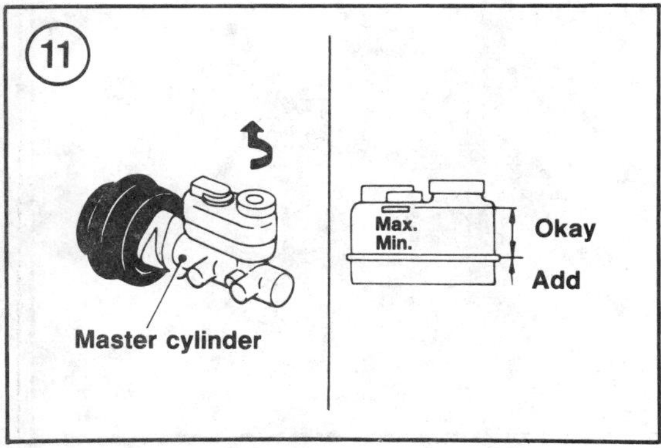

caps and check electrolyte level. See **Figure 9**. It should be up to the bottom of the wells as shown. Top up with distilled water if necessary. Do not overfill. Do not add electrolyte to a battery in service.

5. Check fluid in the windshield washer tank. See **Figure 10**. It should be kept full. Use windshield washer solvent, following the manufacturer's instructions.

> *CAUTION*
> *Do not use radiator antifreeze in the washer tank. The runoff may damage the car's paint.*

6. Check fluid level in the brake master cylinder (**Figure 11**). Since the reservoir is translucent, this can be done at a glance. Fluid should be up to the MAX line. If low, top up with brake fluid marked DOT 3 or DOT 4.

> *CAUTION*
> *Do not remove the reservoir cap unless topping up fluid. Clean the area around the cap before removal.*

7. Check tire pressures (**Table 8**). This should be done when the tires are cold (after driving less than one mile). When the tires heat up from driving, the air in them expands and gives false high-pressure readings.

SCHEDULED MAINTENANCE

This section includes scheduled maintenance for gasoline engines as well as scheduled chassis and body maintenance for all models. Scheduled maintenance for diesel engines is covered separately in this chapter.

Engine Oil and Filter

If the car is given normal use, change the oil when recommended in **Table 2**. If it is used for stop-and-go driving, in dusty areas, left idling for long periods or used to tow a trailer, change the oil when recommended in **Table 4**.

Use an oil recommended in **Table 6** and **Table 7**. The rating (SE or SF) is usually printed on top of the can (**Figure 12**).

To drain the oil and change the filter, you will need:

a. Drain pan.
b. Oil can spout or can opener and funnel.
c. Filter wrench.
d. Drain plug wrench.
e. 5 quarts of oil.
f. Oil filter.

There are several ways to discard the old oil safely. The easiest is to pour it from the drain pan into a gallon bleach or milk bottle. The oil can be taken to a service station for recycling or, where permitted, thrown in your household trash.

1. Warm the engine to operating temperature, then shut it off.

> **WARNING**
> *During the next step, move your hand away quickly once the drain plug is loose. Otherwise, hot oil may run down your arm.*

2. Put the drain pan under the drain plug (**Figure 13**). Remove the plug and let the oil drain for at least 10 minutes.
3. Unscrew the oil filter (**Figure 13**) counterclockwise. Use a filter wrench if the filter is too tight to remove by hand.
4. Wipe the gasket surface on the engine block clean with a lint-free cloth.
5. Coat the neoprene gasket on the new filter with clean engine oil. See **Figure 14**.
6. Screw the filter onto the engine *by hand* until the gasket just touches the engine block. At this point, there will be a very slight resistance when turning the filter.
7. Tighten the filter 1/2 turn more *by hand*. If the filter wrench is used, the filter will probably be overtightened. This will cause an oil leak.
8. Install the oil pan drain plug. Tighten it securely.
9. Remove the oil filler cap (**Figure 13**).
10. Pour oil into the engine. Capacity is listed in **Table 9**.
11. Start the engine and let it idle. The instrument panel oil pressure light will remain on for 15-30 seconds, then go out.

> **CAUTION**
> *Do not race the engine to make the oil pressure light go out. It takes time for the oil to reach all areas of the engine and racing it could damage dry parts.*

12. While the engine is running, check the drain plug and oil filter for leaks.
13. Turn the engine off. Let the oil settle for several minutes, then check the level on the dipstick (**Figure 15**). Add oil if necessary to bring the level up to the "H" mark, but *do not* overfill.

Brake Inspection

1. Check brake pads for wear and check calipers for leaks as described in Chapter Eleven.

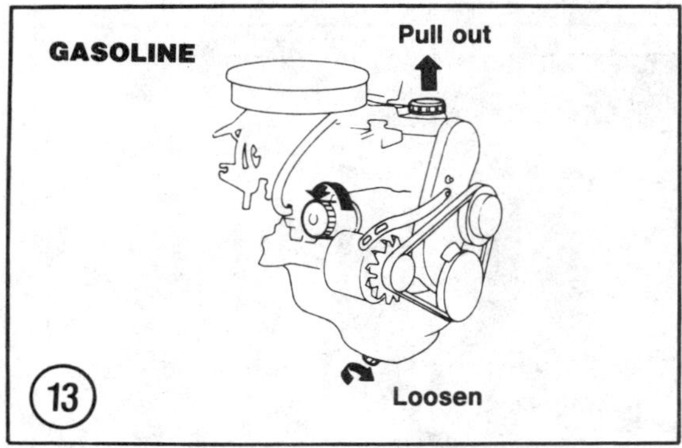

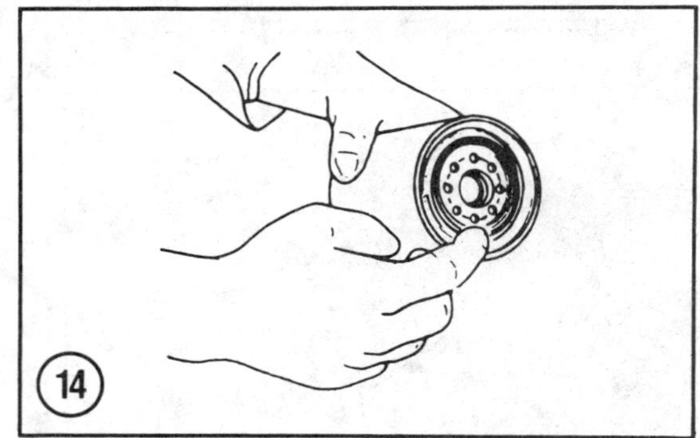

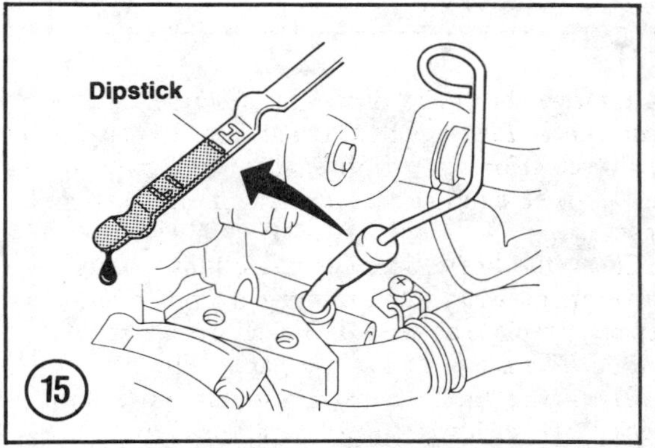

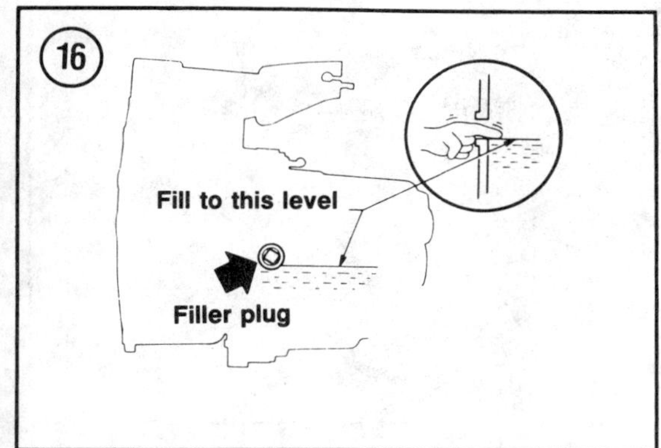

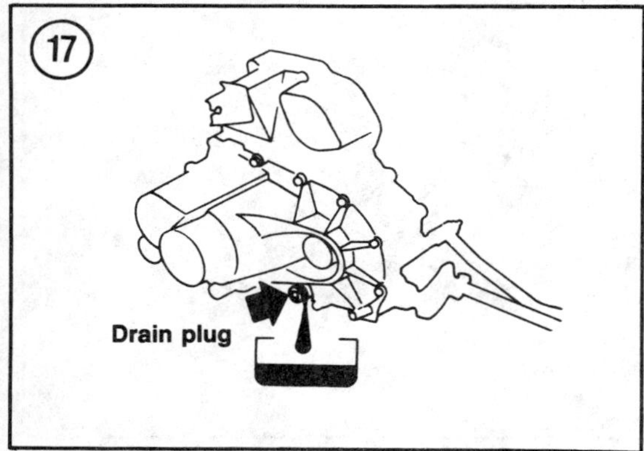

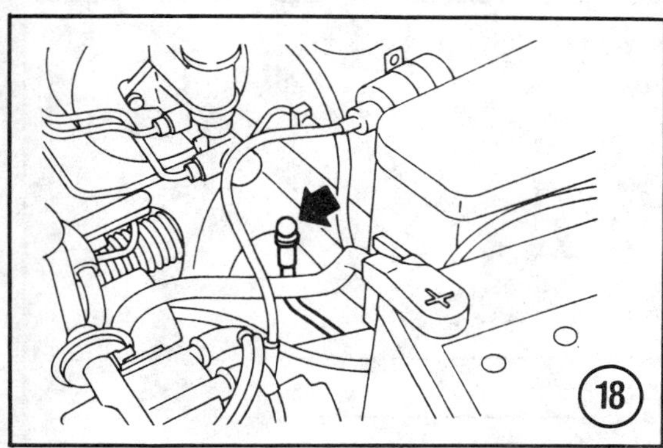

Manual Transaxle Oil Check

1. Park the car on a level surface.
2. With the engine off, remove the filler plug from the side of the transaxle. See **Figure 16**. Oil should be up to the bottom of the filler hole. Top up if necessary with an oil recommended in **Table 6** and **Table 7**.

Manual Transaxle Oil Change

1. Drive the car until the engine warms to normal operating temperature. This warms the transaxle oil.
2. Park the car on a level surface.
3. Place a pan beneath the transaxle drain plug.
4. Remove the transaxle drain plug (**Figure 17**). Let the oil drain for at least 10 minutes, then reinstall the plug.
5. Remove the filler plug (**Figure 16**). Fill the transaxle with an oil recommended in **Table 6** and **Table 7**. Capacity is listed in **Table 9**. Oil level should be up to the bottom of the filler hole.
6. Reinstall the filler plug. Drive the car a short distance, then check the transaxle for oil leaks.

Automatic Transaxle Fluid Check

1. Warm the engine to normal operating temperature, then drive the car for approximately 5 minutes in stop-and-go conditions. This warms the transaxle fluid.

> *NOTE*
> *If it is not possible to drive the car, the fluid level can be check on the dipstick's "COLD" scale after warming up the engine. However, it must be rechecked on the dipstick's "HOT" scale to ensure accuracy.*

> *NOTE*
> *If the car has been driven for a long distance at high speeds, in stop-and-go traffic during hot weather or is pulling a trailer, it will not be possible to obtain an accurate fluid level reading. Let the fluid cool for approximately 30 minutes before checking the level.*

2. Move the shift lever from PARK through all the gear positions, then back to PARK.
3. With the engine idling, remove the dipstick (**Figure 18**). Check fluid level on the dipstick scale (**Figure 19**).
4. If the level is low, add fluid through the dipstick tube (**Figure 20**). Use Dexron type automatic transmission fluid. Do not use any other type.

2. Remove the brake drums as described under *Rear Wheel Bearings* in Chapter Ten. Check the rear brakes for worn linings, damaged parts or leaky wheel cylinders as described in Chapter Eleven.
3. Check the brake lines for leaks, kinks, cracks, corrosion or wear from rubbing on other parts. Repair or replace as needed. Brake lines are shown in the *Brake Lines* section of Chapter Eleven.
4. Check the brake booster vacuum hose and check valve as described in Chapter Eleven.

> *CAUTION*
> *Do not overfill the transaxle. Overfilling can cause the fluid to foam, resulting in wear or damage.*

Automatic Transaxle Fluid Change

1. Warm the engine to normal operating temperature, then drive the car for approximately 5 minutes in stop-and-go conditions. This warms the transaxle fluid.

2. Park the car on a level surface.

3. Place a pan of at least 8 qt. capacity beneath the transaxle, then remove the drain plug (**Figure 21**).

4. Let the transaxle drain for 10 minutes or more, then reinstall the drain plug.

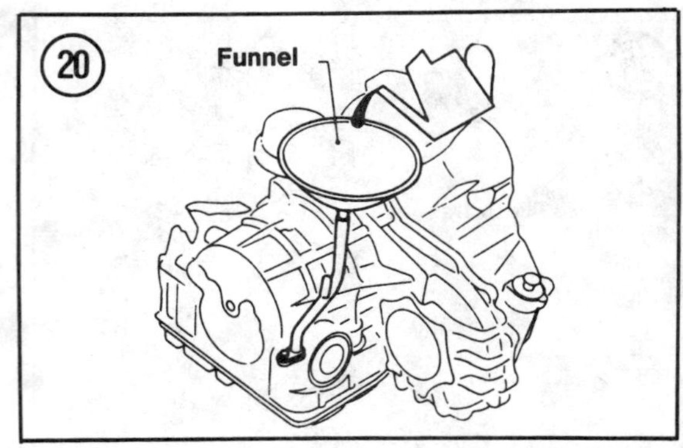

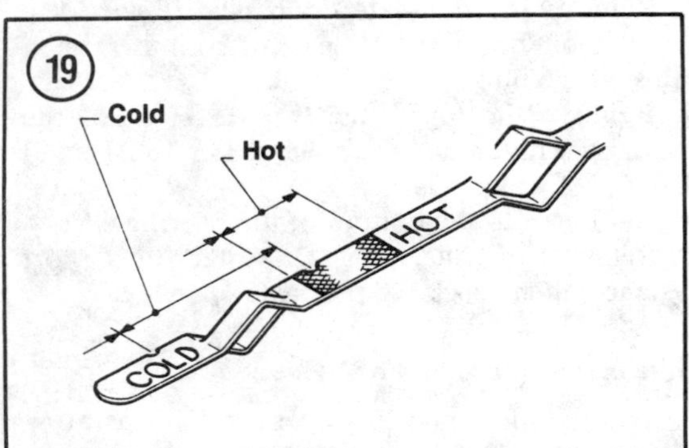

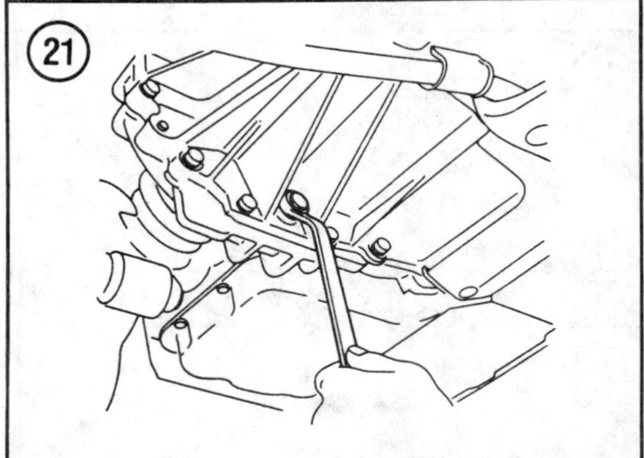

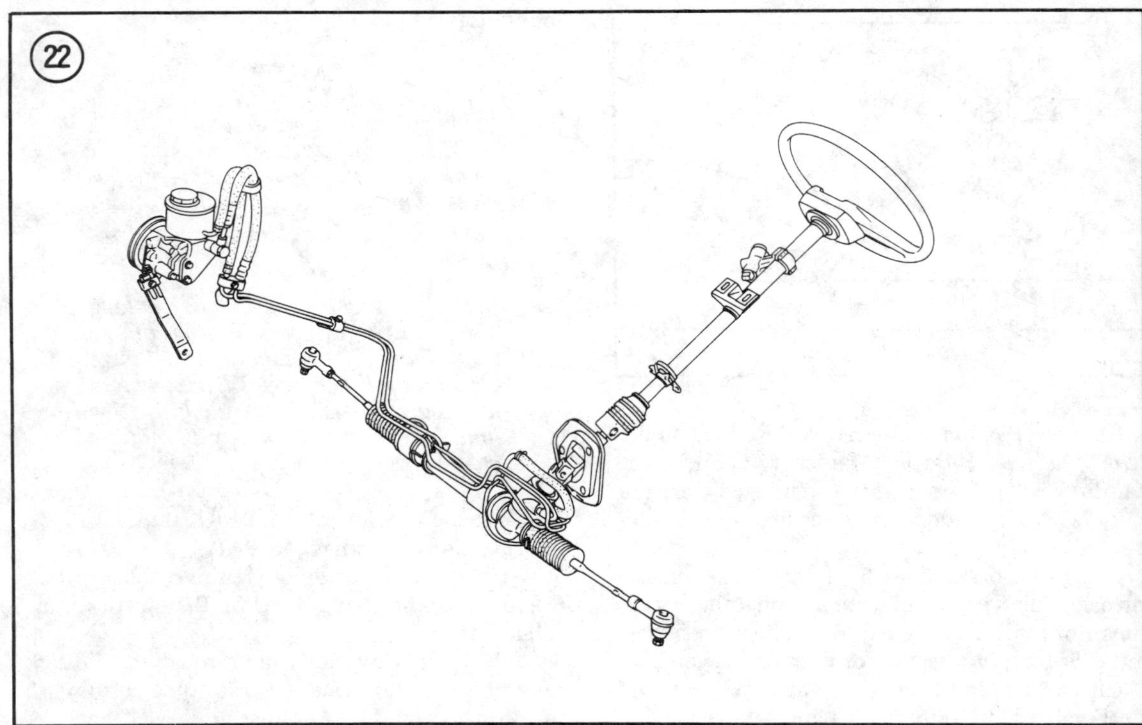

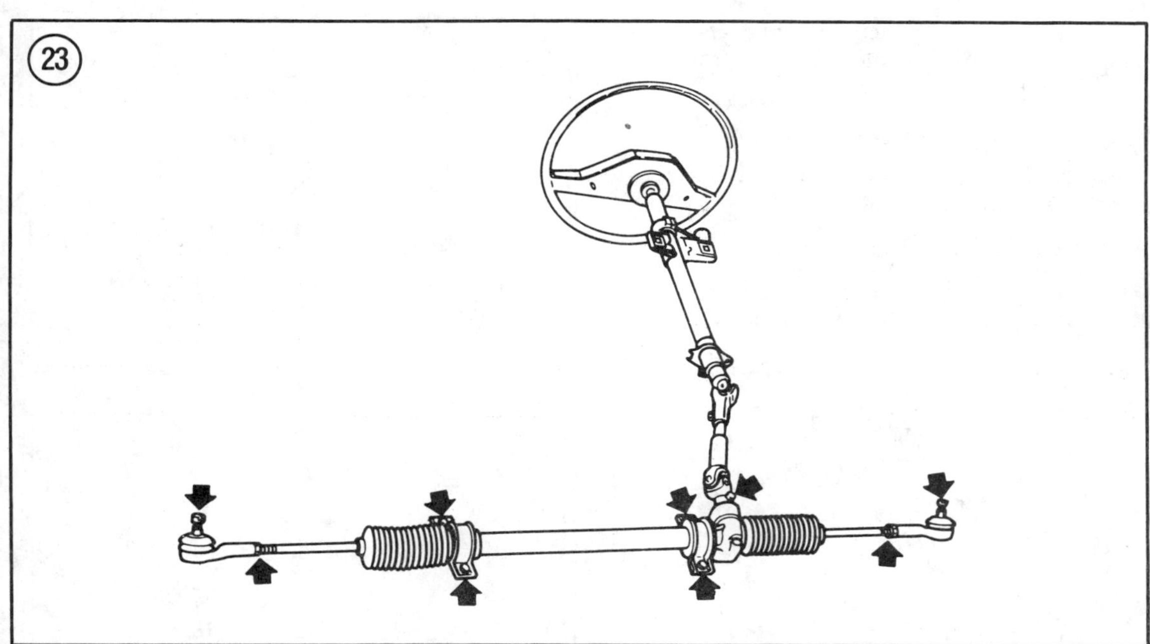

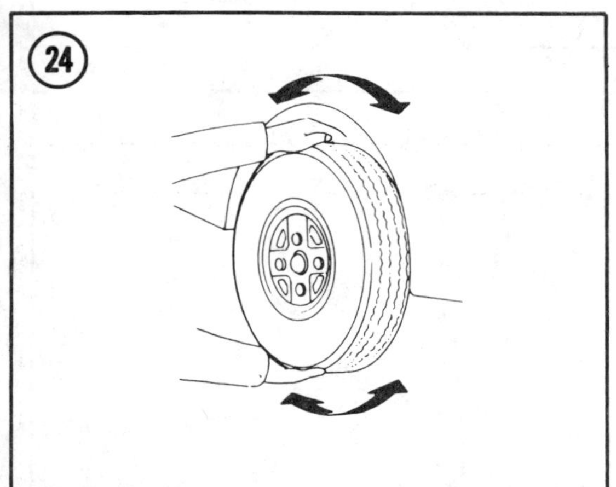

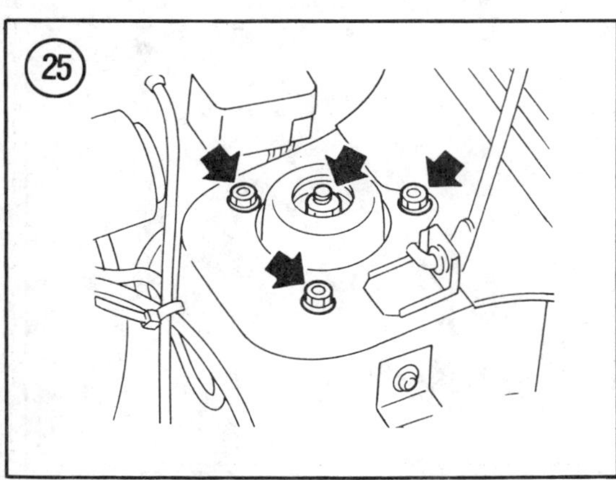

5. Add transaxle fluid through the dipstick tube (**Figure 20**). Use Dexron type automatic transmission fluid only. Do not use any other type. Capacity is listed in **Table 9**.

6. Check fluid level as described in this chapter.

Power Steering Line and Hose Inspection

Check the power steering lines and hoses (**Figure 22**) for cracks, kinks, leaks and wear from rubbing on other parts. Make sure the lines are securely fastened in their clips. Repair or replace as needed.

NOTE
If lines must be disconnected, top up fluid and bleed the system as described in Chapter Nine.

**Steering Linkage and
Front Suspension Inspection**

1. Check the steering linkage (**Figure 23**) for loose, damaged or worn parts. Tighten or replace as needed.

2. Set the handbrake. Securely block both rear wheels so the car will not roll in either direction.

3. Jack up the front end of the car and place it on jackstands.

4. Grasp each front tire at top and bottom and try to twist it. See **Figure 24**. There should not be any play. If there is, inspect ball-joints and front wheel bearings as described in Chapter Nine.

5. Check suspension nuts and bolts for looseness. See **Figure 25** and **Figure 26** (front) or **Figure 27**

and **Figure 28** (rear). Tighten loose nuts and bolts to specifications in Chapter Eleven (front) or Chapter Ten (rear).

Front Wheel Bearing Inspection

Clean, repack and adjust front wheel bearings as described in Chapter Nine.

Hinges, Latches, and Locks

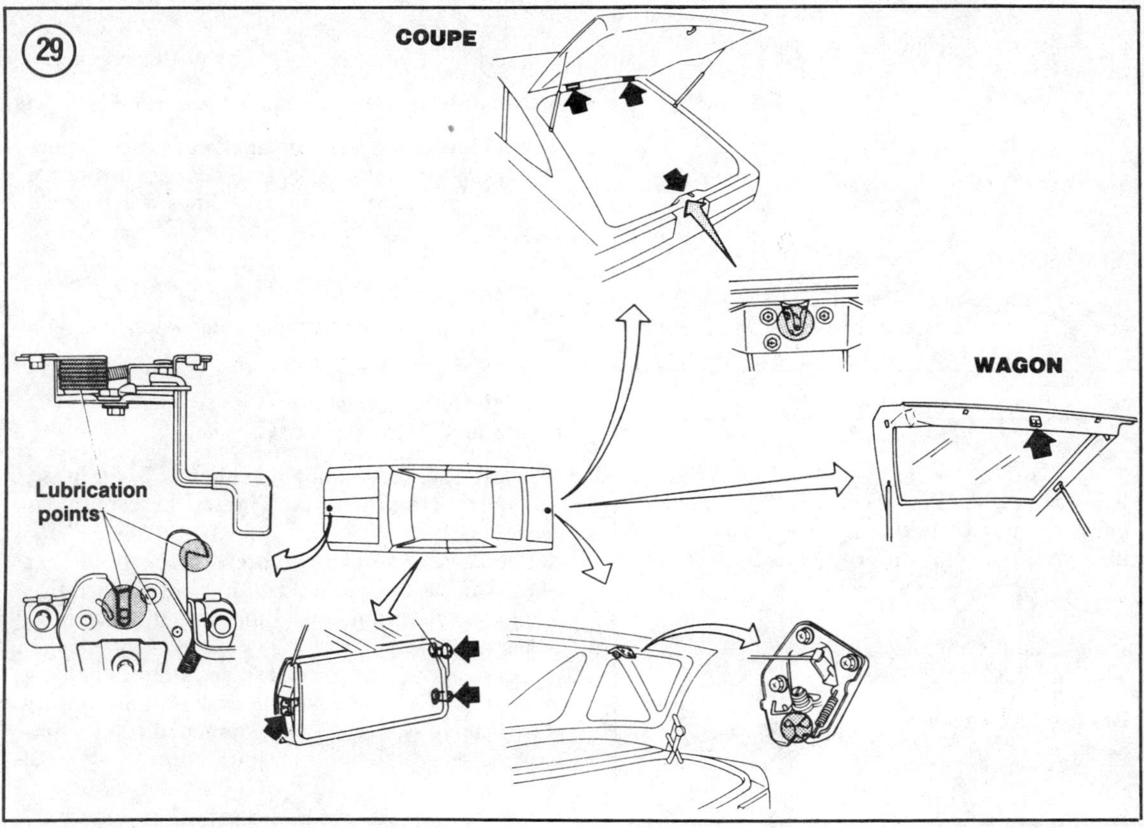

Referring to **Figure 29**, lightly grease the hood latch and trunk or tailgate lock with molybdenum

27

26

28

29

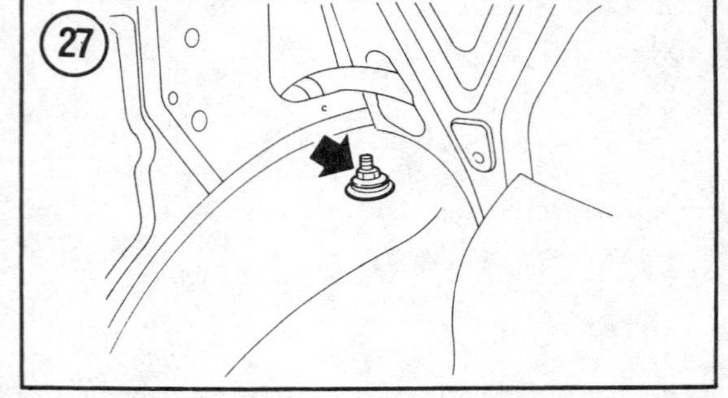

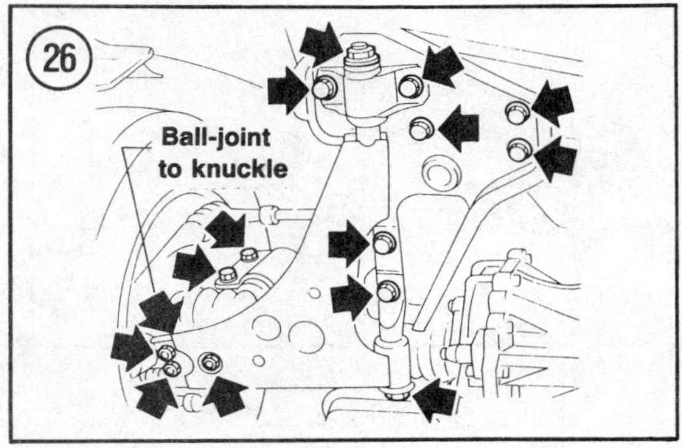

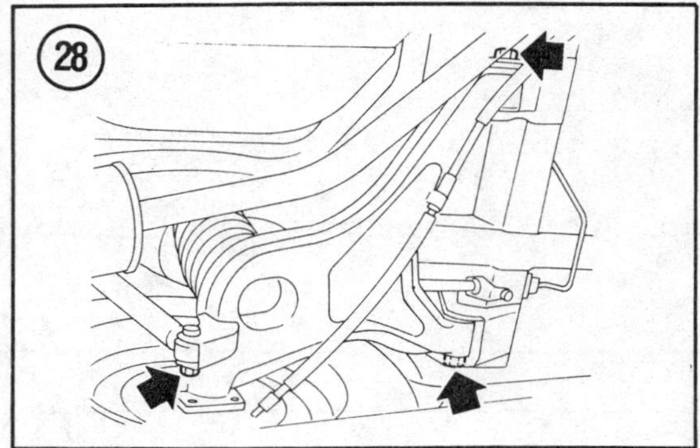

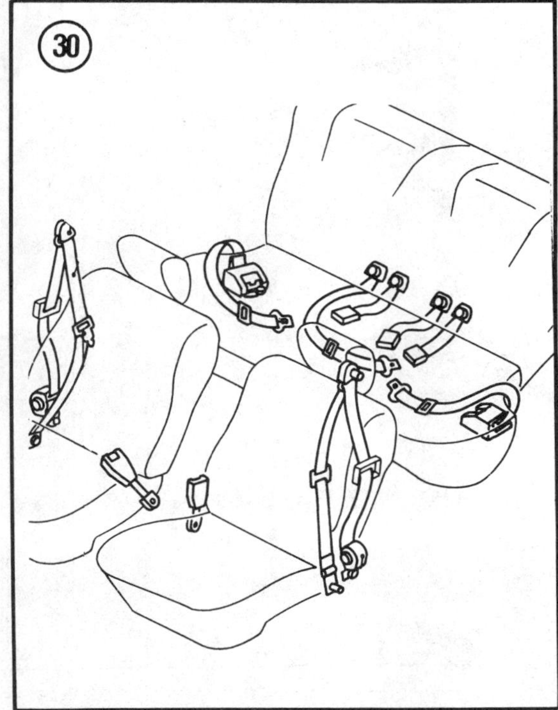

disulfide grease. Apply 1-2 drops of oil to hinges on doors, hood and trunk. Lubricate striker plates with a non-staining stick lube such as Door Ease. Lubricate lock tumblers by applying a thin coat of Lubriplate, lock oil or graphite to the key. Insert and work the lock several times. Wipe the key clean.

Exhaust System Inspection

Check the exhaust system for loose fasteners and corroded or damaged mufflers and pipes. See Chapter Five. Tighten or replace as needed.

Seat Belts

Check seat belts and mounting hardware for wear, damage or deterioration. See **Figure 30**. Replace parts if their condition is in doubt. Seat belts should be replaced as a set if the car is involved in a collision or rollover.

Tune-up

Tune up the engine at specified intervals; refer to *Tune-up* in this chapter.

Brake Fluid Change

Pump out all the old brake fluid and replace it with new fluid. Refer to *Brake Bleeding* in Chapter Eleven.

Drive Belt Inspection

1. Check drive belts for cracks, wear or fraying. Replace belts that show these conditions.

2. Check belt tension. Press on the belt midway between pulleys as shown in **Figure 31**. They should deflect the amount specified in **Table 10**.

> *CAUTION*
> *Be especially careful not to overtighten drive belts marked with a blue label and the word "Bando." These belts tighten when heated during engine operation. If overtightened while cold, they can damage pulleys and other parts.*

3. To adjust an alternator belt, loosen the alternator mounting and adjusting bolts (**Figure 32**). Pry the alternator away from the engine to tighten the belt or push it toward the engine to loosen. Then tighten the mounting and adjusting bolts.

4. To adjust a power steering pump belt loosen the lockbolt (**Figure 31**). Turn the adjusting bolt clockwise to tighten the belt or counterclockwise to loosen it, then tighten the lockbolt.

5. To adjust an air conditioner belt, loosen the idler pulley locknut (**Figure 31**). Turn the double nuts to tighten or loosen the belt as needed, then tighten the locknut.

Air Cleaner Element Replacement

To replace the element, remove the air cleaner cover. Lift out the element (**Figure 33**), install a new one and reinstall the cover.

Induction Valve Filter Replacement

This procedure does not apply to MPG models or 1983 California cars.

To replace the filter, remove the air induction valve case from the side of the air cleaner. See **Figure 34**. Take out the old filter, install a new one and reinstall the case.

Choke Inspection

1. Remove the air cleaner.

2. With the engine cold, floor the throttle cable. The choke valve should close.

3. Push the choke valve with a finger. It should open without sticking or binding.

4. If the choke did not perform as described in Step 2 or Step 3, clean the choke linkage with an aerosol carburetor cleaner.

5. On Canadian cars, make sure the choke coil index mark aligns with the center mark on the

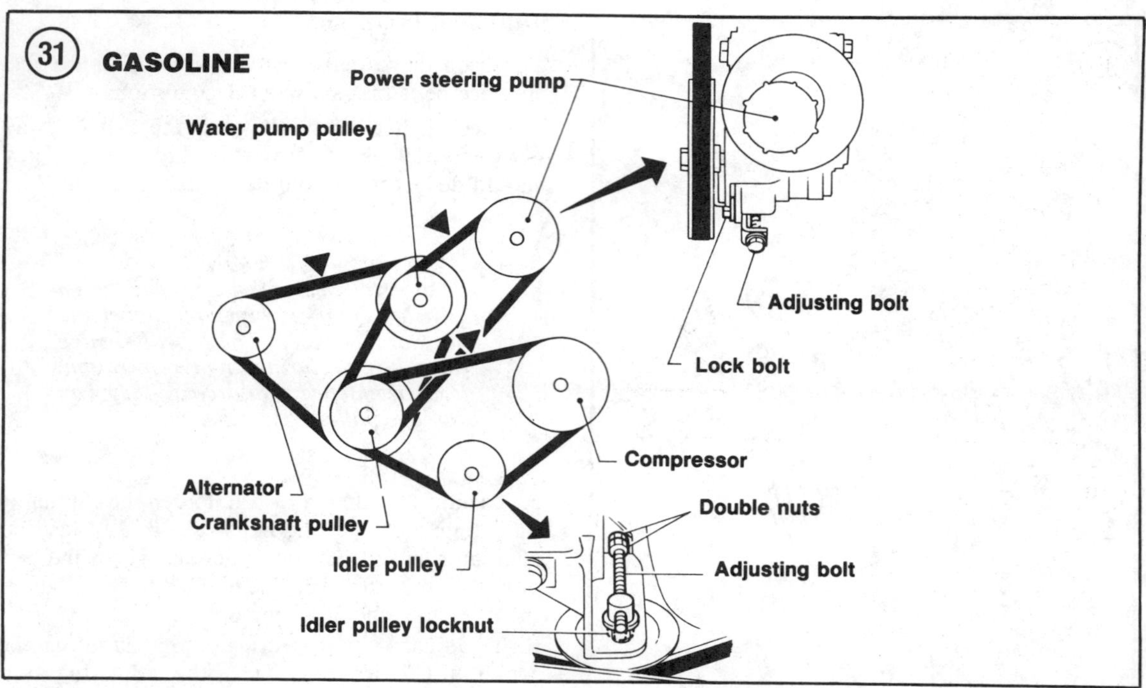

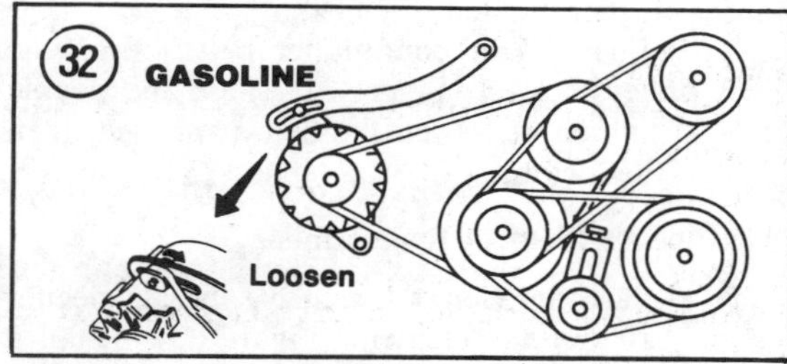

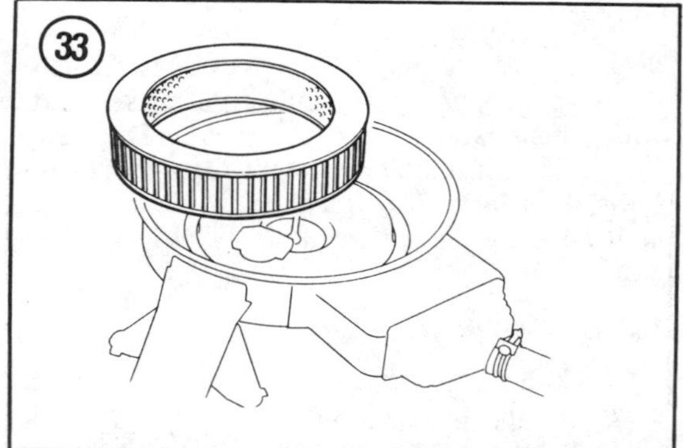

choke housing. See **Figure 35**. If the marks are not aligned, loosen the choke coil retaining ring and reposition the choke coil. See Chapter Five for details.

Vapor Line Inspection

1. Check evaporative emission control system lines for looseness, cracks, kinks, corrosion or damage from rubbing on other parts of the car. Tighten or replace as needed.
2. Check the fuel tank cap gasket for damage or deterioration. Replace as needed.
3. Check the carbon canister (**Figure 36**) for damage. Replace as needed.
4. Check for fuel smells around the car. Fuel smells, vapor locking or a deformed fuel tank indicate problems with the evaporative emission control system. If any of these conditions are found, have the system tested by a dealer or mechanic familiar with Nissan emission controls.

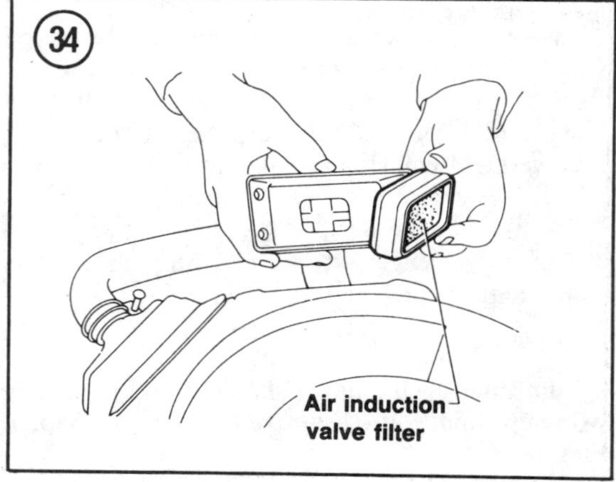

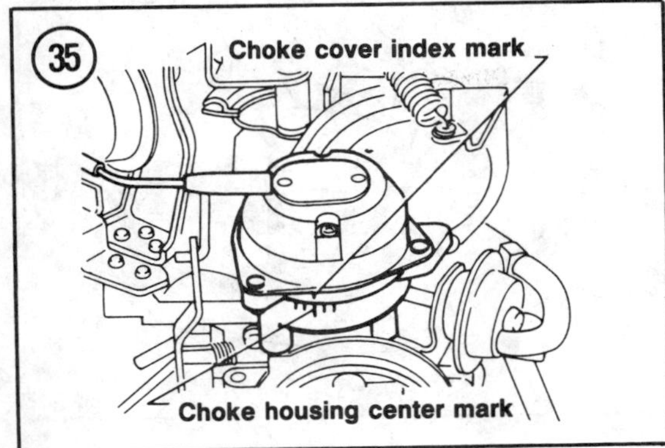

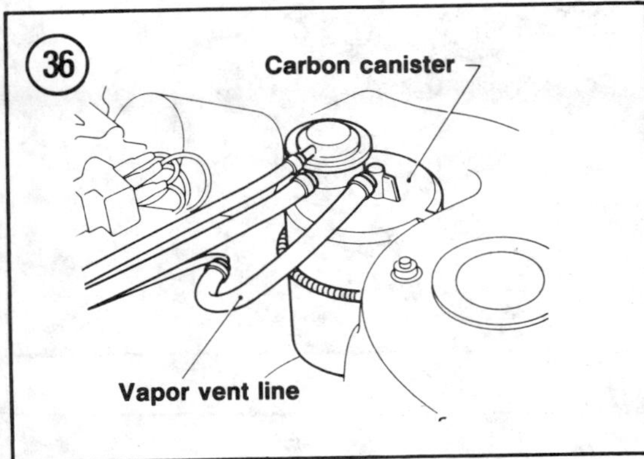

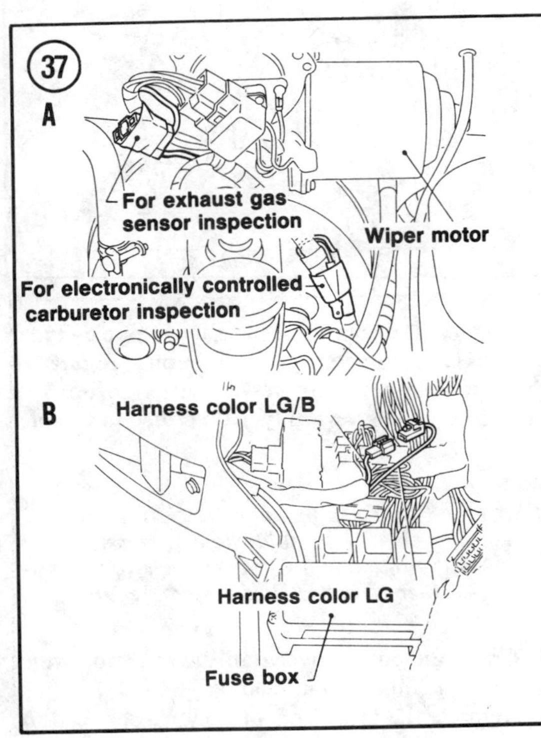

Fuel Line Inspection

Check fuel lines for looseness, cracks, kinks, corrosion or damage from rubbing on other parts of the car. See Chapter Five. Tighten or replace as needed.

Coolant Change

Drain, flush and refill the cooling system as described in Chapter Six.

ATC Air Cleaner Inspection

Inspect the automatic temperature control air cleaner as described in the *Air Cleaner* section of Chapter Five.

Exhaust Gas Sensor Inspection

This procedure applies to MPG models and 1983 California cars.

1. Connect the wiring connector for the exhaust gas sensor test. Make sure the wiring connector for the electronically controlled carburetor test is disconnected. See **Figure 37**.
2. Warm the engine until the temperature gauge needle points to the middle of the gauge.
3. Run the engine at about 2,000 rpm for approximately 5 minutes.
4. Make sure the inspection lamp on the instrument panel is off.
5. Connect the wiring connector for the electronically controlled carburetor inspection.
6. Make sure the inspection lamp on the instrument panel flashes on and off at least 5 times in 10 seconds.

7. If the system has performed as described so far, it is okay. Unplug the wiring connectors for the exhaust gas sensor and electronically controlled carburetor inspection. Disconnect the warning light by unplugging its wiring connector (**Figure 37B**). The light need not be tested. If the system has not performed as described, have it tested further by a dealer or mechanic familiar with Nissan emission controls.

Suspension and Steering Linkage Ball-joint Inspection

Ball-joints should be check for looseness, grease leaks or damaged dust boots. See **Figure 38**. Replace ball-joints that show these conditions.

Fuel Filter Replacement

The fuel filter (mounted on the right-hand side of the engine compartment) should be replaced if it becomes clogged. This is most likely to happen in areas with consistently bad weather or in extremely hot or cold temperatures.

To replace the filter, disconnect the inlet and outlet lines (**Figure 39**). Pull the filter out of its bracket, install a new one and reconnect the lines.

PCV Filter Replacement

The PCV filter should be replaced if it becomes clogged. This is most likely to happen in areas with consistently bad weather or in extremely hot or cold temperatures.

To replace the filter, remove the air cleaner cover. Take the filter out of its pocket on the side of the air cleaner, install a new filter and reinstall the cover.

GASOLINE ENGINE TUNE-UP

Under normal conditions, a tune-up should be done at the intervals specified in **Table 2**. More frequent tune-ups may be needed under the severe service conditions listed in **Table 4**.

Since different engine systems interact, a tune-up should be done in the following order:

a. Compression check.
b. Valve adjustment.
c. Ignition system work.
d. Carburetor adjustment.

The compression test need not be done periodically. It is used to locate problems if the engine is running badly.

Valve adjustment should be done at each tune-up.

Spark plugs should be replaced at alternate tune-ups on U.S. models and at each tune-up on Canadian cars.

The distributor cap, rotor and ignition wires should be inspected at alternate tune-ups.

Idle speed should be adjusted at each tune-up on U.S. models. U.S. models do not require periodic adjustment of ignition timing or idle mixture.

Ignition timing, idle speed and mixture adjustment should be done at each tune-up on Canadian cars.

Compression Test

There are 2 types of compression test: "wet" and "dry." These tests are interpreted together to isolate problems in cylinders and valves. The dry compression test is done first. Test as follows.

1. Warm the engine to normal operating temperature.
2. Remove the spark plugs.

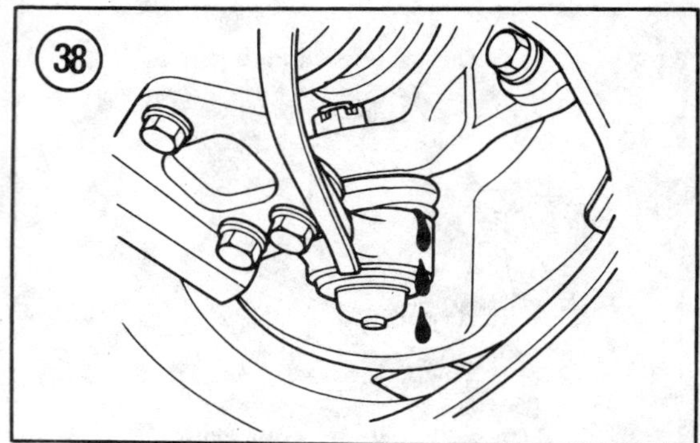

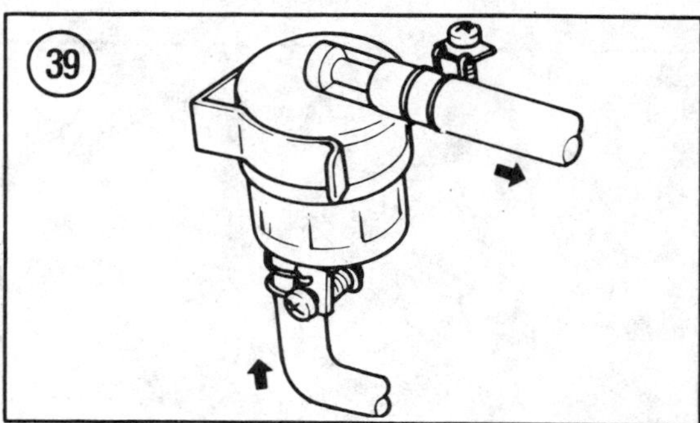

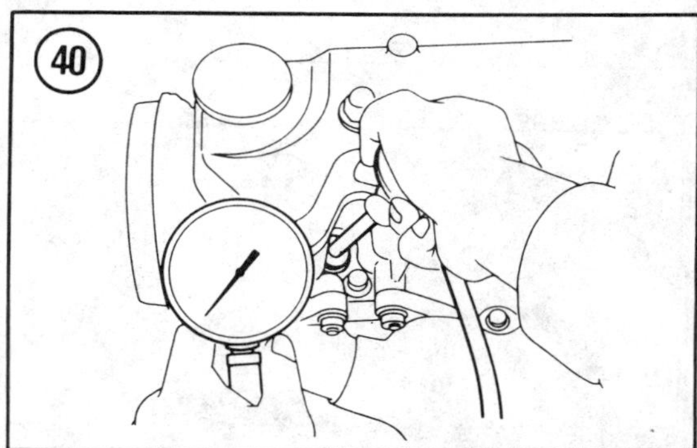

3. Connect the compression tester to one cylinder following manufacturer's instructions. **Figure 40** shows a hand-held compression tester in use. You can also use the screw-in type described in Chapter One.

> *NOTE*
> *Hand-held compression testers require 2 people, one to hold the compression tester and one to crank the engine. Screw-in compression testers require only one person.*

4. Crank the engine over until there is no further increase in compression reading.
5. Remove the tester and write down the reading.

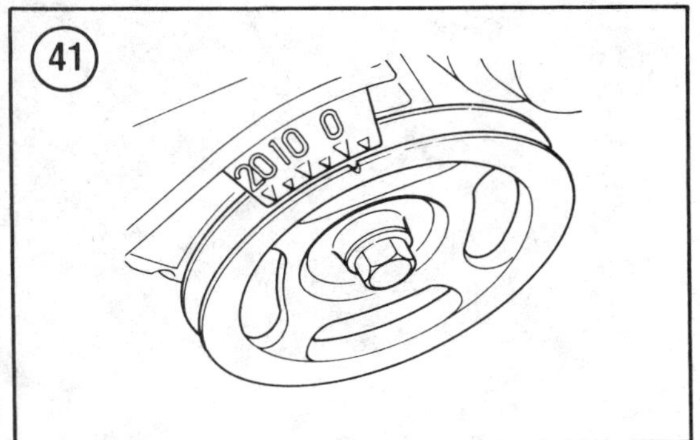

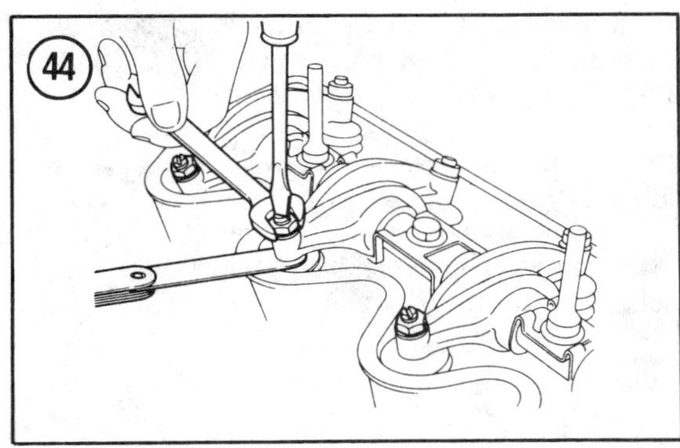

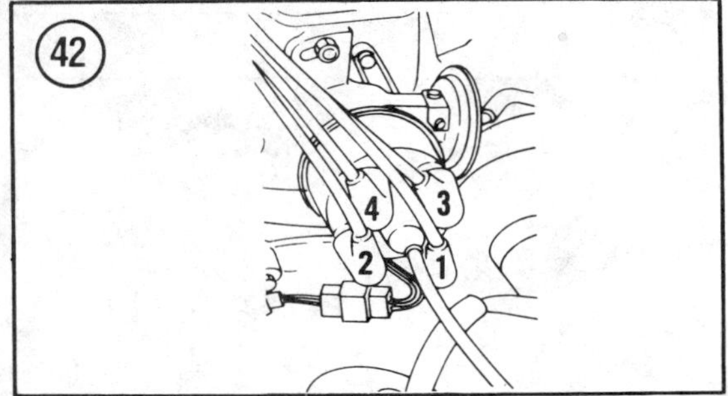

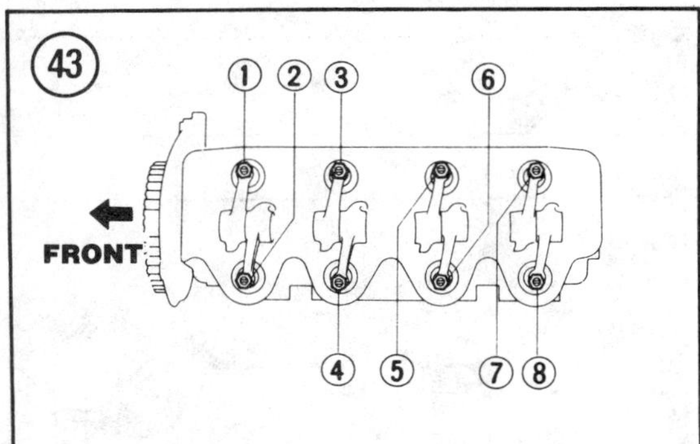

6. Repeat Steps 3-5 for each cylinder. Compare results with **Table 11** in this chapter.

When interpreting the results, actual readings are not as important as the differences in readings. Low readings, although they may be even, are a sign of wear. Low readings in 2 adjacent cylinders may indicate a defective head gasket. An excessive difference in readings indicates worn or broken rings, leaky or sticking valves, a defective head gasket or a combination of all.

If the dry compression test indicates a problem, isolate the cause with a wet compression test. This is done in the same way as the dry compression test, except that about one tablespoon of oil is poured down the spark plug holes before performing Steps 3-6. If the wet compression readings are much greater than the dry readings, the trouble is probably due to worn or broken rings. If there is little difference between wet and dry readings, the trouble is probably due to leaky or sticking valves. If 2 adjacent cylinders are low and the wet and dry readings are close, the head gasket may be damaged.

Valve Adjustment

1. Find valve clearance specifications in **Table 11**.
2. Warm the engine until the temperature needle points to the middle of the gauge, then turn it off.
3. Remove the spark plugs. This makes it easier to turn the engine.

> *CAUTION*
> *See **Spark Plug Removal** in this chapter for correct removal procedures.*

4. Remove the air cleaner.
5. Remove the valve cover.
6. Turn the engine to place No. 1 cylinder at top dead center on its compression stroke. When this occurs, the crankshaft pulley notch will align with the 0 degree mark on the timing scale. See **Figure 41**. In addition, the distributor rotor will point to No. 1 terminal in the distributor cap (**Figure 42**).

> *NOTE*
> *Be sure to remove the distributor cap and check rotor position. The notch and 0 degree mark also line up when No. 4 piston is at top dead center on its compression stroke.*

7. Measure clearances on valves No. 1, 2, 3 and 6 (**Figure 43**). To measure clearance, insert a feeler gauge between rocker arm and valve stem as shown in **Figure 44**. The feeler gauge should fit with a very light drag.
8. To adjust clearance, loosen the locknut (**Figure 44**). Turn the adjusting screw with a screwdriver to change clearance, then tighten the locknut.

9. Turn the engine one full turn (clockwise, viewed from the crankshaft pulley end), so the pulley notch aligns with the 0 degree mark on the timing scale.

10. Check clearance of the remaining valves and adjust as needed.

11. Install the valve cover and air cleaner. If the spark plugs are to be replaced, leave them out; if not, install them.

Spark Plug Removal

1. Blow out any foreign matter from around spark plugs with compressed air. Use a compressor if you have one. Another method is to use a can of compressed inert gas, available from photo stores. If the area around the spark plugs is greasy, clean the engine with engine cleaner.

> *CAUTION*
> *When spark plugs are removed, dirt from around the plugs can fall into the spark plug holes. This can cause expensive engine damage.*

2. Mark spark plug wires with the cylinder numbers so you can reconnect them properly. **Figure 45** shows the distributor cap terminal numbers. Spark plugs are numbered from 1 to 4, counting from the crankshaft pulley end of the engine.

> *NOTE*
> *To make labels, wrap a small strip of masking tape around each wire.*

3. Disconnect spark plug wires. Pull off by grasping the connector, *not* the wire. See **Figure 46**. Pulling on the wire may break it.

> *CAUTION*
> *If the boots seem to be stuck, twist them 1/2 turn to break the seal. Do not pull on boots with pliers. The pliers could cut the insulation, causing an electrical short.*

4. Remove the plugs with a 13/16 in. spark plug socket. Keep the plugs in order so you know which cylinder they came from.

5. Examine each spark plug. Compare its condition with the illustrations in Chapter Two. Spark plug condition indicates engine condition and can warn of developing trouble.

6. Discard the plugs. Although they could be cleaned, regapped and reused if in good condition, they seldom last very long; new plugs are inexpensive and far more reliable.

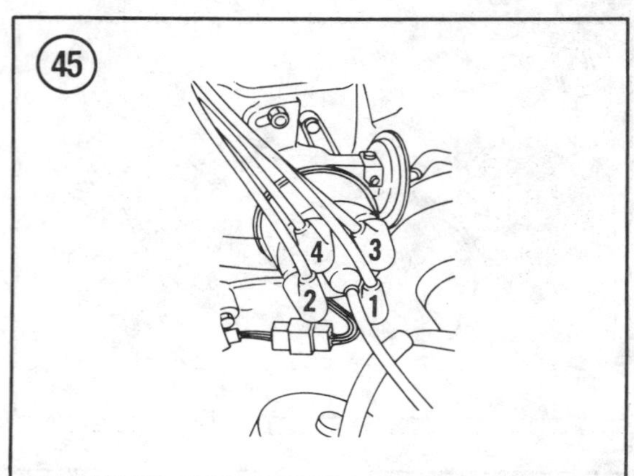

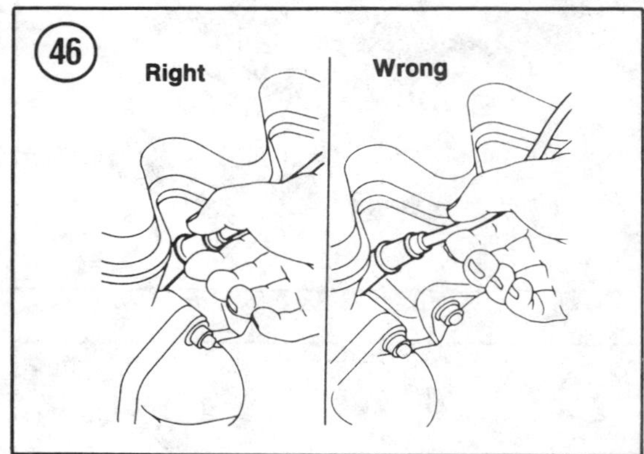

Spark Plug Gapping and Installation

New plugs should be carefully gapped to ensure a reliable, consistent spark. Use a special spark plug tool with a wire gauge. See **Figure 47** or **Figure 48**.

1. Remove the plugs from the boxes. See if the small end pieces (**Figure 49**) are screwed on. If not, install them.

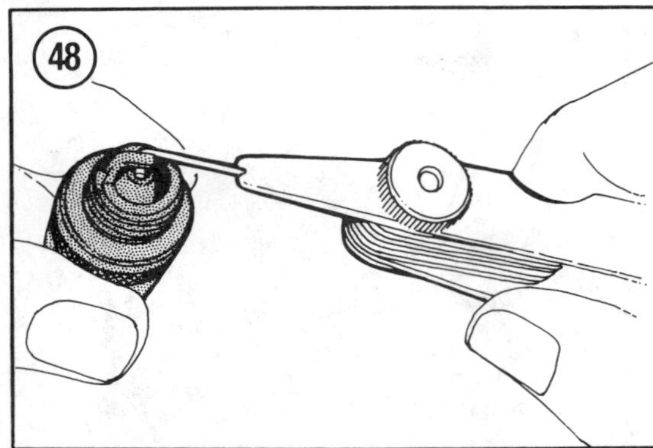

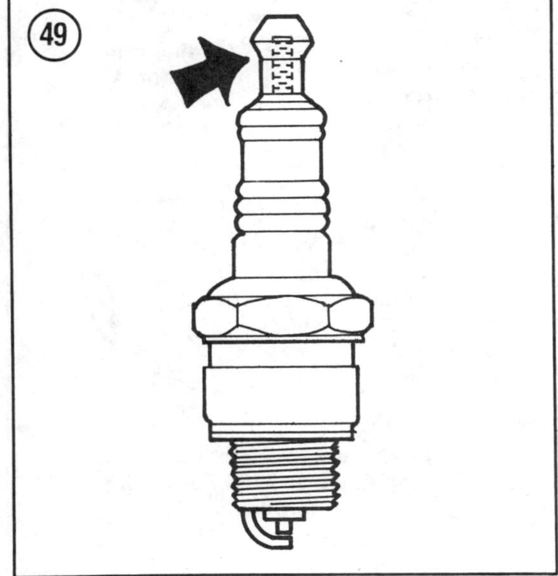

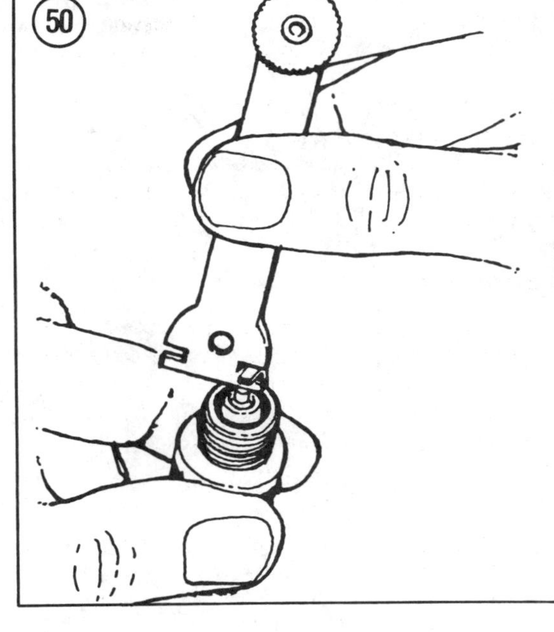

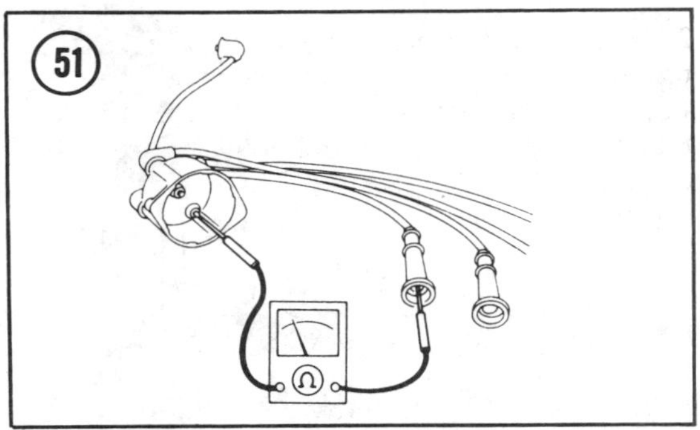

2. Find the correct spark plug gap for your car in **Table 11**. Insert the correct diameter wire gauge between the spark plug electrodes. See **Figure 48**. If the gap is correct, there will be a slight drag as the wire is pulled through. If there is no drag or if the wire won't pull through, bend the side electrode with the gapping tool (**Figure 50**) to change the gap.

3. Put a small amount of aluminum anti-seize compound on the first few threads of each spark plug.

4. Crank the starter for about 5 seconds to blow away any dirt around the spark plug holes.

5. Screw each plug in by hand until it seats. Very little effort is required. If force is necessary, the plug is cross-threaded. Unscrew it and try again.

6. Tighten the spark plugs. If you have a torque wrench, tighten to 20-29 N•m (14-22 ft.-lb.). If not, tighten the plug with fingers, then tighten an additional 1/4-1/2 turn with the plug wrench.

> *CAUTION*
> *Do not overtighten. This prevents the plugs from seating.*

Distributor Cap, Wires and Rotor

1. Pry back the distributor cap clips and remove the cap.

2. If you have an ohmmeter, connect it between each wire end and distributor cap terminal (**Figure 51**). Resistance should be 30,000 ohms or less. If it is higher, remove the wire and test it separately. If resistance is still too high, replace the wire. If not, replace the distributor cap and rotor as a set.

3. If you don't have an ohmmeter, check the distributor cap terminals for dirt or corrosion. See **Figure 52**. Clean or replace as needed.

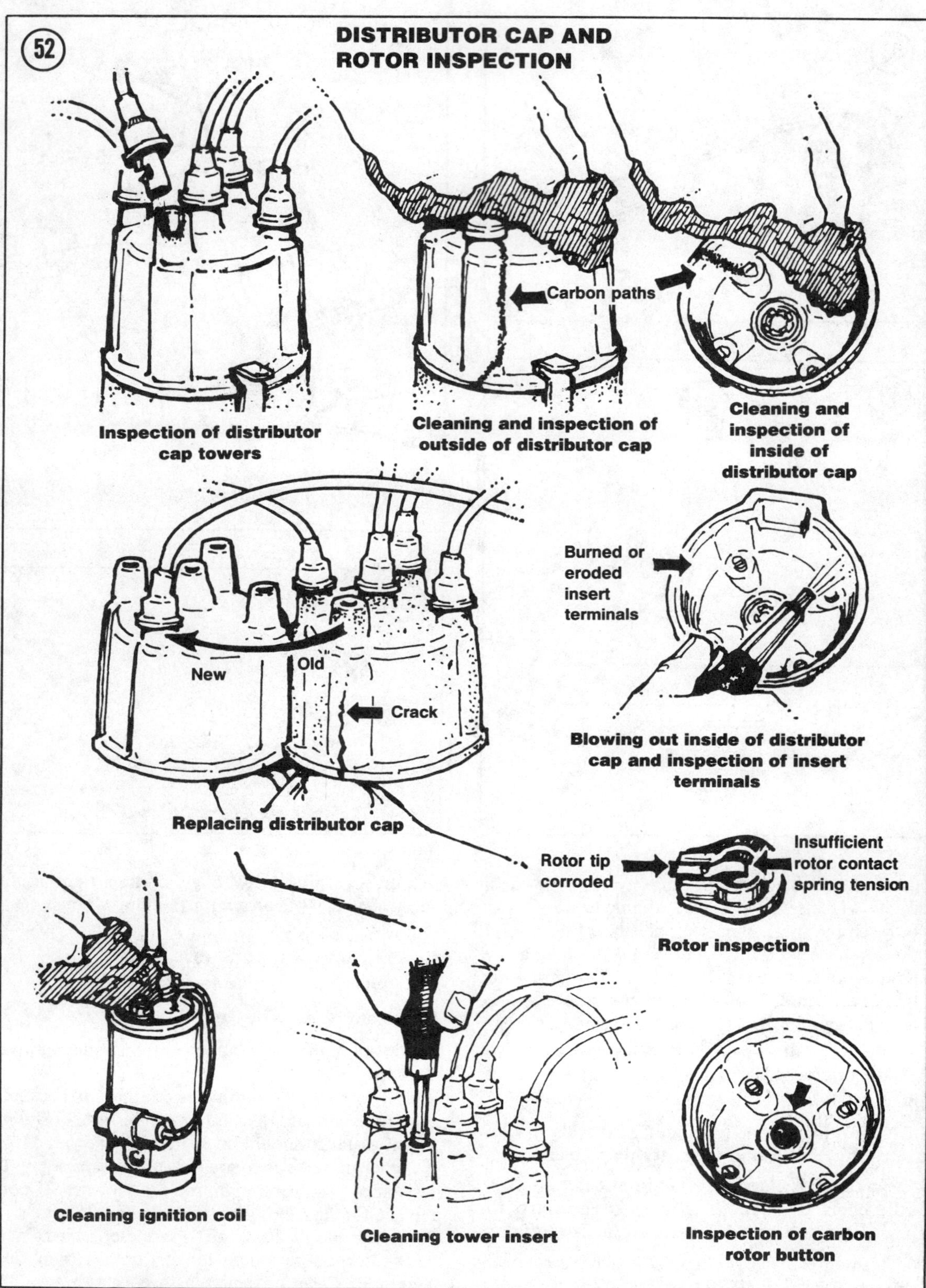

Inspection of distributor cap towers

Cleaning and inspection of outside of distributor cap

Cleaning and inspection of inside of distributor cap

Replacing distributor cap

Blowing out inside of distributor cap and inspection of insert terminals

Rotor inspection

Cleaning ignition coil

Cleaning tower insert

Inspection of carbon rotor button

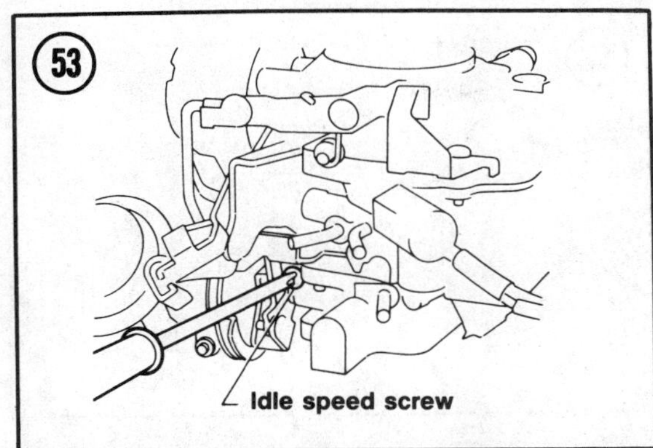

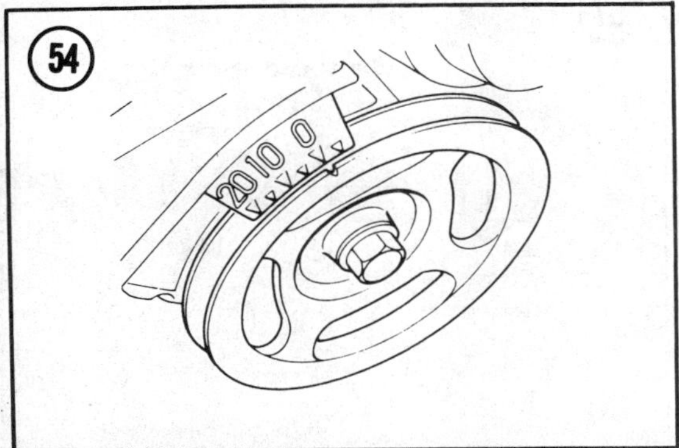

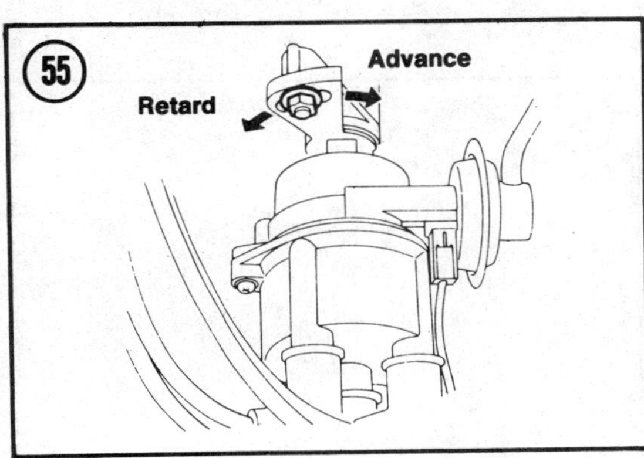

4. Replace the wires if the insulation is melted, brittle or cracked.

5. Check the rotor for burns, cracks or wear. Replace the cap and rotor as a set if these conditions can be seen.

6. Install the rotor. Install the distributor cap and reconnect the wires. Be sure they are connected to the right terminals. **Figure 45** identifies distributor cap terminals. Spark plugs are numbered from 1 to 4, counting from the crankshaft pulley end of the engine.

Ignition Timing Adjustment

Periodic ignition timing adjustment is not required on U.S. cars or Canadian MPG models. This procedure can be used to check timing if the engine is performing poorly or if the distributor has been removed from the engine.

1. Warm the engine to normal operating temperature, then shut it off.

2. Connect a timing light and tune-up tachometer to the engine.

3. Start the engine and let it idle. Compare idle speed with **Table 11**. Adjust if necessary by turning the idle speed screw (**Figure 53**).

> *WARNING*
> *During the next step, keep your hands and hair away from all belts and pulleys. Under the timing light, then may appear to be standing still. They are actually spinning at more than 10 times every second and can cause serious injury.*

4. Point the timing light at the timing marks (**Figure 54**). The notch in the crankshaft pulley should align with the timing mark for your engine (specified in **Table 11**).

> *WARNING*
> *During the next step, do not touch the thick wires running to the distributor cap. This can cause a painful shock, even if the insulation is in perfect condition.*

5. If timing is incorrect, loosen the distributor locknut (**Figure 55**). Turn the distributor to change timing, then tighten the locknut.

Idle Speed Adjustment

This procedure applies to all U.S. cars and Canadian MPG models. It is done under the following conditions:

   a. All electrical equipment (lights, radio, etc.) off.

   b. Air conditioner off (if so equipped).

   c. Radiator fan off (if the fan is running, wait until it stops).

1. Warm the engine until the temperature needle points to the middle of the gauge.

2. Connect a tune-up tachometer to the engine, following manufacturer's instructions.

3. Set the handbrake. Securely block both front wheels so the car will not roll in either direction.

4. Make sure the transaxle is in NEUTRAL.

5. Open the hood and let the engine idle for 2 minutes. Race the engine 2 or 3 times at 2,000-3,000 rpm, then let it idle again.

6. If equipped with an automatic transaxle, shift to DRIVE.

7. Check idle speed on the tachometer and compare with **Table 11**. Adjust if necessary by turning the idle speed screw (**Figure 53**).

Idle Speed, Ignition Timing and Idle Mixture Adjustment

This procedure applies to Canadian non-MPG models. It is done under the following conditions.

  a. Engine oil and coolant up to proper levels.

  b. Valve clearance adjusted to specifications.

  c. Spark plugs, distributor cap, rotor and plug wires in good condition.

  d. All electrical accessories (lights, radio, etc.) off.

  e. Front wheels in straight-ahead position (if equipped with power steering).

  f. Air conditioner off (if so equipped).

  g. Radiator fan off (if the fan is running, wait until it stops).

> *NOTE*
> *Setting the idle mixture requires a CO meter and specially modified screwdriver. If you don't have these tools, have idle mixture adjusted by a dealer or other qualified mechanic.*

1. Warm the engine until the temperature needle points to the middle of the gauge.

2. Connect a tune-up tachometer to the engine, following manufacturer's instructions.

3. Set the handbrake. Securely block both front wheels so the car will not roll in either direction.

4. Make sure the transaxle is in NEUTRAL.

5. Open the hood. Disconnect the air induction hose from the air cleaner and cap or plug the hose. See **Figure 56**.

6. Start the engine and let it idle for 2 minutes. During this time, disconnect and plug the distributor vacuum hose.

7. Rev the engine 2 or 3 times at 2,000-3,000 rpm, then let it idle.

8. Compare idle speed with **Table 11**. Adjust if necessary by turning the idle speed screw (**Figure 57**).

> *WARNING*
> *During the next step, keep your hands and hair away from all belts and pulleys. Under the timing light, they may appear to be standing still. They are actually spinning at more than 10 times every second and can cause serious injury.*

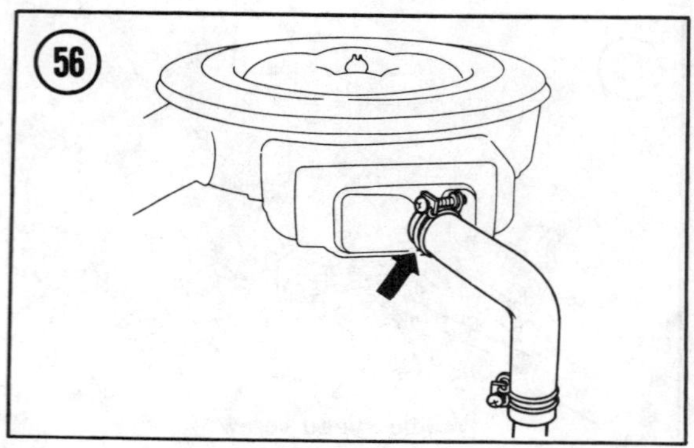

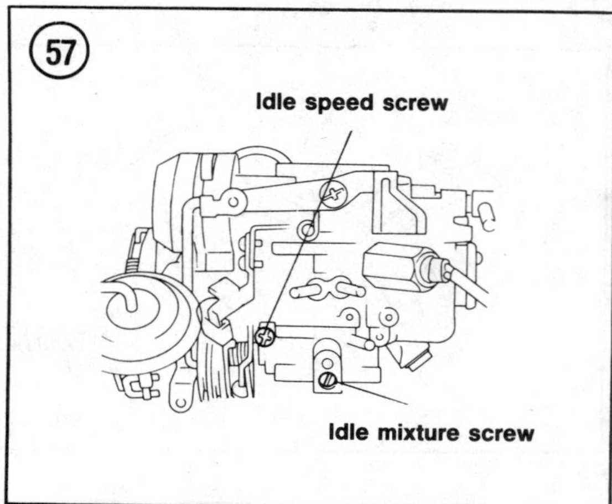

9. Point the timing light at the timing marks (**Figure 54**). The notch in the crankshaft pulley should align with the timing mark for your engine (specified in **Table 11**).

> *WARNING*
> *During the next step, do not touch the thick wires running to the distributor cap. This can cause a painful shock, even if the insulation is in perfect condition.*

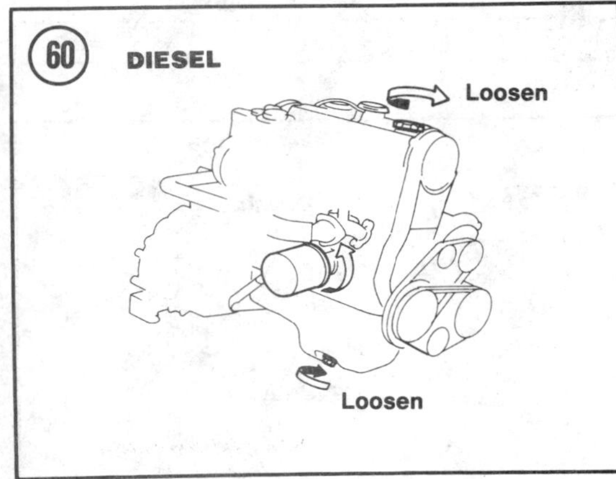

10. If timing is incorrect, loosen the distributor locknut (**Figure 55**). Turn the distributor to change timing, then tighten the locknut.

11. Unplug the distributor vacuum hose and connect it to the distributor.

12. Check idle speed on the tachometer and compare with **Table 11**. Adjust if necessary by turning the idle speed screw (**Figure 57**).

NOTE
The next step requires a CO meter. If you don't have one, have the step done by a dealer or other qualified mechanic.

13. Rev the engine at 2,000-3,000 rpm 2 or 3 times, then let it idle.

14. Insert the CO meter into the tailpipe and note CO percentage. If not within specifications, turn the idle mixture screw (**Figure 57**). The screw is equipped with a limiter cap so a modified screwdriver such as Nissan tool part No. KV10108300 (**Figure 58**) will be required to turn the screw.

15. Once CO percentage is within specifications, reconnect the induction hose to the air cleaner. Recheck idle speed as described in this section and adjust as needed.

DIESEL ENGINE MAINTENANCE

This section describes maintenance procedures for diesel engines. Chassis and body maintenance procedures for diesel-equipped cars are described under *Scheduled Maintenance* in this chapter.

Engine Oil and Filter

If the car is given normal use, change the oil when recommended in **Table 3**. The filter should be changed at every oil change during the first 15,000 miles, then at alternate oil changes.

If the car is used for stop-and-go driving, in dusty areas, left idling for long periods or used to tow a trailer, change the oil and filter when recommended in **Table 4**.

Use an oil recommended in **Table 6** and **Table 7**. The rating (SE or SF) is usually printed on top of the can (**Figure 59**).

To drain the oil and change the filter, you will need:

  a. Drain pan.
  b. Oil can spout or can opener and funnel.
  c. Filter wrench.
  d. Drain plug wrench.
  e. 4 quarts of oil (5 quarts if the filter is being replaced).
  f. Oil filter.

There are several ways to discard the old oil safely. The easiest is to pour it from the drain pan into a gallon bleach or milk bottle. The oil can be taken to a service station for recycling or, where permitted, thrown in your household trash.

1. Warm the engine to operating temperature, then shut it off.

WARNING
During the next step, move your hand away quickly once the drain plug is loose. Otherwise, hot oil may run down your arm.

2. Put the drain pan under the drain plug (**Figure 60**). Remove the plug and let the oil drain for at least 10 minutes.

3. Unscrew the oil filter (**Figure 60**) counterclockwise. Use a filter wrench if the filter is too tight to remove by hand.

4. Wipe the gasket surface on the engine block clean with a lint-free cloth.

5. Coat the neoprene gasket on the new filter with clean engine oil. See **Figure 61**.

6. Screw the filter onto the engine *by hand* until the gasket just touches the engine block. At this point, there will be a very slight resistance when turning the filter.

7. Tighten the filter 1/2 turn more *by hand*. If the filter wrench is used, the filter will probably be overtightened. This will cause an oil leak.

8. Install the oil pan drain plug. Tighten it securely.

9. Remove the oil filler cap (**Figure 60**).

10. Pour oil into the engine. Capacity is listed in **Table 9**.

11. Start the engine and let it idle. The instrument panel oil pressure light will remain on for 15-30 seconds, then go out.

> *CAUTION*
> *Do not race the engine to make the oil pressure light go out. It takes time for the oil to reach all areas of the engine and racing it could damage dry parts.*

12. While the engine is running, check the drain plug and oil filter for leaks.

13. Turn the engine off. Let the oil settle for several minutes, then check the level on the dipstick (**Figure 62**). Add oil if necessary to bring the level up to the "H" mark, but *do not* overfill.

Drive Belt Inspection

1. Check drive belts (**Figure 63**) for cracks, fraying or deterioration. Replace belts that show these conditions.

2. Push on the belts midway between pulleys and note how far they deflect. Compare with **Table 10**.

3. To adjust an alternator belt on an engine without an idler pulley, loosen the alternator mounting and adjusting bolts. See **Figure 64**. Pry

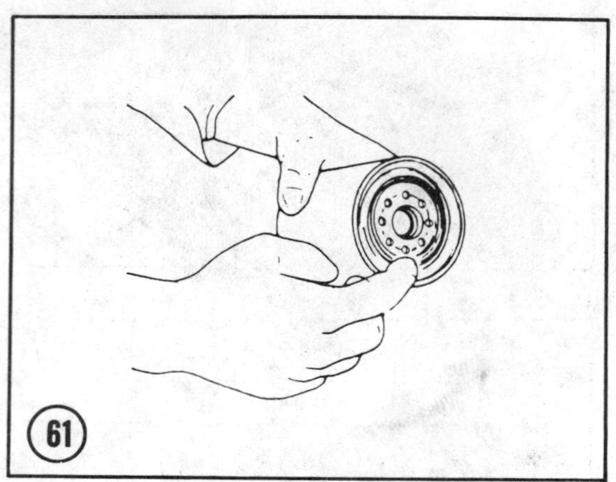

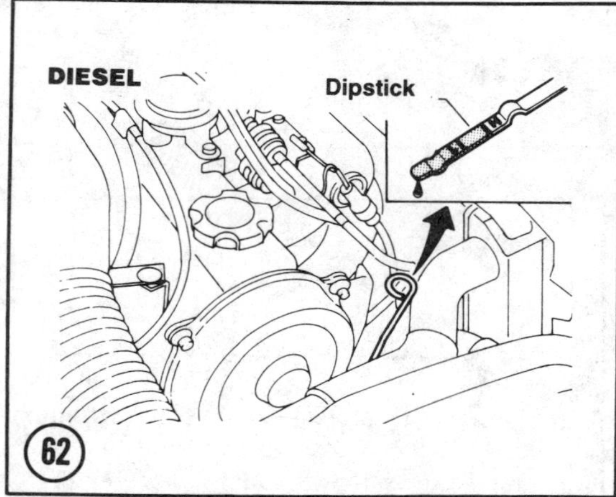

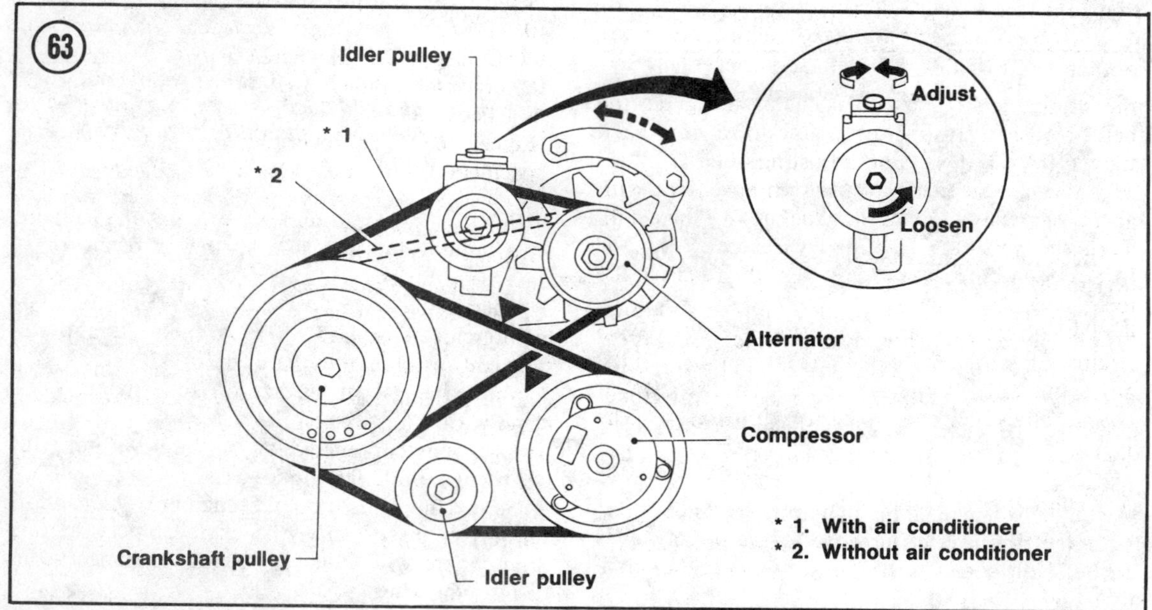

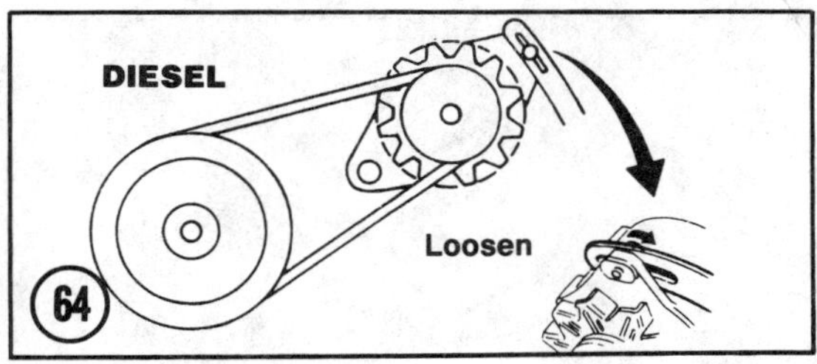

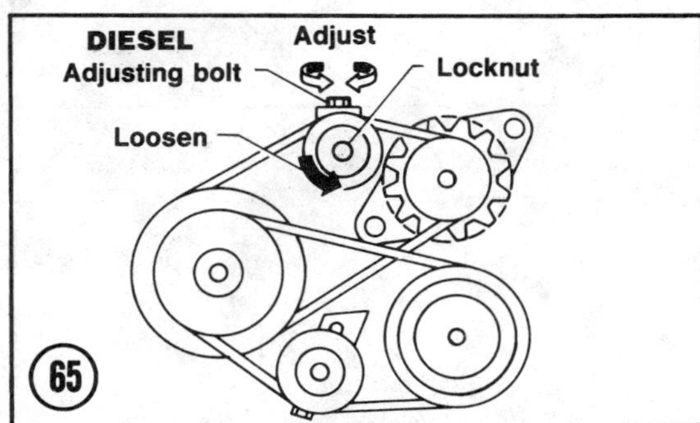

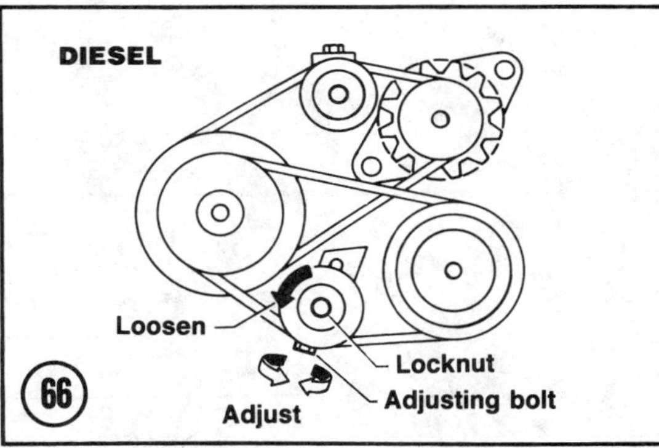

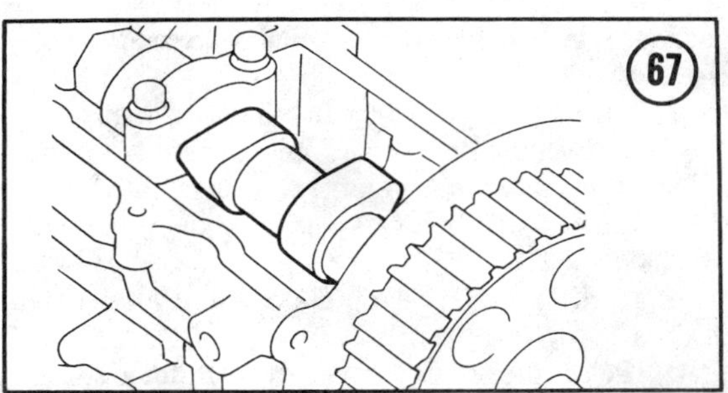

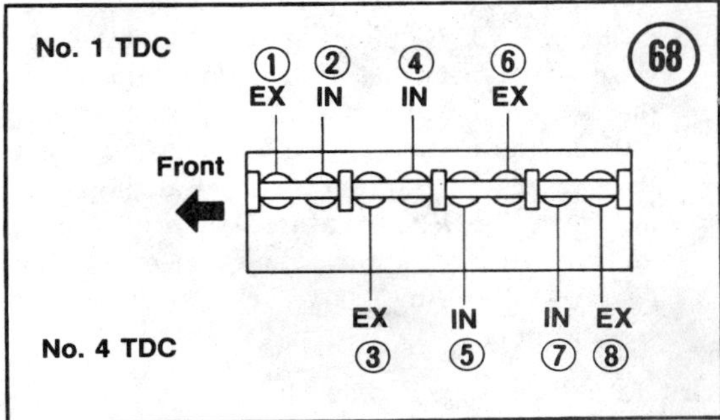

the alternator away from the engine to tighten the belt or push it toward the engine to loosen. Then tighten the mounting and adjusting bolts.

3. To adjust an alternator belt on an engine with an idler pulley, loosen the locknut (**Figure 65**). Turn the adjusting bolt clockwise to tighten the belt or counterclockwise to loosen, then tighten the locknut.

4. To adjust an air conditioner belt (if so equipped), loosen the locknut (**Figure 66**). Turn the adjusting bolt clockwise to tighten the belt or counterclockwise to loosen, then tighten the locknut.

Injection Nozzle Inspection

This procedure requires special equipment and should be done by a dealer or mechanic familiar with diesel engines.

Valve Clearance Check and Adjustment

Valve clearance can be checked with a feeler gauge. Adjustment requires special tools and should be done by a dealer, although the procedure is described in this chapter.

1. Warm the engine to normal operating temperature.

2. Remove the valve cover.

3. Turn the engine so No. 1 cylinder is at top dead center on its compression stroke. When this occurs, the cam lobes will be positioned as shown in **Figure 67**. Cylinders are numbered 1 to 4, counting from the crankshaft pulley end of the engine.

4. Check the clearances of valves 1, 2, 4 and 6 (**Figure 68**). To check, find valve clearance specifications in **Table 11**. Slip a feeler gauge of the specified thickness between the cam lobe and lifter as shown in **Figure 69**. The gauge should slide in with a very light drag.

5. If clearance is incorrect, write down the number of each valve that has incorrect clearance.

6. Turn the engine so No. 4 cylinder is at top dead center on its compression stroke. When this occurs, the No. 4 cam lobes will be positioned as shown in **Figure 67**. Check clearances of valves 3, 5, 7 and 8 (**Figure 68**). Write down the number of each valve that has incorrect clearances.

7. Adjust valves by replacing the valve shim (**Figure 70**). Although clearances can be checked as described in Steps 3-6, clearance adjustment is done one cylinder at a time, with each cylinder at top

dead center on its compression stroke. Adjust as follows:

a. Turn the engine so each cylinder comes to top dead center on its compression stroke. When this occurs, the cam lobes for the cylinder being adjusted will be postioned as shown in **Figure 67**.

b. Recheck valve clearances on the cylinder that is at top dead center.

c. If clearance is too small, use a thinner shim.

d. If clearance is too large, use a thicker shim.

e. Compress the valve spring with Nissan tool part No. KV11102600 (**Figure 71**). Pull out the shim with a magnet as shown. Shim thickness is marked on the underside of the shim (**Figure 70**). If these aren't visible, measure shim thickness with a micrometer. Calculate the difference between measured valve clearance and specified clearance, then select a shim which will bring valve clearance within specifications.

Air Cleaner Element Replacement

To remove the air cleaner element, remove the cover from the air cleaner housing and take the element out. Without allowing debris to enter the engine, clean the inside of the housing and cover with compressed air. Install the new element and reinstall the cover.

Fuel Line and Rubber Hose Inspection

Check fuel lines and rubber hoses for loose connections, cracks, deterioration and wear from rubbing on other parts. Tighten or replace as needed.

Fuel Filter Replacement

1. Disconnect the sensor wire from the bottom of the filter (**Figure 72**).

2. Unscrew the filter and take it out. Use an oil filter wrench if the filter is difficult to remove.

3. Screw on a new filter and tighten by hand only. Do not tighten with a filter wrench or the gasket will leak.

4. Bleed the fuel system as described in this chapter.

Coolant Change

Drain, flush and refill the cooling system as described in Chapter Six.

Idle Speed Adjustment

This procedure requires special tools and should be done by a dealer or other qualified diesel mechanic.

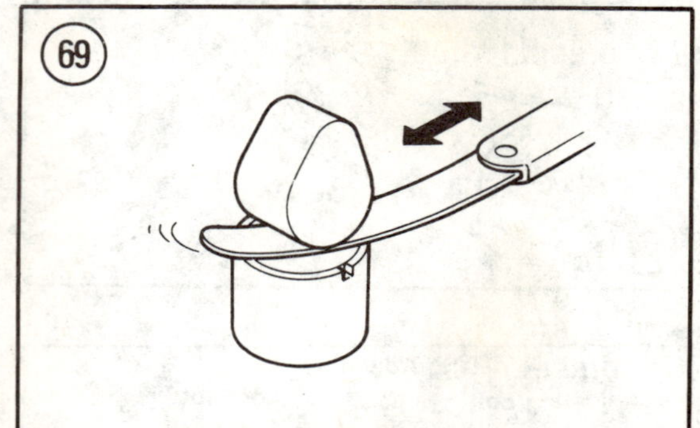

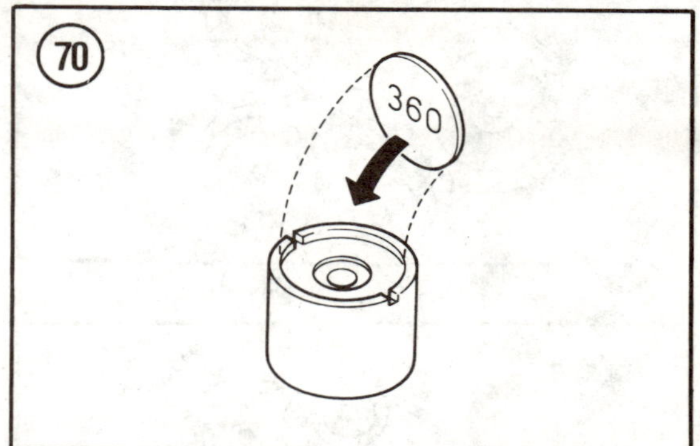

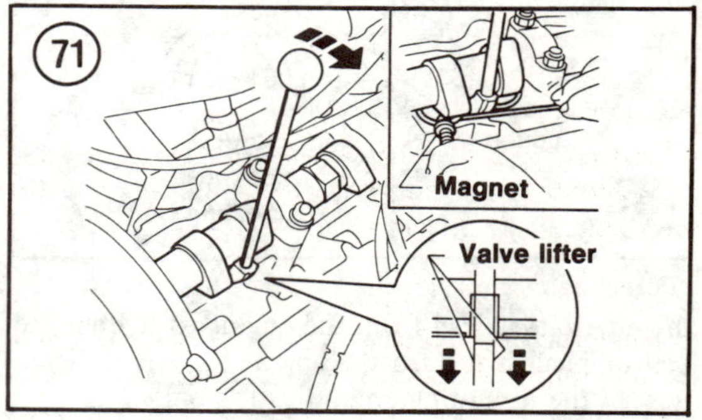

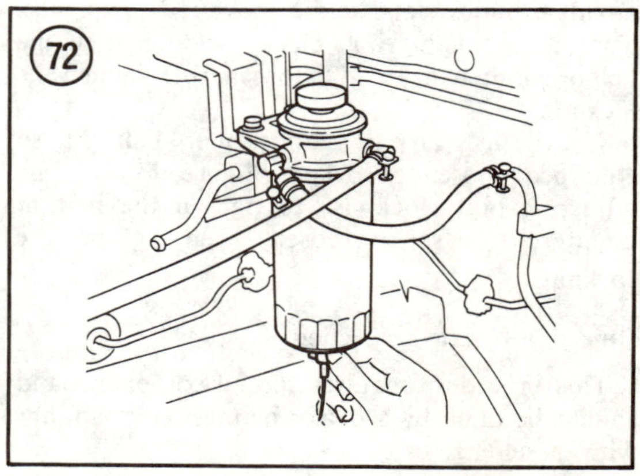

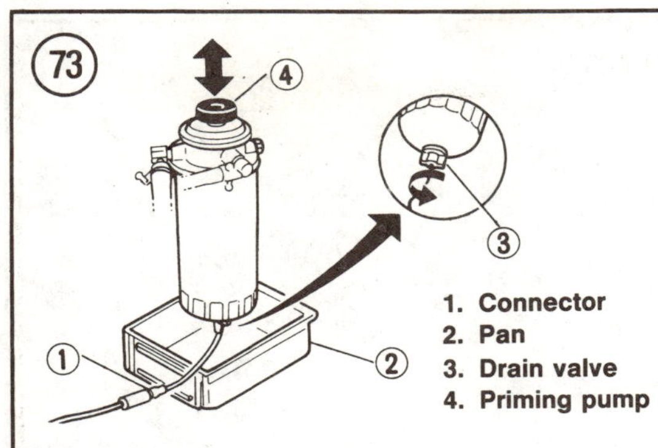

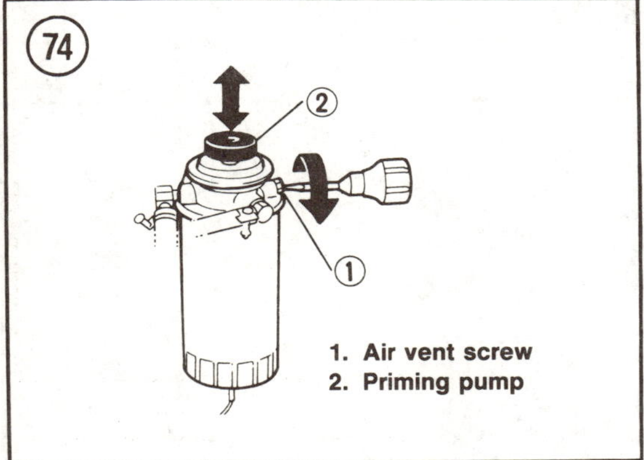

Injection Timing Adjustment

This procedure requires special tools and should be done by a dealer or other qualified diesel mechanic.

Timing Belt Replacement

This procedure requires special tools and should be done by a dealer or other qualified diesel mechanic.

Fuel System Water Removal

Water should be removed from the fuel system whenever the instrument panel warning light comes on.
1. Unplug the wiring connector from the bottom of the fuel filter. See **Figure 73**.
2. Place a pan under the drain valve (**Figure 73**).
3. Loosen the drain valve, push the priming pump up and down by hand until all water has been removed, then tighten the drain valve.
4. Reconnect the wiring connector to the bottom of the fuel filter.
5. Bleed the fuel system as described in this chapter.

Fuel System Bleeding

This should be done whenever the fuel filter is replaced, whenever water is drained from the fuel system or if the fuel tank is run completely dry.
1. Loosen the air vent screw (**Figure 74**).
2. Push the priming pump up and down by hand until no more bubbles emerge from the air vent screw, then tighten the air vent screw.
3. Start the engine. If it doesn't run smoothly, rev the engine 2 or 3 times.

GENERAL MAINTENANCE

The following procedures do not have recommended specific service intervals of miles or time. However, they are important and should be done periodically, such as when cleaning the car or before going on a trip.

Tires and Wheels

1. Check tires for cuts, punctures or excessive wear. If the tires are worn, compare the wear patterns with the illustrations in Chapter Two. Have alignment and balance problems corrected by a dealer or front-end shop.
2. If you haven't done so at the most recent fuel stop, check tire pressures and compare them with **Table 8**. Adjust pressures as needed.
3. Make sure wheel lug nuts are tight.
4. Drive the car and check for vibration, pulling to one side or steering wheel shaking. If any of these conditions are found, have wheel alignment and balance checked by a dealer or front-end shop.

Windshield

Make sure the glass is clean. Check for pits or cracks.

Wipers

1. Check wiper blades for deterioration or cracks. Replace wiper blades that show these conditions. To remove a blade, lift the wiper arm and push the release lever as shown in **Figure 75**. Take the blade out, install a new one and lower the wiper arm.
2. Test the windshield wipers and washers to make sure they work properly. Repair them as needed, referring to Chapter Seven.

Fluid Leaks

Check under the car for fluid leaks. Repair as needed.

> *NOTE*
> *Water dripping from the air conditioner after use is normal.*

Doors and Hood

Make sure the doors and hood work smoothly and latch securely. Make sure the hood safety catch keeps the hood from opening when the cable is pulled to release the hood latch. Lubricate as needed, referring to *Hinges, Latches, and Locks* in this chapter.

Lights

1. Turn on the headlights. Have an assistant operate the turn signals, hazard flashers and brake lights. Walk around the car and make sure all the lights work.
2. Sit in the car and make sure all the warning lights and buzzers or chimes work.

Defroster

Warm the engine to normal operating temperature. Make sure the defroster blows hot air onto the windshield.

Mirrors

Make sure mirrors are clean and securely fastened.

Steering Wheel

With the car stopped, check steering wheel free play (**Figure 76**). If it is more than 35 mm (1 3/8 in.), check the steering mechanism for wear or damage, referring to Chapter Nine.

Throttle Pedal

With the engine off, floor the pedal. It should move smoothly, without sticking or binding. If not, check the cable as described in Chapter Five.

Clutch Pedal

Check pedal free play as described in Chapter Eight. Adjust as needed.

Brakes

1. Road test the brakes and make sure they stop the car securely, without pulling to one side. The pedal should feel firm and not travel too close to the floor. If in doubt, check pedal free play as described in Chapter Eleven.

2. Park the car on a hill. Make sure the handbrake holds the car with the transmission in NEUTRAL. If it doesn't, adjust or repair the handbrake as described in Chapter Eleven.

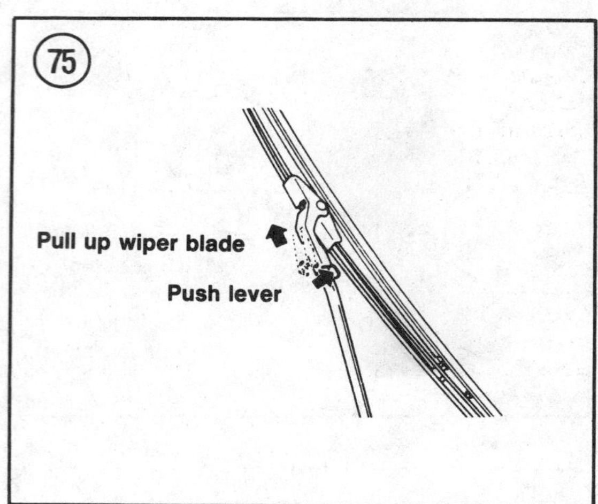

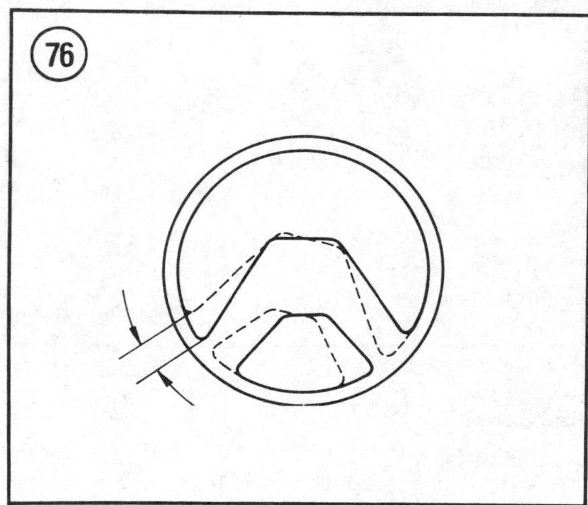

Automatic Transaxle PARK Mechanism

If equipped with an automatic transaxle, park the car on a hill. Make sure the transaxle holds the car when it is placed in PARK with the handbrake off. If not, adjust the shift linkage as described in Chapter Eight. If this doesn't solve the problem, have the transaxle repaired by a dealer or shop familiar with automatic transaxles.

Cooling System

Check cooling system hoses for loose connections, cracks or deterioration as described in Chapter Six. Tighten or replace as needed.

Underbody

Make sure the underbody is free of corrosives such as road salt. In areas where salt is used on the roads, the underbody should be flushed clean with water at the end of each winter.

Table 1   FUEL STOP CHECKS

Engine oil	Check level on dipstick
Coolant	Check level in reservoir
Battery	Check condition
Brake master cylinder	Check fluid level
Tire pressures	Check

Table 2   SCHEDULED MAINTENANCE

Every 7,500 miles (6 months)	• Engine oil and filter change
Every 15,000 miles (12 months)	• Brake inspection • Manual transaxle oil level check • Automatic transaxle fluid level check • Power steering line and hose inspection • Steering linkage and suspension inspection • Front wheel bearing inspection • Hinges, latches, locks lubrication • Exhaust system inspection • Seat belt inspection • Tune-up
Every 30,000 miles (24 months)	• Drive belt inspection • Air cleaner element replacement • Induction valve filter replacement* • Choke inspection • Vapor line inspection • Fuel line inspection • Coolant change • ATC air cleaner inspection • Exhaust gas sensor inspection • Brake fluid change
Every 60,000 miles (48 months)	• Suspension and steering linkage ball-joint inspection
As needed (see text)	• PCV filter replacement • Fuel filter replacement

*Does not apply to MPG models.

Table 3   DIESEL ENGINE MAINTENANCE

Every 7,500 miles (6 months)	• Engine oil change
Every 15,000 miles (12 months)	• Oil filter change • Drive belt inspection • Injection nozzle inspection • Valve clearance adjustment
Every 30,000 miles (24 months)	• Air cleaner element replacement • Fuel line inspection and rubber hose inspection • Fuel filter replacement • Coolant change • Idle speed adjustment • Injection timing adjustment
Every 60,000 miles	• Timing belt replacement
As needed (see text)	• Fuel system water removal • Fuel system bleeding

Table 4   SEVERE SERVICE MAINTENANCE

Interval	Procedure	Notes
As needed	• Air cleaner element replacement	3
	• Air induction valve filter replacement	3
Every 3,000 miles (3 months)	• Engine oil and filter (gasoline)	1, 2, 3, 5
Every 3,750 miles (3 months)	• Engine oil (diesel)	1, 2, 3, 5
	• Oil filter change (diesel)[9]	1, 2, 3, 5
Every 7,500 miles (6 months)	• Oil filter change (diesel)[9]	1, 2, 3, 5
	• Brake inspection	1, 3, 5, 6, 7
	• Steering linkage and suspension inspection	7
	• Ball-joint inspection	
	• Axle shaft boot inspection	4, 6, 7
	• Hinges, latches, locks lubrication	6
	• Exhaust system inspection	
Every 15,000 miles (12 months)	• Brake fluid change	8
Every 30,000 miles (24 months)	• Manual transaxle oil change	5, 7
	• Automatic transaxle fluid change	5, 7

1. Frequent short trips.
2. Extended idling.
3. Dust.
4. Extremely hot or cold weather.
5. Towing a trailer.
6. Road salt or other corrosive materials.
7. Rough or muddy roads.
8. Humid areas or mountains.
9. On diesels, change the oil filter @ every oil change during the first 15,000 miles, then @ alternate oil changes.

Table 5   GENERAL MAINTENANCE

Tires and wheels
Windshield
Wipers
Fluid leaks
Doors and hood
Lights
Defroster
Mirrors
Steering wheel
Throttle pedal
Clutch pedal
Brakes
Automatic transaxle PARK mechanism
Cooling system
Underbody

Table 6 RECOMMENDED LUBRICANTS AND FLUIDS

Engine oil	
Gasoline	
Non-MPG models	API Service SF
MPG models	API Service SF or SE
Diesel	API Service SE/CC, SF/CC, SE/CD, SF/CD or CD

(continued)

Table 6 RECOMMENDED LUBRICANTS AND FLUIDS (continued)

Manual transaxle oil	API GL-4
Automatic transaxle fluid	DEXRON type ATF
Power steering fluid	DEXRON type ATF
Multipurpose grease	NLGI No. 2
Brake fluid	DOT 3
Antifreeze	Ethylene glycol type
Gasoline	
All U.S., Canadian MPG	Unleaded, 87 octane*
Canadian non-MPG	Leaded or unleaded, 87 octane
Diesel fuel	
Above -7° C	
(20° F)	No. 2 diesel, 42 cetane**
Below -7° C	
(20° F)	No. 1 diesel, 42 cetane**

*This is an average of Research and Motor octane numbers. The equivalent Research octane number is 91.
**An equivalent blended diesel fuel may be used, depending on temperature conditions in a specific area. If in doubt, check with the service station operator.

Table 7   LUBRICANT VISCOSITIES

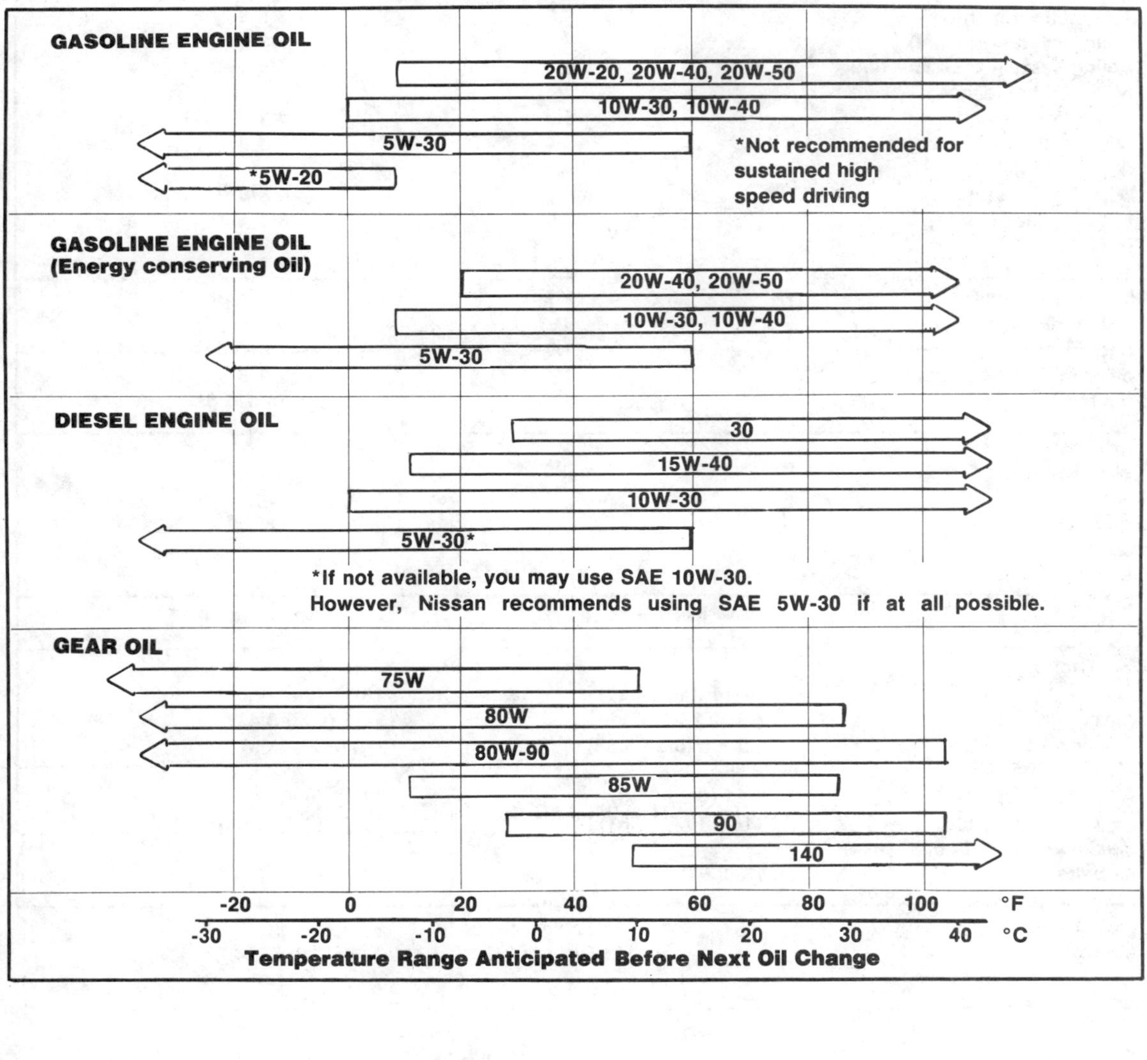

Table 8 TIRE PRESSURES

1982	
155-13, 6.15-13, front and rear	24 psi
155SR-13, 175/70SR-13, front and rear	26 psi
1983	
155SR-13 front	
With E15 and diesel engine	28 psi
With E16 engine	26 psi
155SR-13 rear	26 psi
175/70SR-13 front and rear	26 psi
P155/80D-13 spare	35 psi

Table 9 APPROXIMATE REFILL CAPACITIES

	Liters	Quarts
Cooling system (gasoline)		
Manual transmission	4.7	5
Automatic transmission	5.3	5 5/8
Cooling system (diesel)	7	7 3/8
Cooling system reservoir tank	0.7	3/4
Engine oil (gasoline)		
With filter change	3.9	4 1/8
Without filter change	3.4	3 5/8
Engine oil (diesel)		
With filter change	4.1	4 3/8
Without filter change	3.5	3 3/4
Transaxle		
4-speed manual	2.3	4 7/8 pt.
5-speed manual	2.7	5 3/4 pt.
Automatic	6	6 3/8
Windshield washer tank	1.5	1 5/8
Power steering system	1	1 1/8
Fuel tank	50	13 1/4 gal.

Table 10 DRIVE BELT DEFLECTION

	New belt, mm (in.)	Used belt, mm (in.)
Gasoline engine		
Alternator belt	10-14 (0.39-0.55)	13-17 (0.51-0.67)
Air conditioner belt	7-9 (0.28-0.35)	9-11 (0.35-0.43)
Power steering belt	6.5-8.5 (0.25-0.33)	7-9 (0.28-0.35)
Diesel engine		
Alternator belt	9-11 (0.35-0.43)	11-13 (0.43-0.51)
Air conditioner belt	11-13 (0.43-0.51)	12-14 (0.47-0.55)
Maximum deflection, all belts	16 (0.63)	16 (0.63)

Table 11 TUNE-UP SPECIFICATIONS

Engine compression	
Standard	12.7 kg/cm² (181 psi)
Minimum	10 kg/cm² (142 psi)
Valve clearance (gasoline)	
Warm engine	0.28 mm (0.011 in.)
Cold engine	0.22 mm (0.009 in.)
Valve clearance (diesel)	
Intake	0.2-0.3 mm (0.008-0.012 in.)
Exhaust	0.4-0.5 mm (0.016-0.020 in.)
Spark plug type (NGK brand)	
Standard type (U.S.)	BPR5ES-11
Hot type (U.S.)	BPR4ES-11
Cold type (U.S.)	BPR6ES-11
Standard type (Canada)	BPR5ES
Hot type (Canada)	BPR4ES
Cold type (Canada)	BPR6ES
Spark plug gap	
U.S.	1.0-1.1 mm (0.039-0.043 in.)
Canada	0.8-0.9 mm (0.031-0.035 in.)
Firing order	1-3-4-2 counterclockwise
Ignition timing (at idle speed)*	
1982	
U.S. manual	2 ±2° ATDC
Canadian manual (non-MPG)	4 ±2° ATDC
Canadian manual (MPG)	2 ±2° ATDC
Automatic	6 ±2° ATDC
1983	
Non-MPG	5 ±2° ATDC*
MPG	2 ±2° ATDC*
Idle speed	
Manual (except MPG)	750 ±50 rpm
Automatic	650 ±50 rpm
MPG	700 ±50 rpm
Idle mixture (Canadian non-MPG only)	2 ±1 per cent

* On U.S. models and Canadian MPG models, disconnect and plug the distributor vacuum line.

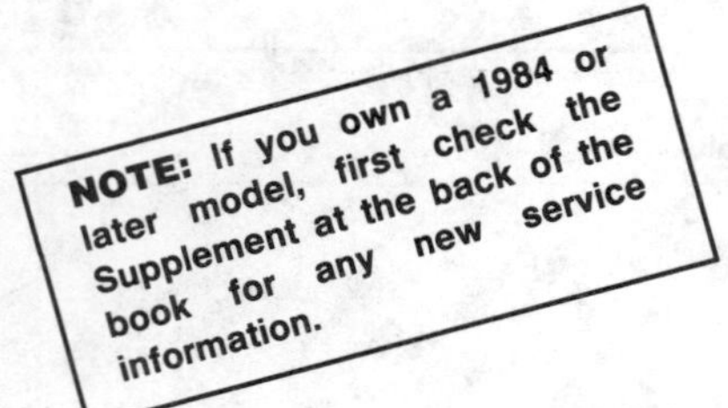

CHAPTER FOUR

ENGINE

The Sentra uses a 4-cylinder overhead cam gasoline engine as standard equipment. The E15 engine is used on all 1982 models, as well on 1983 MPG models. The E16, engine mechanically the same as the E15 except for a longer stroke, is used on 1983 non-MPG cars. The CD17 4-cylinder diesel engine is optional. Diesel engine repairs should be done by a dealer or a repair shop equipped to handle diesel engines.

Specifications and tightening torques for the gasoline engines are listed in **Table 1** and **Table 2** at the end of the chapter.

ENGINE REMOVAL

The engine and transaxle are removed as a unit, then separated. **Figure 1** and **Figure 2** show disconnection points. Refer to them as needed for this procedure.

1. Remove the hood as described in Chapter Twelve.
2. Remove the battery and its support bracket (**Figure 1**).
3. Remove the air cleaner.

> *CAUTION*
> *Stuff a clean rag into the carburetor to keep out dirt and small parts.*

4. Drain the cooling system as described in Chapter Six.

> *WARNING*
> *Antifreeze is poisonous and may attract animals. Do not leave the drained coolant where it can be reached by children or pets.*

5. Remove the radiator and fan as described in Chapter Six.
6. Remove the power steering and air conditioning drive belts (if so equipped) as described under *Drive Belts* in Chapter Three.
7. If equipped with power steering, detach the pump from the engine as described in Chapter Nine. Tie the pump back out of the way. Do not disconnect the pump hoses.

> *WARNING*
> *Do not disconnect the air conditioning compressor hoses during the next step. Air conditioning refrigerant creates freezing temperatures when it evaporates. This can cause frostbite if it touches skin and blindness if it touches the eyes. If discharged near an open flame, the refrigerant forms poisonous gas.*

8. If equipped with air conditioning, detach the compressor from the engine and tie it back out of the way. See **Figure 3**. Do not disconnect the compressor hoses.
9. Detach the front exhaust pipe from the manifold. See **Figure 4**.
10. If equipped with a manual transaxle, detach the shift linkage from the transaxle. See **Figure 5**. Disconnect the neutral switch and back-up lamp wires.
11. If equipped with automatic transaxle, detach the shift control cable from the transaxle. See **Figure 6**. Unplug the inhibitor switch wiring connector.

ENGINE COMPARTMENT

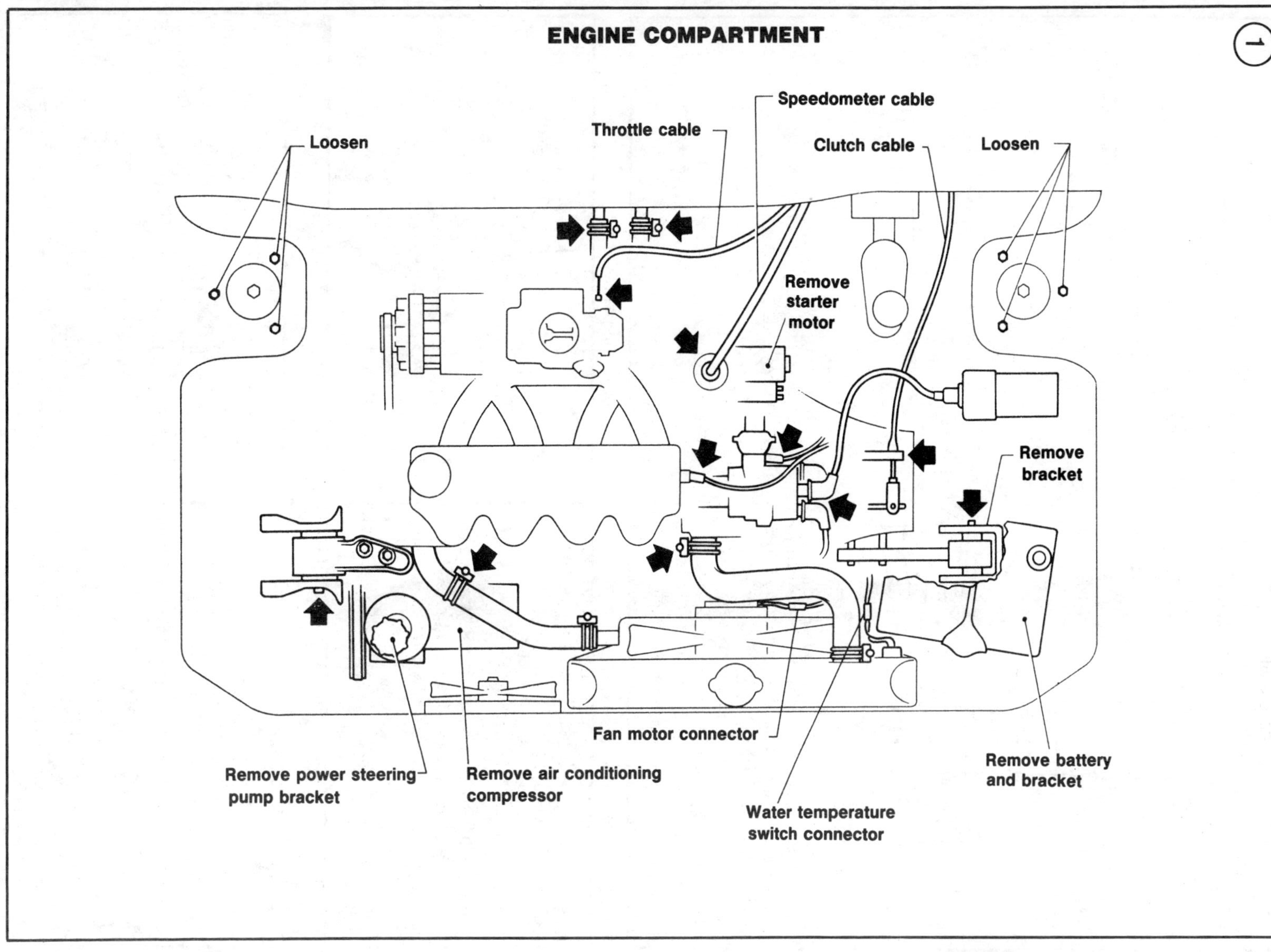

2

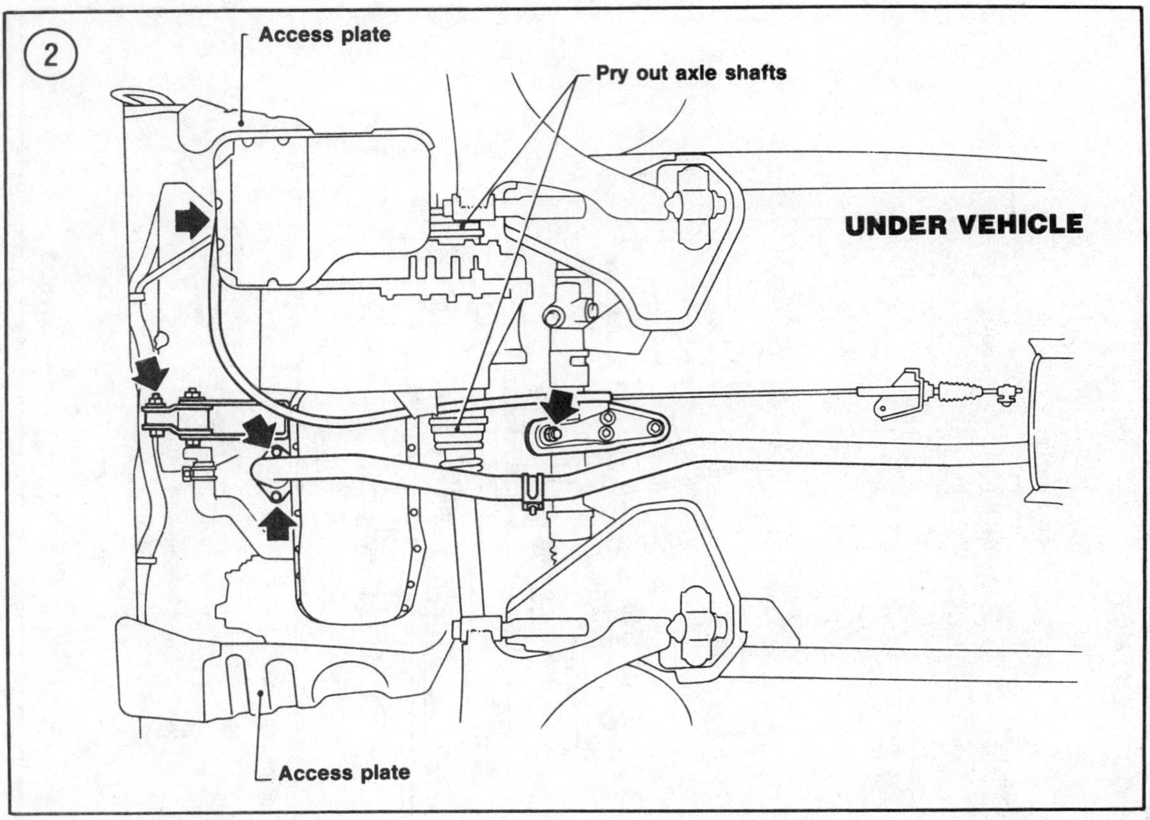

Access plate
Pry out axle shafts
UNDER VEHICLE
Access plate

3

5

4

6

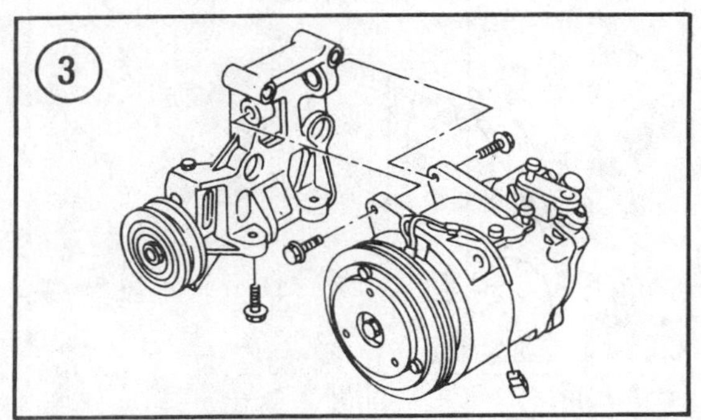

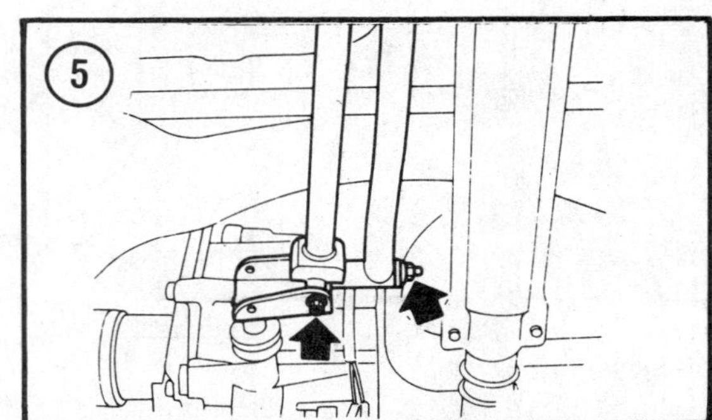

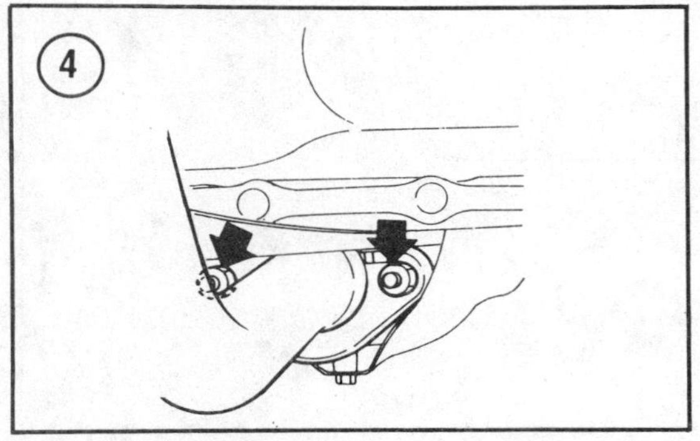

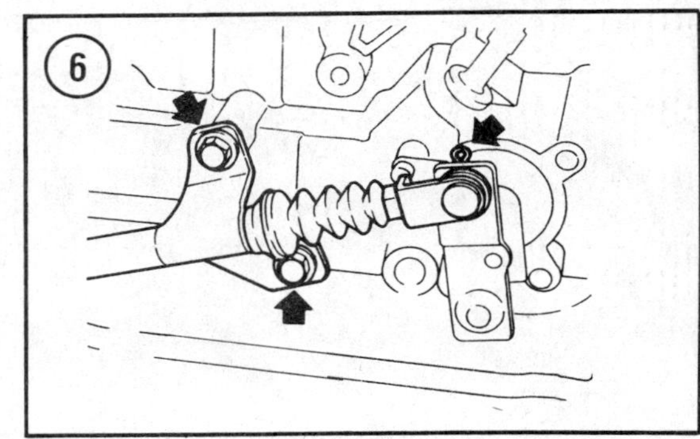

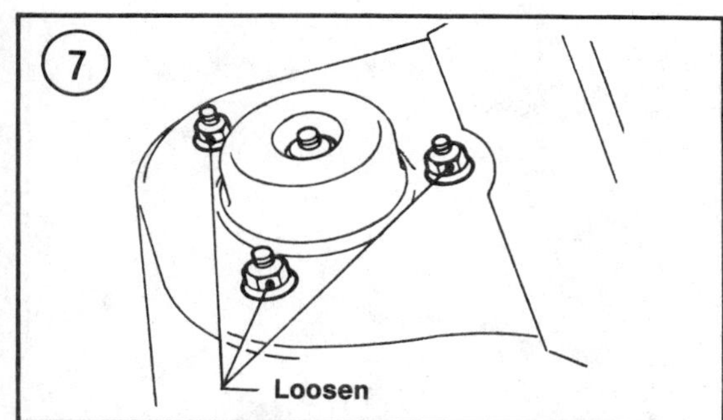

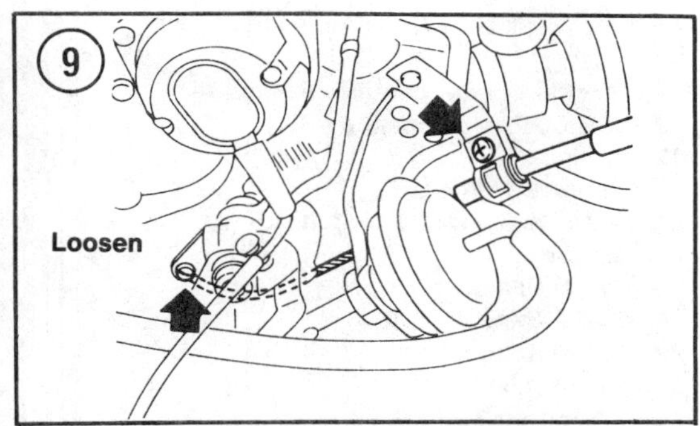

12. Remove the suspension ball-joints as described in Chapter Nine.

13. Loosen, but do not remove, the mounting nuts at the top of the struts. See **Figure 7**.

14. Remove the access plate from each wheel well. See **Figure 2**.

15. Pry the axle shafts out of the transaxle. See **Figure 8**.

16. If equipped with a manual transaxle, detach the clutch cable from the withdrawal lever as described in Chapter Eight.

17. Detach the speedometer cable and pinion from the transaxle.

CAUTION
Plug the speedometer pinion hole with a clean rag to keep dirt out of the transaxle.

18. Disconnect the throttle cable from the carburetor. See **Figure 9**.

19. Remove the starter (**Figure 1**).

20. Disconnect emission control vacuum and air lines connecting the engine to the body. See *Emission Controls* in Chapter Five.

21. Disconnect the distributor and alternator wires.

22. Unplug all wiring connectors securing the engine to the car body. See **Figure 10** (1982) or **Figure 11** (1983).

23. Disconnect the inlet line from the fuel pump (**Figure 12**). Plug the line so it won't drip gasoline and create a fire hazard.

CAUTION
At this point, there should not be any hoses, linkages or wires attaching the engine and transaxle to the car. Recheck this to make sure nothing can hamper engine removal.

24. Attach a hoist to the engine sling brackets (**Figure 13**). Portable hydraulic crane type hoists, available from rental dealers, are easy to use and don't require an upper support such as rafters.

25. Raise the hoist just enough to support the engine, but not enough to place tension on the engine and transaxle mounts.

26. Detach the engine and transaxle mounts (**Figure 14**).

CAUTION
Do not let the engine and transaxle strike equipment on the engine compartment sidewalls during the next step. Use special care not to strike the master cylinder or brake lines.

27. Hoist the engine and transaxle out of the engine compartment as shown in **Figure 15**.

ENGINE/TRANSAXLE SEPARATION

To separate a manual transaxle from the engine, remove the mounting bolts and take it off.

To remove an automatic transaxle from the engine, turn the torque converter and remove the torque converter-to-drive plate bolts. Then remove the mounting bolts and take the transaxle off the engine. See *Automatic Transaxle Removal* in Chapter Nine for details.

ENGINE INSTALLATION

Installation is the reverse of removal, plus the following.

1. Fasten the engine and transaxle securely to their mounts before tightening anything else.

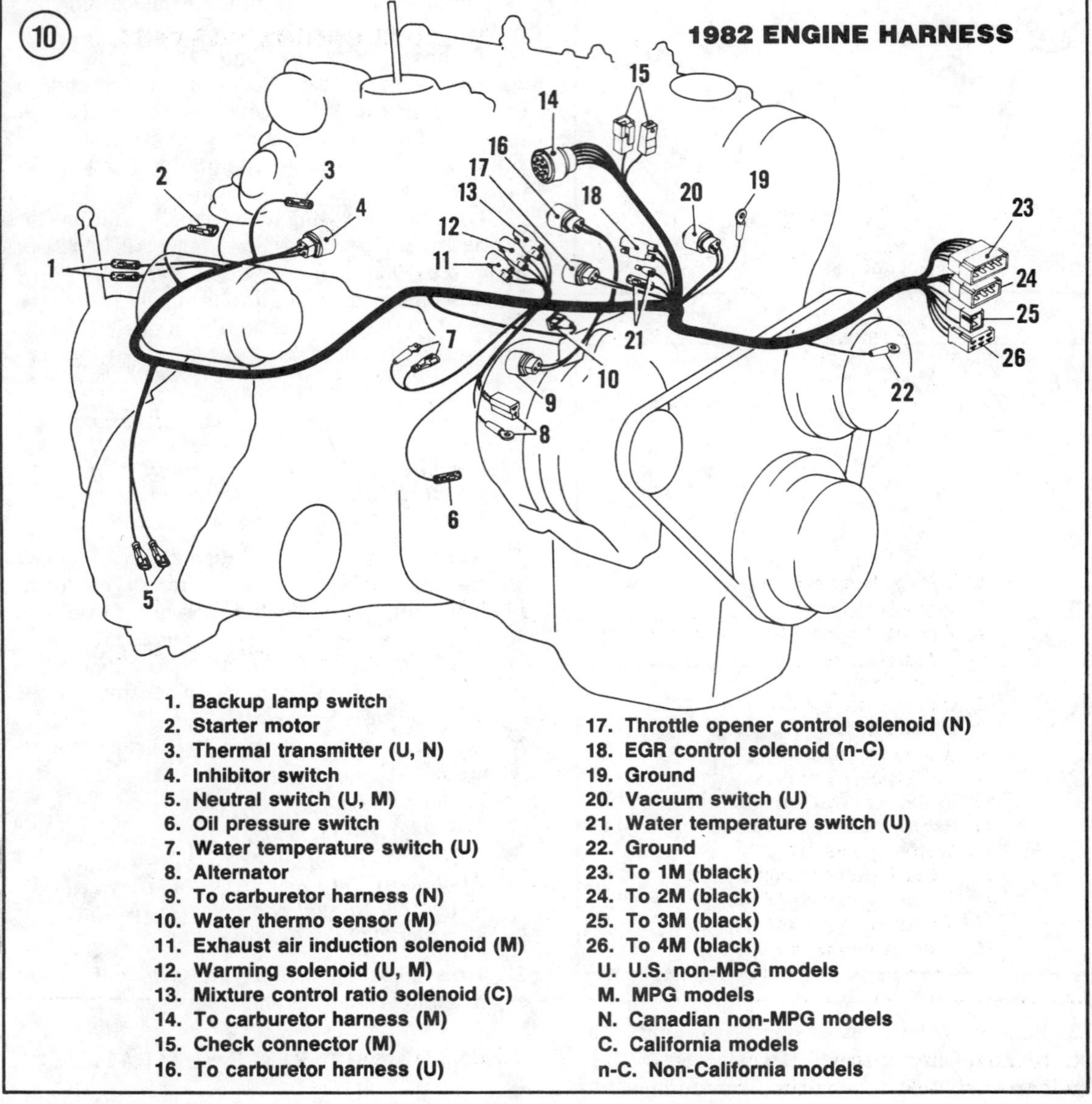

1. Backup lamp switch
2. Starter motor
3. Thermal transmitter (U, N)
4. Inhibitor switch
5. Neutral switch (U, M)
6. Oil pressure switch
7. Water temperature switch (U)
8. Alternator
9. To carburetor harness (N)
10. Water thermo sensor (M)
11. Exhaust air induction solenoid (M)
12. Warming solenoid (U, M)
13. Mixture control ratio solenoid (C)
14. To carburetor harness (M)
15. Check connector (M)
16. To carburetor harness (U)
17. Throttle opener control solenoid (N)
18. EGR control solenoid (n-C)
19. Ground
20. Vacuum switch (U)
21. Water temperature switch (U)
22. Ground
23. To 1M (black)
24. To 2M (black)
25. To 3M (black)
26. To 4M (black)
U. U.S. non-MPG models
M. MPG models
N. Canadian non-MPG models
C. California models
n-C. Non-California models

2. Fill the engine and transaxle with oils recommended in Chapter Three.

3. Fill the cooling system with a 50/50 mixture of ethylene glycol-based antifreeze and water.

4. Check throttle linkage adjustment as described in Chapter Five.

5. If equipped with an automatic transaxle, check shift linkage adjustment as described in Chapter Nine.

DISASSEMBLY CHECKLISTS

These checklists tell how much of the engine to remove and disassemble to do a specific type of service (such as a valve job). They will prevent unnecessary work and make sure nothing is left out.

To use the checklists, remove and inspect each part mentioned. Then go through the checklists backwards, installing the parts. Each major part is covered under its own heading in his chapter unless otherwise noted.

Decarbonizing or Valve Service

1. Remove the intake and exhaust manifolds.
2. Remove the rocker arms and camshaft.
3. Remove the cylinder head.

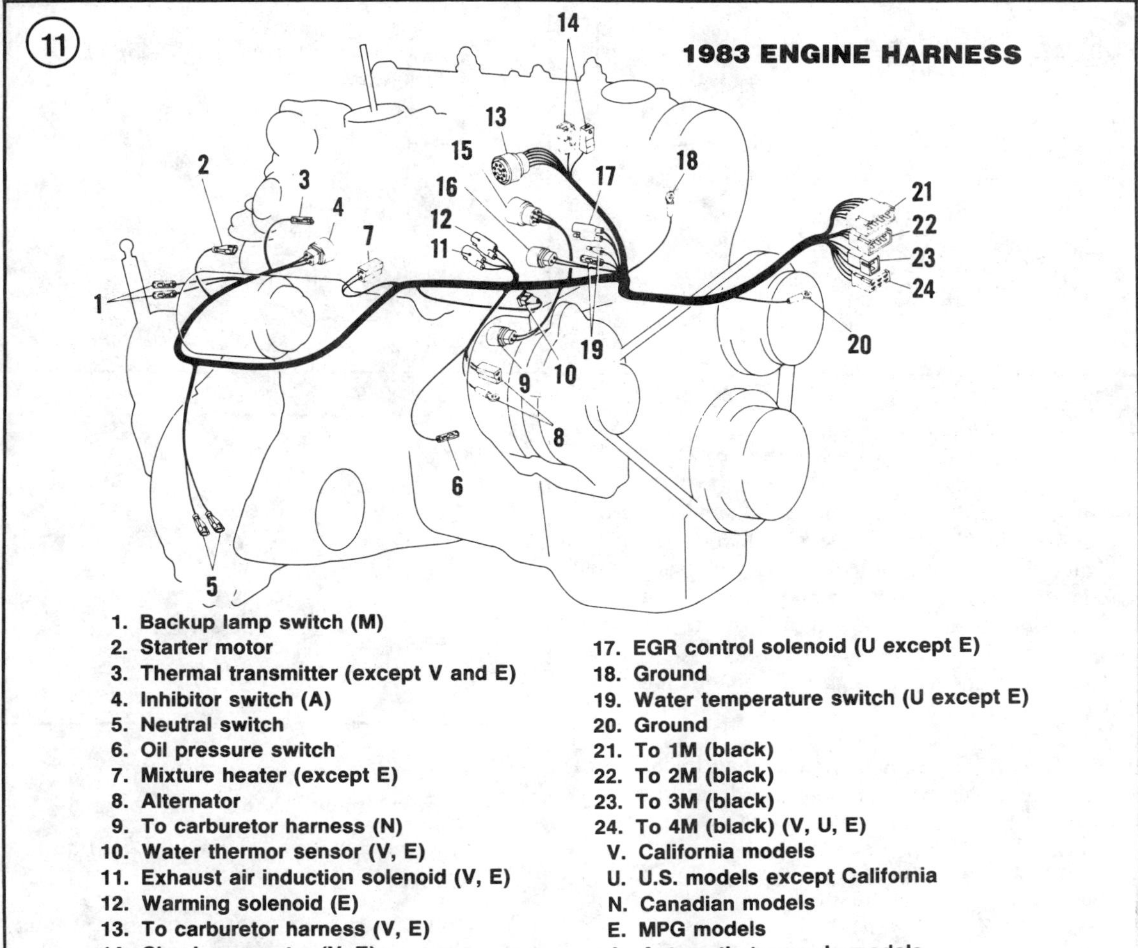

4. Remove and inspect valves. Inspect valve guides and seats, repairing or replacing as necessary.
5. Assemble by reversing Steps 1-4.

Valve and Ring Service

1. Perform Steps 1-4 of *Decarbonizing or Valve Service.*
2. Remove the oil pan.
3. Remove the pistons together with the connecting rods.
4. Remove the piston rings. It is not necessary to separate the pistons from the connecting rods unless a piston, connecting rod or piston pin needs repair or replacement.
5. Assemble by reversing Steps 1-4.

General Overhaul

During overhaul, the following parts are normally taken to a machine shop for inspection and service:
  a. Cylinder block.
  b. Cylinder head.
  c. Crankshaft.
  d. Piston/connecting rod assemblies.
  e. Flywheel or torque converter drive plate.
1. Remove the engine and transaxle and separate them as described in this chapter.
2. Remove the clutch (Chapter Eight) from manual transaxle cars.
3. Remove the engine outer parts. See **Figure 16** and **Figure 17**.

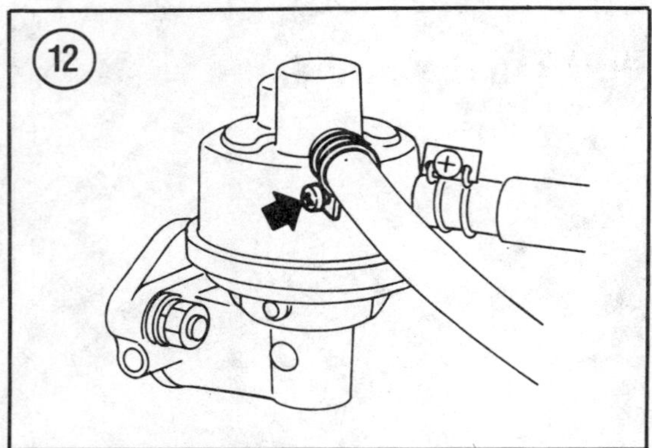

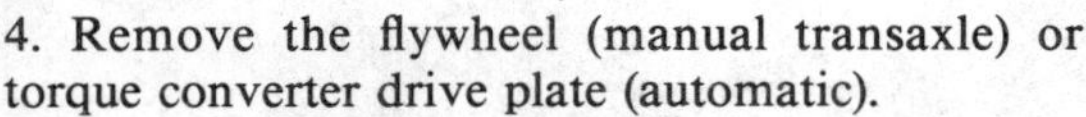

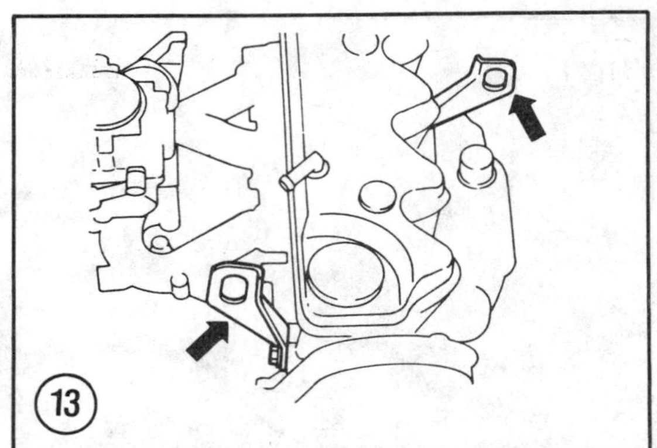

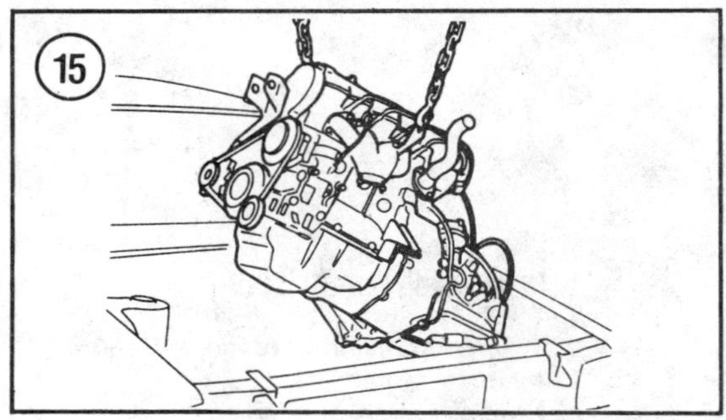

4. Remove the flywheel (manual transaxle) or torque converter drive plate (automatic).
5. Remove the engine rear plate (**Figure 18**).
6. If available, place the engine in a stand. **Figure 19** shows the Nissan engine stand and adapter designed for use with the E-series engines. Similar stands are available from rental dealers. The stand isn't absolutely necessary, but will make the job much easier.
7. Check the engine for signs of coolant and oil leaks.
8. Clean the outside of the engine.
9. Remove the intake and exhaust manifolds.
10. Remove the water pump as described in Chapter Six.
11. Remove the oil pan and pump.
12. Remove the timing belt and sprockets.
13. Remove the rocker assembly.
14. Remove the camshaft.
15. Remove the jackshaft.
16. Remove the cylinder head.
17. Remove the pistons and connecting rods.
18. Remove the rear seal housing (**Figure 20**).
19. Remove the crankshaft.
20. Inspect the cylinder block.
21. Assemble by reversing these steps.

INTAKE AND EXHAUST MANIFOLDS

Intake Manifold Removal/Installation

1. Disconnect all emission control lines and hoses securing the intake manifold to the engine and body. See *Emission Controls* in Chapter Five.
2. Unplug the electrical connectors securing the intake manifold to the engine and body. See **Figure 10** (1982) or **Figure 11** (1983).
3. Disconnect the fuel inlet and return lines from the carburetor. Plug the lines so they won't drip gasoline and create a fire hazard.
4. Drain about one gallon of coolant from the radiator.

WARNING
Antifreeze is poisonous and may attract animals. Do not leave the drained coolant where it can be reached by children or pets.

5. Disconnect the water hoses from the intake manifold.

CAUTION
The intake manifold should come off easily during the next step. If not, make sure all fasteners have been removed. Do not force the manifold off.

6. Remove the intake manifold fasteners, referring to **Figure 16**. Take the manifold off the engine, together with the vacuum line bracket.
7. If necessary, remove the carburetor and emission control system parts from the manifold, referring to **Figure 16**.
8. Installation is the reverse of removal. Use a new gasket. Tighten the manifold fasteners to specifications at the end of the chapter.

Exhaust Manifold Removal/Installation

NOTE
If the exhaust manifold fittings and hardware are corroded, soak them with penetrating oil such as WD-40 before trying to loosen them.

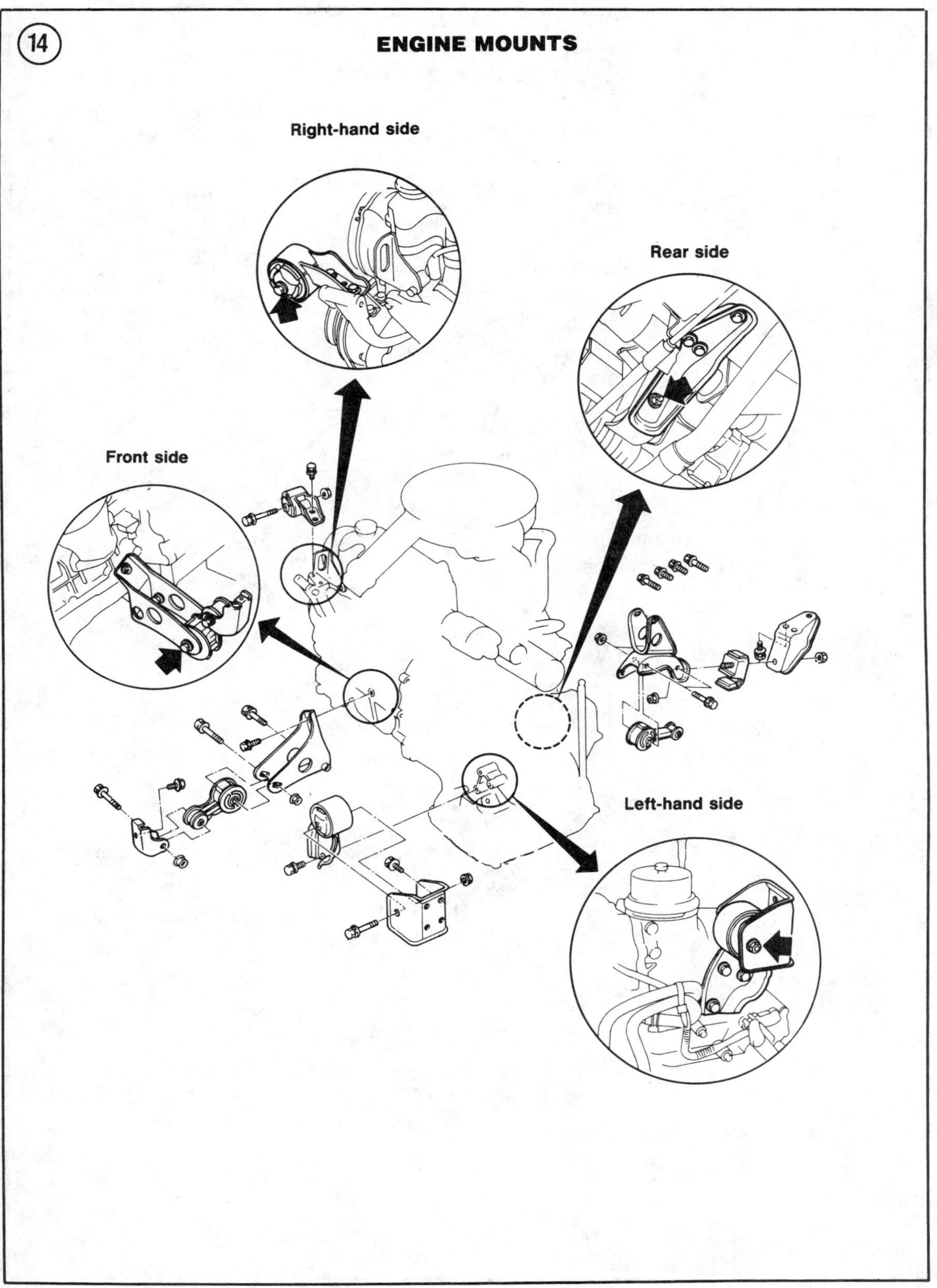
14
ENGINE MOUNTS
Right-hand side
Rear side
Front side
Left-hand side

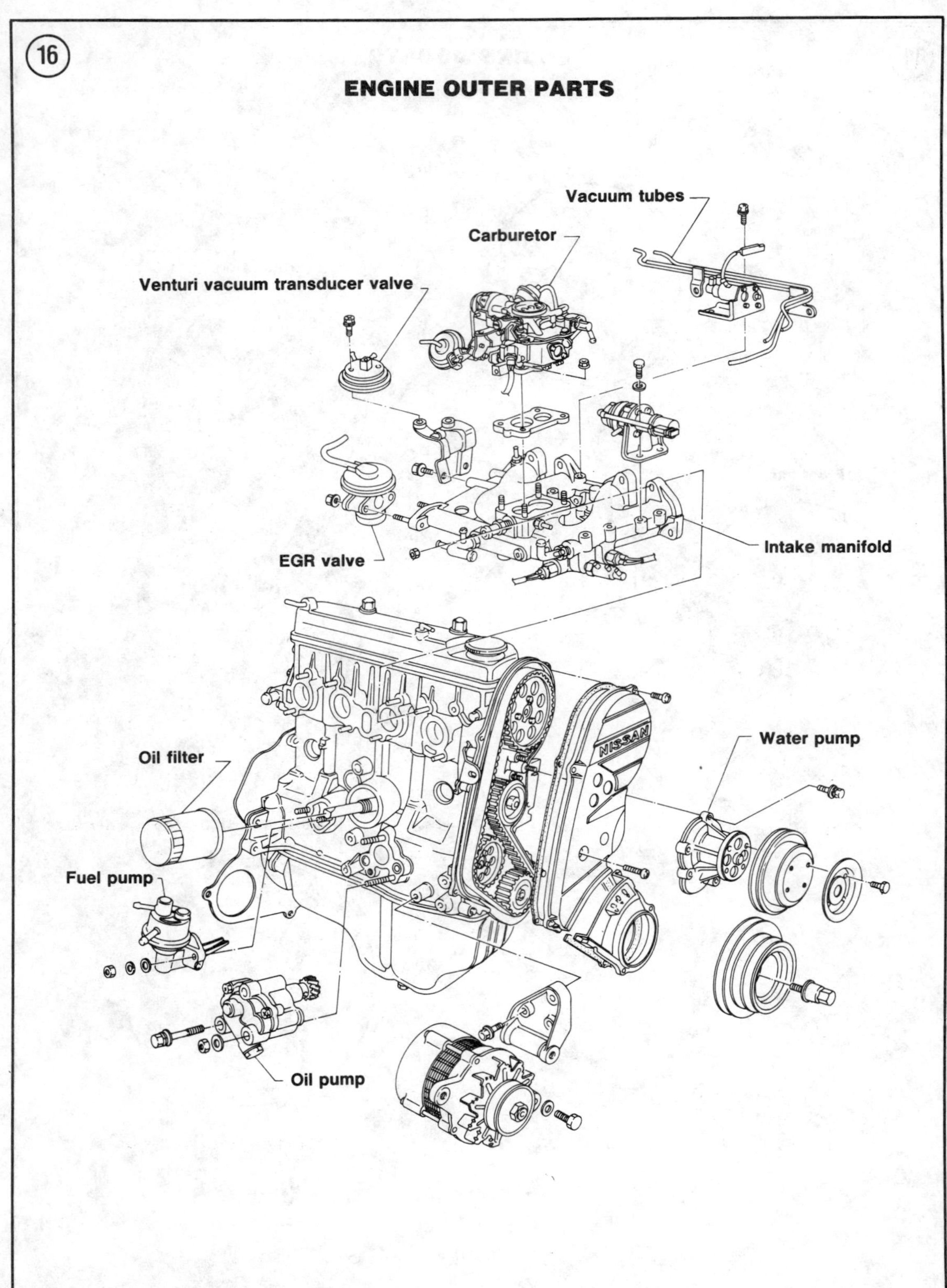

16
ENGINE OUTER PARTS
Vacuum tubes
Carburetor
Venturi vacuum transducer valve
EGR valve
Intake manifold
Oil filter
Water pump
NISSAN
Fuel pump
Oil pump

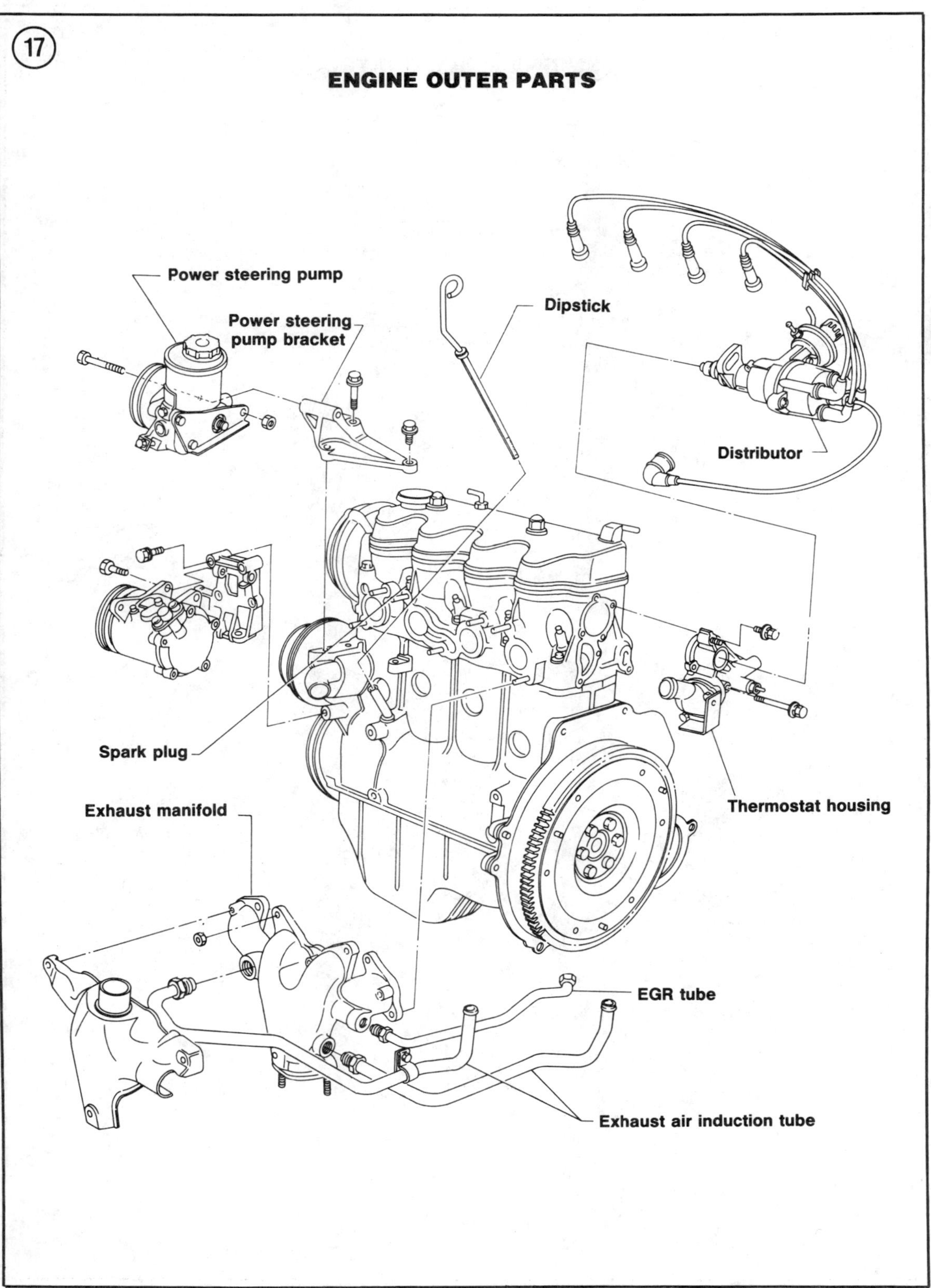
17
ENGINE OUTER PARTS
Power steering pump
Power steering pump bracket
Dipstick
Distributor
Spark plug
Thermostat housing
Exhaust manifold
EGR tube
Exhaust air induction tube
4

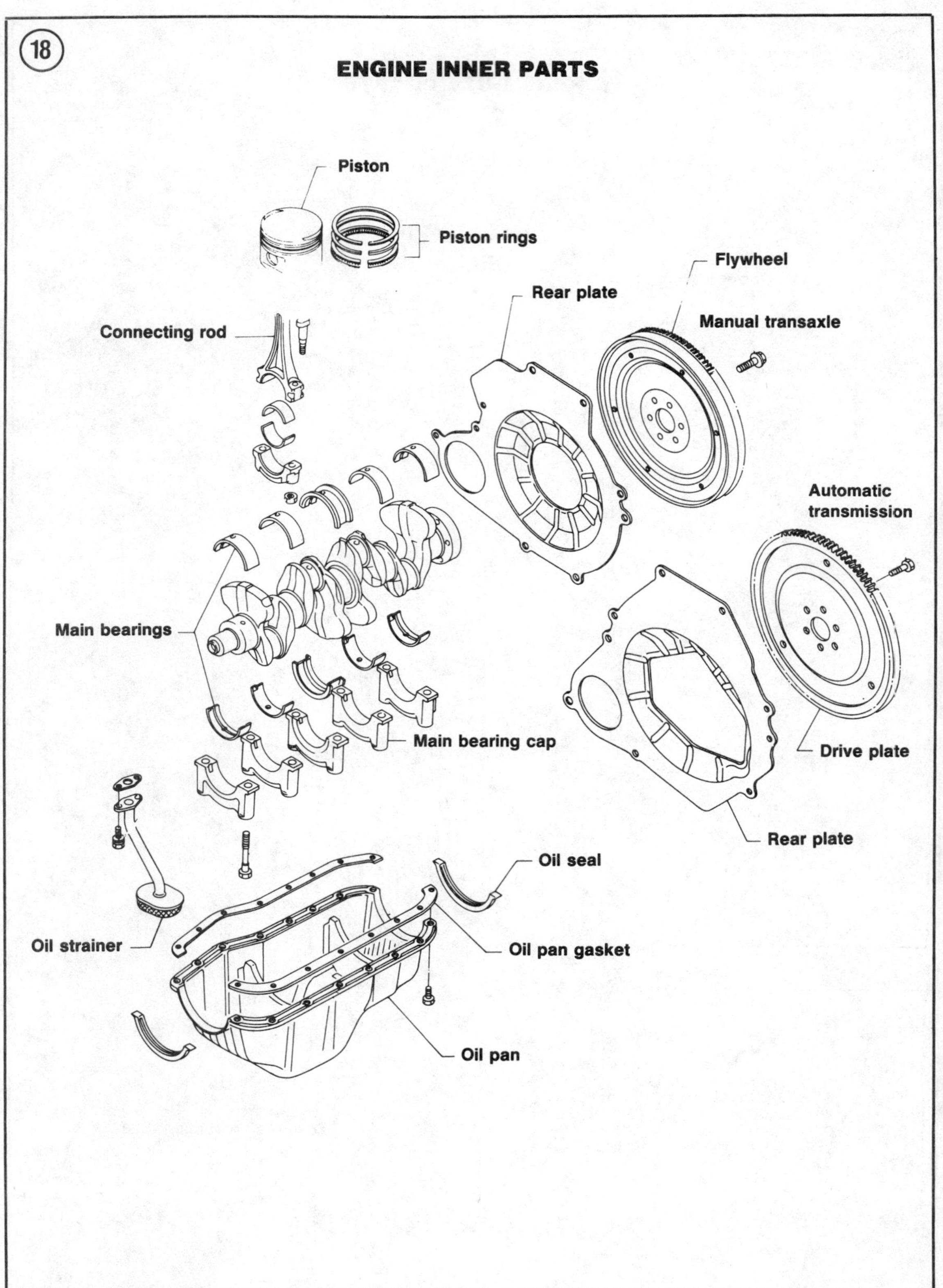
18
ENGINE INNER PARTS
Piston
Piston rings
Flywheel
Rear plate
Manual transaxle
Connecting rod
Automatic transmission
Main bearings
Main bearing cap
Drive plate
Rear plate
Oil seal
Oil pan gasket
Oil strainer
Oil pan

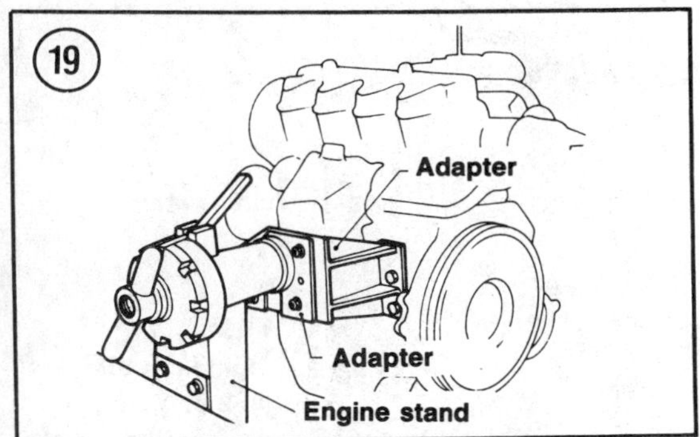

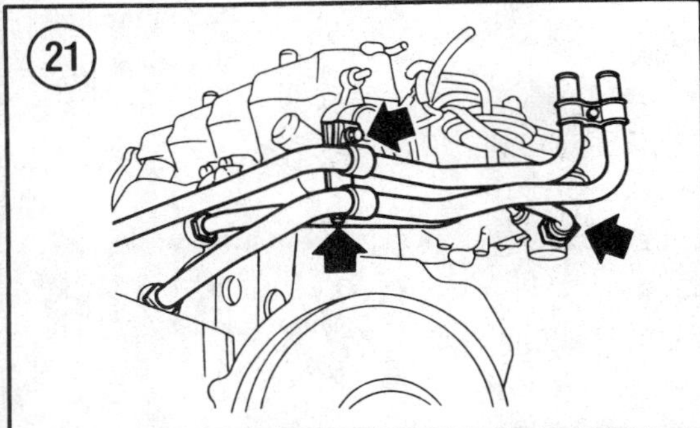

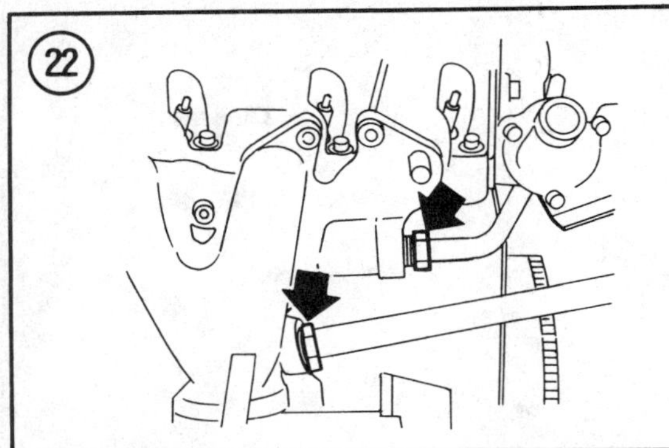

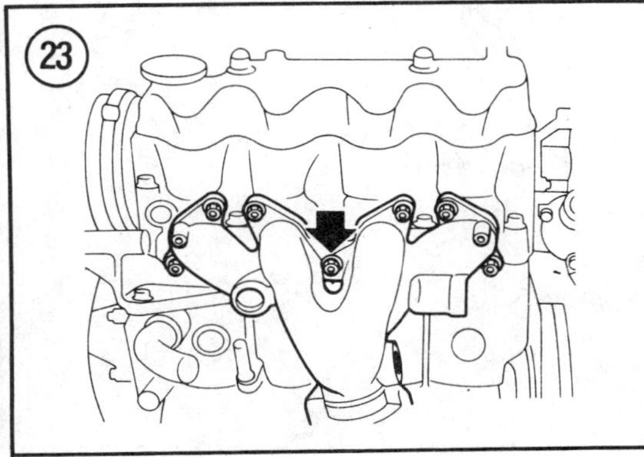

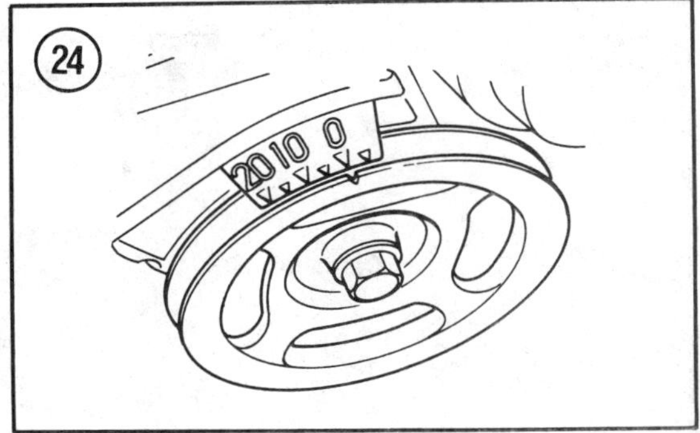

1. Remove the air cleaner.

2. Detach the air induction system tubes from the engine. Disconnect the EGR tube from the EGR valve. See **Figure 21**.

3. Disconnect the air induction tubes and the EGR tube from the exhaust manifold. See **Figure 22**.

4. Remove the exhaust manifold heat shield (**Figure 17**).

CAUTION
The exhaust manifold should come off
easily during the next step. If not, make
sure all fasteners have been removed.
Do not force the manifold off.

5. Remove the exhaust manifold fasteners (**Figure 23**). Take the manifold off the engine.

6. Installation is the reverse of removal. Tighten all fasteners to specifications (**Table 2**). The center nut (**Figure 23**) is of a different diameter than the others.

Inspection

1. Thoroughly clean the manifold in solvent. While cleaning, check for cracks or other obvious damage. Replace damaged manifolds.

2. Check the manifold's gasket surface for warpage with a machinist's straightedge. This can be done inexpensively by a machine shop. Have the manifold resurfaced by a machine shop if warped.

TIMING BELT

Removal

1. Turn the engine so No. 1 cylinder is at top dead center on its compression stroke. When this occurs, the zero degree mark on the timing scale will align with the notch in the crankshaft pulley. See **Figure 24**. In addition, the distributor rotor will point to No. 1 terminal in the distributor cap (**Figure 25**).

NOTE
Be sure to remove the distributor cap
and check rotor position as well as the

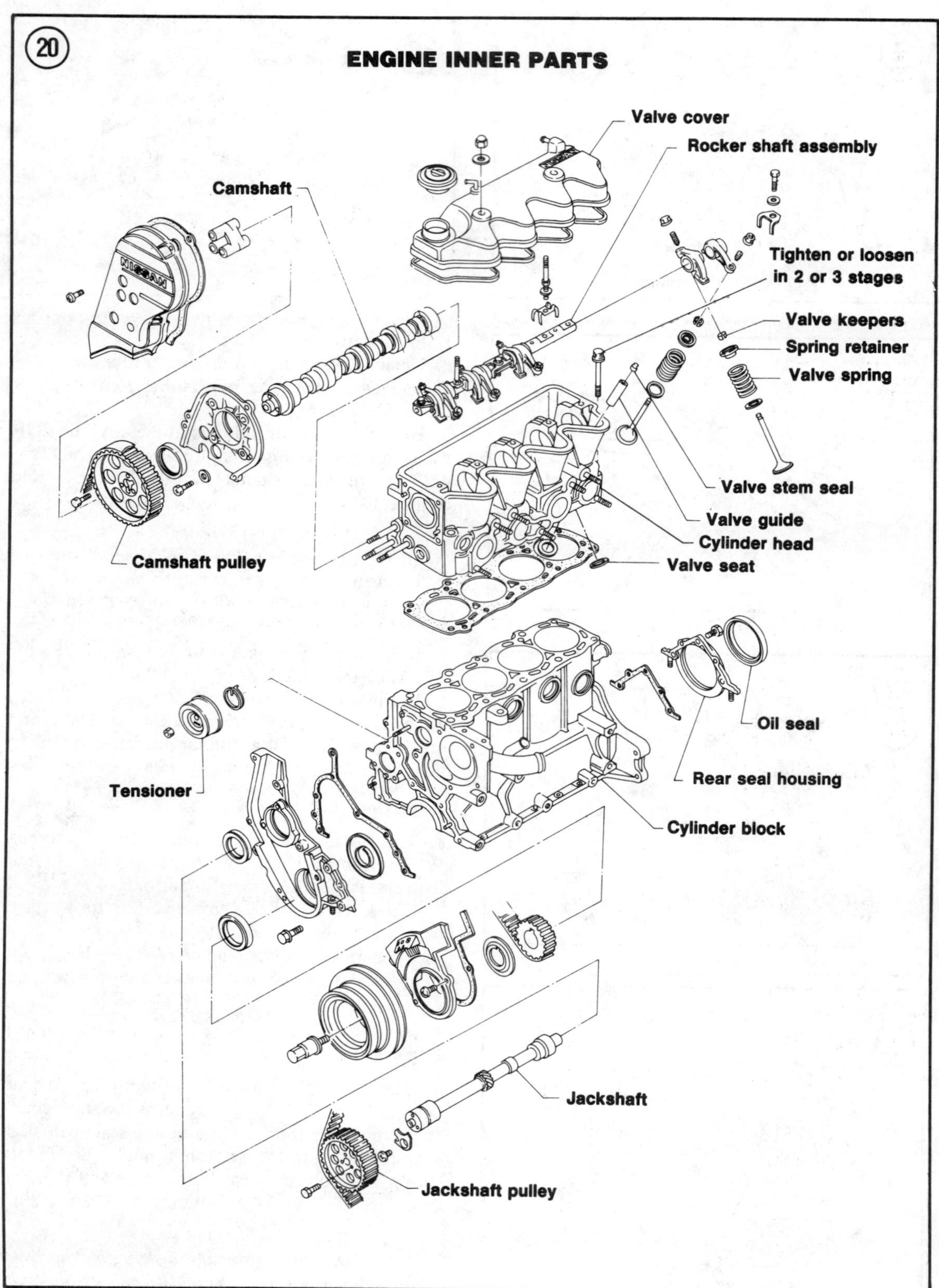

20
ENGINE INNER PARTS
Valve cover
Rocker shaft assembly
Camshaft
Tighten or loosen
in 2 or 3 stages
Valve keepers
Spring retainer
Valve spring
Valve stem seal
Valve guide
Cylinder head
Camshaft pulley
Valve seat
Oil seal
Tensioner
Rear seal housing
Cylinder block
Jackshaft
Jackshaft pulley

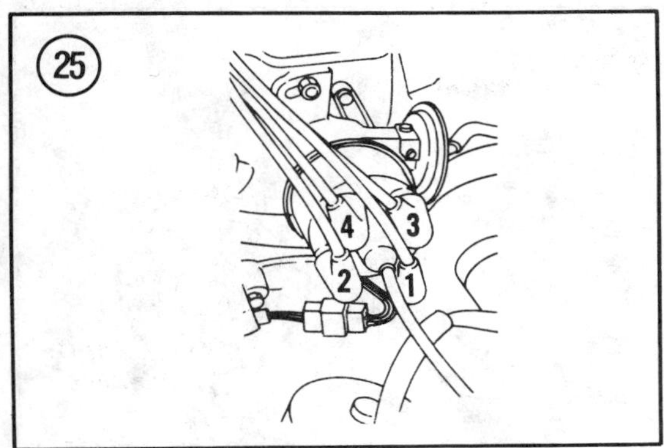

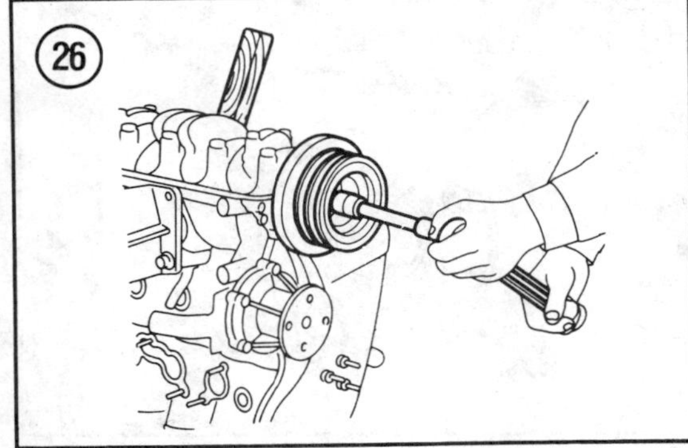

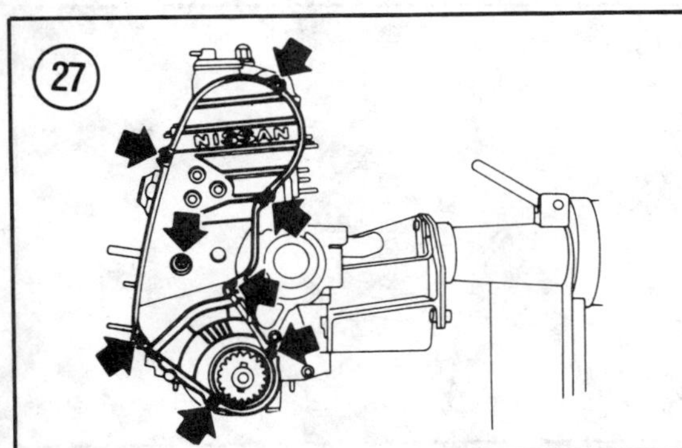

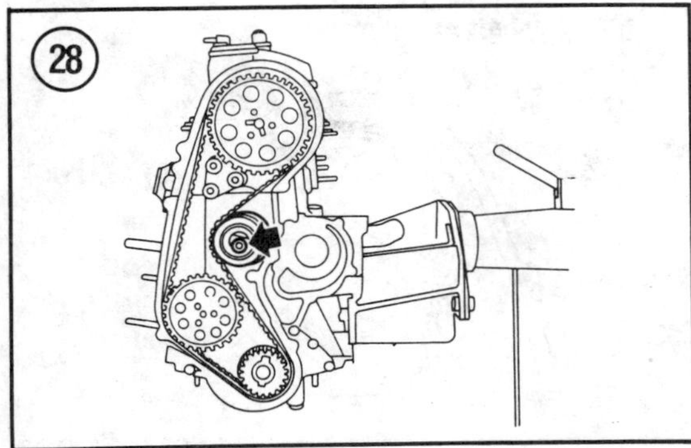

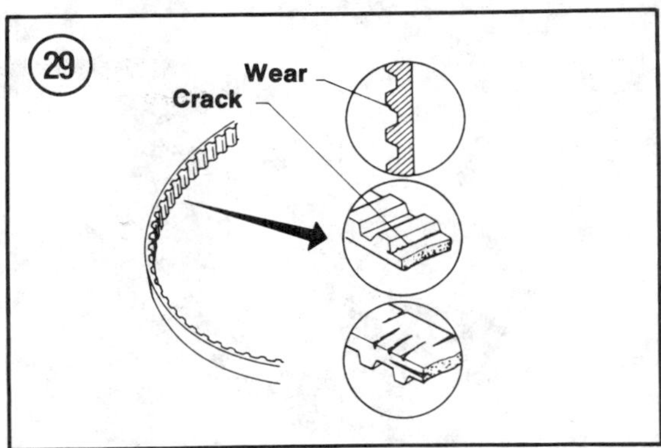

timing marks. The timing marks also align when No. 4 cylinder is at top dead center on its compression stroke.

2. Remove the drive belts as described under *Drive Belts* in Chapter Three.

3. Remove the water pump pulley.

4. Remove the crankshaft pulley (**Figure 26**). Take the spacer off the crankshaft.

5. Remove the timing belt upper and lower covers (**Figure 27**).

6. Remove the tensioner pulley (**Figure 28**).

7. Mark an arrow on the timing belt to indicate the direction of rotation (clockwise, viewed from the crankshaft pulley end of the engine).

8. Take the belt off the pulleys.

> *CAUTION*
> *Do not turn the camshaft or crankshaft once the timing belt has been removed. This will force the valves against the piston tops.*

Inspection

1. Check the belt for oil or water saturation. Replace the belt if it has been saturated.

> *NOTE*
> *If oil has leaked onto the belt, replace the crankshaft and jackshaft oil seals. See **Oil Seals** in this chapter.*

2. Check the belt for cracks, wear or damaged grooves. See **Figure 29**. Replace it if these conditions can be seen.

3. Check the pulleys for wear or damage. Replace worn or damaged pulleys.

   a. To remove a camshaft or jackshaft pulley, remove the bolts and take the pulley off. **Figure 30** shows the camshaft pulley bolts. The jackshaft pulley arrangement is basically the same.

   b. To remove a crankshaft pulley, slide it off the crankshaft as shown in **Figure 31**. If the pulley

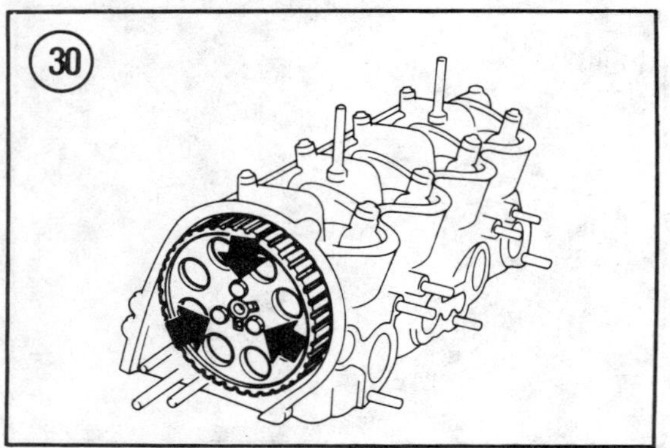

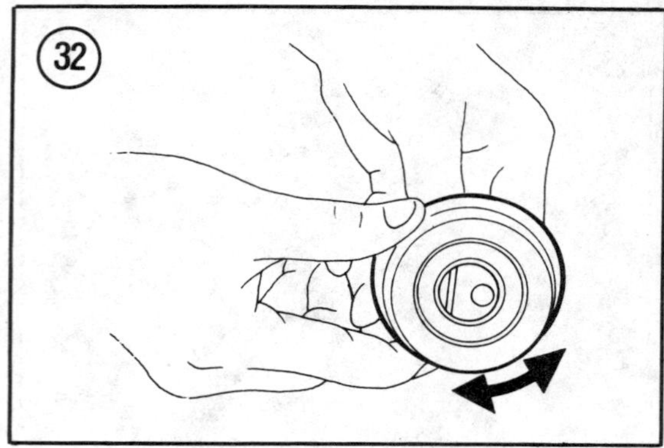

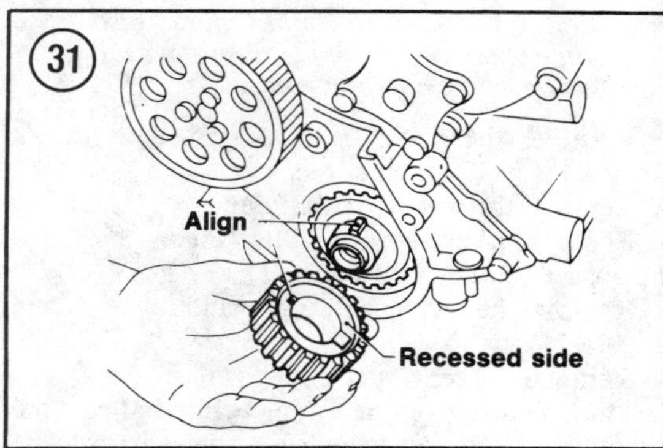

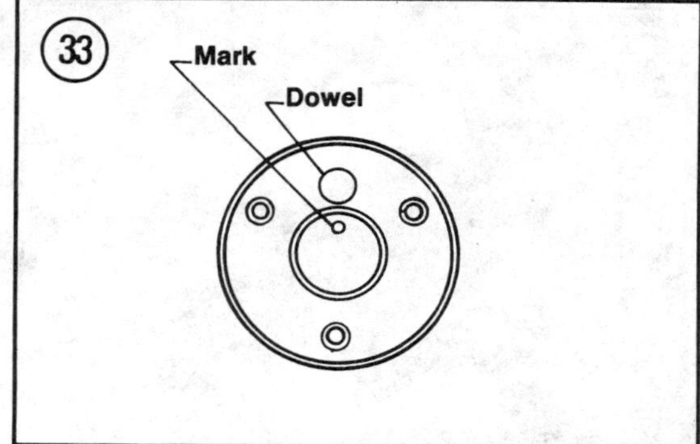

is difficult to remove, use a gear puller (available from rental dealers) or pry it gently with 2 large screwdrivers.

4. Rotate the tensioner pulley by hand (**Figure 32**). It should turn smoothly. Replace the tensioner pulley if it sticks or turns roughly.

Installation

1. If the camshaft pulley was removed, make sure the camshaft dowel aligns with the mark as shown in **Figure 33**.

2. If the pulleys were removed, install them. Tighten the camshaft and jackshaft pulley bolts to specifications (**Table 2**). Install the crankshaft pulley with its recessed side toward the engine as shown in **Figure 31**. Align the pulley notch with the crankshaft Woodruff key and push the pulley on.

> *CAUTION*
> *Do not turn the camshaft while tightening the pulley bolts. This will force the valves against the pistons.*

2. Make sure the crankshaft pulley is positioned as shown in **Figure 34**.

3. Make sure the camshaft pulley mark is aligned with the mark on the inner cover as shown in **Figure 35**.

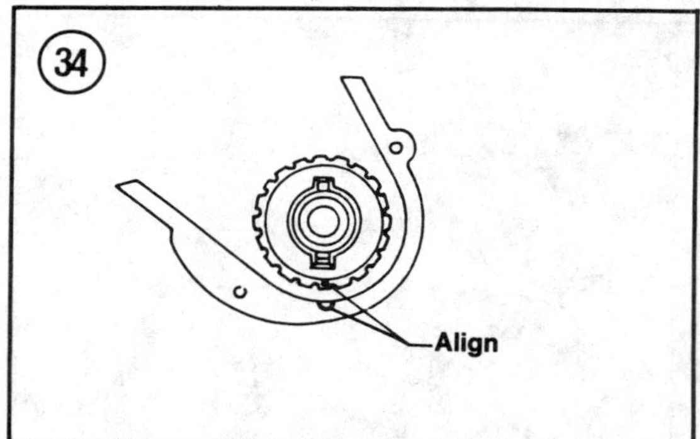

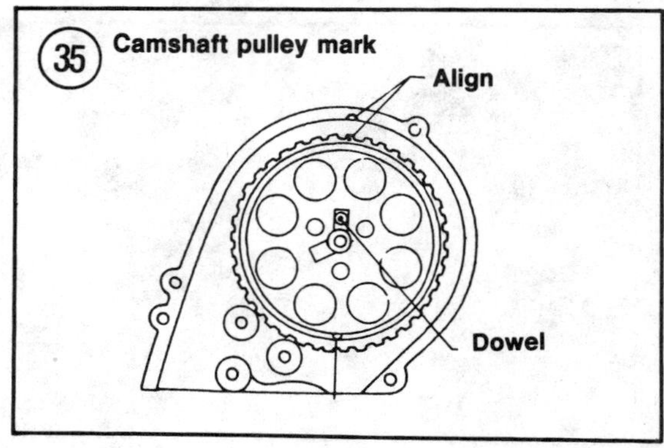

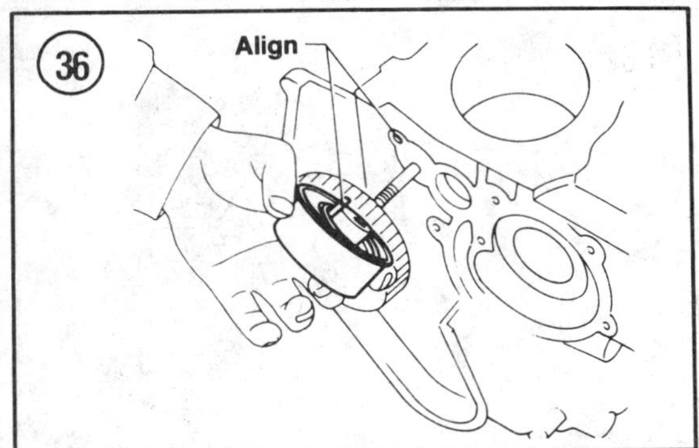

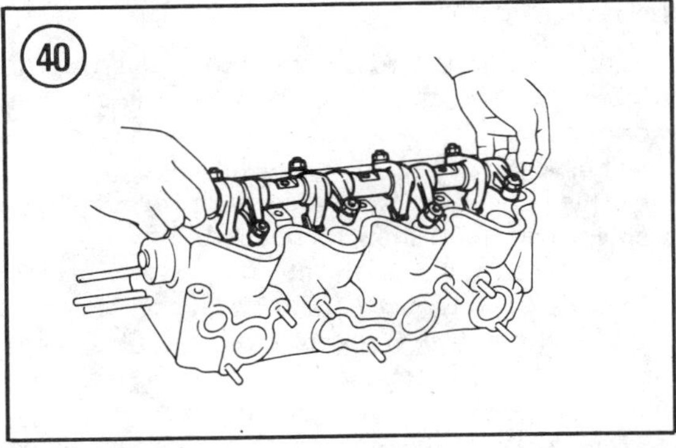

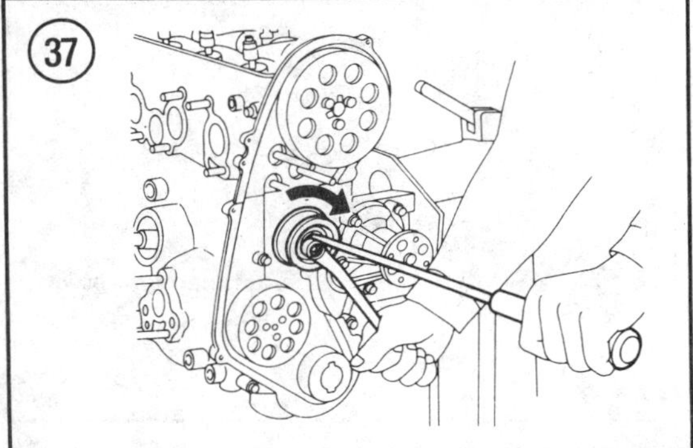

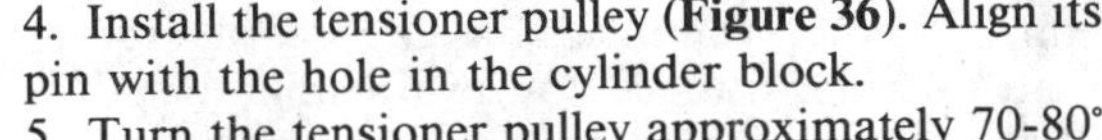

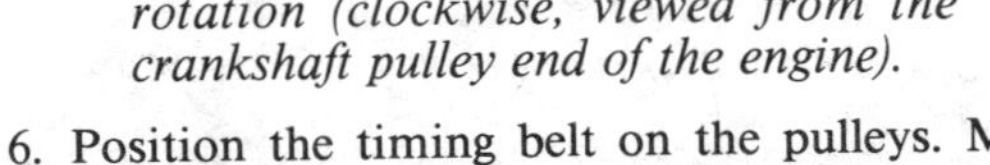

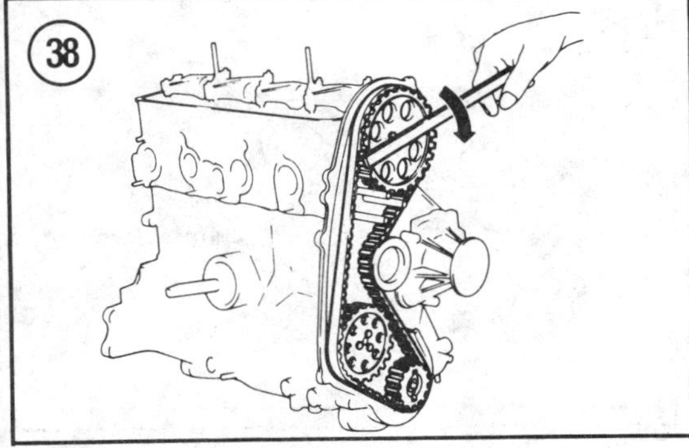

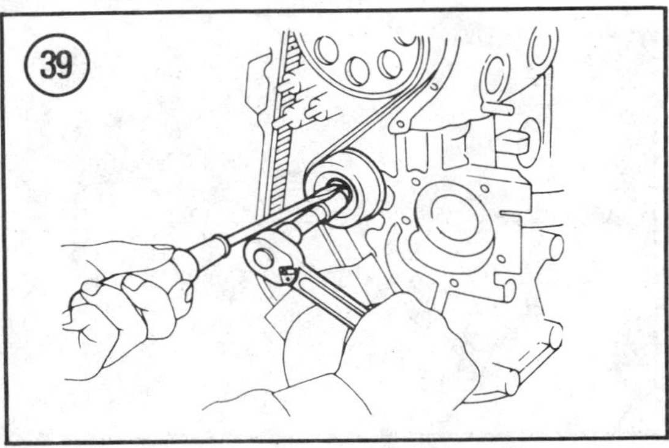

4. Install the tensioner pulley (**Figure 36**). Align its pin with the hole in the cylinder block.

5. Turn the tensioner pulley approximately 70-80° clockwise (**Figure 37**). Hold it from turning as shown and tighten the locknut.

> *CAUTION*
> *If installing a used timing belt, make sure the arrow mark made during removal points in the direction of rotation (clockwise, viewed from the crankshaft pulley end of the engine).*

6. Position the timing belt on the pulleys. Make sure the belt cogs engage the pulley cogs securely.

7. Loosen the tensioner pulley locknut and let the tensioner pulley move outward to tighten the timing belt.

8. Place a heavy screwdriver or similar tool between 2 of the camshaft pulley bolts as shown in **Figure 38**. Turn the pulley approximately 2 notches (20°) clockwise.

9. Hold the tensioner from turning as shown in **Figure 39** and tighten the locknut.

10. Install the upper and lower belt covers.

11. Install the crankshaft and water pump pulleys.

12. Install and tighten the drive belts as described in Chapter Three.

ROCKER ASSEMBLY

Removal/Installation

1. Remove the air cleaner.

2. Remove the rocker cover and gasket.

3. Detach the rocker assembly from the cylinder head and lift it off. See **Figure 40**.

4. Installation is the reverse of removal. Be sure the rocker shaft oil hole faces downward when installed. See **Figure 41**. The cutout in the center retainer faces toward the exhaust manifold. See **Figure 42**. Tighten all nuts and bolts to specifications (**Table 2**). Adjust valve clearances as described in Chapter Three.

Inspection

1. Disassemble the rocker assembly, referring to **Figure 43**. Lay the parts in order on a clean workbench.
2. Thoroughly clean all parts in solvent. While cleaning, check for obvious wear or damage. Replace parts that show these conditions.
3. Slide each rocker arm into its position on the rocker shaft. Grasp each end of the rocker arm and try to twist it. Any rocking motion (not sliding) indicates a worn rocker arm or shaft. Replace the rocker arm or shaft, whichever is worn.
4. Liberally coat the rocker shaft with clean engine oil, then install the brackets, springs and rocker arms. Assemble the rocker assembly so the rocker shaft oil hole will face downward when installed (**Figure 41**) and the cutout in the center bracket will face the exhaust manifold (**Figure 42**).

CAMSHAFT

Removal/Installation

1. Remove the timing belt and camshaft pulley as described in this chapter.
2. Remove the rocker assembly as described in this chapter.
3. Set up a dial indicator as shown in **Figure 44**. Pry the camshaft back and forth and note the reading. This is camshaft end play. If it exceeds specifications (**Table 1**, end of chapter), check the cylinder head cover and camshaft for wear after the camshaft is removed. Replace whichever part is worn.
4. Remove the cylinder head cover (**Figure 45**).
5. Carefully pull out the camshaft (**Figure 46**). Rotate the camshaft while pulling to ease removal.
6. Carefully pry out the camshaft oil seal. Tap in a new seal with its lip facing into the engine. Use a block of wood to spread the hammer's force so the seal won't tilt sideways and jam.
7. Installation is the reverse of removal. Liberally apply clean engine oil to the camshaft journals and lobes, as well as to the bearing surfaces in the cylinder head. After installation, make sure the camshaft dowel aligns with the mark as shown in **Figure 47**.

Inspection

The following steps can be done inexpensively by a machine shop if you don't have the necessary measuring equipment.
1. Measure the camshaft bearing bores in the cylinder head with a bore gauge. See **Figure 48**. Measure camshaft bearing journal diameter with a micrometer and calculate the difference between

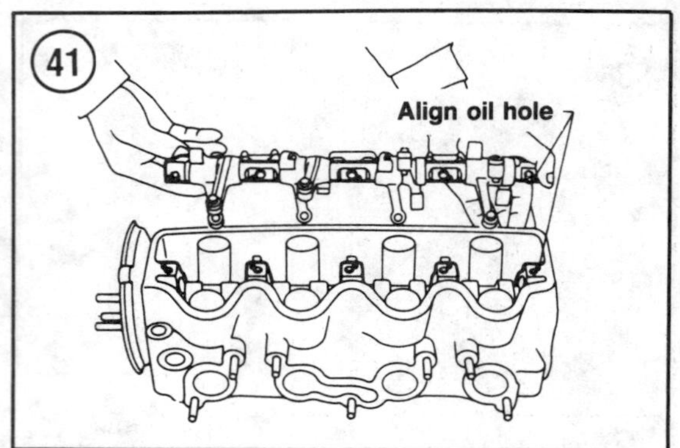

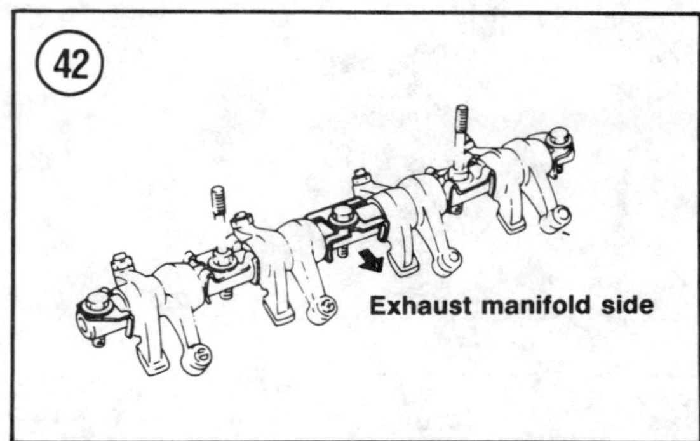

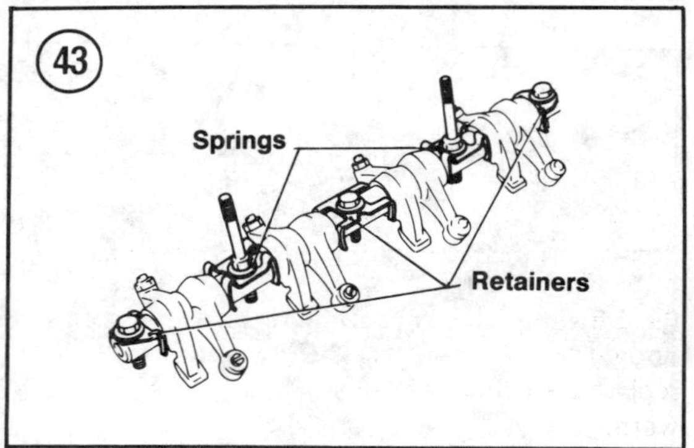

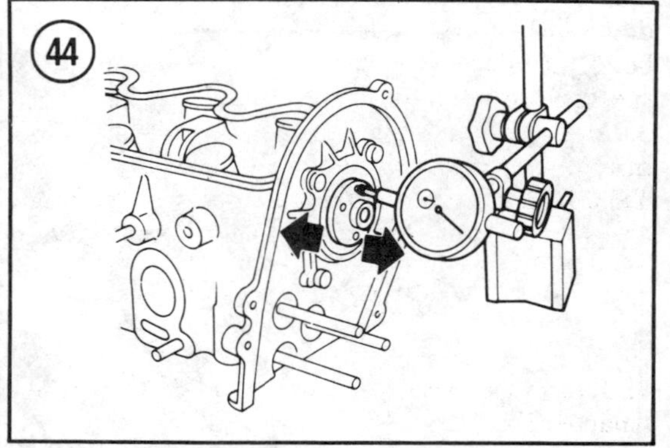

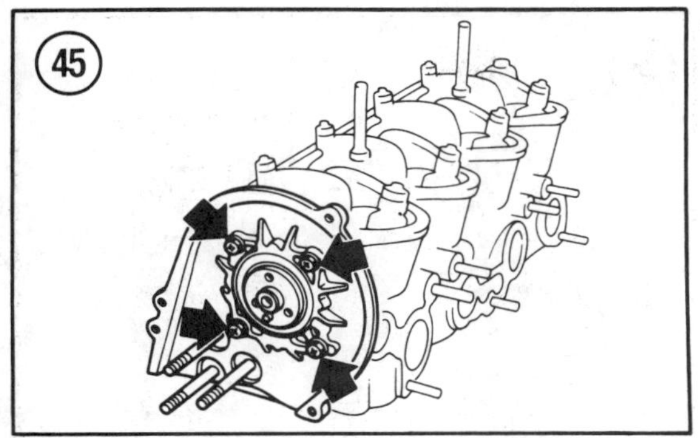

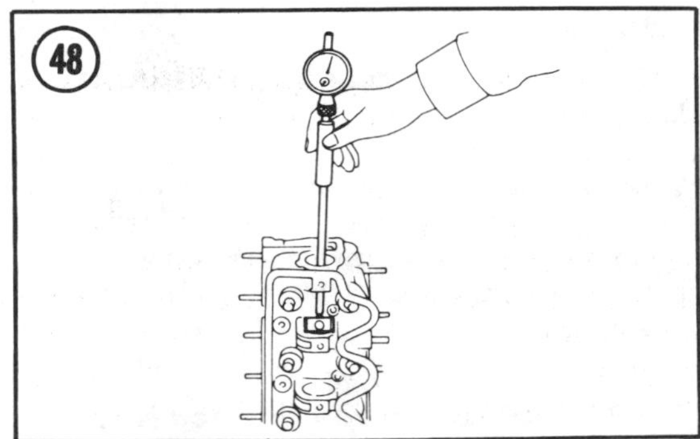

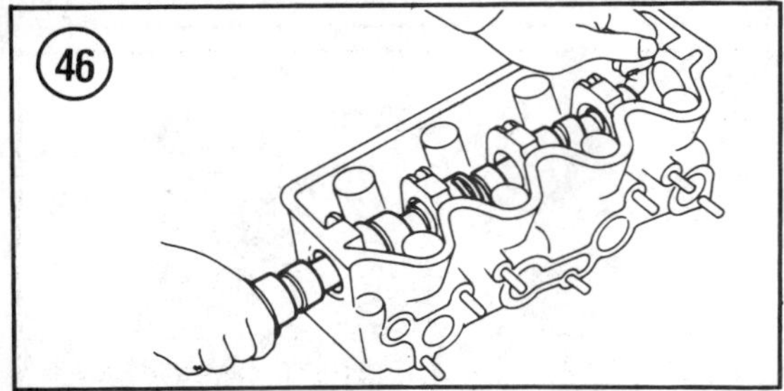

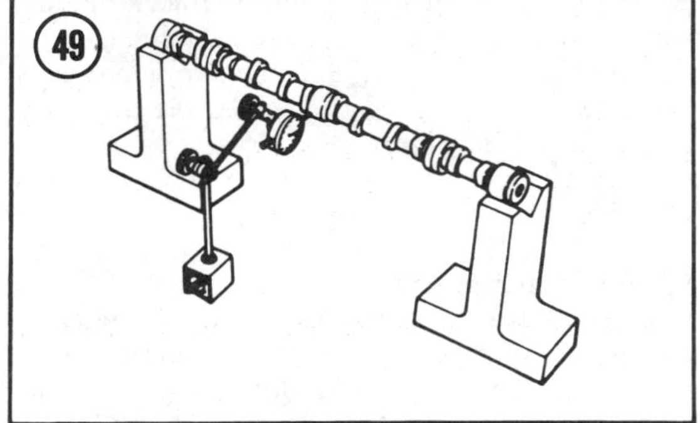

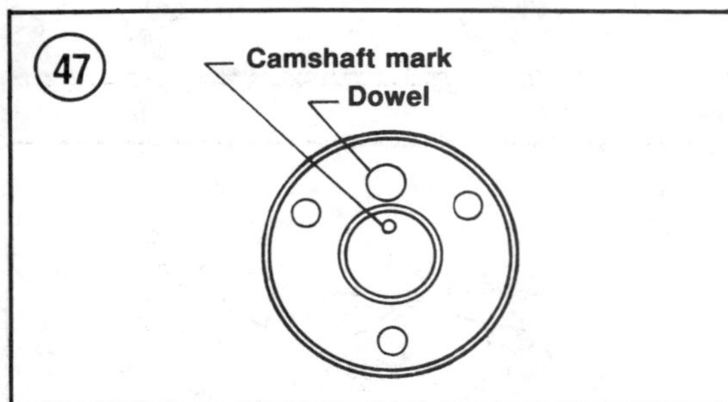

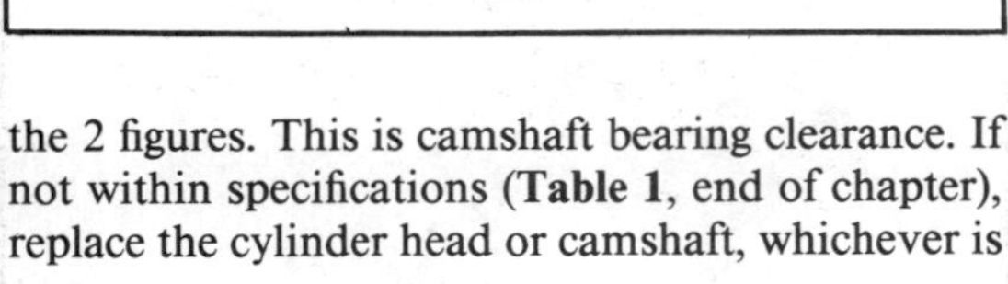

the 2 figures. This is camshaft bearing clearance. If not within specifications (**Table 1**, end of chapter), replace the cylinder head or camshaft, whichever is worn.

2. Place the camshaft between accurate centers, such as V-blocks or a lathe. See **Figure 49**. Set up a dial indicator as shown and measure camshaft bend. Replace the camshaft if bend exceeds specifications (end of chapter).

3. Measure camshaft lobe height with a micrometer and compare with specifications in **Table 1**. Replace the camshaft if any of the lobes are worn beyond specifications.

CYLINDER HEAD

Removal

1. Drain the cooling system as described in Chapter Six.

2. Disconnect the coolant hose and heater hose from the thermostat housing on the cylinder head.

3. Remove the distributor (Chapter Seven).

4. Remove the intake and exhaust manifolds as described in this chapter.

5. Remove the timing belt as described in this chapter.

6. If you plan to remove the rocker arms and camshaft from the head, do it now, referring to procedures in this chapter. The rocker assembly, camshaft and camshaft pulley can be left on the head if desired.

7. Disconnect the engine ground wire from the right rear corner of the cylinder head. Disconnect the temperature sender wires from the thermostat housing end of the head.

8. Remove the cylinder head bolts. Loosen the bolts in 2 or 3 stages, in the order shown in **Figure 50**, to prevent warping the head.

NOTE
There are 3 lengths of head bolts. Label them so they can be reinstalled in the right location.

9. Lift the head off the engine (**Figure 51**). If it is difficult to remove, try tapping gently with a rubber mallet. Do not pry the head loose. This will damage the ports or gasket surface.

Inspection

1. Check the cylinder head for water leaks before cleaning.

2. Clean the cylinder head thoroughly in solvent. While cleaning, check for cracks or other visible damage. Look for corrosion or foreign material in oil or water passages. Clean the passages with a stiff spiral wire brush, then blow them out with compressed air.

> *NOTE*
> *If the head is hard to clean, have it bead blasted by a machine shop.*

3. Check the cylinder head bottom (block mating) surface for flatness. Place an accurate straightedge along its surface (**Figure 52**). If there is any gap, measure it with a feeler gauge. Measure along the lines shown in **Figure 53**. If the gap exceeds specifications, have the head resurfaced by a machine shop.

4. Check studs in the cylinder head for damage. Replace damaged studs.

5. Check threaded holes in the head for wear or damage. If worn or damaged, have a thread insert installed in the hole by a machine shop.

Decarbonizing

1. Without removing valves, remove all deposits from the combustion chambers, intake ports and exhaust ports. Use a wire brush dipped in solvent or make a scraper out of hardwood. Be careful not to scratch or gouge the combustion chambers.

2. After all carbon is removed from the combustion chambers and ports, clean the entire head in solvent.

3. Clean away all carbon on the piston tops. Do not remove the carbon ridge at the top of the cylinder bore.

Installation

1. If you haven't already done so, clean all traces of old gasket from the cylinder head and block.

> *CAUTION*
> *Do not scratch or gouge the head or block mating surfaces while cleaning.*

2. Make sure there is no foreign material on cylinder head and block mating surfaces, in the cylinders or in oil or water passages.

3. Install a new head gasket on the block. Never reuse a head gasket. Do *not* use gasket sealer on the head gasket.

4. Position the cylinder head on the block.

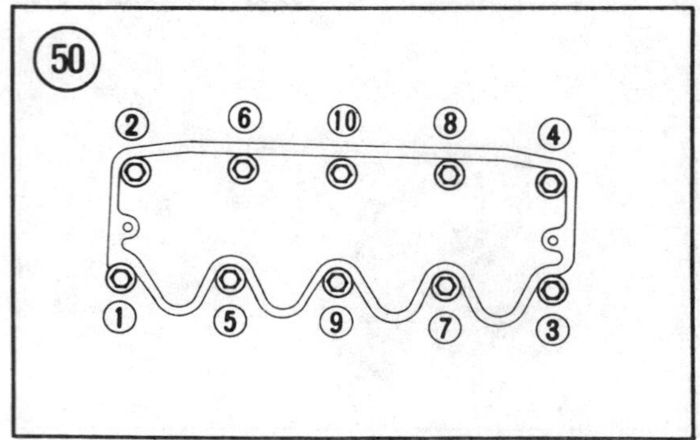

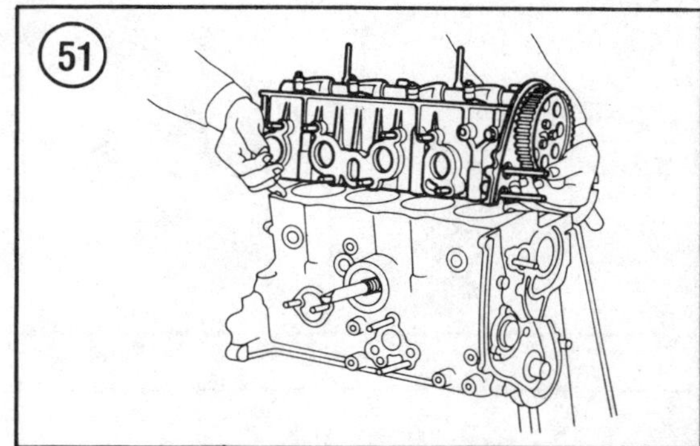

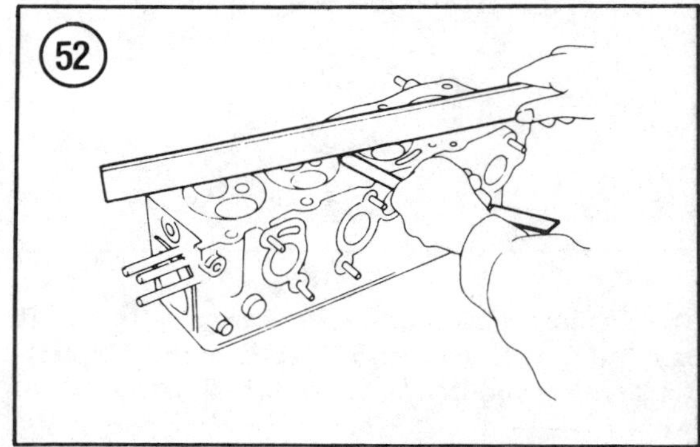

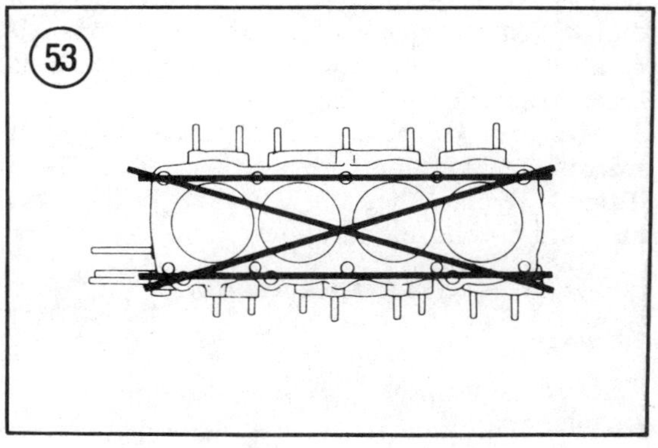

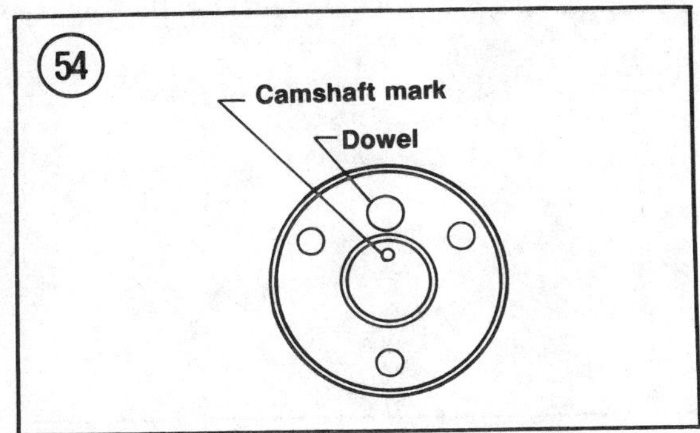

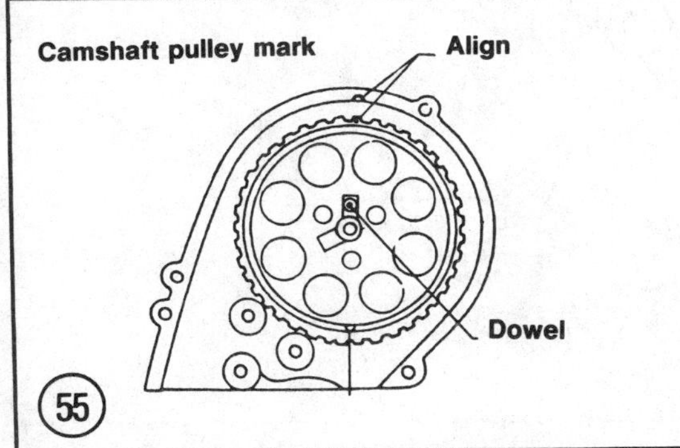

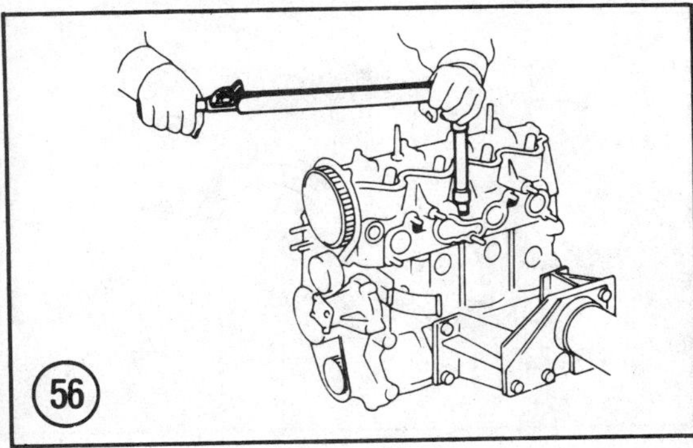

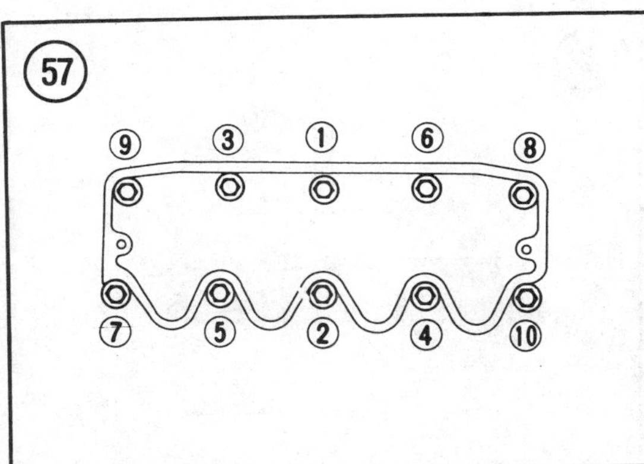

> *CAUTION*
> *If the camshaft is in the head, make sure the dowel aligns with the mark as shown in **Figure 54**. If the pulley is on the camshaft, make sure the pulley and cylinder head cover marks align as shown in **Figure 55**. Do not rotate the camshaft and crankshaft separately or the valves will be forced against the pistons.*

5. Install the cylinder head bolts according to the labels made during removal. See **Figure 56**. Tighten the bolts in 2 stages, in the order shown in **Figure 57**.
  a. In the first stage, tighten the bolts to 39-44 N•m (29-33 ft.-lb.).
  b. In the second stage, tighten the bolts to 69-74 N•m (51-54 ft.-lb.).
6. Install the camshaft and rocker assembly (if removed).
7. Install the timing belt as described in this chapter.
8. Install the motor mount.
9. After installation, warm up the engine. Retighten the cylinder head bolts to 69-74 N•m (51-54 ft.-lb.) in the order shown in **Figure 57**.

VALVES AND VALVE SEATS

Some of the following procedures must be done by a dealer or machine shop, since they require special knowledge and expensive machine tools. Others, while possible for the home mechanic, are difficult or time-consuming. A general practice among those who do their own service is to remove the cylinder head, perform all disassembly except valve removal and take the head to a machine shop for inspection and service. Since the cost is low in relation to the required effort and equipment, this is usually the best approach, even for experienced mechanics.

Valve Removal

1. Remove the rocker arms, camshaft and cylinder head as described in this chapter.
2. Temporarily install the rocker shaft. Compress each valve spring with a compressor such as Nissan tool part No. KV101072SO (**Figure 58**). Remove the valve keepers and release the spring tension. Remove the spring retainer, valve spring and spring seat.

> *CAUTION*
> *Remove any burrs from valve stem grooves before removing the valves. Otherwise the valve guides will be damaged.*

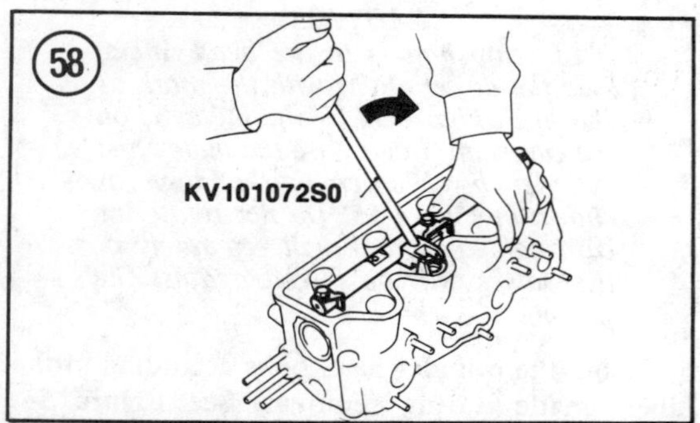

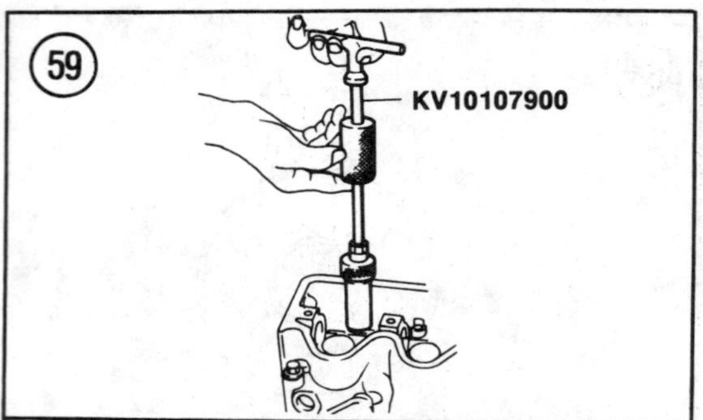

3. Remove the valve stem seals from the guides with a puller such as Nissan tool part No. KV10107900 (**Figure 59**).

Valve and Valve Guide Inspection

1. Clean the valves with a wire brush and solvent. Discard cracked, warped or burned valves.

2. Measure valve stems at top, center and bottom for wear. See **Figure 60**. A machine shop can do this when the valves are ground. Also measure the length of each valve and the diameter of each valve head.

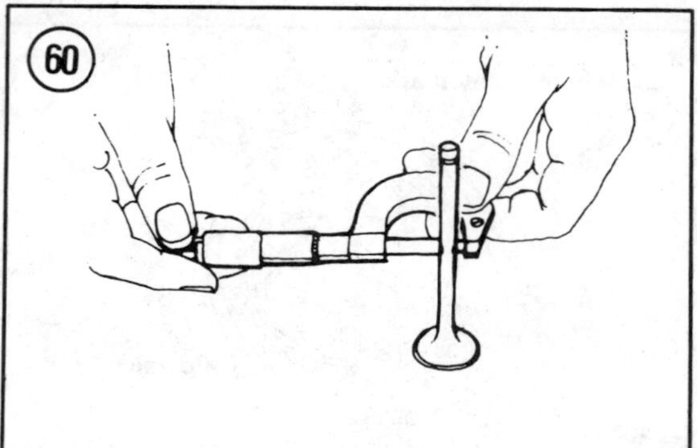

3. The valve faces and stem ends should be resurfaced when the valves are ground. No more than 0.2 mm (0.008 in.) may be removed from valve stem ends. Valve faces may not be ground thinner than 0.5 mm (0.020 in.).

4. Remove all carbon and varnish from valve guides with a stiff spiral wire brush.

> *NOTE*
> *The next step assumes that all valve stems have been measured and are within specifications. Replace valves that have worn stems before performing this step.*

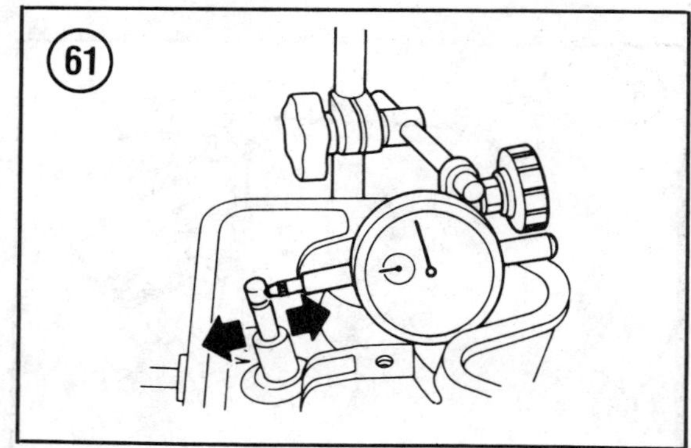

5. Insert each valve into the guide from which it was removed. Set up a dial indicator as shown in **Figure 61**. Hold the valve just slightly off its seat and rock it back and forth in a direction parallel with the rocker arms. This is the direction in which the greatest wear normally occurs. If the valve stem rocks more than approximately 0.2 mm (0.008 in.), the valve guide is probably worn.

6. If there is any doubt about valve guide condition after performing Step 5, measure the valve guide at top, center and bottom with a bore gauge.

7. Measure valve spring free length and compare with specifications. Replace springs that are too long or too short. Measure spring bend with a square (**Figure 62**). Replace springs bent beyond specifications.

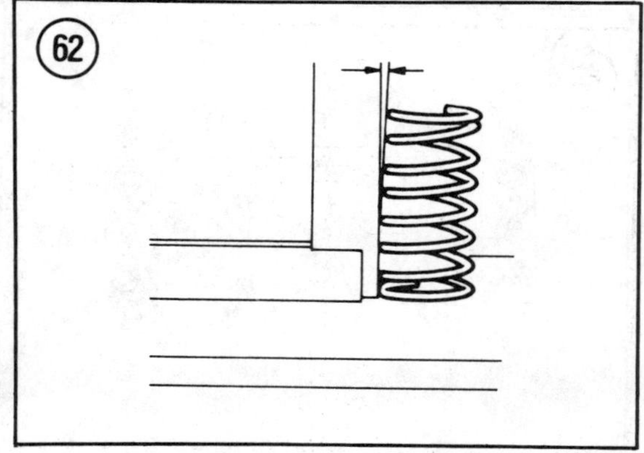

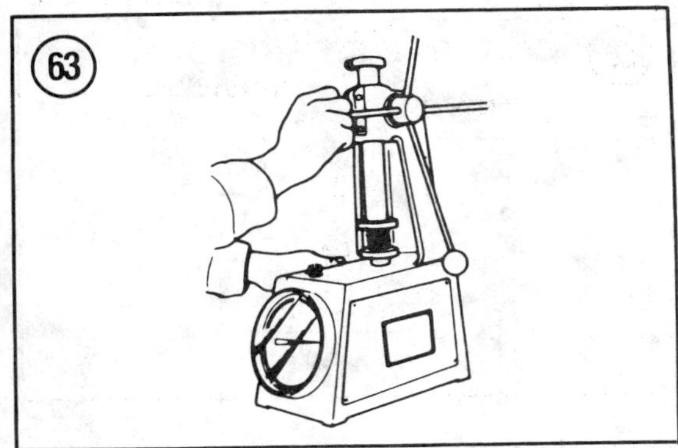

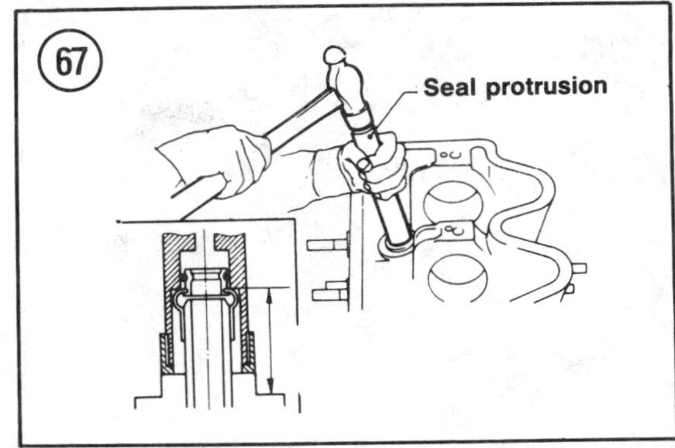

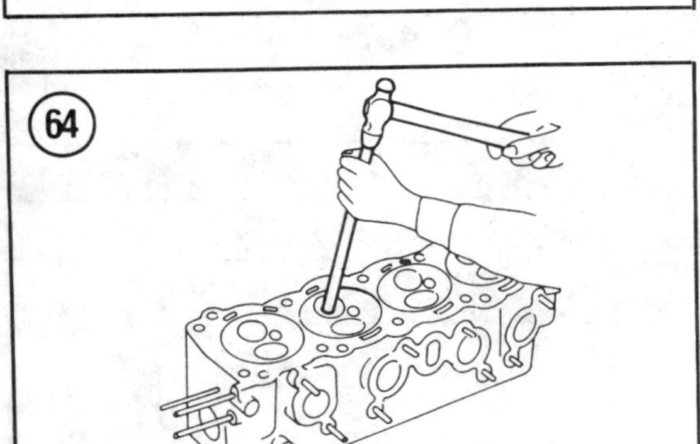

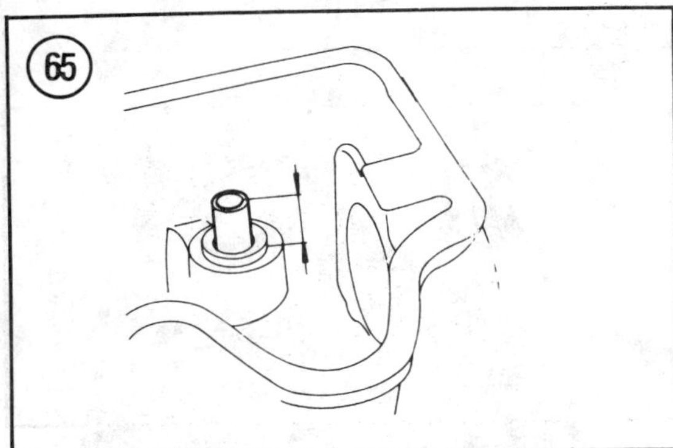

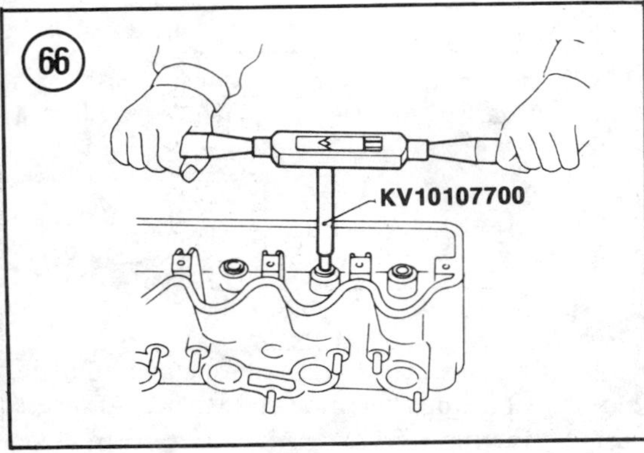

8. Test the valve springs under load on a spring tester (**Figure 63**). Replace weak springs.

9. Inspect valve seats. If worn or burned, they must be reconditioned. This is a job for a dealer or machine shop, although the procedure is described in this chapter.

Valve Guide Replacement

This procedure requires special tools. If you do not have the necessary equipment, take the job to a dealer or machine shop.

NOTE
The next step will be easier if the cylinder head is heated first.

1. Drive out guides from the combustion chamber side with a press or a hammer and drift (**Figure 64**).

2. Let the cylinder head cool to room temperature, then ream the valve guide holes in the head with Nissan tool part No. ST11081000.

3. Heat the cylinder head to 150-160° C (300-320° F). Press or drive in new guides until they protrude from the head the distance specified in **Table 1**. See **Figure 65**.

4. Ream the guides with Nissan tool part No. KV10107700 (**Figure 66**).

5. Install new valve stem seals on the guides with a drift such as Nissan tool part No. KV10107500 (**Figure 67**). Tap the seals in until they protrude the distance specified in **Table 1**.

Valve Seat Reconditioning

1. Cut the valve seats to specified dimensions, using a cutter or special stone. See **Figure 68** (intake) or **Figure 69** (exhaust).

2. Hand lap the valves to the seats with valve grinding compound. After lapping, remove all traces of compound.

3. Coat the corresponding valve face with Prussian blue dye.

4. Insert the valve into the valve guide.

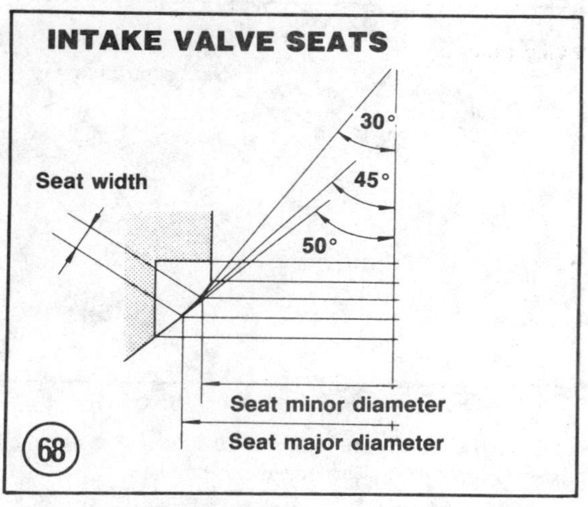

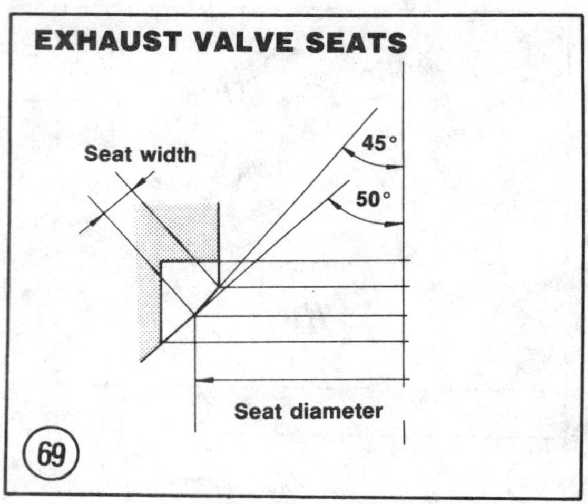

5. Rotate the valve under light pressure approximately 1/4 turn.

6. Lift the valve out. If it seats properly, the dye will transfer evenly to the valve face.

Valve Installation

1. Coat the valves with oil and install them in the cylinder head.

2. Install the valve spring seats, springs and spring retainers. The closely spaced valve spring coils face the cylinder head. The widely spaced coils face upward, away from the head.

3. Compress the valve springs and install the keepers.

OIL PAN

Removal/Installation

1. Set the handbrake. Securely block both rear wheels so the car will not roll in either direction.

2. Jack up the front end of the car and place it on jackstands.

3. Drain the oil as described in Chapter Three.

4. Remove the front exhaust tube. See *Exhaust System* in Chapter Five for details.

5. Unbolt the oil pan from the engine and take it off.

6. Clean all traces of old gasket and sealer from the engine and oil pan.

7. Installation is the reverse of removal. Use a new gasket. Apply small amounts of gasket sealer to the points shown in **Figure 70**. Tighten the oil pan bolts evenly to specifications (**Table 2**).

Inspection

1. Thoroughly clean the oil pan in solvent. If the pan is difficult to clean, a machine shop can boil it out for a nominal fee.

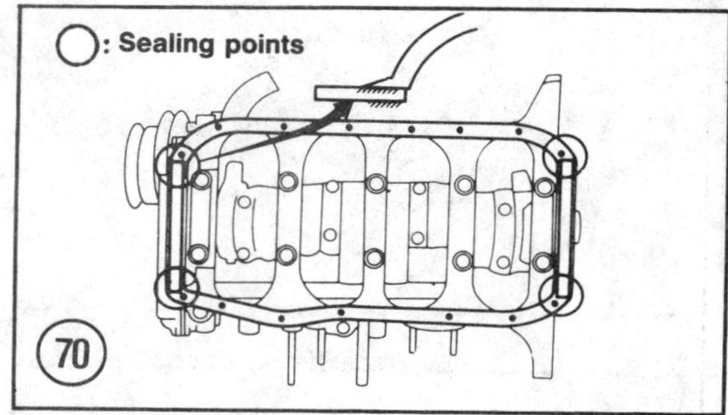

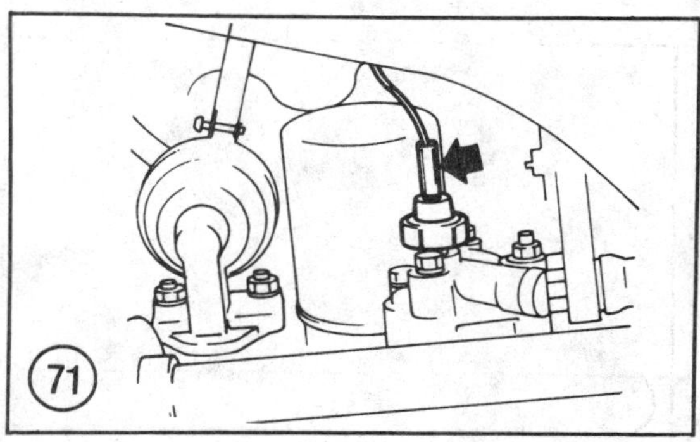

2. Check the oil pan for cracks, dents or a damaged gasket surface. Straighten or replace as needed.

OIL PUMP

Removal

1. Remove the alternator belt as described under *Drive Belts* in Chapter Three.

2. Remove the alternator mounting and adjusting bar bolts. Lay the alternator aside to provide access to the oil pump.

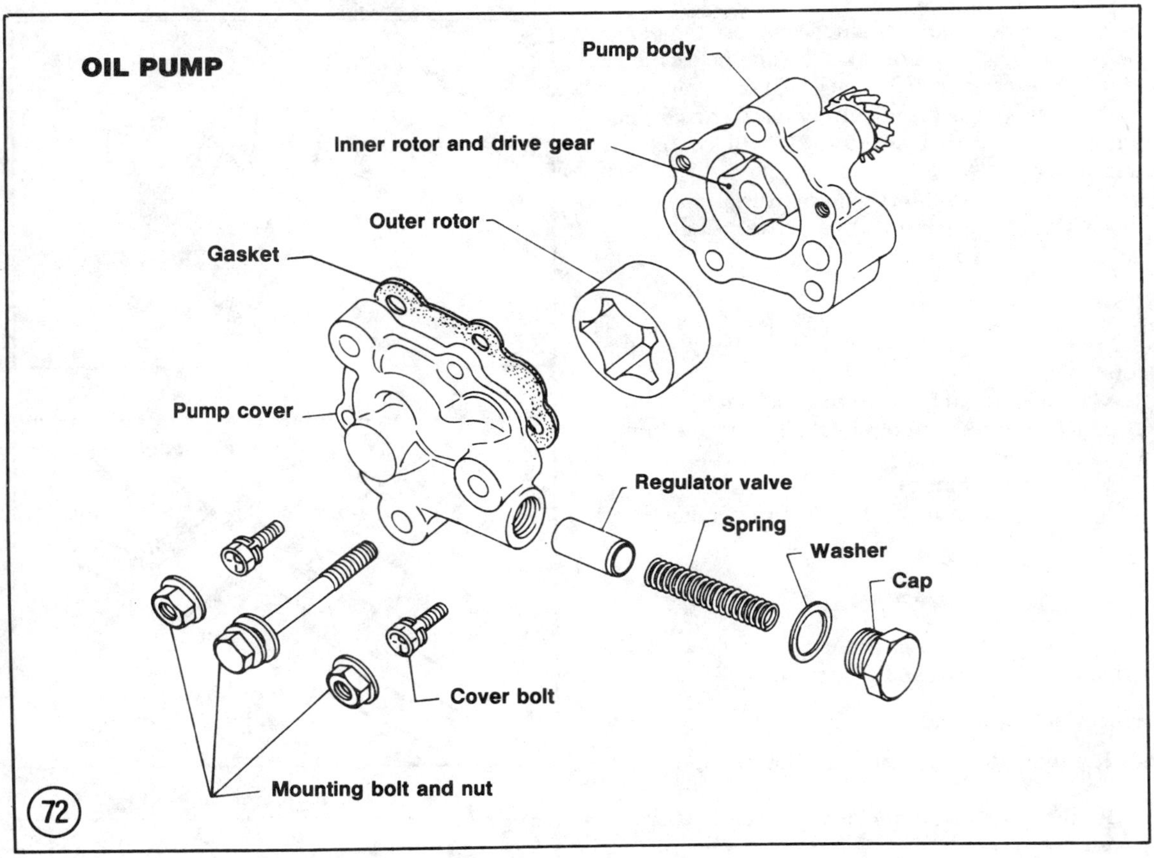

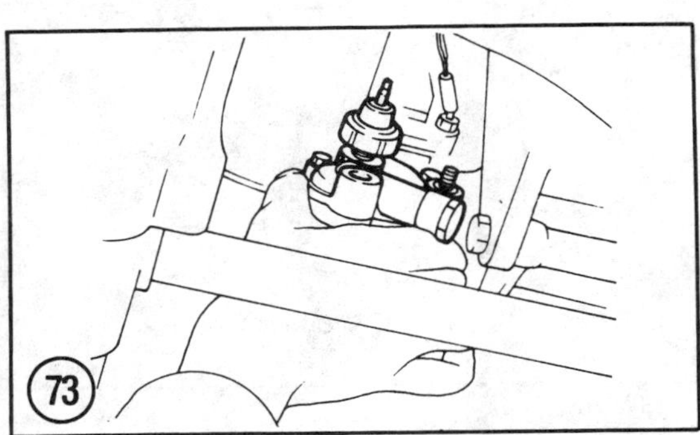

72

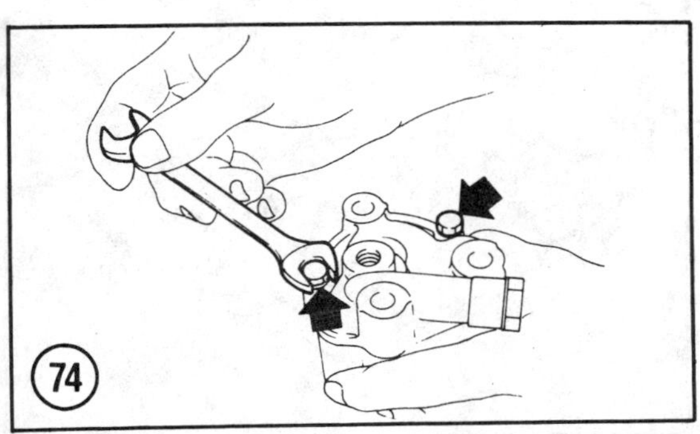

73

74

3. Unplug the oil pressure sender wire (**Figure 71**).
4. Remove the oil pump mounting nuts and bolt (**Figure 72**).
5. Remove the oil pump and its gasket as shown in **Figure 73**.

Inspection

Refer to **Figure 72** for this procedure.
1. Remove the pump cover bolts (**Figure 74**). Take the cover and gasket off.
2. Remove the outer rotor. The inner rotor and shaft cannot be removed.
3. Unscrew the regulator valve cap. Remove the washer, spring and regulator valve.
4. Thoroughly clean all parts in solvent. While cleaning, check for visible wear or damage. If the pump body, rotors or shaft are worn or damaged, replace the oil pump as an assembly. If the regulator valve, spring, washer or cap is worn or damaged, replace the valve set.
5. Measure rotor tip clearance (1, **Figure 75**) and outer rotor-to-body clearance (2). Compare with specifications in **Table 1**. If either clearance is not within specifications, replace the oil pump.

6. Place an accurate straightedge across the pump body and rotors (**Figure 76**). Measure the clearance between rotors and feeler gauge (3) or pump body and feeler gauge (4). If either clearance is not within specifications (**Table 1**), replace the oil pump.

7. Coat the pump rotors with oil. Install the cover and gasket. Tighten the cover bolts to specifications (**Table 2**).

Installation

Installation is the reverse of removal, plus the following.

1. Coat the oil pump drive gear and shaft with oil.

2. Pour oil into the pump inlet and turn the pump by hand several times.

3. Use a new pump gasket.

4. Tighten the nuts and bolt to specifications (**Table 2**).

JACKSHAFT

The jackshaft, mounted in the cylinder block, drives the oil pump and fuel pump.

Removal/Installation

1. Remove the oil pump as described in this chapter.

2. Remove the fuel pump as described in Chapter Five.

3. Remove the timing belt as described in this chapter.

4. Remove the timing belt pulleys from the crankshaft and jackshaft.

5. Remove the cylinder block cover and oil seal collar (**Figure 77**).

6. Remove the jackshaft locate plate (**Figure 78**).

7. Carefully pull the jackshaft out of the engine. See **Figure 79**. Rotate the jackshaft while pulling to ease removal.

8. Installation is the reverse of removal. Apply clean engine oil to the jackshaft journals, oil pump drive gear and fuel pump lobe.

Inspection

1. Clean the jackshaft and its locate plate in solvent. While cleaning, check the jackshaft and locate plate for obvious wear or damage. Replace as needed.

> *NOTE*
> *The next step can be done by a machine shop if you don't have the necessary equipment.*

2. Measure jackshaft journal diameter with a micrometer. Measure jackshaft bushing diameter

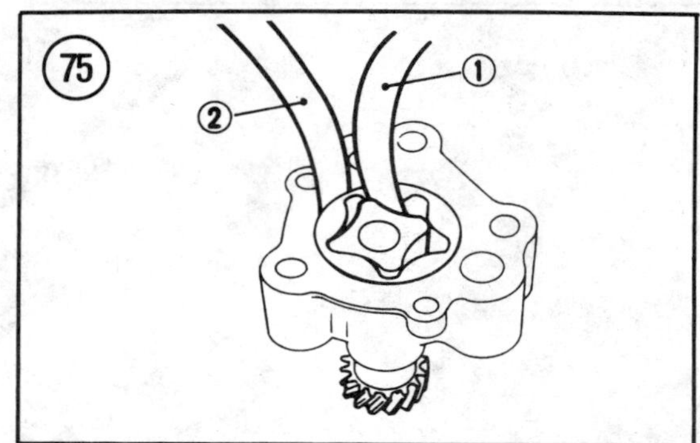

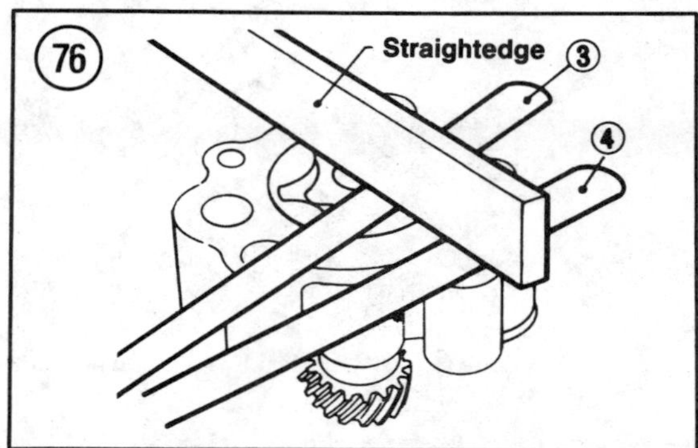

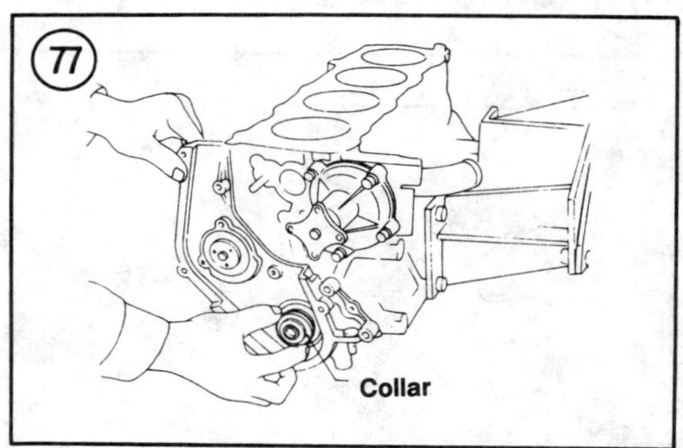

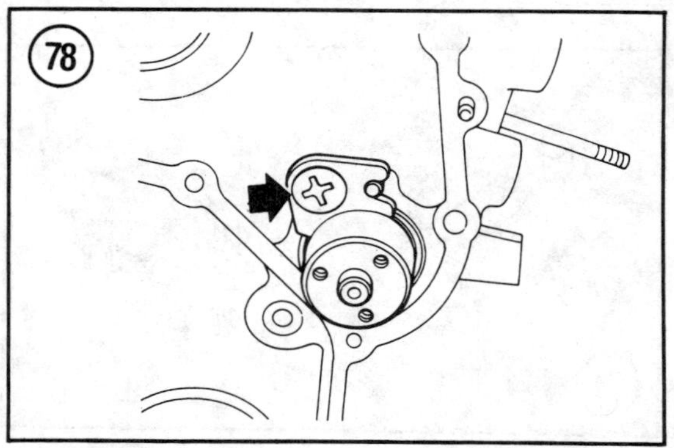

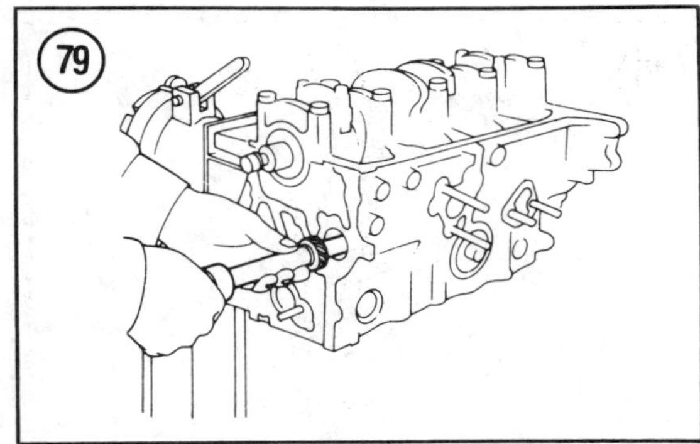

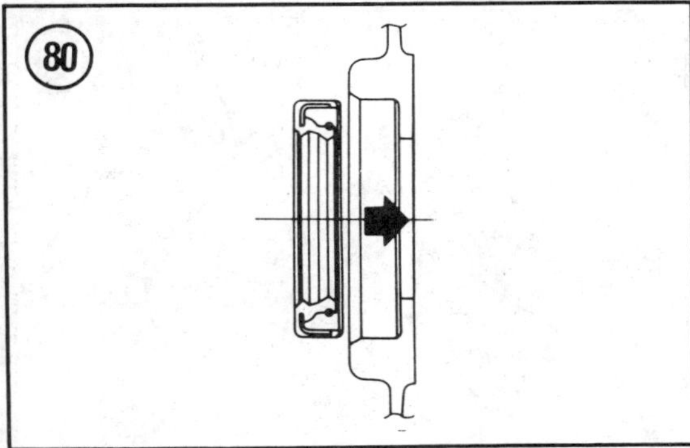

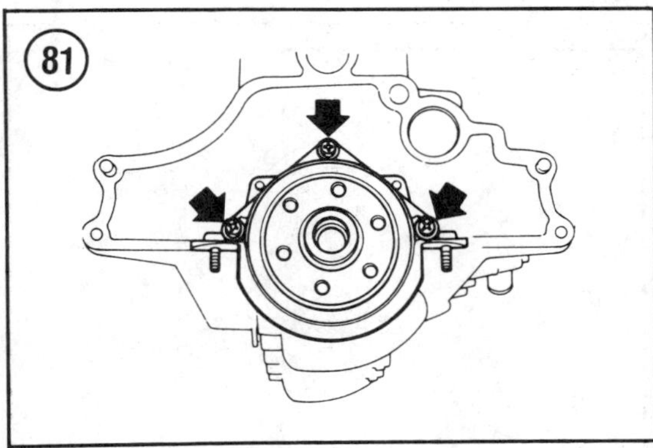

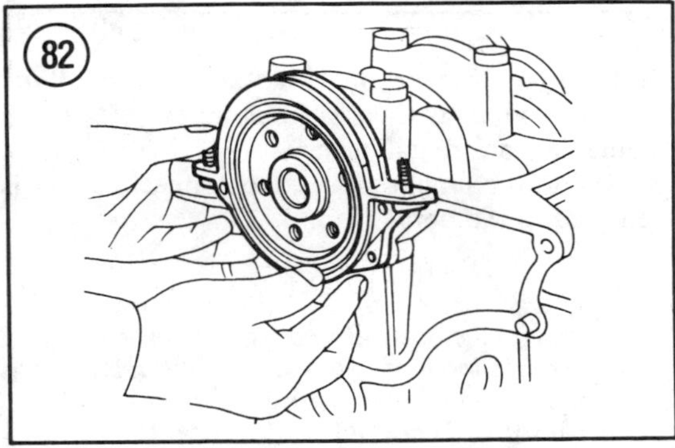

with a bore gauge. If the difference between the 2 measurements (jackshaft bushing clearance) exceeds specifications in **Table 1**, have the jackshaft bushings replaced by a machine shop.

OIL SEAL REPLACEMENT

Oil seals are used on the camshaft, jackshaft and on the front and rear ends of the crankshaft.

Camshaft Oil Seal

This is described under *Camshaft* in this chapter.

Crankshaft Front Seal and Jackshaft Seal

1. Remove the timing belt as described in this chapter.
2. Remove the crankshaft and jackshaft pulleys as described under *Timing Belt* in this chapter.
3. Remove the cylinder block cover (**Figure 77**).
4. Carefully pry the oil seals out of the cylinder block cover.
5. Tap new seals in so their lips will face into the engine when installed. See **Figure 80**. Use a block of wood to spread the hammer's force so the seal won't tilt sideways and jam.
6. Install the cylinder block cover, pulleys and timing belt as described in this chapter.

Crankshaft Rear Oil Seal

1. Remove the transaxle (Chapter Eight).
2. Remove the oil pan as described in this chapter.
3. Remove the oil seal retainer and gasket (**Figure 81**).
4. Carefully pry the old oil seal out of the housing. Do not scratch or gouge any metal surfaces.
5. Tap a new seal in so its lip will face into the engine when installed. See **Figure 80**. Use a block of wood to spread the hammer's force so the seal won't tilt sideways and jam.
6. Coat the oil seal lip and the oil seal contact surface on the crankshaft with oil.
7. Install the oil seal retainer (**Figure 82**). Use a new gasket, coated on both sides with a thin layer of gasket sealer.
8. Install the oil pan as described in this chapter.
9. Install the transaxle as described in Chapter Eight.

FLYWHEEL

Removal/Inspection/Installation

1. Remove the transaxle as described in Chapter Eight.
2. Remove the oil pan as described in this chapter.

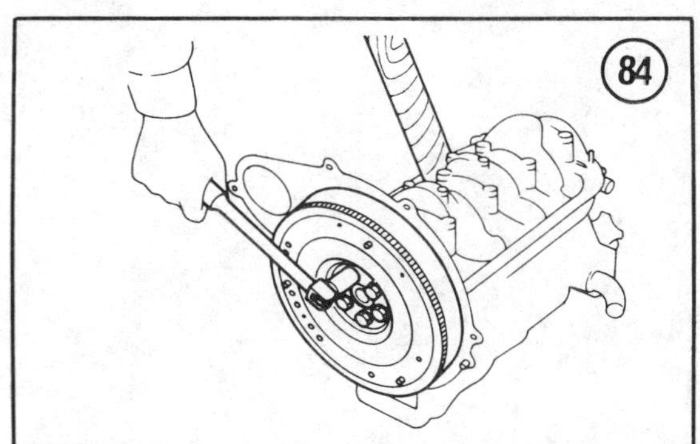

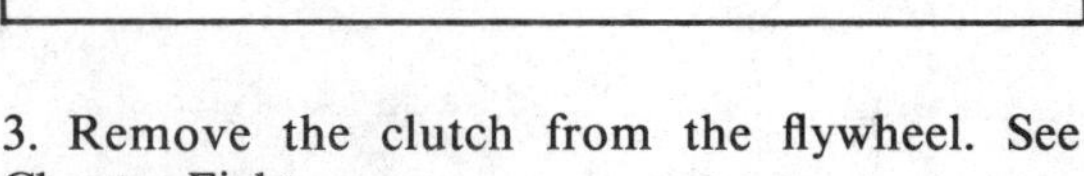

3. Remove the clutch from the flywheel. See Chapter Eight.

4. Check the flywheel for scoring and wear. If the surface is glazed or slightly scratched, have it resurfaced by a machine shop. Replace the flywheel if damage is serious.

5. Measure flywheel runout with a dial indicator as shown in **Figure 83**. Replace or resurface the flywheel if runout exceeds specifications in **Table 1**.

6. Inspect the flywheel ring gear teeth. If the teeth are chipped, broken or excessively worn, have a new ring gear shrunk onto the flywheel by a machine shop.

CAUTION
Do not hold the flywheel from turning with a locking tool that secures the ring gear teeth.

7. Insert a wooden hammer handle between the crankshaft and cylinder block to keep the flywheel from turning. See **Figure 84**. Remove the flywheel bolts and take the flywheel off.

8. Installation is the reverse of removal. Tighten flywheel bolts to specifications (end of chapter). Tighten gradually in a diagonal pattern.

TORQUE CONVERTER DRIVE PLATE

The torque converter drive plate, used with automatic transaxles, is bolted to the crankshaft in the same manner as the flywheel.

Drive plate runout is measured in the same manner as flywheel runout. Replace the drive plate if runout exceeds specifications (**Table 1**). The drive plate must also be replaced if the ring gear is damaged or worn excessively.

PISTON/CONNECTING ROD ASSEMBLIES

Piston Removal

1. Remove the cylinder head and oil pan as described in this chapter.

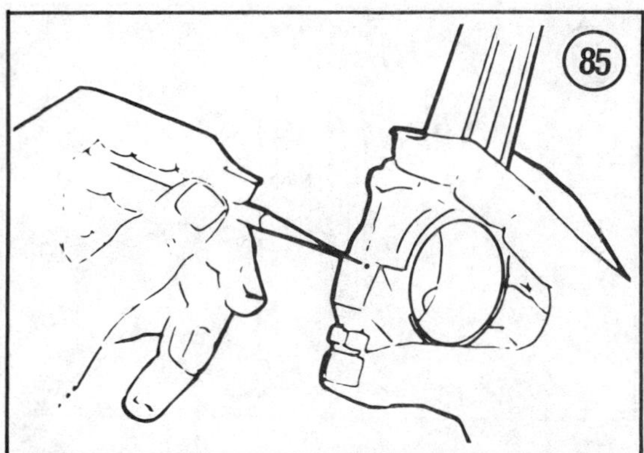

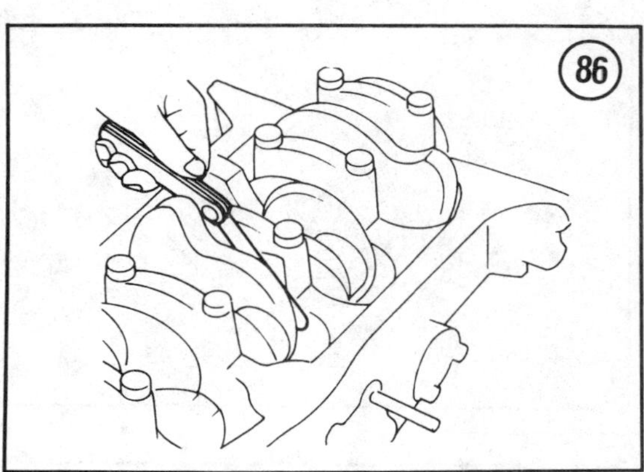

2. Remove the carbon ridge at the top of the cylinder bores with a ridge reamer. These are available from rental dealers.

3. Rotate the crankshaft so the connecting rod is centered in the bore.

NOTE
*Check for identifying marks stamped on connecting rod and cap. If the rods are not marked with cylinder numbers, make your own number marks as shown in **Figure 85**.*

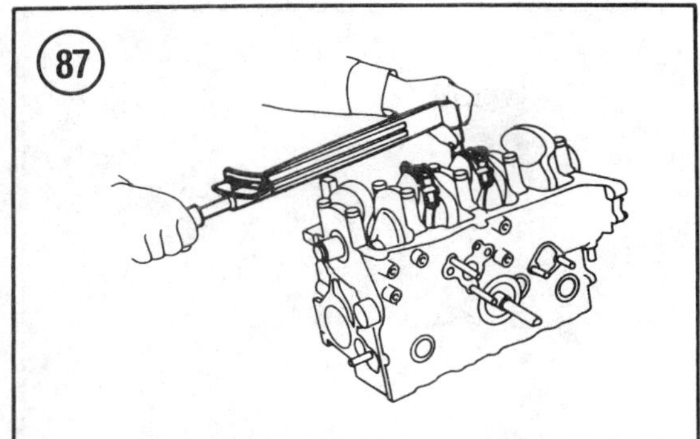

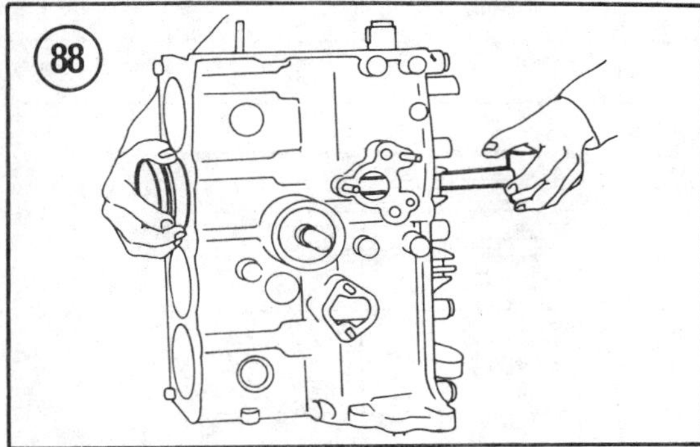

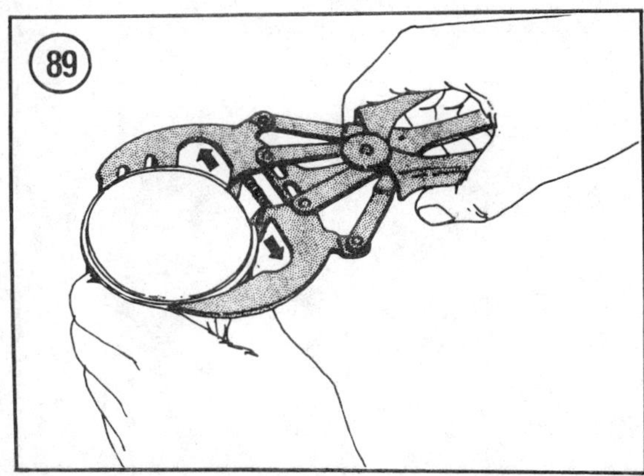

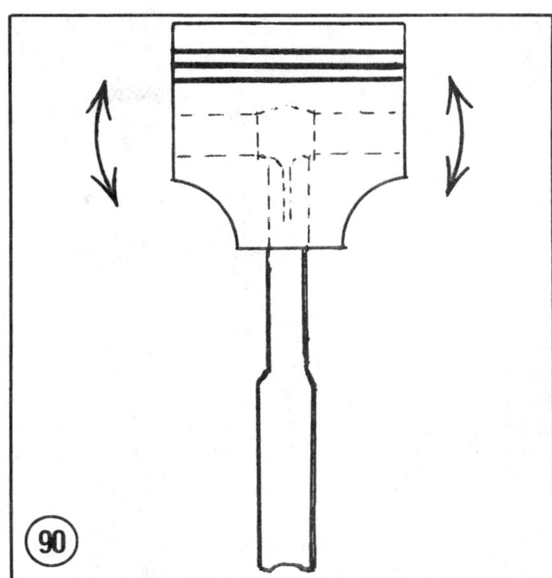

4. Insert a feeler gauge between the connecting rod big end and crankshaft and measure the clearance (**Figure 86**). Replace the connecting rod if clearance exceeds specifications (end of chapter).

5. Remove the nuts securing the connecting rod cap (**Figure 87**). Lift off the cap, together with the lower bearing half.

6. Push the piston and connecting rod out of the bore with a wooden hammer handle or taped screwdriver. See **Figure 88**.

7. Remove the piston rings with a ring remover (**Figure 89**).

Piston Pin Removal/Installation

The piston pins are press-fitted to the connecting rods and hand-fitted to the pistons. Removal requires a press and support stand. This is a job for a dealer or machine shop equipped to fit the pistons to the pins and install the pistons and pins on the connecting rods.

To check for wear, place each piston/connecting rod assembly in a vise and twist the piston (**Figure 90**). Any rocking motion (not sliding) indicates a worn piston, pin or connecting rod small end bore.

Piston Clearance Check

This procedure should be done at room temperature. Cylinder walls must be clean and dry.

1. Insert a piston without rings upside down into the cylinder bore.

2. Insert a 0.04 mm (0.0016 in.) feeler gauge into the cylinder bore. See **Figure 91**.

3. Pull up on the feeler gauge with a spring scale as shown. The force required to pull the feeler gauge out should range from 0.5-1.5 kg (1.1-3.3 lb.).

   a. If the required force is less than specified, piston clearance is excessive. Measure piston diameter as described in this chapter to determine whether the piston is worn.

   b. If the required force is more than specified, piston clearance is insufficient.

   c. If piston clearance is excessive due to worn cylinder bores, the cylinders must be rebored and oversized pistons installed.

4. Repeat the procedure for all 4 cylinders and pistons.

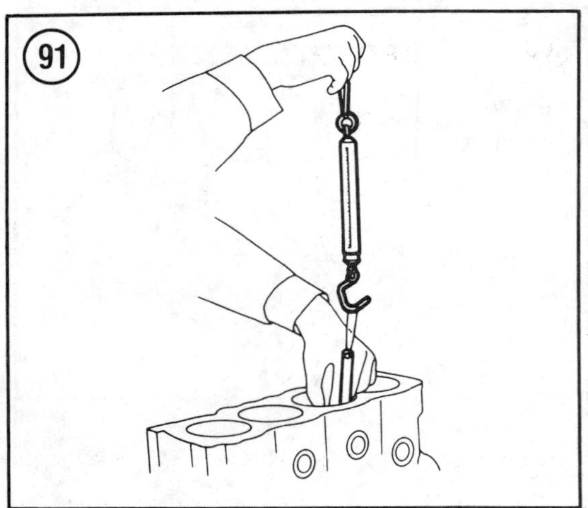

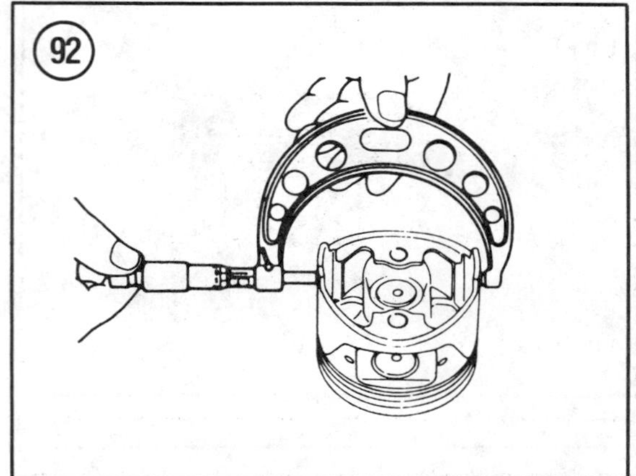

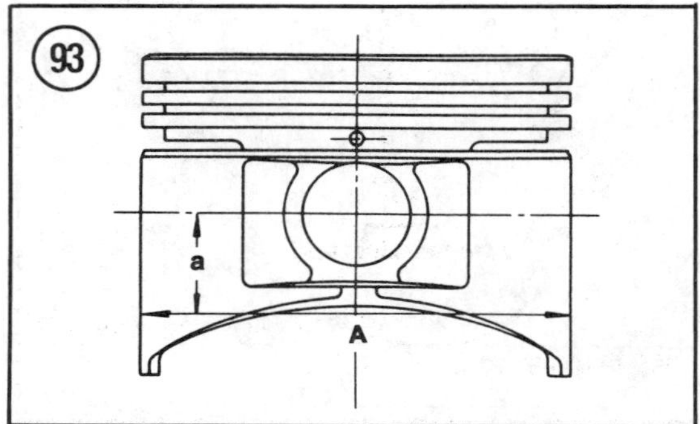

Piston Diameter Measurement

Measure piston diameter with a micrometer as shown in **Figure 92**. Measure at a point 17.5 mm (0.689 in.) above the piston skirt and at right angles to the piston pin bore. See **Figure 93**. Compare with specifications at the end of the chapter. Replace worn pistons.

Piston Ring Fit/Installation

1. Check the ring gap of each piston ring. To do this, position the ring at the top or bottom of the ring travel area and square it by tapping gently with an inverted piston.

> *NOTE*
> *If the cylinders have not been rebored, check the gap at the bottom of the ring travel, where the cylinder is least worn.*

2. Measure ring gap with a feeler gauge as shown in **Figure 94**. Compare with specifications at the end of the chapter.
3. Check side clearance of the rings as shown in **Figure 95**. Place the feeler gauge alongside the ring all the way into the groove. Specifications are listed in **Table 1**.
4. Using a ring expander tool, carefully install the oil control ring, then the compression rings. Oil rings consist of 3 segments. The wavy segment goes between the flat segments to act as a spacer. See **Figure 96**. The top sides of both compression rings are marked and must be up.
5. Position the ring gaps as shown in **Figure 97**.

Connecting Rod Inspection

Have connecting rod straightness checked by a dealer or machine shop. Compare with specifications for bend and twist (**Table 1**).

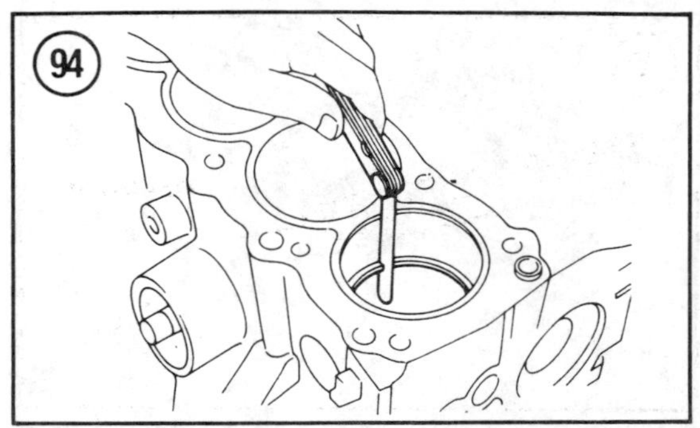

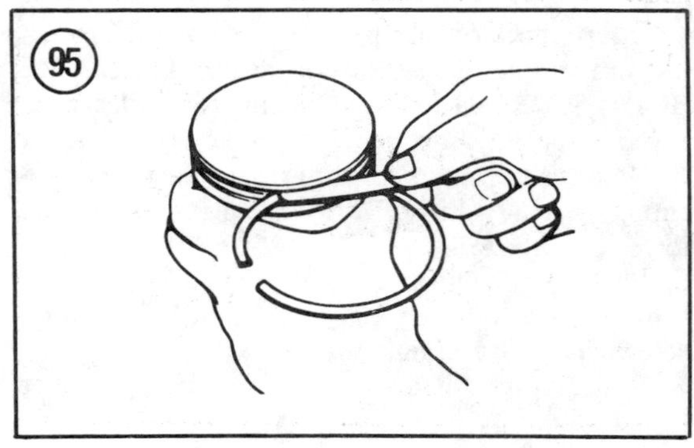

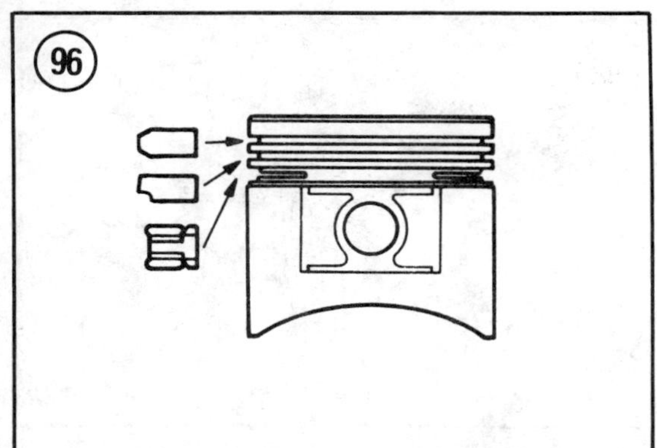

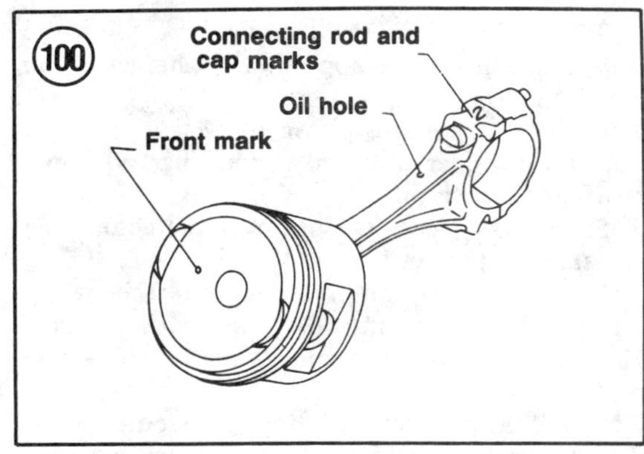

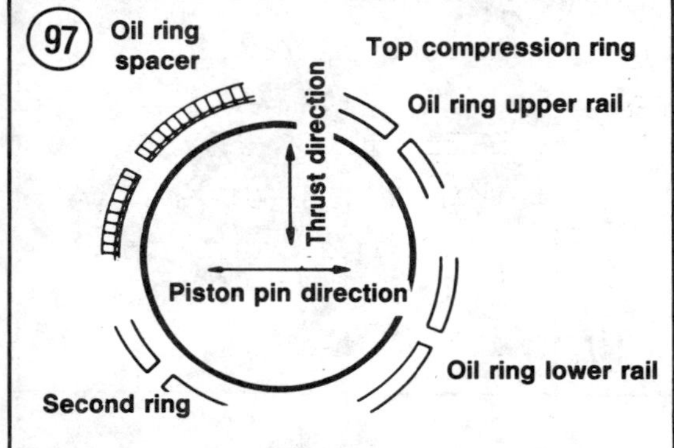

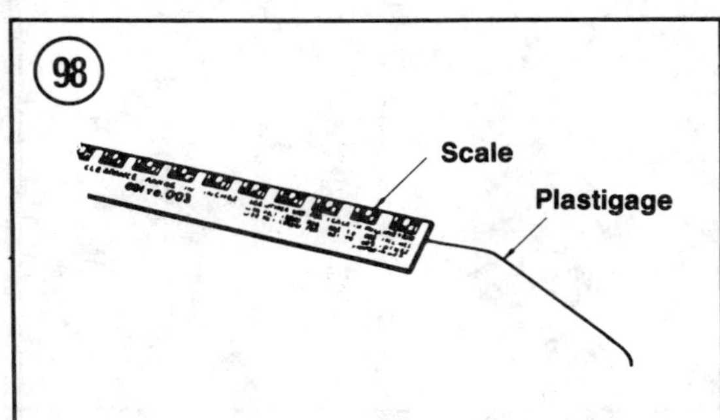

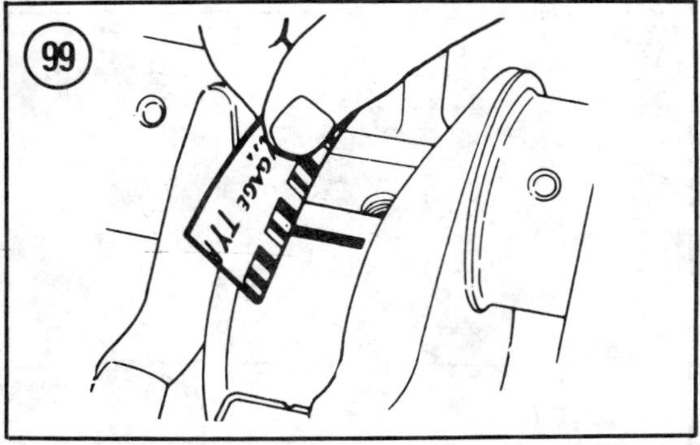

Connecting Rod Bearing Clearance Measurement

1. Place connecting rods and upper bearing halves on the proper crankpins (connecting rod journals).
2. Cut a piece of Plastigage (**Figure 98**) the width of the bearing. Place the Plastigage on the crankpin, then install the lower bearing half and cap.

> *NOTE*
> *Do not place Plastigage over the crankpin oil hole.*

3. Install the connecting rod cap. Make sure the identifying marks are on the same side. Tighten the connecting rod cap to specifications (end of chapter). Do not rotate the crankshaft while the Plastigage is in place.
4. Remove the connecting rod cap. Bearing clearance is determined by comparing the width of the flattened Plastigage to the markings on the envelope (**Figure 99**). If clearance is excessive, the crankshaft must be reground and undersize bearings installed.

Installing Piston/Connecting Rod Assembly

1. Make sure the pistons are correctly installed on the connecting rods. The front mark in the piston (**Figure 100**) goes toward the crankshaft pulley end of the engine. The oil hole in the connecting rod big end goes toward the right-hand side of the engine (viewed from the flywheel end). The cylinder number marks also go toward the right-hand side.
2. Be sure the ring gaps are positioned as shown in **Figure 97**.

> *CAUTION*
> *During the next step, be sure the oil hole in the bearing aligns with the oil hole in the connecting rod. If it doesn't, the cylinder walls will be damaged by lack of lubrication when the engine runs.*

3. Thoroughly clean the bearings, including the back sides. Install the upper bearing halves in the connecting rods.

4. Immerse the entire piston in clean engine oil. Coat the cylinder wall and connecting rod upper bearing half with oil.

5. Slide short pieces of hose over the connecting rod studs to protect the crankshaft.

6. Slide a ring compressor over the rings. Compress the rings into the grooves. See **Figure 101**. Ring compressors are available from tool rental dealers.

7. Install the piston/connecting rod assembly in its cylinder as shown in **Figure 101**. Tap lightly with a wooden hammer handle to insert the piston. Be sure the connecting rod number corresponds to the cylinder number (counting from the crankshaft pulley of the engine).

CAUTION
Use extreme care not to let the connecting rod nick the crankpin.

8. Remove the hose from the connecting rod studs.

9. Place the bearings in the connecting rod cap. Coat the crankpins and bearings with clean engine oil.

10. Install the connecting rod cap. Make sure the identifying marks on the rod and cap are on the same side (**Figure 100**).

11. Tighten the cap nuts to specifications (end of chapter). See **Figure 102**.

12. Check connecting rod big end play as described under *Piston Removal*, Step 4.

CRANKSHAFT

Removal

1. Remove the engine as described in this chapter.

2. Remove the flywheel or torque converter drive plate as described in this chapter.

3. Remove the drive belts. See Chapter Three.

4. Remove the timing belt as described in this chapter.

5. Remove the oil pan.

6. Remove the crankshaft front and rear oil seals as described in this chapter.

7. Remove the connecting rod caps.

8. Set up a dial indicator as shown in **Figure 103**. Pry the crankshaft to the front and rear with a screwdriver and note the reading. This is crankshaft end play. If it exceeds specifications (end of chapter), replace the center bearings. These are included in the main bearing set.

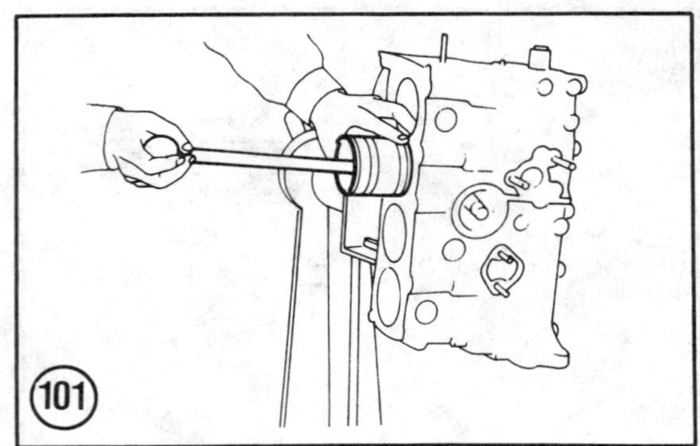

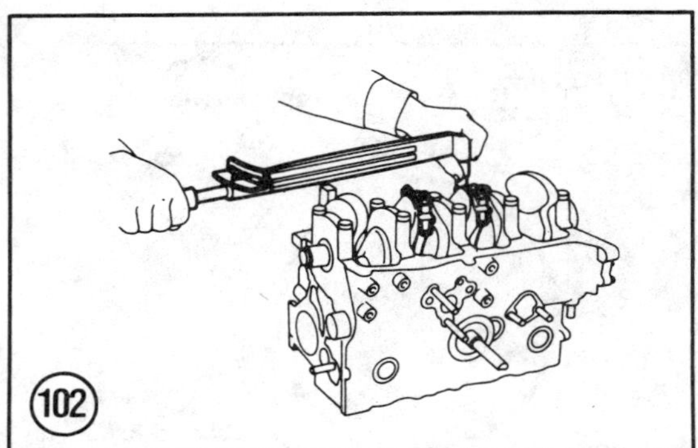

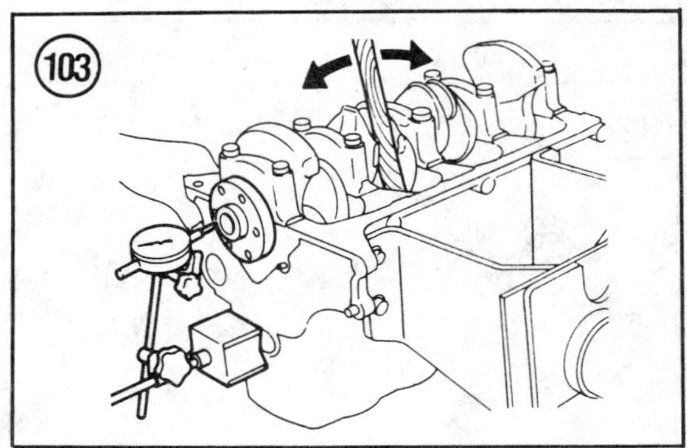

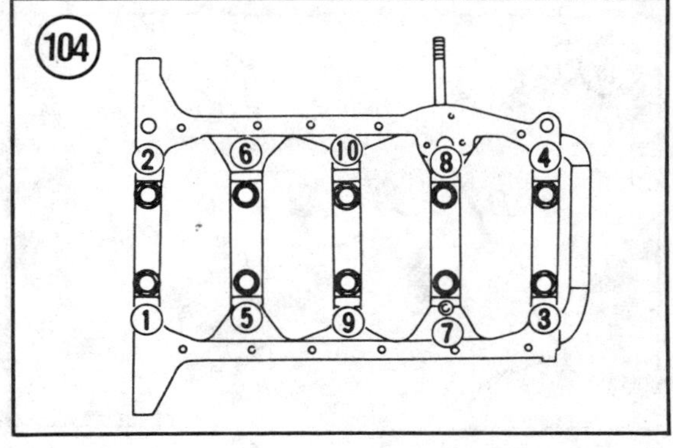

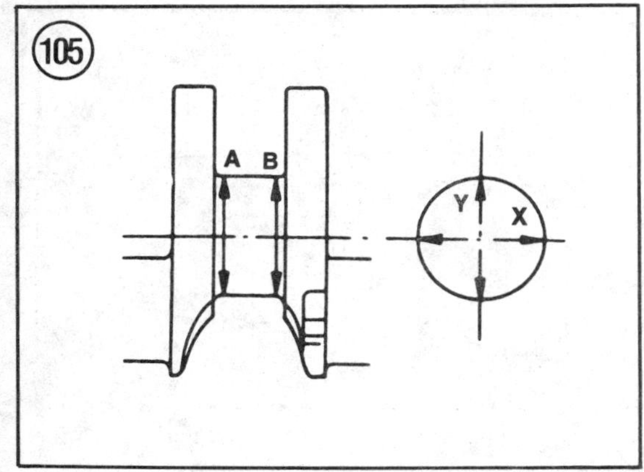

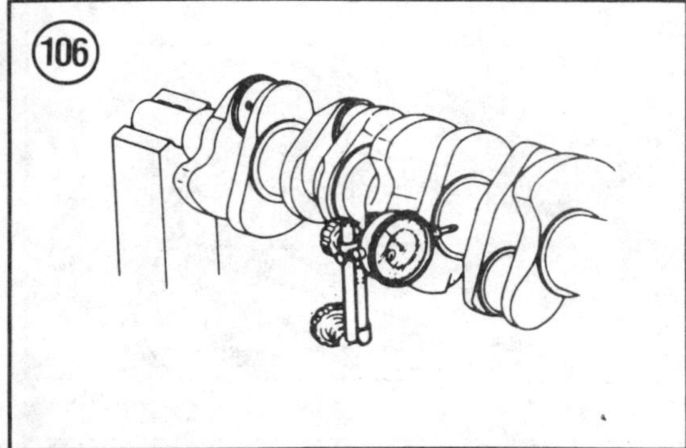

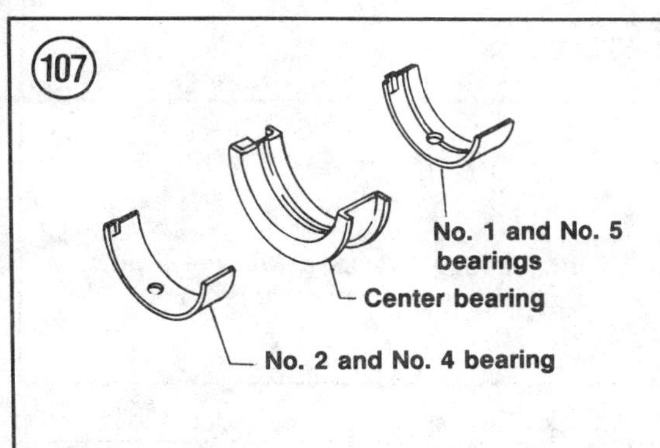

9. Check the main bearing caps for number marks facing the crankshaft pulley end of the engine. If they are not visible, clean the main bearing caps with a wire brush. If the marks are still not visible, make your own.

10. Unbolt the main bearing caps (**Figure 104**). Loosen the caps in 2 or 3 stages in the order shown.

11. Place the caps in order on a clean workbench.

12. Lift the crankshaft out of the engine. Lay the crankshaft, main bearings and bearing caps in order on a clean workbench.

Inspection

1. Clean the crankshaft thoroughly with solvent. Blow out the oil passages with compressed air.

NOTE
If you do not have precision measuring equipment, have a machine shop perform Step 2 and Step 3.

2. Check crankpins and main bearing journals for wear, scoring and cracks. Check all journals against specifications (end of chapter) for out-of-roundness, taper and wear. See **Figure 105**. Have the crankshaft reground if necessary.

3. Check the crankshaft for bending. Mount the crankshaft between accurate centers (such as V-blocks or a lathe) and rotate it one full turn with a dial indicator contacting the center journal. See **Figure 106**. The crankshaft must be reground if bent beyond specifications.

Main Bearing Clearance Measurement

Main bearing clearance is measured in the same manner as connecting rod bearing clearance, described in this chapter. Excessive clearance requires that the bearings be replaced, the crankshaft be reground or both.

Installation

1. Thoroughly clean bearings, including the back sides.

CAUTION
During the next step, be sure the bearing oil holes line up with the block oil holes. Otherwise the crankshaft will run wihout lubrication and be ruined.

2. Install the bearings in the cylinder block and bearing caps. The center bearing is flanged (**Figure 107**). Bearings No. 1 and 5 are grooved and interchangeable. Bearings No. 2 and 4 are smooth and interchangeable. Make sure the bearing locating tangs are correctly positioned in the cylinder block and bearing cap grooves.

3. Coat the bearings freely with clean engine oil. Lay the crankshaft in the block. Coat the crankshaft journals with engine oil.

4. Install the bearing caps and tighten the cap bolts slightly. See **Figure 108**. Make sure the number marks on the caps face the crankshaft pulley end of the engine. Make sure the number marks are in order, starting with the crankshaft pulley end of the engine.

5. Gently push the crankshaft toward front and rear of the engine to verify that the bearings and caps are properly aligned and seated.

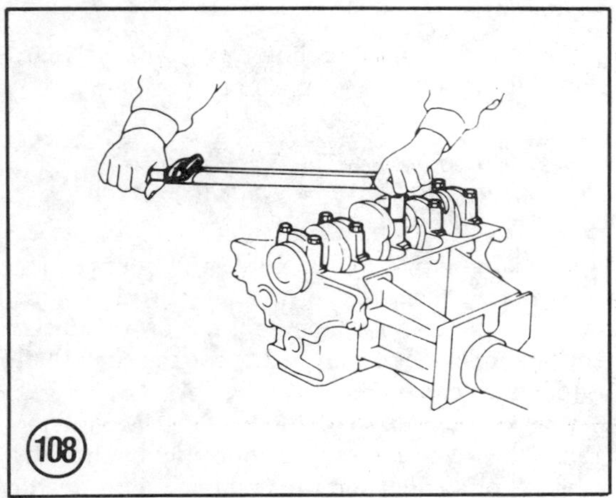

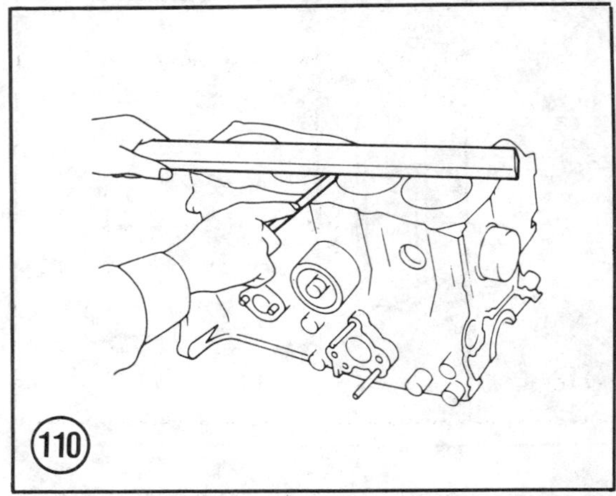

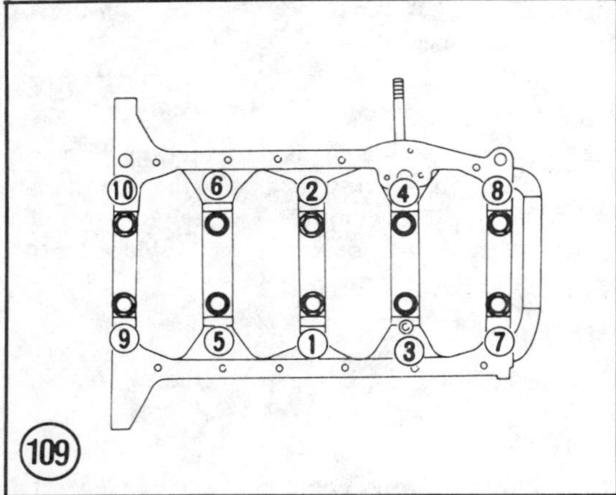

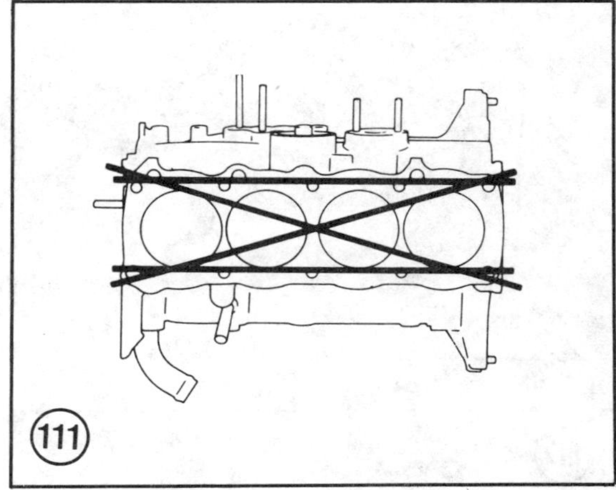

6. Tighten the cap bolts to specifications (end of chapter). Tighten gradually in 2 or 3 stages, in the order shown in **Figure 109**. Rotate the crankshaft during tightening to make sure it isn't binding. If the crankshaft becomes hard to turn, stop and find out why before continuing. Check for foreign material on bearings and journals. Make absolutely certain that bearings are the correct size, especially if the crankshaft has been reground. Never use undersize bearings if the crankshaft has not been reground.

7. Recheck crankshaft end play (**Figure 103**).

CYLINDER BLOCK INSPECTION

1. Clean the block thoroughly with solvent and check all freeze plugs for leaks. Replace any freeze plugs that are suspect. It is a good idea to replace all of them. While cleaning, check oil and water passages for sludge, dirt and corrosion. If the passages are very dirty, the block should be boiled out by a machine shop.

NOTE
Block boiling necessitates replacement of all freeze plugs. However, a block dirty enough to need boiling almost certainly needs these parts replaced anyway.

2. Examine the block for cracks.

3. Check flatness of the cylinder block's top surface. Use an accurate straightedge as shown in **Figure 110**. Measure along the lines shown in **Figure 111**. Have the block resurfaced if it is warped more than specified in **Table 1**.

4. Measure the cylinder bores for out-of-roundness or excessive wear with a bore gauge (**Figure 112**). Measure at the points shown in **Figure 113**, in front-to-rear and side-to-side directions. Compare measurements to specifications at the end of the chapter. If the cylinders exceed maximum tolerances, they must be rebored. Reboring is also necessary if the cylinder walls are badly scuffed or scored.

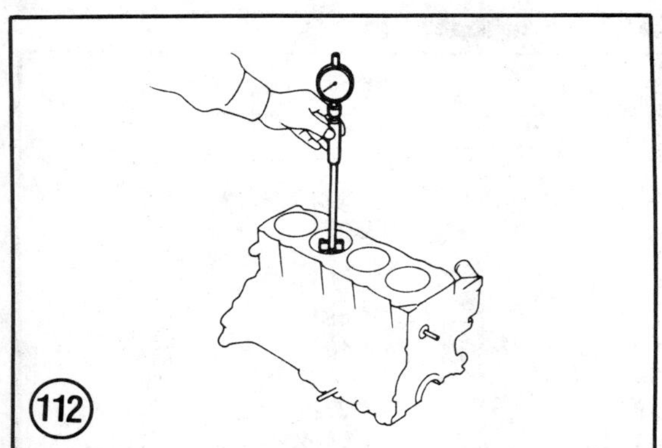

(112)

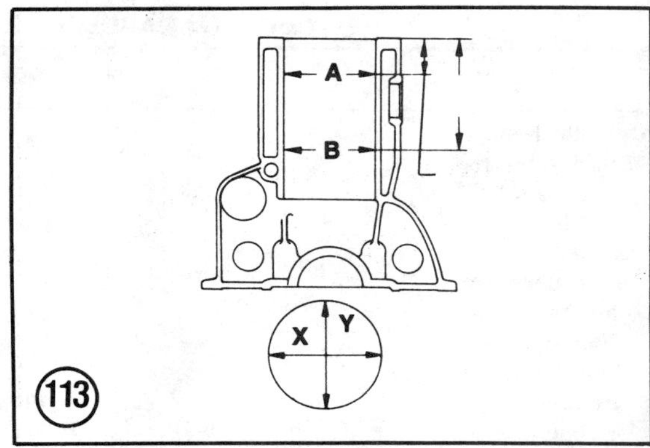

(113)

4

Tables are on the following pages.

Table 1 GASOLINE ENGINE SPECIFICATIONS

	mm	in.
Cylinder head		
Surface warp		
Standard	0.05 or less	0.002 or less
Maximum	0.1	0.004
Valves		
Head diameter		
Intake	37	1.457
Exhaust	30	1.181
Stem length, 1982		
Intake	118.5-118.9	4.67-4.68
Exhaust	117.85-118.25	4.64-4.66
Stem length, 1983		
E15 intake	118.4-119.0	4.66-4.69
E15 exhaust	117.75-118.35	4.64-4.66
E16 intake	116.4-117.0	4.58-4.61
E16 exhaust	115.75-116.35	4.56-4.58
Stem diameter		
Intake	6.970-6.985	0.2744-0.2750
Exhaust	6.945-6.960	0.2734-0.2740
Face angle	45° 15'-45° 45'	
Head edge thickness, minimum	0.5	0.020
Stem end grinding limit	0.2	0.008
Valve springs		
Free height	46.7	1.8386
Assembled height/load	39.2/23.43 kg	1.543/51.66 lb.
Maximum bend	2.0	0.079
Valve guides		
Outer diameter		
Original equipment	12.033-12.044	0.4737-0.4742
Replacement guides	12.256-12.274	0.4825-0.4832
Inner diameter (finished size)	7.005-7.020	0.2758-0.2764
Guide hole diameter in cylinder head		
Original equipment	11.970-11.988	0.4713-0.4720
For replacement guides	12.200-12.211	0.4803-0.4807
Valve guide interference fit	0.045-0.074	0.0018-0.0029
Stem-to-guide clearance		
Intake, standard	0.02-0.05	0.0008-0.0020
Exhaust, standard	0.045-0.075	0.0018-0.0030
Maximum, all guides	0.1	0.004
Valve seats		
Seat width		
Intake	1.5	0.059
Exhaust	1.8	0.071
Seat major diameter (intake)	36.5-36.7	1.437-1.445
Seat minor diameter (intake)	34.4-34.6	1.354-1.362
Seat diameter (exhaust)	29.5-29.7	1.161-1.169
Camshaft		
Bearing clearance, standard		
Journals 1, 3, 5	0.035-0.076	0.0014-0.0030
Journals 2 and 4	0.078-0.119	0.0031-0.0047
Bearing clearance, maximum		
Journals 1, 3, 5	0.15	0.0059
Journals 2 and 4	0.20	0.0079
Bearing inner diameter	42.000-42.025	1.6535-1.6545

(continued)

Table 1 GASOLINE ENGINE SPECIFICATIONS (continued)

	mm	in.
Camshaft (cont.)		
Bend (total indicator reading)		
Standard	0.02 or less	0.0008 or less
Maximum	0.1	0.004
End play		
Standard	0.15-0.29	0.0059-0.0114
Maximum	0.04	0.016
Lobe height		
Intake	35.884-36.143	1.4128-1.4226
Exhaust	35.64-35.89	1.4031-1.4130
Lobe wear, maximum	0.20	0.0079
Jackshaft		
Journal-to-bearing clearance	0.020-0.098	0.0008-0.0039
Bearing inner diameter		
Front	32.020-32.085	1.2606-1.2632
Rear	28.620-28.685	1.1268-1.1293
Journal outer diameter		
Front	31.987-32.000	1.2593-1.2598
Rear	28.587-28.600	1.1255-1.1260
End play	0.045-0.105	0.0018-0.0041
Fuel pump cam height	27.8-27.9	1.094-1.098
Pistons		
Diameter (dimension A)	75.967-76.017	2.9908-2.9928
Measuring point (dimension a)	17.5	0.689
Available oversizes	0.02, 0.50	0.0008, 0.0197
Piston pin hole diameter	19.003-19.012	0.7481-0.7485
Piston pin diameter	18.995-19.000	0.7478-0.7480
Piston pin-to-piston clearance	0.008-0.012	0.0003-0.0005
Piston-to-connecting rod interference fit	0.017-0.038	0.0007-0.0015
Piston clearance in block	0.023-0.043	0.0009-0.0017
Piston rings		
Side clearance, standard		
Top ring	0.040-0.073	0.0016-0.0029
Second ring	0.030-0.063	0.0012-0.0025
Oil ring	0.050-0.145	0.0020-0.0057
Side clearance, maximum*	0.2	0.008
Ring gap, standard		
Top ring	0.20-0.35	0.0079-0.0138
Second ring	0.15-0.30	0.0059-0.0118
Oil ring rails	0.30-0.90	0.0118-0.0354
Ring gap, maximum*	1.0	0.039
Connecting rods		
Center-to-center distance	140.5	5.53
Bend or twist**	0.05	0.002
Piston pin hole diameter	18.962-18.978	0.7465-0.7472
Big end play		
Standard	0.10-0.37	0.0040-0.0146
Maximum	0.5	0.020
Crankshaft		
Main bearing journal diameter	49.943-49.964	1.9663-1.9671
Crankpin diameter	39.954-39.974	1.5730-1.5738
Journal center to crankpin center distance	41	1.61

(continued)

Table 1 GASOLINE ENGINE SPECIFICATIONS (continued)

	mm	in.
Crankshaft (cont.)		
Out-of-roundness or taper		
Standard	0.01 or less	0.0004 or less
Maximum	0.03	0.0012
Bend		
Standard	0.05 or less	0.002 or less
Maximum	0.1	0.0039
End play		
Standard	0.05-0.18	0.0020-0.0071
Maximum	0.3	0.0118
Main bearing clearance, non-MPG models		
Bearings 1 and 5 (standard)	0.031-0.076	0.0012-0.0030
Bearings 2, 3 and 4		
(standard)	0.031-0.092	0.0012-0.0036
All bearings (maximum)	0.10	0.0039
Main bearing clearance, MPG models		
Bearings 1, 3 and 5		
(standard)	0.047-0.076	0.0019-0.0030
Bearings 2 and 4 (standard)	0.031-0.092	0.0012-0.0036
All bearings (maximum)	0.1	0.004
Connecting rod bearing clearance		
Standard	0.030-0.060	0.0012-0.0024
Maximum	0.1	0.004
Flywheel warp, maximum	0.15	0.0059
Drive plate runout, maximum	0.5	0.020
Cylinder block		
Measuring point A	20	0.79
Measuring point B	100	3.94
Surface warp		
Standard	0.05 or less	0.002 or less
Maximum	0.10	0.0039
Bore diameter		
Standard	76.00-76.05	2.9921-2.9941
Maximum	76.20	3.000
Out-of-roundness	0.015 or less	0.006 or less
Taper	0.02 or less	0.0008 or less
Difference between bores	0.05 or less	0.002 or less

*Applies to compression rings only.
**Per 100 mm (3.94 in.) of connecting rod length.

Table 2   TIGHTENING TORQUES

Fastener	N•m	ft.-lb.
External parts		
Air conditioning compressor		
bracket to engine	26-34	20-25
Air conditioning compressor		
to bracket	26-34	20-25
Alternator bracket bolt	9.1-11.8	7-9
Alternator to adjusting bar bolt	16-21	12-15
Crankshaft pulley bolt	113-147	83-108
EGR valve to EGR tube	39-59	29-43

(continued)

Table 2   TIGHTENING TORQUES (continued)

Fastener	N·m	ft.-lb.
External parts (cont.)		
Exhaust air induction tube nut	39-59	29-43
Fuel pump nuts	9.1-11.8	7-9
Manifold nuts	16-21	12-15
Engine mount bracket to block	29-39	22-29
Engine mount bracket to head	16-21	12-15
Oil pump nuts	9.1-11.8	7-9
Oil pump bolt	9.1-11.8	7-9
Power steering pump bracket to engine	26-34	20-25
Power steering pump to bracket	31-42	23-31
Spark plugs	15-20	11-14
Splash shield screws	3.7-5.0	3-4
Thermostat housing bolts	3.7-5.0	3-4
Water pump bolts	9-14	6.5-10.0
Internal parts		
Camshaft pulley bolts	6-8	5-6
Connecting rod nuts	31-37	23-27
Cylinder head bolts		
First step	39-44	29-33
Second step	69-74	51-54
Cylinder block front cover	3.7-5.0	3-4
Cylinder head front cover	3.7-5.0	3-4
Drive plate bolts	93-103	69-76
Flywheel bolts	78-88	58-65
Jackshaft pulley bolts	6-8	5-6
Main bearing cap bolts	49-59	36-43
Oil pan bolts and nuts	3.7-5.0	3-4
Oil pan drain plug	35-47	26-35
Oil strainer bolts	6.3-8.3	4.6-6.1
Rocker arm locknuts	16-21	12-15
Rocker shaft bolts	16-21	12-15
Tensioner locknut	16-21	12-15
Valve cover nuts	4-8	3-6

4

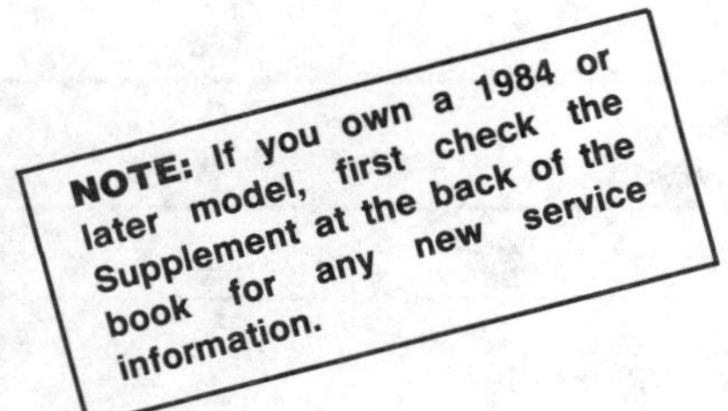

FUEL, EXHAUST AND EMISSION CONTROL SYSTEMS

This chapter provides service procedures for the gasoline fuel system (air cleaner, fuel pump and carburetor), as well as the fuel tank and lines, exhaust system, throttle linkage and emission control systems for gasoline and diesel-engined models. **Table 1** is at the end of the chapter.

The diesel fuel injection system contains expensive, precision-made parts. Service requires special tools and skills and extreme standards of cleanliness. Refer all service other than specified in Chapter Three to a dealer or qualified specialist.

AIR CLEANER

The Sentra uses an automatic temperature control air cleaner. See **Figure 1**. When underhood temperature is less than 38° C (100° F), a flap valve blocks the normal air inlet and hot air is drawn from around the exhaust manifold. This improves combustion of the fuel-air mixture. When underhood temperature is above 53° C (127° F), the flap valve moves to block the hot air intake. Cool air is then drawn through the normal inlet.

A defective ATC air cleaner may cause engine stalling or hesitation, increased fuel consumption or loss of power. The ATC system should be inspected at intervals specified in Chapter Three.

The air cleaner also includes an idle compensator. This is a valve which opens at high idle temperatures, admitting extra air into the intake manifold to compensate for overrich fuel mixtures.

ATC System Test

1. With the engine cold (underhood temperature less than 38° C/100° F), look down the air inlet with a mirror as shown in **Figure 2**. The flap valve should be blocking the inlet.

2. Have an assistant race the engine several times. The flap valve should move each time the engine is raced.

3. Warm the engine to normal operating temperature while watching the flap valve. It should move gradually to block the hot air intake and open the inlet to cool air.

4. If the system has performed as described so far, it is okay. If not, perform the following steps to isolate the cause.

5. Let the engine cool until underhood temperature is less than 38° C (100° F).

6. With the engine idling, disconnect the vacuum hose from the vacuum motor. See **Figure 3**. Place a thumb over the hose and feel for vacuum:

   a. If vacuum is present, the vacuum lines and temperature sensor are okay.

   b. If vacuum is very weak or not present, inspect the vacuum lines. If these are in good condition and properly connected, replace the temperature sensor.

7. Connect another vacuum line to the vacuum motor and apply vacuum. The flap valve should move. If it doesn't move, push the valve with a finger to make sure it isn't stuck. If the valve isn't

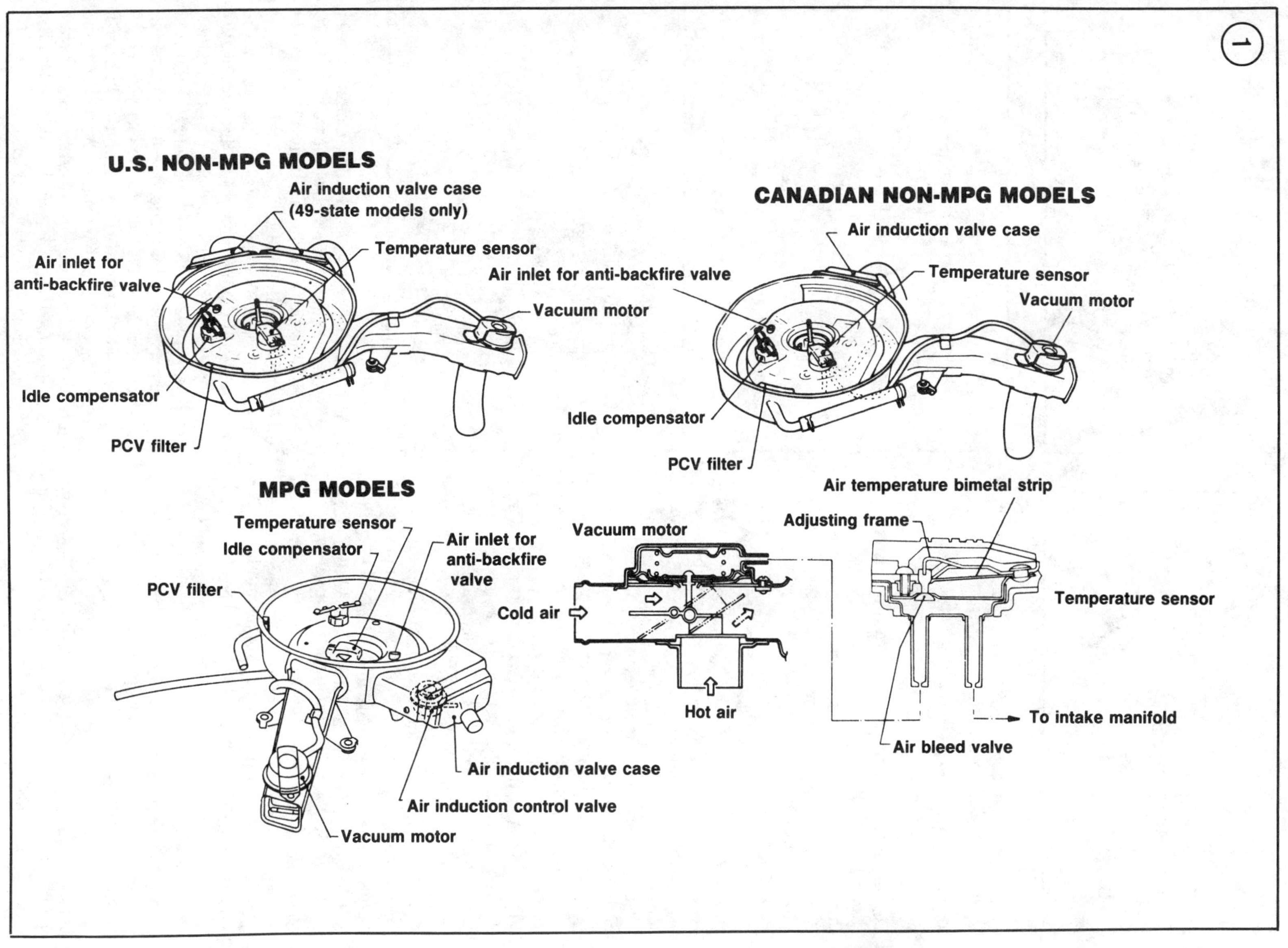
U.S. NON-MPG MODELS
Air induction valve case
(49-state models only)
Temperature sensor
Air inlet for
anti-backfire valve
Vacuum motor
Idle compensator
PCV filter
CANADIAN NON-MPG MODELS
Air induction valve case
Air inlet for anti-backfire valve
Temperature sensor
Vacuum motor
Idle compensator
PCV filter
Air temperature bimetal strip
Adjusting frame
Temperature sensor
To intake manifold
Air bleed valve
MPG MODELS
Temperature sensor
Idle compensator
PCV filter
Air inlet for
anti-backfire
valve
Vacuum motor
Cold air
Hot air
Air induction valve case
Air induction control valve
Vacuum motor

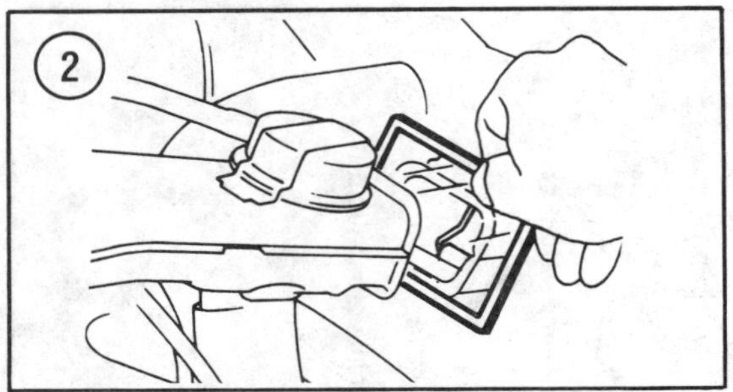

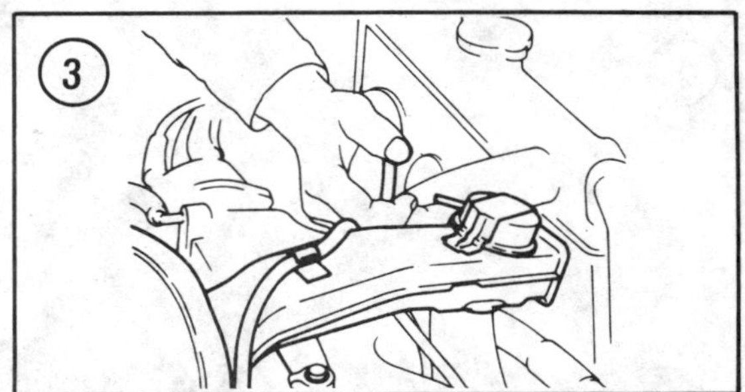

stuck, but doesn't move when vacuum is applied, replace the vacuum motor.

Idle Compensator Test

1. Make sure underhood temperature is below the compensator operating temperatures listed in **Table 1**.
2. Remove the air cleaner cover.
3. Disconnect the idle compensator hose from the intake manifold.
4. Block each idle compensator valve in turn and suck on the hose. See **Figure 4**. It should not be possible to suck air through the hose. If it is, replace the idle compensator as an assembly.
5. Warm the engine to normal operating temperature.
6. Place a thermometer next to the idle compensator as shown in **Figure 5**. Heat the idle compensator with a heat gun or similar tool while watching the thermometer. The idle compensator valves should open and emit a hissing sound as they reach the opening temperature specified in **Table 1**. If either valve fails to open at the specified temperature, replace the idle compensator.

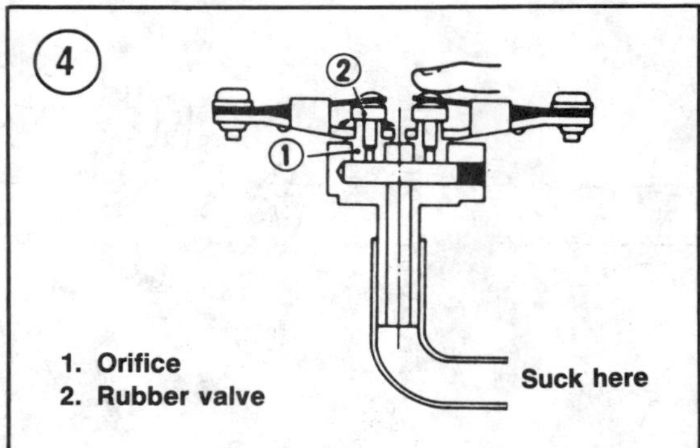

FUEL PUMP

On-car Test

1. Disconnect the fuel inlet line from the carburetor. Using a T-fitting, connect a fuel pressure gauge into the line as close to the carburetor as possible.
2. Start the engine and run it at varying speeds. Compare the pressure reading on the **gauge** to specifications in **Table 1**:
   a. If fuel pressure is insufficient, replace the fuel pump.
   b. If fuel pressure is within specifications, perform the following steps.
3. Disconnect the T-fitting from the carburetor and fuel line.
4. Place the end of the carburetor's fuel inlet line in a graduated container of at least one quart capacity.

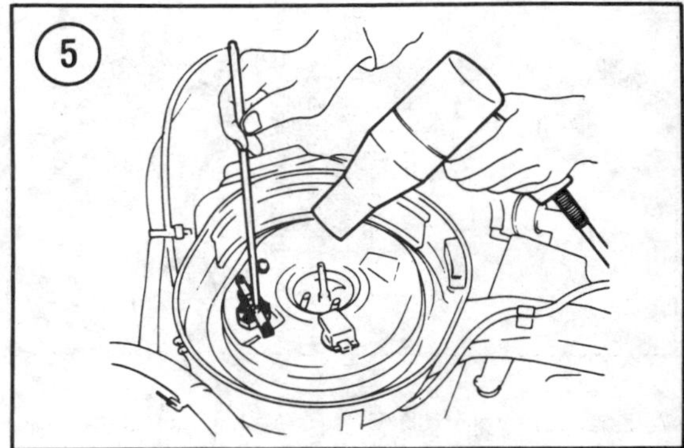

5. Start the engine and let it idle (there is enough fuel in the carburetor float bowl for this). After 30 seconds, note the amount of fuel in the container and compare with **Table 1**:
   a. If the specified amount of fuel is in the container, the fuel pump and lines are okay.
   b. If there is insufficient fuel in the container, perform the next steps to isolate the problem.
6. Disconnect the fuel pump inlet line (**Figure 6**). Connect a length of fuel line to the fuel pump inlet port and place the other end of the line in a container of gasoline. This allows the fuel pump to draw fuel from a source of fuel other than the car's tank and will tell you whether the problem is in the fuel pump or in the lines and filter.

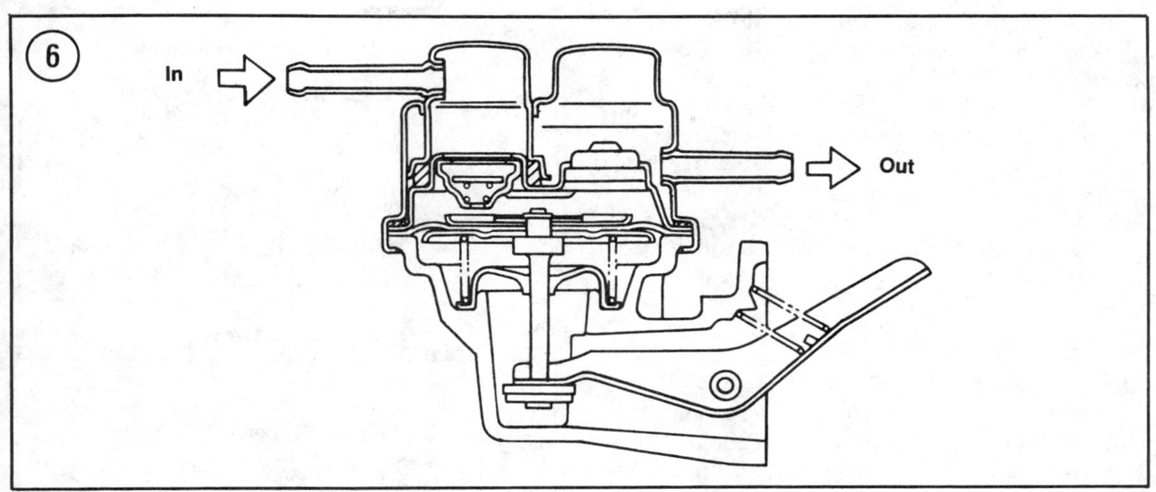

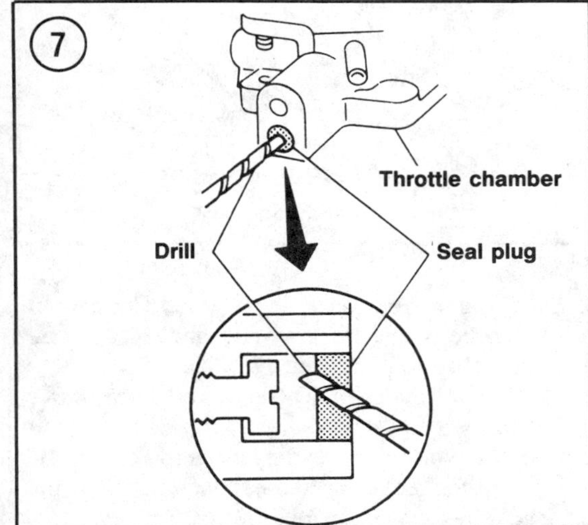

7. Start the engine and let it idle. Again, note the amount of fuel in the graduated container after 30 seconds of idling:
  a. If the amount is correct, the fuel pump is okay. Check for a clogged fuel filter or fuel line.
  b. If the amount is below specifications, replace the fuel pump.

Off-car Test

1. With the fuel pump removed from the engine, connect the fuel pump inlet port to a fuel source (such as a can of gasoline) with a length of fuel line.
2. Hold the fuel pump about one meter (3 ft.) above the fuel source. Operate the pump lever by hand. The pump should quickly draw fuel from the fuel source. If not, replace it.

Removal/Installation

1. With a container handy to catch dripping gasoline, disconnect the inlet and outlet lines from the pump.
2. Remove the pump mounting nuts, lockwashers and washers.
3. Take the pump off the engine, together with its spacer and gaskets.
4. Clean all traces of old gasket and sealer from the fuel pump and spacer.
5. Installation is the reverse of removal. Use new gaskets, coated on both sides with gasket sealer. Tighten the fuel pump mounting nuts to 9-12 N•m (7-9 ft.-lb.).

CARBURETOR

All models use a 2-barrel, downdraft carburetor with an electrically heated automatic choke.

Idle Mixture Adjustment (U.S. and MPG Models)

This procedure should be done only after the carburetor has been overhauled or the car has failed an emissions test. A CO meter is required and the idle mixture screw seal must be drilled out of the carburetor.

Periodic idle adjustments are described in Chapter Three.

> *CAUTION*
> *During the next step, keep metal shavings out of the carburetor. Do not scratch metal surfaces with the drill. Do not drill in far enough to hit the idle mixture screw.*

1. With the carburetor off the engine, drill out the mixture screw plug (**Figure 7**). Then pry the plug out.

2. Install the carburetor on the engine.

3. Adjust ignition timing and idle speed as described in Chapter Three.

4. Turn the idle mixture screw to obtain the correct CO percentage (**Table 1**, end of chapter). If the correct percentage can't be obtained, overhaul or replace the carburetor.

5. Turn off the engine. Position a new plug over the mixture screw and drive it in with a suitable tool. See **Figure 8**.

Automatic Choke Inspection

Start this procedure with a cold engine.

1. Remove the air cleaner cover. Have an assistant floor the throttle pedal and watch the choke valve. It should close automatically. If not, check the choke linkage for binding and clean or repair it as needed.

2. Push the choke valve with a finger. It should move smoothly, without sticking or binding. If not, clean or repair the choke linkage.

3. Make sure the choke cover mark is lined up with the choke housing index mark. See **Figure 9**.

4. Check the choke heater source wiring for breaks or bad connections, referring to wiring diagrams at the end of the book.

5. Warm the engine to normal operating temperature. Make sure the choke valve opens all the way. If it does, the choke system is okay. If not, test the choke coil, choke heater circuit and choke relay as described in this chapter.

Choke Coil Test

Disconnect the choke wire. Connect an ohmmeter between the choke wire and carburetor body. It should indicate a low resistance. If the ohmmeter indicates infinity, replace the choke chamber (U.S. and MPG models) or choke coil (Canadian models).

Choke Heater Circuit Test

1. Locate the function check connector above the fuse block in the passenger compartment. See **Figure 10**.

2. With the engine off, connect an ohmmeter between the gray-red and black wire terminals. It should indicate continuity (little or no resistance):

   a. If the ohmmeter indicates continuity, the choke heater circuit is okay.

   b. If the ohmmeter indicates no continuity (infinite resistance), check the heater circuit wiring for breaks or bad connections. **Figure 10** shows a schematic of the heater circuit.

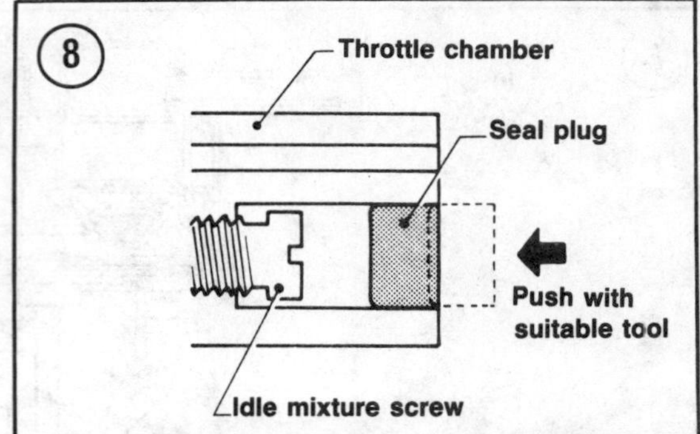

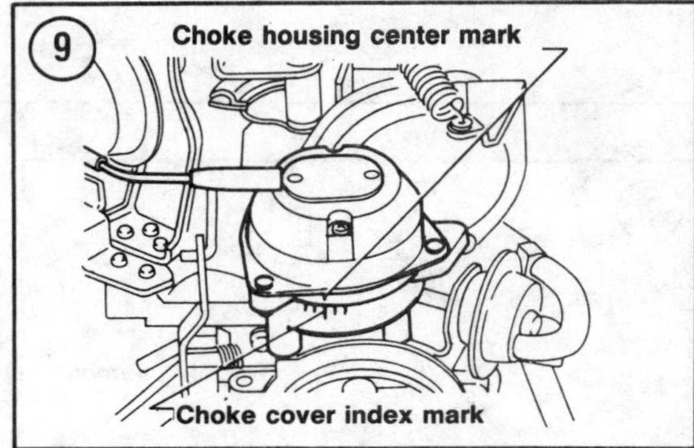

3. Start the engine and let it idle. Connect a voltmeter between the gray-red and black wire terminals. It should indicate 12 volts:

   a. If the voltmeter indicates 12 volts, the heater circuit is okay.

   b. If the voltmeter reading is zero, check the wiring for breaks or bad connections. Test the choke relay as described in this chapter.

Choke Relay Test

1. Locate the choke relay on the relay box in the engine compartment. See **Figure 11**.

2. Remove the relay and identify its terminals. See **Figure 12**.

3. Connect an ohmmeter between terminals No. 3 and 6 (**Figure 13**). It should indicate continuity (zero ohms).

4. Connect the ohmmeter between terminals No. 4 and 5 (**Figure 13**). It should indicate infinite resistance.

5. Connect the positive terminal of the car's battery to terminal No. 2 with a length of wire. See **Figure 14**. Connect the battery negative terminal to terminal No. 1. With the battery connected, the ohmmeter should indicate infinite resistance when connected between terminals No. 3 and 6. It

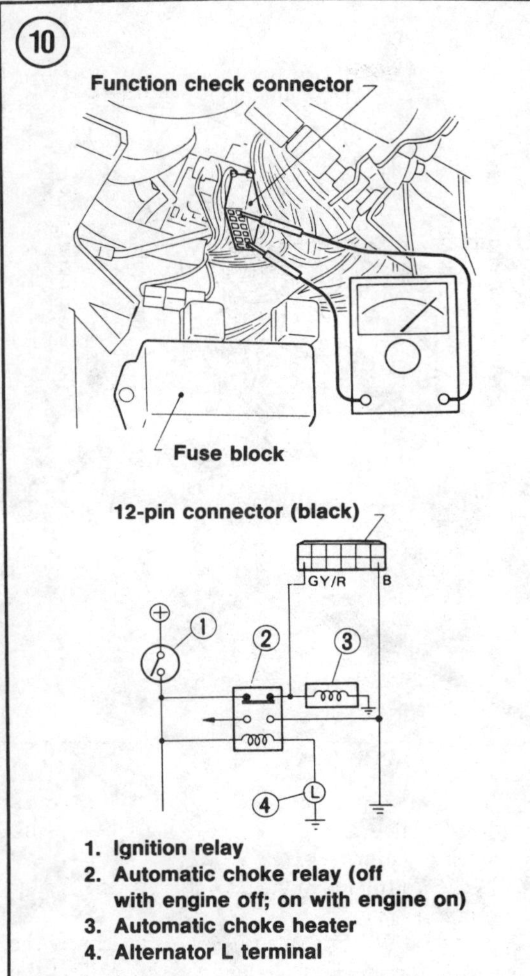

should indicate zero ohms when connected between terminals No. 4 and 5.

6. If the relay doesn't perform as described, replace it.

Carburetor Removal/Installation

1. Remove the air cleaner as described in this chapter.

2. Disconnect the fuel inlet and return lines. Plug the lines so they won't drip gasoline and create a fire hazard.

3. Unplug the wiring connectors for automatic choke, anti-dieseling solenoid, throttle valve switch (if so equipped) and mixture heater (if so equipped).

4. Label and disconnect the carburetor vacuum lines.

5. Remove the carburetor mounting nuts. Take the carburetor and spacer off the intake manifold.

CAUTION
Stuff a clean rag into the intake manifold opening to prevent parts from falling in.

6. Installation is the reverse of removal. Use new gaskets.

Carburetor Disassembly

Refer to the following illustrations.
   a. MPG models—**Figure 15**.
   b. 1982 non-MPG models—**Figure 16**.
   c. 1983 California models (except MPG)—**Figure 17**.
   d. 1983 non-California models (except MPG)—**Figure 18**.
During disassembly, observe the following.

1. When removing jets, note their location and the number stamped in each jet.

2. Make sure wrenches and screwdrivers fit exactly.

3. Lay all parts in order to ease reassembly.

4. Do not remove throttle shafts, throttle plates or the choke plate. On U.S. models, do not remove the choke coil from the housing.

5. Do not remove linkage parts from the throttle shafts unless they are bent or otherwise damaged. Be sure replacement parts are available before removing.

Carburetor Inspection

1. Thoroughly clean all parts in solvent, aerosol carburetor cleaner or parts cleaner except the following:
   a. Diaphragms.
   b. Anti-dieseling solenoid.
   c. Choke cover.
   d. Throttle valve switch (if so equipped).
   e. Air-fuel ratio solenoid (if so equipped).
   f. Float.
Wipe these parts clean with a rag moistened in solvent.

2. Replace all parts in the repair kit, no matter what the apparent condition of the old parts.

NOTE
Some aftermarket repair kits are designed to apply to several carburetors and may include parts not used on your carburetor.

3. Blow out jets and passages with compressed air. If a compressor is not available, use aerosol carburetor cleaner. These usually include a plastic tube which fits into the can's nozzle, making it easy to blow cleaner through jets and passages.

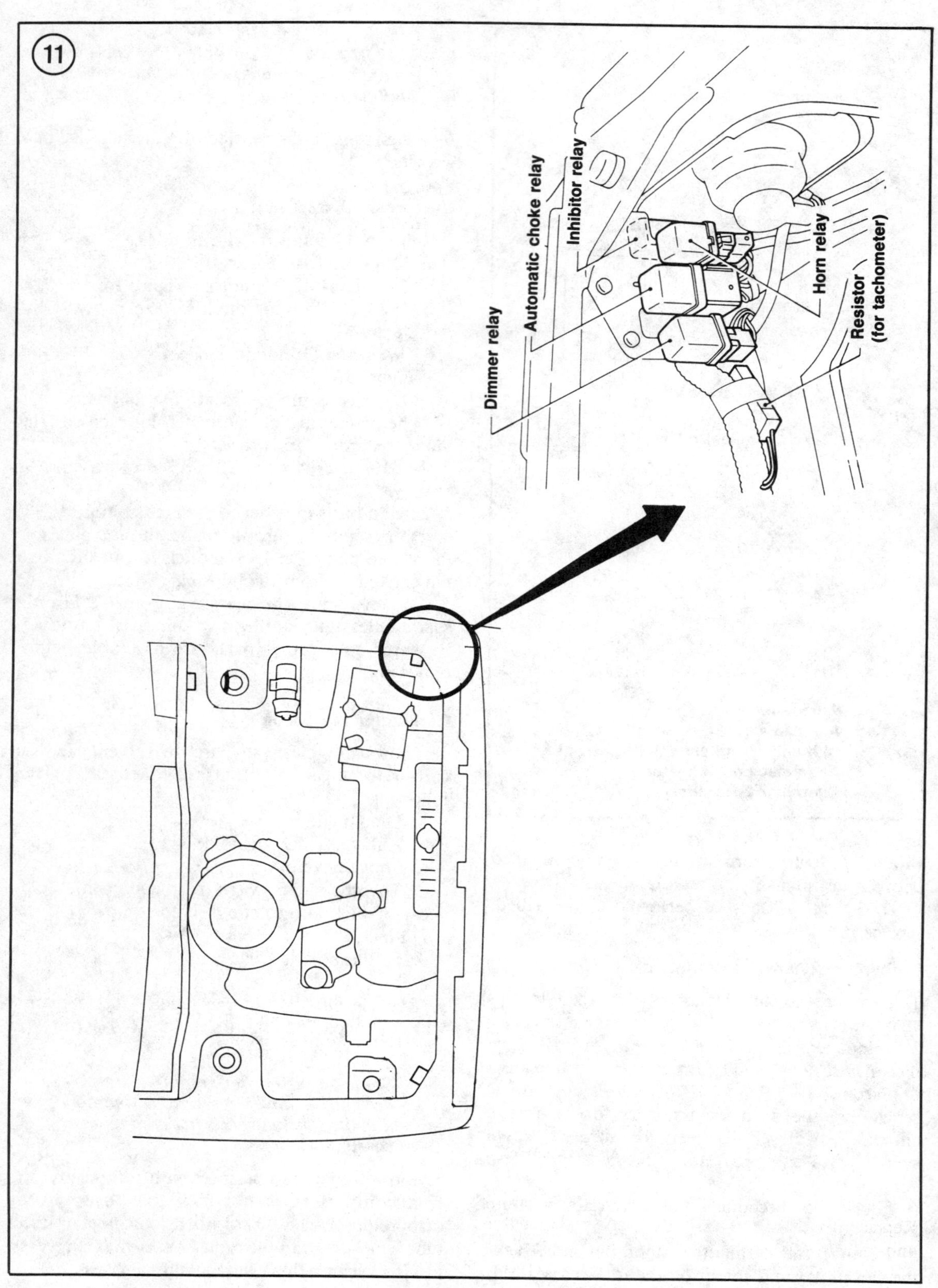
11
Dimmer relay
Automatic choke relay
Inhibitor relay
Horn relay
Resistor
(for tachometer)

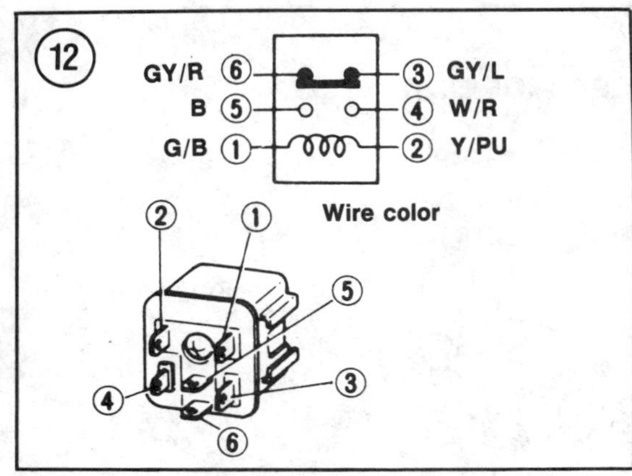

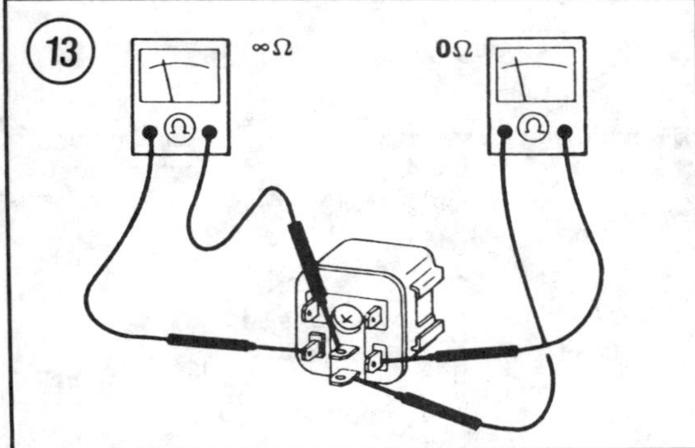

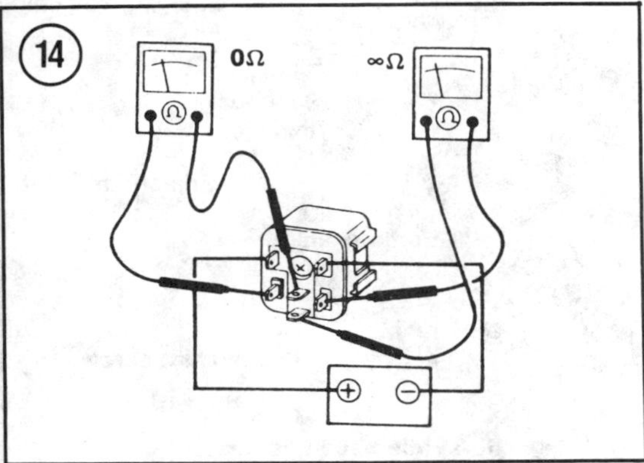

4. Check the needle valve and seat for wear. Replace if wear can be seen. If a new needle valve and seat are included in the repair kit, replace the old ones no matter what their apparent condition.

5. Hold the float next to your ear, shake it and listen for liquid inside. If this can be heard, replace the float.

6. Check all castings for cracks. Replace cracked castings.

7. Check the accelerator pump piston seal for wear, damage or deterioration. Replace as needed.

8. Check the idle mixture screw for wear at the tip. Replace the screw if wear is detected.

9. Test the choke diaphragm, throttle opener diaphragm (except 1983 California), secondary throttle opener diaphragm (1983 California) and air conditioner actuator diaphragm (1983 California, if so equipped). To do this, push on the diaphragm connecting rod and hold the vacuum fitting closed with a finger. The connecting rod should stay pushed in for at least 15 seconds. If it doesn't, replace the diaphragm.

10. Test the anti-dieseling solenoid (if so equipped). Connect the solenoid's wire terminals to the car's battery terminals with lengths of wire. The solenoid should click each time the wire is connected and disconnected. If not, replace the solenoid.

Carburetor Assembly

Assembly is the reverse of disassembly, plus the following.

1. Use new gaskets and O-rings.

NOTE
On carburetors with an air-fuel ratio solenoid (all MPG models, 1983 California non-MPG models), replace the solenoid O-ring with a new one whenever the solenoid is removed. The slightest damage to the O-ring will cause the solenoid to malfunction. Lubricate the solenoid O-ring with petroleum jelly just before installation.

2. Be sure the jets and air bleeds are installed in the holes from which they were removed. Refer to the numbers written down during disassembly. If in doubt, refer to **Table 1** at the end of the chapter.

3. After assembly, adjust float level, fast idle, choke housing (Canada only) and dashpot (if so equipped).

Float Level Adjustment

1. If the carburetor is still on the car, start the engine and let it idle. Fuel level should be approximately halfway up the sight glass (**Figure 19**). If not, remove the choke chamber from the carburetor and adjust the float.

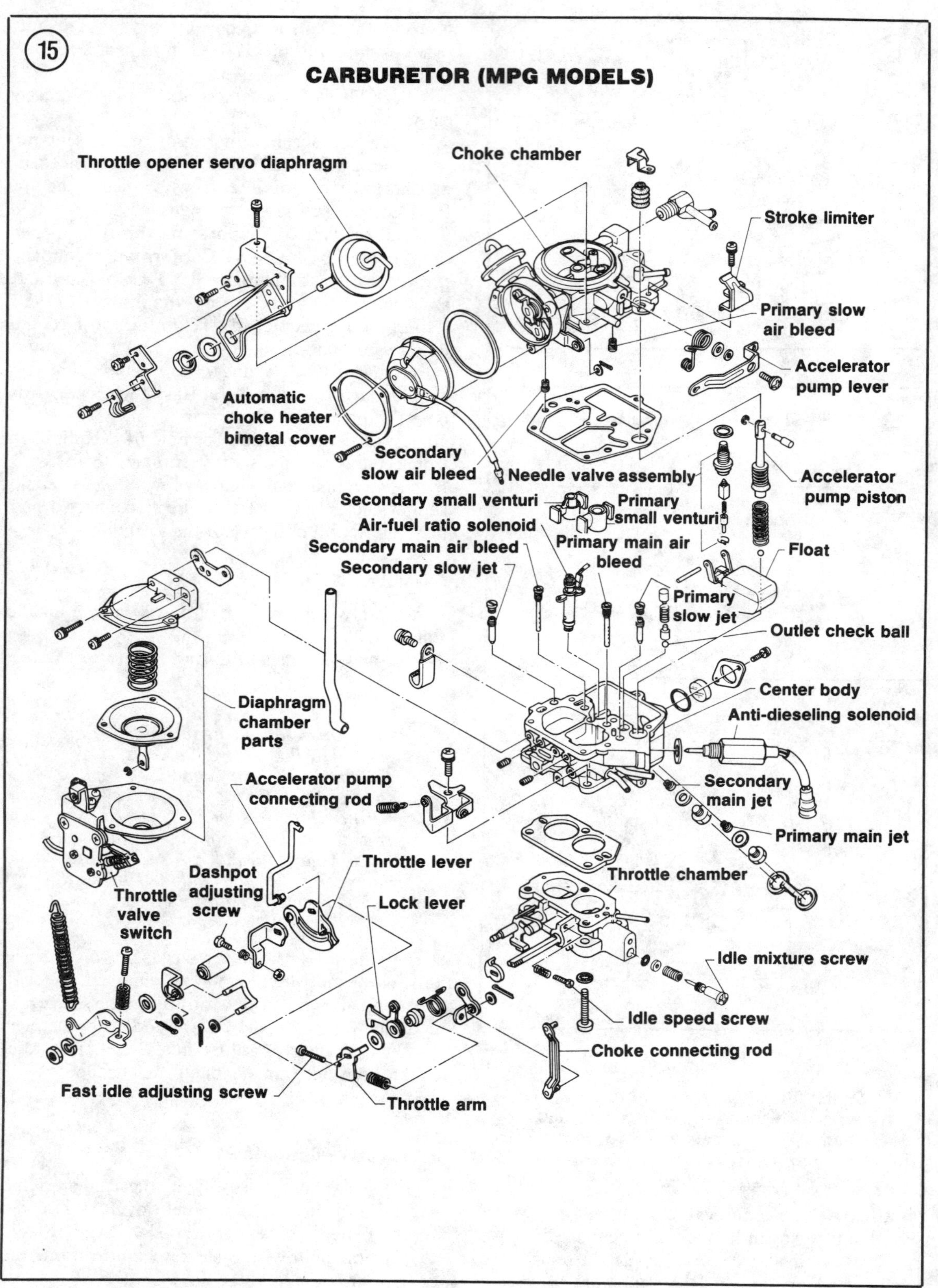

15
CARBURETOR (MPG MODELS)
Throttle opener servo diaphragm
Choke chamber
Stroke limiter
Primary slow air bleed
Accelerator pump lever
Automatic choke heater bimetal cover
Secondary slow air bleed
Needle valve assembly
Secondary small venturi
Primary small venturi
Air-fuel ratio solenoid
Primary main air bleed
Secondary main air bleed
Secondary slow jet
Accelerator pump piston
Float
Primary slow jet
Outlet check ball
Center body
Anti-dieseling solenoid
Diaphragm chamber parts
Accelerator pump connecting rod
Secondary main jet
Primary main jet
Throttle lever
Throttle chamber
Dashpot adjusting screw
Lock lever
Throttle valve switch
Idle mixture screw
Idle speed screw
Choke connecting rod
Fast idle adjusting screw
Throttle arm

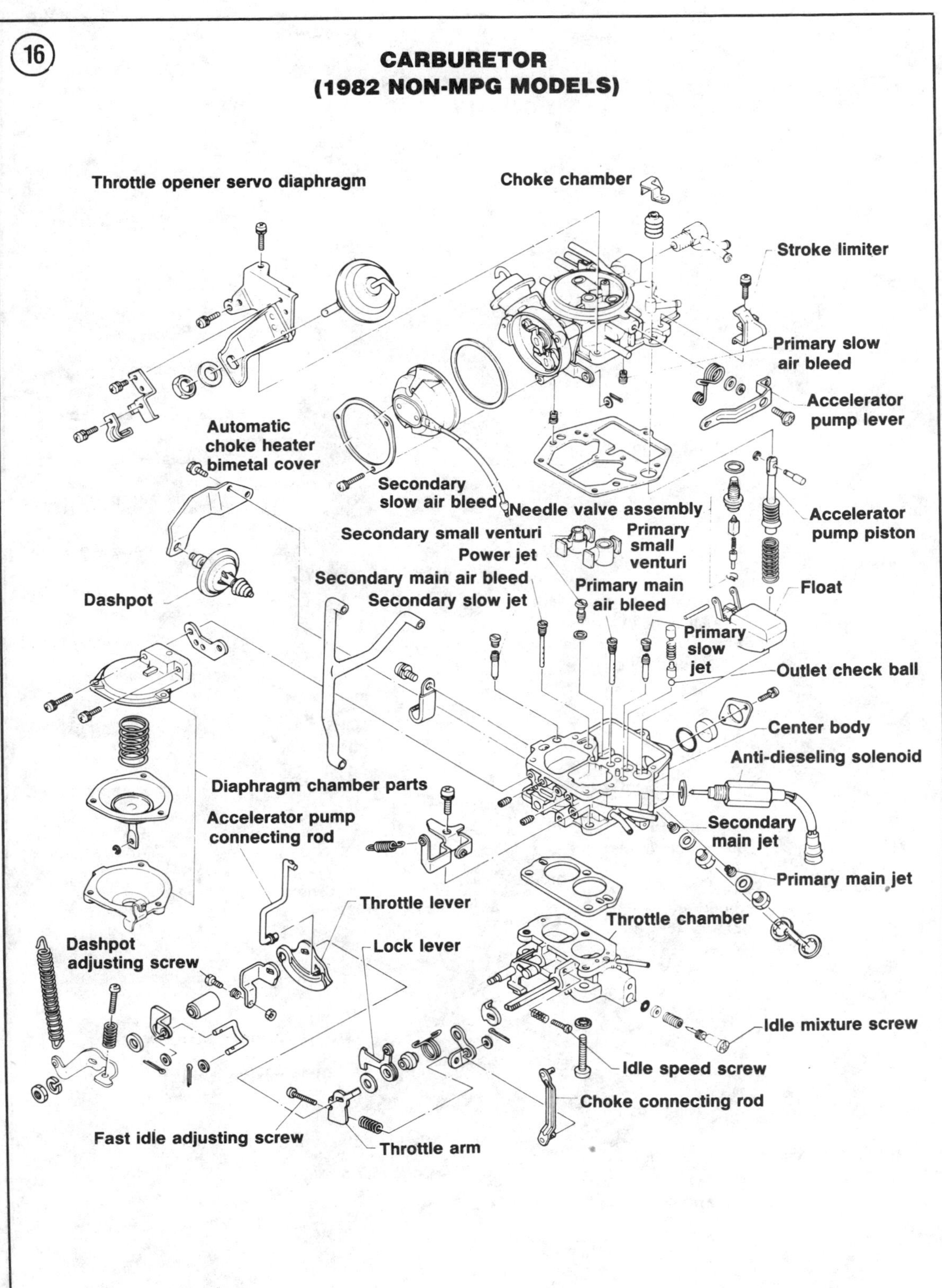

16
CARBURETOR
(1982 NON-MPG MODELS)
Throttle opener servo diaphragm
Choke chamber
Stroke limiter
Primary slow air bleed
Accelerator pump lever
Automatic choke heater bimetal cover
Secondary slow air bleed
Needle valve assembly
Accelerator pump piston
Secondary small venturi
Primary small venturi
Power jet
Primary main air bleed
Secondary main air bleed
Secondary slow jet
Primary main air bleed
Float
Dashpot
Primary slow jet
Outlet check ball
Center body
Anti-dieseling solenoid
Diaphragm chamber parts
Accelerator pump connecting rod
Secondary main jet
Throttle lever
Primary main jet
Dashpot adjusting screw
Lock lever
Throttle chamber
Idle mixture screw
Idle speed screw
Choke connecting rod
Fast idle adjusting screw
Throttle arm
5

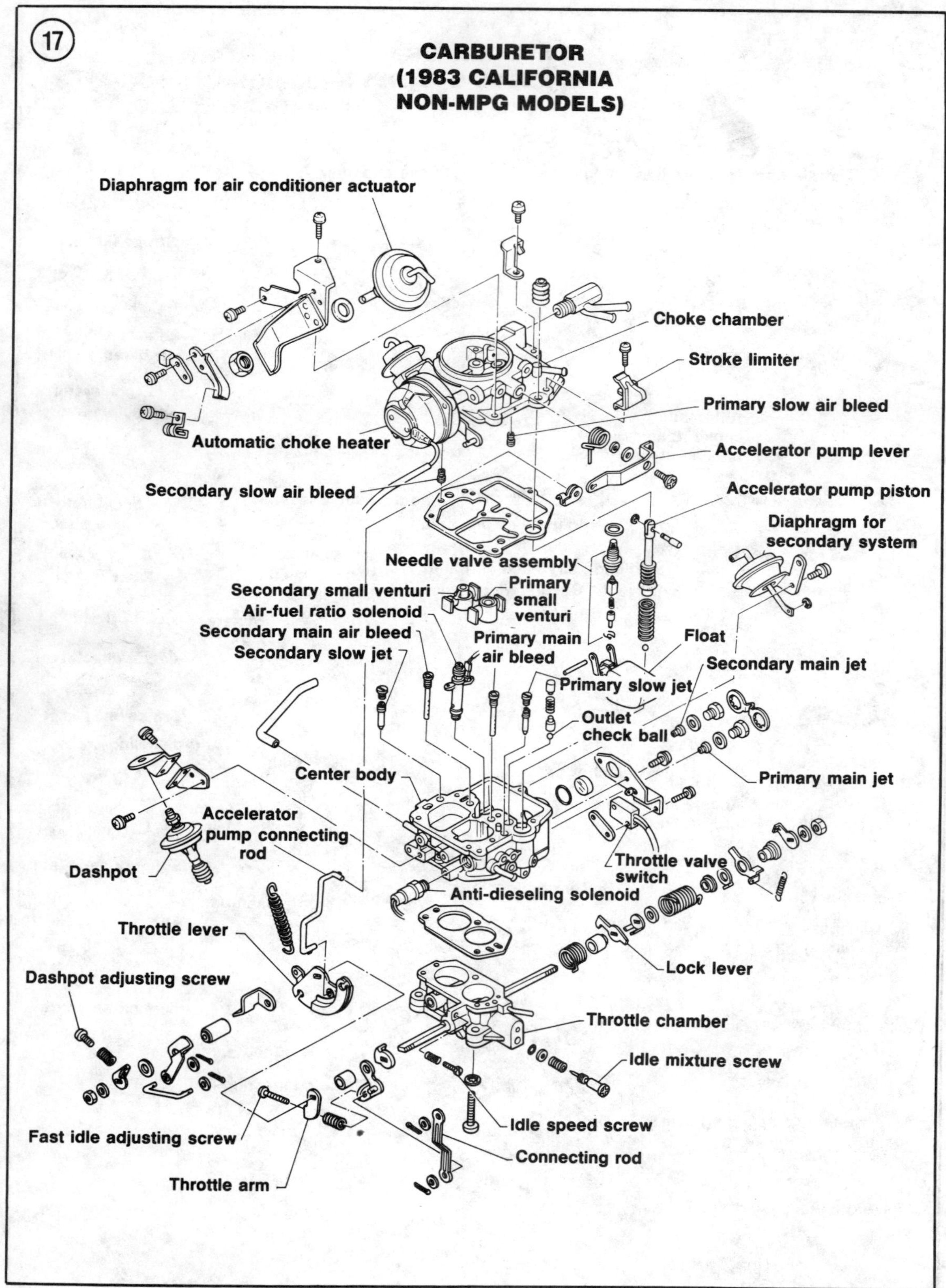
17
CARBURETOR
(1983 CALIFORNIA
NON-MPG MODELS)
Diaphragm for air conditioner actuator
Choke chamber
Stroke limiter
Primary slow air bleed
Automatic choke heater
Accelerator pump lever
Accelerator pump piston
Secondary slow air bleed
Diaphragm for
secondary system
Needle valve assembly
Secondary small venturi
Primary
small
venturi
Air-fuel ratio solenoid
Secondary main air bleed
Secondary slow jet
Primary main
air bleed
Float
Secondary main jet
Primary slow jet
Outlet
check ball
Primary main jet
Center body
Accelerator
pump connecting
rod
Throttle valve
switch
Dashpot
Anti-dieseling solenoid
Throttle lever
Lock lever
Dashpot adjusting screw
Throttle chamber
Idle mixture screw
Fast idle adjusting screw
Idle speed screw
Connecting rod
Throttle arm

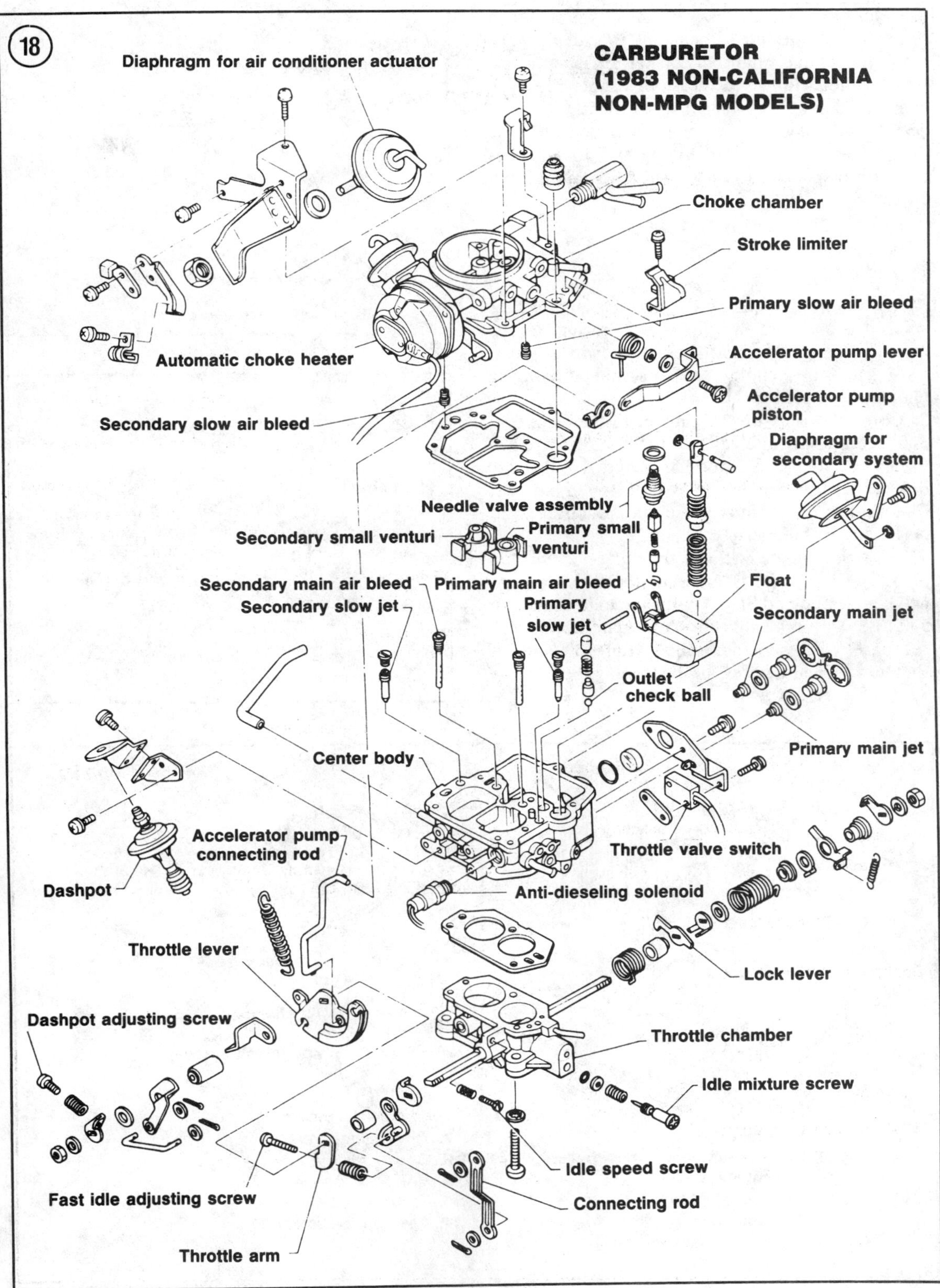
18
Diaphragm for air conditioner actuator
CARBURETOR
(1983 NON-CALIFORNIA
NON-MPG MODELS)
Choke chamber
Stroke limiter
Primary slow air bleed
Accelerator pump lever
Automatic choke heater
Accelerator pump piston
Diaphragm for secondary system
Secondary slow air bleed
Needle valve assembly
Secondary small venturi
Primary small venturi
Float
Secondary main air bleed
Secondary slow jet
Primary main air bleed
Primary slow jet
Secondary main jet
Outlet check ball
Center body
Primary main jet
Accelerator pump connecting rod
Throttle valve switch
Dashpot
Anti-dieseling solenoid
Throttle lever
Lock lever
Dashpot adjusting screw
Throttle chamber
Idle mixture screw
Idle speed screw
Fast idle adjusting screw
Connecting rod
Throttle arm
5

2. Hold the choke chamber upside down as shown in **Figure 20**. Measure dimension "H" (the distance from the choke chamber gasket surface to the float). If not within specifications (**Table 1**, end of chapter), bend the float seat to adjust it.

3. Lift the float and measure dimension "h" (the distance between the needle valve and float seat). If not within specifications, bend the float stopper to adjust it.

Fast Idle Adjustment

Fast idle is the speed at which the engine runs when it is cold and the choke is operating. As the engine warms, idle speed drops to normal.

1. Warm the engine to normal operating temperature, then turn it off.

2. Connect a tune-up tachometer to the engine.

3. Place the fast idle cam on the second step. See **Figure 21**. On U.S. models, move the throttle linkage and turn the choke plate by hand. On Canadian cars, remove the choke cover and position the choke arm by hand.

4. Start the engine without touching the throttle pedal. If the pedal is touched, the fast idle cam will be released and Step 3 will have to be repeated.

5. Note the reading on the tachometer and compare with specifications (**Table 1**, end of chapter). Adjust if necessary by turning the fast idle screw (**Figure 21**).

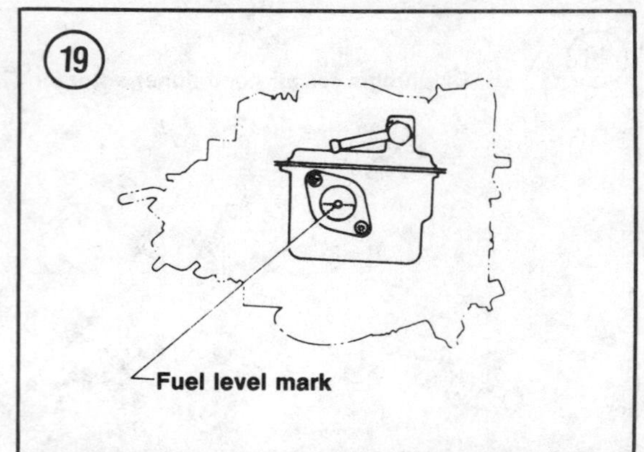

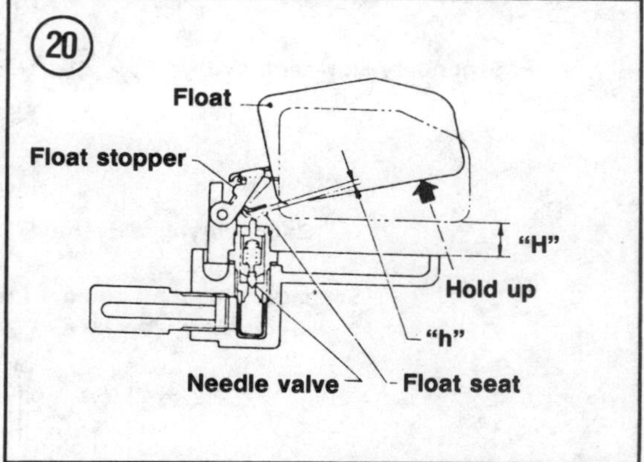

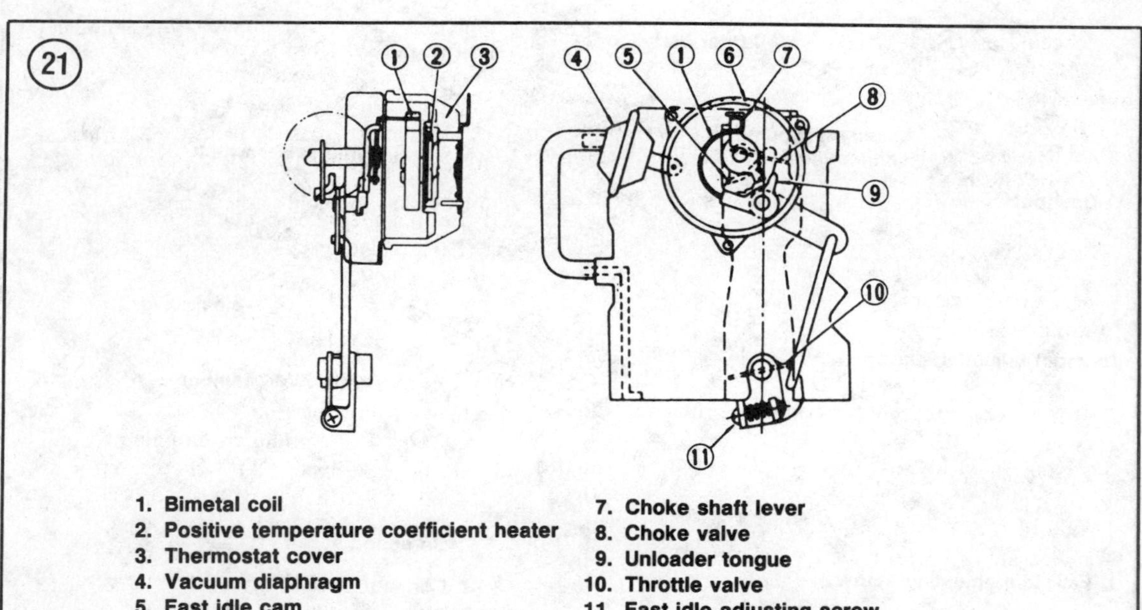

1. Bimetal coil
2. Positive temperature coefficient heater
3. Thermostat cover
4. Vacuum diaphragm
5. Fast idle cam
6. Choke cover index mark
7. Choke shaft lever
8. Choke valve
9. Unloader tongue
10. Throttle valve
11. Fast idle adjusting screw

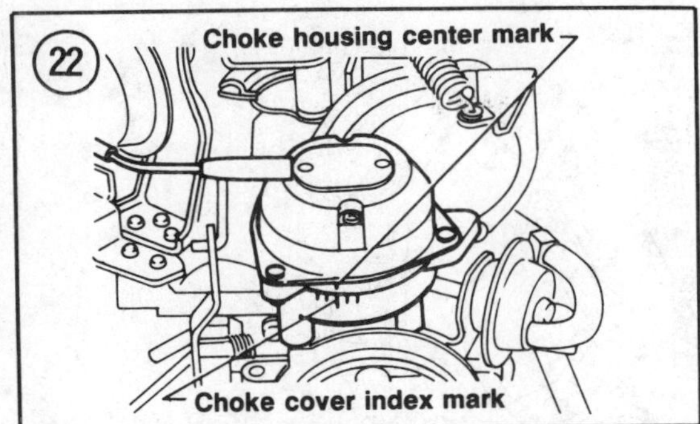

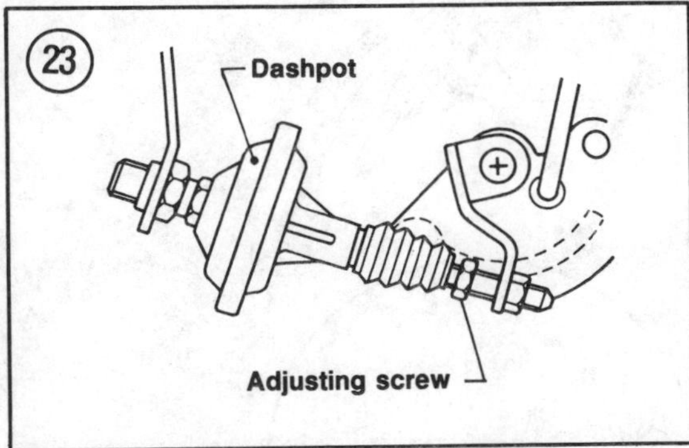

Choke Housing Adjustment

This procedure applies to Canadian cars only. The choke housing on U.S. models is not adjustable.

1. Check the match marks on choke cover and housing (**Figure 22**). The choke cover mark should align with the center mark on the housing.
2. To adjust, remove the choke cover retaining ring. Reposition the choke cover and install the retaining ring.

Dashpot Adjustment

The engine must be properly tuned up and running well for this procedure.

1. Warm the engine to normal operating temperature.
2. Connect an accurate tune-up tachometer to the engine.
3. Move the throttle linkage by hand until the dashpot just touches the stopper lever. See **Figure 23**. Note the tachometer reading. If not within specifications (**Table 1**, end of chapter), turn the adjusting screw to correct it.

FUEL TANK AND LINES

Figure 24 shows the fuel tank and lines.

Fuel Tank Removal/Installation

1. Siphon the fuel from the tank.
2. Remove the access plate and unplug the tank gauge unit's wiring connector. See **Figure 25**.
3. Detach the fuel filler tube and ventilation tube from the tank (**Figure 25**).
4. Disconnect the outlet, return and vapor hoses from the metal lines. See **Figure 25**.
5. Remove the tank mounting bolts and take the tank out.
6. Installation is the reverse of removal.

Gauge Unit Removal/Installation

1. Remove the access plate and unplug the gauge unit connector (**Figure 25**).
2. Remove the gauge unit lockplate (**Figure 24**). Tap the lockring counterclockwise with a hammer and screwdriver, then lift it off and take out the gauge unit and O-ring.
3. Installation is the reverse of removal. Use a new O-ring.

Gauge Unit and Thermistor Test

The gauge unit operates the fuel gauge. The thermistor operates the fuel warning light.

1. Remove the gauge unit as described in this chapter.
2. Connect an ohmmeter between gauge unit terminals No. 1 and 3 (**Figure 26**). Raise and lower the float and note the ohmmeter reading at each float position. If not within specifications, replace the gauge unit.
3. Set up the test circuit shown in **Figure 27**. Dip the thermistor in water as shown. The test lamp should stay out.
4. Remove the thermistor from the water. The test lamp should come on after approximately 3 minutes.
5. If the thermistor doesn't perform as described, replace the gauge unit.

EXHAUST SYSTEM

To remove and install exhaust system parts, refer to the following illustrations:

   a. 1982 U.S., 1982 Canada MPG, 1983 U.S. (gasoline)—**Figure 28**.
   b. 1982 Canada except MPG, 1983 Canada (gasoline)—**Figure 29**.
   c. All 1983 diesel models—**Figure 30**.

The main muffler-to-rear exhaust tube connection on diesels and Canadian non-MPG models is sealed with Nissan muffler sealer. Separate and reconnect it as follows.

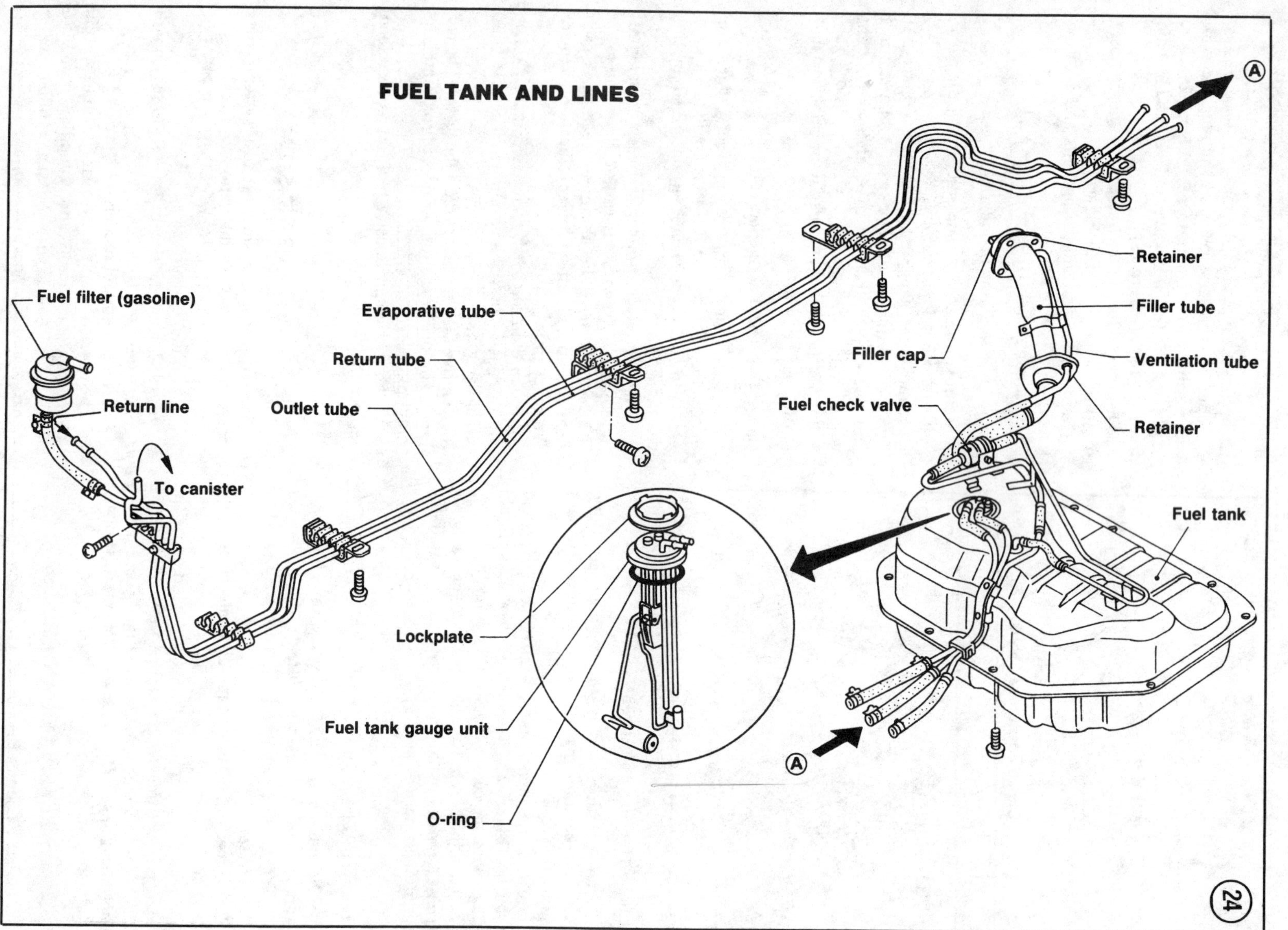
FUEL TANK AND LINES
24
A
Retainer
Filler tube
Ventilation tube
Retainer
Fuel tank
Filler cap
Fuel check valve
Fuel filter (gasoline)
Return line
To canister
Evaporative tube
Return tube
Outlet tube
Lockplate
Fuel tank gauge unit
O-ring
A

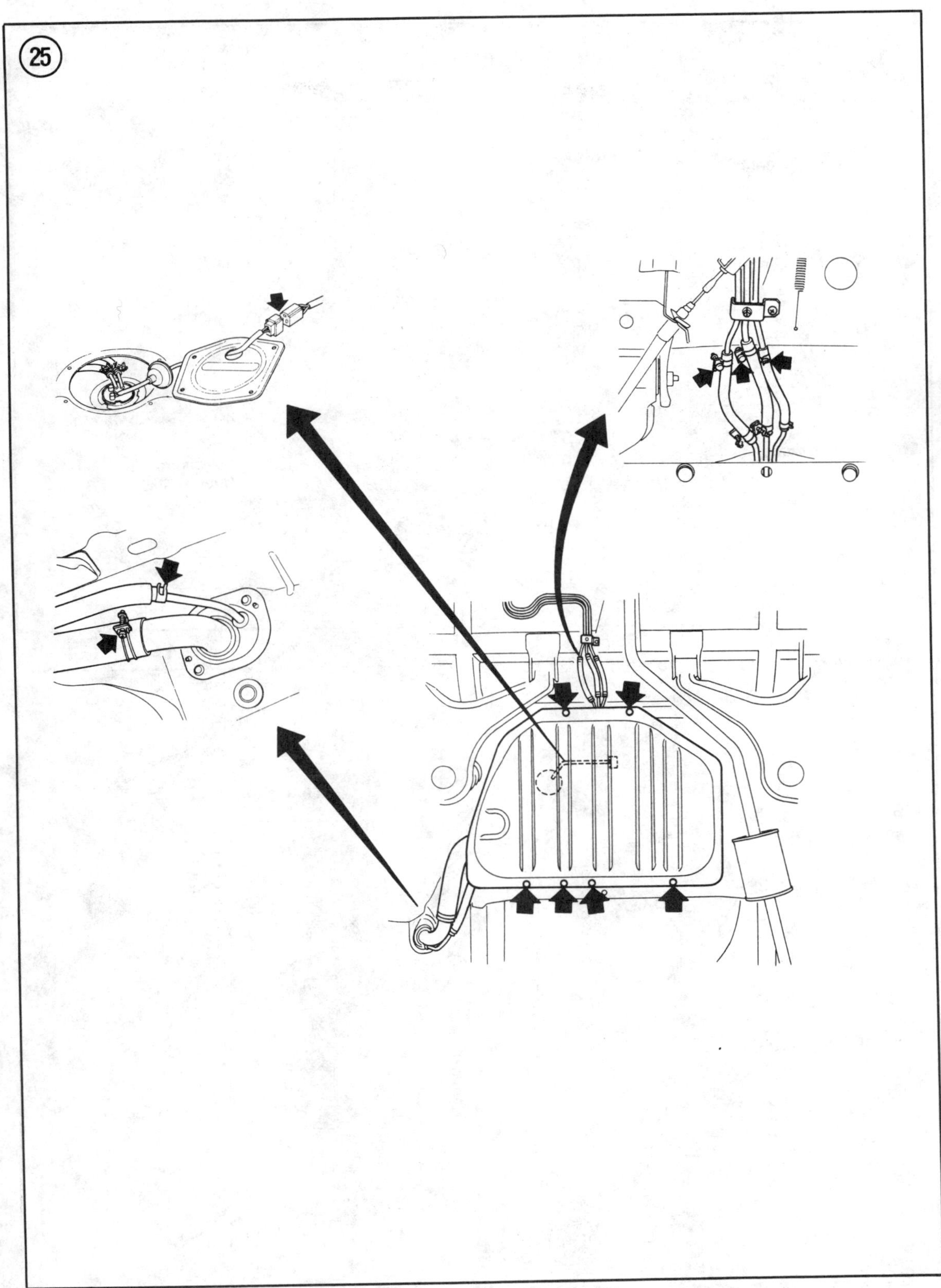

26
Full (10 ohms) 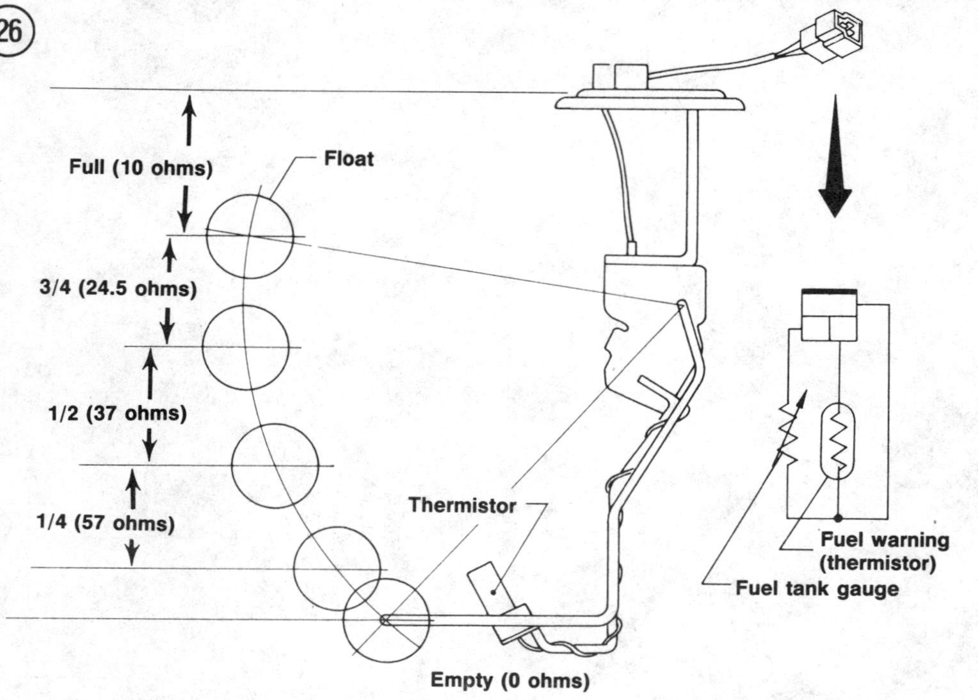
Float
3/4 (24.5 ohms)
1/2 (37 ohms)
1/4 (57 ohms)
Thermistor
Empty (0 ohms)
Fuel warning
(thermistor)
Fuel tank gauge

27
Battery 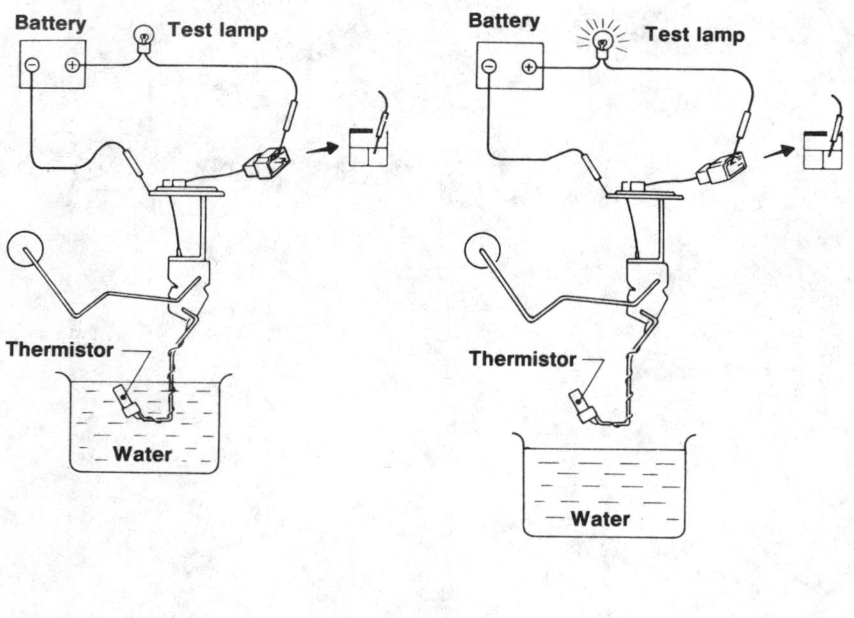
Test lamp
Battery
Test lamp
Thermistor
Thermistor
Water
Water

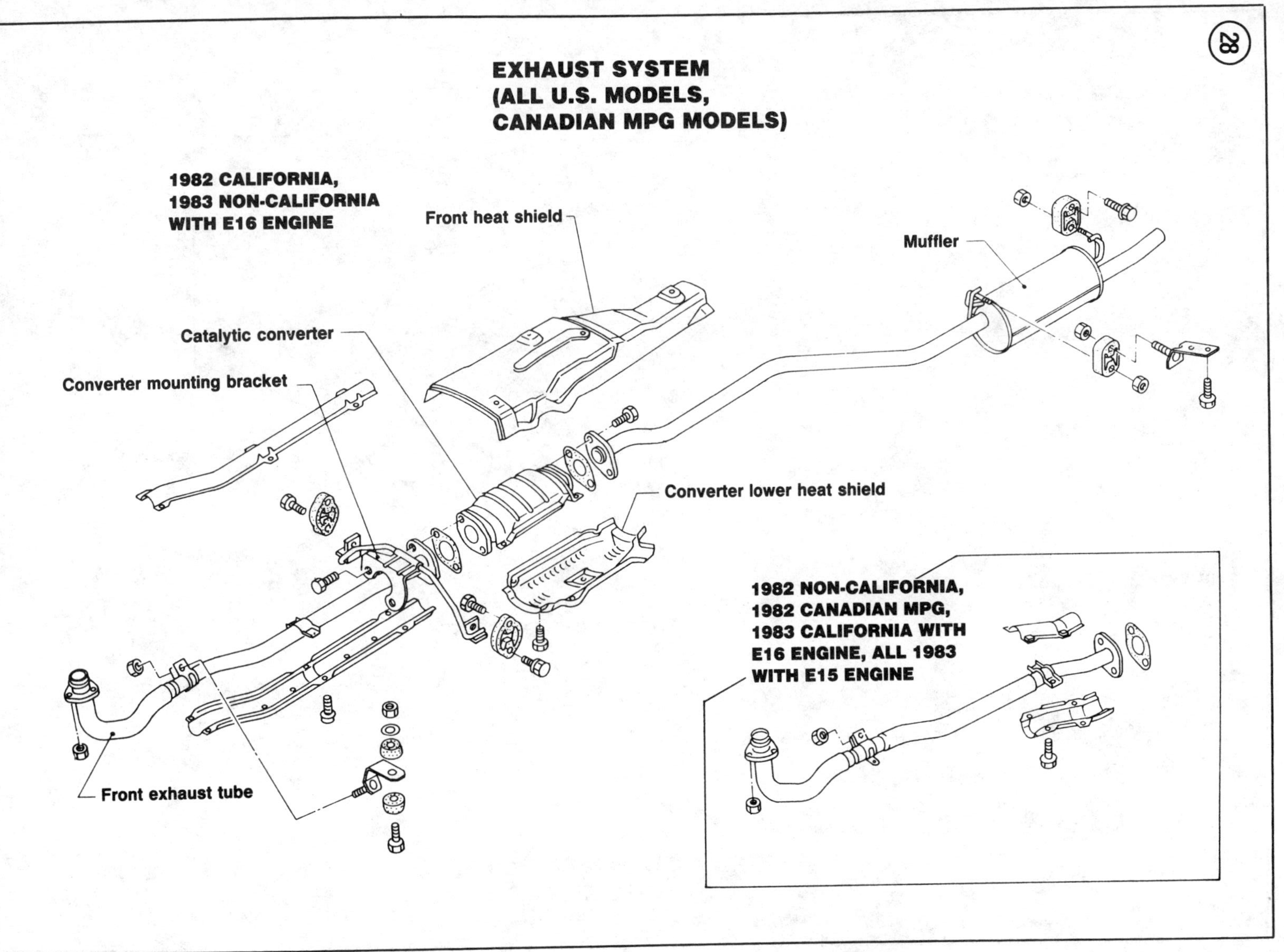

28
EXHAUST SYSTEM (ALL U.S. MODELS, CANADIAN MPG MODELS)
1982 CALIFORNIA, 1983 NON-CALIFORNIA WITH E16 ENGINE
Front heat shield
Muffler
Catalytic converter
Converter mounting bracket
Converter lower heat shield
1982 NON-CALIFORNIA, 1982 CANADIAN MPG, 1983 CALIFORNIA WITH E16 ENGINE, ALL 1983 WITH E15 ENGINE
Front exhaust tube
5

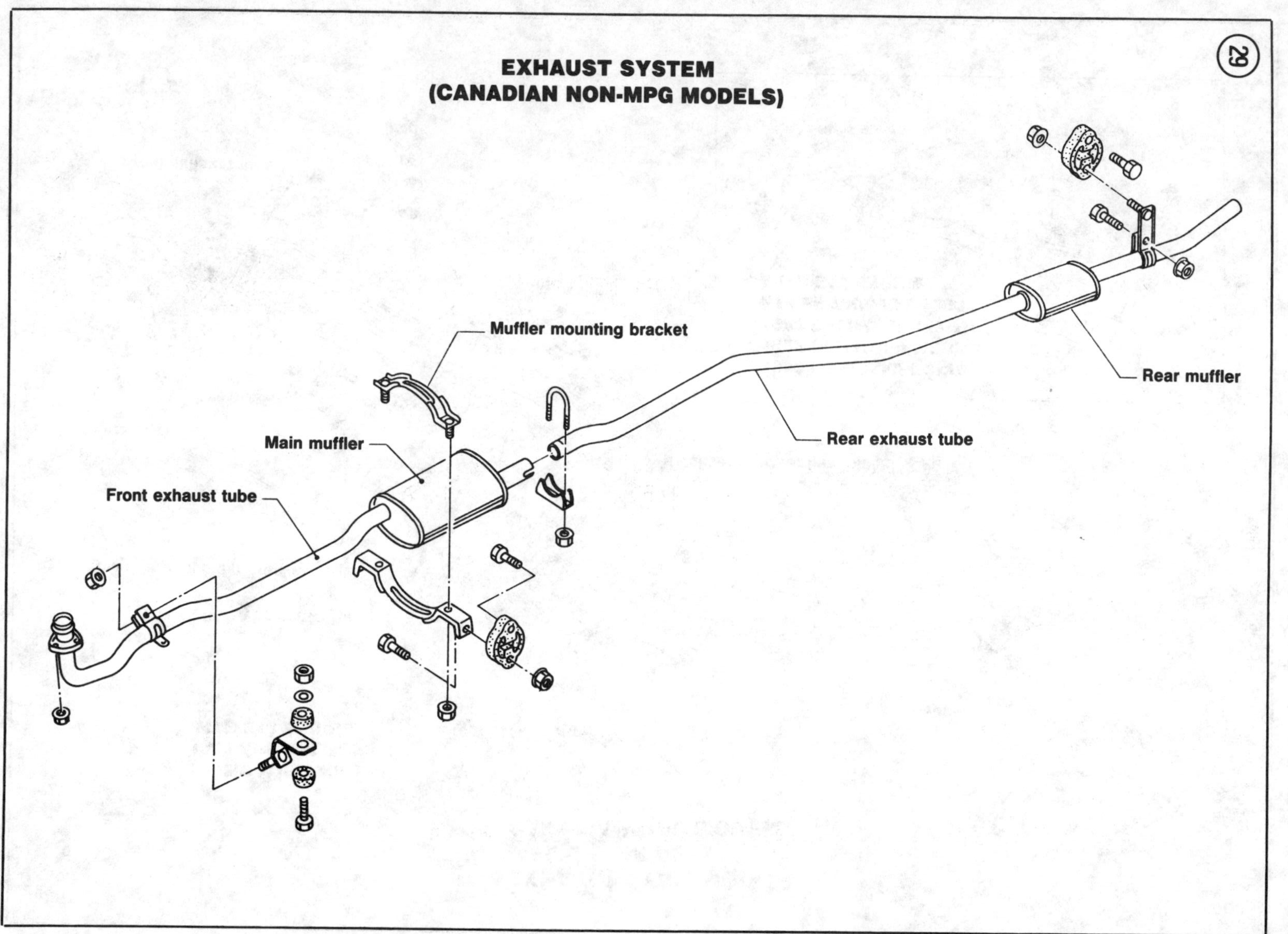
EXHAUST SYSTEM
(CANADIAN NON-MPG MODELS)
Rear muffler
Rear exhaust tube
Muffler mounting bracket
Main muffler
Front exhaust tube

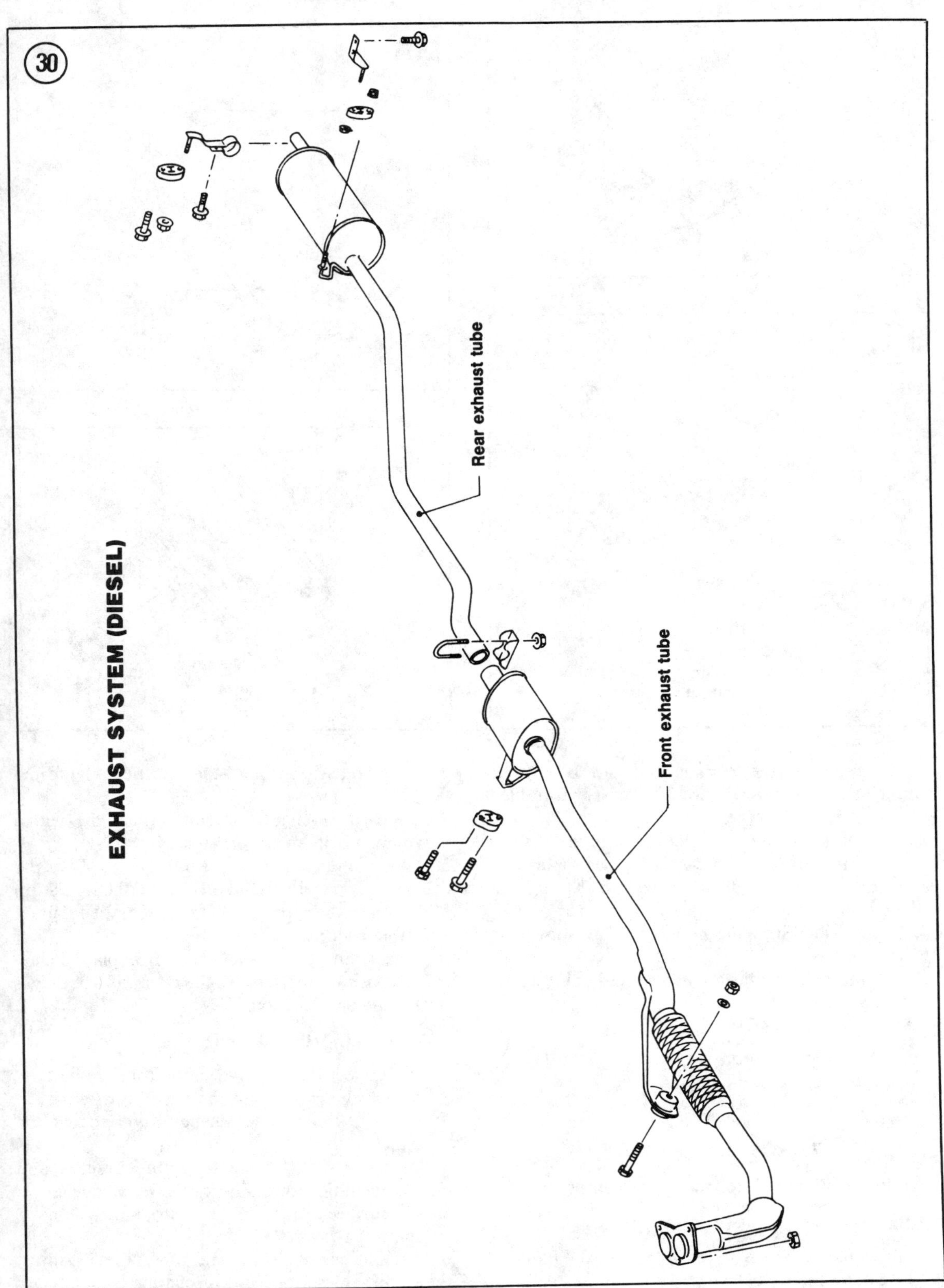

30
EXHAUST SYSTEM (DIESEL)
Rear exhaust tube
Front exhaust tube
5

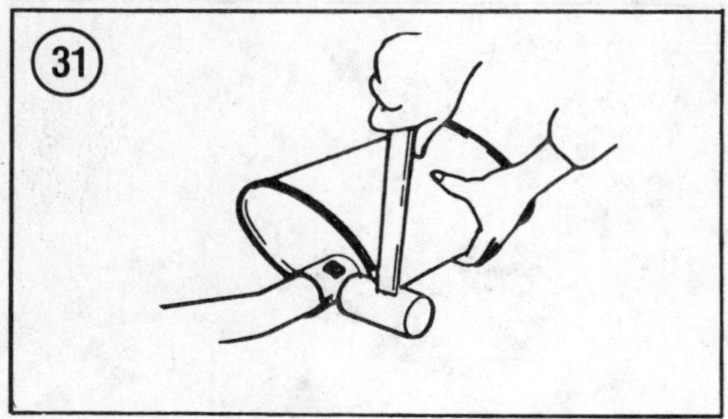

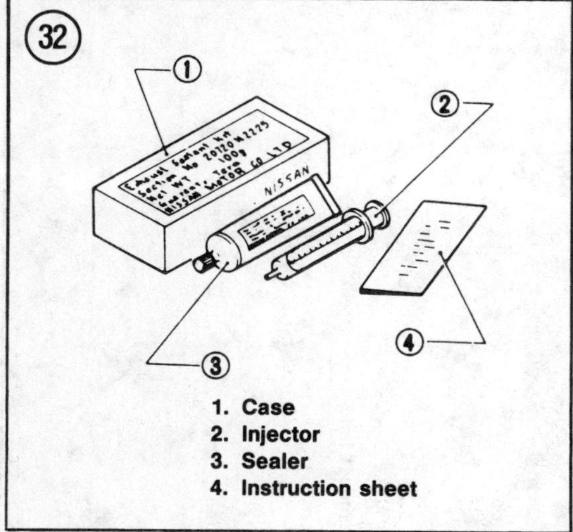

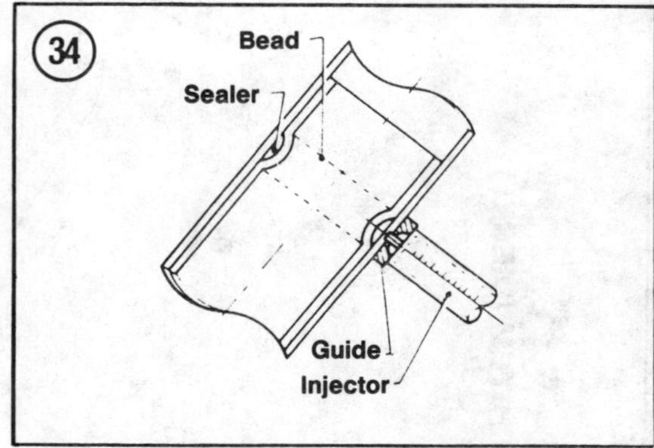

1. To separate the connection, tap it with a hammer as shown in **Figure 31**. Twist the muffler to free it from the pipe.

2. To reattach the connection, use a Nissan exhaust kit (part No. 20702-N2225). See **Figure 32**.

3. Insert the muffler all the way into the stopper (**Figure 33**). Position the clamp as shown.

4. Inject sealer into the connection as shown in **Figure 34**.

5. Let the engine idle for at least 10 minutes to cure the sealer.

> *CAUTION*
> *Do not accelerate rapidly for 20-30 minutes.*

THROTTLE LINKAGE

Refer to **Figure 35** for these procedures.

Adjustment

1. Disconnect the negative cable from the battery.

2. Remove the air cleaner.

3. Have an assistant hold the throttle pedal to the floor.

4. On gasoline-engined models, push the choke valve open if it isn't open already.

5. Loosen the cable clamp (**Figure 36**). Move the cable so the pedal will have 1-2 mm (0.04-0.08 in.) of free play when the pedal is released, then tighten the cable clamp.

6. Release the pedal and check free play (**Figure 36**). Reposition the cable in the clamp if free play is not within specifications.

Cable Removal/Installation

1. Disconnect the negative cable from the battery.

2. Detach the cable from the top of the pedal.

3. Remove the plastic washer that secures the grommet to the firewall.

4. Disconnect the cable from the bracket and carburetor (injection pump on diesel engines).

5. Withdraw the cable into the engine compartment.

6. Installation is the reverse of removal. Adjust the cable as described in this chapter.

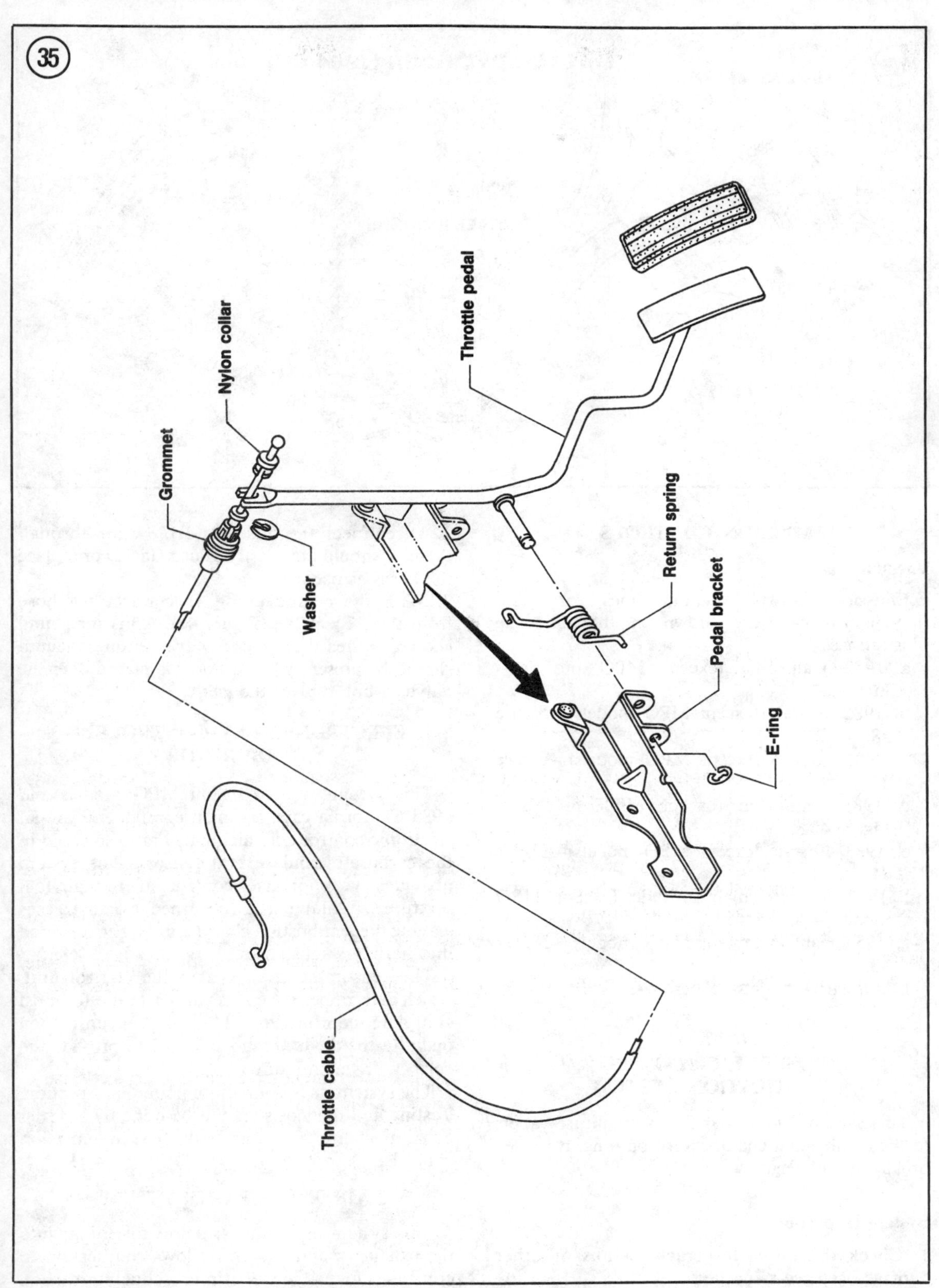
35
Nylon collar
Grommet
Throttle pedal
Washer
Return spring
Pedal bracket
E-ring
Throttle cable
5

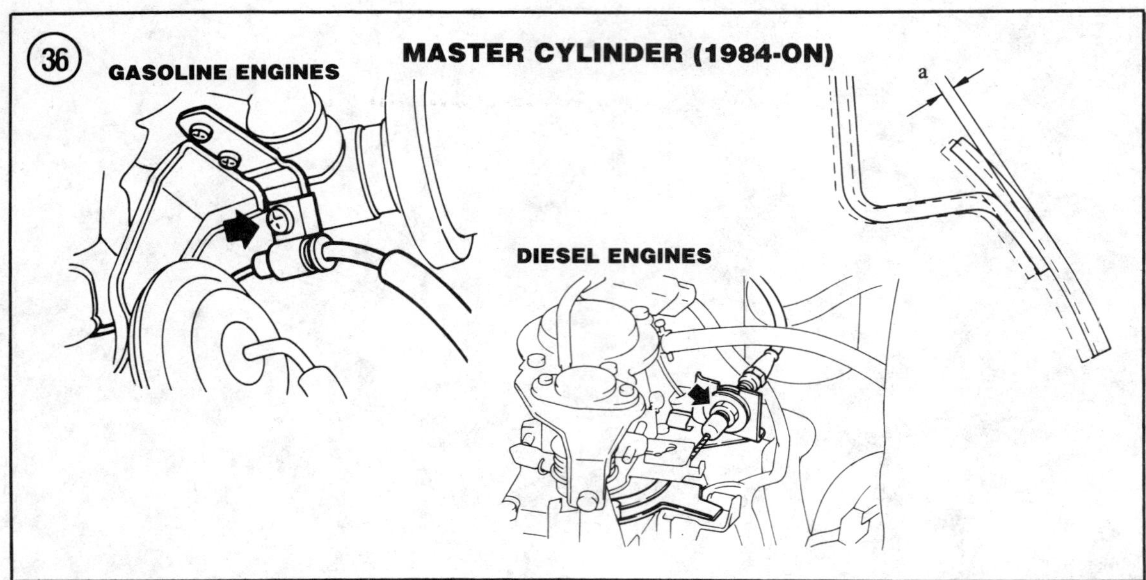

EMISSION CONTROLS

Vacuum Lines

Emission control vacuum lines for gasoline-engined cars are shown in the following illustrations.

a. 1982 California (except MPG models)—**Figure 37**.

b. 1982 49-state (except MPG models)—**Figure 38**.

c. 1982 Canada (except MPG models)—**Figure 39**.

d. 1983 California (except MPG models)—**Figure 40**.

e. 1983 49-state (except MPG models)—**Figure 41**.

f. 1983 49-state high altitude (except MPG models)—**Figure 42**.

g. 1983 Canada (except MPG models)—**Figure 43**.

h. All MPG models—**Figure 44**.

POSITIVE CRANKCASE VENTILATION SYSTEM

This system (**Figure 45**) routes crankcase vapors to the combustion chambers for burning. It is used on all gasoline engines.

System Inspection

1. Check the hoses for cracks, kinks or other damage. Replace as needed.

2. Disconnect the hoses and blow air through them. It should flow easily. If not, unclog or replace the hoses as needed.

3. With the engine idling, disconnect the hose from the PCV valve (**Figure 46**). A hissing sound should be heard from the valve. Strong vacuum should be present when a finger is placed over the valve. If not, replace the valve.

ELECTRONICALLY CONTROLLED CARBURETOR

This system is used on all MPG models and 1983 California cars. Its main components are an electronic control unit, an air-fuel ratio solenoid in the carburetor and several sensors. The system provides very precise control of the air-fuel mixture, so that partially burned exhaust gases leaving the combustion chambers can be converted into harmless substances.

The sensors send signals to the control unit, which determines the correct air-fuel ratio for most complete combustion. The control unit then operates the air-fuel ratio solenoid to provide the correct air-fuel mixture.

The system does not require periodic inspection. Testing and diagnosis should be done by a dealer or a mechanic familiar with Nissan emission controls.

AIR INDUCTION SYSTEM

This system uses exhaust pulses to pull air into the exhaust manifold. This allows combustion to continue for a longer time, reducing carbon

37
EMISSION CONTROL SYSTEM
(1982 NON-MPG CALIFORNIA)
Oxidation catalytic converter
Exhaust manifold
EGR tube
Air induction tube
Distributor
Vacuum switching valve
(catalyst warmup system)
Mixture ratio control solenoid
To air cleaner
Vacuum switch
Venturi vacuum
transducer
Vacuum delay
valve
EGR control valve
Thermal
vacuum valve
Air induction valve
Throttle opener
To idle
compensator
and automatic
temperature
control sensor
Carburetor
Anti-
backfire
valve
To air
cleaner
Altitude
compensator
Carbon canister
From fuel tank
Ported vacuum (distributor)
Ported vacuum (EGR and canister)
Venturi vacuum
Manifold vacuum
Air
Canister purge
Vent air

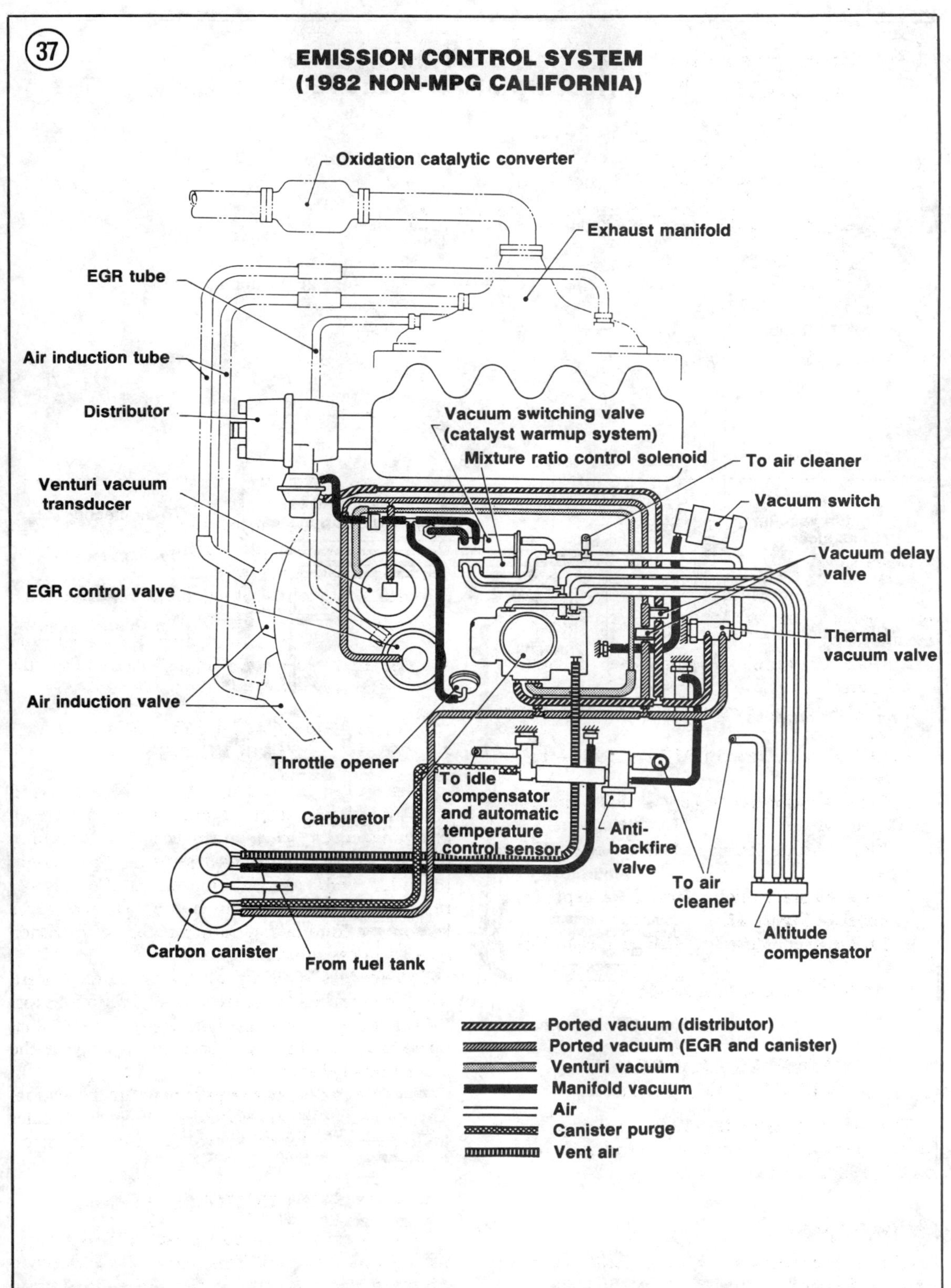

5

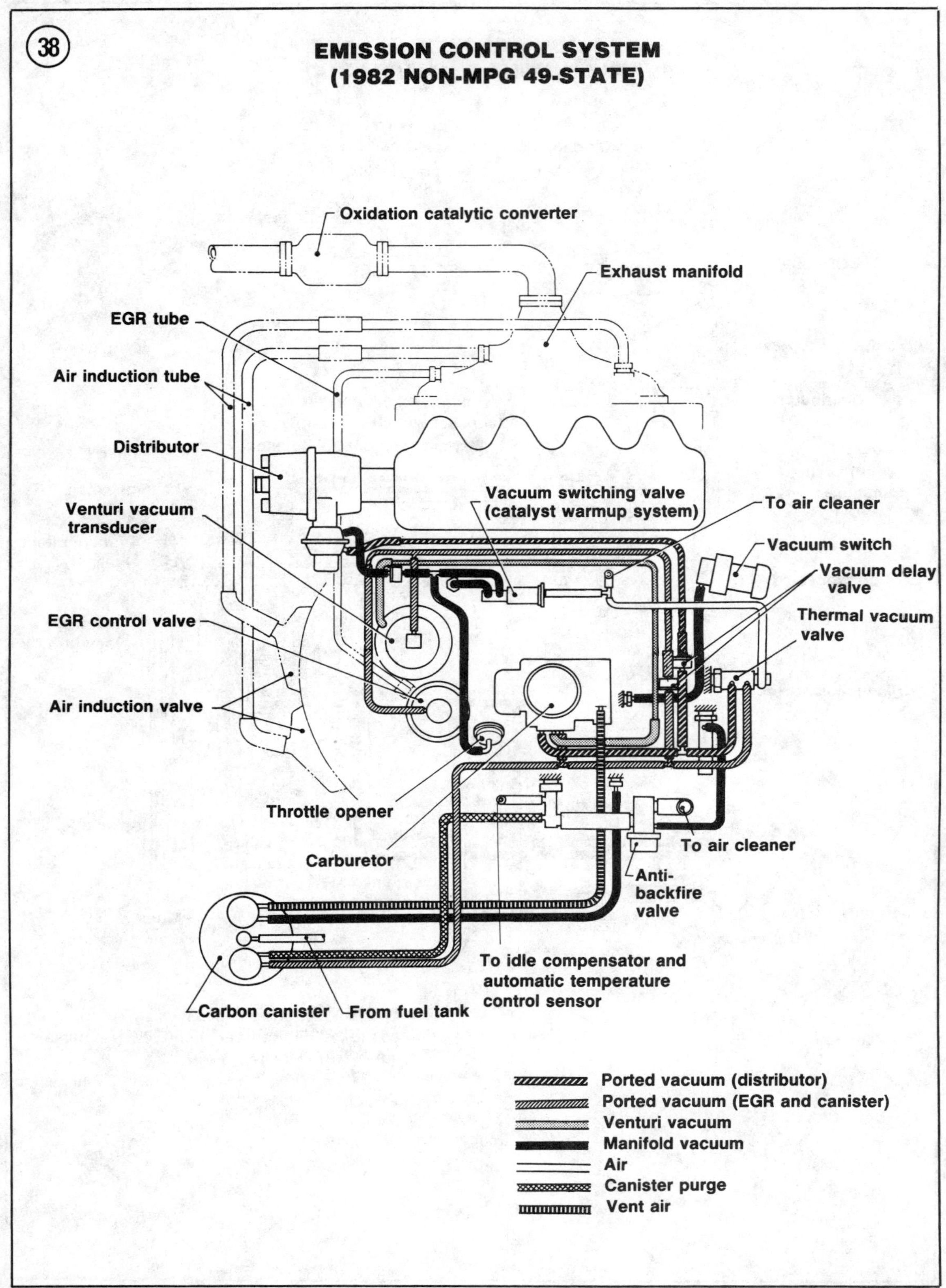
38
EMISSION CONTROL SYSTEM
(1982 NON-MPG 49-STATE)
Oxidation catalytic converter
Exhaust manifold
EGR tube
Air induction tube
Distributor
Vacuum switching valve
(catalyst warmup system)
To air cleaner
Venturi vacuum
transducer
Vacuum switch
Vacuum delay
valve
Thermal vacuum
valve
EGR control valve
Air induction valve
Throttle opener
To air cleaner
Carburetor
Anti-
backfire
valve
To idle compensator and
automatic temperature
control sensor
Carbon canister
From fuel tank
Ported vacuum (distributor)
Ported vacuum (EGR and canister)
Venturi vacuum
Manifold vacuum
Air
Canister purge
Vent air

39
EMISSION CONTROL SYSTEM
(1982 NON-MPG CANADA)
Exhaust manifold
Air induction tube
EGR tube
Distributor
To air cleaner
Throttle opener control system solenoid
Carburetor
Throttle opener
Throttle opener control system control valve
EGR control valve
Thermal vacuum valve
Air induction valve
To air cleaner
Anti-backfire valve
To idle compensator and automatic temperature control sensor
To fuel tank
Carbon canister
Ported vacuum (distributor)
Ported vacuum (EGR and canister)
Manifold vacuum
Air
Canister purge

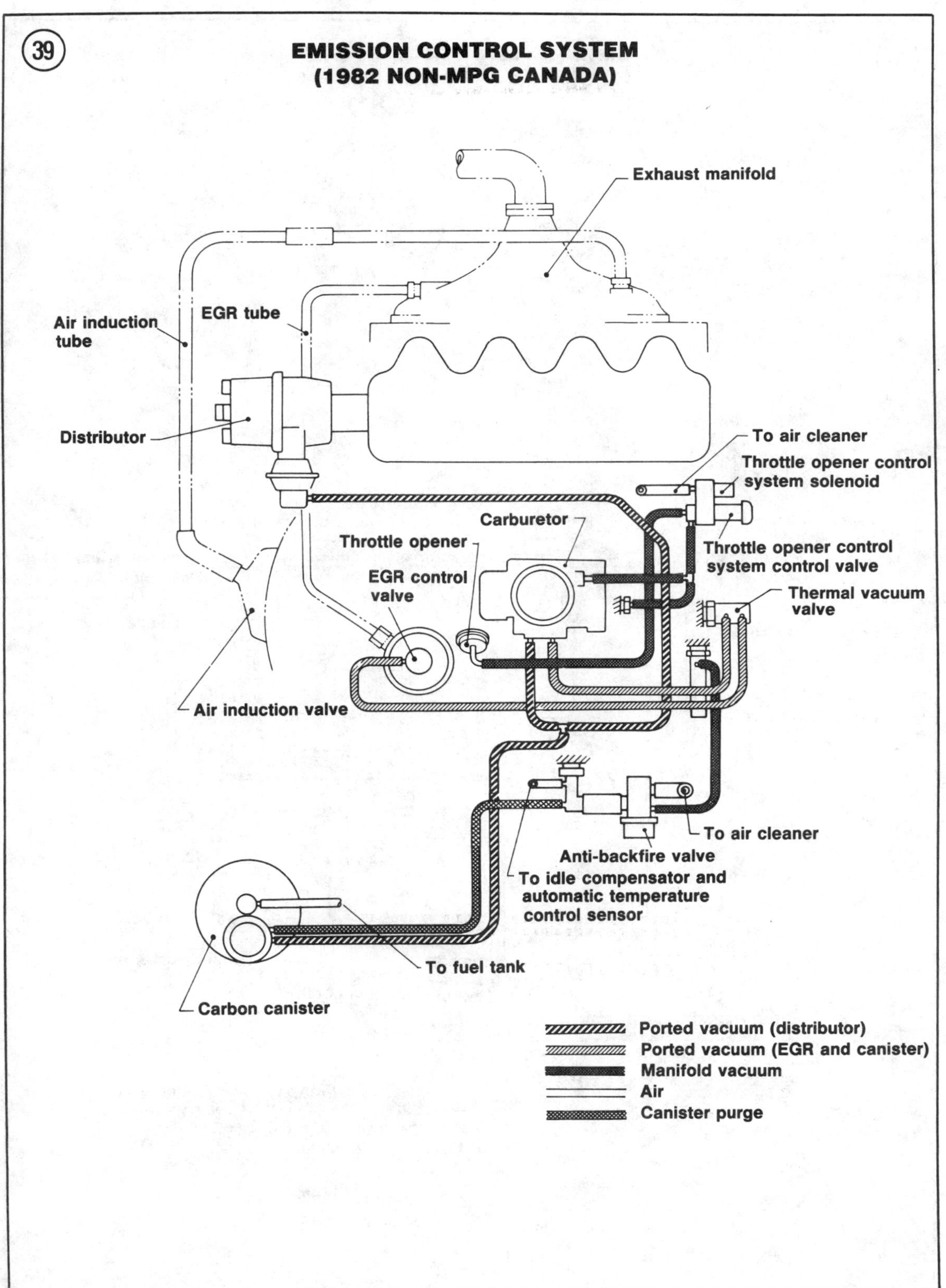

5

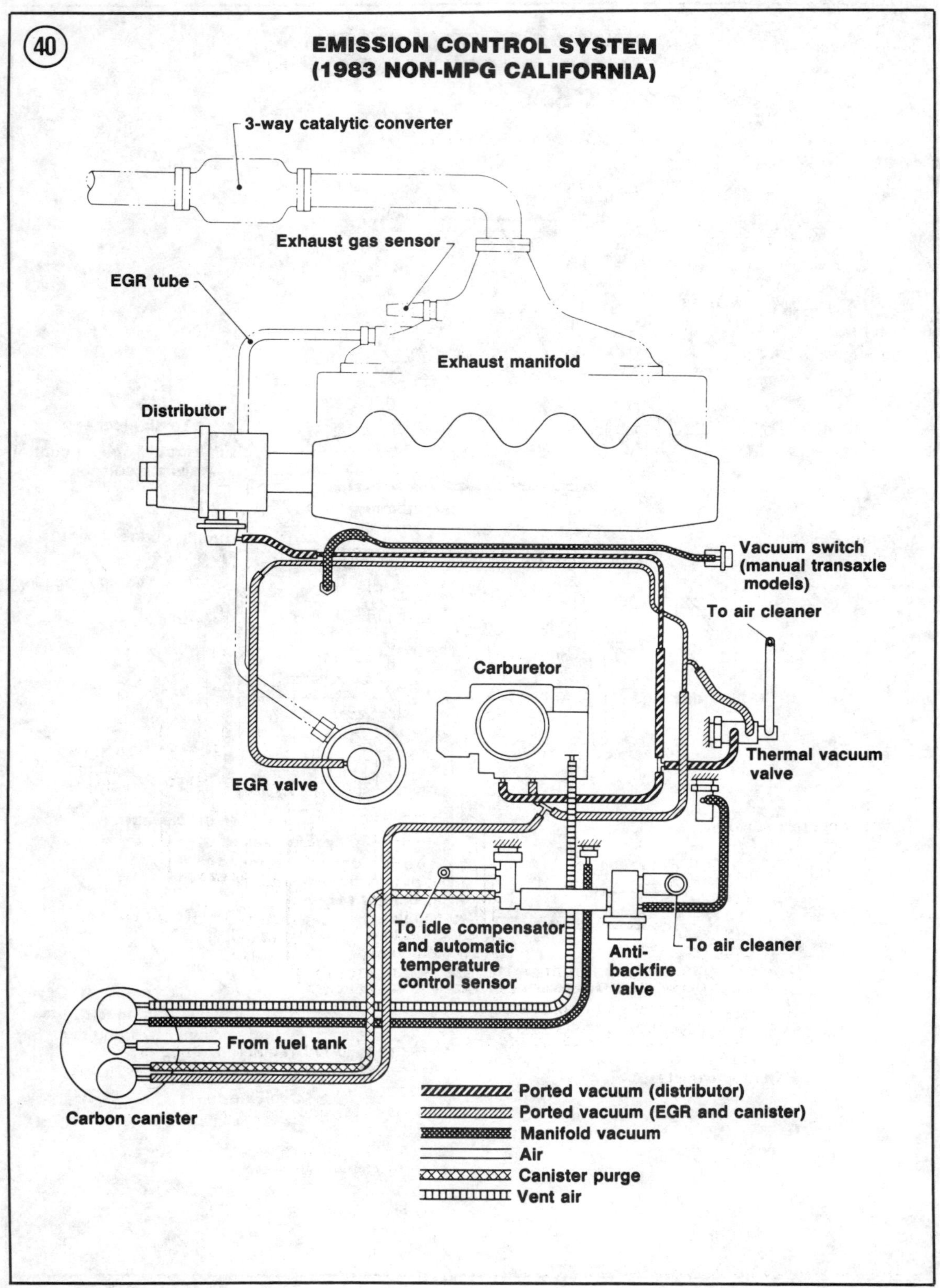

40
EMISSION CONTROL SYSTEM
(1983 NON-MPG CALIFORNIA)
3-way catalytic converter
Exhaust gas sensor
EGR tube
Exhaust manifold
Distributor
Vacuum switch
(manual transaxle
models)
To air cleaner
Carburetor
Thermal vacuum
valve
EGR valve
To idle compensator
and automatic
temperature
control sensor
Anti-
backfire
valve
To air cleaner
From fuel tank
Carbon canister
Ported vacuum (distributor)
Ported vacuum (EGR and canister)
Manifold vacuum
Air
Canister purge
Vent air

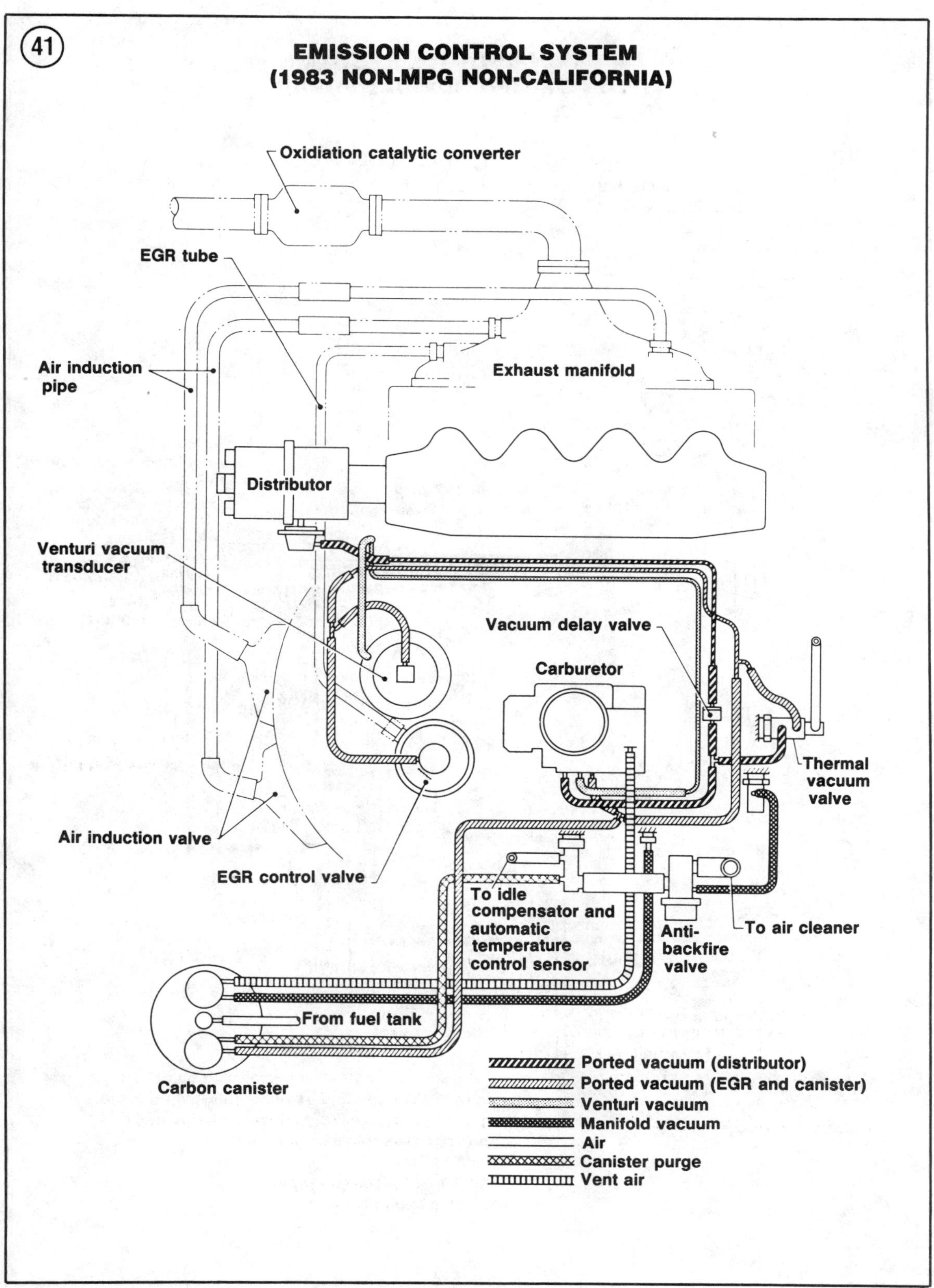
41
EMISSION CONTROL SYSTEM
(1983 NON-MPG NON-CALIFORNIA)
Oxidiation catalytic converter
EGR tube
Air induction pipe
Exhaust manifold
Distributor
Venturi vacuum transducer
Vacuum delay valve
Carburetor
Thermal vacuum valve
Air induction valve
EGR control valve
To idle compensator and automatic temperature control sensor
Anti-backfire valve
To air cleaner
From fuel tank
Carbon canister
Ported vacuum (distributor)
Ported vacuum (EGR and canister)
Venturi vacuum
Manifold vacuum
Air
Canister purge
Vent air

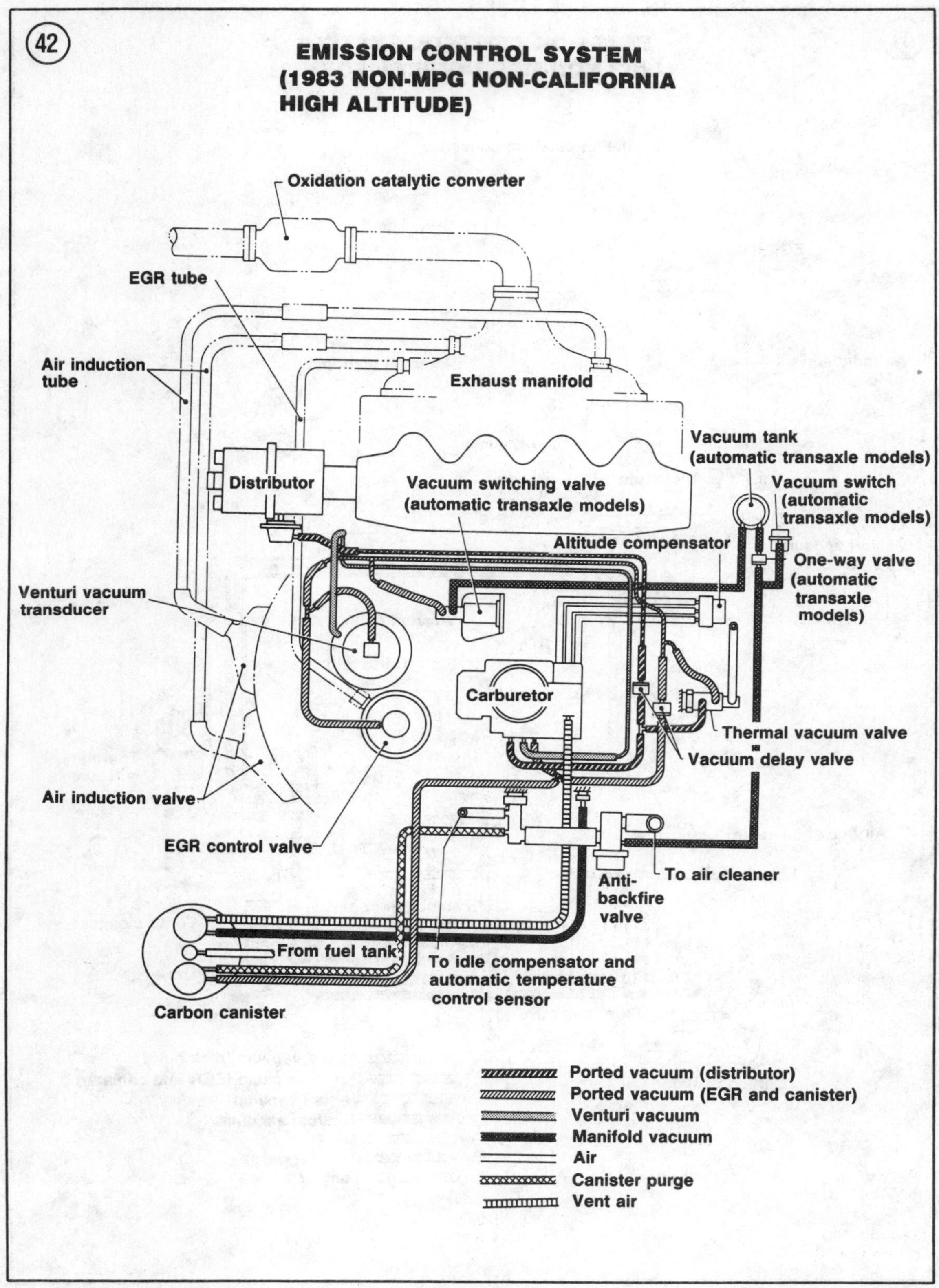

42
EMISSION CONTROL SYSTEM
(1983 NON-MPG NON-CALIFORNIA
HIGH ALTITUDE)
Oxidation catalytic converter
EGR tube
Air induction tube
Exhaust manifold
Vacuum tank (automatic transaxle models)
Vacuum switch (automatic transaxle models)
Distributor
Vacuum switching valve (automatic transaxle models)
Altitude compensator
One-way valve (automatic transaxle models)
Venturi vacuum transducer
Carburetor
Thermal vacuum valve
Vacuum delay valve
Air induction valve
EGR control valve
To air cleaner
Anti-backfire valve
From fuel tank
To idle compensator and automatic temperature control sensor
Carbon canister
Ported vacuum (distributor)
Ported vacuum (EGR and canister)
Venturi vacuum
Manifold vacuum
Air
Canister purge
Vent air

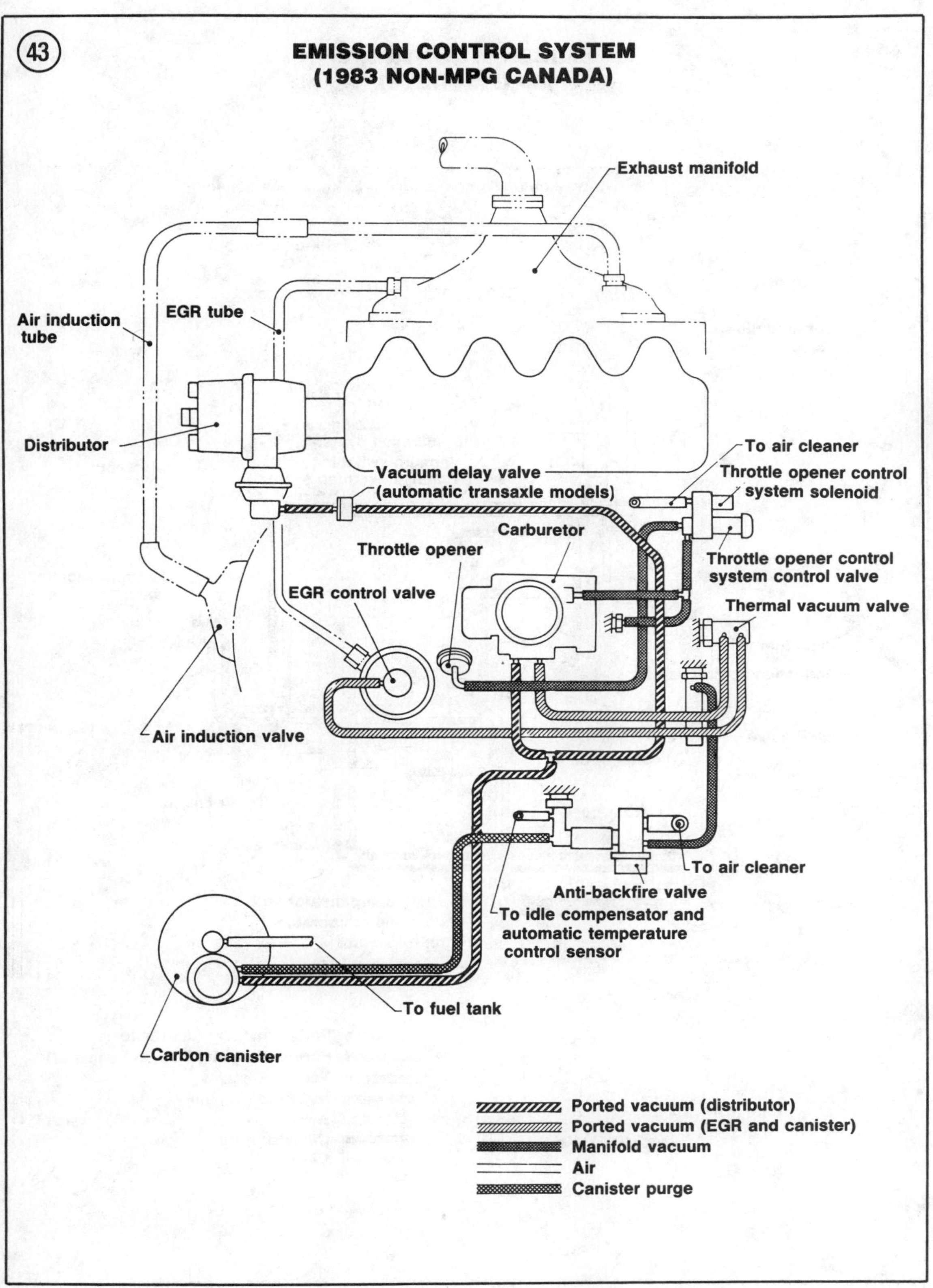
43
EMISSION CONTROL SYSTEM
(1983 NON-MPG CANADA)
Exhaust manifold
Air induction tube
EGR tube
Distributor
To air cleaner
Throttle opener control system solenoid
Vacuum delay valve
(automatic transaxle models)
Carburetor
Throttle opener control system control valve
Throttle opener
Thermal vacuum valve
EGR control valve
Air induction valve
To air cleaner
Anti-backfire valve
To idle compensator and automatic temperature control sensor
To fuel tank
Carbon canister
Ported vacuum (distributor)
Ported vacuum (EGR and canister)
Manifold vacuum
Air
Canister purge

5

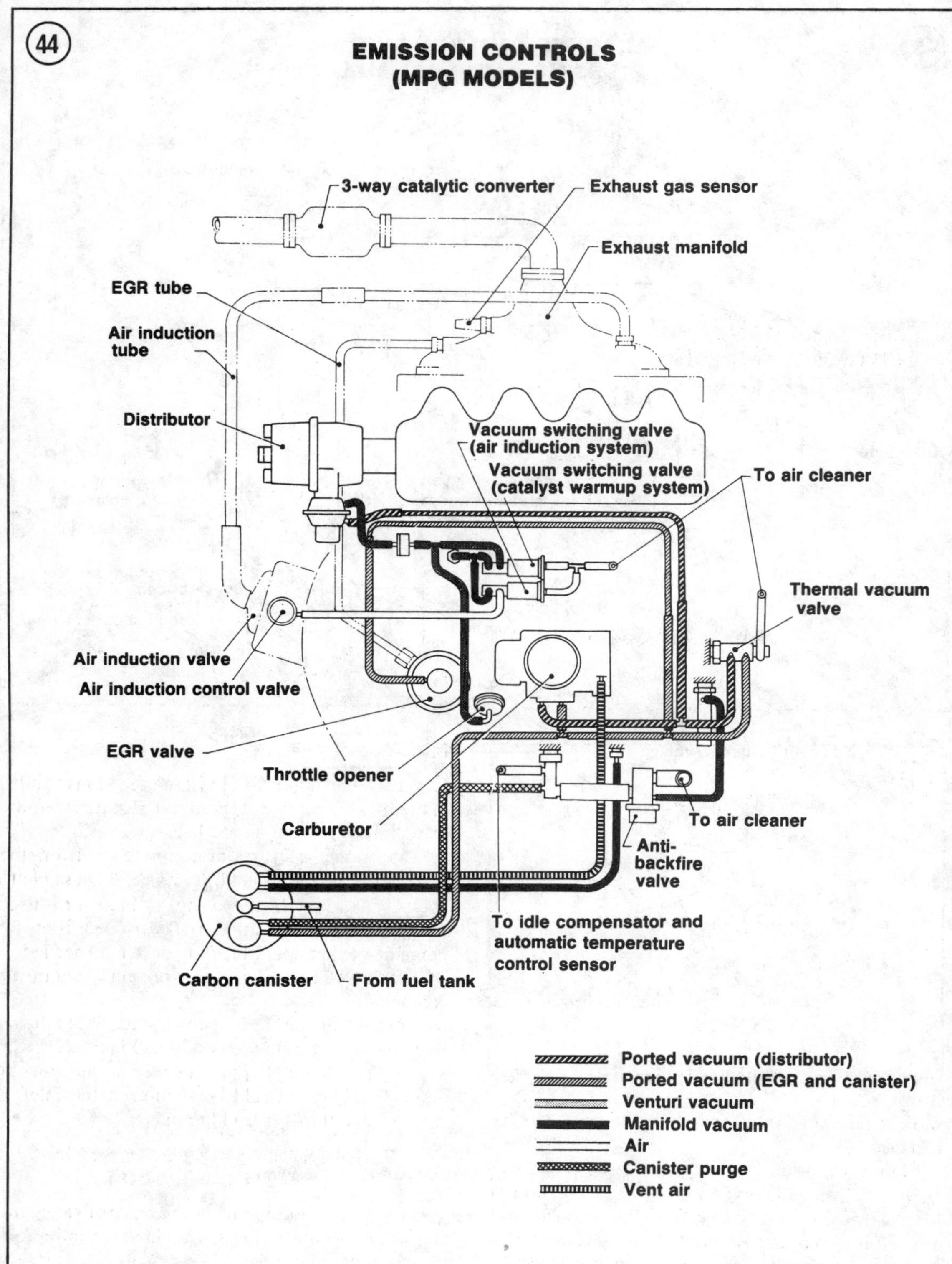

44
EMISSION CONTROLS
(MPG MODELS)
3-way catalytic converter
Exhaust gas sensor
Exhaust manifold
EGR tube
Air induction tube
Distributor
Vacuum switching valve
(air induction system)
Vacuum switching valve
(catalyst warmup system)
To air cleaner
Thermal vacuum valve
Air induction valve
Air induction control valve
EGR valve
Throttle opener
Carburetor
To air cleaner
Anti-backfire valve
To idle compensator and automatic temperature control sensor
Carbon canister
From fuel tank
Ported vacuum (distributor)
Ported vacuum (EGR and canister)
Venturi vacuum
Manifold vacuum
Air
Canister purge
Vent air

45

POSITIVE CRANKCASE VENTILATION SYSTEM (GASOLINE ENGINES)

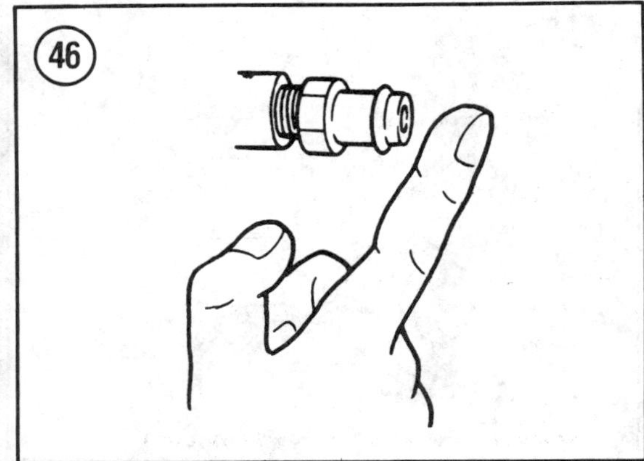

46

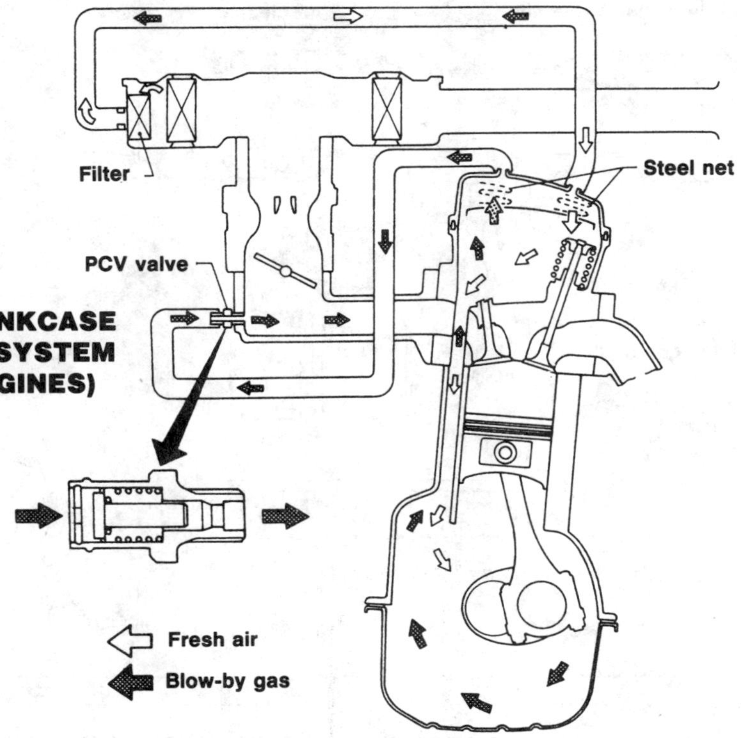

monoxide and unburned hydrocarbon in the exhaust.

Figure 47 shows the system used on 1982 non-MPG model and 1983 non-California models (except MPG). The system on MPG models and 1983 California cars is part of the electronically controlled carburetor system. Inspection on these models should be done by a dealer or mechanic familiar with Nissan emission controls.

Inspection

1. Check the hoses for loose connections, kinks, flattening, cracks or deterioration. Tighten, reroute or replace the hoses as needed.
2. Disconnect the air induction hose from the metal tube. See **Figure 48**. It should be possible to suck air from the hose, but not to blow air into it.
3. Check the air induction valve and filter for clogging or damage. Clean or replace as needed.
4. Warm the engine to normal operating temperature.
5. Remove the air cleaner cover and place a finger over the anti-backfire valve inlet (**Figure 49**). Run the engine at 3,000 rpm and release the throttle suddenly. There should be suction at the inlet. If not, replace the anti-backfire valve.

EXHAUST GAS RECIRCULATION SYSTEM (GASOLINE)

This system routes part of the exhaust gases into the combustion chambers. This lowers combustion temperature, reducing oxides of nitrogen in the exhaust. **Figure 50** shows the 1982 systems. **Figure 51** shows the 1983 designs.

5

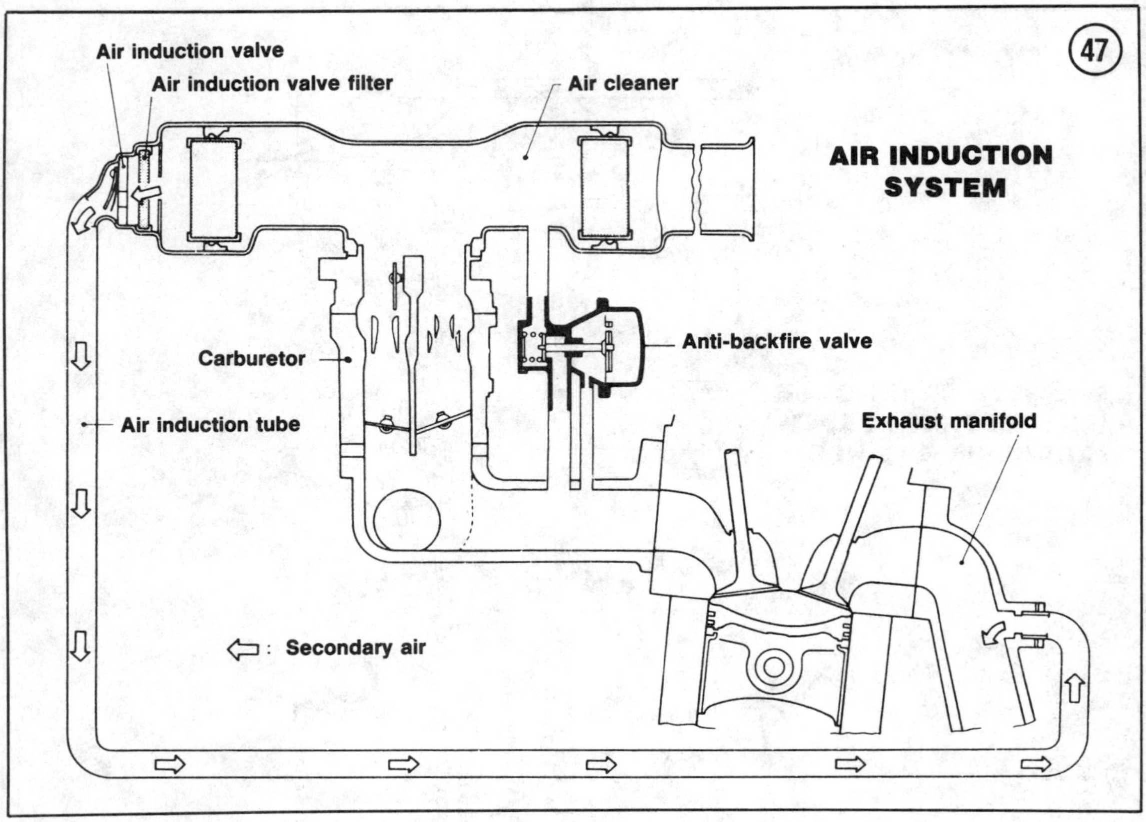

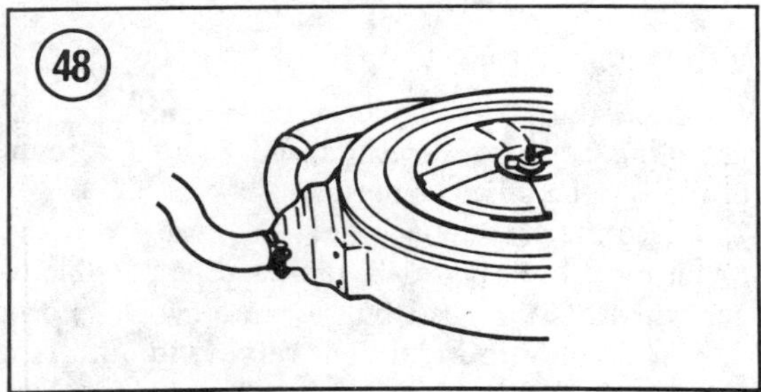

Figure 47

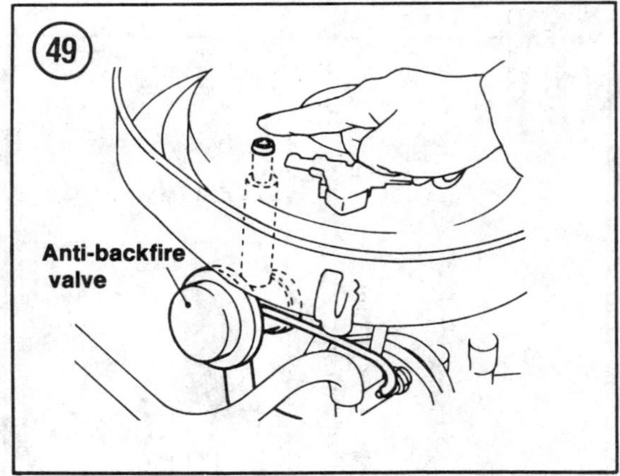

Figure 48

Figure 49

Inspection

1. Check the system for visible defects such as loose or cracked hoses. Tighten or replace as needed.

> *WARNING*
> *During the next steps, do not let your finger get caught between the EGR valve diaphragm and body.*

2. With the engine off, reach beneath the EGR valve and lift its diaphragm. See **Figure 52**. It should rise smoothly, without sticking or binding.

3. Make sure engine coolant temperature is less than 50° C (122° F).

4. Start the engine. Move the throttle to raise engine speed to 3,000-3,500 rpm. Place a finger under the EGR valve and make sure it does not move.

5. Warm the engine to normal operating temperature.

6. Again, run the engine at 3,000-3,500 rpm and place a finger beneath the EGR valve. This time, the valve diaphragm should rise.

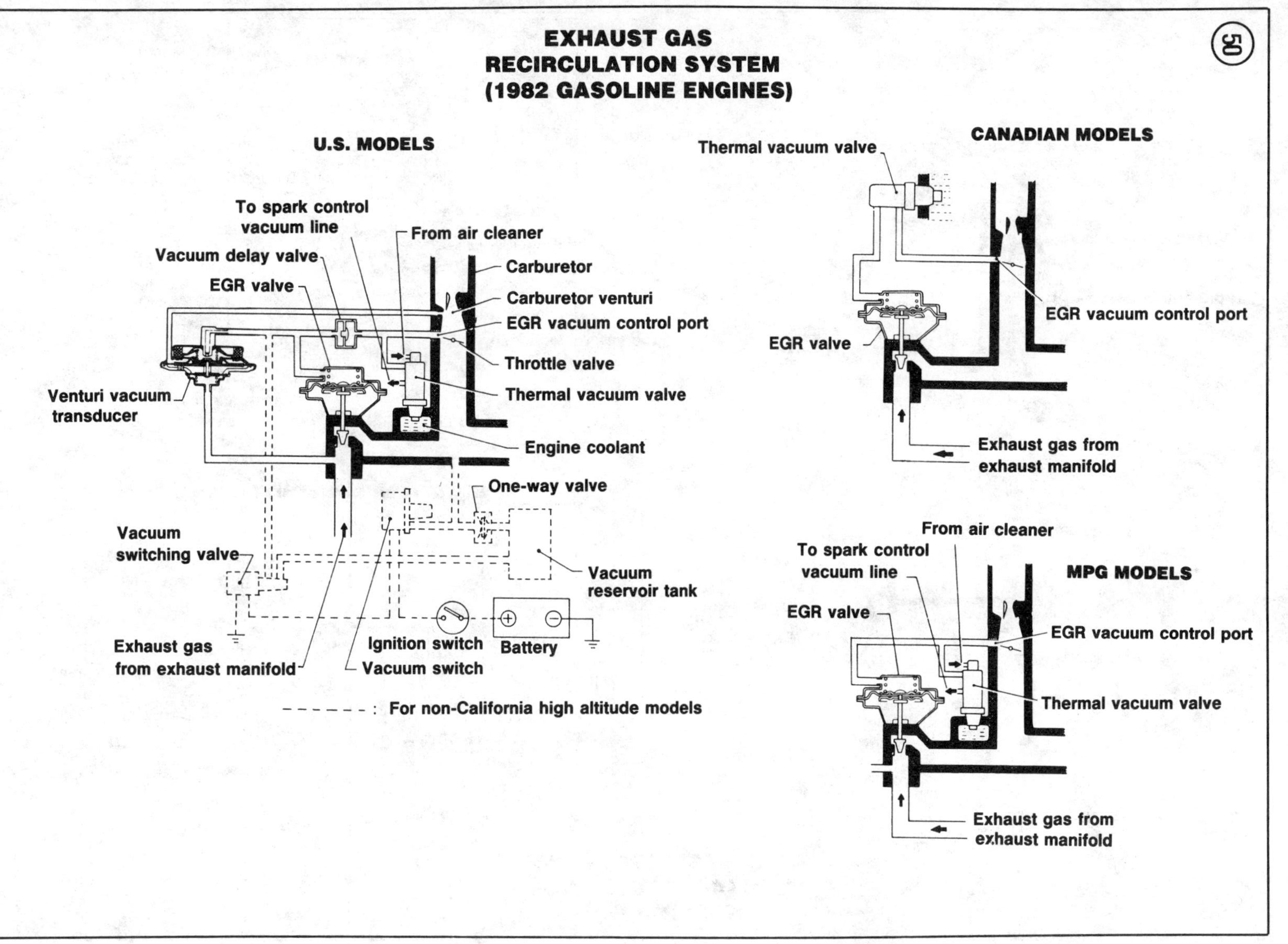
50

EXHAUST GAS
RECIRCULATION SYSTEM
(1982 GASOLINE ENGINES)

U.S. MODELS

To spark control vacuum line
From air cleaner
Vacuum delay valve
EGR valve
Carburetor
Carburetor venturi
EGR vacuum control port
Throttle valve
Thermal vacuum valve
Venturi vacuum transducer
Engine coolant
One-way valve
Vacuum switching valve
Vacuum reservoir tank
Exhaust gas from exhaust manifold
Ignition switch
Vacuum switch
Battery

- - - - - : For non-California high altitude models

CANADIAN MODELS

Thermal vacuum valve
EGR vacuum control port
EGR valve
Exhaust gas from exhaust manifold

MPG MODELS

From air cleaner
To spark control vacuum line
EGR valve
EGR vacuum control port
Thermal vacuum valve
Exhaust gas from exhaust manifold

5

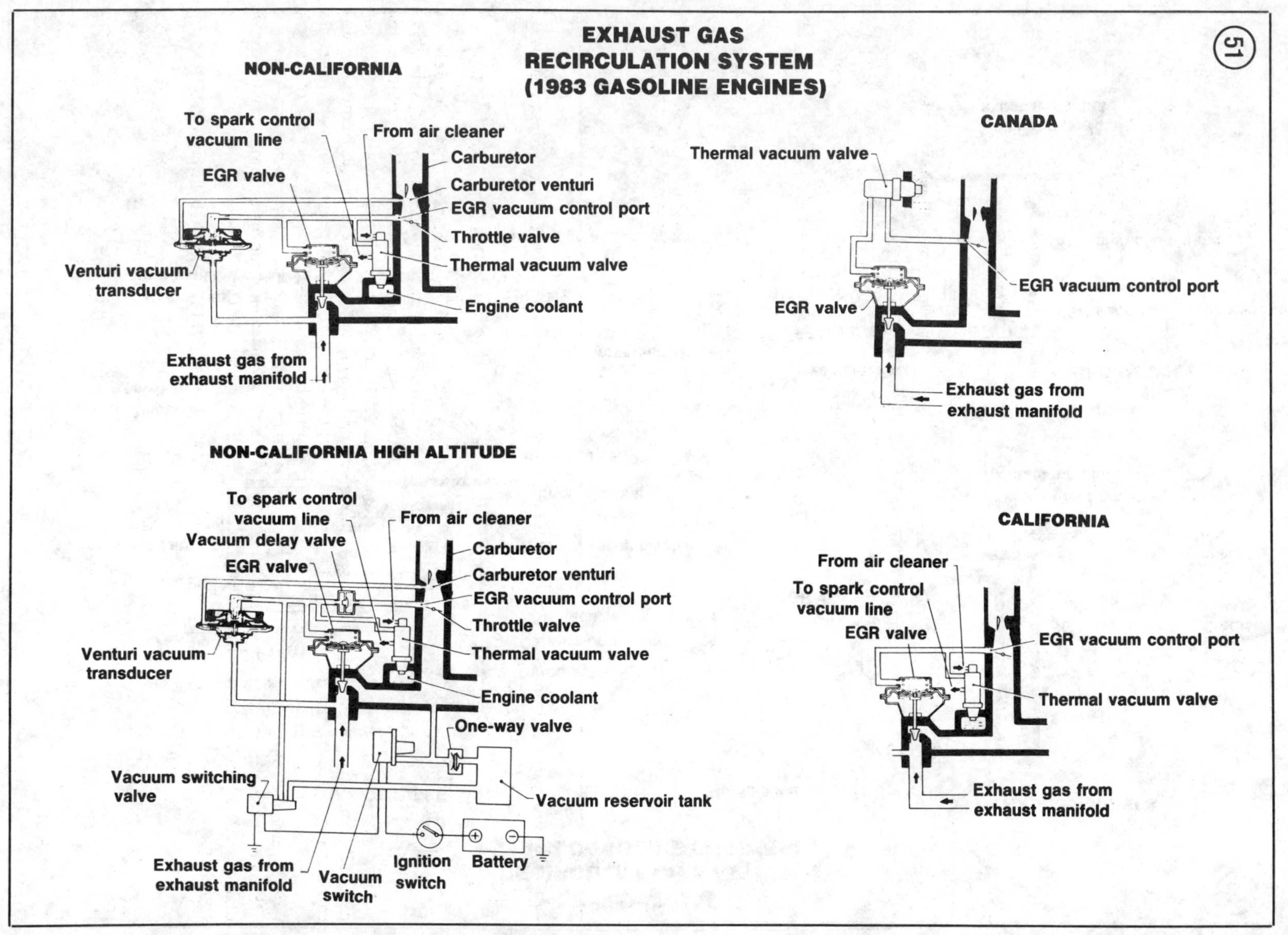

51
EXHAUST GAS
RECIRCULATION SYSTEM
(1983 GASOLINE ENGINES)
NON-CALIFORNIA
To spark control vacuum line
From air cleaner
Carburetor
Carburetor venturi
EGR vacuum control port
Throttle valve
Thermal vacuum valve
EGR valve
Venturi vacuum transducer
Engine coolant
Exhaust gas from exhaust manifold
CANADA
Thermal vacuum valve
EGR vacuum control port
EGR valve
Exhaust gas from exhaust manifold
NON-CALIFORNIA HIGH ALTITUDE
To spark control vacuum line
Vacuum delay valve
From air cleaner
Carburetor
Carburetor venturi
EGR vacuum control port
Throttle valve
Thermal vacuum valve
EGR valve
Venturi vacuum transducer
Engine coolant
One-way valve
Vacuum switching valve
Vacuum reservoir tank
Exhaust gas from exhaust manifold
Vacuum switch
Ignition switch
Battery
CALIFORNIA
From air cleaner
To spark control vacuum line
EGR valve
EGR vacuum control port
Thermal vacuum valve
Exhaust gas from exhaust manifold

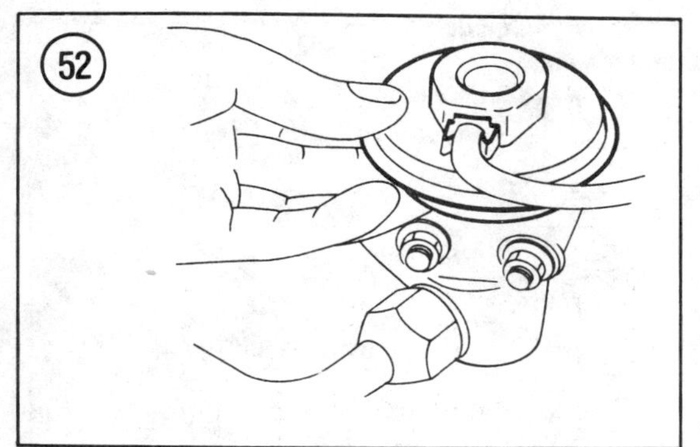

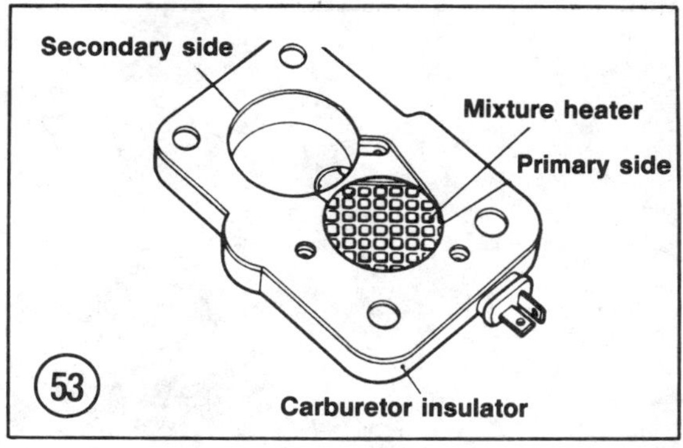

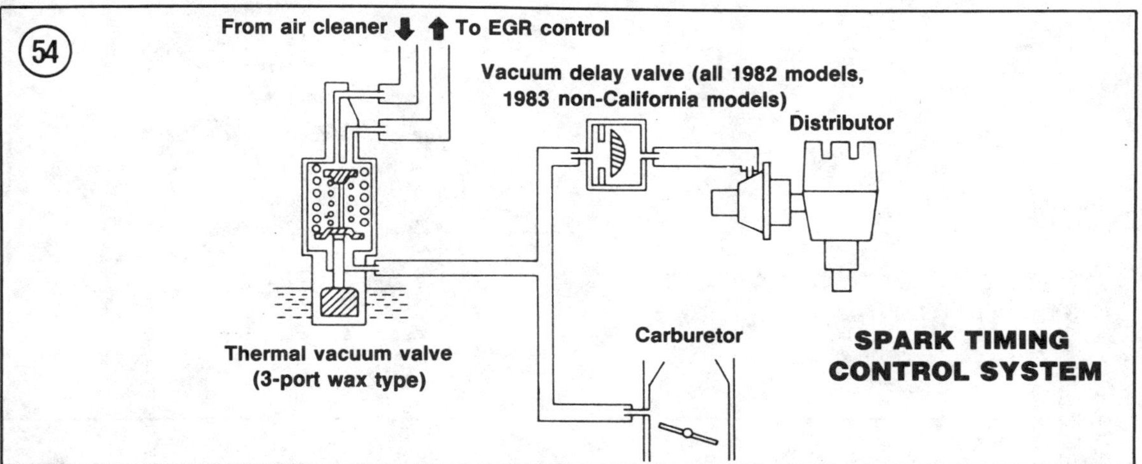

7. If the EGR valve did not perform as described in this test, have the EGR system tested further by a dealer or mechanic familiar with Nissan emission controls.

MIXTURE RATIO RICH-LEAN EXCHANGE SYSTEM

This system is used on 1982 California non-MPG models. It uses a solenoid in the carburetor to give precise control of the air-fuel ratio. The ratio varies according to engine temperature and vehicle speed.

System inspection is complicated and should be done by a dealer or mechanic familiar with Nissan emission controls.

FUEL SHUTOFF SYSTEM

This system uses the carburetor anti-dieseling solenoid to cut off fuel flow to the carburetor during high-speed deceleration, when intake manifold vacuum is at high levels. This improves fuel economy. Periodic inspection is not required. System testing and diagnosis should be done by a dealer or mechanic familiar with Nissan emission controls.

MIXTURE HEATING SYSTEM

This system is used on 1983 models. A honeycomb heating unit in the primary side of the carburetor insulator (**Figure 53**) preheats the air-fuel mixture entering the engine during cold-engine operation. This reduces emissions and improves driveability. The system requires no periodic inspection. If it is suspected of causing poor performance when the engine is cold, have it tested by a dealer or mechanic familiar with Nissan emission controls.

SPARK TIMING CONTROL SYSTEM

This system (**Figure 54**) controls spark timing under various driving conditions to reduce emissions of unburned hydrocarbons and oxides of nitrogen.

System Test

Start this test with a cold engine.

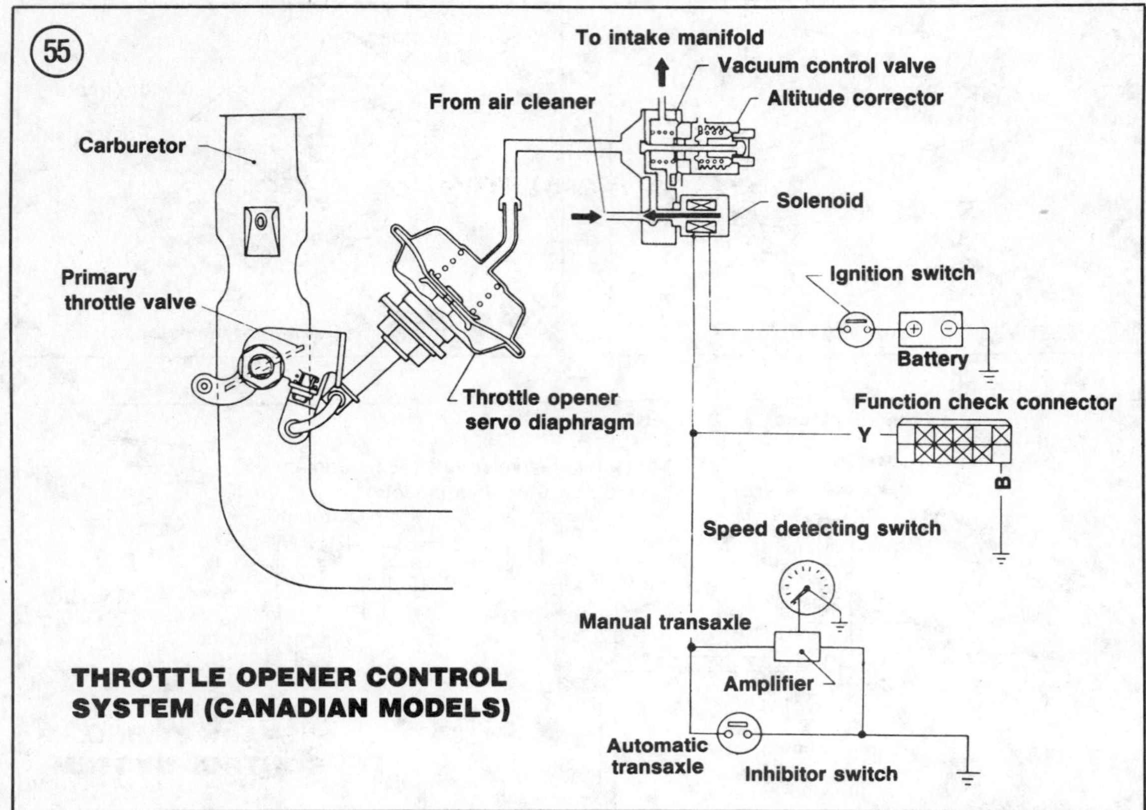

1. Make sure the system's vacuum lines are properly connected and in good condition. Tighten or replace as needed.
2. Measure coolant temperature with a thermometer. Note whether is is above or below 10° C (50° F).
3. Connect a timing light to the engine.

> *WARNING*
> *Keep your hands and hair away from belts and pulleys during the next step. They may appear to be standing still or moving slowly under the timing light. They are actually turning at more than 10 times every second and can cause serious injury.*

4. Start the engine and let it idle. Note ignition timing.
5. Let the engine idle until it warms up. Watch ignition timing:
  a. If coolant temperature in Step 2 was below 10° C (50° F), ignition timing should retard, then advance as the engine warms up.
  b. If coolant temperature in Step 2 was above 10° C (50° F), ignition timing should advance as the engine warms up.

6. If the system didn't perform as described during this test, have it tested further by a dealer or mechanic familiar with Nissan emission controls.

THROTTLE OPENER CONTROL SYSTEM

This system (**Figure 55**) is used on Canadian cars. It opens the throttle slightly during deceleration, when the fuel mixture entering the engine is normally too lean to burn. This allows combustion to continue, reducing emissions of unburned hydrocarbons.

The system may be at fault if the engine idles too rapidly and will not drop to a normal idle. If this is the case, have the system tested by a dealer or mechanic familiar with Nissan emission cotrols.

EVAPORATIVE EMISSION CONTROL SYSTEM

This system (**Figure 56**) controls the emission of fuel vapor to the atmosphere. It should be inspected at periodic intervals as described in Chapter Three.

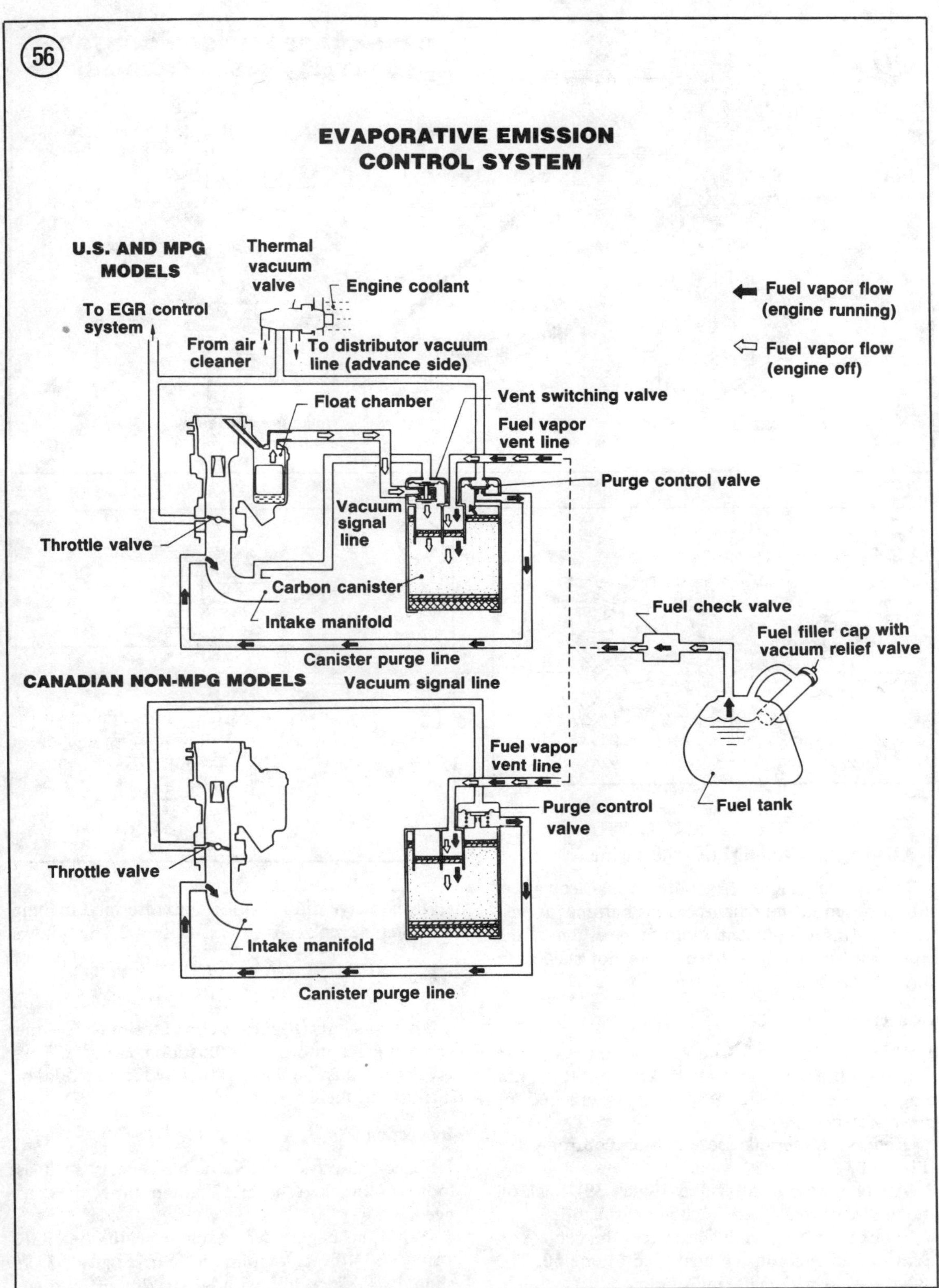

56

EVAPORATIVE EMISSION
CONTROL SYSTEM

U.S. AND MPG MODELS

Thermal vacuum valve
Engine coolant
To EGR control system
From air cleaner
To distributor vacuum line (advance side)
Float chamber
Vent switching valve
Fuel vapor vent line
Purge control valve
Vacuum signal line
Throttle valve
Carbon canister
Intake manifold
Canister purge line

Fuel vapor flow (engine running)
Fuel vapor flow (engine off)

Fuel check valve
Fuel filler cap with vacuum relief valve
Fuel tank

CANADIAN NON-MPG MODELS
Vacuum signal line
Fuel vapor vent line
Purge control valve
Throttle valve
Intake manifold
Canister purge line

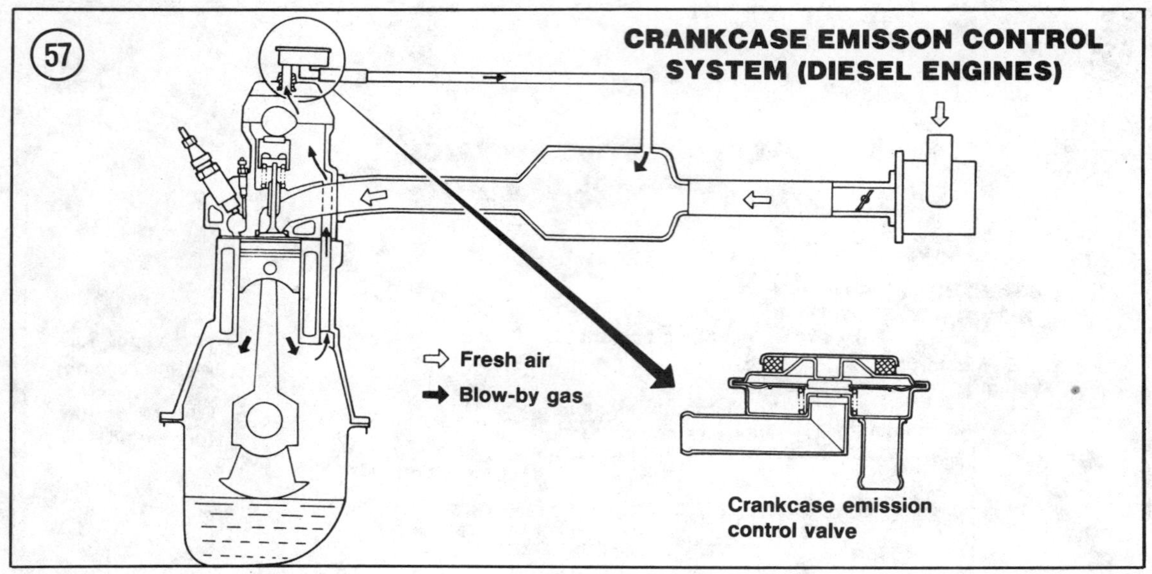

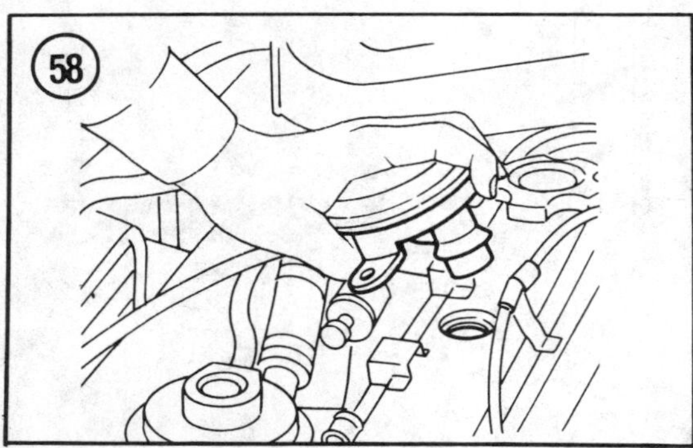

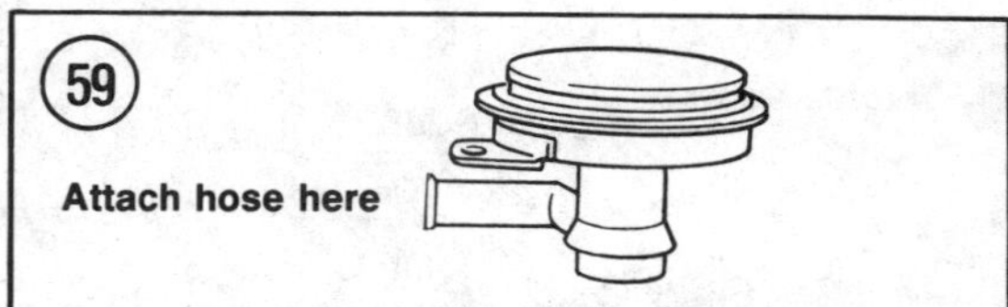

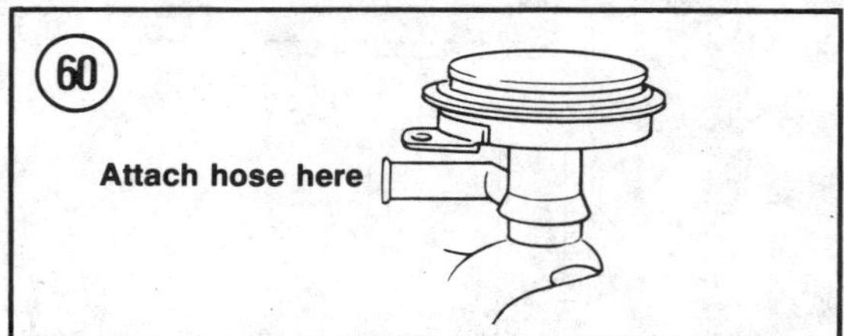

CRANKCASE VENTILATION
SYSTEM (DIESEL)

This system (**Figure 57**) routes crankcase vapors into the combustion chambers for burning, as well as providing a constant internal pressure in the crankcase so that air and dirt are not sucked in through the crankshaft oil seals.

Inspection

1. Remove the system hose. Blow out the hose with compressed air and make sure it is not clogged. Replace the hose if it is cracked or deteriorated.
2. Remove the crankcase emission control valve (**Figure 58**).
3. Attach a hose to the valve (**Figure 59**). Suck on the hose and make sure air flows through it.
4. Block the fitting on the bottom of the valve with a finger and suck on the hose. See **Figure 60**. The valve should make clicking sounds.

5. If the valve didn't perform as described in Step 3 or Step 4, replace it.

EXHAUST GAS RECIRCULATION
SYSTEM (DIESEL)

This system (**Figure 61**) routes part of the exhaust gases into the combustion chambers. This lowers combustion temperature, reducing oxides of nitrogen in the exhaust.

Inspection

1. Check the system for visible defects such as loose or cracked hoses. Tighten or replace as needed.
2. With the engine off, reach beneath the EGR valve and lift its diaphragm. See **Figure 62**. It should rise smoothly, without sticking or binding.

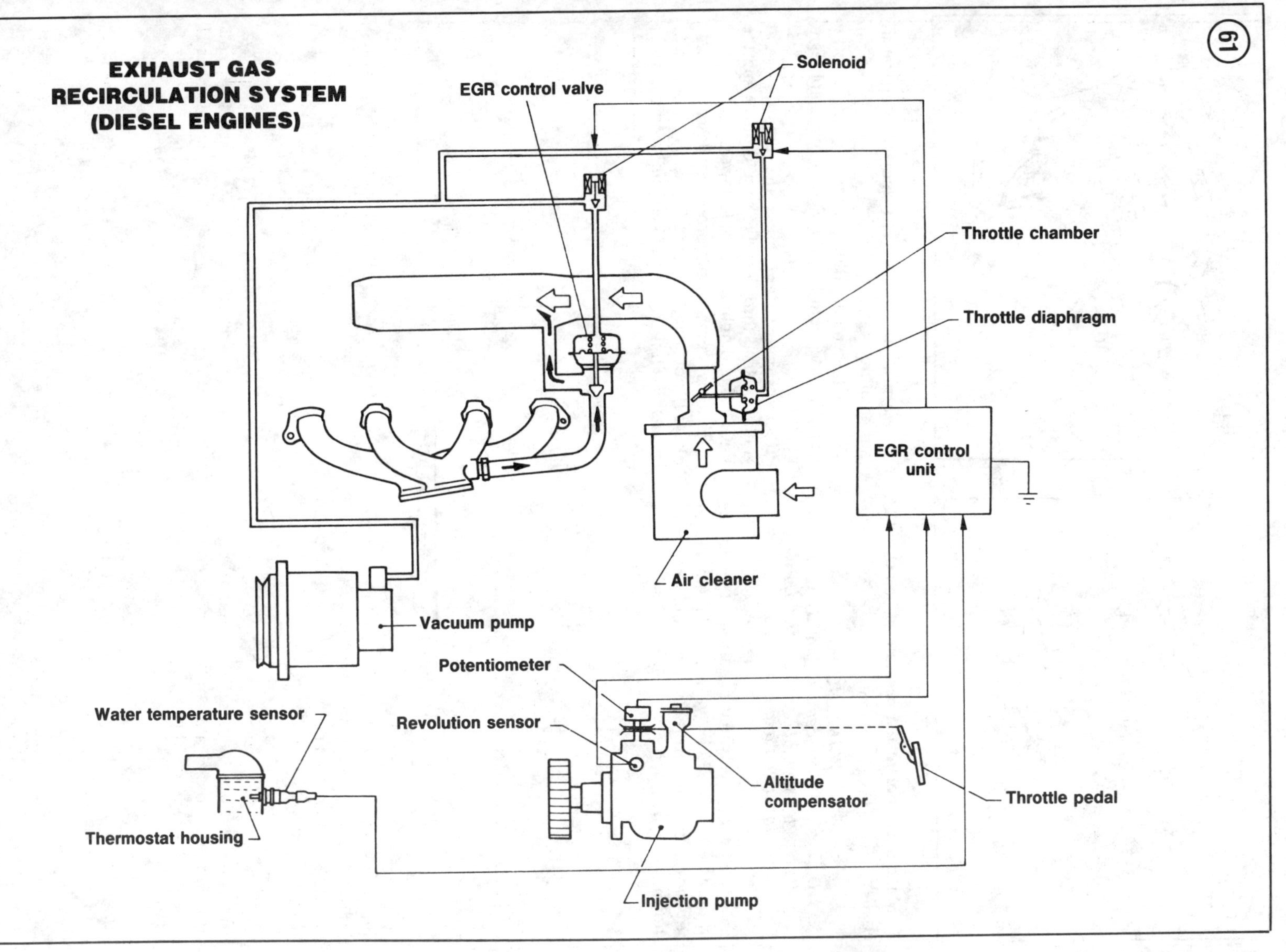
61
EXHAUST GAS
RECIRCULATION SYSTEM
(DIESEL ENGINES)
EGR control valve
Solenoid
Throttle chamber
Throttle diaphragm
EGR control unit
Air cleaner
Vacuum pump
Potentiometer
Revolution sensor
Water temperature sensor
Altitude compensator
Throttle pedal
Thermostat housing
Injection pump
5

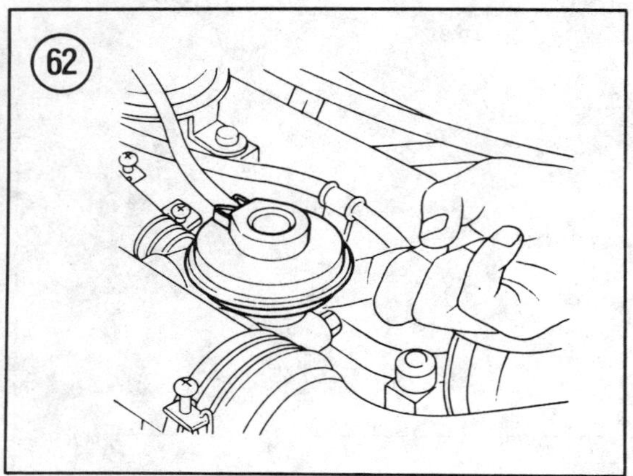

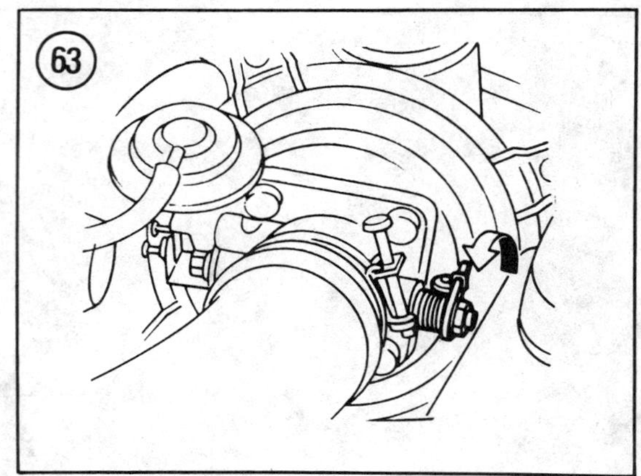

3. Make sure coolant temperature is below 40° C (104° F).

> *WARNING*
> *During the next steps, do not let your finger get caught between the EGR valve diaphragm and body.*

4. Start the engine. Have an assistant press the throttle pedal. The EGR valve diaphragm should not move, but the throttle valve should move as shown in **Figure 63**.

5. Warm the engine to normal operating temperature.

6. With the engine idling, make sure the throttle valve is closed, but that the EGR valve diaphragm rises.

7. Have an assistant press the throttle pedal gradually. The throttle valve should move and the EGR valve diaphragm should lower.

8. If the system has performed as described, it is okay. If not, have it tested further by a dealer or mechanic familiar with Nissan emission controls.

Table 1 FUEL SYSTEM SPECIFICATIONS

Idle compensator operating temperatures	
No. 1 valve	60-70° C (140-158° F)
No. 2 valve	70-80° C (158-176° F)
1982 jets and air bleeds	
Primary main jet	
California manual	115
California automatic	114
49-state manual	117
49-state automatic	115
Canada	100
MPG	98
Secondary main jet	
U.S.	125
Canada	130
MPG	135
Primary main air bleed	
California	80
49-state	60
Canada	70
MPG	60
Secondary main air bleed	
U.S.	80
Canada	60
MPG	80
Primary slow jet	
U.S.	45
Canada	43
MPG	43
Secondary slow jet	
U.S.	50
Canada	80
MPG	55
Primary slow air bleed	
California manual	210
California automatic	190
49-state	190
Canada	170
MPG	160
Secondary slow air bleed	
California	70
49-state	60
Canada	100
MPG	80
Power jet	
California manual	38
California automatic	35
49-state	38
Canada	40
MPG	—
Solenoid controlled slow air bleed	
(MPG only)	220
Solenoid controlled fuel orifice	
(MPG only)	70

(continued)

Table 1 FUEL SYSTEM SPECIFICATIONS (continued)

1983 jets and air bleeds	
Primary main jet	
California	91
49-state	106
Canada	100
MPG	98
Secondary main jet	
California	130
49-state	133
Canada	135
MPG	140
Primary main air bleed	
California	105
49-state	100
Canada	110
MPG	60
Secondary main air bleed	
U.S.	60
Canada	60
MPG	80
Primary slow jet (all)	43
Secondary slow jet	
California	70
49-state	55
Canada	65
MPG	55
Primary slow air bleed	
California	170
49-state	185
Canada	180
MPG	160
Secondary slow air bleed	
California	80
49-state	100
Canada	100
MPG	80
Power jet	
California	—
49-state	35
Canada	35
MPG	—
Solenoid controlled slow air bleed	
California	220
49-state	—
Canada	—
MPG	220
Solenoid controlled fuel orifice	
California	70
49-state	—
Canada	—
MPG	70

(continued)

Table 1 FUEL SYSTEM SPECIFICATIONS (continued)

Carburetor CO percentage	
1982 non-MPG	
Measurement standard*	4% or less
Adjustment standard*	1.5 +1.0, -0.7%
1982 MPG	
Measurement standard*	2-6%
Adjustment standard*	4+/-1%
1983 California	
Measurement standard*	1-5%
Adjustment standard*	3+/-1%
1983 MPG	
Measurement standard*	2-6%
Adjustment standard	4+/-1%
1983 49-state, non-MPG	
Measurement standard*	4% or less
Adjustment standard*	1.5 +0, -0.7%
Float adjustment	
Dimension "H"	12 mm (0.47 in.)
Dimension "h"	1.3-1.7 mm (0.051-0.067 in.)
1982 fast idle speed	
California	2,300-3,100
49-state	2,400-3,200
Canada manual	1,900-2,700
Canada automatic	2,400-3,200
1983 fast idle speed	
California manual	2,600-3,400
California automatic	2,900-3,700
49-state manual	2,400-3,200
49-state automatic	2,700-3,500
Canada manual	1,900-2,700
Canada automatic	2,400-3,200
MPG	2,400-3,200
Fuel pump pressure	19.6-26.5 kPa (2.8-3.8 psi)
Fuel pump capacity (30 seconds)	650 cc (22 fl. oz.) or more
Dashpot adjusting speed	2,300-2,500 rpm

*Automatic transaxle in DRIVE.

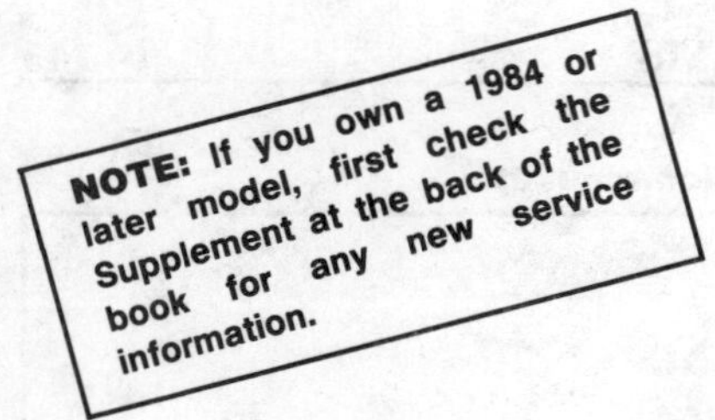

CHAPTER SIX

COOLING, HEATING AND AIR CONDITIONING SYSTEM

The Sentra uses a centrifugal water pump to propel coolant through the radiator, engine and heater. An electric fan pulls air through the radiator to cool the coolant. A thermostat blocks coolant flow to the radiator when the engine is cold to speed warmup.

Table 1 and **Table 2** are the end of the chapter.

COOLING SYSTEM FLUSHING

The recommended coolant is a 50/50 mixture of ethylene glycol-based antifreeze and water. This protects the system from freezing to approximately -35° C (-31° F). Concentration can be checked with a coolant hydrometer. These are available inexpensively from car parts stores.

The system should be drained, flushed and refilled at intervals specified in Chapter Three. If desired, a chemical flushing agent may be used prior to the flushing method described here. **Figure 1** shows the gasoline cooling system. **Figure 2** shows the diesel system.

1. Coolant can stain concrete and harm plants. Park the car over a gutter or similar area.
2. Turn the heater control on the instrument panel to WARM.
3. Open the tap at the bottom of the radiator. **Figure 3** shows the radiator used with gasoline engines. The diesel radiator is similar.
4. On diesel engines, remove the cylinder block drain plug (**Figure 4**).

5. After the system has finished draining, close the tap (and reinstall the drain plug on diesels).
6. Remove the thermostat as described in this chapter. Temporarily reinstall the water outlet elbow.
7. Disconnect the top and bottom hoses from the radiator. See **Figure 5** (gasoline) or **Figure 6** (diesel).
8. Disconnect the heater hoses from the engine.
9. Connect a garden hose to one of the heater hoses. This does not have to be a positive fit, as long as most of the water enters the heater hose. Run water into the heater hose until clear water flows from the other hose.
10. Insert the hose into the top radiator hose. Run water into the hose until clear water flows from the bottom hose.
11. Insert the hose into the hose fitting at the bottom of the radiator. Run water into the radiator until clear water flows from the top fitting.
12. Turn off the water. Let the engine, radiator and heater drain.
13. Connect the hoses to the engine and radiator.
14. Fill the cooling system with a 50/50 mixture of ethylene glycol-based antifreeze and water, even if you live in an area that doesn't require this degree of freeze protection. The antifreeze makes a good corrosion inhibitor. Cooling system capacity is listed in **Table 1** at the end of the chapter. On gasoline engines, fill the radiator with coolant to 20-30 mm

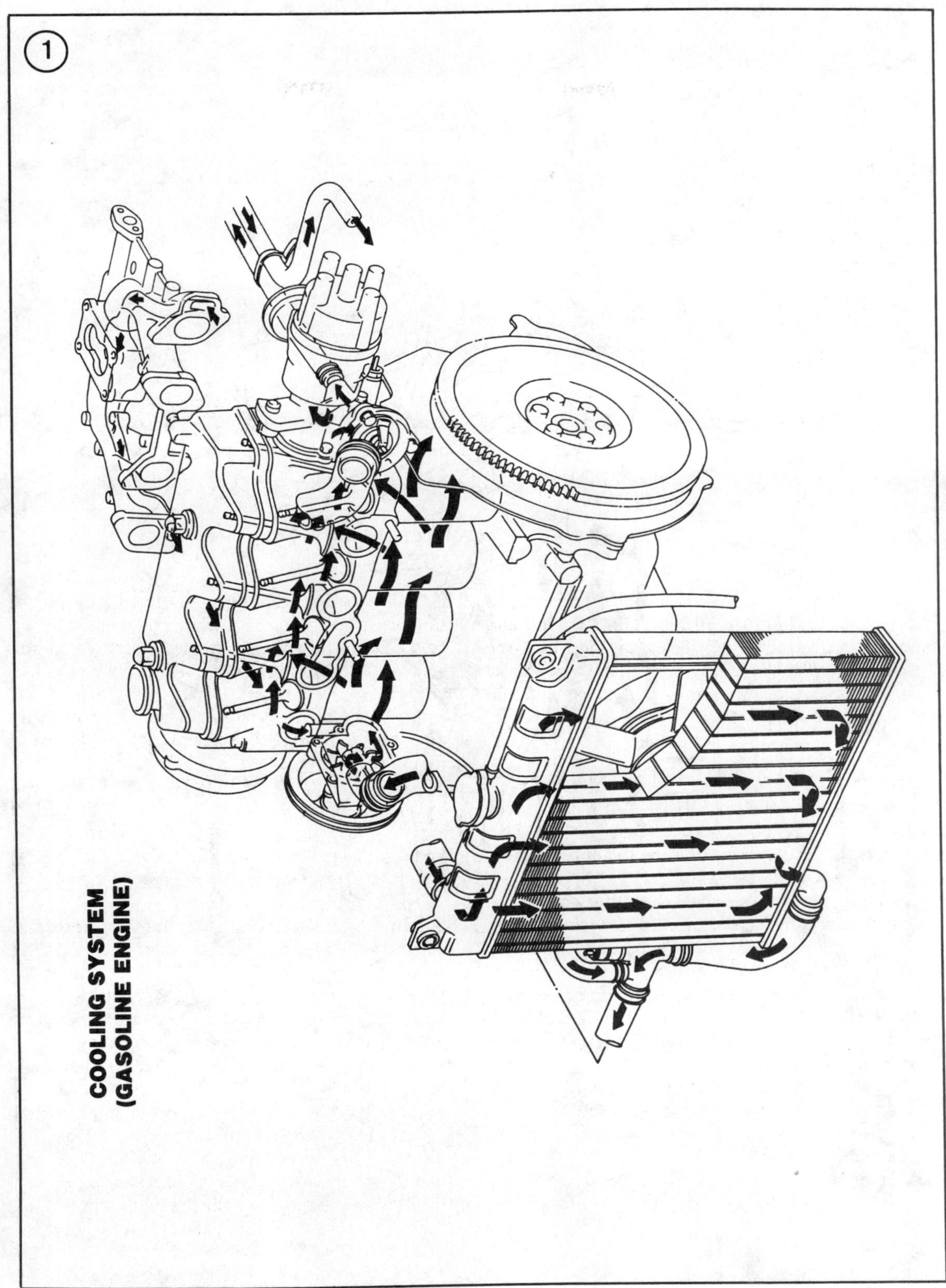

1
COOLING SYSTEM
(GASOLINE ENGINE)

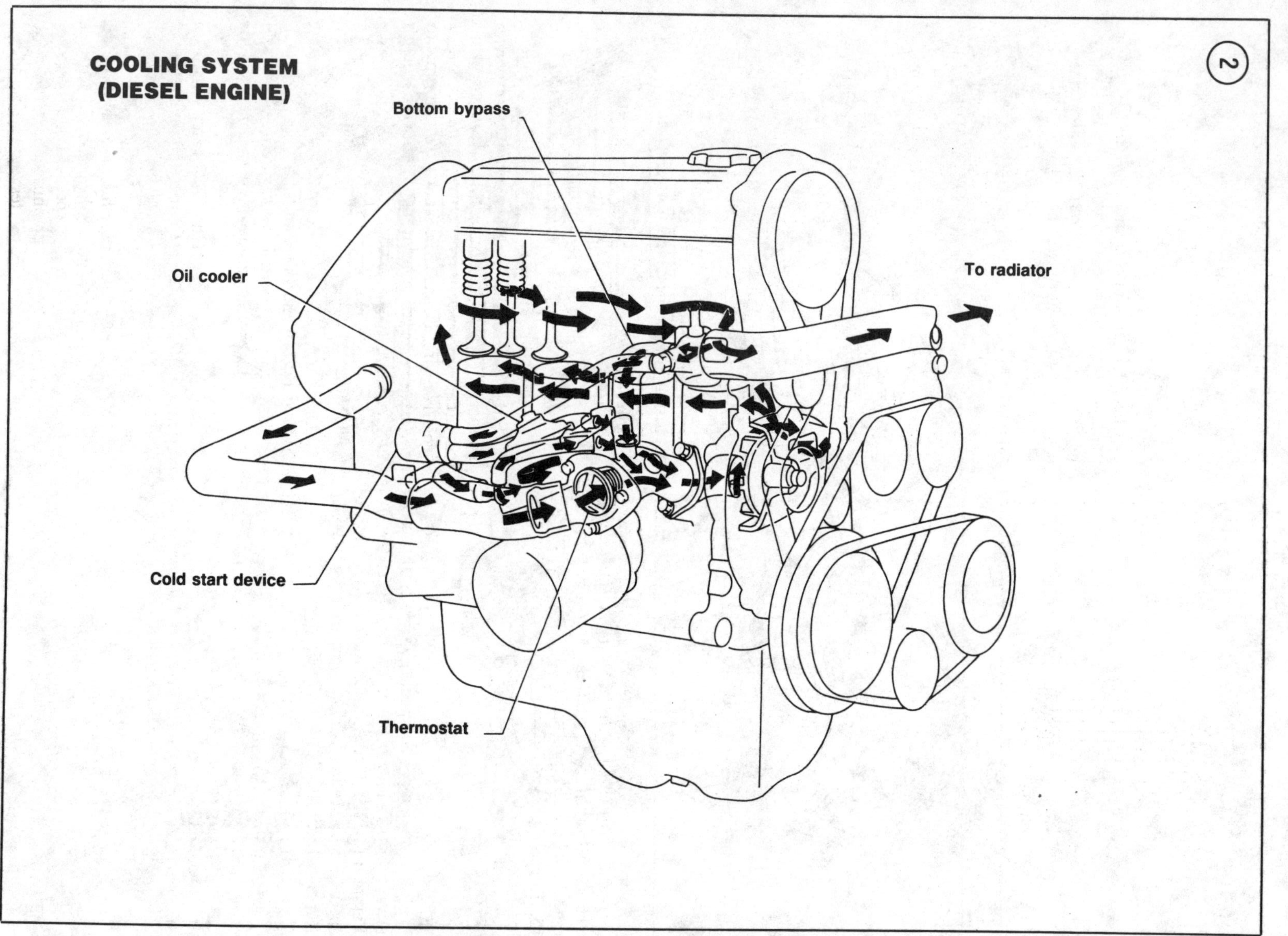

2
COOLING SYSTEM
(DIESEL ENGINE)
Bottom bypass
Oil cooler
To radiator
Cold start device
Thermostat

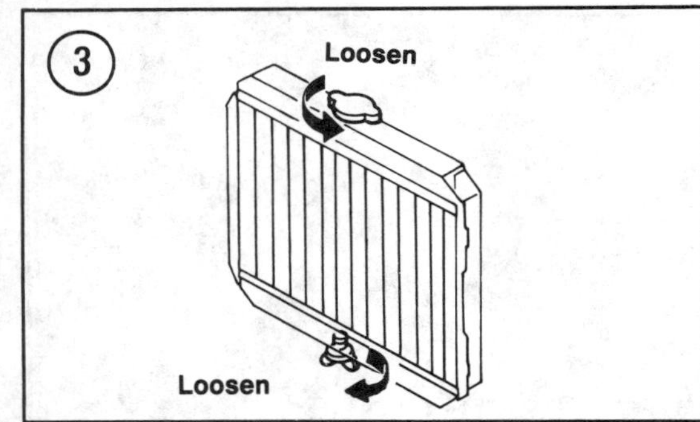

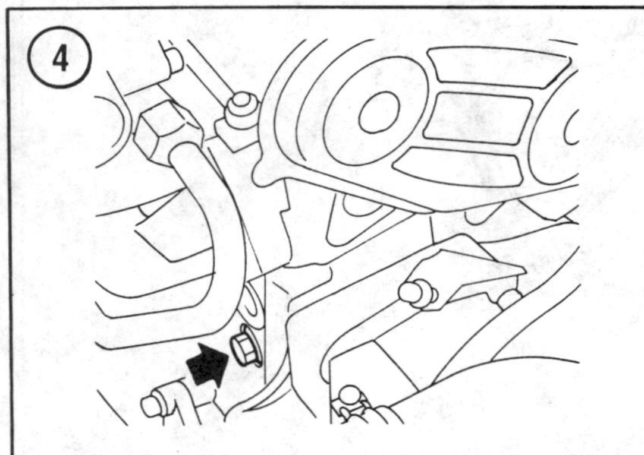

(3/4-1 1/4 in.) below the filler neck. On diesel engines, fill to the bottom of the filler neck. On all models, fill the reservoir tank to the "MAX" mark.
15. Run the engine for several minutes and check for leaks. Recheck coolant level and top off as needed.

HOSES

Hoses should be inspected periodically and always before a long trip. See **Figure 5** (gasoline) or **Figure 6** (diesel). Check hoses for cracks, extreme softness, crumbling rubber and mildew stains. Replace hoses that show these conditions.

CAUTION
If a hose's condition is in doubt, play it safe and replace it. It is most likely to fail during driving, when the heated coolant is trying to expand. Replacing a hose under roadside working conditions can be a truly miserable job.

NOTE
When buying new hoses, look at the hose ends and make sure there is reinforcing fabric imbedded in the rubber. Unreinforced hoses are weaker than reinforced ones.

Check all hose connections for leaks. Tighten or replace clamps as needed.

RADIATOR AND FAN

Radiator Inspection

1. Check the radiator fins and tubes for clogging or damage. Carefully straighten bent fins with a fingernail. Clean bugs, dirt, etc., from the fins with a soft brush or compressed air. If leaks can be seen in the tubes, have the radiator recored by a radiator shop.
2. Check the radiator seams for leaks. Small leaks can be soldered. Larger leaks can be brazed. Leak repairs can be done inexpensively by a radiator shop if you don't have the necessary equipment.

Removal/Installation

1. Drain the radiator as described under *Cooling System Flushing* in this chapter.
2. Disconnect the hoses from the radiator. See **Figure 5** (gasoline) or **Figure 6** (diesel).
3. Remove the radiator mounting bolts. Lift the radiator and fan out.
4. If necessary, remove the fan mounting bolts and take the fan off.
5. Installation is the reverse of removal.

Fan Motor Test

WARNING
If the fan is working, it will run during the next step. Keep your hands and hair out of the way.

If the fan fails to operate, unplug its wiring connector (**Figure 7**). Connect the green-red wire's terminal to the battery positive terminal with a length of wire. Connect the black wire's terminal to the battery negative terminal. If the fan doesn't run, replace the fan motor.

Fan Switch Test

1. Drain the radiator as described under *Cooling System Flushing* in this chapter.
2. Unplug the switch wiring connector and unscrew the water temperature switch from the radiator.
3. Immerse the switch in water with a thermometer (**Figure 8**). Connect an ohmmeter or a test lamp like the one shown in **Figure 9** between the switch terminals.
4. With the water cold, the ohmmeter should show infinite resistance or the test lamp should stay out.
5. Heat the water above specified fan operating temperature (**Table 1**). The ohmmeter should show little or no resistance or the test lamp should light.

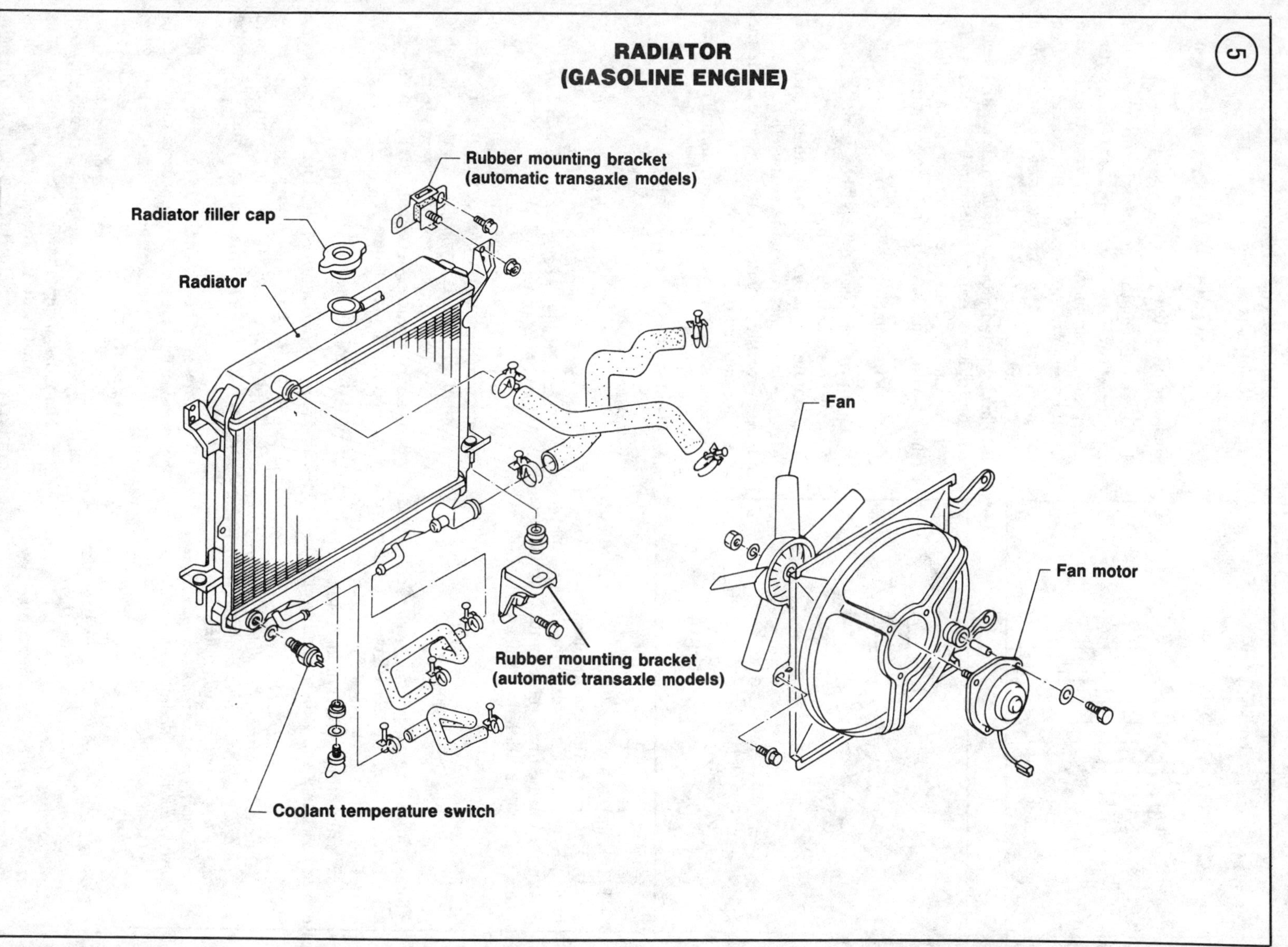

5
RADIATOR
(GASOLINE ENGINE)
Rubber mounting bracket
(automatic transaxle models)
Radiator filler cap
Radiator
Fan
Fan motor
Rubber mounting bracket
(automatic transaxle models)
Coolant temperature switch

⑥

RADIATOR
(DIESEL ENGINE)

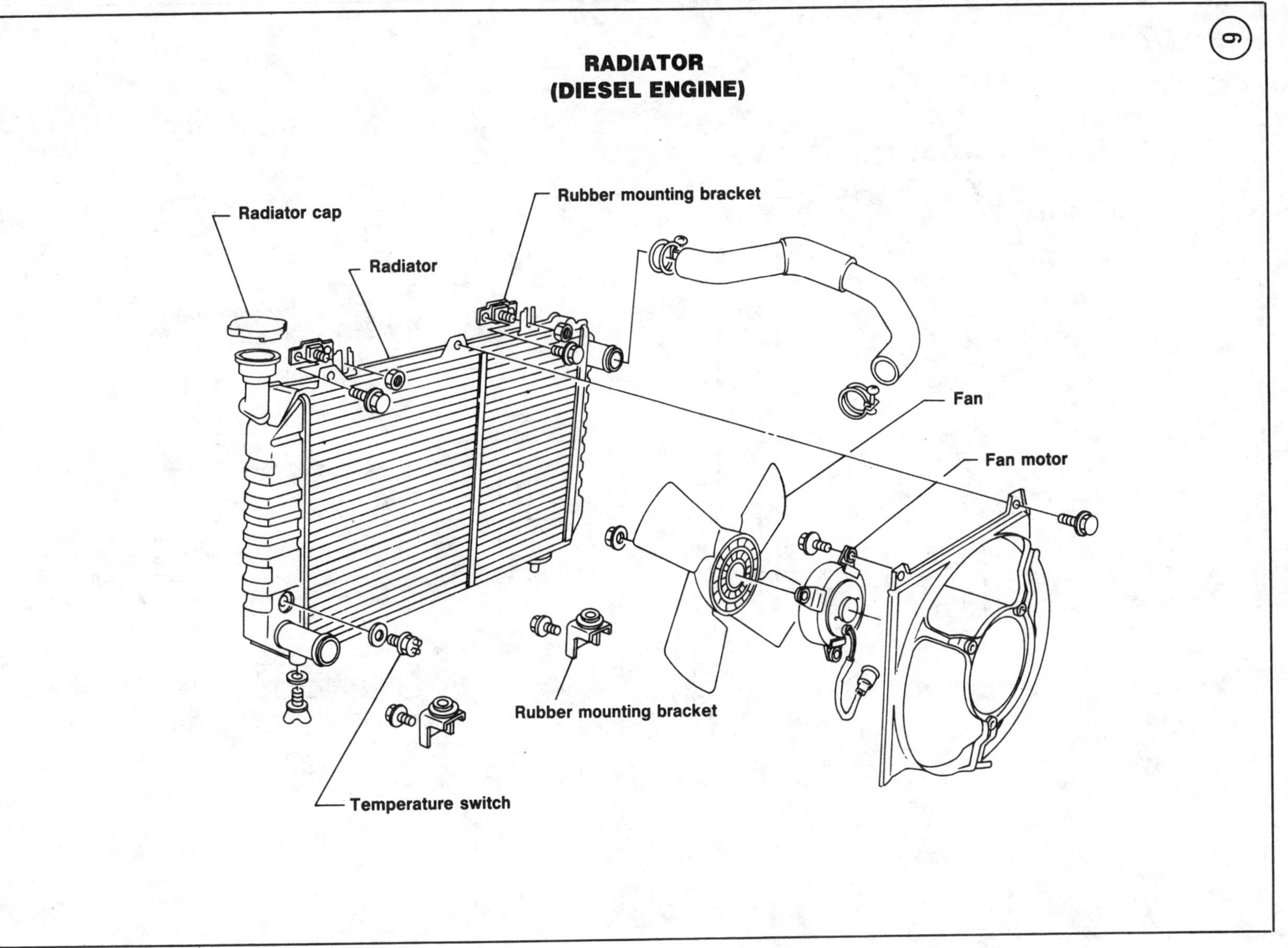

6

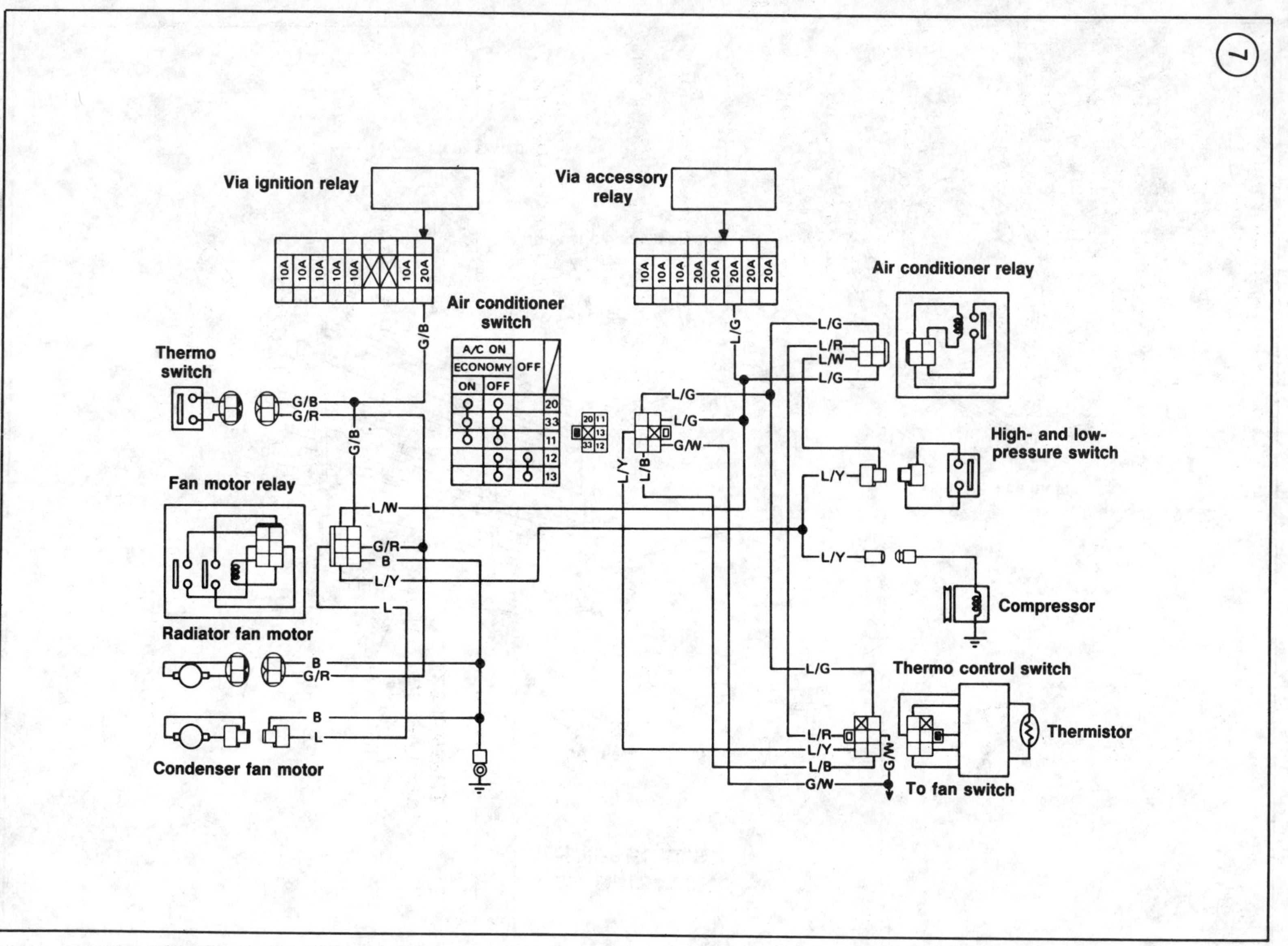
7
Via ignition relay
Via accessory relay
Air conditioner relay
Thermo switch
Air conditioner switch
High- and low-pressure switch
Fan motor relay
Radiator fan motor
Condenser fan motor
Compressor
Thermo control switch
Thermistor
To fan switch
10A
10A
10A
10A
10A
10A
20A
10A
10A
10A
20A
20A
20A
20A
20A
A/C ON
ECONOMY OFF
ON OFF
20
33
11
12
13
G/B
G/B
G/B
G/R
G/R
G/R
B
L/W
L/Y
L
B
G/R
B
L
L/G
L/G
L/G
L/G
L/R
L/W
L/G
L/Y
L/B
G/W
L/Y
L/Y
L/G
L/R
L/Y
L/B
G/W
G/W

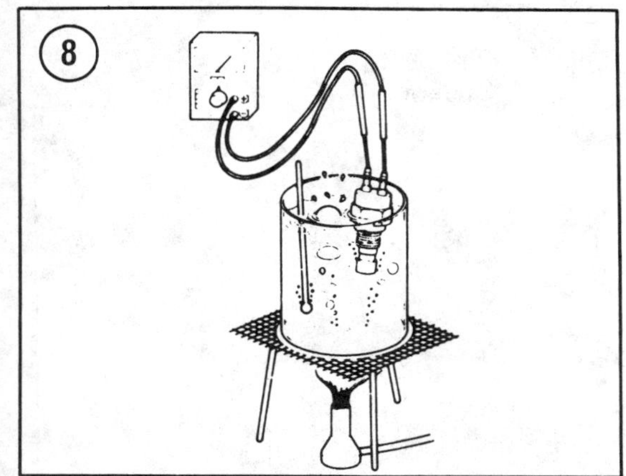

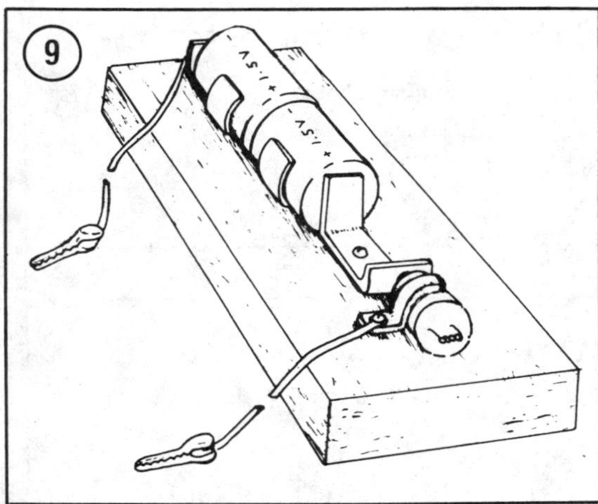

6. If the water temperature switch does not perform as described, replace it.

THERMOSTAT

The thermostat blocks water flow to the radiator when the engine is cold. As the engine warms up, the thermostat gradually opens, allowing water to circulate through the radiator. See **Figure 10** (gasoline) or **Figure 11** (diesel).

If the engine overheats quickly but coolant level is normal and the fan works, the thermostat is probably stuck shut. If so, it must be replaced.

Removal and Testing

1. Make sure the engine is cool.
2. Drain about one gallon of coolant from the radiator. If the coolant is clean, save it for reuse.

WARNING
Ethylene glycol is poisonous and may attract animals. Do not leave the coolant where it is accessible to pets or children.

3. Detach the hose from the water outlet elbow. See **Figure 12**.
4. Remove the water outlet elbow (**Figure 13**). Lift out the thermostat.
5. Place the thermostat in a pan of water with a thermometer (**Figure 14**).

NOTE
Suspend the thermostat with wire so it doesn't touch the bottom or sides of the pan.

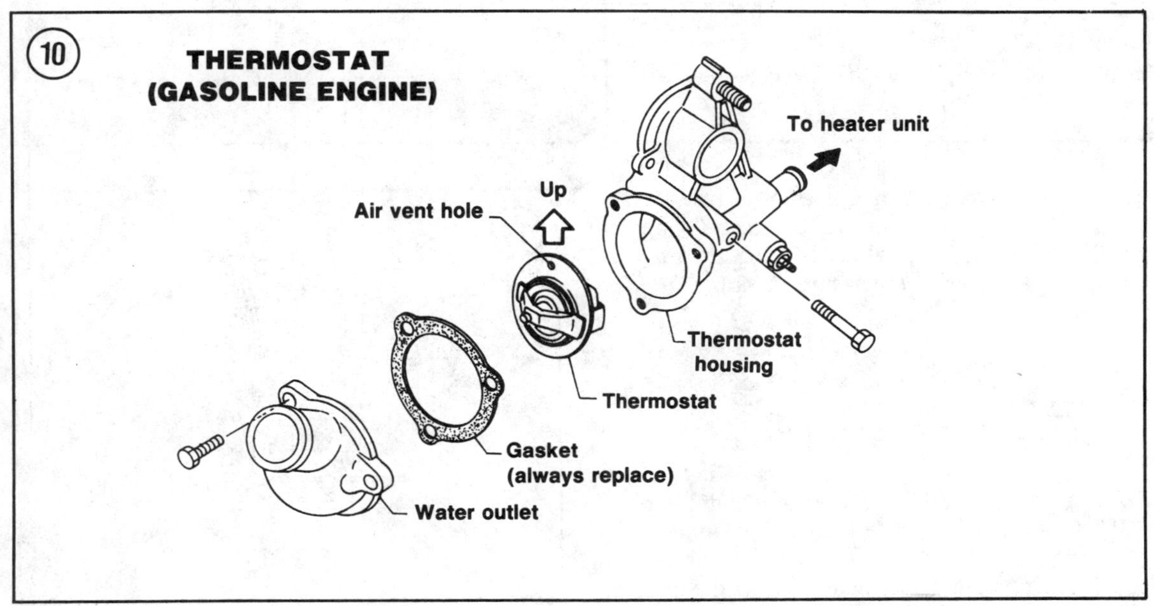

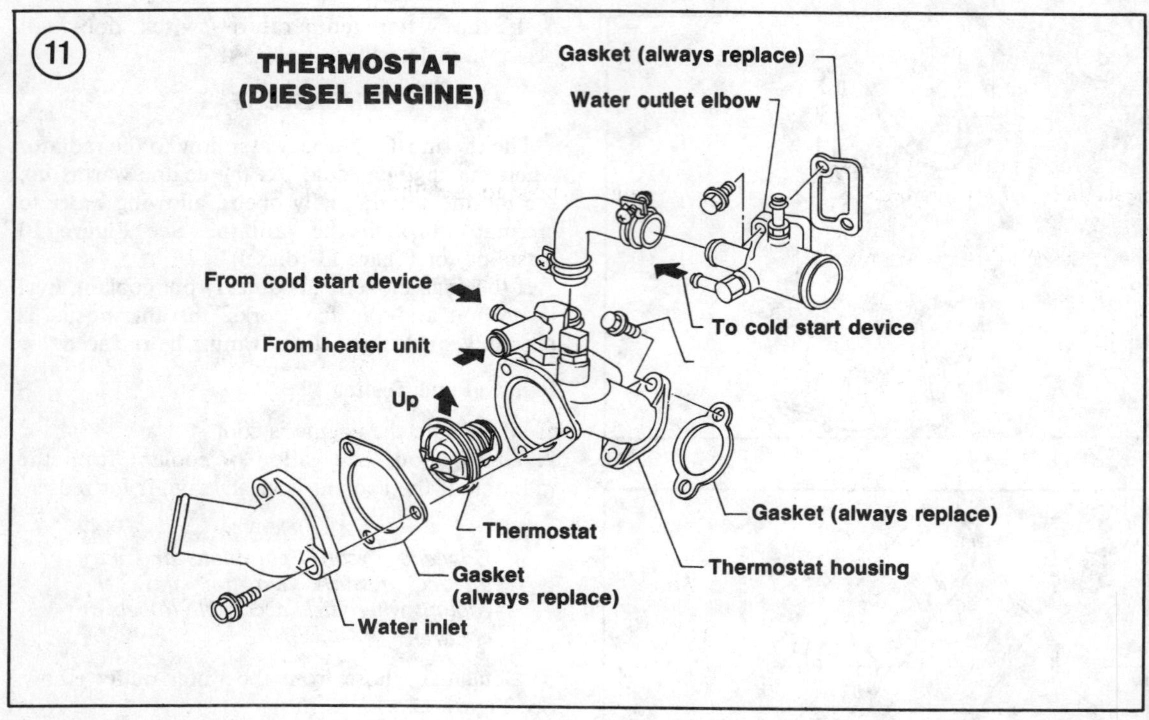

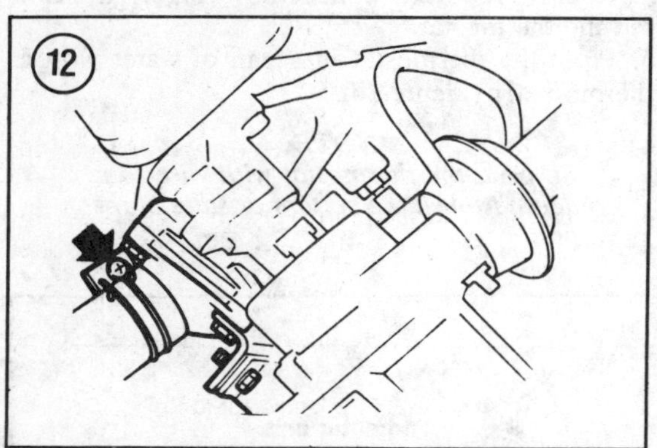

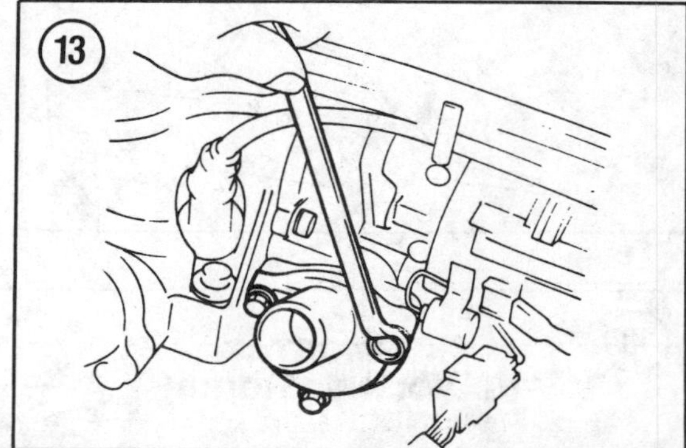

6. Heat the water until the thermostat just begins to open, then note the water temperature. Compare with specifications in **Table 1**. If the thermostat opens at the wrong temperature or fails to open, replace it.

> *NOTE*
> *Actual opening temperature may vary slightly from that specified. This does not indicate a defective thermostat.*

7. Measure maximum lift of the thermostat valve. To do this, mark a screwdriver at a point 8 mm (5/16 in.) from the tip. The screwdriver is used as a measuring device. Heat the water to the valve opening temperature specified in **Table 1**. Measure

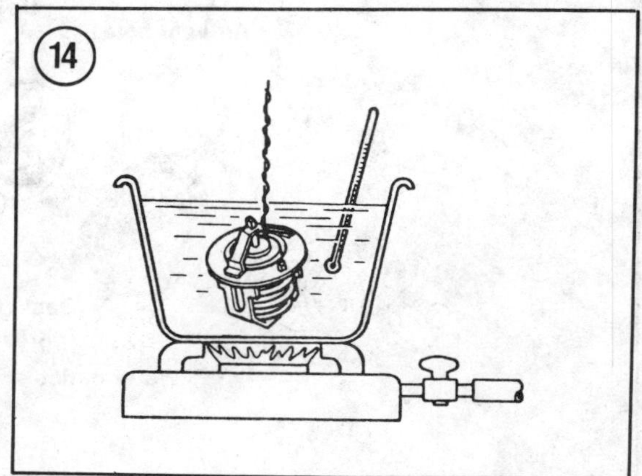

the valve opening with the marked screwdriver. If it is less than 8 mm (5/16 in.), replace the thermostat.

Installation

1. If a new thermostat is being installed, test it as described in the preceding section. A new thermostat may be defective and testing it will save the time and trouble required to remove it later.

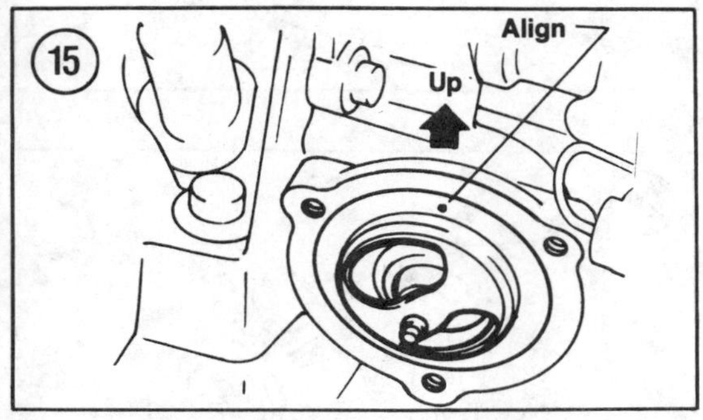

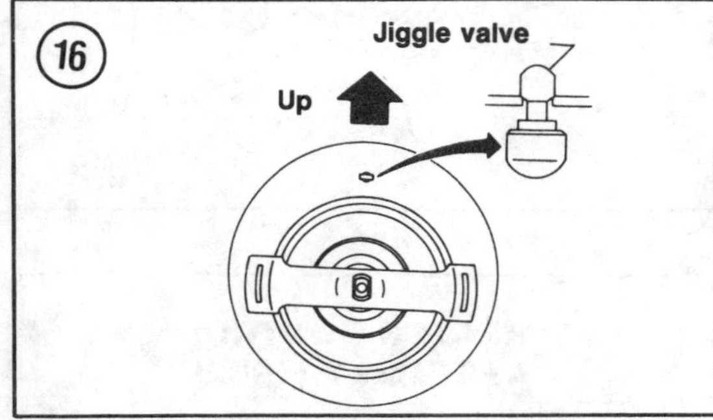

2. Position the thermostat in the engine. Make sure the jiggle valve or air vent is upward. See **Figure 15** (gasoline) or **Figure 16** (diesel).
3. Install the water outlet elbow. Use a new gasket, coated on both sides with gasket sealer.
4. Tighten the elbow securing nuts. Reconnect the hose to the elbow.

WATER PUMP

A defective water pump may warn of failure by making noise. A water leak from behind the pulley indicates a worn water pump seal.

This section applies to gasoline engine water pumps only. Removing the diesel water pump requires removing the timing belt. This should be done by a dealer or other qualified diesel mechanic.

Removal/Installation (Gasoline Engine)

1. Drain the radiator as described in this chapter.

> *WARNING*
> *Ethylene glycol is poisonous and may attract animals. Do not leave the coolant where it is accessible to children or pets.*

2. If equipped with power steering, detach the power steering pump from the engine and lay it aside. See Chapter Nine. It is not necessary to disconnect the pump hoses.
3. Remove the alternator belt as described in Chapter Three. Push the alternator toward the engine as far as it will go.
4. Remove the water pump pulley (**Figure 17**).
5. Remove the water pump mounting bolts (**Figure 18**) and take the pump off.

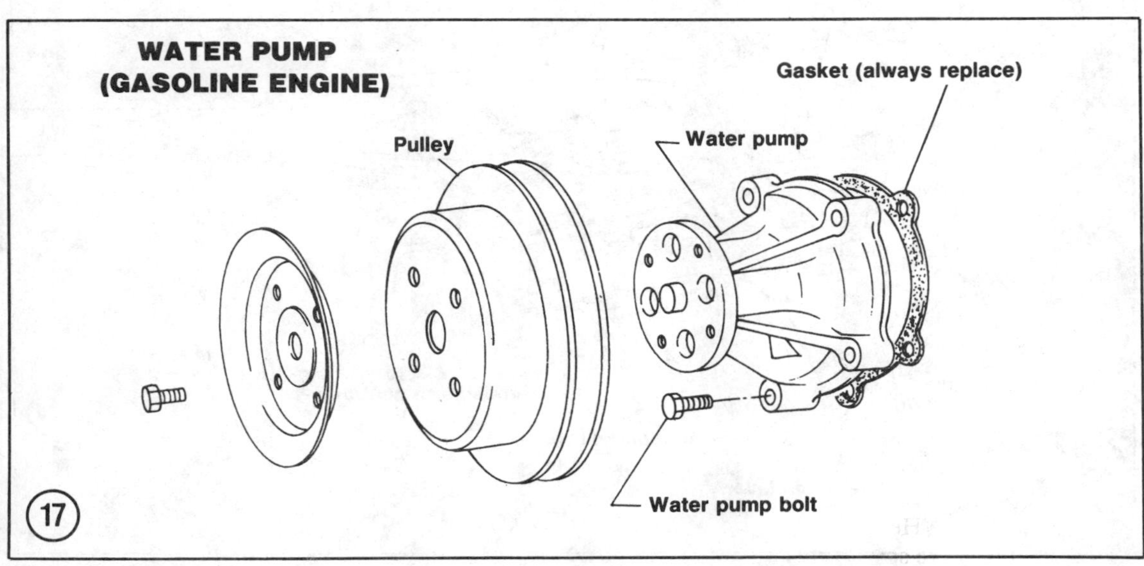

6. Remove all traces of old gasket and sealer from the water pump mounting surface on the engine.

7. Installation is the reverse of removal. Use a new gasket, coated on both sides with gasket sealer. Tighten all fasteners to specifications (**Table 2**). Adjust the alternator belt (and power steering belt, if so equipped) as described in Chapter Three.

Inspection

1. Check the water pump vanes (**Figure 19**) for corrosion or damage. Replace the water pump if the vanes are damaged or corroded more than slightly.

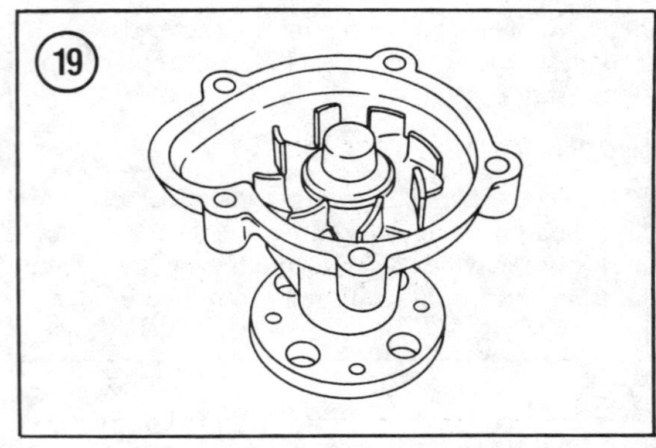

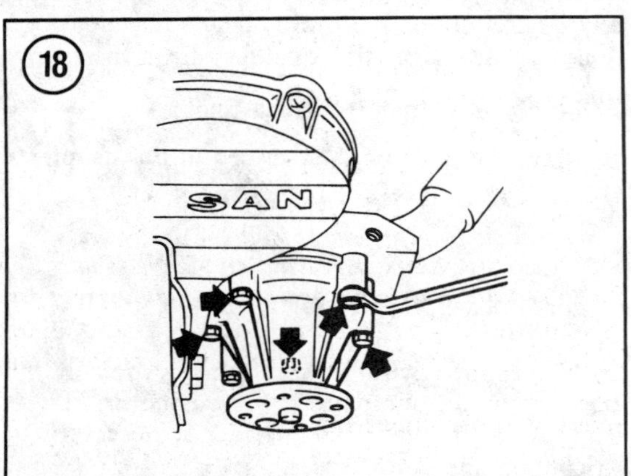

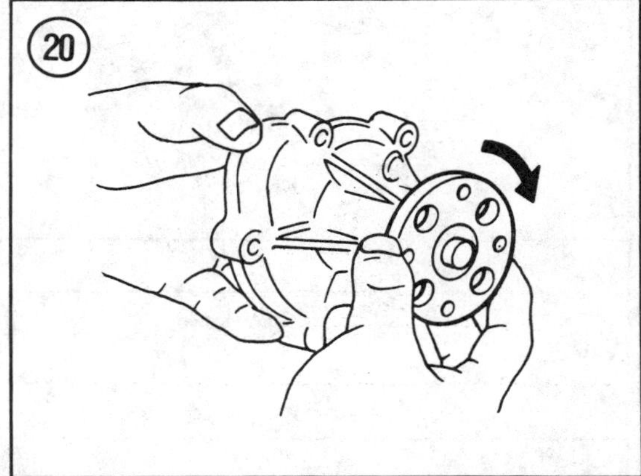

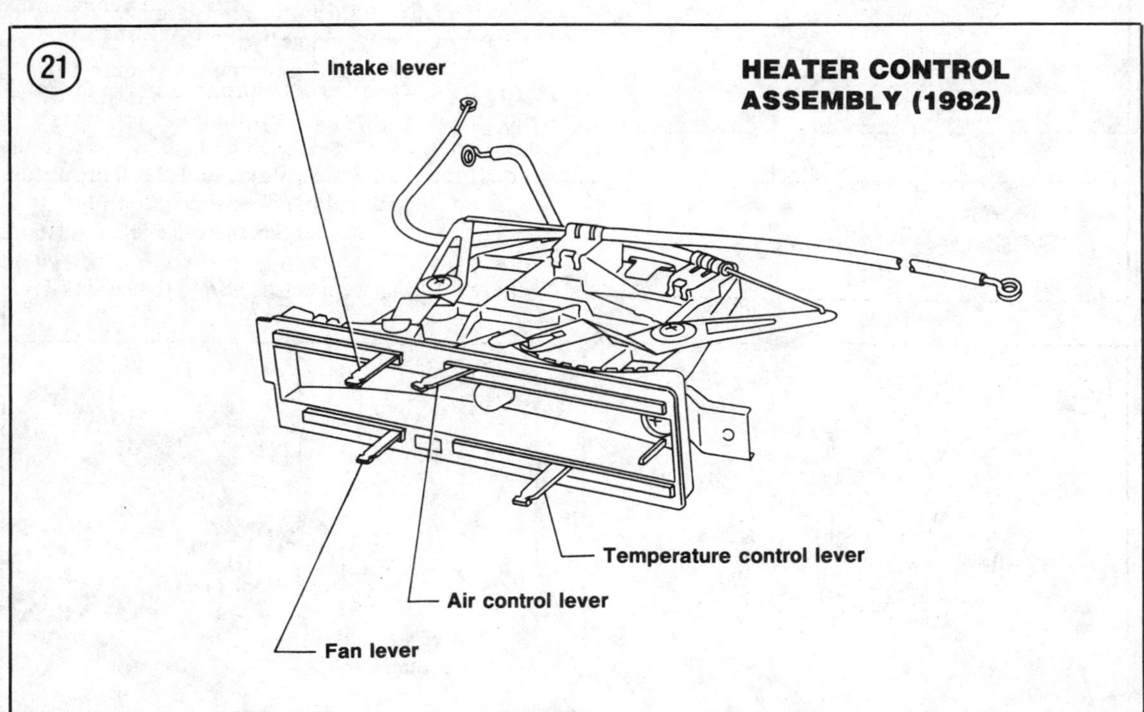

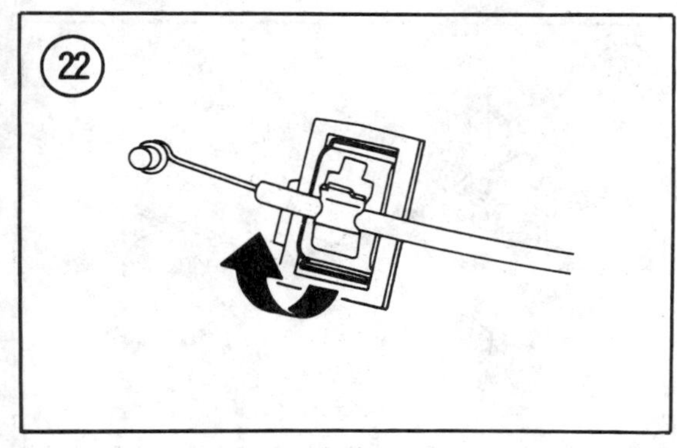

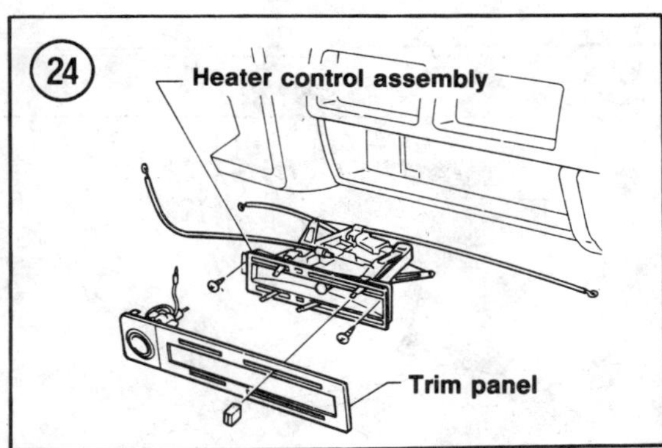

2. Turn the water pump flange by hand and check for rough bearing movement. See **Figure 20**. If movement is rough or if there is more than slight end play in the bearing, replace the water pump.

HEATER

Control Assembly Removal/Installation (1982)

Figure 21 shows the control assembly.

1. Unfasten the cable clips (**Figure 22**) and disconnect the cables from the doors on the heater unit.

2. Unplug the control assembly wiring connector.

3. Pull off the heater knobs (**Figure 23**). Compress the retainer prongs on the control assembly trim panel and take the panel out.

4. Remove the control assembly mounting screws (**Figure 24**). Take the assembly out.

5. Installation is the reverse of removal. Adjust the cables as described in this chapter.

Cable Adjustment (1982)

1. Place the intake lever in the RECIRC position (MAX A/C if equipped with air conditioning). Set the intake door at the recirculating position (**Figure 25**). Connect the control cable to the link lever and secure the cable with the clip. Make sure the control knob moves smoothly.

2. Place the temperature lever in the COLD position. Move the air mix door in the direction of the arrow (**Figure 26**). Connect the temperature control rod to the lever, then secure the cable with the clip.

3. Pull the water valve control rod in the direction shown in **Figure 27** so that the clearance is approximately 2 mm (0.08 in.), then connect the rod to the door lever. Make sure the temperature lever on the control panel moves smoothly.

4. Place the air control lever in the DEF position. Move the link lever in the direction shown in **Figure 28**, then connect the cable to the link lever

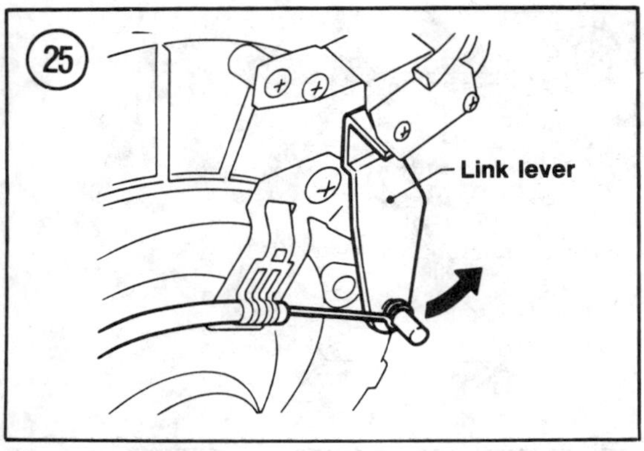

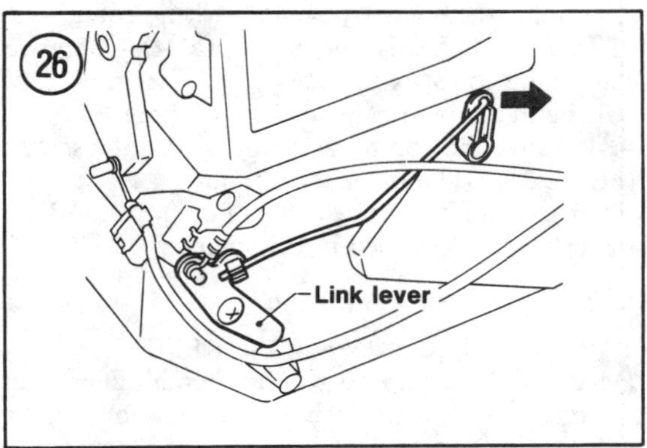

and secure it with the clip. Make sure the air control lever moves smoothly.

Blower Motor Removal/Installation (1982)

1. Remove the lower cover from the instrument panel as described in Chapter Twelve.
2. Unplug the blower motor wiring connector.
3. Remove the lower casing screws (**Figure 29**). Take the casing out.
4. Remove the blower motor mounting screws and take the motor out.
5. Installation is the reverse of removal.

Heater Unit Removal/Installation (1982)

1. Drain the cooling system as described in this chapter.
2. Working in the engine compartment, disconnect the heater hoses from the heater unit.
3. Remove the instrument panel as described in Chapter Twelve.
4. Remove the heater control assembly as described in this chapter.
5. Place a plastic sheet such as a painting dropcloth on the car floor to catch drips.
6. Remove the heater unit fasteners (**Figure 30**). Remove the heater unit into the passenger compartment and take it out of the car.
7. Installation is the reverse of removal. Fill the cooling system as described in this chapter.

Heater Core Removal/Installation (1982)

To remove the heater core, remove the heater unit as described in this chapter. Disassemble the case and take the core out, referring to **Figure 31**. Installation is the reverse of removal.

Control Assembly Removal/Installation (1983)

Figure 32 shows the control assembly.
1. Unfasten the cable clips (**Figure 33**) and disconnect the cables from the doors on the heater unit.
2. Unplug the control assembly wiring connector.
3. Pull off the heater knobs (**Figure 34**). Compress the retainer prongs on the control assembly trim panel and take the panel out.
4. Remove the control assembly mounting screws (**Figure 35**). Take the assembly out.
5. Installation is the reverse of removal. Adjust the cables as described in this chapter.

Cable Adjustment (1983)

1. Place the intake lever in the RECIRC position (MAX A/C if equipped with air conditioning). Set the intake door at the recirculating position (**Figure 36**). Connect the control cable to the link lever and

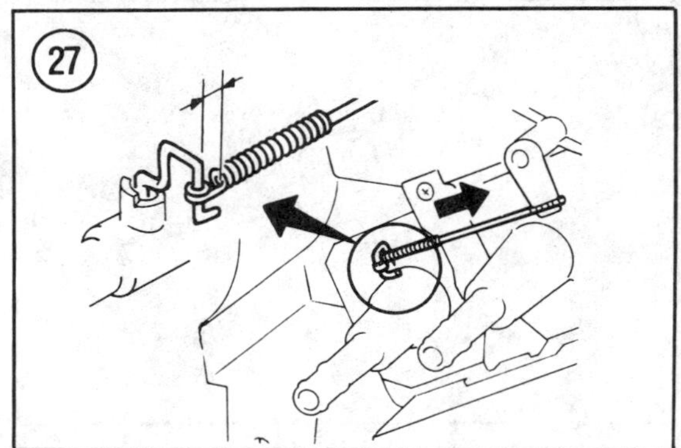

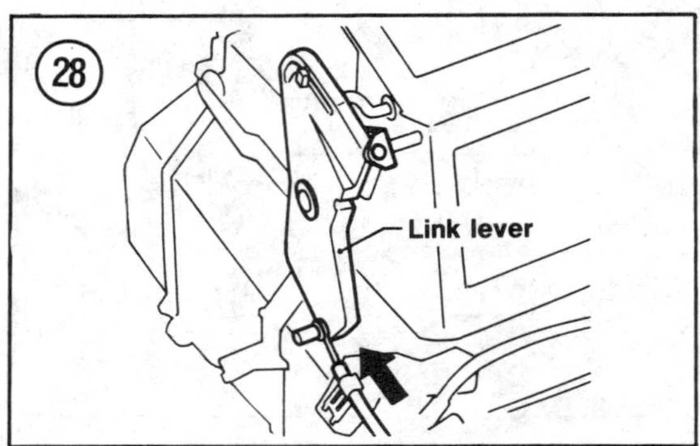

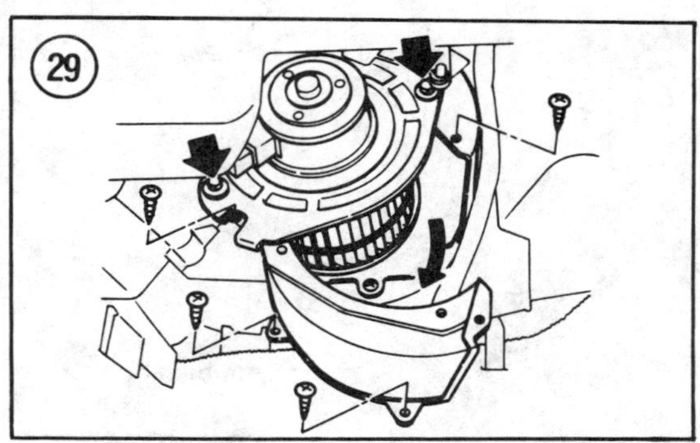

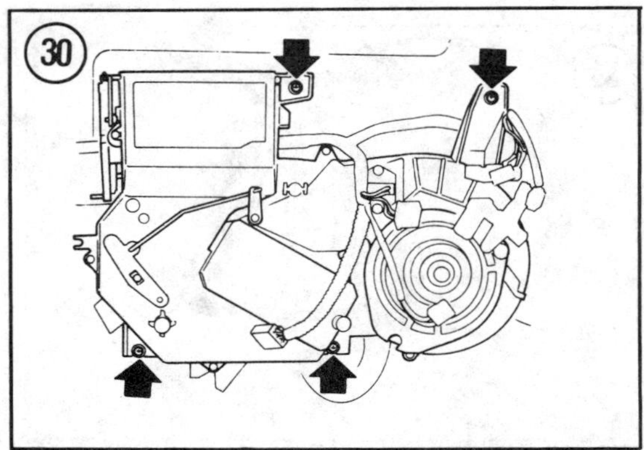

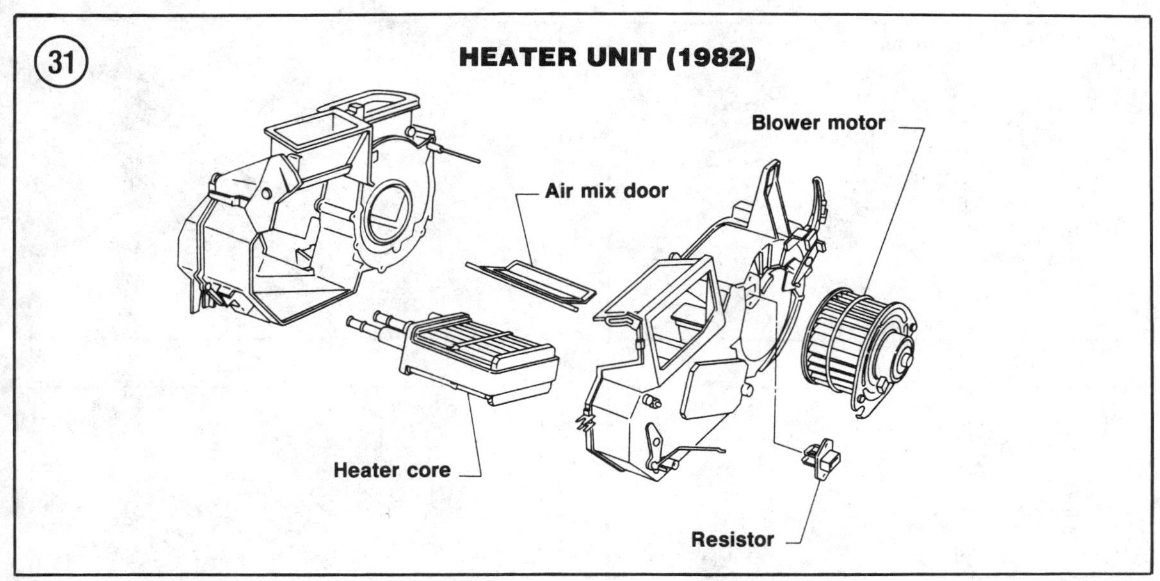
31
HEATER UNIT (1982)
Blower motor
Air mix door
Heater core
Resistor

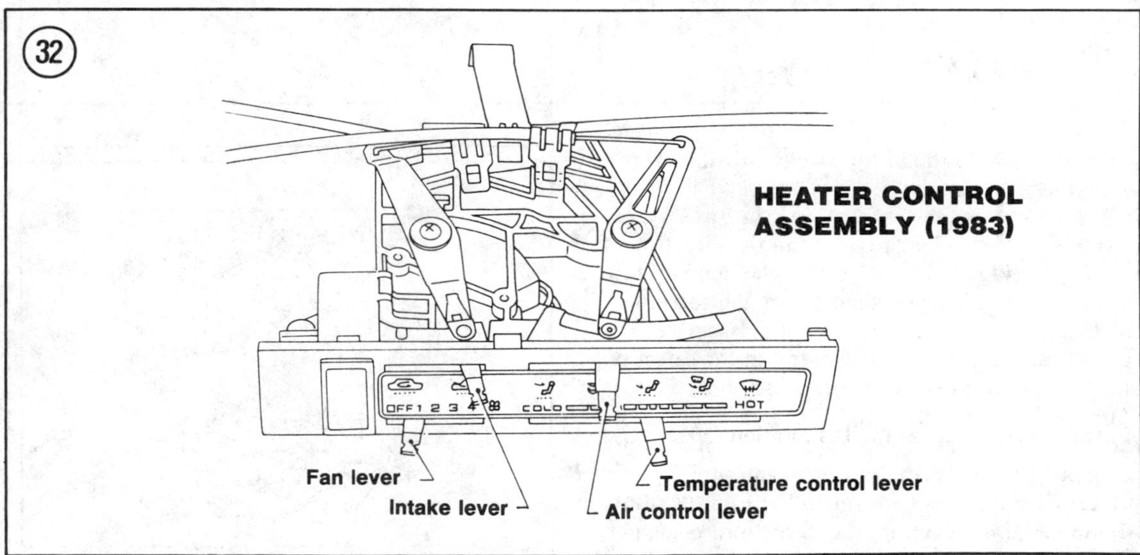
32
HEATER CONTROL
ASSEMBLY (1983)
OFF 1 2 3 4
COLD
HOT
Fan lever
Intake lever
Air control lever
Temperature control lever

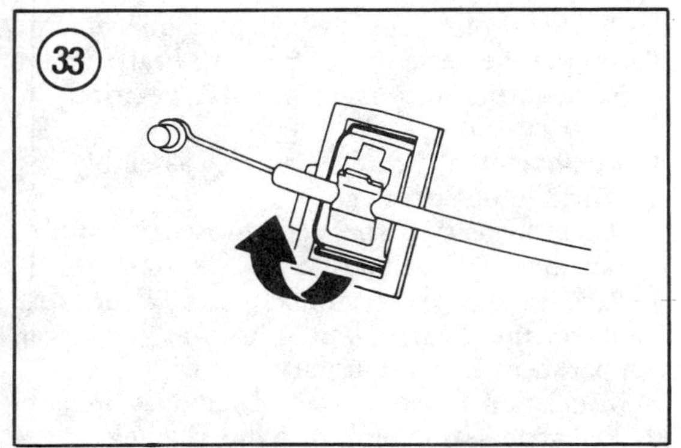
33

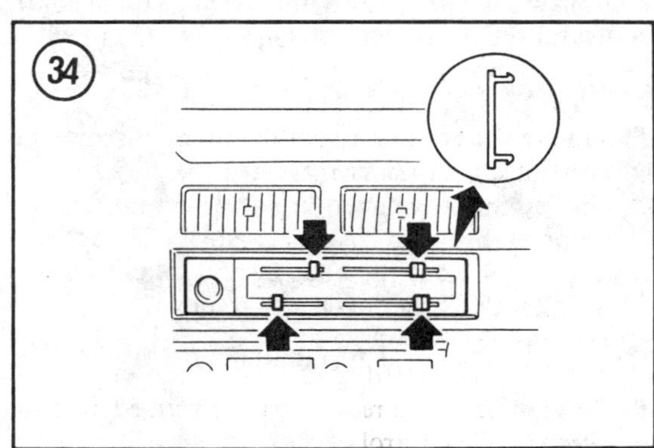
34

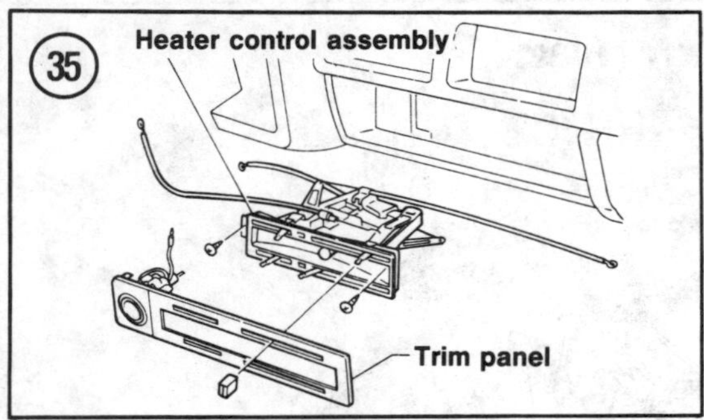

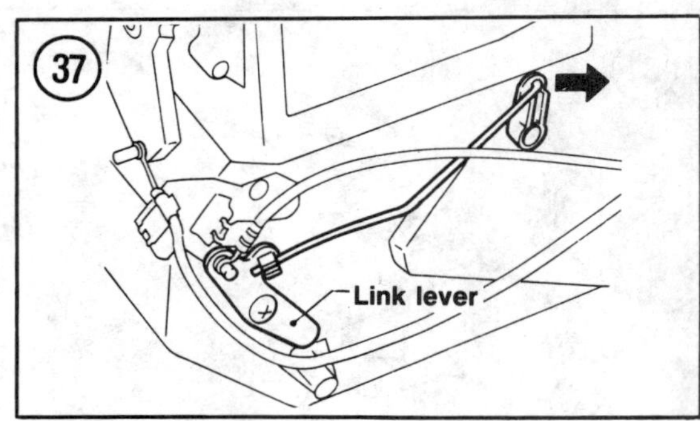

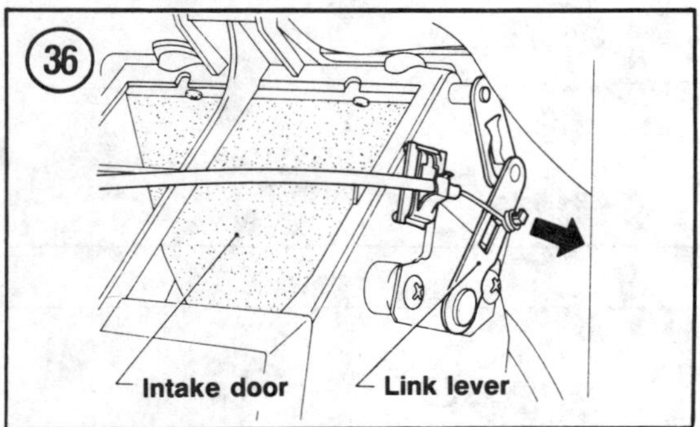

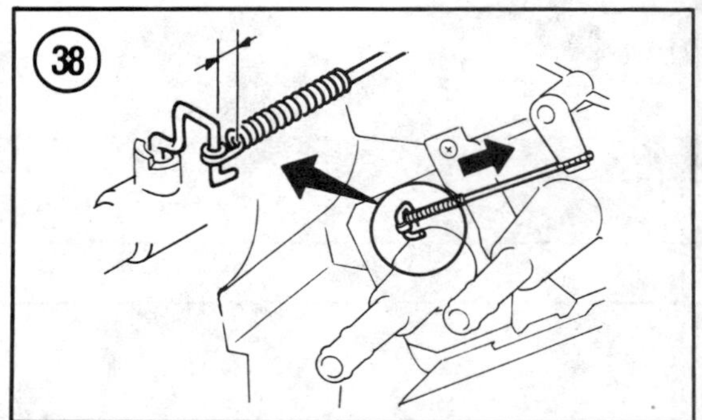

secure the cable with the clip. Make sure the control knob moves smoothly.

2. Place the temperature lever in the COLD position. Move the air mix door in the direction of the arrow (**Figure 37**). Connect the temperature control rod to the lever, then secure the cable with the clip.

3. Pull the water valve control rod in the direction shown in **Figure 38** so that the clearance is approximately 2 mm (0.08 in.), then connect the rod to the door lever. Make sure the temperature lever on the control panel moves smoothly.

4. Place the air control lever in the DEF position. Move the link lever in the direction shown in **Figure 39**, then connect the cable to the link lever and secure it with the clip. Make sure the air control lever moves smoothly.

Blower Motor Removal/Installation (1983)

1. Remove the lower cover from the instrument panel as described in Chapter Twelve.
2. Unplug the blower motor wiring connector.
3. Remove the lower cover (**Figure 40**). Detach the blower motor from the housing and take it out.
4. Installation is the reverse of removal.

Heater Unit Removal/Installation (1983)

1. Drain the cooling system as described in this chapter.

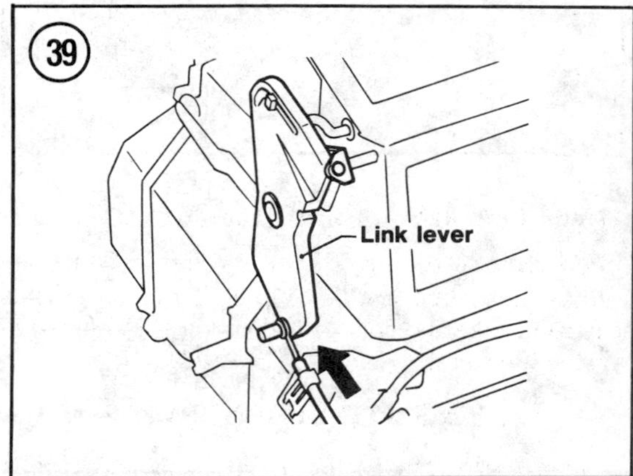

2. Working in the engine compartment, disconnect the heater hoses from the heater unit.
3. Remove the instrument panel as described in Chapter Twelve.
4. Remove the heater control assembly as described in this chapter.
5. Place a plastic sheet such as a painting dropcloth on the car floor to catch drips.
6. Remove the heater unit fasteners (**Figure 41**). Remove the heater unit into the passenger compartment and take it out of the car.
7. Installation is the reverse of removal. Fill the cooling system as described in this chapter.

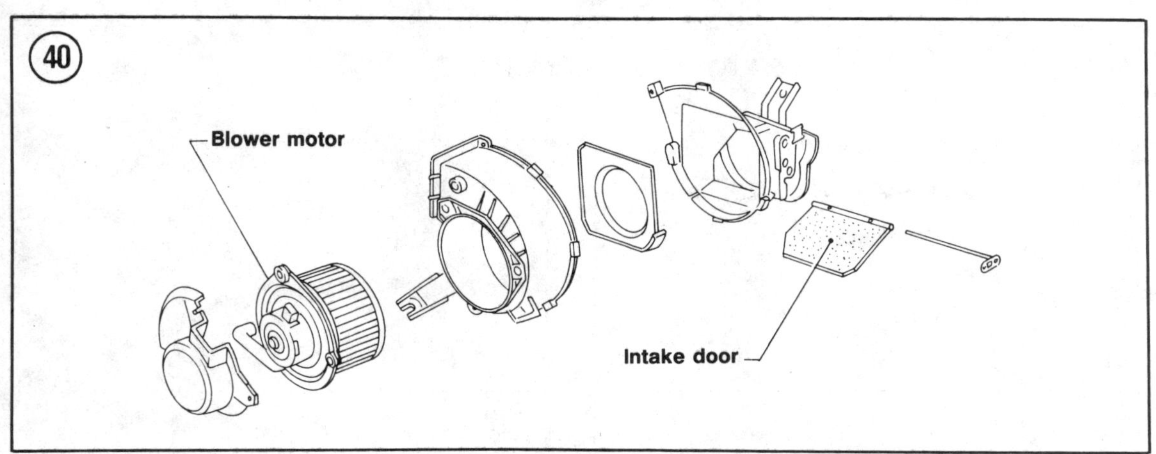

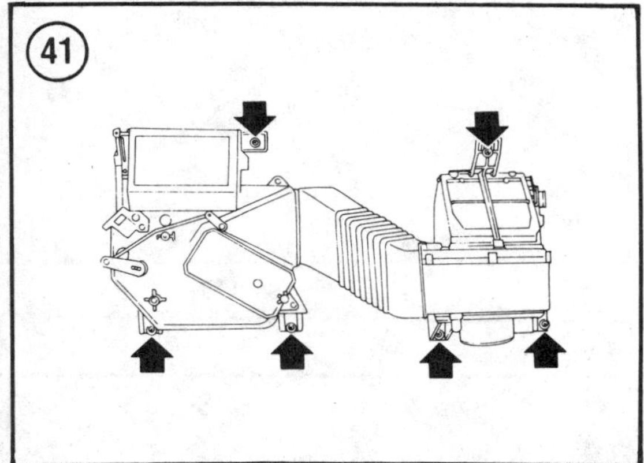

Heater Core Removal/Installation (1983)

To remove the heater core, remove the heater unit as described in this chapter. Disassemble the case and take the core out, referring to **Figure 42**. Installation is the reverse of removal.

AIR CONDITIONING

This section covers the maintenance and minor repairs that can prevent or correct most air conditioning problems. Major repairs require special training and tools and should be left to a dealer or air conditioning shop.

SYSTEM OPERATION

Figure 43 and **Figure 44** show the system parts.

These 5 basic components are common to all air conditioning systems:
   a. Compressor.
   b. Condenser.
   c. Receiver/drier.
   d. Expansion valve.
   e. Evaporator.

WARNING
*The components, connected with high-pressure hoses and tubes, form a closed loop. The refrigerant in the system is under very high pressure. It can cause frostbite if it touches skin and blindness if it touches the eyes. If discharged near a flame, the refrigerant forms poisonous gas. If the refrigerant can is hooked up wrong, it can explode. For these reasons, **read this entire section** before working on the system.*

Figure 45 is a schematic of the system. For practical purposes, the cycle begins at the compressor. The refrigerant, in a warm, low-pressure vapor state, enters the low-pressure side of the compressor. It is compressed to a high-pressure hot vapor and pumped out of the high-pressure side to the condenser.

Air flow through the condenser removes heat from the refrigerant and transfers the heat to the outside air. As the heat is removed, the refrigerant condenses to a warm, high-pressure liquid.

The refrigerant then flows to the receiver/drier where moisture is removed and impurities are filtered out. The refrigerant is stored in the receiver/drier until it is needed. The receiver/drier incorporates a sight glass that permits visual monitoring of the condition of the refrigerant as it flows. From the receiver/drier, the refrigerant then flows to the expansion valve. The expansion valve is thermostatically controlled and meters refrigerant to the evaporator. As the refrigerant leaves the expansion valve it changes from a warm, high-pressure liquid to a cold, low-pressure liquid.

In the evaporator, the refrigerant removes heat from the passenger compartment air that is blown across the evaporator's fins and tubes. In the process, the refrigerant changes from a cold,

(42) **HEATER UNIT (1983)**

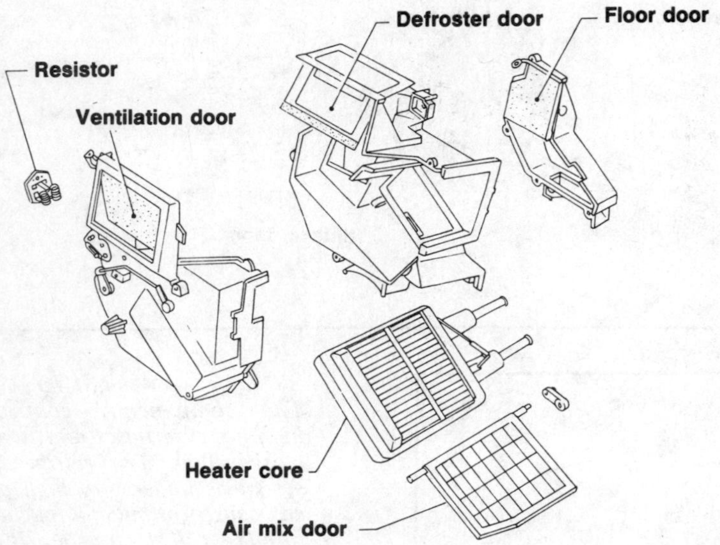

(43) **AIR CONDITIONING SYSTEM PARTS**

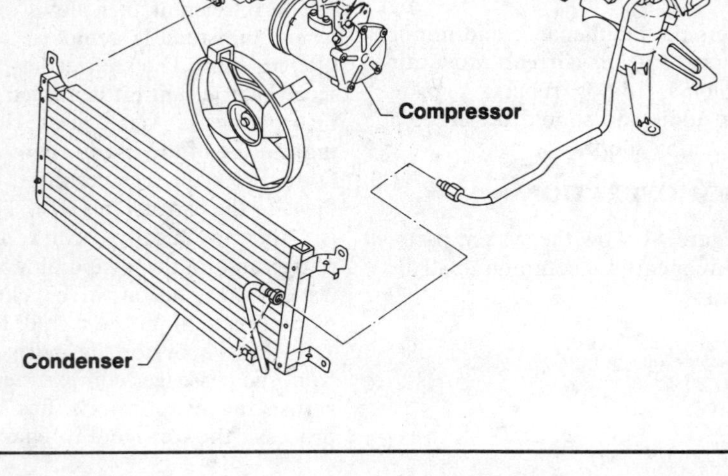

AIR CONDITIONING SYSTEM PARTS

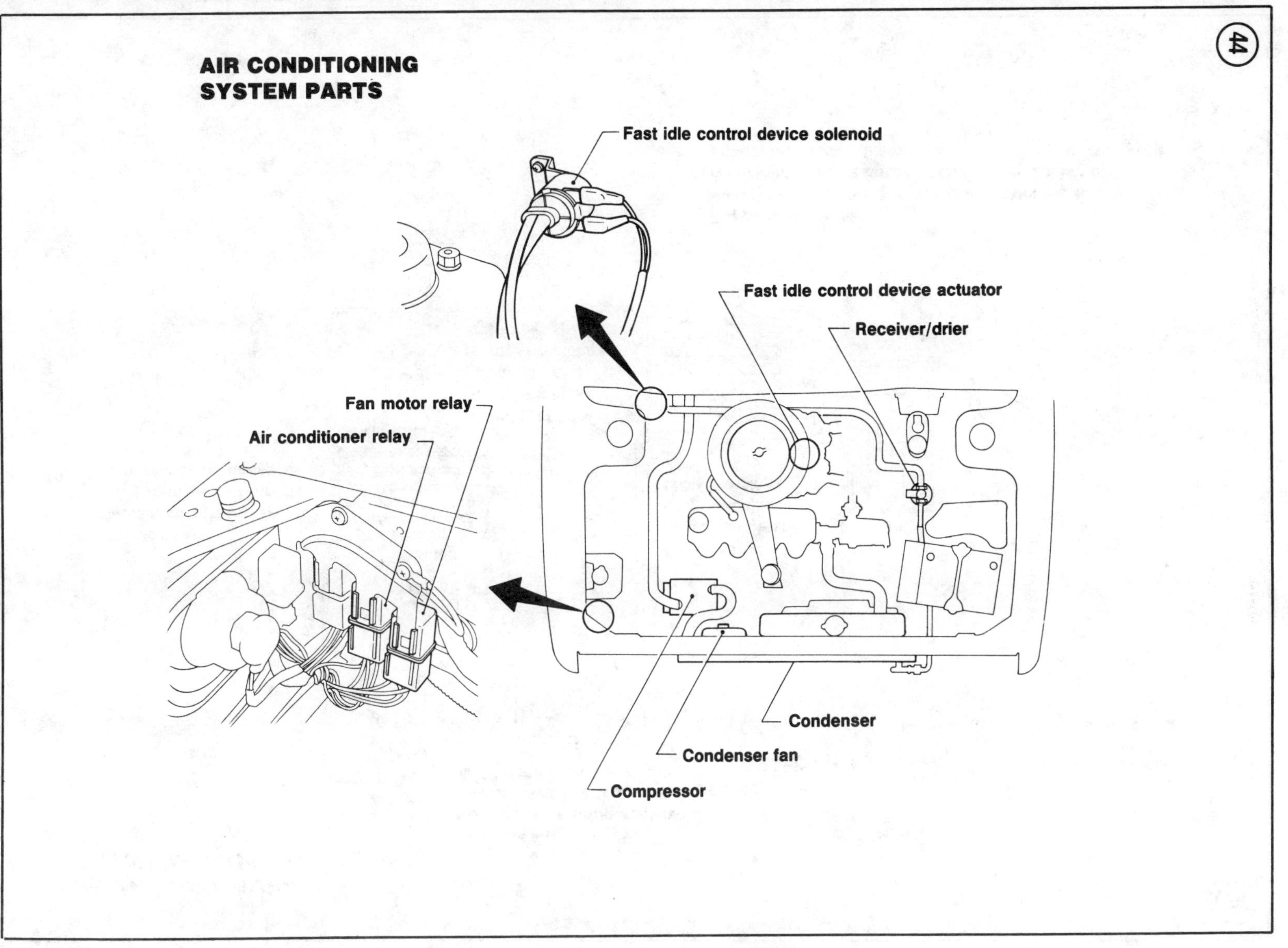

AIR CONDITIONING SCHEMATIC

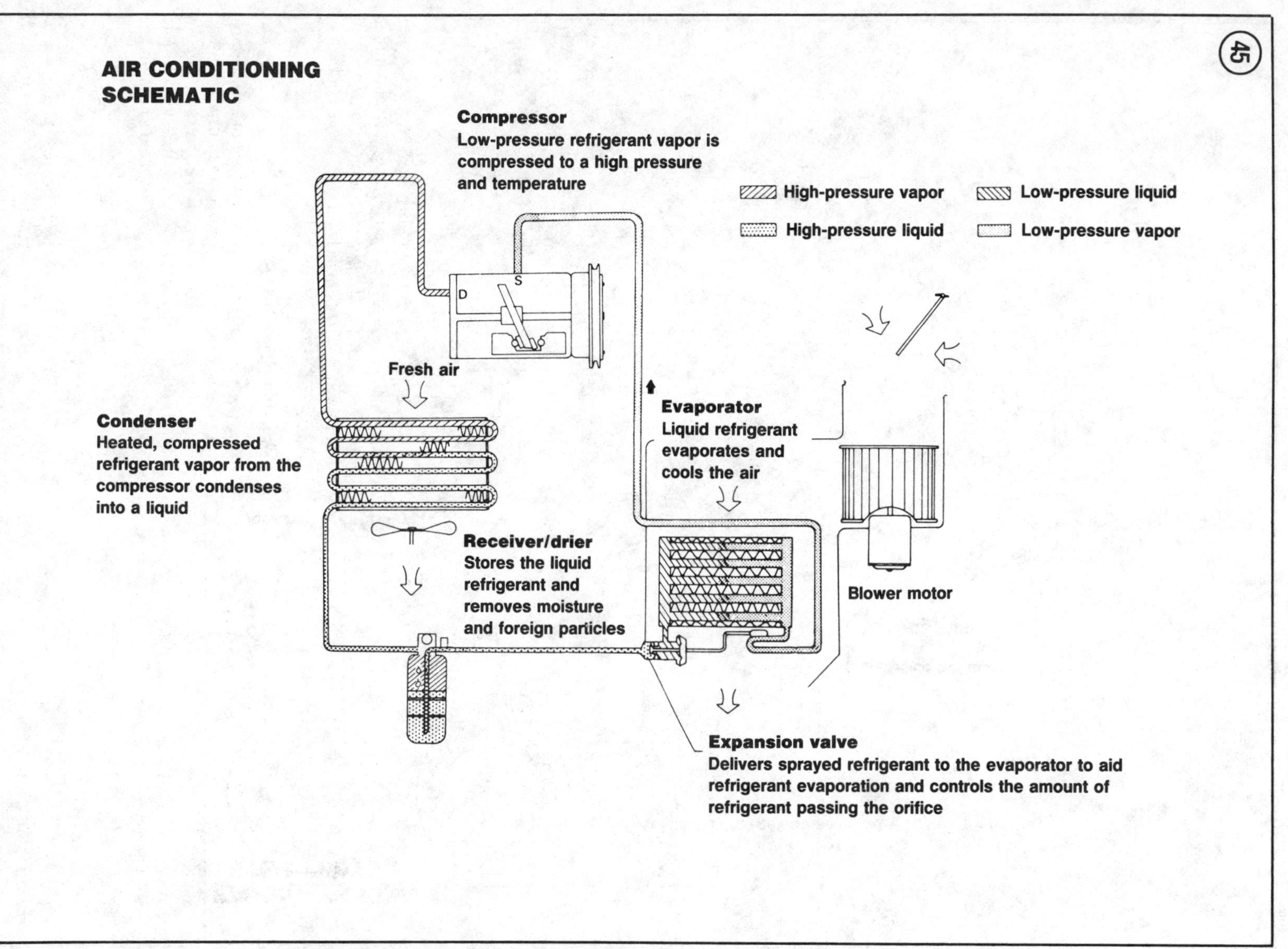

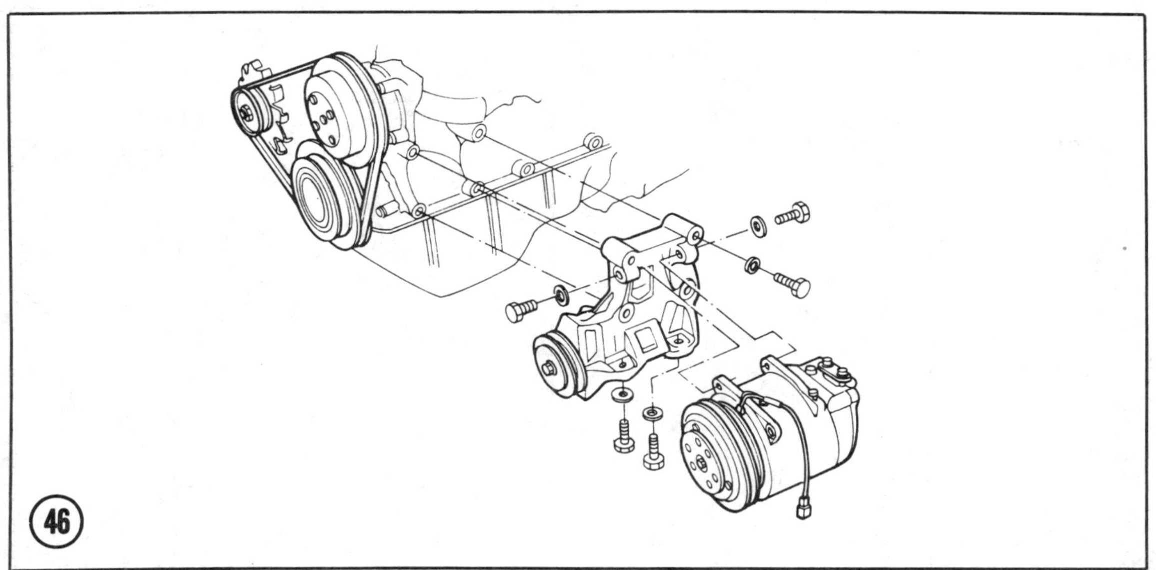

(46)

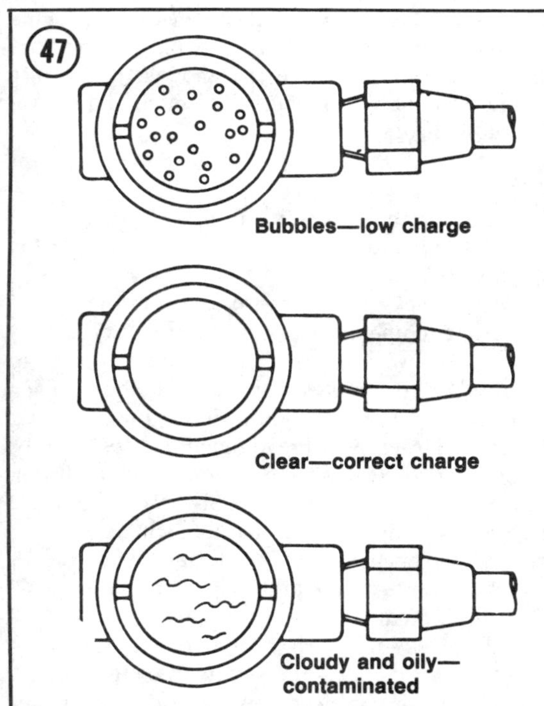

(47)

low-pressure liquid to a warm, high-pressure vapor. The vapor flows back to the compressor, where the cycle begins again.

GET TO KNOW YOUR VEHICLE'S SYSTEM

With **Figure 43** and **Figure 44** as a guide, locate each of the following components in turn:

a. Compressor.
b. Condenser.
c. Receiver/drier.
d. Expansion valve.
e. Evaporator.

Compressor

The compressor is located on the front of the engine, like the alternator, and is driven by a V-belt. See **Figure 46**. The large pulley on the front of the compressor contains an electromagnetic clutch. This activates and operates the compressor when the air conditioning is switched on.

Condenser

The condenser is mounted in front of the radiator. Air passing through the fins and tubes removes heat from the refrigerant in the same manner it removes heat from the engine coolant as it passes through the radiator.

Receiver/Drier

The receiver/drier is a small tank-like unit, mounted in the right front corner of the engine compartment. It incorporates a sight glass (**Figure 47**) through which refrigerant flow can be seen. The refrigerant's appearance is used to troubleshoot the system.

Expansion Valve

The expansion valve is located between the receiver/drier and the evaporator. It is mounted on the cooling unit in the passenger compartment.

Evaporator

The evaporator is located in the passenger compartment, inside the cooling unit. Warm air is blown across the fins and tubes, where it is cooled and dried and then ducted into the passenger compartment.

ROUTINE MAINTENANCE

Preventive maintenance of the air conditioning system is easy; at least once a month, even in cold weather, start your engine, turn on the air conditioner and operate it at each of the control settings. Operate the air conditioner for about 5 minutes. This will ensure that the compressor seal does not deform from sitting in the same position for a long period of time. If this occurs, the seal is likely to leak.

The efficiency of the air conditioning system also depends in great part on the efficiency of the cooling system. This is because some of the heat from the condenser passes through the radiator. If the cooling system is dirty or low on coolant, it may be impossible to operate the air conditioner without overheating. Inspect the coolant. If necessary, flush and refill the cooling system as described in this chapter.

With an air hose and a soft brush, clean the radiator and condenser fins and tubes to remove bugs, leaves and other imbedded debris.

Check drive belt tension as described in Chapter Three.

If the condition of the cooling system thermostat is in doubt, test it as described in this chapter.

Once you are sure the cooling system is in good condition, the air conditioning system can be inspected.

Inspection

1. Clean all lines, fittings and system components with solvent and a clean rag. Pay particular attention to the fittings; oily dirt around connections almost certainly indicates a leak. Oil from the compressor will migrate through the system to the leak. Carefully tighten the connection, but don't overtighten and strip the threads. If the leak persists, it will soon be apparent once again as oily dirt accumulates. Clean the sight glass with a clean, dry cloth.
2. Clean the condenser fins and tubes with a soft brush and an air hose or with a high-pressure stream of water from a garden hose. Remove bugs, leaves and other imbedded debris. Carefully straighten any bent fins with a screwdriver, taking care not to puncture or dent the tubes.

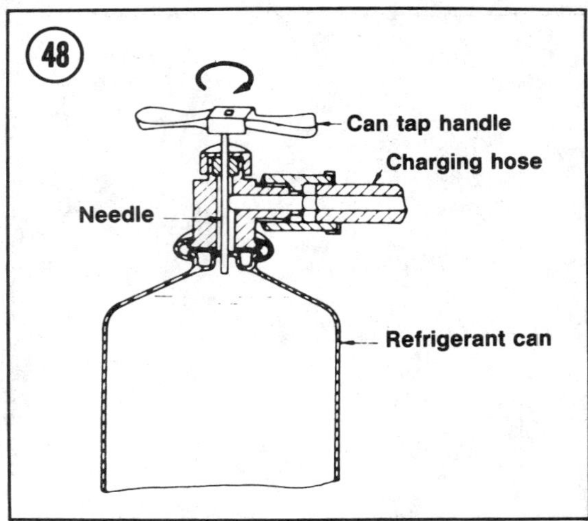

3. Start the engine and check the operation of the blower motor and the compressor clutch by turning the controls on and off. If either the blower or the clutch fails to operate, shut off the engine and check the fuses. If they are blown, replace them. If not, remove them and clean the fuse holder contacts. Then check the clutch and blower operation again.

Testing

1. Place the transmission in NEUTRAL (manual transmission) or PARK (automatic). Set the handbrake.
2. Start the engine and run it at a fast idle.
3. Set the temperature control to its coldest setting and the blower to high. Allow the system to operate for 10 minutes with the doors open. Then shut them and set the blower on its lowest setting.
4. Check air temperature at the outlet. It should be noticeably colder than the surrounding air. If not, the refrigerant level is probably low. Check the sight glass as described in the following step.
5. Run the engine at a fast idle and switch on the air conditioning. Look at the sight glass (**Figure 47**) and check for the following:
   a. Bubbles—the refrigerant level is low.
   b. Oily or cloudy—the system is contaminated. Have it serviced by a dealer or air conditioning shop.
   c. Clear glass—either there is enough refrigerant, too much or the system is so close to empty it can't make bubbles. If there is no difference between the inlet and outlet air temperatures, the system is probably near empty. If the system does blow cold air, it either has the right amount of refrigerant or too much. To tell which, turn off the air conditioner while

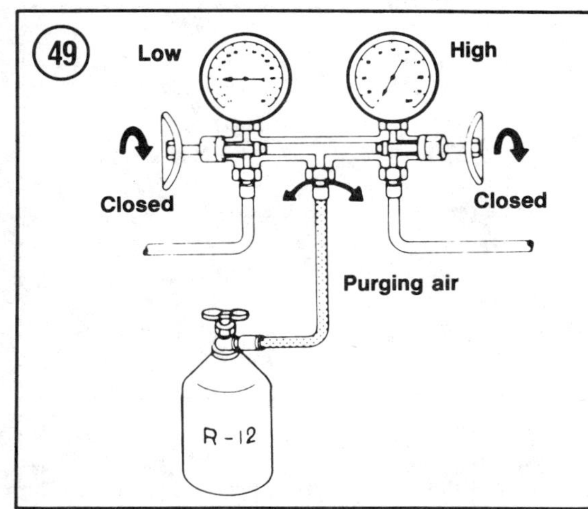

watching the sight glass. If the refrigerant foams, then clears up, the amount is correct. If it doesn't foam, but stays clear, there is too much.

REFRIGERANT

The air conditioning system uses a refrigerant called dichlorodifluoromethane or R-12.

WARNING
R-12 creates freezing temperatures when it evaporates. This can cause frostbite if it touches skin and blindness if it touches the eyes. If discharged near an open flame, R-12 forms poisonous gas. If the refrigerant can is hooked up to the pressure side of the compressor, it may explode. Always wear safety goggles when working with R-12.

Charging

This section applies to partially discharged or empty air conditioning systems. If a hose has been disconnected or any internal part of the system exposed to air, the system should be evacuated and recharged by a dealer or air conditioning shop. Recharge kits are available from auto parts stores. Be sure the kit includes a gauge set.

NOTE
Gauge sets are expensive, but so is having the system professsionally recharged. Compare the price of a gauge set with the cost of a professional charging job before proceeding.

1. Carefully read and understand the gauge manufacturer's instructions before charging the system.

WARNING
During the next step, water temperature must not exceed 40° C (104° F). If it does, the can may explode.

2. Place the refrigerant can in a pan of warm water.
3. Turn the handle of the refrigerant can tap valve all the way counterclockwise to retract the needle. See **Figure 48**.
4. Turn the disc on the can tap valve all the way counterclockwise. Install the valve on the can.
5. Connect the center hose to the can tap valve.
6. Make sure the gauge valves are closed.
7. Turn the can tap valve clockwise to make a hole in the can.
8. Turn the handle all the way counterclockwise to open the hole in the can.
9. Slowly loosen the nut connecting the center hose to the gauge set until hissing can be heard. See **Figure 49**. Let this continue for a few seconds to purge air from the hose, then tighten the nut.

CAUTION
During the next steps, the refrigerant can must remain upright. If it is turned upside down, refrigerant will enter the system as a liquid, which may damage the compressor.

10. Open the low-pressure valve (**Figure 50**). Adjust the valve so the gauge reads no more than 2.8 kg/cm² (40 psi).

CAUTION
Leave the high-pressure valve closed at all times.

11. Run the engine at a fast idle and turn on the air conditioner. Let the system charge until the sight glass is free of air bubbles. See **Figure 47**.

NOTE
If the system is nearly empty, another can of refrigerant will be needed. Attach it as described in the following steps.

12. Close the low-pressure valve.
13. Remove the can tap valve and attach a new can. Don't make a hole in the new can yet.
14. Slightly loosen the can tap valve disc. Barely open the low-pressure valve for a few seconds to purge air from the hose. Close the low-pressure valve, then tighten the can tap valve disc.
15. Turn the can tap valve handle clockwise to make a hole in the can. Let the system charge until the sight glass is free of air bubbles.
16. Once the system is fully charged, close the low-pressure valve.

6

17. Close the can tap valve. Very slowly loosen the charge line to allow any remaining refrigerant to escape.

> *WARNING*
> *Wear gloves and safety goggles to prevent frostbite and blindness. Do not allow any open flame near the refrigerant or poisonous gas may be formed.*

18. Turn off the engine. Cover the compressor service valve fittings with a shop rag, then quickly disconnect them.

19. Install the caps on the service valves.

TROUBLESHOOTING

If the air conditioner fails to blow cold air, the following steps will help locate the problem.

1. First, stop the car and look at the control settings. One of the most common air conditioning problems occurs when the temperature is set for maximum cold and the blower is set on low. This promotes ice buildup on the evaporator fins and tubes, particularly in humid weather. Eventually, the evaporator will ice over completely and restrict air flow. Turn the blower on high and place a hand over an air outlet. If the blower is running but there is little or no air flowing through the outlet, the evaporator is probably iced up. Leave the blower on high and turn the temperature control off or to its warmest setting and wait. It will take 10-15 minutes for the ice to start melting.

2. If the blower is not running, the fuse may be blown, there may be a loose wiring connection or the motor may be burned out. First, check the fuse block for a blown or incorrectly seated fuse. Then check the wiring for loose connections.

3. Shut off the engine and inspect the compressor drive belt. If loose or worn, tighten or replace. See Chapter Three.

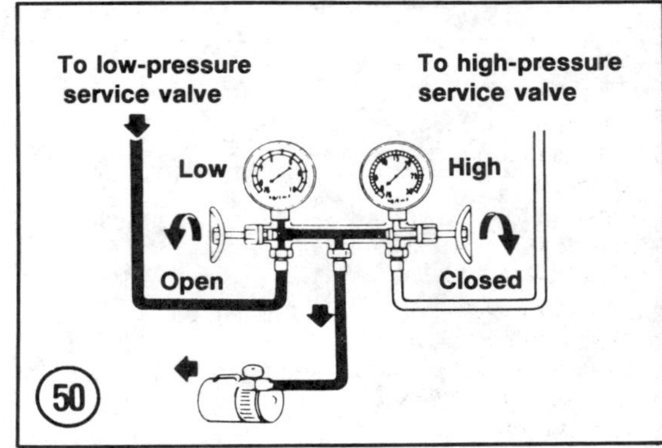

4. Start the engine. Check the compressor clutch by turning the air conditioning on and off. If the clutch does not activate, its fuse may be blown or the evaporator temperature-limiting switches may be defective. If the fuse is defective, replace it. If the fuse is not the problem, have the system checked by a dealer or air conditioning shop.

5. If the system checks out okay to this point, start the engine, turn on the air conditioner and watch the refrigerant through the sight glass. If it fills with bubbles after a few seconds, the refrigerant level is low. If the sight glass is oily or cloudy, the system is contaminated and should be serviced by a shop as soon as possible. Corrosion and deterioration occur very quickly and if not taken care of at once will result in a very expensive repair job.

6. If the system still appears to be operating as it should but air flow into the passenger compartment is not cold, check the condenser and cooling system radiator for debris that could block air flow. Recheck the cooling system as described under *Inspection* in this chapter.

7. If the preceding steps have not solved the problem, take the car to a dealer or air conditioning shop for service.

Table 1   COOLING SYSTEM SPECIFICATIONS

Cooling system capacity	
Gasoline	
Manual transmission	4.7 liters (5 qt.)
Automatic transmission	5.3 liters (5 5/8 qt.)
Diesel	7 liters (7 3/8 qt.)
Reservoir tank capacity	0.7 liters (3/4 qt.)
Thermostat opening temperature	
Cold-weather type	88° C (190° F)
Standard type	82° C (180° F)
Warm-weather type*	76.5° C (170° F)
Thermostat maximum opening temperature	
Cold-weather type	100° C (212° F)
Standard type	95° C (203° F)
Warm-weather type*	90° C (194° F)
Fan operating temperature	90° C (194° F)

*1982 only.

Table 2   TIGHTENING TORQUES

Fastener	N•m	ft.-lb.
Water outlet elbow bolts (gasoline)	8-11	6-8
Water pump bolts (gasoline)	9-14	6.5-10.0
Water inlet elbow bolts (diesel)	16-21	12-15

6

ELECTRICAL SYSTEM

This chapter provides service procedures for the battery, charging system, starter, lights, switches, windshield wipers and washers, fuses and fusible links, turn indicators, instruments, gasoline engine ignition system and horn. **Table 1** and **Table 2** are at the end of the chapter.

BATTERY

Care and Inspection

Some of the following steps apply to unsealed batteries, which are used on some MPG models. This type has filler caps through which water is periodically added. Maintenance-free batteries have no filler caps and do not require the addition of water.

1. Disconnect the negative and then the positive battery cable and remove the battery.

2. Clean the top of the battery with a baking soda and water solution. Scrub it with a stiff bristle brush. Wipe the battery clean with a cloth moistened in ammonia or baking soda solution.

> *CAUTION*
> *Keep cleaning solution out of battery cells or the electrolyte will be seriously weakened.*

3. Clean battery terminals with a stiff wire brush or one of the many tools made for this purpose.

4. Check entire battery case for cracks, clogged vents or a warped case. See **Figure 1**. Replace batteries that show these conditions.

5. On maintenance-free batteries, check the condition indicator (**Figure 2**). If it is blue (**Figure 3**), the battery is properly charged. If it is transparent (**Figure 4**), the battery needs to be recharged.

6. Install the battery and reconnect the battery cables (first positive and then negative).

> *CAUTION*
> *Be sure the battery cables are connected to the proper terminals. Connecting the battery backwards can damage the alternator.*

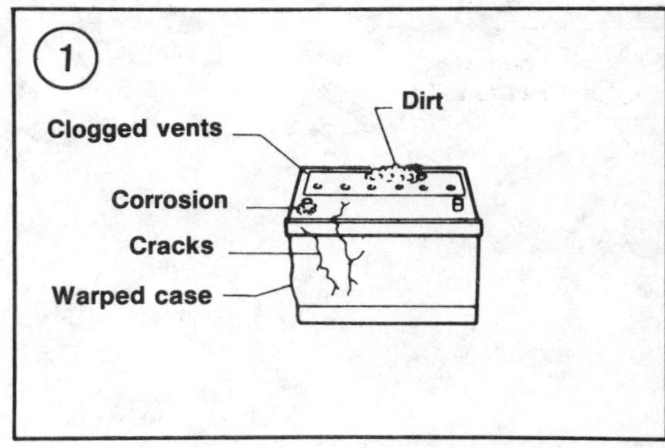

7. Coat the battery connections with Vaseline or light mineral grease after tightening.

8. If the battery has removable filler caps, check electrolyte level. Top up with distilled water if necessary.

Testing (Unsealed Batteries)

Hydrometer testing is the best way to check battery condition. Use a hydrometer with numbered graduations from 1.100-1.300 rather than one with just color-coded bands. To use the hydrometer, squeeze the rubber ball, insert the tip in the cell and release the ball (**Figure 5**).

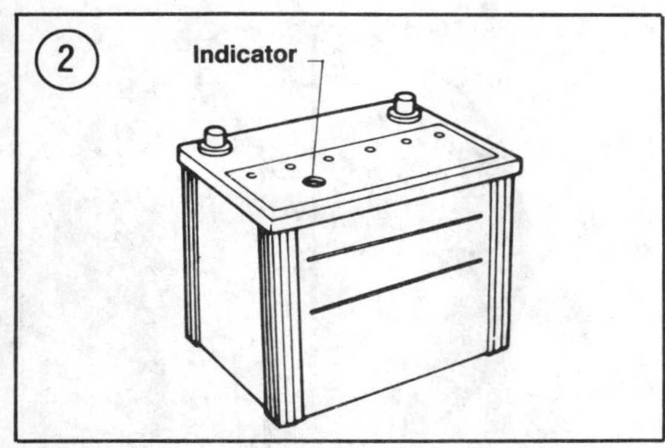

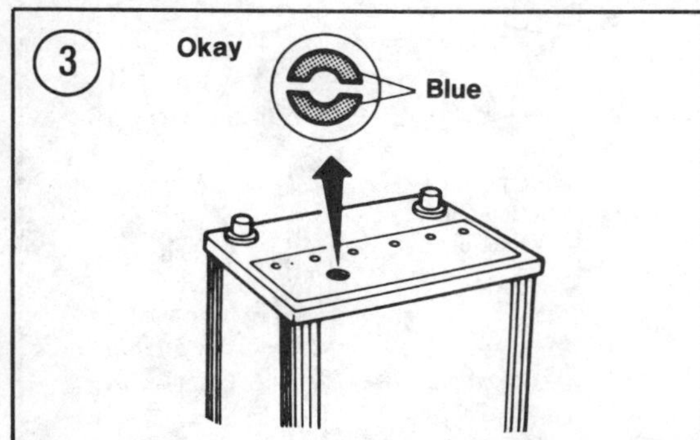

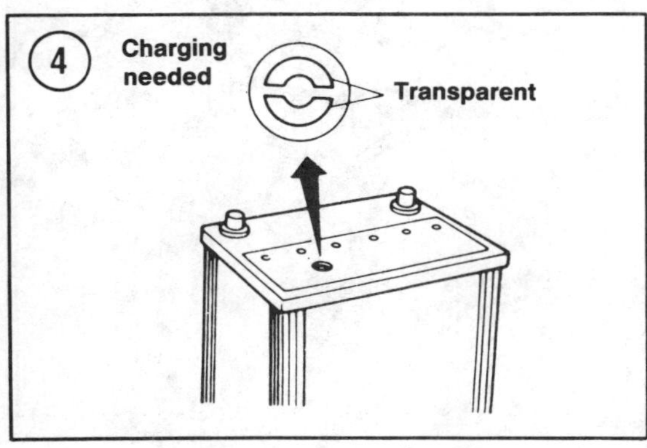

Draw enough electrolyte to float the weighted float inside the hydrometer. Note the number in line with the surface of the electrolyte. This is the specific gravity for the cell. Return the electrolyte to the cell from which it came.

The specific gravity of the electrolyte in each battery cell is an excellent indicator of that cell's condition. A fully charged cell will read 1.260 or more at 20° C (68° F). If the cells test below 1.200, the battery must be recharged. Charging is also necessary if the specific gravity of the cell varies more than 0.025 from cell to cell.

NOTE
For every 10° F above 80° (25° C) electrolyte temperature, add 0.004 to specific gravity reading. For every 10° below 80° F (25° C), subtract 0.004.

Charging

The battery need not be removed from the car for charging. Just make certain that the area is well ventilated and that there is no chance of sparks or flames occurring near the battery.

WARNING
Charging batteries give off highly explosive hydrogen gas. If this explodes, it may spray battery acid over a wide area.

Disconnect the cables from the battery. On unsealed batteries, make sure the electrolyte is fully topped up.

WARNING
Connect the charger to the battery before plugging it in.

Connect the charger to the battery—negative to negative, positive to positive. If the charger output is variable, select a low setting (5-10 amps), set the voltage selector to 12 volts and plug the charger in. If the battery is severely discharged, allow it to charge for at least 8 hours. Batteries that aren't as badly discharged require less charging time. **Table 1** gives approximate charge rates. On unsealed batteries, check charging progress with the hydrometer.

CHARGING SYSTEM

The charging system consists of the battery, alternator with built-in integrated circuit regulator, charge warning lamp and wiring. **Figure 6** is a diagram of the 1982 charging system. **Figure 7** shows the 1983 gasoline system. **Figure 8** shows the diesel version.

Alternator repairs, including regulator replacement, are not practical for home mechanics. If test procedures indicate a defective alternator or regulator, replace the alternator with a new or rebuilt unit.

Charging System Test

Figure 9 is a flow chart which shows how to test the charging system. During the test, it may be necessary to ground the F terminal, which is inside the alternator. To do this on gasoline models, insert a piece of stiff wire into the hole shown in **Figure 10** until it touches the brushes. Attach the other end of the wire to the alternator body. On diesels, remove the vacuum pump from the back of the alternator as described in Chapter Eleven. Insert a piece of stiff wire into the hole shown in **Figure 11** until it touches the brushes. Attach the other end of the wire to the alternator body.

> *WARNING*
> *Do not drive the car unless the vacuum pump is installed and working properly. It supplies vacuum to the brake booster.*

Alternator Removal/Installation

1. Disconnect the negative cable from the battery.
2. Remove the alternator belt as described in Chapter Three.
3. On diesels, remove the vacuum pump from the alternator as described in Chapter Eleven.
4. Disconnect the alternator wires.
5. Remove the alternator mounting and adjusting bolts. Take the alternator off the engine.
6. Installation is the reverse of removal. Adjust the alternator belt as described in Chapter Three.

STARTER

Starter repairs are not practical for home mechanics. The following sections describe testing and replacement.

Testing (On Car)

Figure 12 is a flow chart which tells how to test the starter.

Removal/Installation

1. Disconnect the negative cable from the battery.
2. Disconnect the starter wires.
3. Remove the starter mounting bolts and take the starter out.
4. Installation is the reverse of removal.

Testing (Off Car)

This test will isolate starter problems to the starter motor or starter circuit. It requires a length of wire and a pair of jumper cables.
1. Remove the starter as described in this chapter.
2. Place the starter on a hard surface such a garage floor or driveway.
3. Connect one of the jumper cables from the negative terminal of the car's battery to the starter body. The starter mounting bolt flange is a convenient place to make this connection.

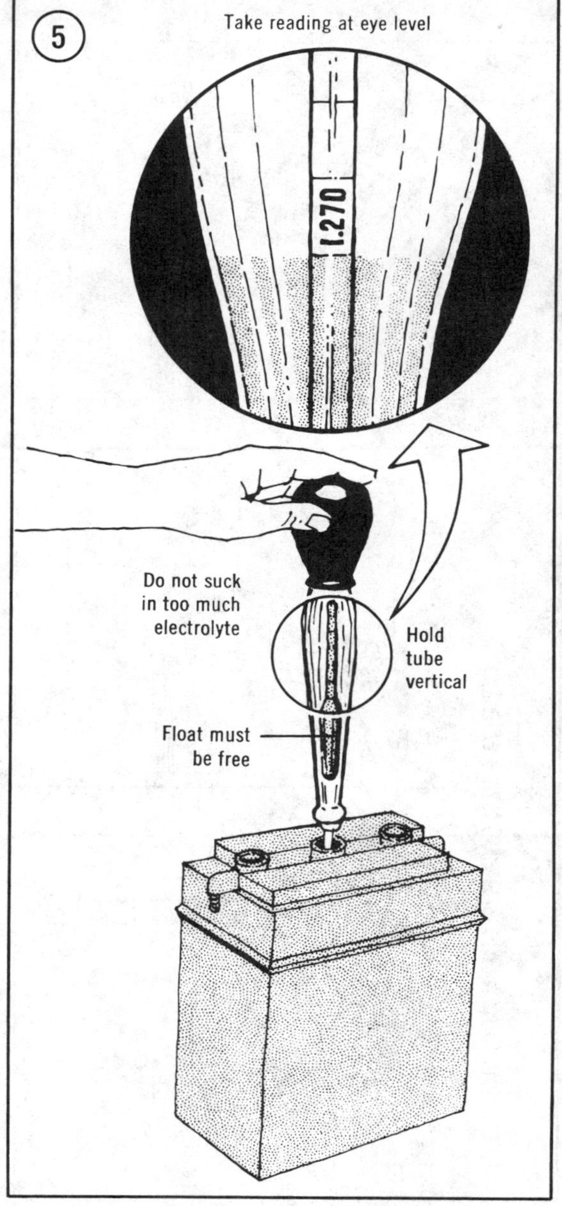

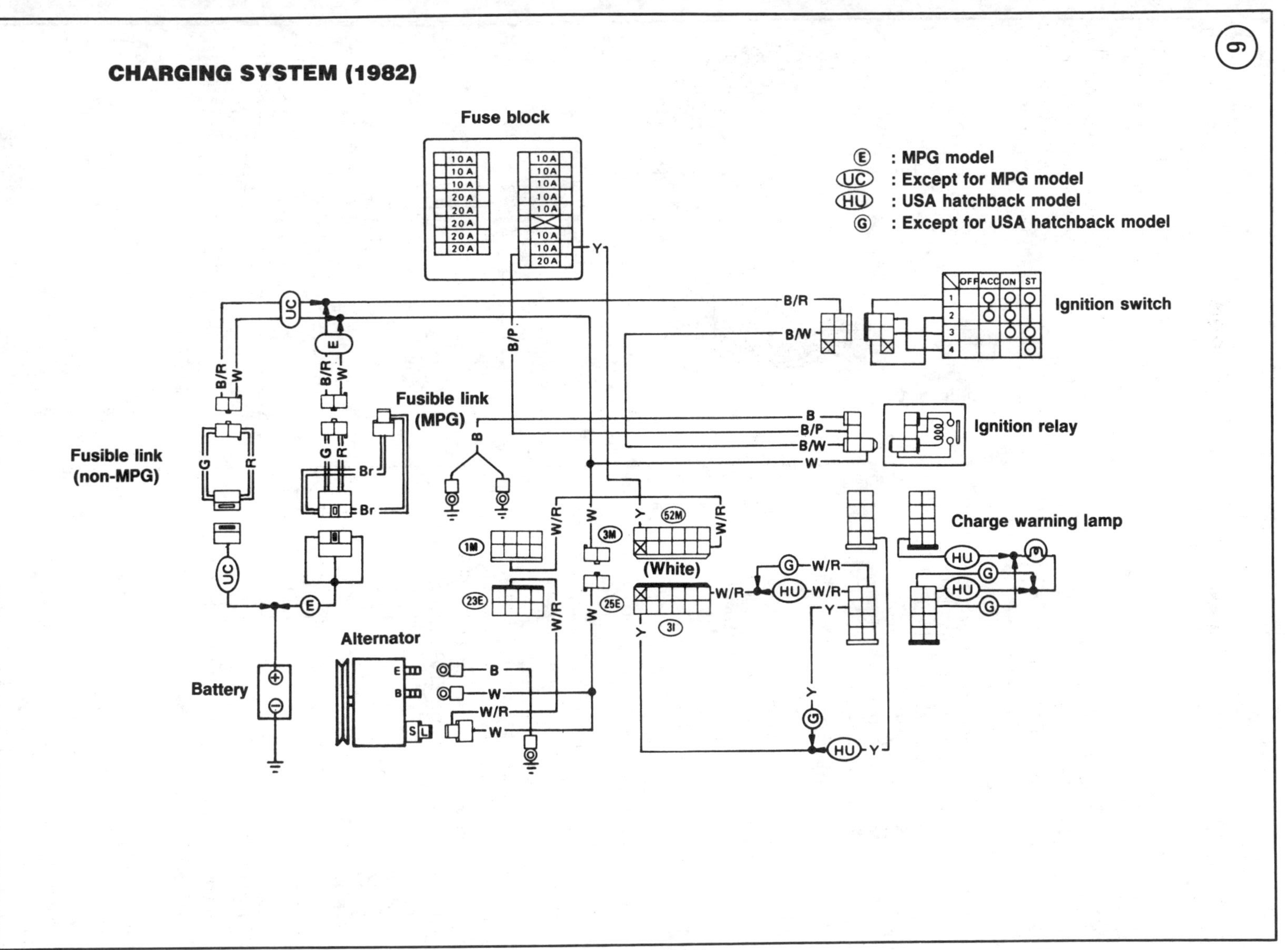
6
7
CHARGING SYSTEM (1982)
Fuse block
E : MPG model
UC : Except for MPG model
HU : USA hatchback model
G : Except for USA hatchback model
10 A
10 A
10 A
20 A
20 A
20 A
20 A
20 A
10 A
10 A
10 A
10 A
10 A
10 A
20 A
Y
B/P
OFF ACC ON ST
1
2
3
4
B/R
B/W
Ignition switch
B
B/P
B/W
W
Ignition relay
UC
E
B/R
W
B/R
W
G R
G R
Br
Br
Fusible link (MPG)
B
Fusible link (non-MPG)
UC
E
Battery
Alternator
E B
B W
W/R
W
S L
W/R
W
1M
23E
W/R
W
3M
W
25E
52M
(White)
31
Y
Y
W/R
G W/R
HU W/R
Y
G
Y
HU Y
Charge warning lamp
HU G
HU G

CHARGING SYSTEM
(1983 GASOLINE ENGINE)

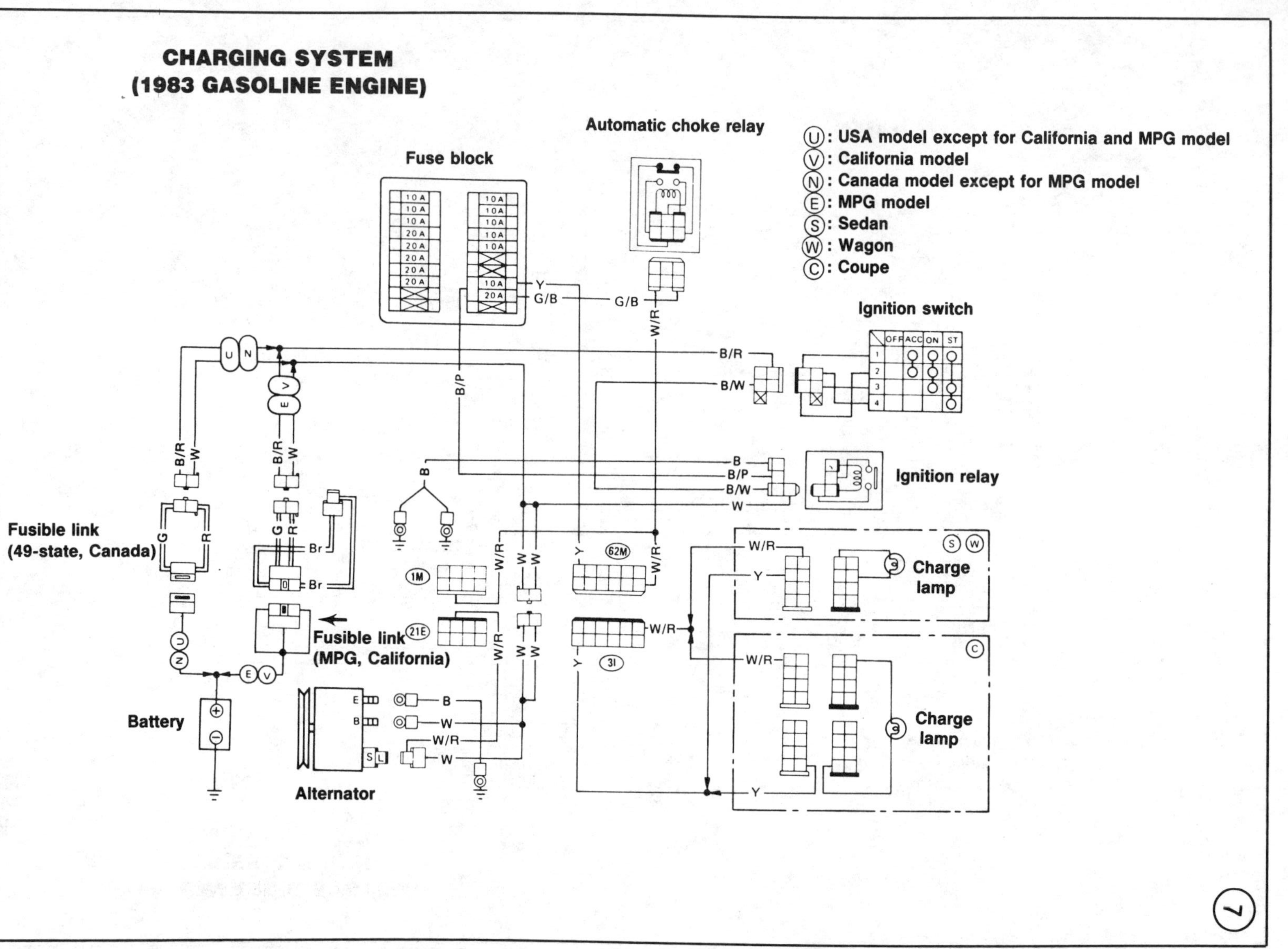

8
CHARGING SYSTEM
(DIESEL ENGINE)
Ignition relay
Fuse block
Ignition switch
Fusible link
Alternator
Battery
Bulb check relay
Charge lamp

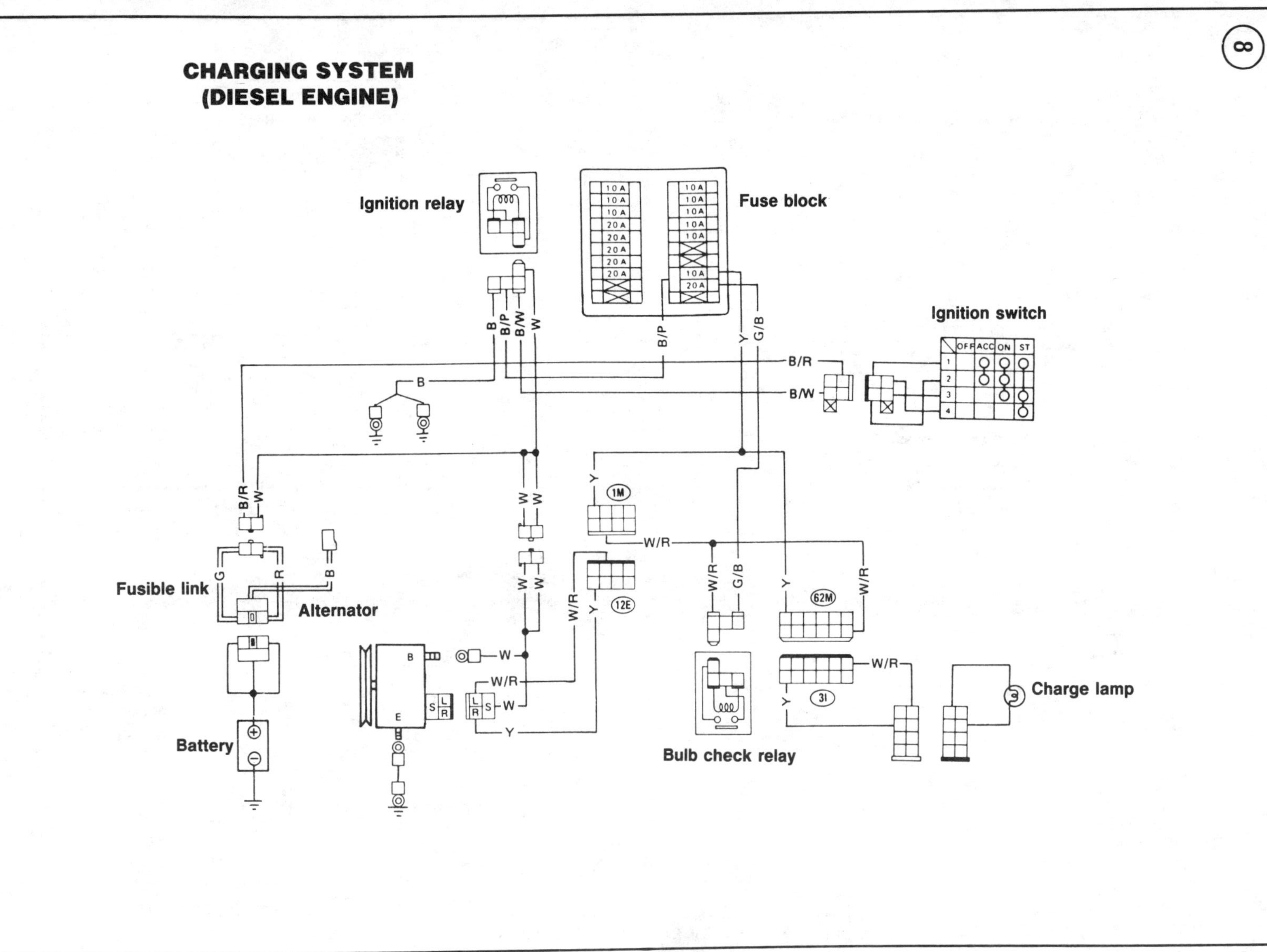

7

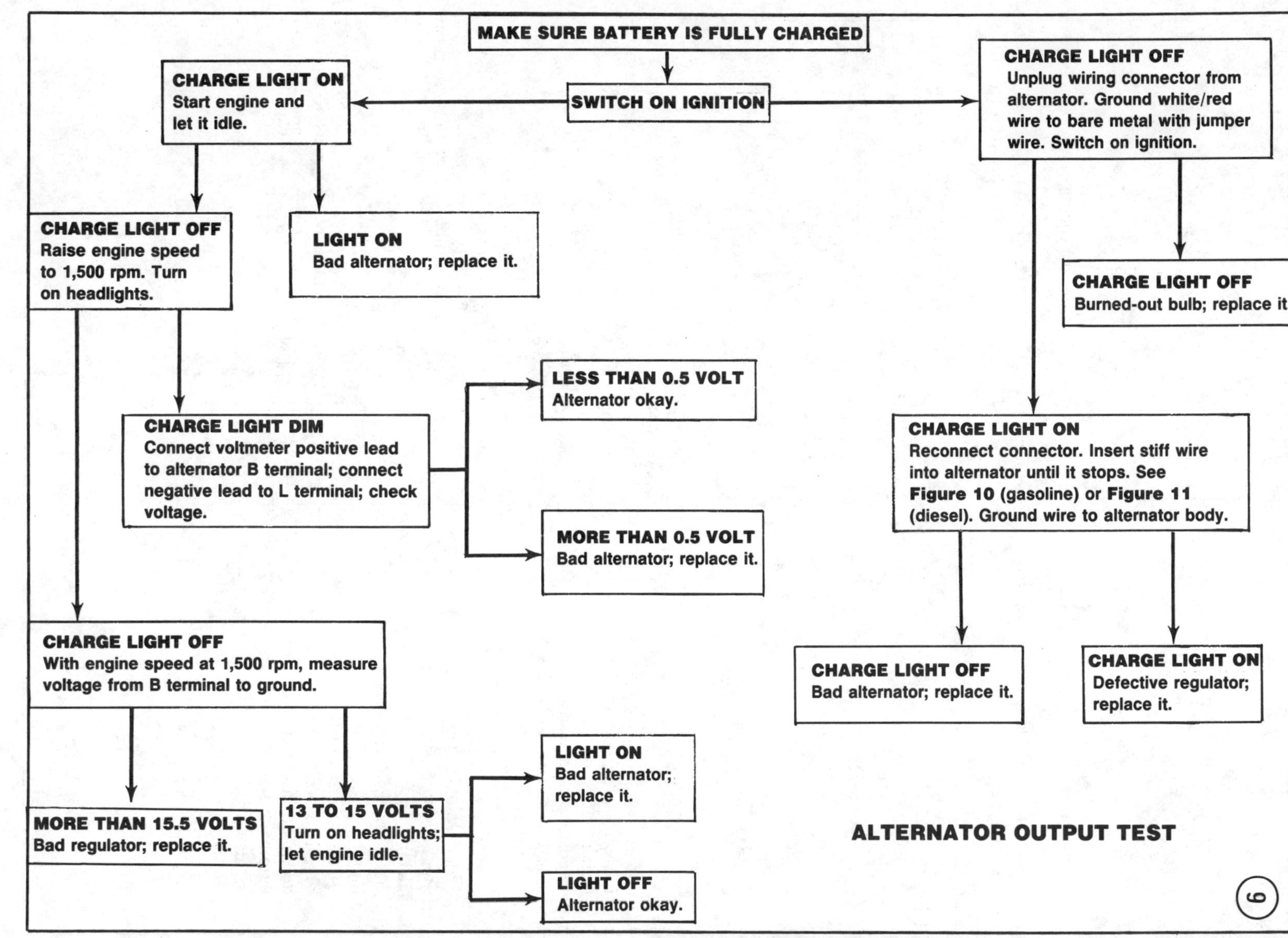

MAKE SURE BATTERY IS FULLY CHARGED
SWITCH ON IGNITION
CHARGE LIGHT ON
Start engine and let it idle.
CHARGE LIGHT OFF
Unplug wiring connector from alternator. Ground white/red wire to bare metal with jumper wire. Switch on ignition.
CHARGE LIGHT OFF
Raise engine speed to 1,500 rpm. Turn on headlights.
LIGHT ON
Bad alternator; replace it.
CHARGE LIGHT OFF
Burned-out bulb; replace it.
CHARGE LIGHT DIM
Connect voltmeter positive lead to alternator B terminal; connect negative lead to L terminal; check voltage.
LESS THAN 0.5 VOLT
Alternator okay.
MORE THAN 0.5 VOLT
Bad alternator; replace it.
CHARGE LIGHT ON
Reconnect connector. Insert stiff wire into alternator until it stops. See Figure 10 (gasoline) or Figure 11 (diesel). Ground wire to alternator body.
CHARGE LIGHT OFF
With engine speed at 1,500 rpm, measure voltage from B terminal to ground.
CHARGE LIGHT OFF
Bad alternator; replace it.
CHARGE LIGHT ON
Defective regulator; replace it.
MORE THAN 15.5 VOLTS
Bad regulator; replace it.
13 TO 15 VOLTS
Turn on headlights; let engine idle.
LIGHT ON
Bad alternator; replace it.
LIGHT OFF
Alternator okay.
ALTERNATOR OUTPUT TEST
9

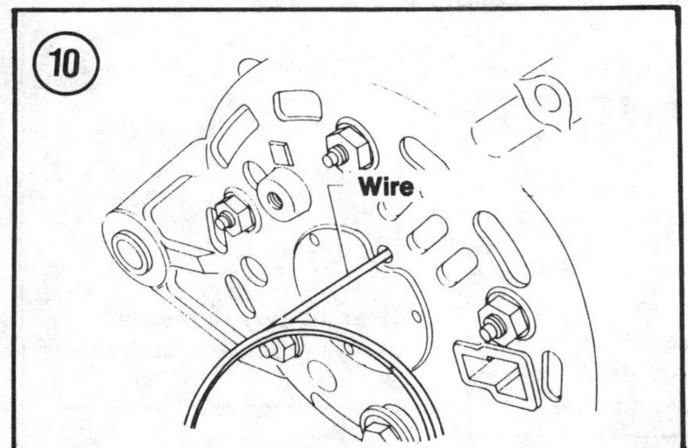

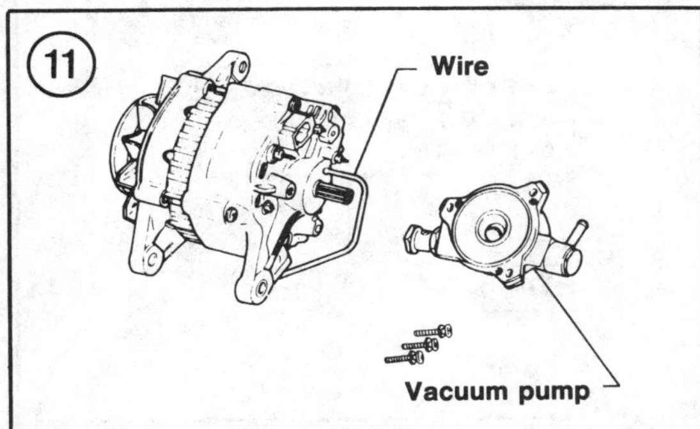

4. Connect the other jumper cable from the positive terminal of the car's battery to the starter B terminal. This is the terminal to which the battery positive cable is connected when the starter is installed in the car.

5. Hold the starter down with a piece of wood. Connect a length of wire between the positive terminal of the car's battery and the S terminal on the starter solenoid. This is the terminal to which the thin wire is connected when the starter is installed in the car. The starter pinion should move out with a firm click. The starter should spin freely and rapidly:

   a. If the starter performs as described in this step, it is good. Check the ignition switch as described in this chapter. If equipped with an automatic transaxle, test the inhibitor switch as described in Chapter Nine. Check the starter wiring.

   b. If the starter doesn't perform as described in this step, replace it as described in this chapter.

LIGHTING SYSTEM

Bulb specifications are listed in **Table 2**.

Headlights

If one headlight fails to work, the cause is probably a bad wiring connection or burned-out bulb. If one headlight is dim, the cause is probably a bad fuse. If the high beams or low beams fail to work or the headlights can't be switched from high beams to low beams or vice versa, test the lighting switch and dimmer relay as described in this chapter.

1. Remove the front parking light screws and take the parking light off. See **Figure 13**.

2. Remove the headlight mounting screws (**Figure 14**). Take the bulb out and unplug the wiring connector.

> *CAUTION*
> *Do not turn the aiming screws (**Figure 15**).*

3. Connect the wiring connector to the new bulb. Position the bulb on the housing and install the mounting screws.

4. Install the clearance light.

5. If necessary, have headlight aim adjusted by a dealer or certified lamp adjusting station.

Front Turn Signals

To replace a bulb, remove the lens securing screws and take off the lens. See **Figure 16**. Press the bulb into its socket and turn counterclockwise to remove. Install in the reverse order.

Front Parking Lights

To replace a bulb, remove the light assembly screws and take the light off. See **Figure 17**. Remove the bulb socket screws and take the socket off. Presss the bulb into its socket and turn counterclockwise to remove. Install in the reverse order.

Side Marker Lights

To replace a bulb, remove the lens securing screws and take off the lens. See **Figure 18**. Pull the bulb out of its socket, push in a new one and reinstall the lens.

Rear Combination Lights

Rear combination lights include rear turn signals, brake-taillights and backup lights. On coupes, they include the license plate lights as well.

> *NOTE*
> *If both brake lights or both taillights fail to work and the bulbs are in good condition, test the brake-taillight sensor as described in this chapter.*

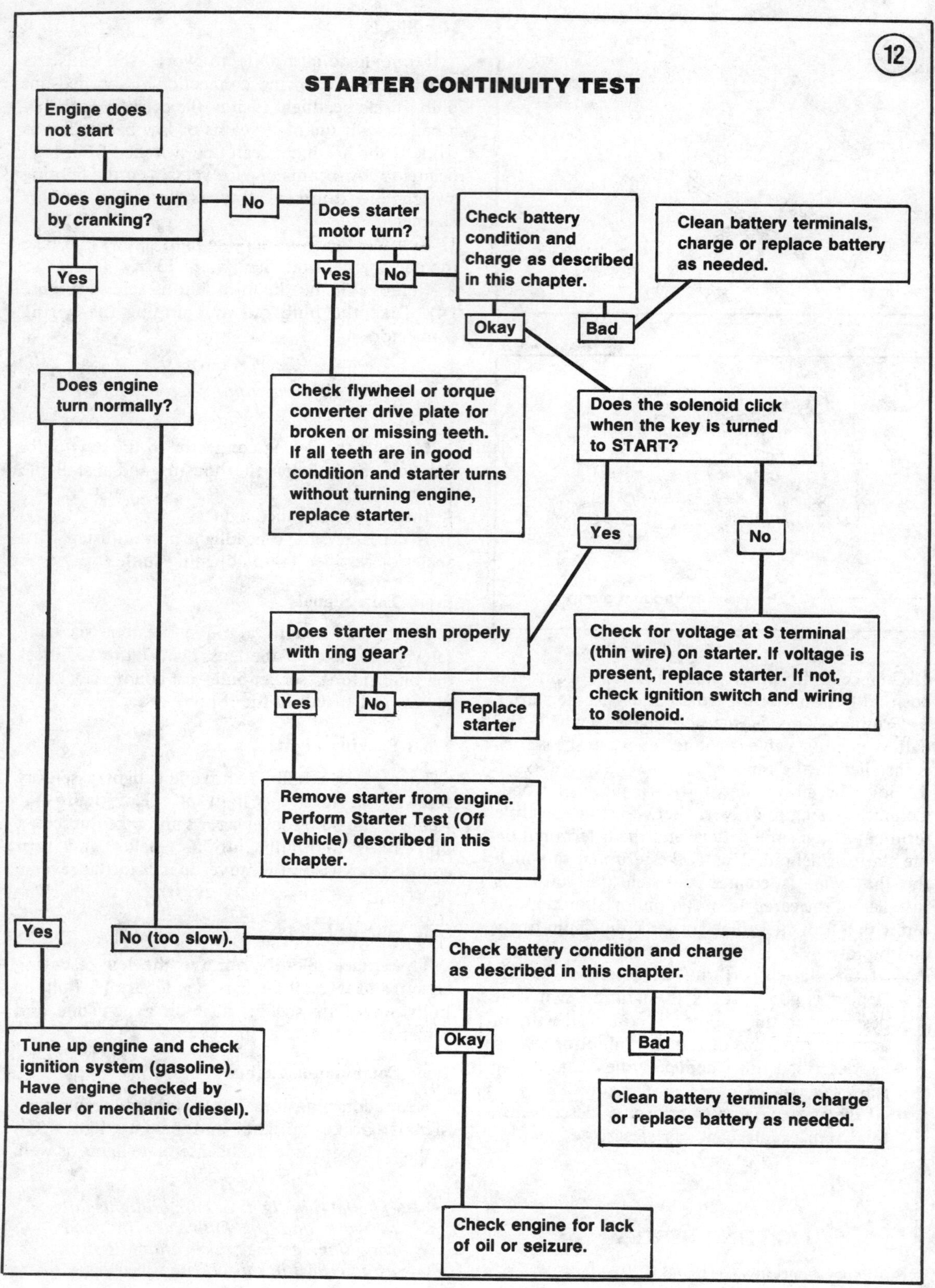
STARTER CONTINUITY TEST
12
Engine does not start
Does engine turn by cranking?
No
Does starter motor turn?
Yes
Yes
No
Check battery condition and charge as described in this chapter.
Clean battery terminals, charge or replace battery as needed.
Okay
Bad
Does engine turn normally?
Check flywheel or torque converter drive plate for broken or missing teeth. If all teeth are in good condition and starter turns without turning engine, replace starter.
Does the solenoid click when the key is turned to START?
Yes
No
Does starter mesh properly with ring gear?
Check for voltage at S terminal (thin wire) on starter. If voltage is present, replace starter. If not, check ignition switch and wiring to solenoid.
Yes
No
Replace starter
Remove starter from engine. Perform Starter Test (Off Vehicle) described in this chapter.
Yes
No (too slow).
Check battery condition and charge as described in this chapter.
Tune up engine and check ignition system (gasoline). Have engine checked by dealer or mechanic (diesel).
Okay
Bad
Clean battery terminals, charge or replace battery as needed.
Check engine for lack of oil or seizure.

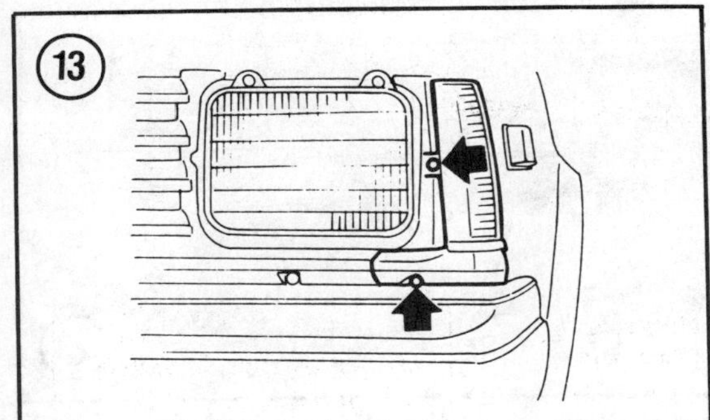

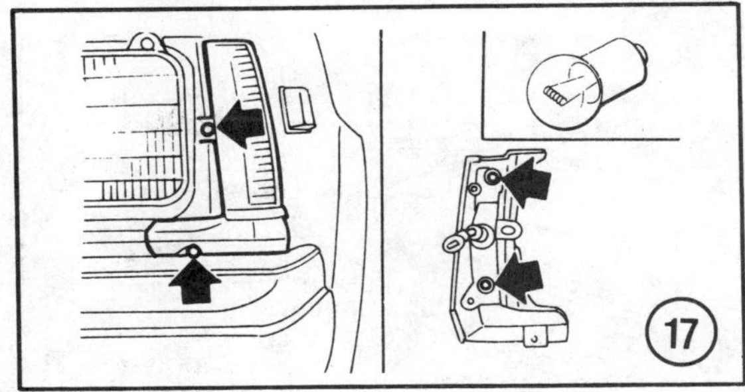

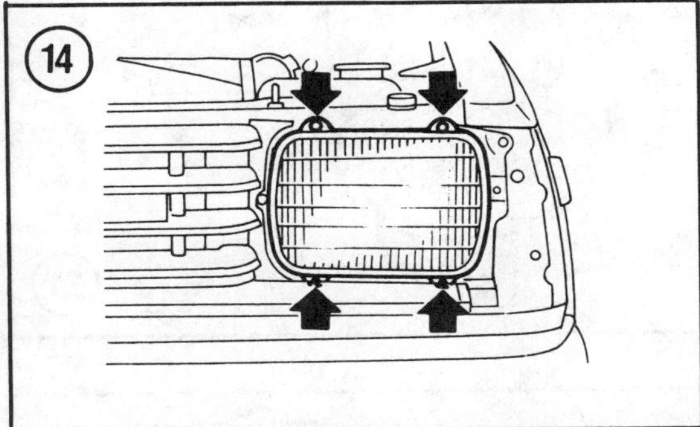

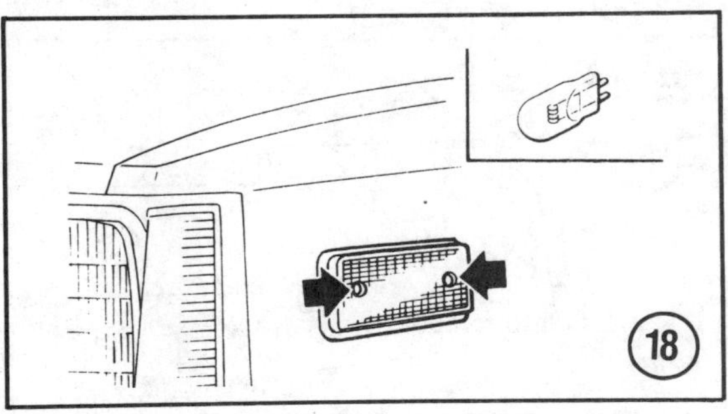

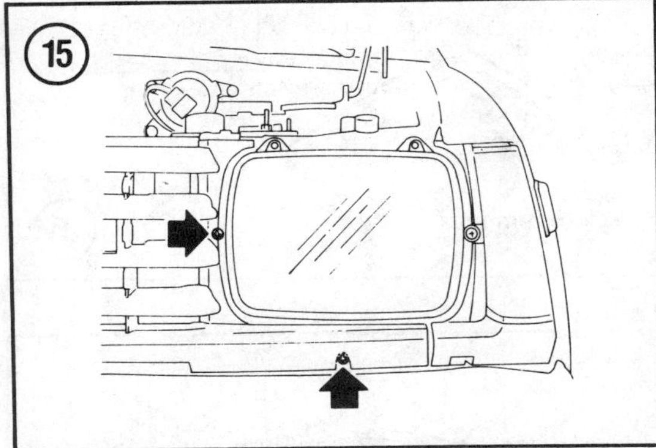

To replace a bulb, remove the access plate. See **Figure 19** (sedan), **Figure 20** (coupe) or **Figure 21** (wagon). On coupes and wagons, twist the bulb holder and take it out. Press the bulb into its socket and turn counterclockwise to remove. Install in the reverse order.

License Plate Lights (Sedan)

To replace a bulb, twist the bulb holder and take it out. See **Figure 22**. Press the bulb into its socket and turn counterclockwise to remove. Install in the reverse order.

License Plate Lights (Wagon)

To replace a bulb, remove the lens securing screws and take off the lens. See **Figure 23**. Press the bulb into its socket and turn counterclockwise to remove. Install in the reverse order.

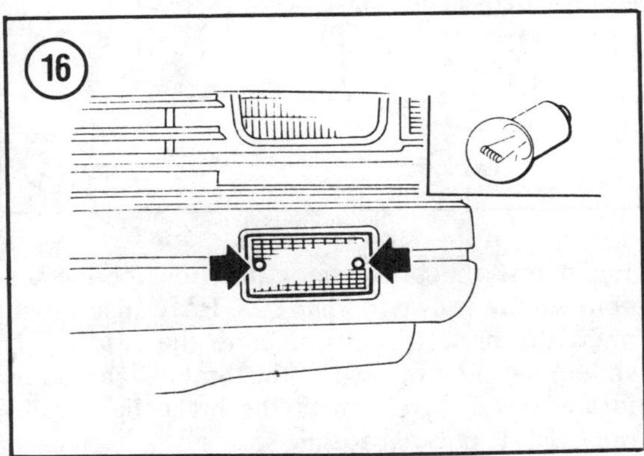

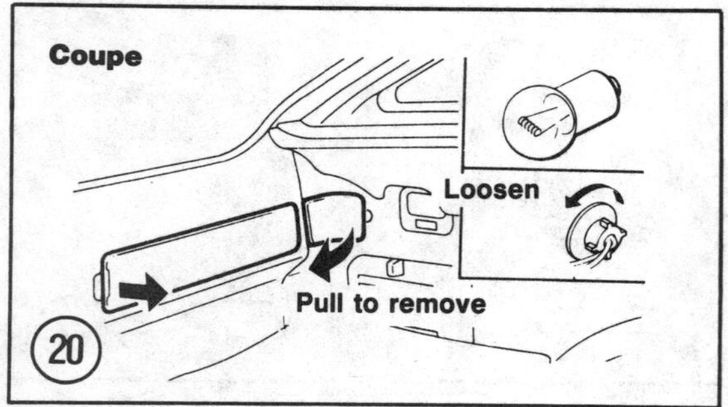

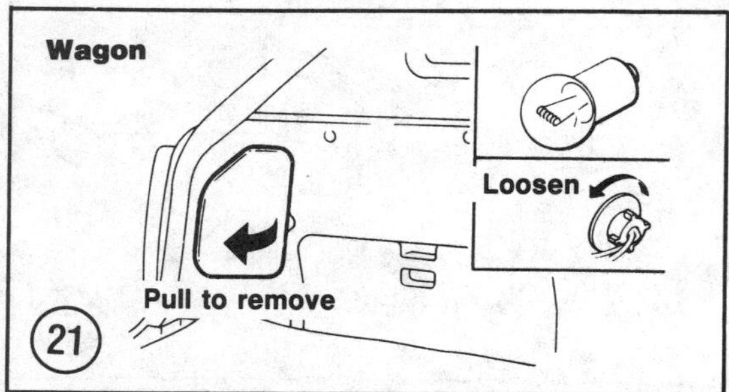

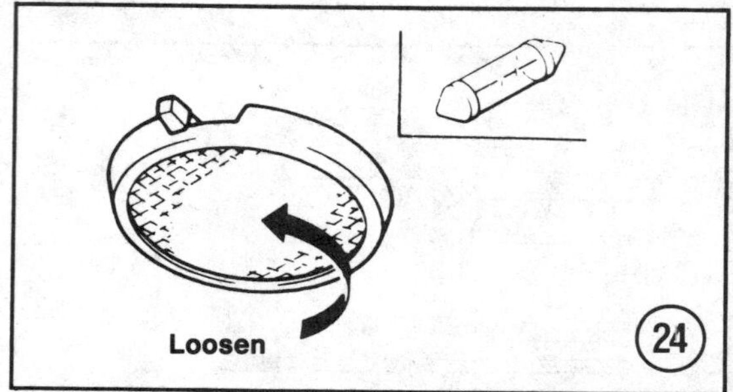

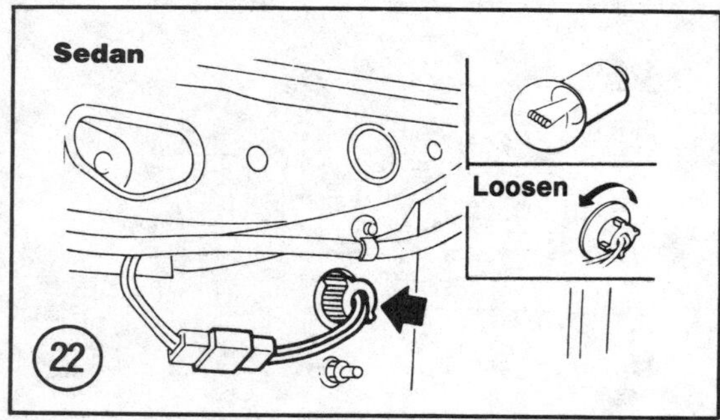

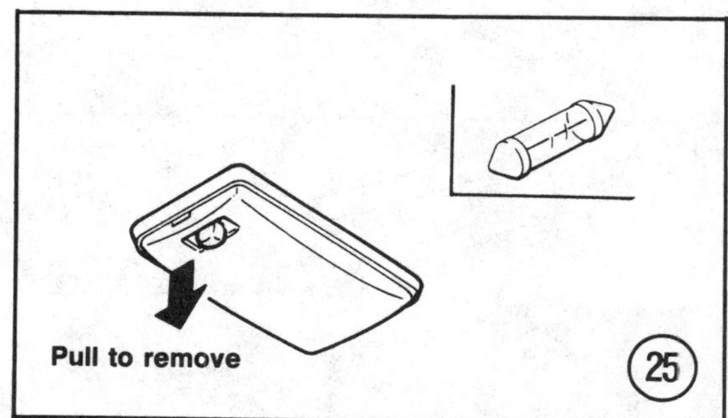

Interior Light

To replace a bulb, remove the lens. See **Figure 24** (round lights) or **Figure 25** (rectangular lights). Pull the bulb out of its holder, install a new one and reinstall the lens.

Luggage Compartment Light (Coupe)

To replace a bulb, remove the lens securing screws and take off the lens. See **Figure 26**. Pull the bulb out of its holder, push in a new one and reinstall the lens.

Brake-Taillight Sensor Test

The brake-taillight sensor is mounted on the left rear combination lamp (**Figure 27**). Before testing, make sure the bulbs are in good condition. Refer to **Table 2** and make sure the correct bulbs are being used.

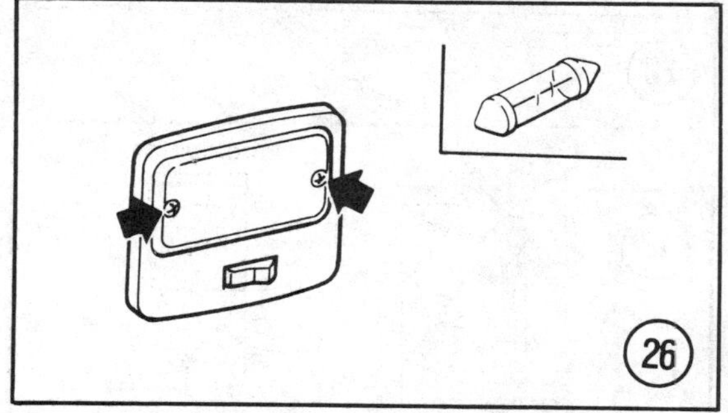

1. To test the brake light function, connect a voltmeter as shown in **Figure 28**. Have an assistant press the brake pedal and note the reading. It should be 12 volts with the brake light bulbs installed and 2 volts with the brake light bulbs removed. If not, replace the sensor.

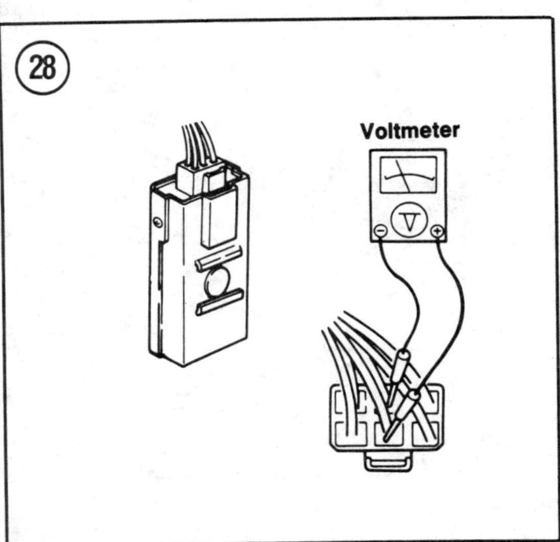

2. To test the taillight function, connect the voltmeter as shown in **Figure 28**. Turn the headlight switch on and note the reading. It should be 12 volts with the taillight bulbs installed and 2 volts with the taillight bulbs removed. If not, replace the sensor.

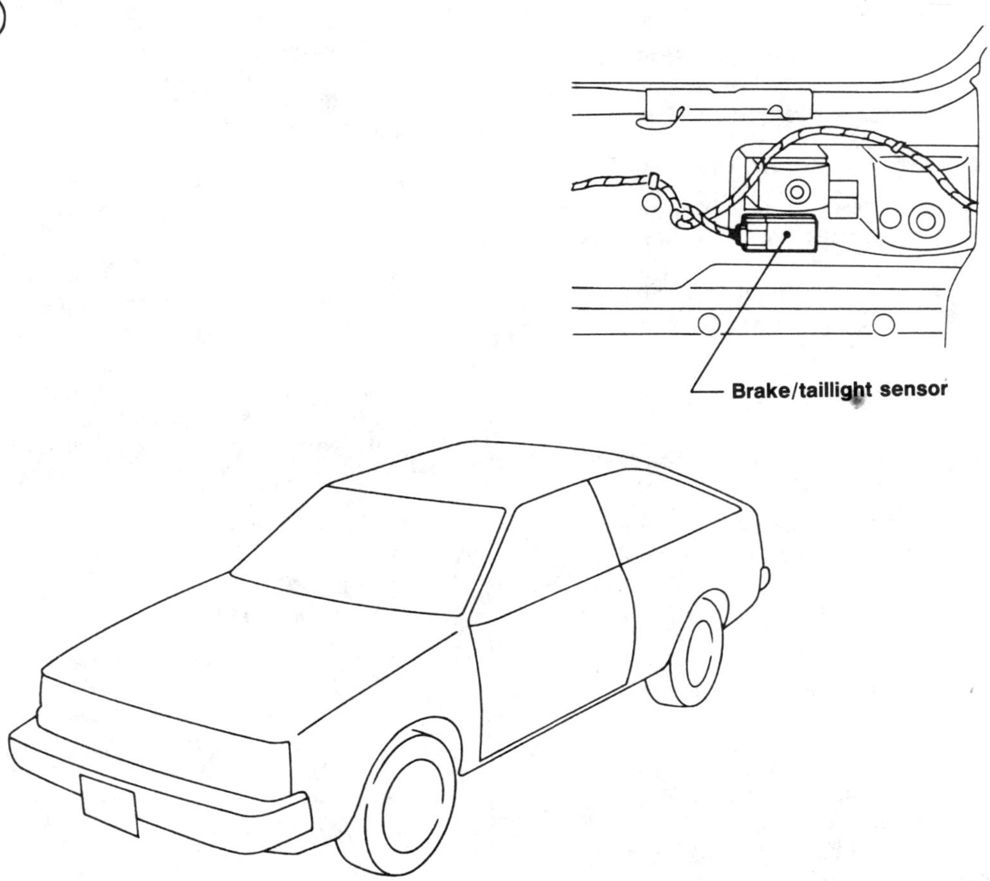

SWITCHES

Switches can be tested with an ohmmeter or a self-powered test lamp like the one shown in **Figure 29**.

Brake Light Switch Test

When the switch is in the normal position (plunger pushed in), there should not be continuity between terminals 1 and 2 (**Figure 30**). When the plunger is released, there should be continuity between the terminals.

Combination Switch Test

The combination switch (**Figure 31**) controls the headlights, wipers, turn signals and horn. To test, remove the switch as described in this chapter. Check switch continuity, referring to **Figure 31**.

Combination Switch Removal/Installation

1. Disconnect the negative cable from the battery.
2. Remove the steering wheel as described in Chapter Nine.
3. Remove the steering column shell (**Figure 32**).
4. Unplug the switch wiring connectors and take the switch off.
5. Installation is the reverse of removal. Align the switch protrusion with the hole in the steering column. See **Figure 33**.

Ignition Switch Test

1. Remove the steering column shell (**Figure 32**).
2. Unplug the wiring connector from the back of the ignition switch (**Figure 34**). To test the key warning function, unplug the key switch wiring connector as well.
3. Test the switch with an ohmmeter or self-powered test lamp. See **Figure 34**.

Ignition Switch Removal/Installation

1. Remove the steering column shell (**Figure 32**).
2. Unplug the wiring connector from the back of the ignition switch (**Figure 34**). Remove the screw that secures the switch to the steering lock (**Figure 35**) and take the switch off.
3. If the key warning switch is defective, replace the steering lock as described in Chapter Nine.
4. Installation is the reverse of removal.

Hazard Flasher Switch Test

Test the switch with an ohmmeter or self-powered test lamp, referring to **Figure 36**.

Hazard Flasher Switch Removal/Installation

1. Unplug the switch wiring connector (**Figure 36**).
2. Remove the switch mounting screws and take the switch out.
3. Installation is the reverse of removal.

Rear Wiper Switch Test

1. Reach behind the instrument panel, squeeze the switch retainer prongs and push it out of the instrument panel.
2. Unplug the switch wiring connector and take it out. To test the switch, refer to **Figure 37**.

WINDSHIELD WIPERS AND WASHERS

Troubleshooting

This section lists wiper problems and possible causes and solutions. Perform the numbered steps in the order listed.

Wipers don't work at all

1. Check the wiper fuse as described in this chapter.
2. Check the wiring for breaks or bad connections, referring to wiring diagrams at the end of the book.
3. Test the wiper switch as described in this chapter.
4. Check the wiper linkage for obstructions, rusted or seized parts or a disconnected rod.
5. Test the wiper motor as described in this chapter.

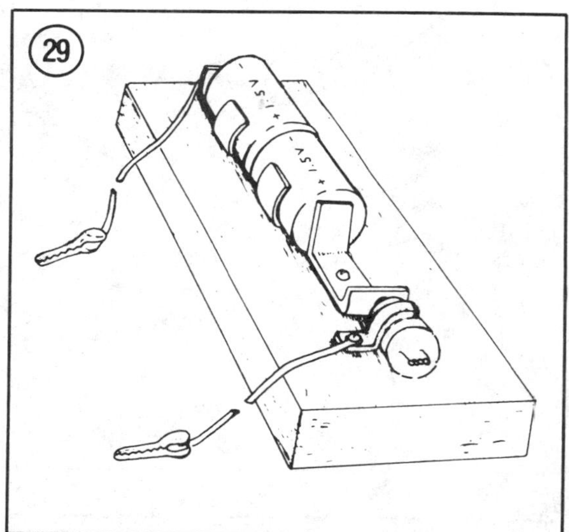

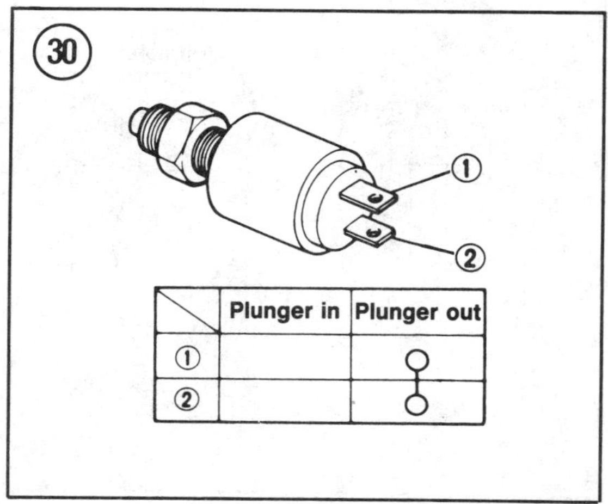

	Plunger in	Plunger out
①		○—●
②		○

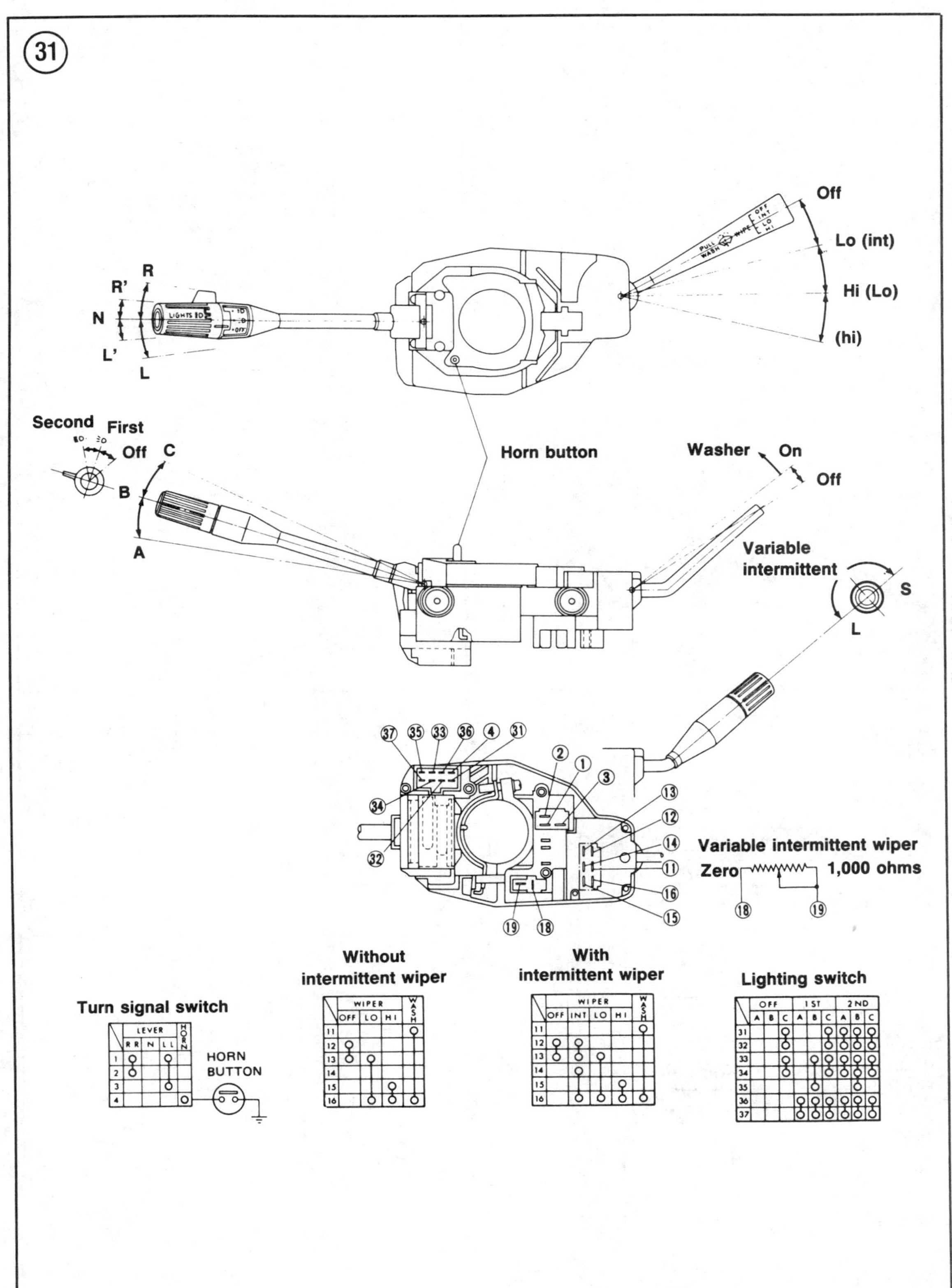

Turn signal switch

	R	R	N	L	L	HORN
1	O			O		
2	O					
3				O		
4						O

HORN BUTTON

Without intermittent wiper

	OFF	LO	HI	WASH
11				O
12	O			
13	O	O		
14				
15			O	
16		O	O	O

With intermittent wiper

	OFF	INT	LO	HI	WASH
11					O
12	O	O			
13	O	O	O		
14		O			
15				O	
16		O	O	O	O

Lighting switch

	OFF A	OFF B	OFF C	1ST A	1ST B	1ST C	2ND A	2ND B	2ND C
31			O			O	O	O	O
32			O			O	O	O	O
33			O		O	O	O	O	O
34			O			O	O	O	O
35					O			O	
36				O	O	O	O	O	O
37				O	O	O	O	O	O

7

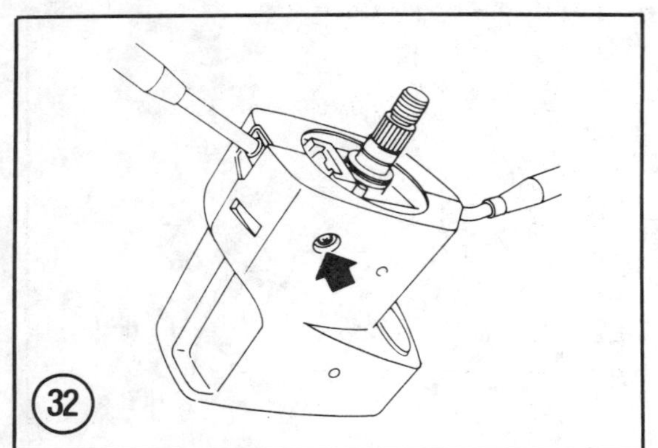

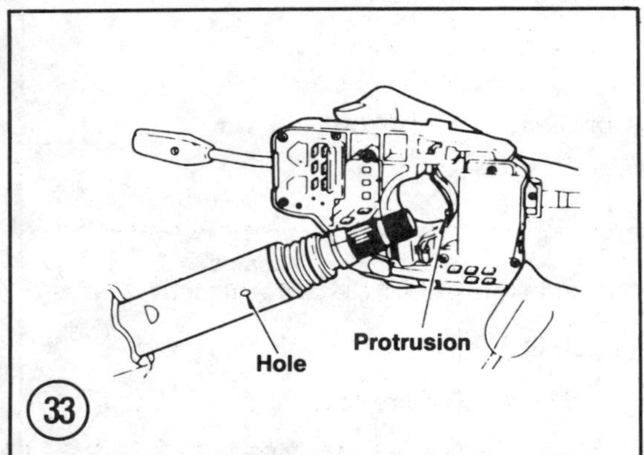

Protrusion
Hole

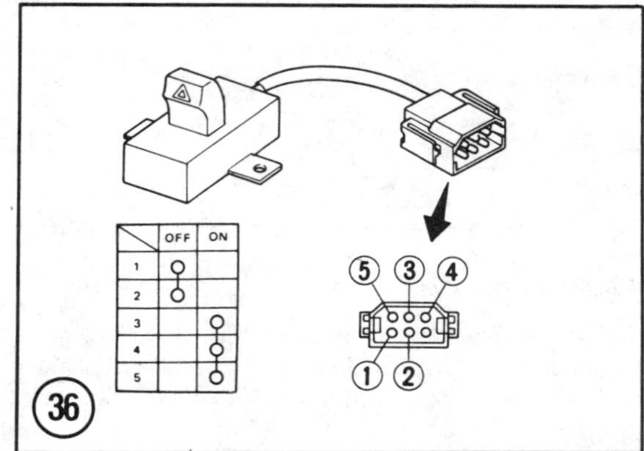

	OFF	ON
1	O	
2	O	
3		O
4		O
5		O

5 3 4
1 2

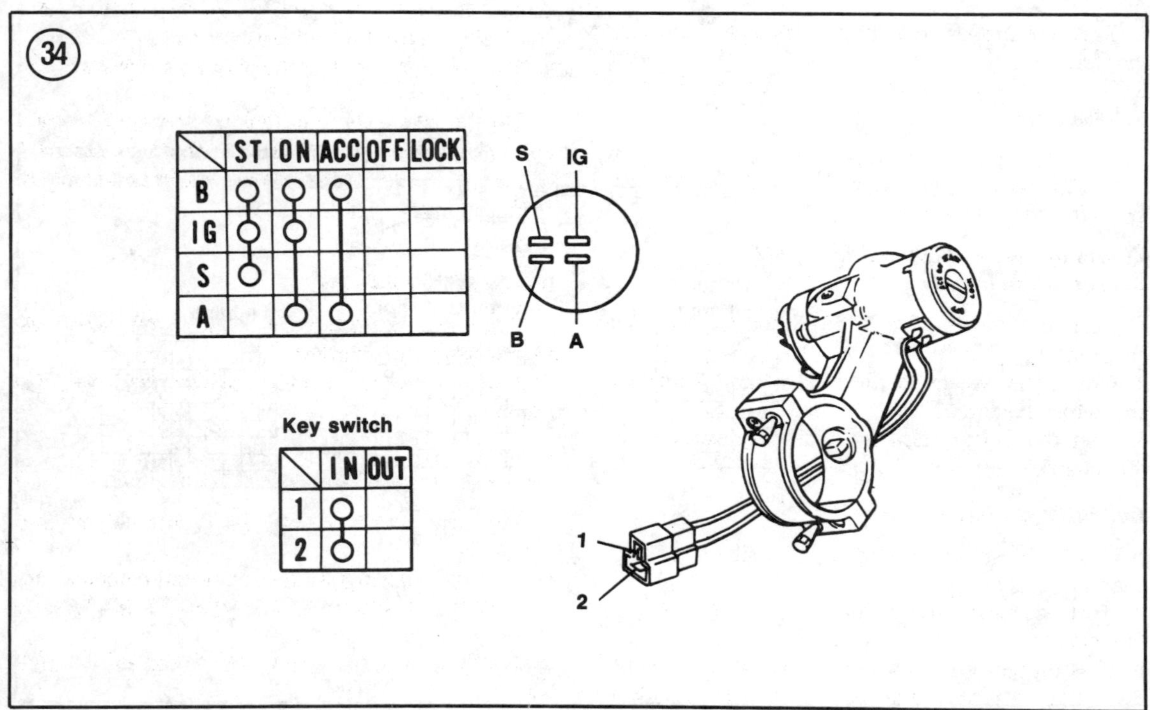

	ST	ON	ACC	OFF	LOCK
B	O	O	O		
IG	O	O			
S	O				
A		O	O		

S   IG

B   A

Key switch

	IN	OUT
1	O	
2	O	

1
2

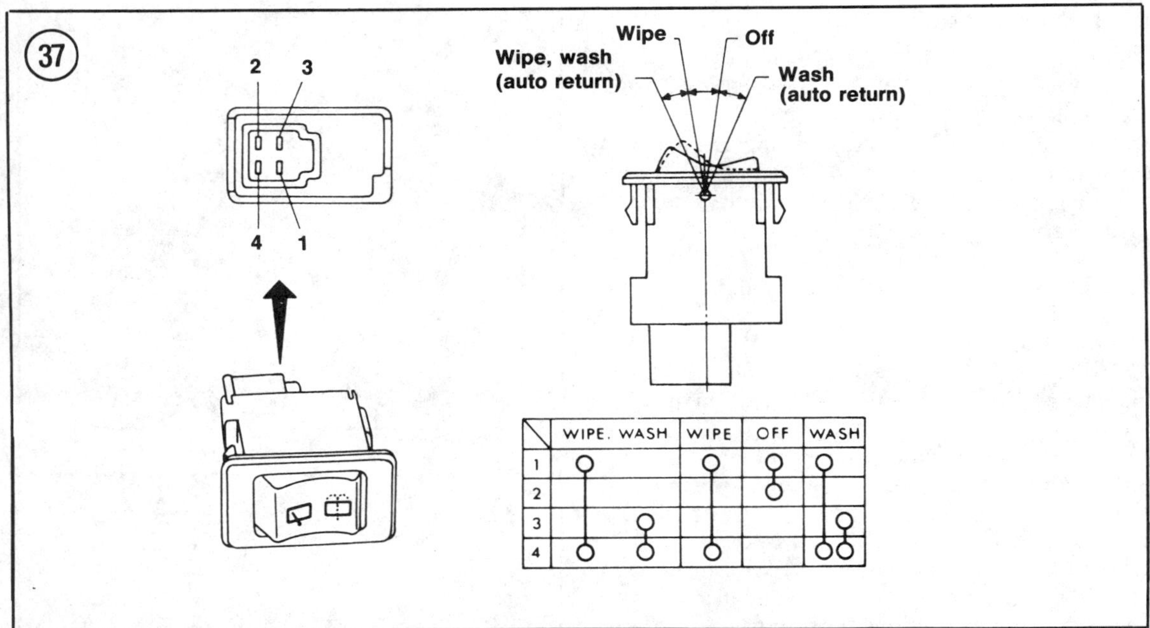

	WIPE. WASH	WIPE	OFF	WASH
1	○	○	○○	○
2			○	
3		○		○○
4	○	○	○	○○

Wipers are too slow

1. Check the battery as described in this chapter.
2. Check the wiring for breaks or bad connections.
3. Test the wiper motor as described in this chapter.

Wipers don't stop correctly

1. Test the wiper switch as described in this chapter.
2. Test the wiper motor as described in this chapter.

NOTE
The next steps apply to cars with intermittent wipers.

Wipers operate at high and low speeds, but not intermittently

1. Test the wiper switch as described in this chapter.
2. Check the wiring to the intermittent amplifier and wiper motor.
3. Test the intermittent amplifier as described in this chapter.

Intermittent speed too short

1. Test the wiper motor as described in this chapter.
2. Test the intermittent amplifier as described in this chapter.
3. If equipped with variable intermittent wipers, test the intermittent time control rheostat (mounted on the combination switch) as described in this chapter.

Intermittent speed too long

1. Check voltage to the wiper motor with a voltmeter. It should be at least 10 volts. If not, check the battery as described in this chapter and check the wiring for bad connections.
2. Test the intermittent amplifier as described in this chapter.
3. If equipped with variable intermittent wipers, test the intermittent time control rheostat (mounted on the combination switch) as described in this chapter.

Wipers do not turn off

1. Test the intermittent wiper amplifier as described in this chapter.
2. Test the wiper switch as described in this chapter.

Intermittent speed is erratic

1. Test the wiper switch as described in this chapter.
2. Check the wiring for breaks or bad connections.
3. Test the intermittent wiper amplifier as described in this chapter.
4. Test the wiper motor as described in this chapter.

Front Wiper Motor Test

This procedure requires an ohmmeter or a self-powered test lamp like the one shown in **Figure 38**.

1. Unplug the wiper motor wiring connector. Connect the positive terminal of the car's battery to the connector's blue wire (wiper motor side, not wiring harness side) with a length of wire.
2. Connect another length of wire between the connector's blue-black wire and ground (bare metal in the engine compartment). The motor should run at low speed.
3. Move the ground wire from the blue-black to the blue-white wire. The motor should run at high speed.
4. With the motor running, connect the ohmmeter or test lamp between the blue-orange wire and the black wire. The ohmmeter should indicate periodic continuity or the test lamp should flash on and off.
5. With the motor off and the wiper blades in the parked position, connect the ohmmeter or test lamp between the black and blue-orange wires. The ohmmeter should show little or no resistance or the test lamp should light.
6. If the wiper motor did not perform as described during any of these steps, replace it.

Rear Wiper Motor Test

This procedure requires an ohmmeter or a test lamp like the one shown in **Figure 38**.

1. Unplug the wiper motor wiring connector.
2. Connect the positive terminal of the car's battery to the blue-black wire in the connector (wiper motor side, not wiring harness side).
3. Connect the blue-yellow wire in the wiring connector to ground (nearby bare metal) with a length of wire. The motor should run.
4. With the motor running, connect the ohmmeter or test lamp between the black wire and blue-red wire in the connector. The ohmmeter should show periodic continuity or the test lamp should flash on and off.
5. Disconnect the length of wire from the connector. With the motor off and the wiper in the parked position, connect the ohmmeter or test lamp between the blue-black and black wires in the wiring connector. The ohmmeter should show continuity (little or no resistance) or the test lamp should light.
6. If the motor doesn't perform as described during these steps, replace it.

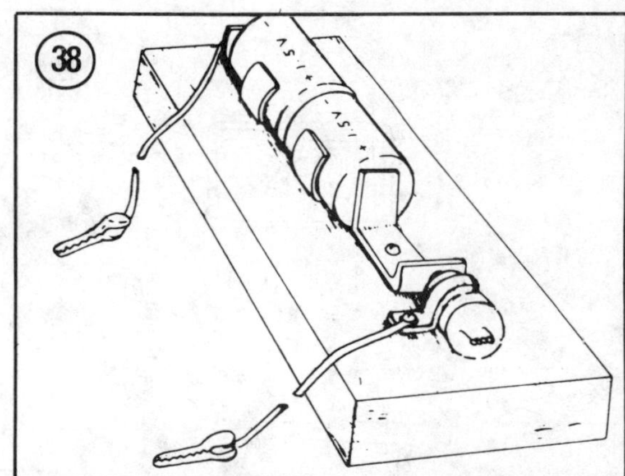

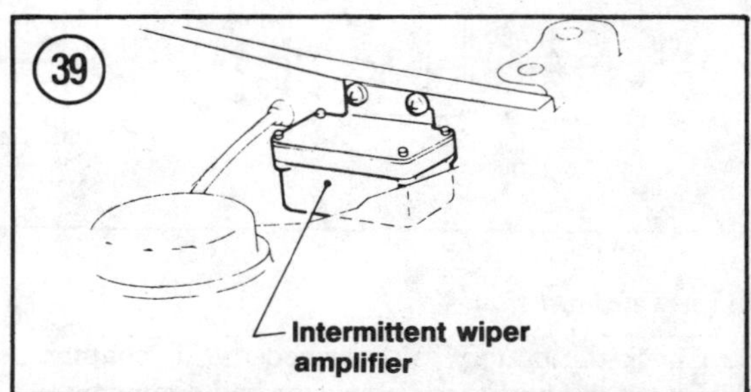

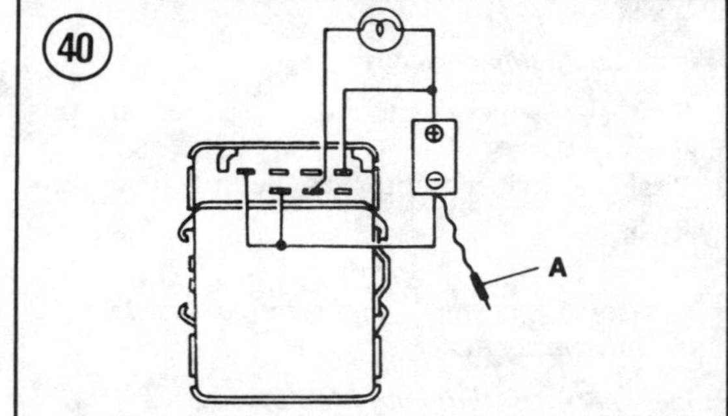

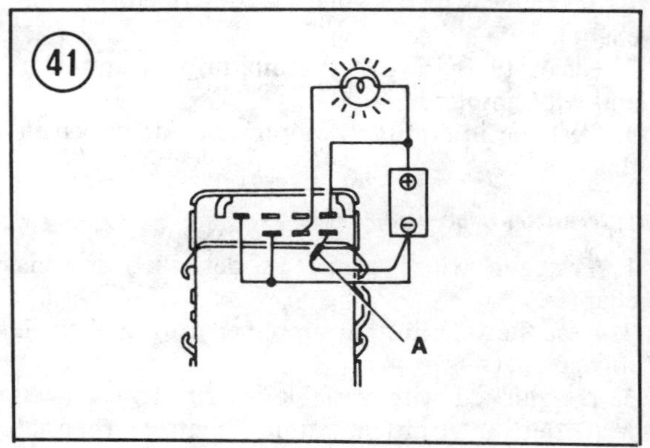

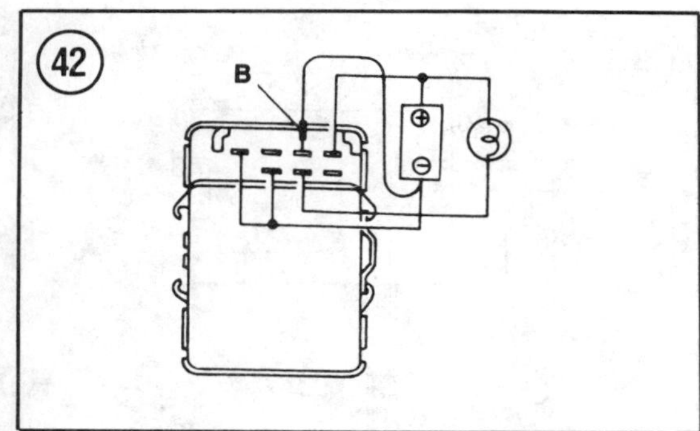

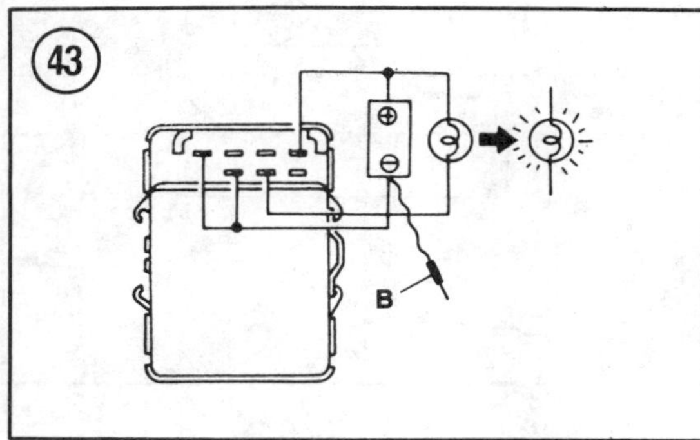

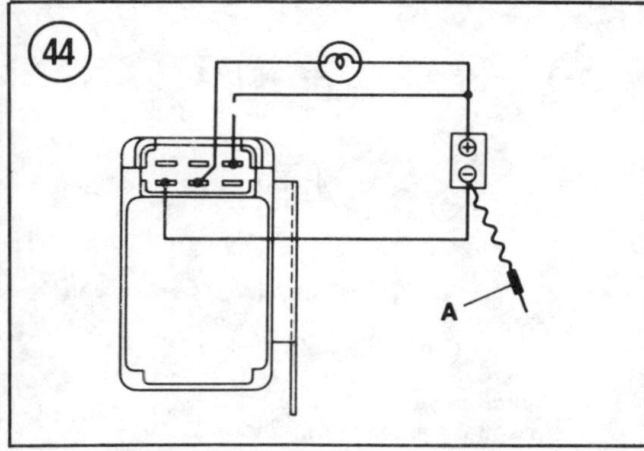

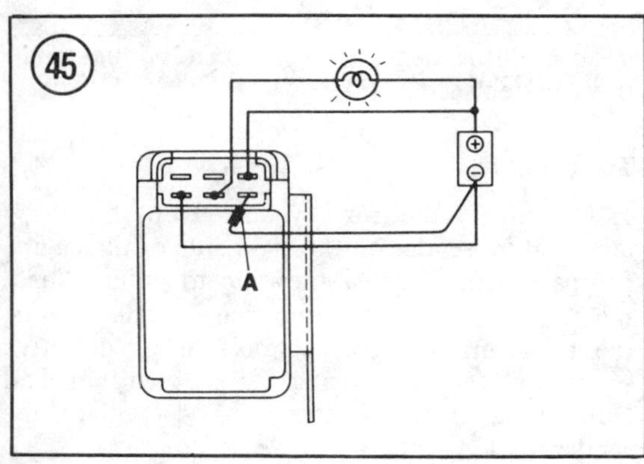

Intermittent Amplifier Test
(With Variable Intermittent Wipers)

1. Locate the intermittent amplifier in the left rear corner of the engine compartment. See **Figure 39**.

CAUTION
Be sure to connect the wires to the proper terminals during the following steps.

2. Set up the test circuit shown in **Figure 40**. Leave the end of wire A disconnected for the time being.
3. Connect wire A to the terminal shown in **Figure 41**. The test lamp should flash on and off.
4. Set up the test circuit shown in **Figure 42**.
5. Disconnect wire B (**Figure 43**). The test lamp should go out, then come back on within a few seconds.
5. If the amplifier doesn't perform as described during these steps, replace it.

Intermittent Amplifier Test
(With Intermittent Wipers)

1. Locate the intermittent amplifier in the left rear corner of the engine compartment. See **Figure 39**.

CAUTION
Be sure to connect the wires to the proper terminals during the following steps.

2. Set up the test circuit shown in **Figure 44**. Leave wire A disconnected for the time being.
3. Connect wire A as shown in **Figure 45**. The test lamp should flash on and off.
4. Move wire A to the terminal shown in **Figure 46**, then disconnect it. The test lamp should light within a few seconds.
5. If the amplifier doesn't perform as described during these steps, replace it.

Washer Motor Test

If the washer motor doesn't run, connect its terminals directly to the car's battery with lengths of wire (blue-black wire to positive terminal; blue-orange wire to negative terminal). The motor should run. If not, replace it.

TURN SIGNAL AND HAZARD FLASHER TROUBLESHOOTING

This section lists turn signal and hazard flasher problems and possible causes and solutions. Perform the numbered steps in the order listed. See *Lighting System* in this chapter for bulb replacement.

Turn Signals Don't Work; Hazard Flashers Do

1. Check the turn signal fuse as described in this chapter.
2. Check the wiring for breaks or bad connections.
3. Test the turn signal switch as described in this chapter.
4. Test the hazard flasher switch as described in this chapter.
5. If the preceding steps haven't located the problem, replace the turn signal flasher unit (**Figure 47**).

Hazard Flashers Work; Turn Signals Don't

1. Check the hazard flasher fuse as described in this chapter.
2. Test the hazard flasher switch as described in this chapter.
3. If the preceding steps haven't solved the problem, replace the hazard flasher unit (**Figure 47**).

Neither Turn Signals nor Hazard Flashers Work

1. Test the hazard flasher switch as described in this chapter.
2. Check the turn signal and hazard flasher wiring for breaks or bad connections.

Flasher Unit Doesn't Click

1. Check with **Table 2** to make sure the correct bulbs are being used.
2. Check the wiring for breaks or bad connections.
3. If the preceding steps haven't located the problem, replace the flasher unit (**Figure 47**).

Lights Flash Too Slow or Too Fast

1. Check with **Table 2** to make sure the correct bulbs are being used.
2. Make sure no bulbs are burned out.
3. Check the wiring for breaks or bad connections.
4. If the preceding steps haven't located the problem, replace the flasher unit (**Figure 47**).

Lights Flash Erratically

1. Check with **Table 2** to make sure the correct bulbs are being used.
2. Make sure no bulbs are burned out.
3. Check the wiring for breaks or bad connections.
4. If the preceding steps haven't located the problem, replace the flasher unit (**Figure 47**).

INSTRUMENT TROUBLESHOOTING

This section lists instrument problems and possible causes and solutions. Perform the numbered steps in the order listed. See Chapter

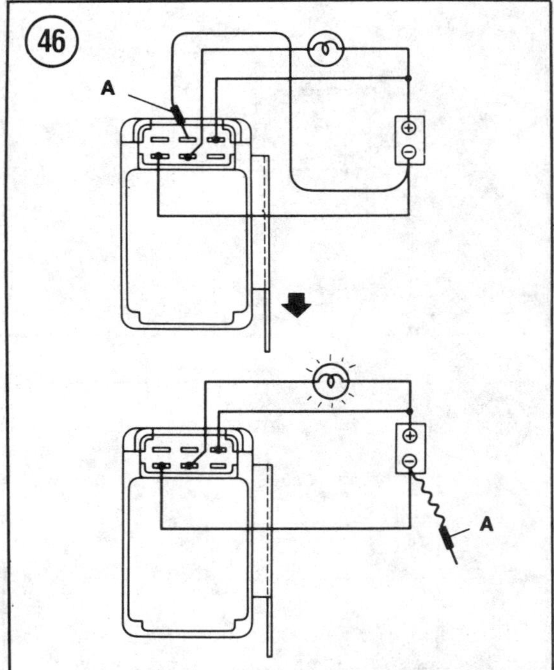

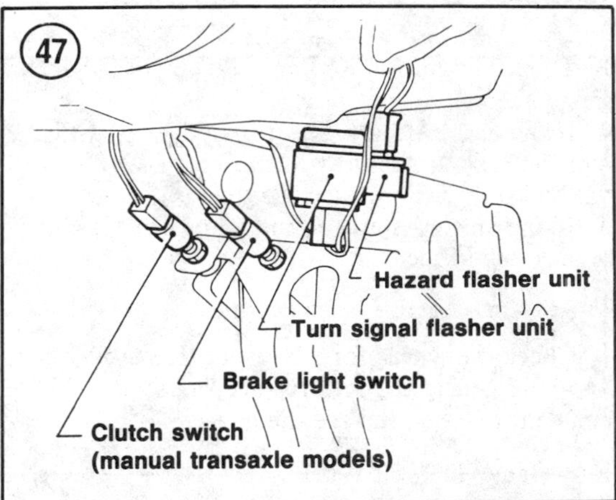

Twelve, *Instrument Panel*, if an individual gauge must be replaced.

Temperature Gauge Doesn't Work

1. Disconnect the wire (yellow-green) from the temperature sender on the right side of the engine compartment. Connect the wire to ground (bare metal on the engine). If the gauge needle moves, the problem is a bad connection or defective sender. Check the wiring for a break or bad connection. If the wiring is good, replace the sender.

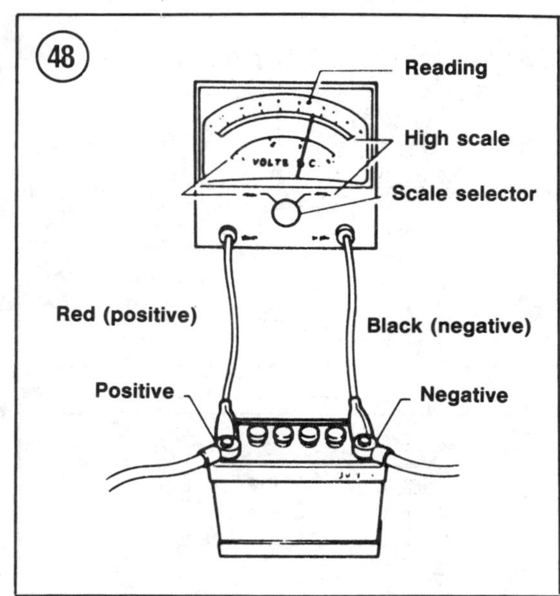

2. If the gauge needle does not move when the sender wire is grounded, replace the gauge.

Temperature Gauge Indicates Maximum at All Times

1. Turn the ignition ON and OFF and watch the gauge needle.
2. If the gauge needle goes to maximum with the ignition ON and returns to the cold position with the ignition OFF, replace the sender.
3. If the needle stays at maximum at all times, replace the gauge.

Temperature Gauge is Inaccurate

1. Check the wiring for a break or bad connection.
2. If the wiring is good, replace the sender. If the problem persists, replace the gauge.

Fuel Gauge Doesn't Work

1. Locate the gauge unit on the fuel tank. See *Fuel Tank and Lines* in Chapter Five.
2. Disconnect the yellow wire from the gauge unit and touch it to nearby bare metal. If the gauge needle moves, replace the gauge unit.
3. If the gauge needle doesn't move, check the wiring for breaks or bad connections.
4. If the gauge unit and wiring are good, replace the fuel gauge.

Speedometer and Odometer Don't Work

1. Check the speedometer cable for loose connections at the speedometer and transaxle.
2. Check for a broken speedometer cable.

3. Check the speedometer pinion on the transaxle for damage.
4. Have the speedometer tested by a speedometer shop.

Speedometer Needle Wavers

1. Check the speedometer cable for loose connections at the speedometer and transaxle.
2. Check the ends of the speedometer cable for damage.
3. Have the speedometer tested by a speedometer shop.

Speedometer Noisy

1. Lubricate the speedometer cable.
2. Check the inner speedometer cable for bends or twisting.
3. Have the speedometer tested by a speedometer shop.

Speedometer or Odometer Inaccurate

Have the speedometer tested and calibrated by a speedometer shop.

IGNITION SYSTEM

All models use a breakerless, magnetic pulse-controlled integrated circuit ignition system.

System Test

This test requires a voltmeter and ohmmeter.
1. Connect the voltmeter between the battery terminals as shown in **Figure 48** and note the reading. This is battery voltage. Write it down for later use.

> *NOTE*
> *The reading should be at least 11.5 volts. If not, inspect the charging system as described in this chapter.*

2. Disconnect the thick wire (coil wire) from the center of the distributor cap. Ground the wire by connecting it to nearby bare metal. Crank the starter and note the voltage reading between battery terminals. Again, write the reading down for later use.

> *NOTE*
> *Voltage while cranking should be at least 9.6 volts. If not, check the battery, charging system and starting system as described in this chapter.*

3. Inspect the distributor cap and ignition wiring as described under *Tune-up* in Chapter Three.
4. Disconnect the wires from the ignition coil and measure coil secondary resistance with the

ohmmeter. See **Figure 49**. It should be 7,300-11,000 ohms. If not within this range, replace the coil. After the test, reconnect the coil wires.

5. Test the power supply circuit. Connect a voltmeter as shown in **Figure 50**. Turn the key to ON, but don't start the engine. The voltmeter should indicate 11.5-12.5 volts. If it is less than this, check the wiring from ignition switch to the integrated circuit (IC) unit inside the distributor.

6. Ground the coil secondary (thick) wire by connecting it to bare metal. Connect the voltmeter as shown in **Figure 50** and crank the starter. The voltage reading should be within one volt of battery cranking voltage (written down during Step 2). It should be at least 8.6 volts. If not, check the ignition switch and the wiring to the integrated circuit unit.

7. Connect the voltmeter as shown in **Figure 51**. Turn the key to ON, but don't start the engine. Voltage should be 11.5-12.5 volts. If so, skip the next step. If not, perform the next step.

8. Test the coil primary circuit. Connect the ohmmeter as shown in **Figure 52**. Resistance should be 0.84-1.02 ohms. If not within this range, replace the ignition coil. If resistance is correct, check the ignition switch as described in this chapter. Also check the wiring from the ignition switch to the integrated circuit (IC) unit inside the distributor.

9. Connect the voltmeter as shown in **Figure 53**. Ground the coil secondary wire (thick wire) to bare metal. Crank the starter and note the voltmeter reading. It should be 0.5 volt or less:

   a. If the reading is 0.5 volt or less, have the IC ignition unit inside the distributor replaced by a dealer or automotive electrical shop.

   b. If the reading is more than 0.5 volt, make sure the distributor is properly grounded to the engine. Check the wiring from chassis ground to the battery. Make sure the battery connections are clean and tight.

Distributor Removal

1. Turn the engine by hand until No. 1 cylinder is at top dead center on its compression stroke. When this occurs, the 0 degree mark on the timing scale will align with the notch in the crankshaft pulley. See **Figure 54**. In addition, the distributor rotor will point to No. 1 terminal in the distributor cap. See **Figure 55**.

> *NOTE*
> *Be sure to remove the distributor cap and check rotor position. The timing*

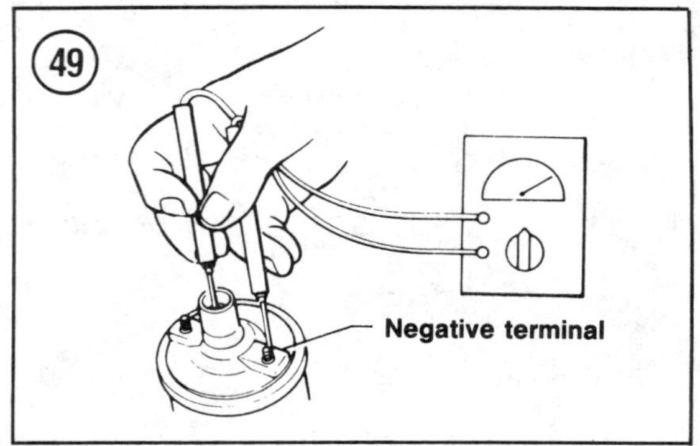

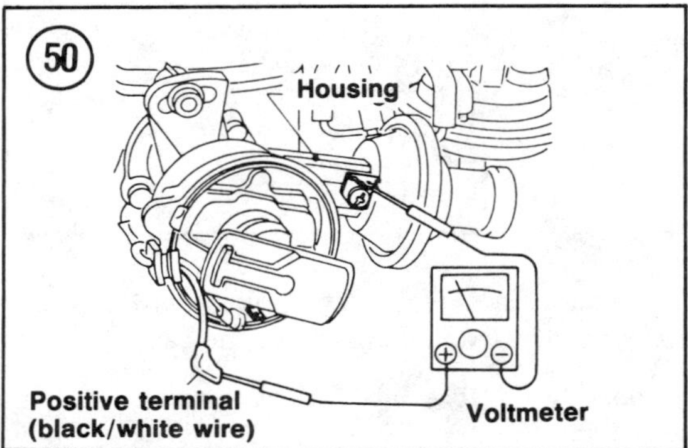

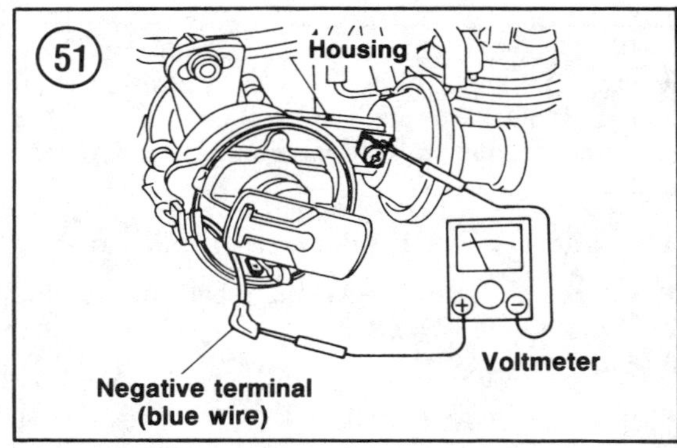

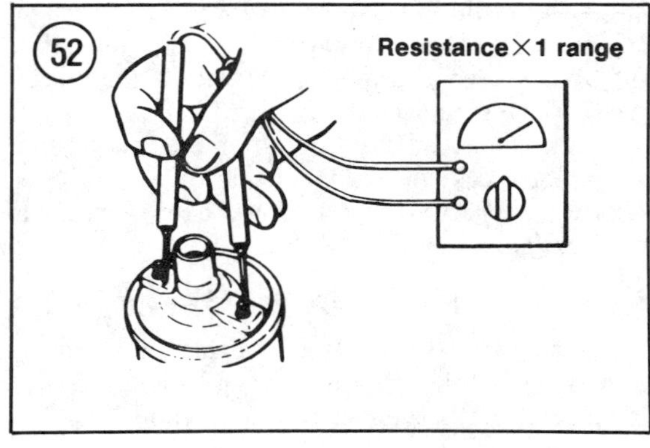

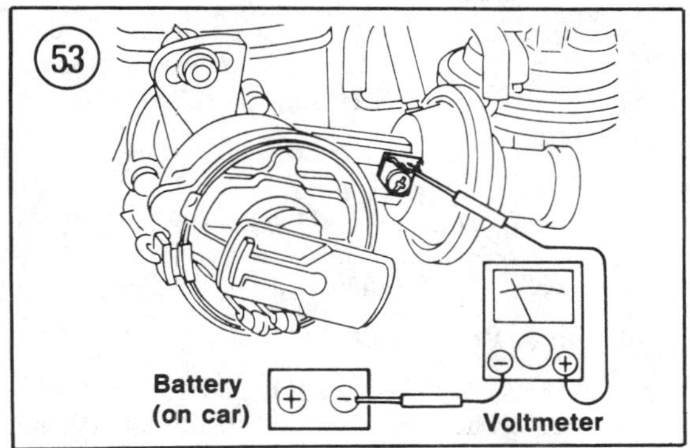

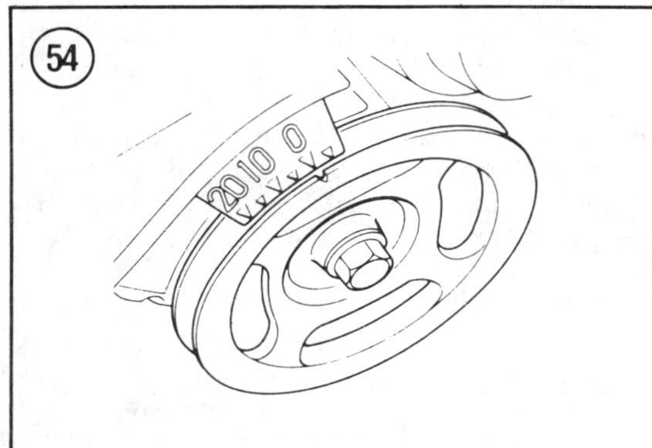

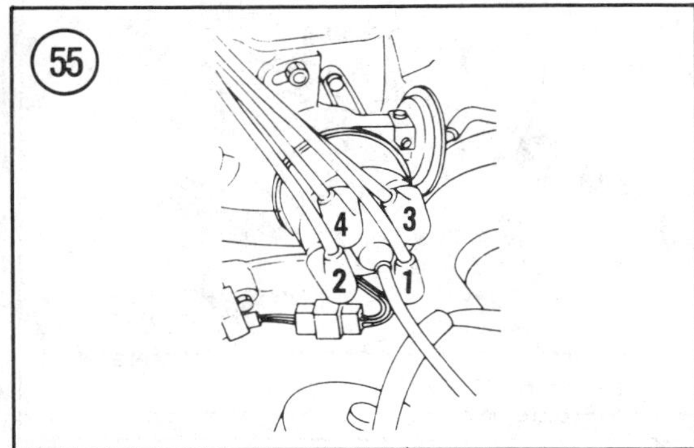

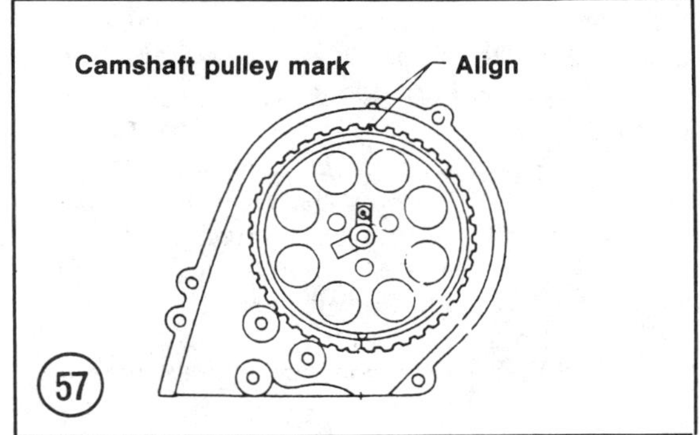

marks also line up when No. 4 cylinder is at TDC on its compression stroke.

2. Unplug the distributor wiring connector.

3. Make alignment marks on the distributor body and engine (**Figure 56**). The marks will ease installation.

4. Remove the distributor locknut (**Figure 56**). Take the distributor out of the engine.

Distributor Installation

1. If the engine has been turned with the distributor out, align the match marks on camshaft pulley and front cover (**Figure 57**). This places No. 1 cylinder at top dead center on its compression stroke.

2. Install the distributor in the engine. Make sure the rotor points to No. 1 terminal position in the distributor cap, then tighten the locknut.

3. Install the distributor cap.

4. Check ignition timing as described in Chapter Three. Adjust as needed.

HORN

There are 2 horns, mounted at the front of the engine compartment. If the horns work, but are not loud enough, make sure the wires are making good contact and the horns are properly grounded to the car body. Horn volume can be adjusted by loosening the locknut and turning the adjusting screw on the back of the horn (**Figure 58**). Tighten the locknut after adjusting.

If only one horn works, check the wiring to the non-working horn. If the horn is receiving current and is grounded properly, it is probably defective. Replace it.

If neither horn works, turn on the headlights to make sure the battery is good. If the battery is okay, check the horn fuse.

If the horn fuse is good, test the horn relay as described in this chapter.

If the relay is good, remove the horn pad as described under *Steering Wheel Removal*, Chapter Nine. Check the horn contacts for burns or other damage.

If the horn stays on all the time, check the horn relay as described in this chapter. Also check the horn button for damaged contacts. The horn button is a switch that grounds the horn relay, causing it to provide current to the horns.

Horn Relay Test

1. Locate the horn relay in the left front corner of the engine compartment. See **Figure 59**. Take the relay out.
2. Identify the relay terminals (**Figure 60**).
3. Connect an ohmmeter or a self-powered test lamp like the one shown in **Figure 61** between terminals 2 and 3. The ohmmeter should show infinite resistance or the test lamp should stay out.
4. Connect the car's battery terminals to relay terminals 1 and 2 with lengths of wire. The ohmmeter should show little or no resistance or the test lamp should light.
5. If the relay doesn't perform as described, replace it.

FUSES AND FUSIBLE LINKS

Fuse Replacement

The fuse block is located under the driver's side of the instrument panel (**Figure 62**). Fuse functions are listed on the fuse block cover.

To replace, pull out the old fuse with the car's fuse puller (**Figure 63**). Push in a new fuse. Be sure the new fuse has the same amperage rating as the old one.

Whenever a fuse blows, find out the cause before replacing. Usually the trouble is a short circuit in the wiring. This may be caused by worn-through insulation or by a wire that works its way loose and touches metal. Carry several spare fuses in the glove compartment.

> *CAUTION*
> *Never substitute metal foil or wire for a fuse. An overload could cause a fire and complete loss of the car.*

Fusible Link Replacement

Fusible links are short sections of thin wire in a thicker wire. They are intended to burn out if an overload occurs, thus protecting the wiring harnesses.

The fusible links are located next to the battery (**Figure 64**). Burned-out fusible links can usually be detected by melted or burned insulation. They may smoke before burning out. Suspect links with no apparent damage can be checked for continuity with an ohmmeter or self-powered test lamp. If a link burns out, unplug it and plug in a new one.

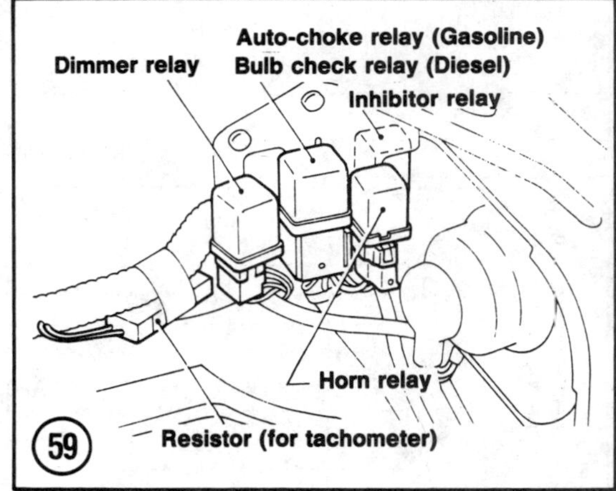

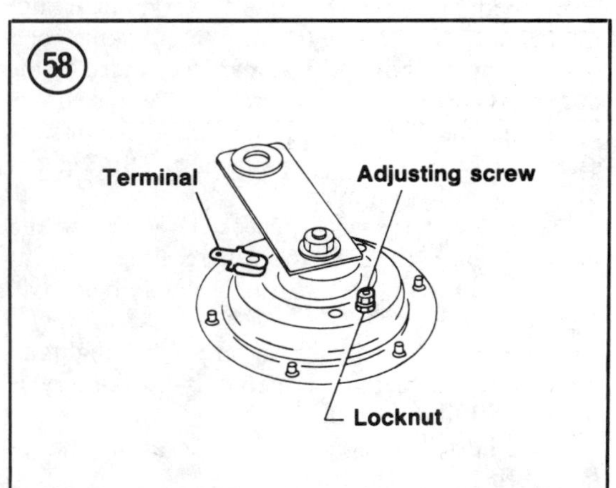

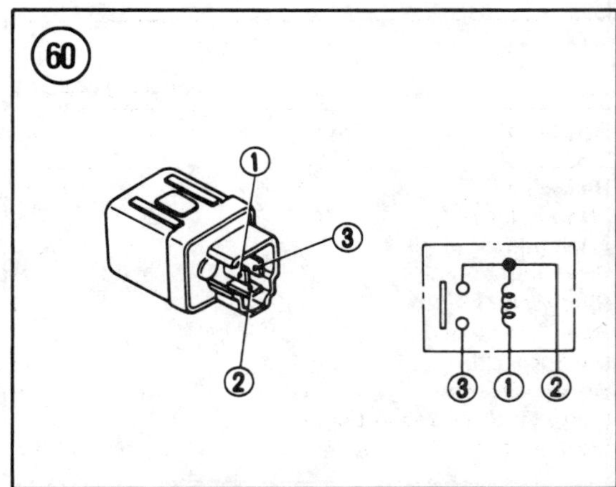

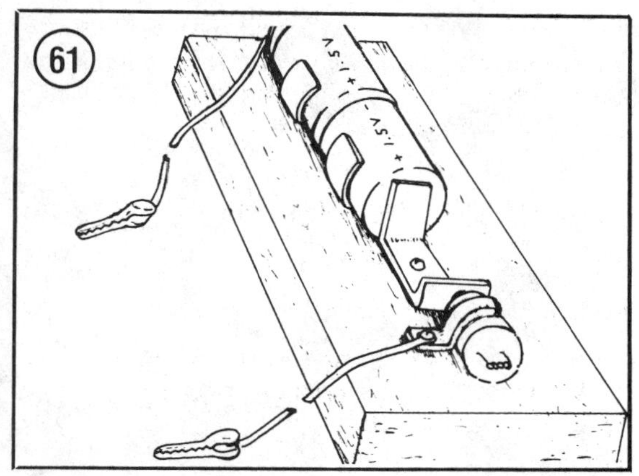

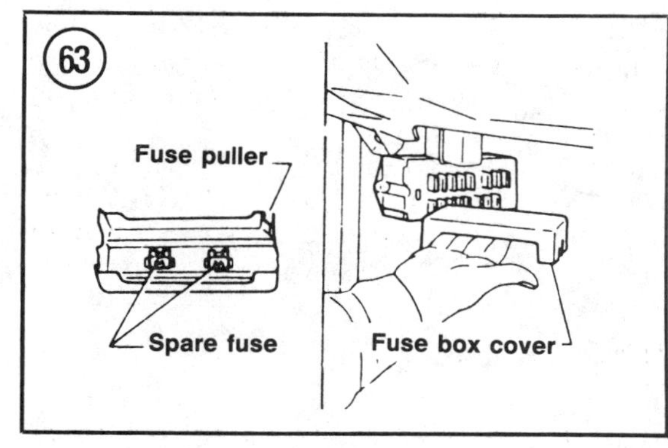

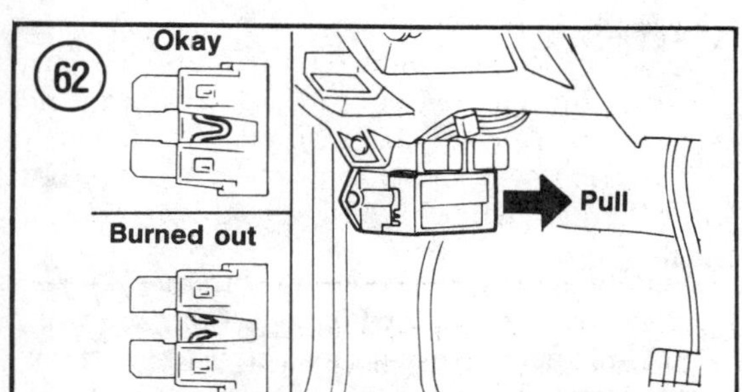

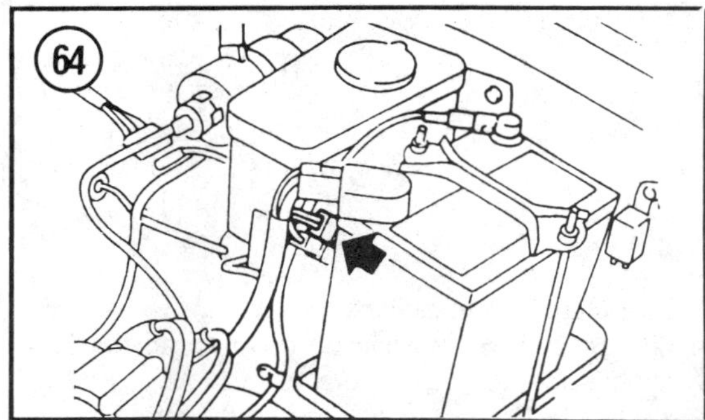

Table 1 APPROXIMATE CHARGE RATES

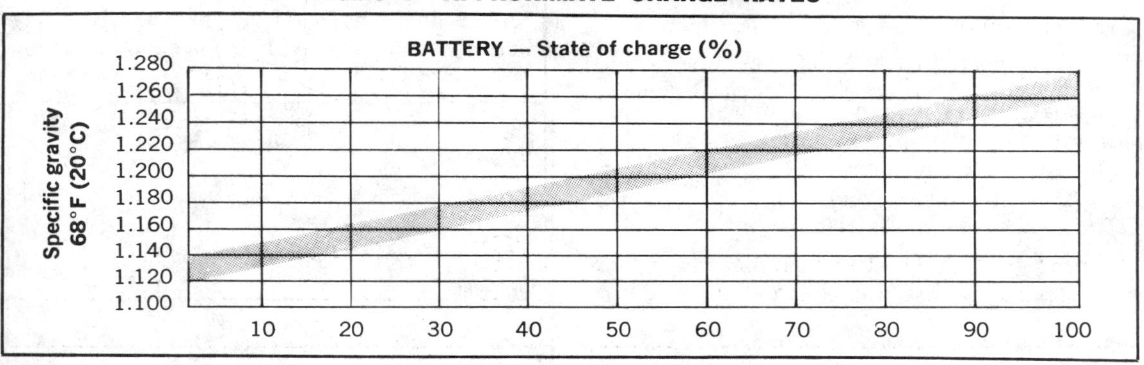

Table 2 BULB SPECIFICATIONS

Application	Wattage	Trade No.
Headlights		
Non-halogen	65/55	–
Halogen	65/35	H6504
Front turn signals	27	1156
Side marker lights	3.4	158
Rear turn signals	27	1156
Backup lights	27	1156
Brake/taillights	27/8	1157
Luggage compartment light	5	–
Interior light	10	–

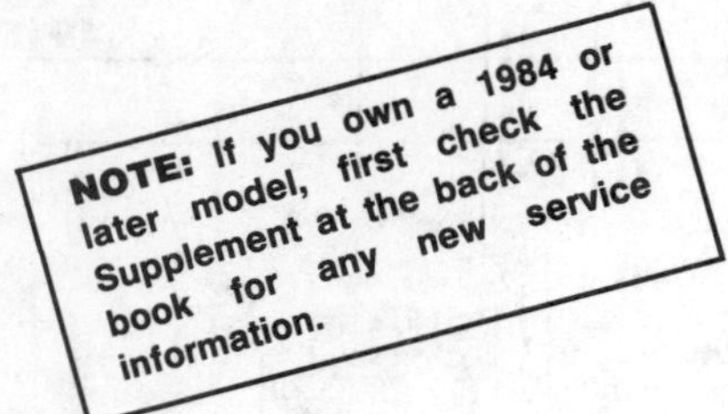

CHAPTER EIGHT

CLUTCH AND TRANSAXLE

This chapter provides all clutch and transaxle service procedures practical for home mechanics. Specifications and tightening torques are listed in **Table 1** and **Table 2** at the end of the chapter.

CLUTCH

The Sentra uses a single dry plate clutch with diaphragm spring. Clutch engagement and disengagement are controlled by the release mechanism, which in turn is controlled by pedal pressure transmitted through a cable.

Major clutch components are the disc, pressure plate, release mechanism and cable.

The release mechanism consists of a bearing, sleeve and withdrawal lever.

Part Identification

Many clutch parts have 2 or more names. To prevent confusion, the following list gives part names used in this chapter and common synonyms.

  a. Withdrawal lever—throw-out arm, release lever.
  b. Pressure plate—pressure plate assembly, clutch cover assembly.
  c. Disc—driven plate.

Pedal Adjustment

1. Check pedal height from the floor. Compare with **Table 1**. If pedal height is incorrect, loosen the pedal stopper locknut (**Figure 1**). Turn the pedal stopper to adjust, then tighten the locknut.

2. Working under the car, check withdrawal lever free play. See **Figure 2** or **Figure 3**. Compare with **Table 1**. If free play is incorrect, adjust by turning the adjuster or locknuts.

3. Press the pedal to the floor and release it. Make sure the pedal moves smoothly without squeaking.

4. As a final check on height and free play adjustments, press the pedal by hand and note the

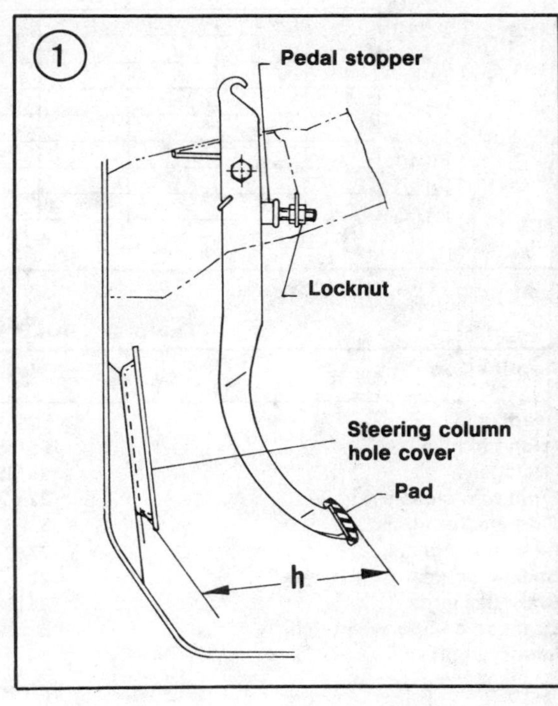

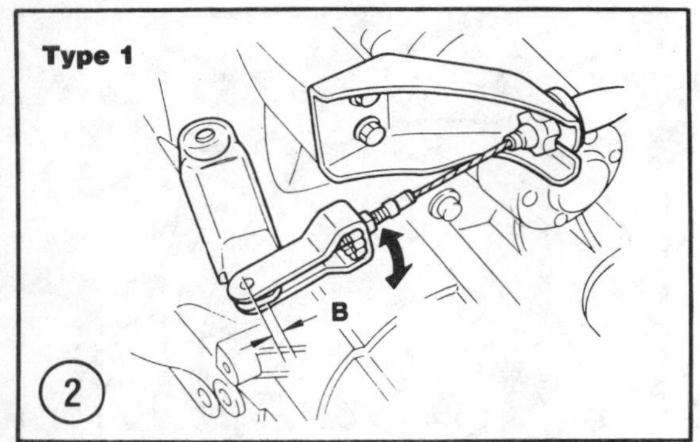

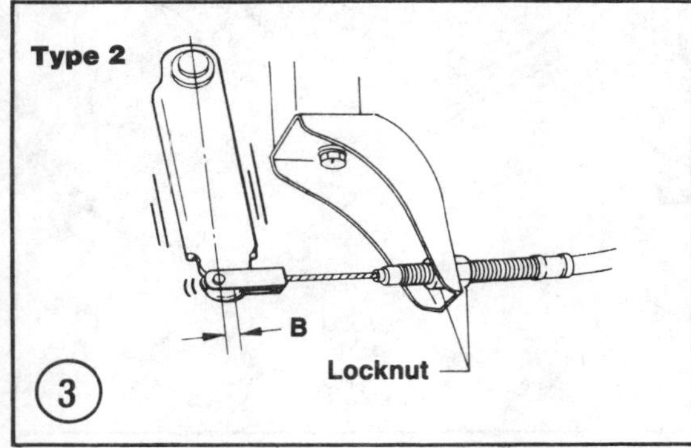

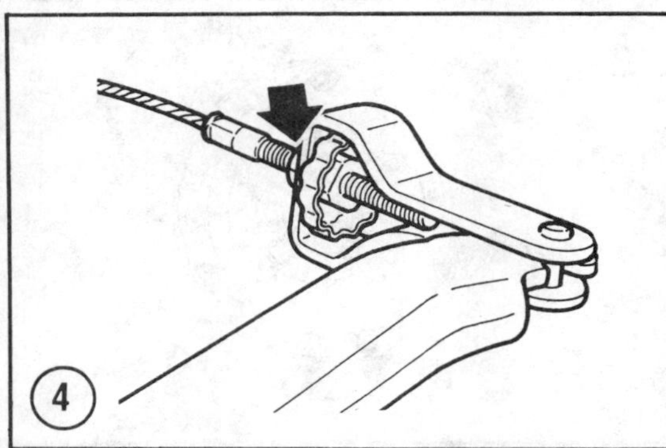

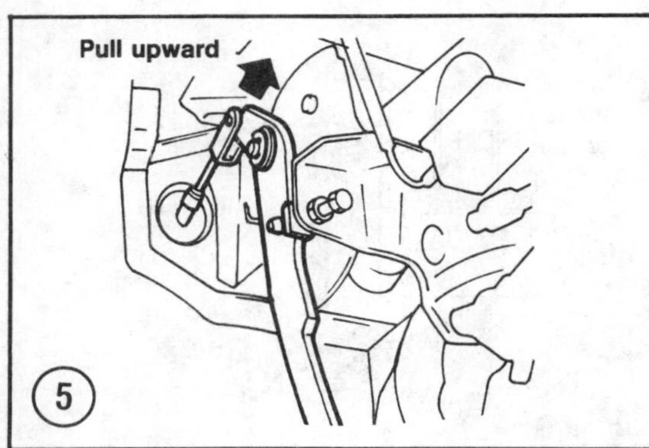

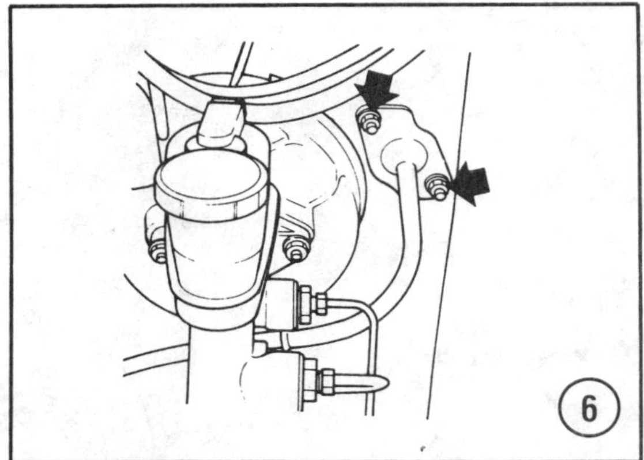

point at which resistance abruptly increases. The distance the pedal travels (free travel) is specified in **Table 1** at the end of the chapter. If free travel is incorrect, recheck pedal height and withdrawal lever free play.

Cable Replacement

1. Working beneath the car, loosen the cable adjuster or locknuts (**Figure 4**). Disconnect the cable from the withdrawal lever.
2. Remove the lower cover from the instrument panel.
3. Disconnect the upper end of the clutch cable from the pedal. See **Figure 5**.
4. Detach the cable housing from the firewall (**Figure 6**) and take the cable out.
5. Installation is the reverse of removal. Check and adjust pedal height and withdrawal lever free play as described in this chapter.

Clutch Removal

The engine and transaxle must be separated to remove the clutch. This can be done either by removing the engine and transaxle and separating them (Chapter Four) or by removing only the transaxle as described in this chapter. If no engine work is planned it is easier to remove just the transaxle. Refer to **Figure 7** for the following procedures.

Once the engine and transaxle have been separated, do the following.
1. Mark the edges of the pressure plate and flywheel so they may be reassembled in the same relative positions.
2. Remove the clutch cover bolts one turn at a time in a diagonal pattern to prevent warping the pressure plate. Take the pressure plate and disc off the flywheel. See **Figure 8**.

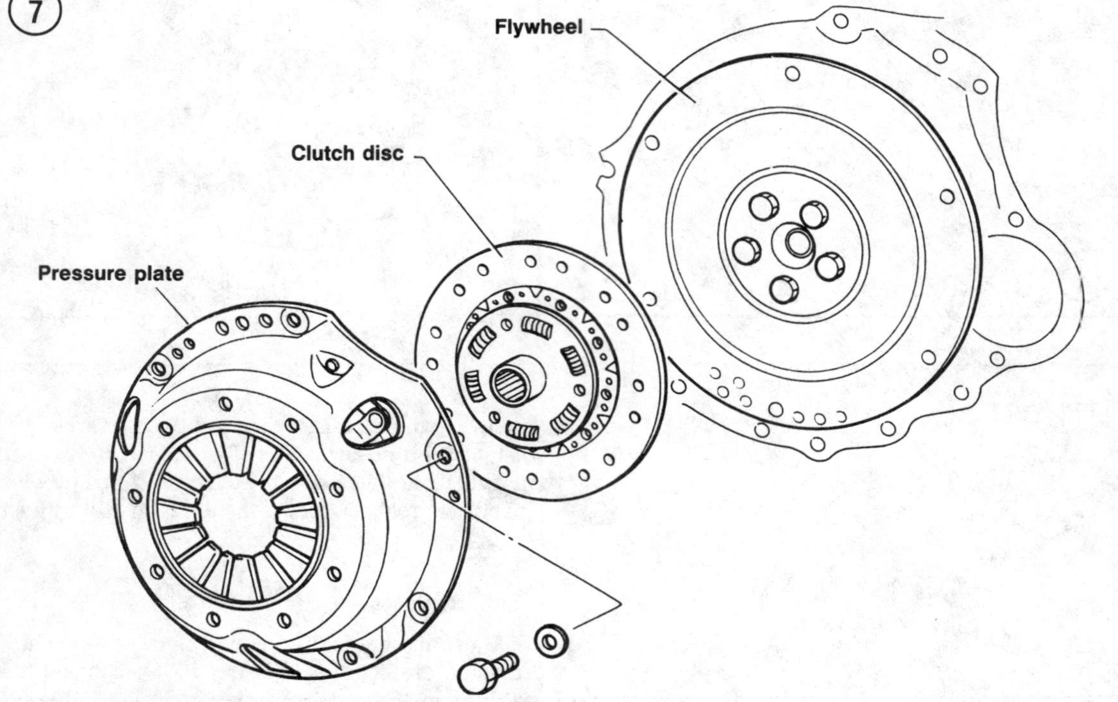

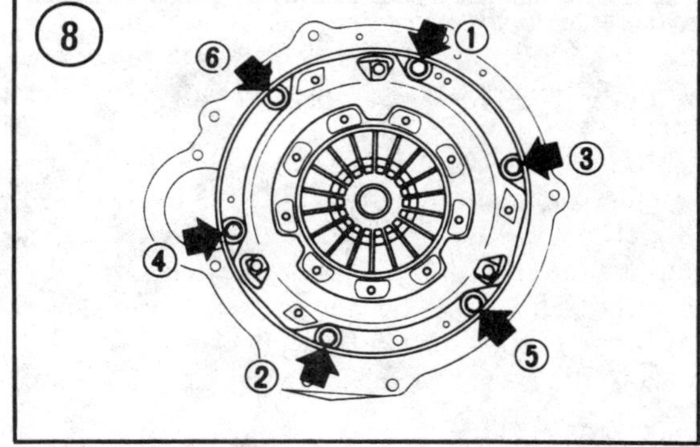

Clutch Disc Inspection

Check the clutch disc for the following:
a. Oil or grease on the facings.
b. Glazed facings.
c. Warped facings.
d. Loose or missing rivets.
e. Facings worn to within 0.3 mm (0.012 in.) of any rivet. Measure with a vernier caliper as shown in **Figure 9** or have the measurement done by a machine shop.
f. Broken springs.
g. Loose fit or rough movement on the transaxle input shaft splines.

Light surface stains may be sanded off and the facings dressed with a wire brush. However, if the facings are soaked with oil or grease, the clutch disc must be replaced. The disc must also be replaced if any of the other defects is present or if the facings are partially worn and a new pressure plate is being installed.

Pressure Plate Inspection

1. Check the pressure plate (**Figure 7**) for:
a. Scoring.
b. Burn marks.
c. Cracks.
Replace the pressure plate if these are found.

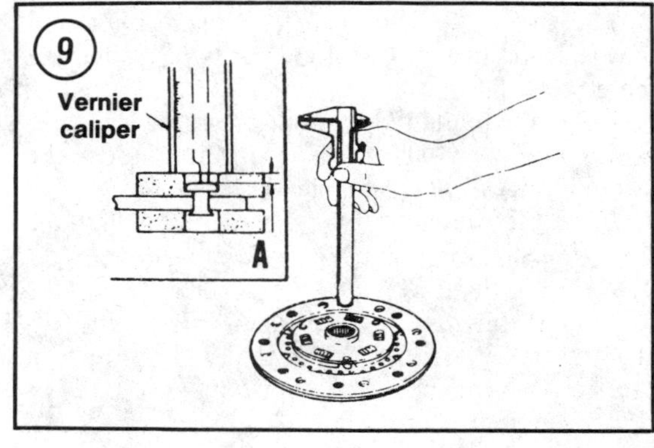

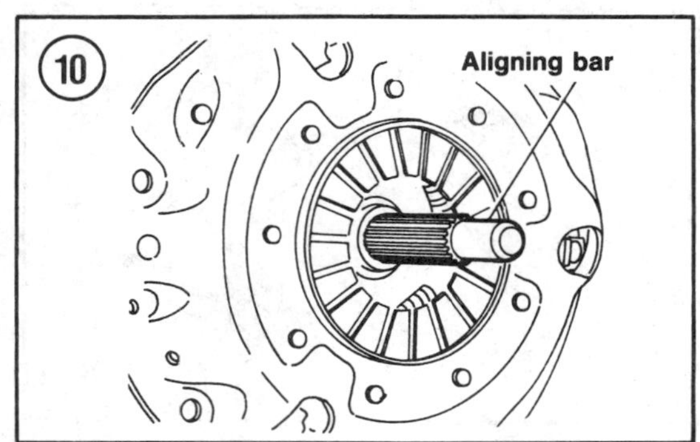

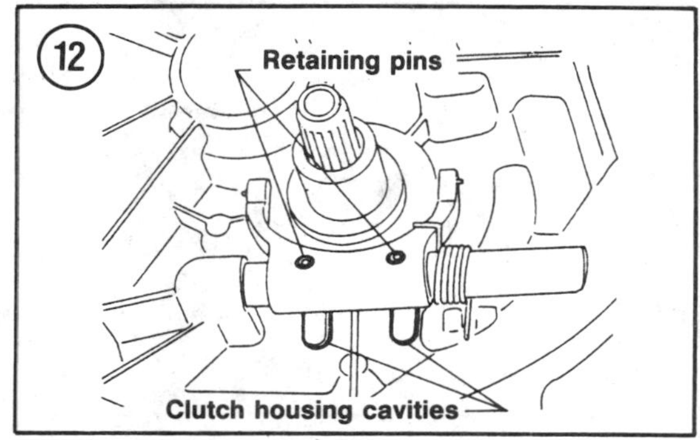

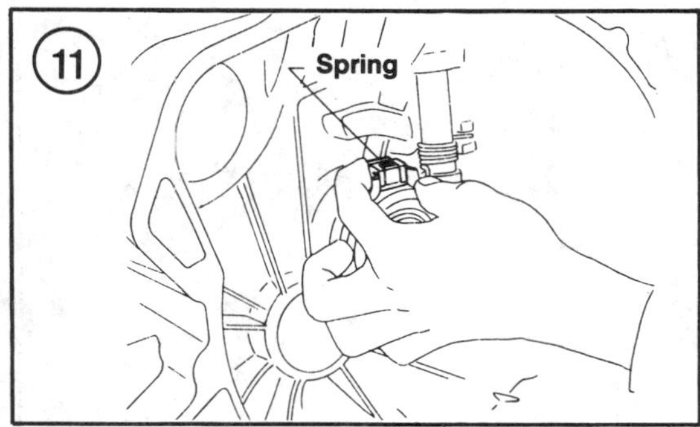

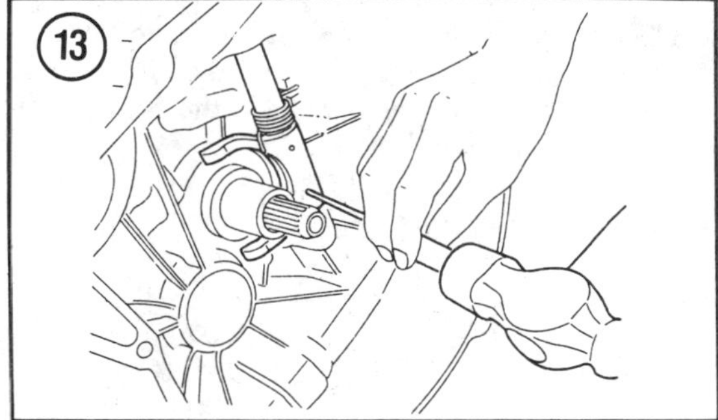

2. Check the diaphragm spring for wear or damage at the release bearing contact surface. Check for bent or broken spring fingers or damaged retracting springs. Replace the pressure plate if these are found.

If the clutch trouble still is not apparent, take the pressure plate and disc to a competent machine shop. Have the disc and pressure plate checked for runout and the diaphragm spring checked for correct finger height. Do not attempt to dismantle the pressure plate or readjust the fingers yourself without the proper tools and experience.

Clutch Installation

1. Be sure your hands are clean.
2. Make sure the disc facings, pressure plate and flywheel are free of oil, grease and other foreign material.
3. Place the clutch disc and presssure plate in position on the flywheel. The protruding side of the disc hub faces away from the flywheel.
4. If the old pressure plate is being reinstalled, be sure the alignment marks on clutch cover and flywheel are lined up.
5. Center the disc and pressure plate with an aligning bar (pilot shaft) such as the one shown in **Figure 10**. Inexpensive aligning bars can be purchased from some foreign car parts stores. An input shaft from a junk transaxle can be used if the factory tool isn't available. Some tool rental dealers and parts stores rent universal aligning bars which can be adapted.
6. Install the clutch cover bolts. Tighten gradually in a diagonal pattern to specifications (**Table 2**).
7. Apply a *light* coat of molybdenum disulfide grease to the splines on clutch hub and transaxle input shaft.

Release Mechanism Removal

As with the clutch, release mechanism removal requires that the engine and transaxle be separated. The release mechanism is mounted in the clutch housing. Either remove the engine and transaxle (Chapter Four) or remove just the transaxle as described in this chapter. If no engine work is planned, it will be easier to remove just the transaxle.

1. Detach the release bearing spring (**Figure 11**) from the release bearing. Take the bearing out.
2. Align the withdrawal lever retaining pins with the clutch housing cavities. See **Figure 12**.
3. Tap out the withdrawal lever retaining pins (**Figure 13**).
4. Pull out the clutch control shaft (**Figure 14**) and take out the withdrawal lever.

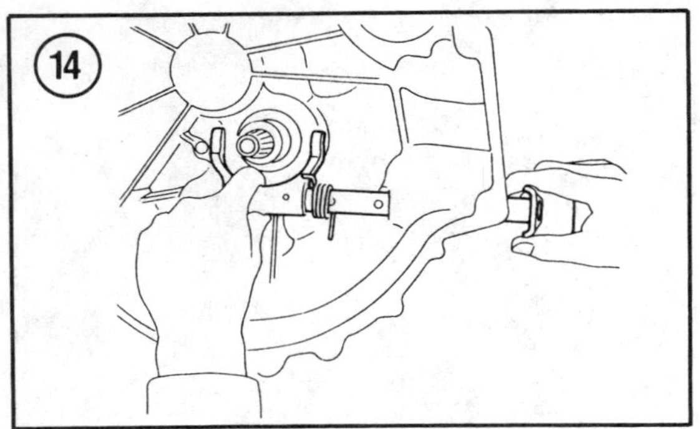

Release Mechanism Inspection

1. Check the release mechanism for the following:
   a. *Wear at the contact point of release bearing and withdrawal lever*—replace the bearing or withdrawal lever if worn.
   b. *Grease leaking from the release bearing*— replace the bearing if this is evident.

> *CAUTION*
> *Do not clean the release bearing in solvent, since it is prelubricated at the factory. Wipe the bearing clean with a lint-free cloth.*

   c. *A worn release bearing*—To check, hold the bearing inner race with fingers and rotate the outer race while applying light pressure to it. If the bearing feels rough or makes noise, replace it.

2. Pry out the clutch control shaft oil seal (**Figure 15**). Coat the oil seal mounting surface with gear oil, then tap in a new seal with a drift the same diameter as the seal. See **Figure 16**.

Release Mechanism Installation

1. Apply a *light* coat of molybdenum disulfide grease to the following points:
   a. Contact points of withdrawal lever and release bearing sleeve.
   b. Inside of release bearing sleeve (**Figure 17**).
2. Apply molybdenum disulfide grease to the end of the clutch control shaft farthest from the lever. Apply multipurpose lithium grease to the end nearest the lever. See **Figure 18**.
3. Position the withdrawal lever in the clutch housing. Slide the shaft in and attach the return spring as shown in **Figure 19**.
4. Apply a light coat of molybdenum disulfide grease to the transaxle input shaft splines and the release bearing sliding surface on the transaxle case. See **Figure 20**.

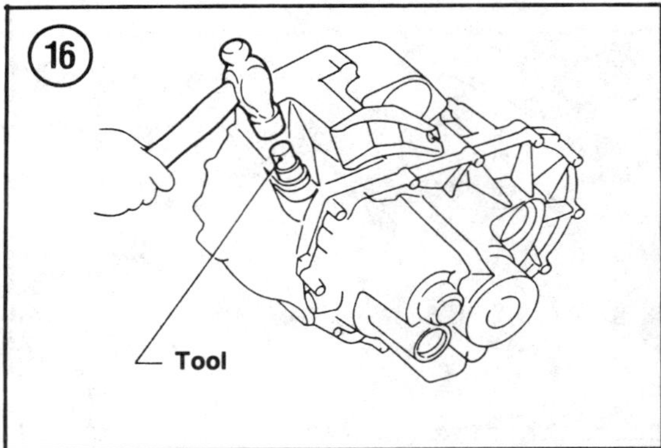

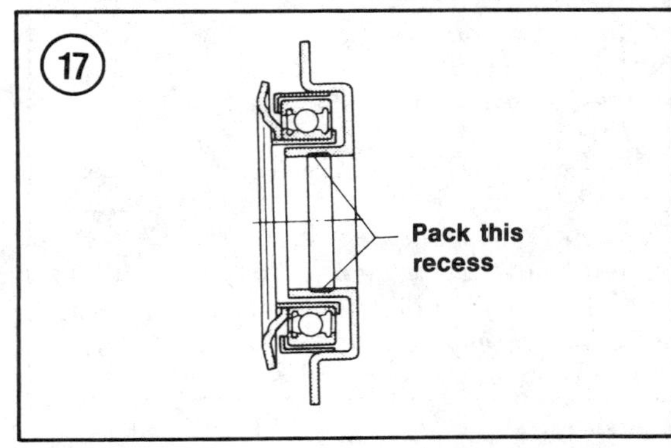

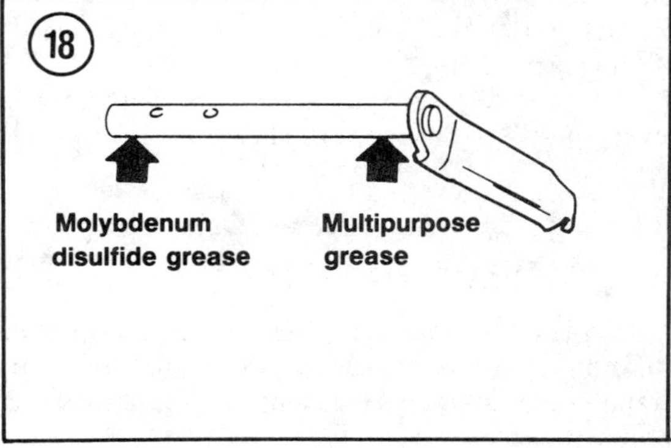

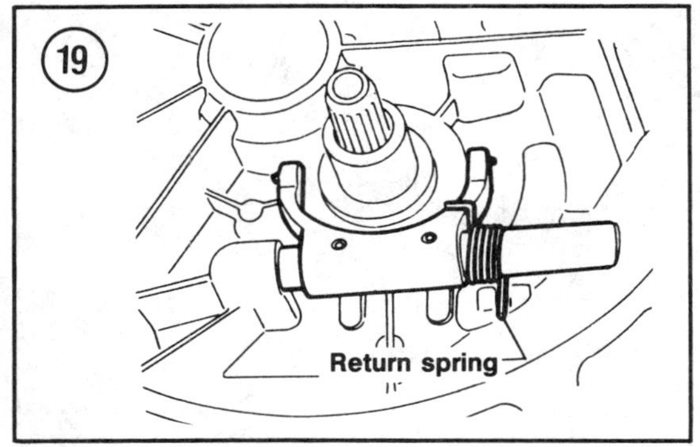

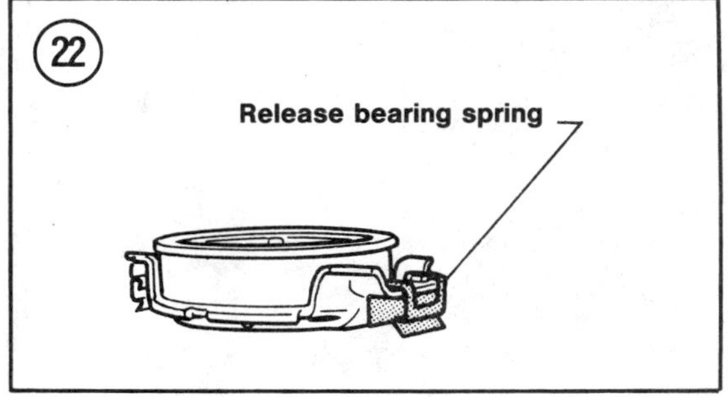

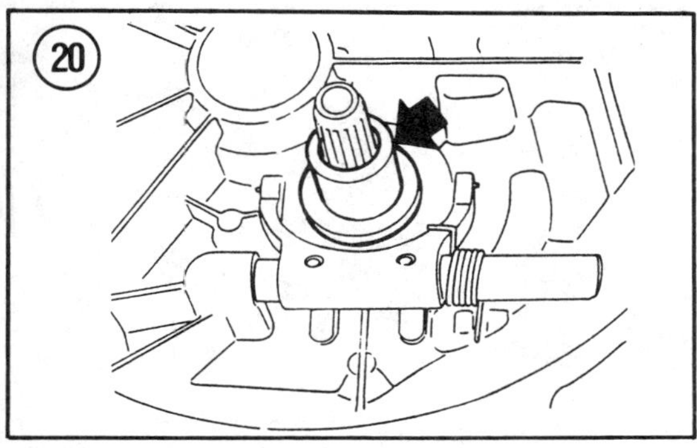

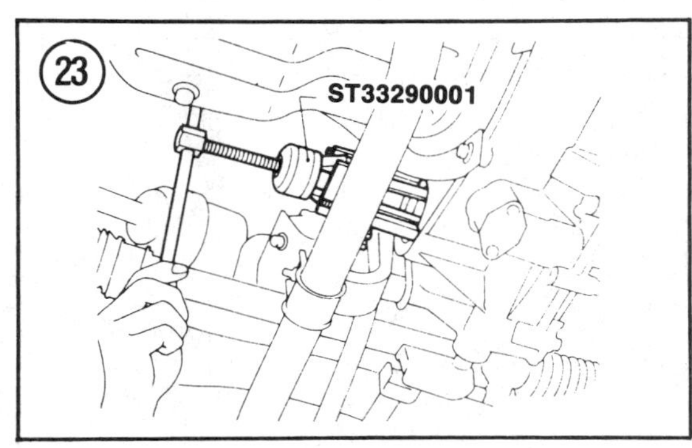

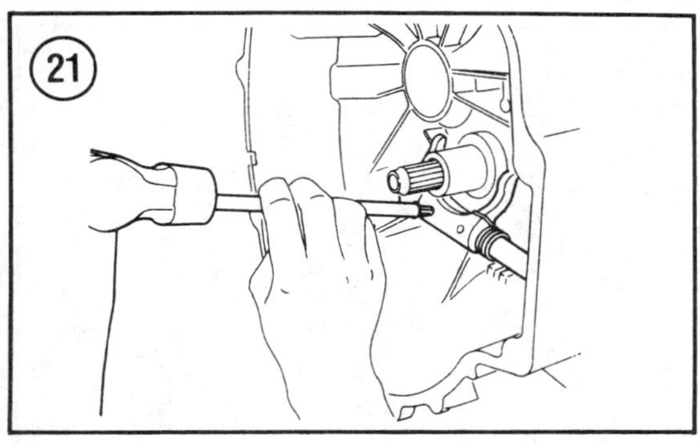

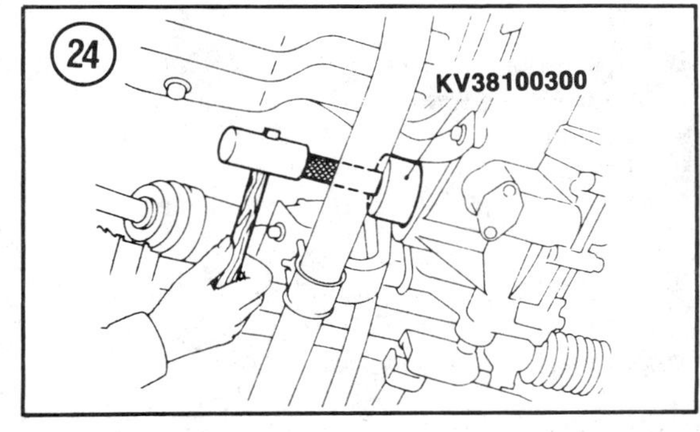

5. Secure the lever to the shaft with the retaining pins. See **Figure 21**.

6. Install the retaining springs on the release bearing. See **Figure 22**.

7. Push the release bearing onto the withdrawal lever. Make sure the springs click and the bearing is securely fastened to the lever.

MANUAL TRANSAXLE

A transaxle consists of a transmission and differential in one housing. A 4-speed manual transaxle is standard equipment. A 5-speed is optional.

This section includes removal and installation procedures for the transaxle, as well as oil seal replacement and complete service procedures for the shift control mechanism. Transaxle repairs require expensive special tools which cannot be duplicated by home mechanics. Repairs should be done by a dealer or properly equipped transmission shop.

Axle Shaft Oil Seals Replacement

1. Drain the transaxle oil as described in Chapter Three.

2. Remove the axle shafts as described in Chapter Nine.

3. Remove the oil seal with a puller such as Nissan tool part No. ST33290001 (**Figure 23**).

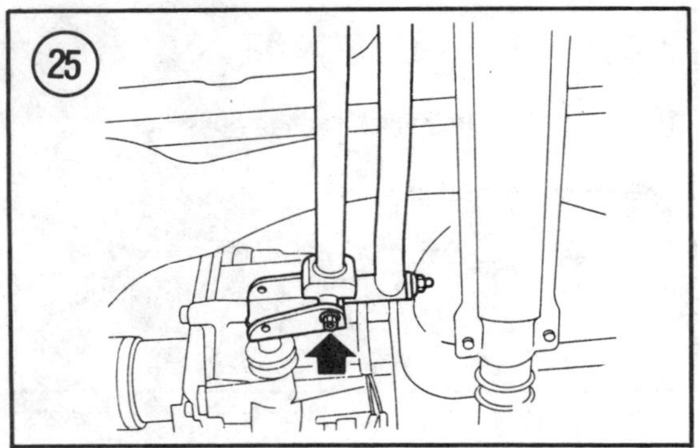

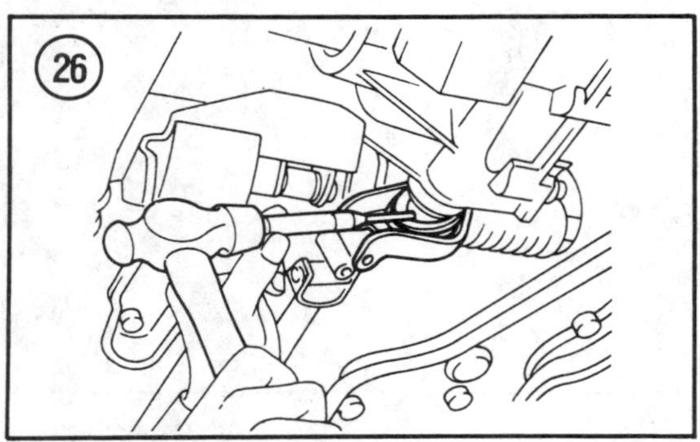

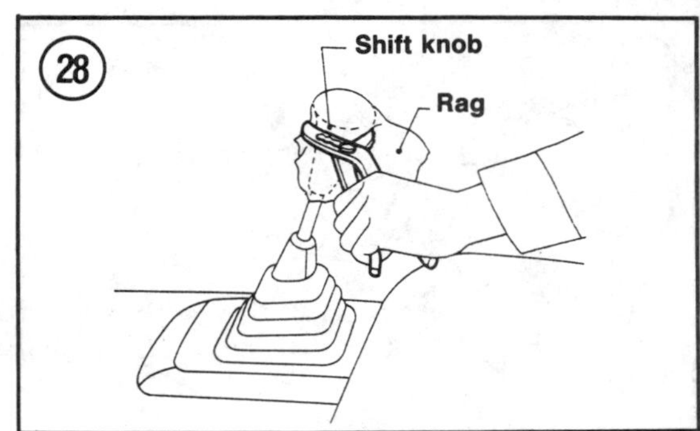

4. Coat the seal mounting surface on the transaxle with gear oil. Tap in a new seal with a drift such as Nissan tool part No. KV38100300 (**Figure 24**).

5. Coat the seal lip with gear oil.

6. Install the axle shafts as described in Chapter Nine.

7. Fill the transaxle with gear oil as described in Chapter Three.

Shift Control Oil Seal Replacement

1. Set the handbrake. Securely block both rear wheels so the car will not roll in either direction.

2. Jack up the front end of the car and place it on jackstands.

3. Detach the shift control rod from the transaxle. See **Figure 25**.

CAUTION
Do not damage the boot during the next step.

4. Tap out the retaining pin and remove the yoke (**Figure 26**).

5. Pry out the old oil seal as shown in **Figure 27**.

6. Coat the seal mounting surface with gear oil, then tap in a new oil seal with a drift (such as a piece of pipe) the same diameter as the seal.

7. Install the yoke and attach the shift control rod.

8. Lower the car and unblock the wheels.

1. Set the handbrake. Securely block both rear wheels so the car will not roll in either direction.

2. Jack up the front end of the car and place it on jackstands.

3. Wrap the shift knob with a thick rag and unscrew it with pliers. See **Figure 28**.

4. Detach the control rod and support rod from the transaxle. See **Figure 29**.

5. Remove the control bracket mounting bolts (**Figure 30**). Lower the shift linkage clear and take it out from under the car.

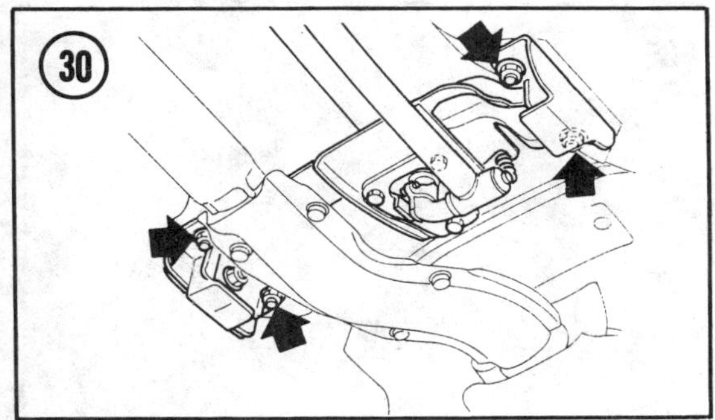

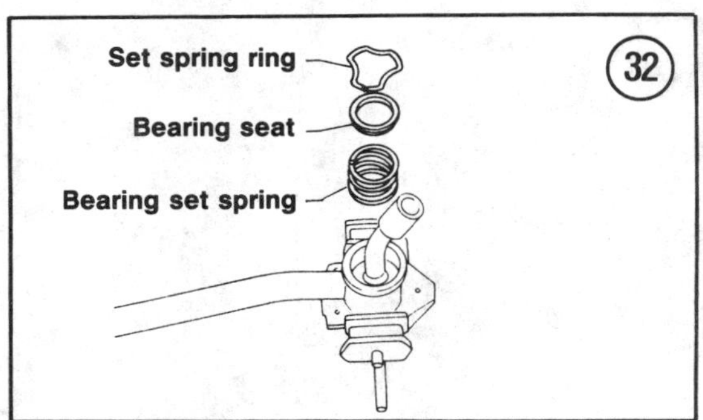

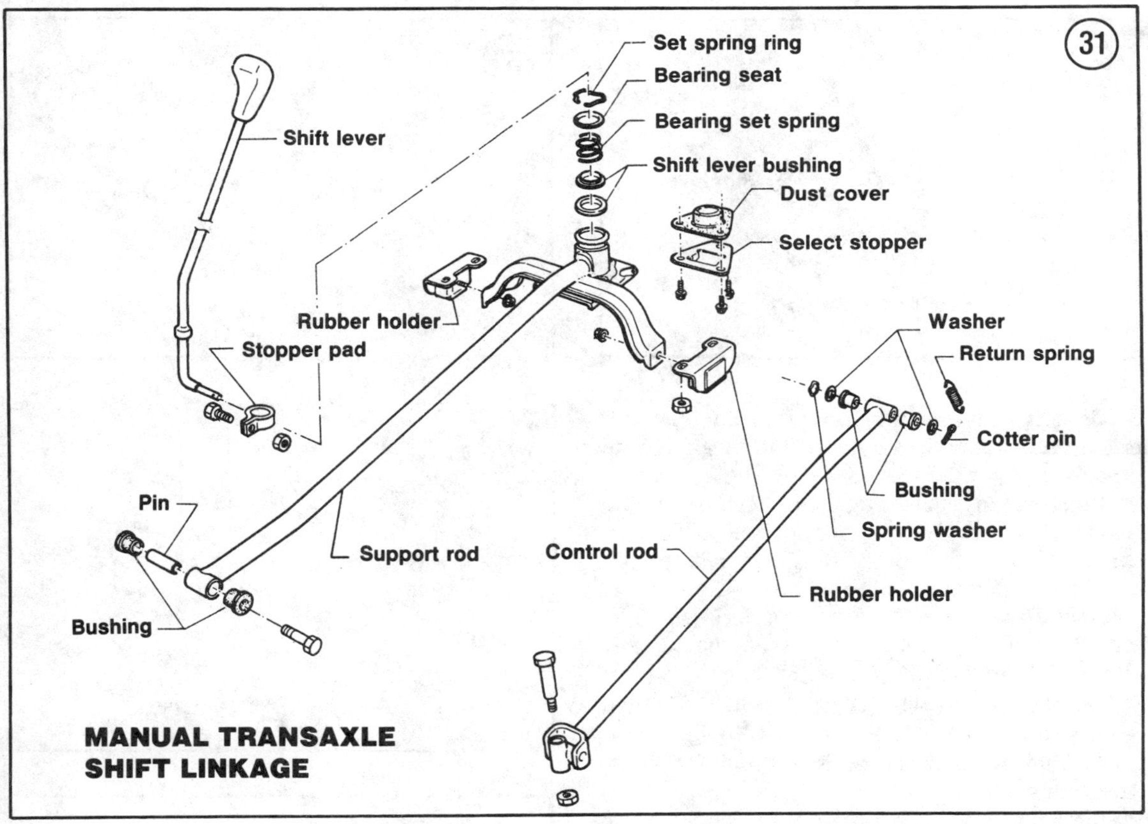

MANUAL TRANSAXLE SHIFT LINKAGE

Shift Linkage Overhaul

Refer to **Figure 31** for this procedure.

1. Remove the shift linkage as described in this chapter.

2. Unhook the return spring. Remove the cotter pin, then detach the control rod from the shift linkage. Discard the cotter pin. It must not be reused.

3. Remove the control lever bracket, set spring ring, bearing set seat and bearing set spring. See **Figure 32**.

4. Remove the rubber holder (**Figure 33**). Remove the screws and take off the dust cover and control lever bearing.

5. Thoroughly clean all parts in solvent. While cleaning, check for wear and damage. Replace worn or damaged parts.

6. Check the set spring, set spring ring and control lever bearing (**Figure 34**) for wear, deformation, cracks or other defects. Replace parts that show these conditions.

7. Check the control rod and support rod bushings for wear, cracks or deterioration. If any of these

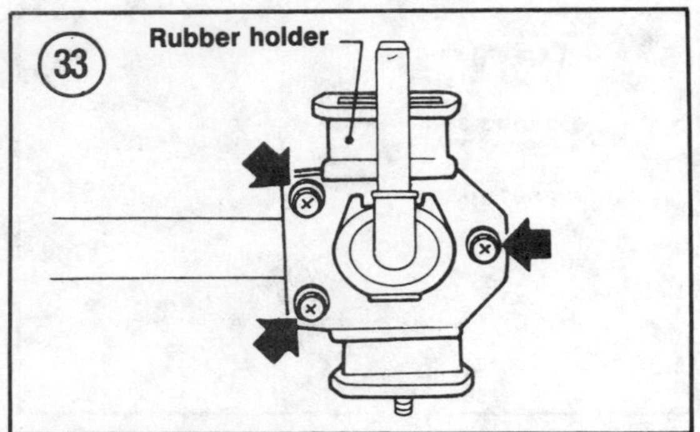

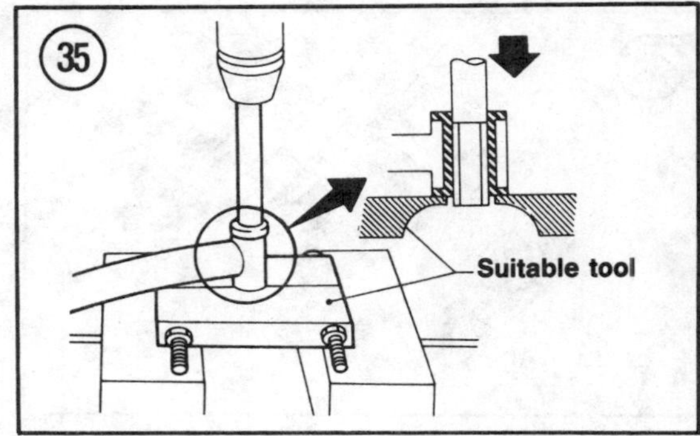

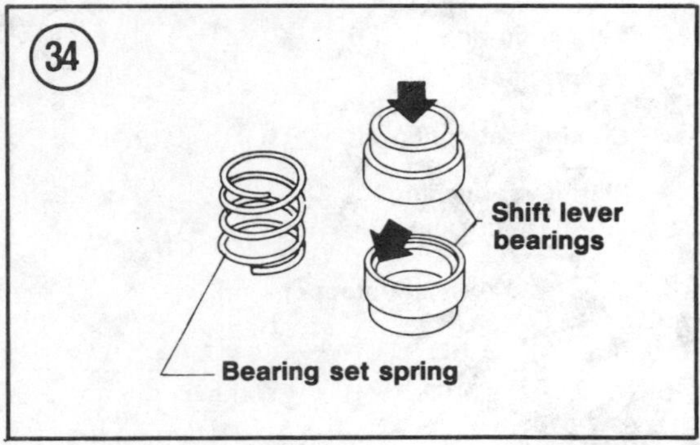

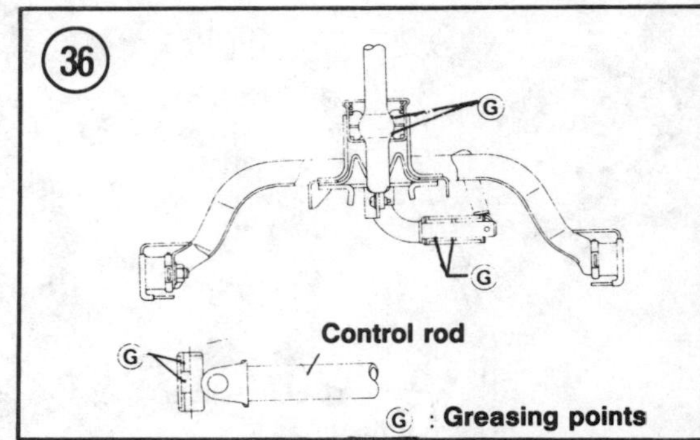

conditions can be seen, have the old bushings pressed out and new ones pressed in by a machine shop. See **Figure 35**.

8. Assemble by reversing Steps 2-4. Note the following:

   a. Apply multipurpose lithium grease to the friction points shown in **Figure 36**.

   b. Install the cotter pin as shown in **Figure 37**.

   c. Position the rubber holders on the support rod as shown in **Figure 38**. Be sure there is no weight on the support rod when positioning the rubber holders.

   d. Install the dust cover securely as shown in **Figure 39**.

Shift Linkage Installation

Installation is the reverse of removal, plus the following.

1. After the linkage is installed, loosen the select stopper mounting bolts (**Figure 40**).

2. Place the shift lever in FIRST.

3. Set the clearance between select stopper and shift lever to one mm (0.039 in.). To do this, move the select stopper as shown in **Figure 41**.

4. Tighten the select stopper mounting bolts.

5. Make sure the shift lever can be shifted to all gear positions without dragging or binding.

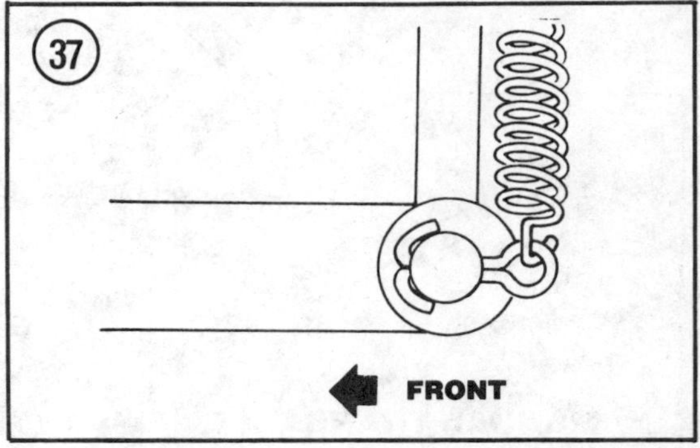

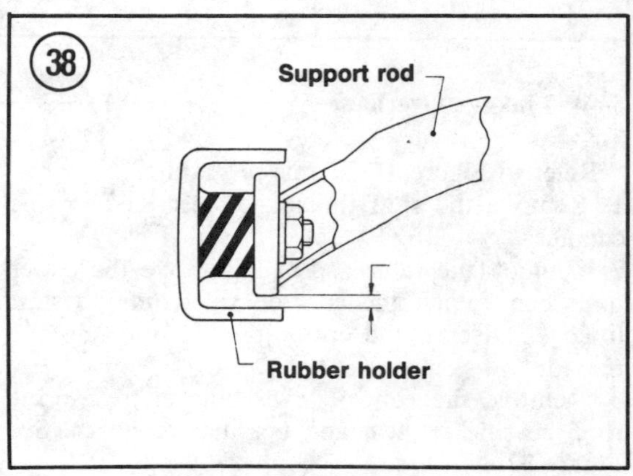

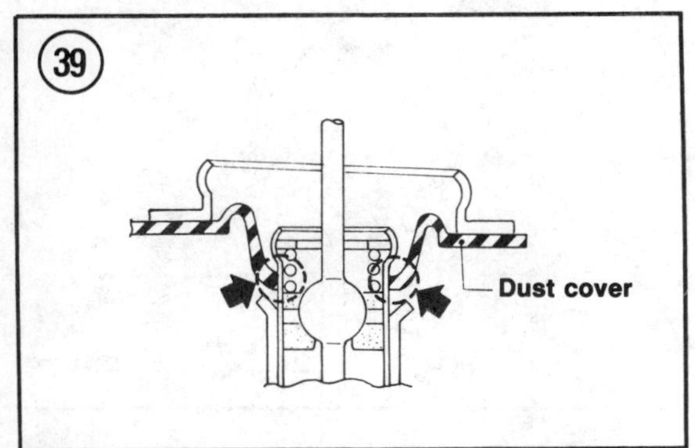

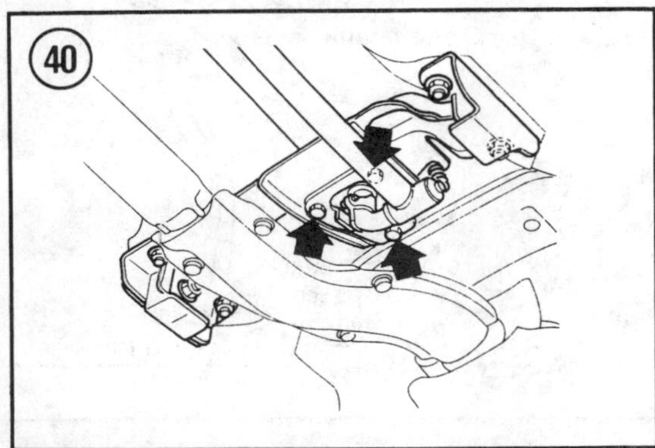

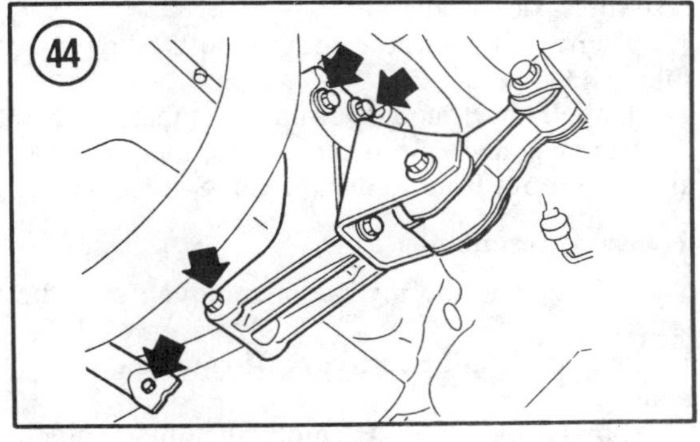

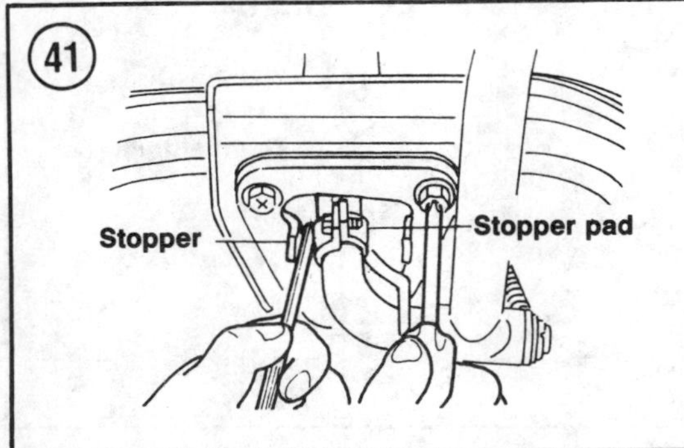

Transaxle Removal/Installation

1. Remove the battery and its mounting plate.
2. Remove the radiator reservoir tank.
3. Drain the transmission oil as described in Chapter Three.
4. Remove the axle shafts as described in Chapter Nine.
5. Remove the access plates from the wheel wells. See **Figure 42**.
6. Detach the support rod and control rod from the transaxle. See **Figure 43**.
7. Place a jack beneath the engine to support it. Use a block of wood between jack and oil pan so the pan won't collapse.
8. Detach the engine gusset from the transaxle and motor mount. See **Figure 44**.
9. Disconnect the clutch cable from the withdrawal lever. See *Cable Replacement* in this chapter.
10. Disconnect the speedometer cable from the transaxle.
11. Unplug the wires from the backup lamp and neutral switches.
12. Place a jack beneath the transaxle to support it. Transmission jacks, available from rental dealers, work well for this. They have cradles which prevent the transaxle from falling. They can also be

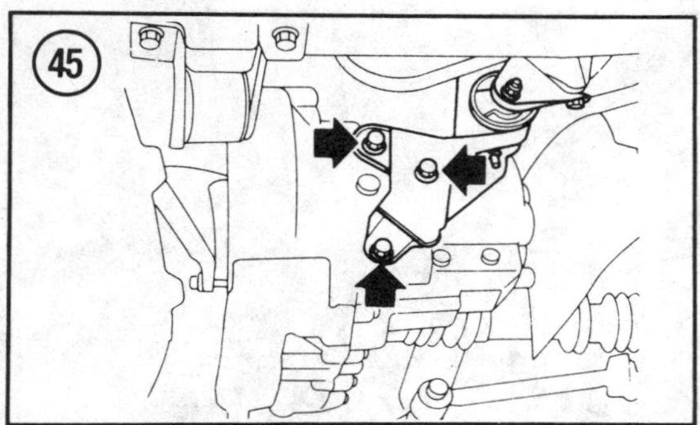

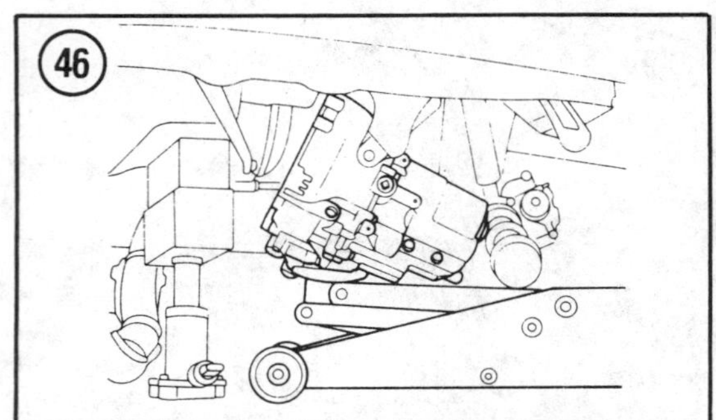

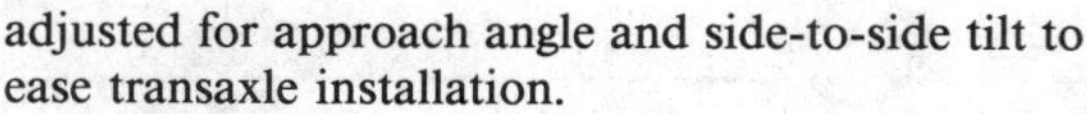

adjusted for approach angle and side-to-side tilt to ease transaxle installation.

13. Remove the motor mount bolts shown in **Figure 45**.

14. Unbolt the transaxle from the engine. Move the transaxle away from the engine, then lower it and take it out from under the car. See **Figure 46**.

Transaxle Installation

Installation is the reverse of removal, plus the following.

1. Clean the mating surfaces of engine and clutch housing.

2. Apply a light coat of molybdenum disulfide grease to the clutch disc splines and input shaft splines.

3. Tighten all fasteners to specifications (**Table 2**).

4. Fill the transaxle with oil as described in Chapter Three.

AUTOMATIC TRANSAXLE

Many automatic transaxle problems can be diagnosed with the simple checks described in this chapter. Major repairs require special tools and should be done by a dealer or transmission shop.

Throttle Cable Adjustment

Improper throttle cable adjustment can cause automatic downshifting to occur too early, too late or not at all.

1. Loosen the throttle cable nuts (A and B, **Figure 47**).

2. Hold the throttle lever in the wide open position. Move the cable fitting (Q, **Figure 48**) all the way in direction T and turn nut B as far as it will go in direction U.

3. Back nut B off 1-1 1/2 turns. Tighten nut A securely in direction T.

4. Release the throttle. Move it from idle to wide open and measure the throttle cable stroke (L, **Figure 49**). It should be 27.4-31.4 mm (1 1/16-1 1/4 in.). If not, recheck the cable adjustment.

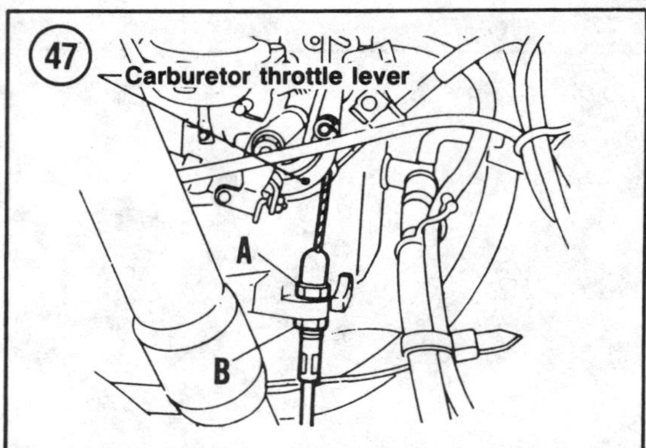

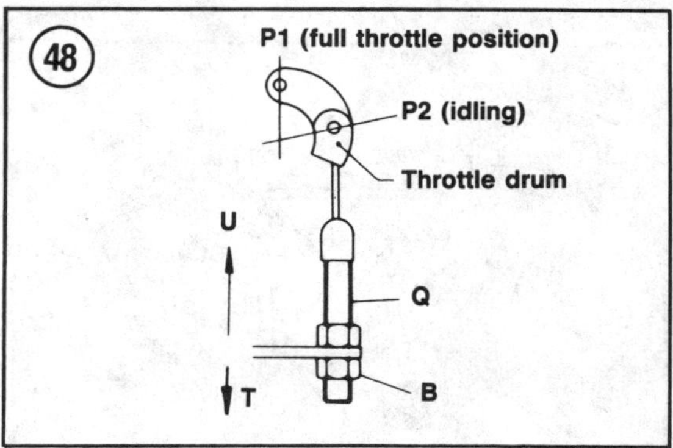

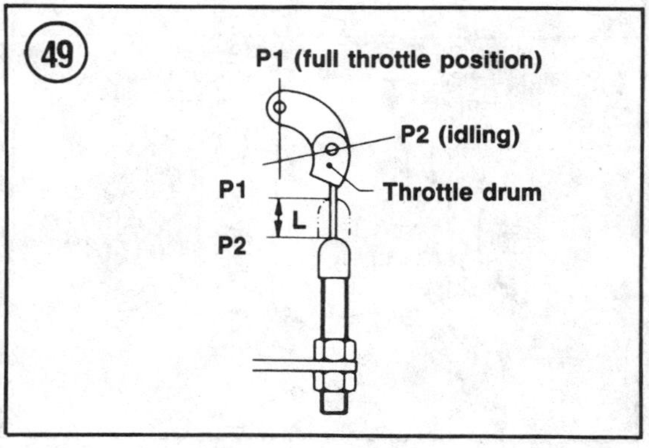

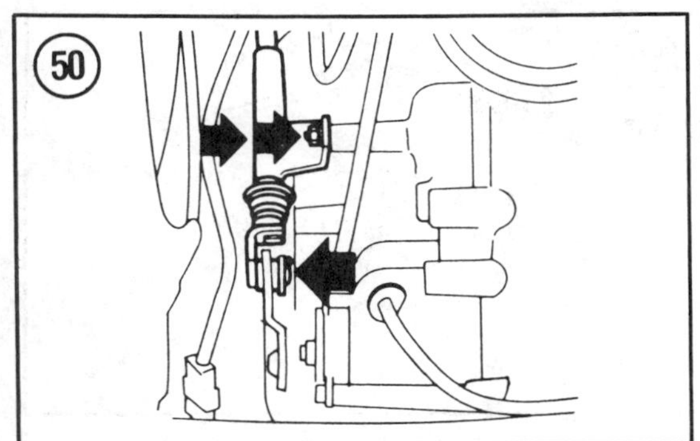

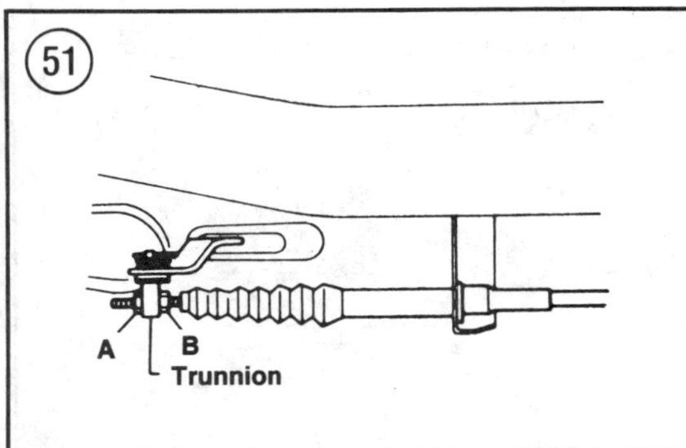

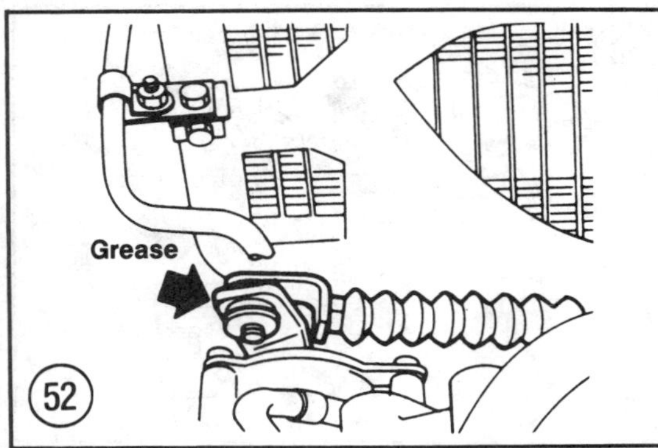

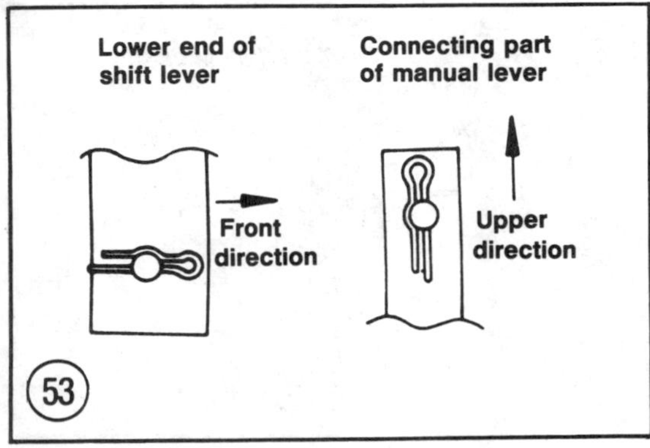

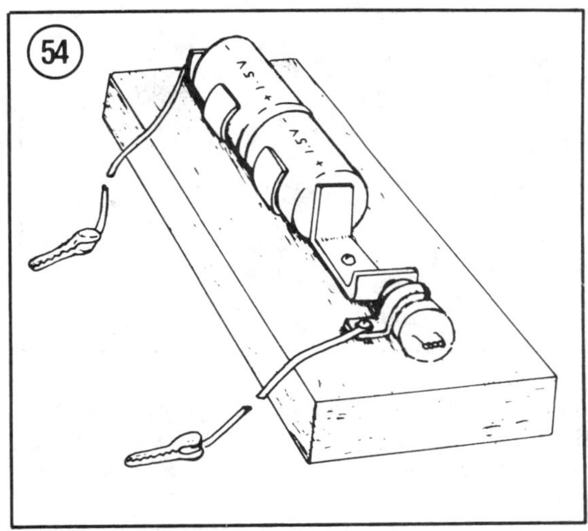

Control Cable Adjustment

1. Check control cable adjustment. Move the shift lever through all the gear positions. You should be able to feel a detent (stopping point) at each position. The shift lever pointer should line up with the indicator at each position. If not, perform the following steps to adjust the cable.

2. Move the lever to PARK. Make sure the transaxle holds the car from moving.

3. Make sure the cable is securely fastened to the transaxle. See **Figure 50**.

4. Loosen the control cable adjusting nuts (**Figure 51**). Let the control cable find its position in relation to the trunnion, then tighten the adjusting nuts.

5. Move the shift lever through the gear positions and back to PARK. Make sure it moves smoothly, without binding.

6. Apply multipurpose grease to the spring washer (**Figure 52**).

7. Make sure the cotter pins at the ends of the cable are positioned correctly. See **Figure 53**. If not, remove them and reinstall them in the correct positions.

Inhibitor Switch Test

The inhibitor switch prevents the engine from starting when the transmission is in any gear except PARK or NEUTRAL. It also operates the backup lights.

This procedure requires an ohmmeter or a test lamp like the one shown in **Figure 54**.

1. Unplug the switch wiring connector (**Figure 55**). With the shift lever in PARK or NEUTRAL, there should be continuity between terminals 1 and 2. An ohmmeter connected between these terminals

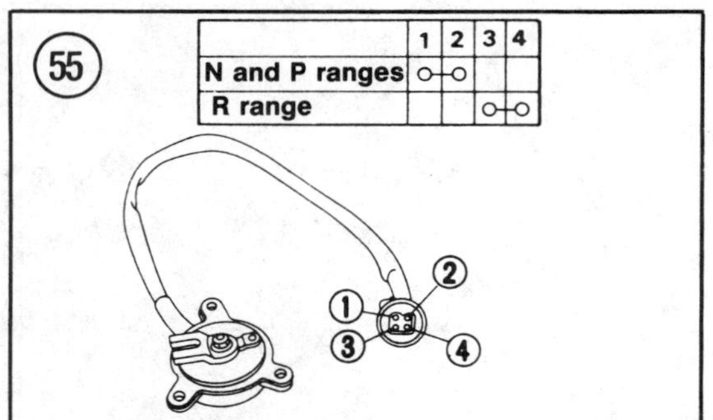

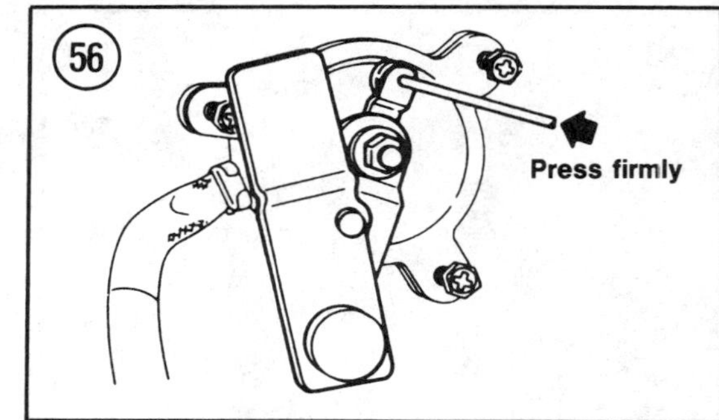

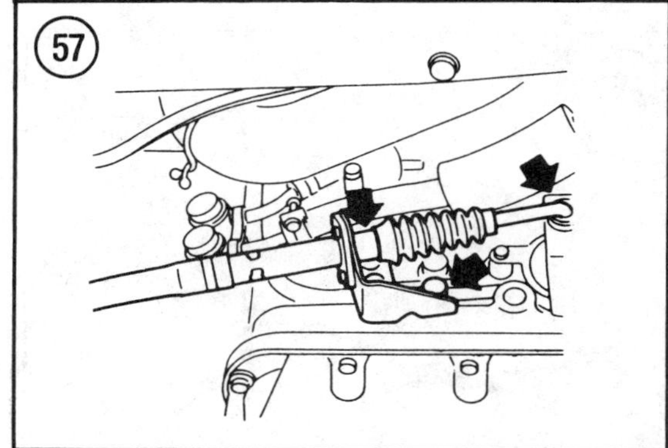

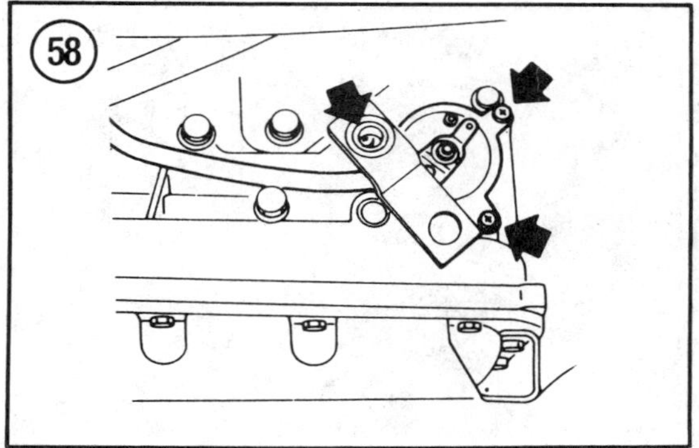

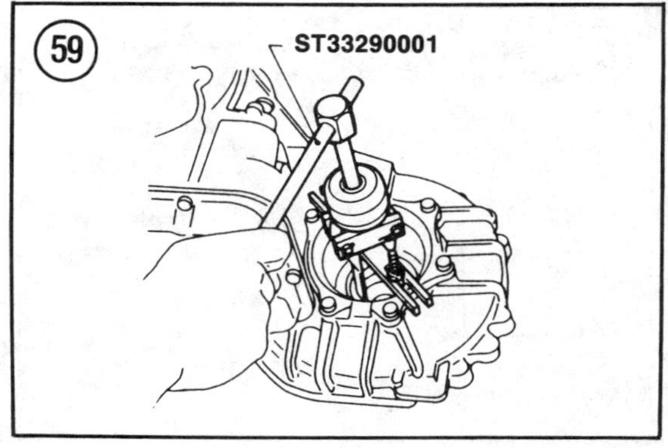

should show little or no resistance or a test lamp should light. There should not be continuity between terminals 1 and 2 in any other gear position.

2. Leave the ohmmeter or test lamp connected to terminals 1 and 2.

3. Locate the manual lever on the side of the transmission. This is the lever to which the lower end of the shift control cable is connected.

4. With the shift lever in NEUTRAL, move the manual lever by hand an equal amount in both directions. The switch should open (the ohmmeter should show infinite resistance or the test lamp go out) at equal distances in both directions. If the switch opens sooner in one direction than the other, adjust the switch as described in this chapter.

5. Place the shift lever in REVERSE. There should be continuity between terminals 3 and 4. There should not be continuity between terminals 3 and 4 with the shift lever in any other gear position.

6. If the switch has continuity when it shouldn't, adjust it as described in this chapter. If it doesn't have continuity at all, replace it as described in this chapter.

Inhibitor Switch Adjustment

1. Before adjusting the switch, adjust the control cable as described in this chapter.

2. Loosen the switch mounting screws.

3. Insert a 2.5 mm (0.098 in.) diameter pin into the adjustment holes in the switch and switch lever. See **Figure 56**. Make sure the holes are aligned as closely as possible, then tighten the switch mounting screws.

Inhibitor Switch Removal/Installation

1. Remove the splash shield from under the front of the car.

2. Disconnect the shift control cable from the manual lever on the side of the transaxle. See **Figure 57**.

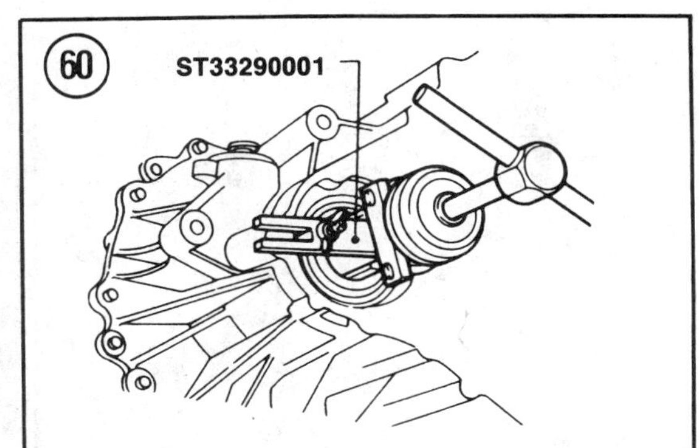

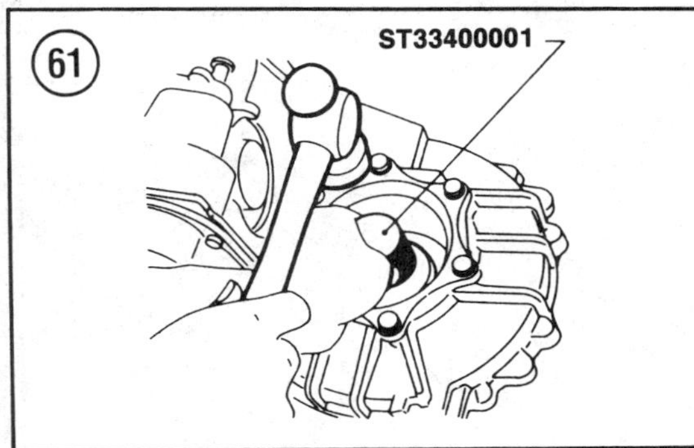

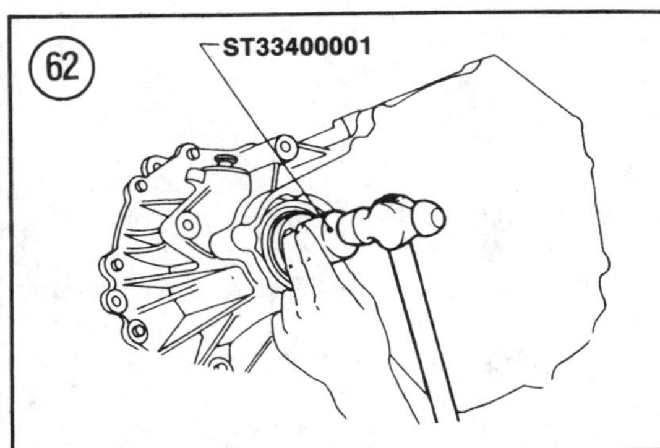

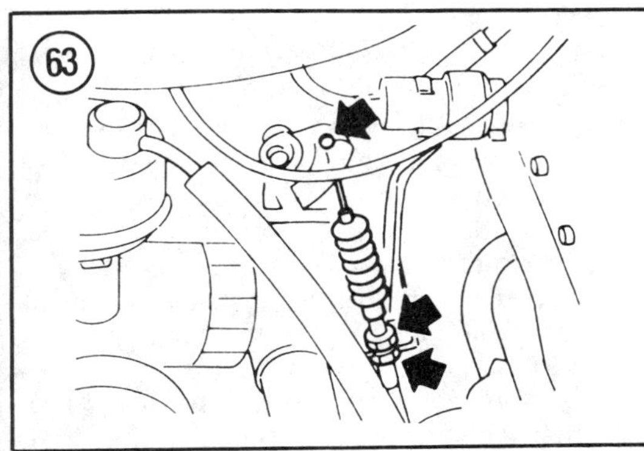

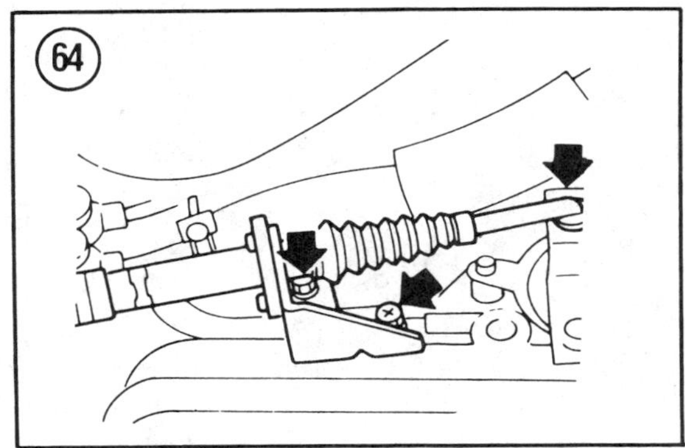

3. Unplug the switch wiring connector. Remove the switch mounting screws (**Figure 58**) and take the switch off.

4. Installation is the reverse of removal. Adjust the switch as described in this chapter.

Oil Seal Replacement

1. Remove the axle shaft from the side on which the seal is being replaced. See *Axle Shafts* in Chapter Nine.

2. Remove the oil seal with a puller such as Nissan tool part No. ST33290001. See **Figure 59** (left side) or **Figure 60** (right side).

3. Coat the seal mounting surface with automatic transmission fluid. Tap in a new seal with a drift such as Nissan tool part No. ST33400001. See **Figure 61** (left side) or **Figure 62** (right side).

4. Install the axle shaft as described in Chapter Nine.

Transaxle Removal

1. Disconnect the negative cable from the battery.

2. If equipped with a diesel engine, remove the air cleaner.

3. Set the handbrake. Securely block both rear wheels so the car will not roll in either direction.

4. Loosen the left front wheel nuts. Jack up the front end of the car, place it on jackstands and remove the left front wheel.

5. Drain the transaxle fluid as described in Chapter Three.

6. Remove the access panel from the left wheel well.

7. Remove the axle shafts as described in Chapter Nine.

8. Disconnect the speedometer cable from the transaxle.

9. Disconnect the throttle cable from the throttle lever. See **Figure 63**.

10. Disconnect the shift control cable from the transaxle. See **Figure 64**.

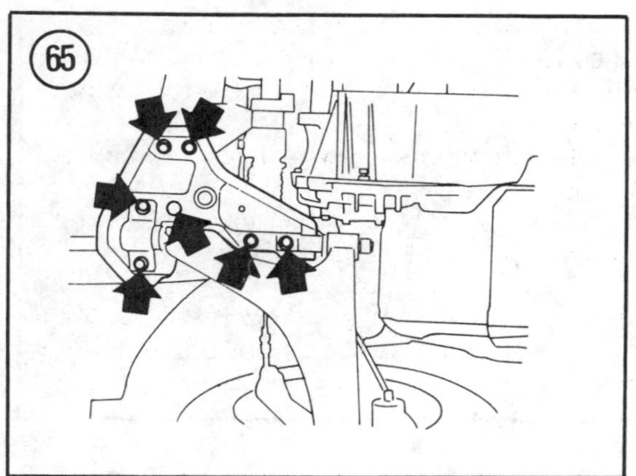

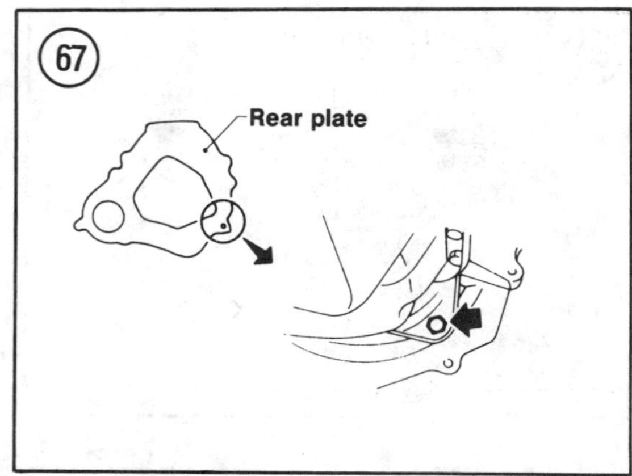

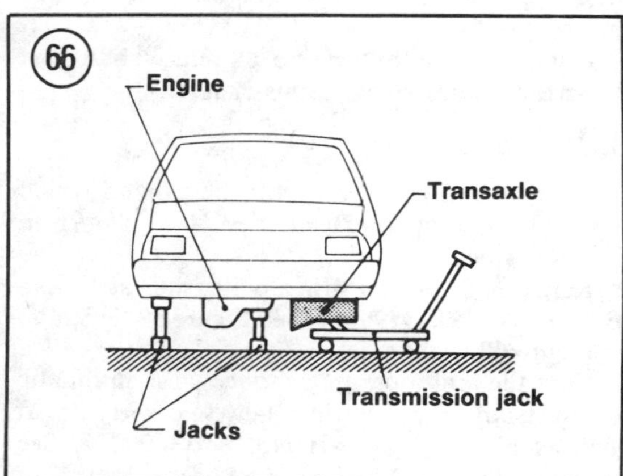

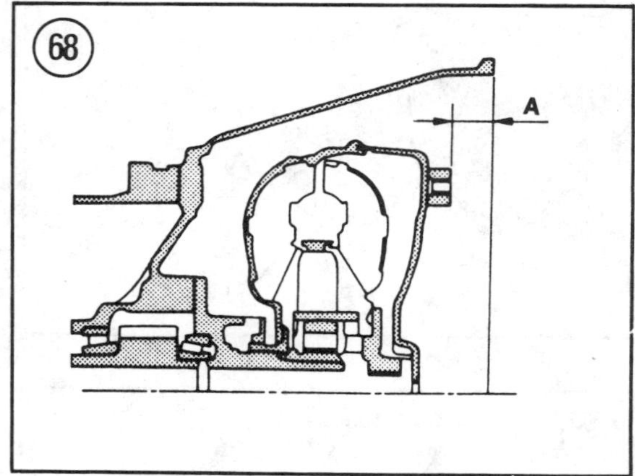

11. Remove the transmission fluid dipstick.

12. If equipped with a diesel engine, remove the left suspension arm and gusset. See **Figure 65**.

CAUTION
During the next step, do not place the jack beneath the oil pan drain plug.

13. Place a jack beneath the engine to support it. Use a block of wood between jack and oil pan so the pan won't collapse.

14. Place a jack beneath the transaxle to support it. See **Figure 66**. Transmission jacks, available from rental dealers, work well for this. They have cradles which prevent the transaxle from falling. They can also be adjusted for approach angle and side-to-side tilt to ease transaxle installation.

15. Disconnect the transaxle fluid cooler tubes from the transaxle. Immediately cap or plug all openings to keep out dirt.

16. If equipped with a diesel engine, remove the engine gusset.

17. Make alignment marks on the torque converter and drive plate in 2 places. Turn the engine to expose the torque converter-to-drive plate bolts (**Figure 67**) and remove the bolts.

18. Remove the motor mount bolts.

19. Remove the starter as described in Chapter Seven.

20. Remove the transaxle-to-engine bolts. Lower the jack beneath the transaxle and remove the transaxle through the left wheel well.

Transaxle Installation

Installation is the reverse of removal, plus the following.

1. If the torque converter was removed from the transaxle, measure distance A, **Figure 68**, to make sure it is installed correctly. It should be at least 21.1 mm (0.831 in.).

2. Align the match marks on torque converter and drive plate. The torque converter can be turned through the hole near the starter mounting flange (**Figure 69**).

3. Apply thread locking agent to the drive plate-to-torque converter bolts. Once the drive

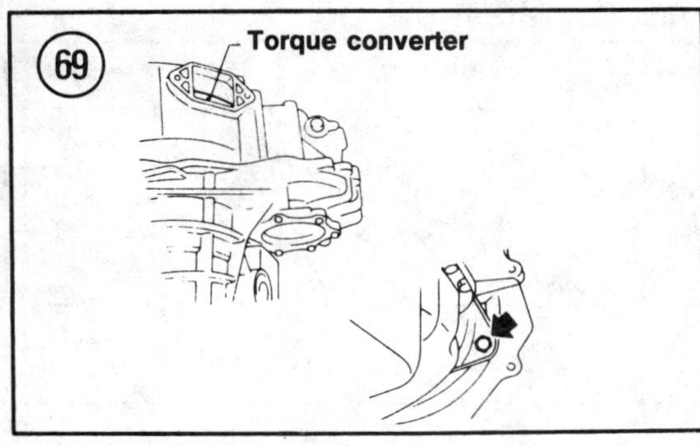

plate is bolted to the torque converter, rotate the engine several turns by hand and make sure the drive plate and torque converter rotate freely, without binding.

4. Fill the transmission with fluid as described in Chapter Three.

5. Adjust the shift control cable and inhibitor switch as described in this chapter.

6. With the engine running, move the shift lever to all gear positions. A slight shock should be felt as the transaxle shifts into each forward and reverse gear.

Tables are on the following page.

Table 1 CLUTCH SPECIFICATIONS

Item	mm	in.
Pedal height		
1982	201-207	7 15/16-8 1/8
1983	194-204	7 5/8-8
Withdrawal lever free play	2-4	3/32-3/16
Pedal free travel	11-21	7/16-13/16

Table 2 TIGHTENING TORQUES

Fastener	N·m	ft.-lb.
Clutch		
Pedal stopper locknut	12-15	9-11
Clutch cable locknut (gasoline)	3-4	2-3
Clutch cable double nuts (diesel)	19-25	14-19
Clutch cable bracket bolts	8-11	6-8
Pressure plate bolts		
1982	16-21	12-15
1983 (7T)*	16-21	12-15
1983 (9T)*	22-29	16-22
Manual transaxle		
Front buffer rod bracket		
To engine	29-39	22-29
To transaxle	16-21	12-15
Left motor mount to transaxle	29-39	22-29
Rear motor mount to body	29-39	22-29
Rear motor mount buffer rod	39-49	29-36
Speedometer pinion gear	3.7-5.0	3-4
Shift control rod to transaxle	6.3-8.3	4.6-6.1
Shift support rod to transaxle	8-12	6-9
Linkage select stopper bolt	3.1-5.0	2.5-3.7
Linkage rubber holder to body	8-12	6-9
Automatic transaxle		
Drive plate to torque converter	49-69	36-51
Converter housing to engine		
M8 bolts	16-22	12-16
M10 bolts	39-49	29-36
Engine to gusset	30-40	22-30
Gusset to converter housing	16-21	12-15

* 7T bolts are indicated by the number 7 stamped in the bolt head. 9T bolts are indicated by the number 9.

CHAPTER NINE

FRONT SUSPENSION, AXLE SHAFTS, WHEEL BEARINGS AND STEERING

The Sentra uses a MacPherson strut front suspension. The shock absorbers and coil springs are combined into single units, mounted to the wheel wells at the top and to the knuckle arms at the bottom. This chapter provides service procedures for the front suspension, wheel bearings, front axle shafts and steering. **Tables 1-3** are at the end of the chapter.

FRONT SUSPENSION

Figure 1 shows the front suspension.

Shock Absorber Replacement

Shock absorber replacement requires a coil spring compressor designed for MacPherson struts. These are available from tool rental dealers.

NOTE
Before changing your own shock absorbers, check the cost of having them replaced at local shops. It may be more practical to have the job done than to do it yourself.

1. Set the handbrake. Securely block both rear wheels so the car will not roll in either direction.
2. Loosen the front wheel nuts. Jack up the front end of the car, place it on jackstands and remove the front wheels.
3. Place a jack beneath the suspension arm to support it.

4. Detach the metal line from the brake hose at the strut. To do this, loosen the flare nut with a flare nut wrench such as Nissan tool part No. GG94310000 (**Figure 2**). Pull out the clip with pliers, then detach the metal line and hose from the bracket on the strut.

WARNING
During the next step, do not remove the center nut at the top of the strut. This could allow the coil spring to fly out and cause serious injury.

5. Remove the strut upper mounting nuts (**Figure 3**).
6. Detach the lower end of the strut from the steering knuckle. See **Figure 4**. Take the strut assembly out.

WARNING
Do not try to improvise the spring compressor mentioned in the next step. This could allow the coil spring to fly out and cause serious injury.

7. Place the strut assembly in a vise. Install the spring compressor and compress the spring just enough so the mounting insulator at the top of the strut can be turned by hand.

WARNING
Be sure the spring compressor is securely positioned on the strut. Otherwise the coil spring could fly out and cause serious injury.

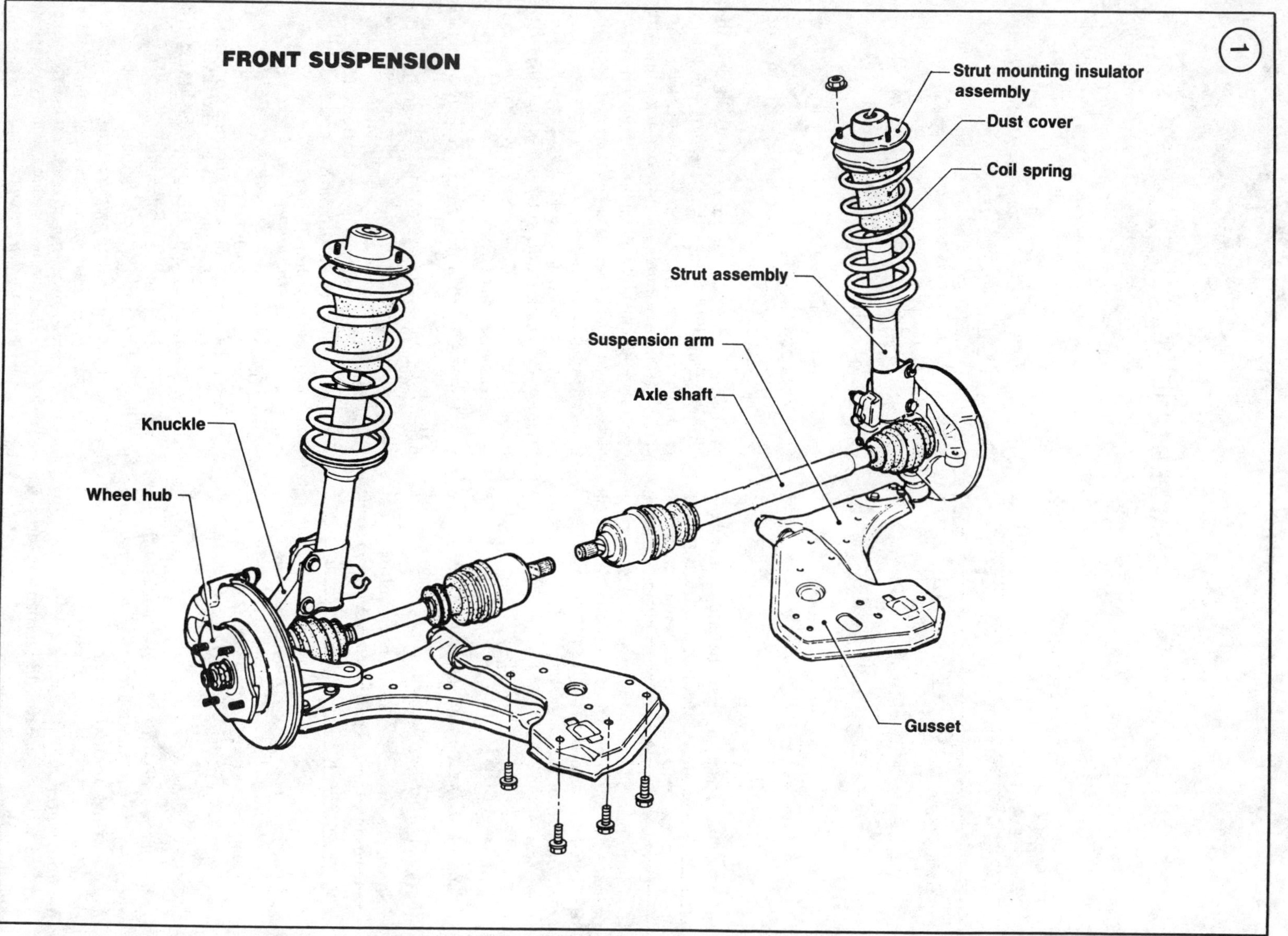
1
FRONT SUSPENSION
Strut mounting insulator assembly
Dust cover
Coil spring
Strut assembly
Suspension arm
Axle shaft
Knuckle
Wheel hub
Gusset

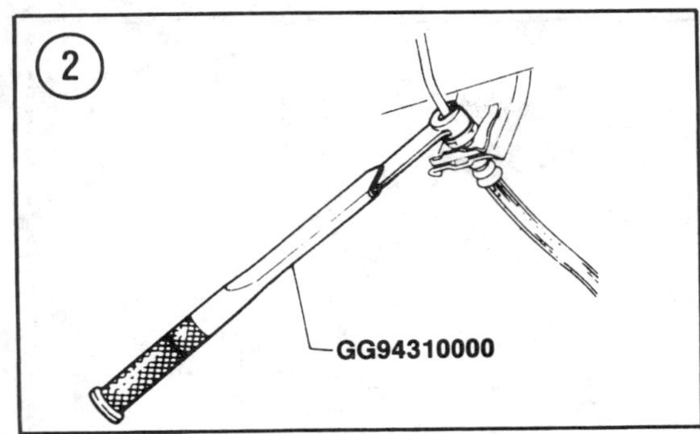

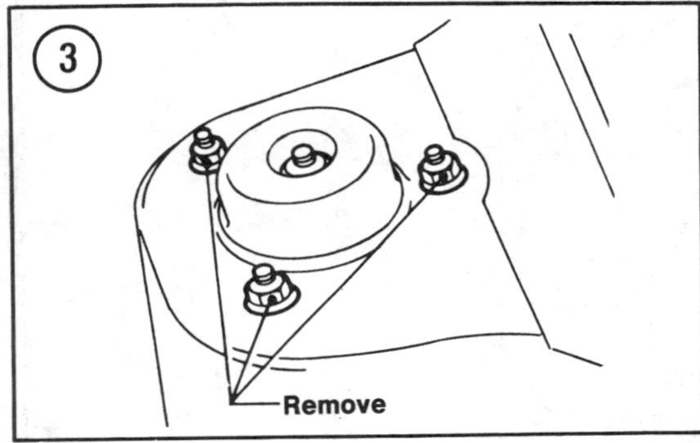

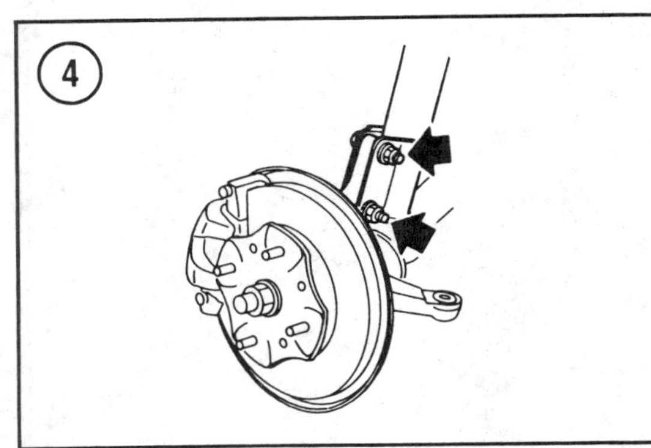

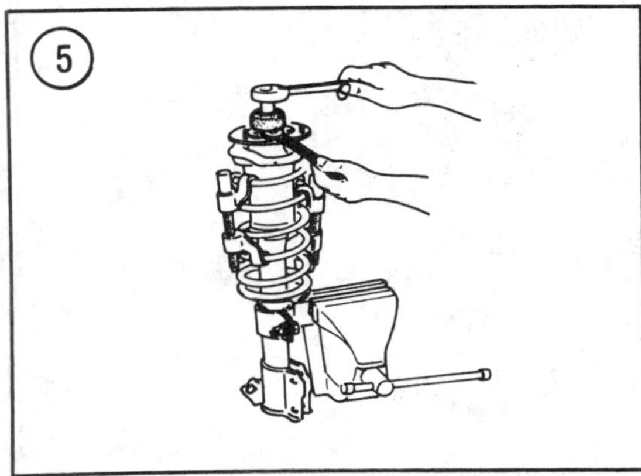

8. Remove the center nut at the top of the strut. See **Figure 5**. Discard the nut. It must not be reused. Release the spring compressor, then remove the spring and related parts. See **Figure 6**.

9. Check all parts for wear and damage. Replace as needed. If oil has been leaking past the piston rod, replace the shock absorber. If a micrometer is available, measure piston rod diameter and runout as shown in **Figure 7**. Replace the strut if diameter and runout are not within specifications (end of chapter).

10. Assemble and install by reversing Steps 1-8. Be sure the lower end of the coil spring is positioned as shown in **Figure 8**. Apply multipurpose lithium grease to the points indicated in **Figure 9**. Use a new self-locking nut at the top of the strut. Tighten all fasteners to specifications (**Table 2**).

Spring Removal/Installation

The spring is combined with the shock absorber into a single unit (strut). To remove or install it, use the shock absorber replacement procedure in this chapter.

Suspension Arm Removal/Installation

1. Set the handbrake. Securely block both rear wheels so the car will not roll in either direction.

2. Loosen the front wheel nuts. Jack up the front end of the car, place it on jackstands and remove the front wheels.

3. Detach the suspension arm from the ball-joint (**Figure 10**). Discard the nuts. They must not be reused.

4. Detach the suspension arm from the body (**Figure 11**), then take it off.

5. Detach the gusset (**Figure 12**) and take it off.

6. Installation is the reverse of removal. Tighten the bushing nuts slightly, then tighten them to specifications with the car's weight on the wheels. Tighten all fasteners to specifications (end of chapter). Have wheel alignment checked by a dealer or front-end shop.

Inspection

1. Check the suspension arm for cracks or dents. Replace it if these are found.

2. Check the suspension arm for rust. Sand off light rust and paint the suspension arm. Replace the suspension arm if rust is serious.

3. Check the suspension arm bushings for wear or deterioration. If these conditions are found, take the rear bushing off the spindle and slide a new one on. Press the front bushing out of the suspension arm as shown in **Figure 13** and press a new one in.

9

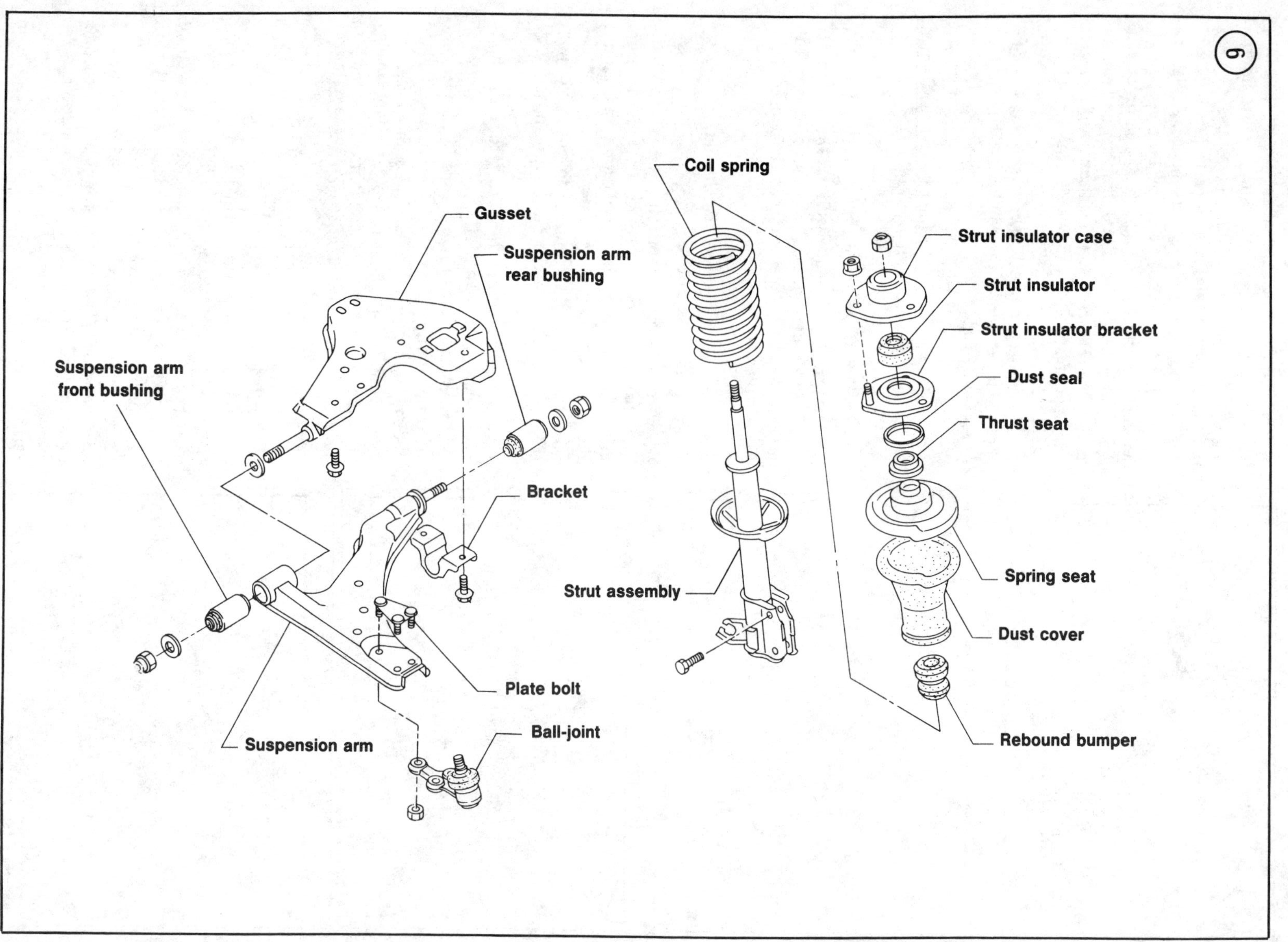
6
Coil spring
Gusset
Suspension arm rear bushing
Suspension arm front bushing
Bracket
Strut assembly
Plate bolt
Suspension arm
Ball-joint
Strut insulator case
Strut insulator
Strut insulator bracket
Dust seal
Thrust seat
Spring seat
Dust cover
Rebound bumper

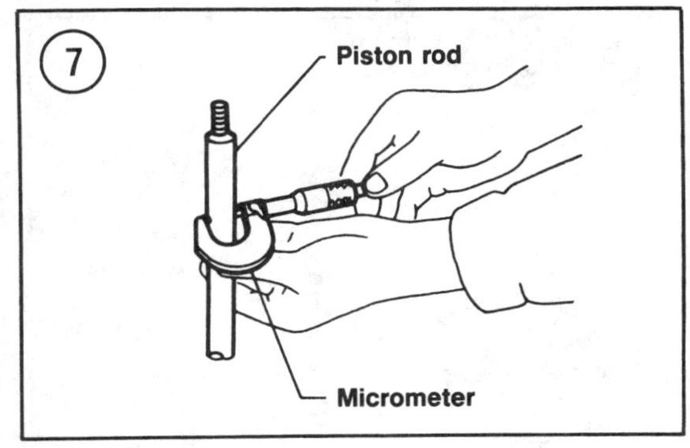
7
Piston rod
Micrometer

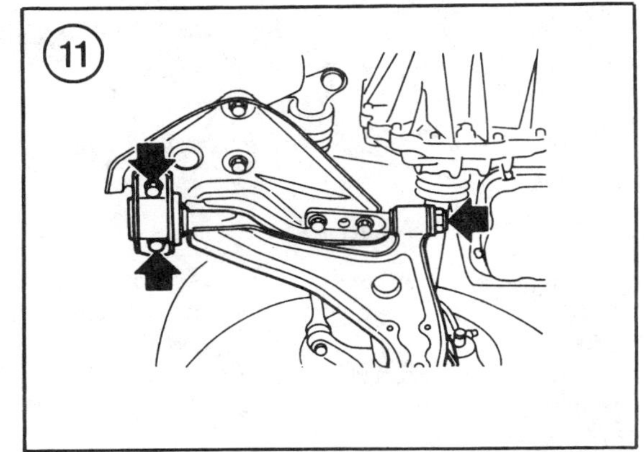
11

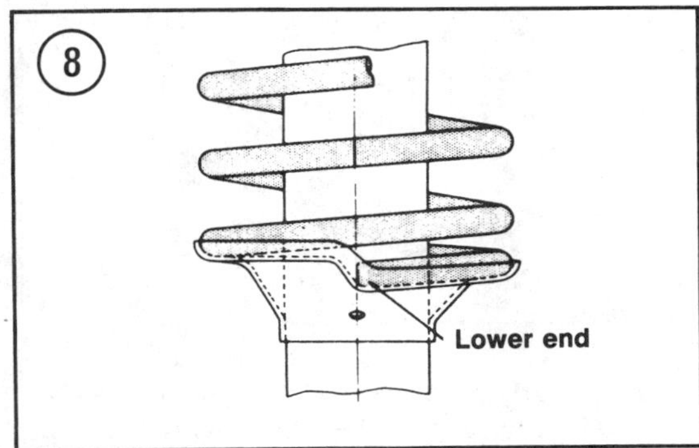
8
Lower end

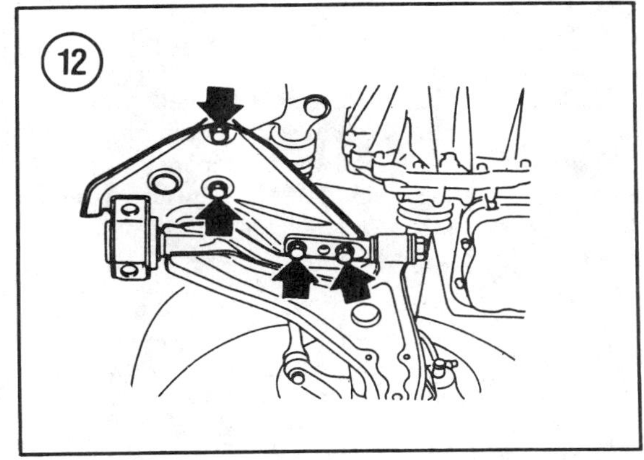
12

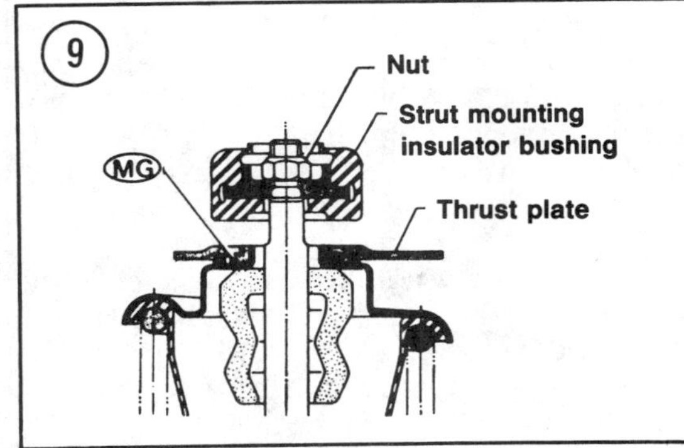
9
Nut
Strut mounting
insulator bushing
MG
Thrust plate

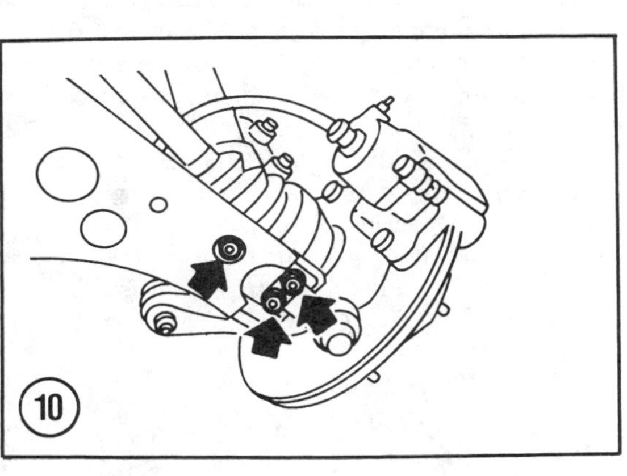
10

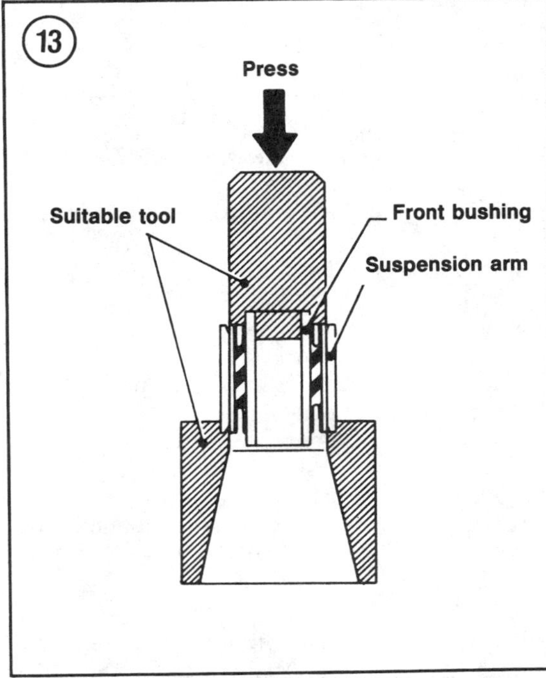
13
Press
Suitable tool
Front bushing
Suspension arm

A machine shop can do this inexpensively if you don't have a press.

CAUTION

Do not let oil or grease touch the bushings.

WHEEL ALIGNMENT

Several suspension angles affect the running and steering of the front wheels. These angles must be properly aligned to prevent excessive wear, as well as to maintain directional stability and ease of steering. The angles are as follows:

a. Caster.

b. Camber.

c. Toe-in.

d. Steering axis inclination.

e. Steering lock angles.

Caster, camber and steering axis inclination are built in and cannot be adjusted. These angles are measured to check for bent suspension parts. Steering lock angles should not be adjusted without a front-end rack. Toe-in can be adjusted as described in this chapter.

WARNING

Some alignment equipment manufacturers produce devices which adjust camber by bending the strut housing. Nissan recommends against the use of this method.

Pre-alignment Check

Adjustment of the steering and various suspension angles is affected by several factors. Perform the following steps before any adjustments are attempted.

1. Check tire pressure and wear. See *Tire Wear Analysis,* Chapter Two.

2. Check play in front wheel bearings. Adjust if necessary.

3. Check play in ball-joints.

4. Check for broken springs.

5. Remove any excessive load.

6. Check shock absorbers.

7. Check steering gear for wear or damage.

8. Check play in steering linkage.

9. Check wheel balance.

10. Check rear suspension for looseness.

Front tire wear patterns can indicate several alignment problems. These are covered under *Tire Wear Analysis,* Chapter Two.

Caster and Camber

Caster is the inclination from vertical of the line through the ball-joints. Positive caster shifts the

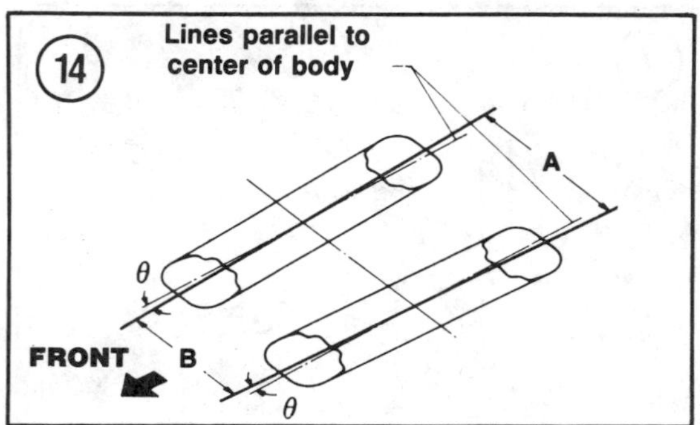

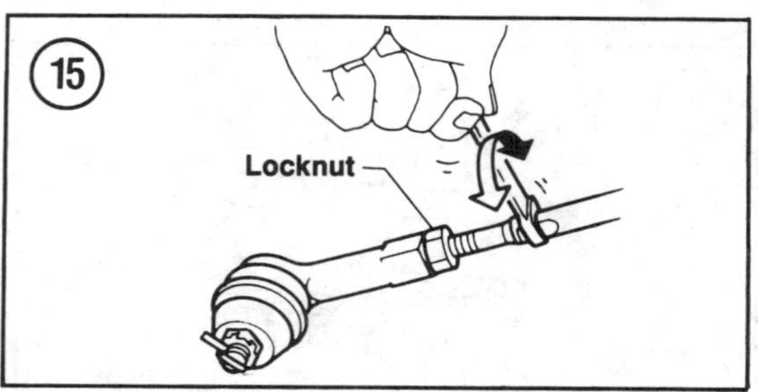

wheel forward; negative caster shifts the wheel rearward. Caster causes the wheels to return to a straight-ahead position after a turn. It also prevents the wheels from wandering due to wind, potholes, or uneven road surfaces.

Camber is the inclination of the wheel from vertical. With positive camber, the top of the tire leans outward. With negative camber, the top of the tire leans inward.

Toe-in

Since the front wheels tend to point outward when the car is moving forward, the distance between the front edges of the tire (B, **Figure 14**) is slightly less than the distance between the rear edges (A) when the car is at rest.

Although toe-in adjustment requires only a simple home-made tool, it usually isn't worth the trouble for home mechanics. Alignment shops include toe-in as part of the alignment procedure, so you probably won't save any money by doing it yourself. The procedure described here can be used for an initial toe-in setting after steering linkage overhaul or suspension repairs.

Toe-in is adjusted under the following conditions:

a. Fuel tank, radiator and engine oil full.

b. Spare tire, jack, tools and floor mats in position.

c. Tires inflated to correct pressure.

d. All dirt and road deposits removed from underbody.

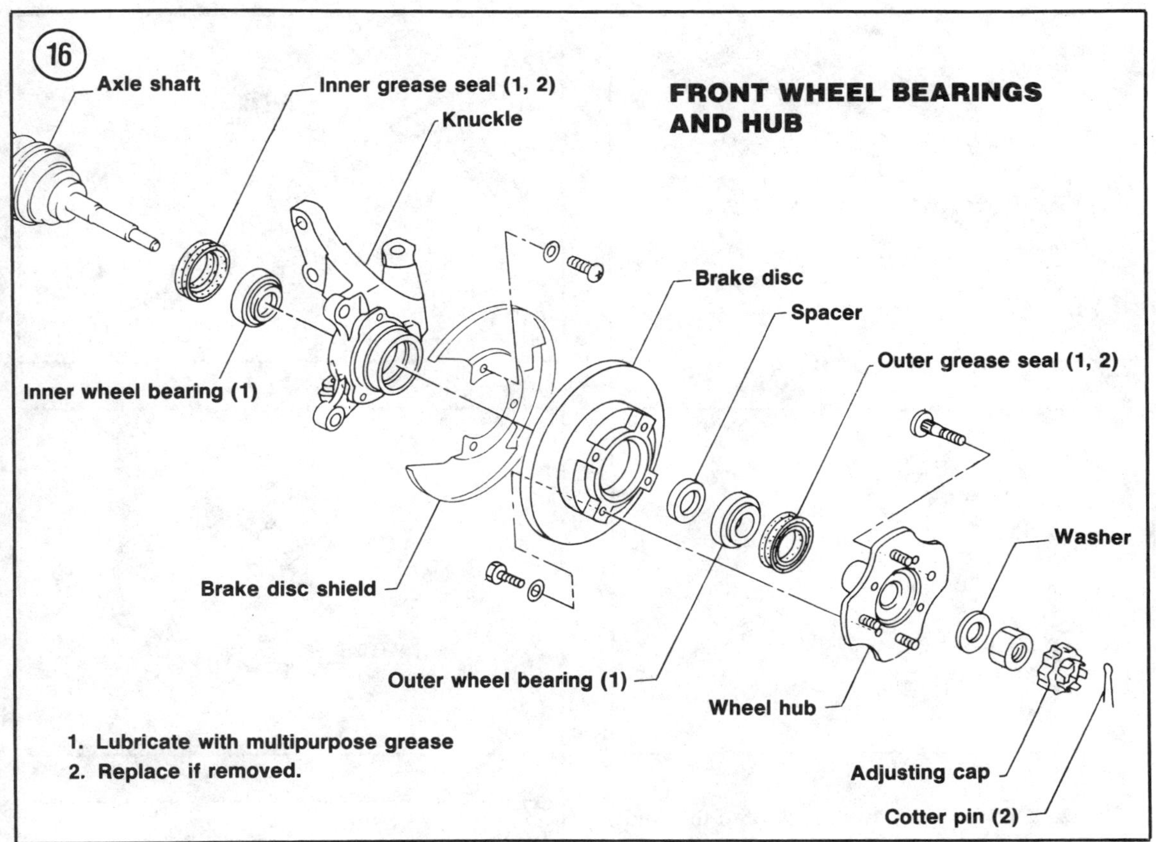

1. With the steering wheel centered, roll forward about 15 ft. onto a smooth, level surface.
2. Mark the center of the tread at the front and rear of each tire.
3. Measure the distance between forward chalk marks (B, **Figure 14**). Use 2 pieces of telescoping aluminum tubing. Telescope the tubing so each end contacts a chalk mark. Using a sharp scribe, mark the small diameter tubing where it enters the large diameter tubing.
4. Measure between the rear chalk marks with the telescoping tubes. Make another mark on the small tube where it enters the large one. The distance between the 2 scribe marks is toe-in.

If toe-in is incorrect, loosen the tie rod locknuts (**Figure 15**). Rotate the tie rods as shown to change toe-in, then tighten the clamps.

NOTE
Rotate the left and right tie rods an equal number of turns.

Steering Axis Inclination

Steering axis inclination is the inward or outward lean of the struts. It is not adjustable.

Steering Lock Angles

When a car turns, the inside wheel makes a smaller circle than the outside wheel. Because of this, the inside wheel turns at a greater angle than the outside wheel. These angles are adjustable, but the job should be left to a dealer or front-end specialist.

WHEEL BEARINGS, HUBS AND AXLE SHAFTS

Refer to **Figure 16** for the following procedures.

Removal

1. Set the handbrake. Securely block both rear wheels so the car will not roll in either direction.
2. Loosen the front wheel nuts. Jack up the front end of the car, place it on jackstands and remove the front wheels.
3. Remove the brake caliper as described in Chapter Eleven.
4. Remove the cotter pin from the adjusting cap. See **Figure 16**.

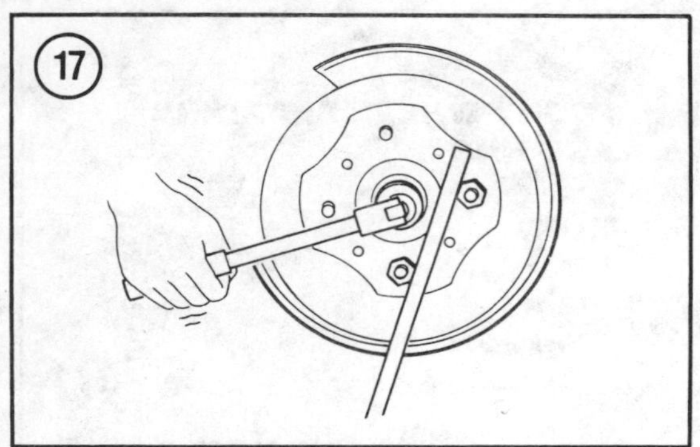

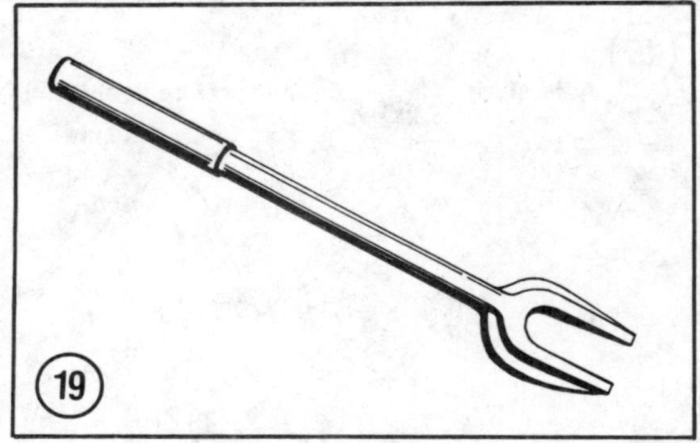

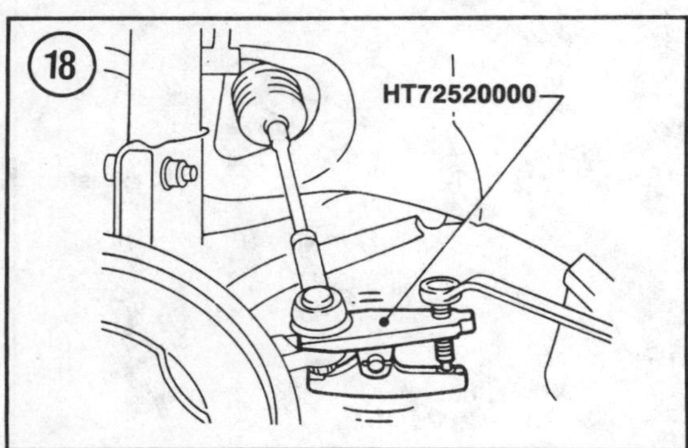

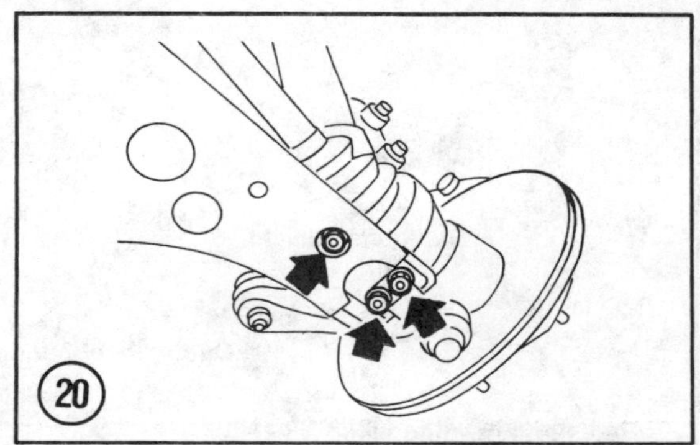

5. Thread 2 of the wheel nuts back onto the studs to protect the threads. Place a bar between the studs to keep the hub from turning as shown in **Figure 17**. Loosen, but do not remove, the wheel bearing nut.

6. Remove the cotter pin and nut from the tie rod stud, then separate the tie rod ball-joint from the knuckle arm. Use a tool such as Nissan tool part No. HT72520000 (**Figure 18**) or a fork-type separator (**Figure 19**). These are available from rental dealers.

7. Remove the ball-joint lower nuts (**Figure 20**). Discard the nuts. They must not be reused.

8. Place a pan beneath the transaxle and drain the oil or fluid.

9. Pry the axle shaft end out of the transaxle. See **Figure 21** (right side) or **Figure 22** (left side).

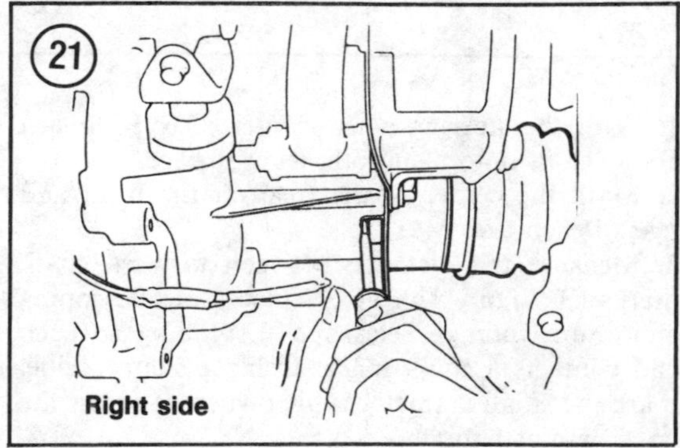

> *CAUTION*
> *Do not pull or hammer the axle shafts*
> *out of the transaxle.*

10. Remove the axle shaft oil seal from the transaxle. Use a puller such as Nissan tool part No. ST33920001 (**Figure 23**). These are available from rental dealers. Axle shaft oil seals must be replaced whenever the axle shafts are removed.

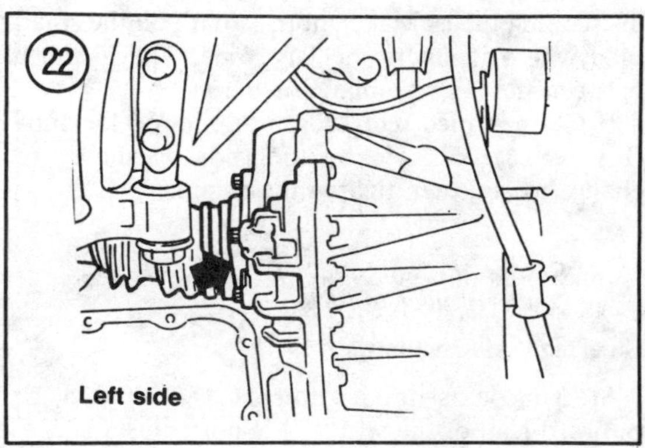

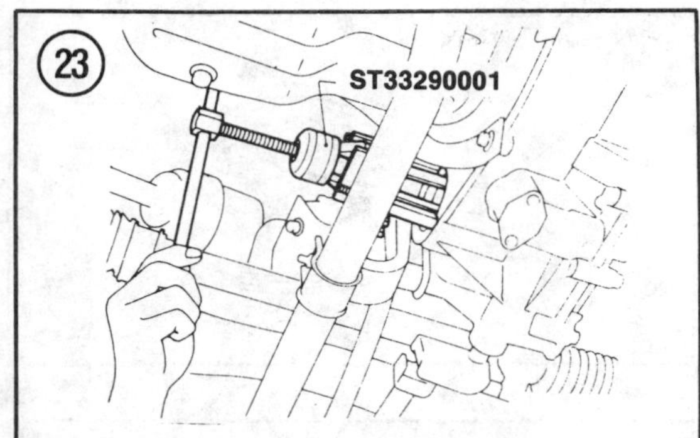

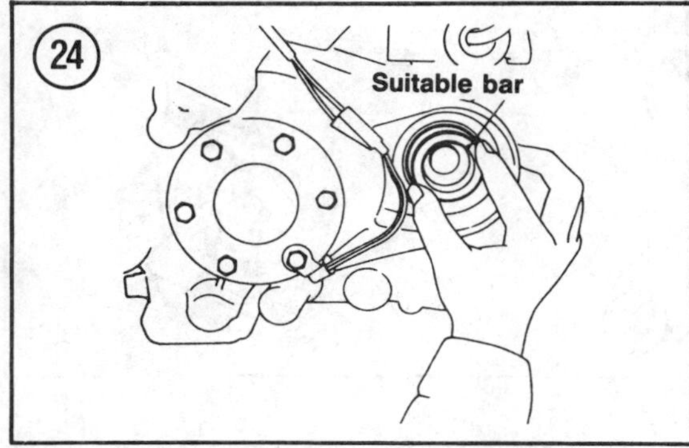

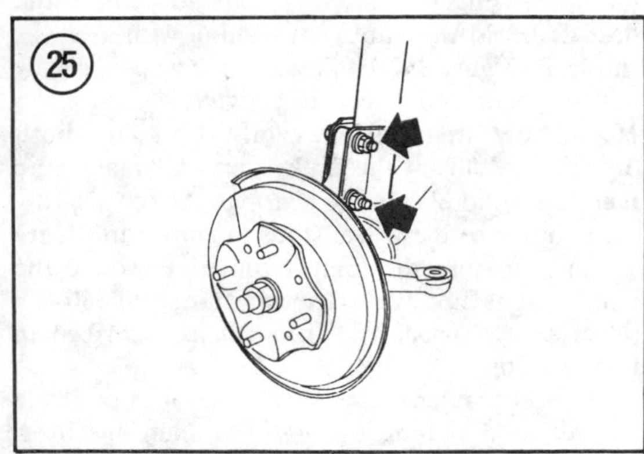

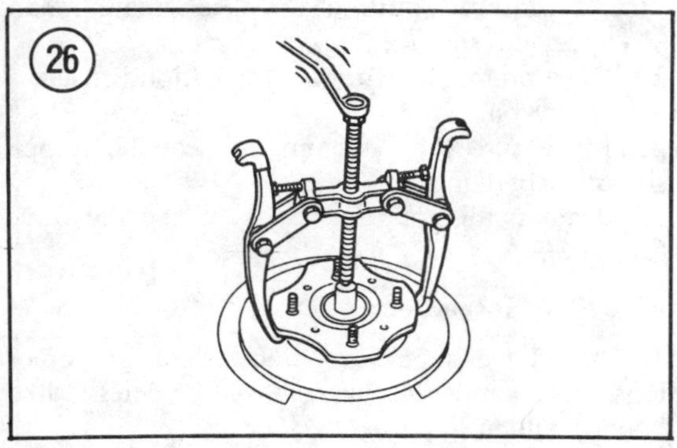

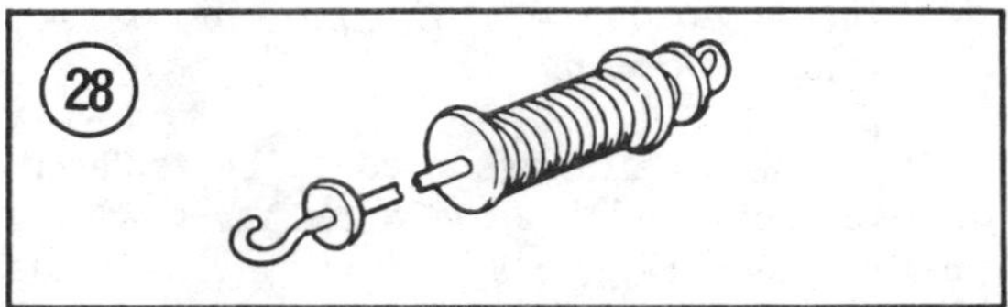

11. Place a suitable bar or similar tool in the transaxle's axle shaft hole to keep the differential side gear from falling out. See **Figure 24**.

12. Hold the knuckle and hub assembly so it won't fall, then detach it from the strut. See **Figure 25**.

13. Remove the wheel bearing nut (which was loosened in Step 5). Separate the hub and axle shaft with a gear puller (**Figure 26**). These are available from rental dealers.

Wheel Bearing Inspection

Refer to **Figure 16** for this procedure.

1. Separate the hub from the knuckle with a slide hammer and adapter such as Nissan tools part Nos. KV40101000 and ST36230000 (**Figure 27** and **Figure 28**). These are available from rental dealers.

2. Unbolt the brake disc from the hub. See **Figure 29**.

> *NOTE*
> *It may cost less to have the next step done by a machine shop than to rent the necessary tools. Compare prices before proceeding.*

3. Remove the outer bearing with a gear puller and bearing splitter as shown in **Figure 30**. These are available from rental dealers.

4. Remove and discard the outer bearing grease seal.

5. Remove the inner bearing, spacer and grease seal.

6. Thoroughly clean all parts with solvent.

7. Check bearing cones and outer races for rust, galling and the bluish tint that indicates overheating. Rotate the bearings and check for roughness and excessive noise. Compare the races and rollers to the defective bearing parts shown in **Figure 31**. Replace any bearings that have similar defects.

NOTE
If either cone or outer race needs to be replaced, replace both the inner and outer cones and their outer races as a set.

NOTE
It may cost less to have the next step done by a machine shop than to rent the necessary tools. Compare prices before proceeding.

8. If the wheel bearings need to be replaced, remove the wheel bearing outer races with a suitable puller (**Figure 32**). These are available from rental dealers. Do not remove outer races unless they are to be replaced.

9. Check the knuckle, hub and brake disc dust shield for cracks or other damage. Replace damaged parts.

10. Tap the bearing outer races into the knuckle until they rest against the stop. See **Figure 33** and **Figure 34**.

11. Select a spacer. If the knuckle is not being replaced, use the old spacer if it is serviceable. If not, use a new spacer with the same identification number (**Figure 35**). If the knuckle is being replaced, measure the distance between the outer races (L1, **Figure 34**). Subtract 0.16 mm (0.0063 in.) from this figure to determine the required spacer thickness. Thicknesses are listed in **Table 3** at the end of the chapter.

12. Pack the bearing cones with multipurpose grease. Drag the bearing through the grease as shown in **Figure 36** and work as much grease as possible between the rollers.

13. Tap in a new grease seal and the inner bearing cone with a suitable drift. See **Figure 37**. Be sure the grease seal lips face in the direction shown. Pack the seal lips with multipurpose lithium grease.

CAUTION
During the next step, let the drift bear against the bearing inner race only. Do not apply force to the rollers or bearing cage.

14. Tap the outer grease seal and bearing onto the hub. See **Figure 38**. Be sure the seal lips face in the direction shown. Pack the seal lips with multipurpose lithium grease.

15. Install the spacer on the hub.

16. Bolt the brake disc to the hub. Tighten the hub bolts evenly to specifications (end of chapter).

17. Slide the axle shaft into the knuckle and hub. Install the wheel bearing nut and tighten it finger-tight.

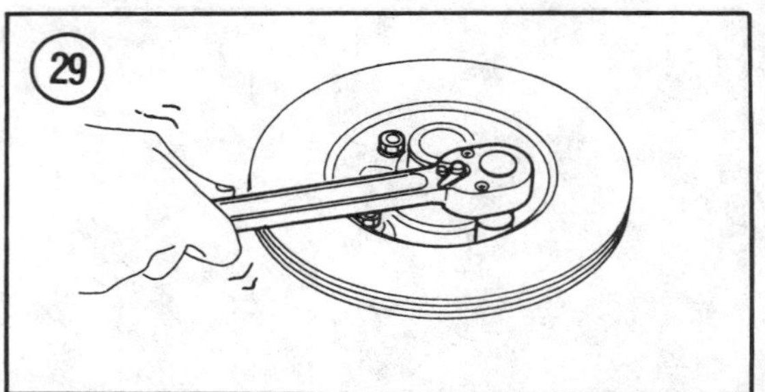

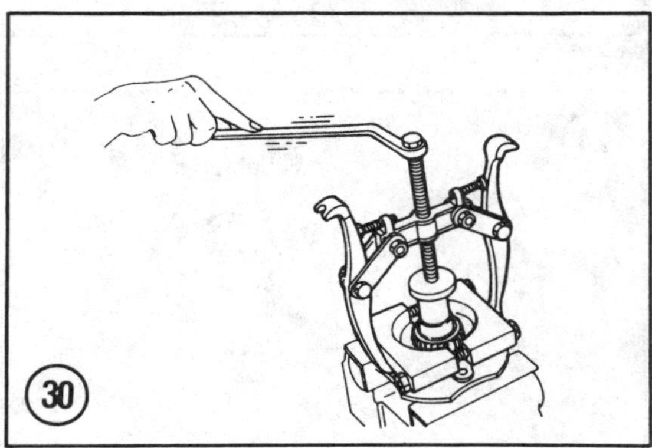

18. Place the axle shaft in a vise. Make sure 2 of the wheel nuts are on the studs to protect the threads. Hold the hub from turning with a bar as shown in **Figure 39**, then tighten the wheel bearing nut to specifications (end of chapter).

19. Rotate the hub several turns in both directions. Pull on the brake disc and make sure there is no end play in the bearings. Attach a spring scale to one of the wheel studs as shown in **Figure 40** and measure the force required to rotate the hub. If it is not within specifications (**Table 1**), select a new spacer and install it as described in this section:

   a. If there is end play in the bearings or if the required pulling force is less than specified, select a thinner spacer.

   b. If required pulling force is greater than specified, select a thicker spacer.

20. Once preload is within specifications, install a new cotter pin.

21. Make sure the disc and hub can be turned smoothly by hand.

22. Tighten all nuts and bolts to specifications (**Table 2**).

Axle Shaft Inspection

1. Check the dust boots for cracks, deterioration or loose boot bands. Replace cracked or deteriorated boots. Tighten loose bands.

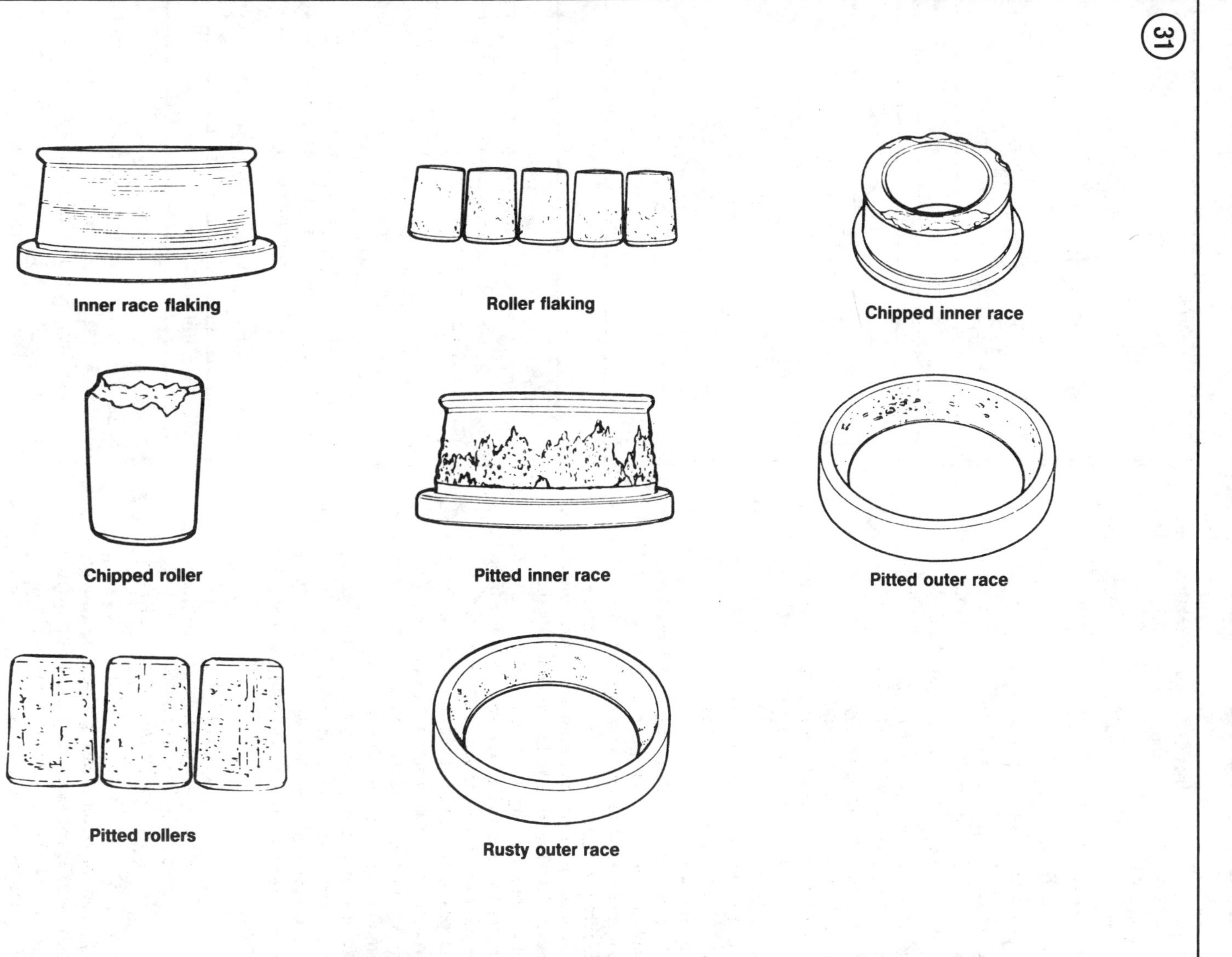

31
Inner race flaking
Roller flaking
Chipped inner race
Chipped roller
Pitted inner race
Pitted outer race
Pitted rollers
Rusty outer race
9

2. Twist the shafts by hand and feel for looseness. If the joints are loose, repair them as described in this chapter.

3. Check the shafts for cracks or signs of twisting. Replace shafts that show these conditions.

Axle Shaft Overhaul

The outer joint cannot be disassembled. If it is defective, the axle shaft must be replaced. If the axle shaft is equipped with a tripod joint at the inner end, the spider assembly can be replaced, but not disassembled. Refer to **Figure 41** for this procedure.

> *NOTE*
> *Before overhaul, buy an axle shaft repair kit from your dealer. The kit contains a special grease which must be used to lubricate the axle shaft. Do not use any other type of grease.*

Tripod joint (inner end)

1. Place the axle shaft in a soft-jawed vise and remove the boot bands. See **Figure 42**.

2. Make match marks on the spider and axle shaft (**Figure 43**).

3. Remove the snap ring from the end of the axle shaft. Take the slide joint housing and slide cover off.

4. Remove the snap ring, then press the tripod off. See **Figure 44**. A machine shop can do this inexpensively if you don't have a press.

5. Remove the axle shaft boot.

> *CAUTION*
> *Do not cut the slide joint housing during the next step.*

6. Cut the edge of the slide joint cover with a hacksaw as shown in **Figure 45**. Carefully bend the cover away from the housing, then take the cover off.

7. Remove and discard the O-ring.

8. Thoroughly clean all parts in solvent and blow dry. While cleaning, check for visible wear or damage. Replace worn or damaged parts.

9. Check the spider assembly for a worn or damaged tripod, rollers, needle bearing and washer. Replace the spider assembly if any of its parts are worn or damaged.

10. Check the slide joint housing for wear or damage. Replace as needed.

11. Apply a coat of the grease contained in the axle shaft repair kit to a new O-ring, then install the O-ring.

12. Install a new slide joint cover. Bend the cover's edge at 2 points 180° apart with a hammer as

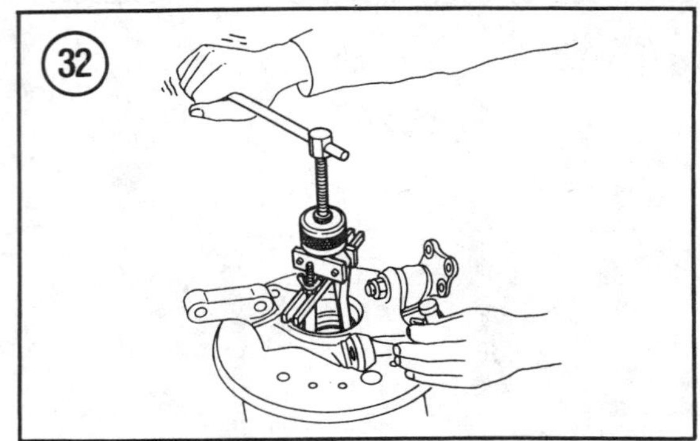

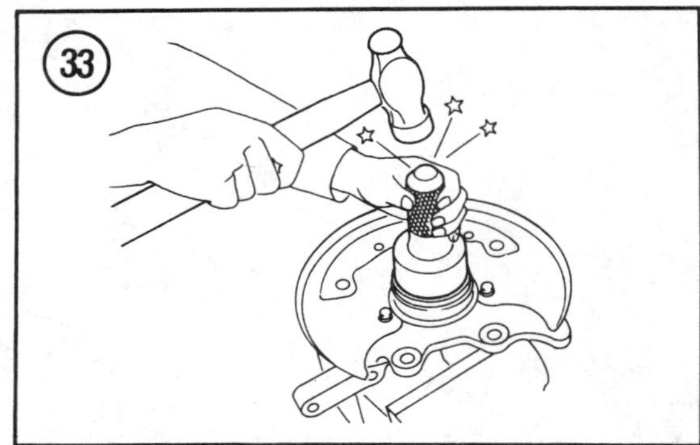

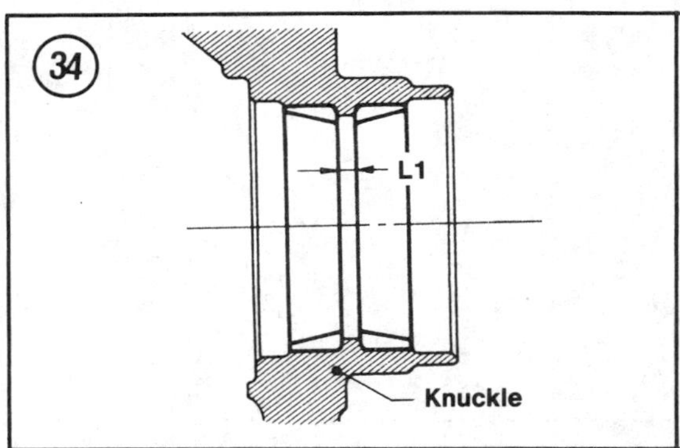

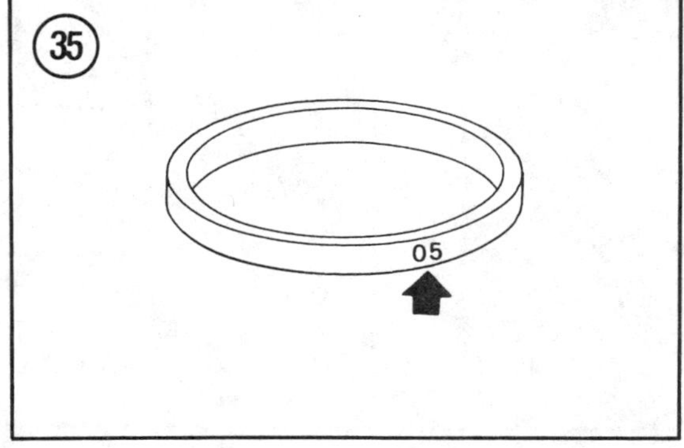

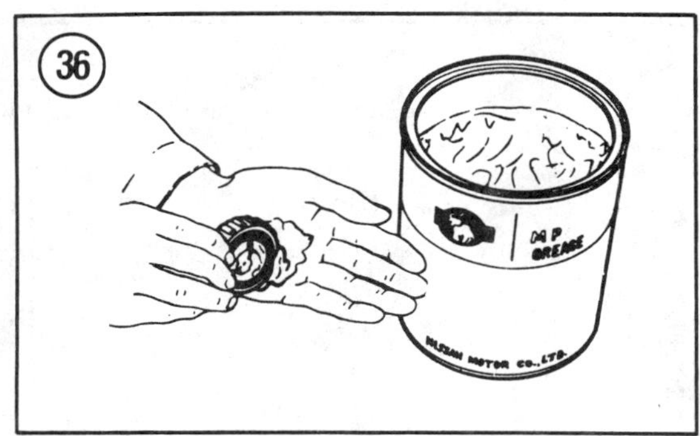

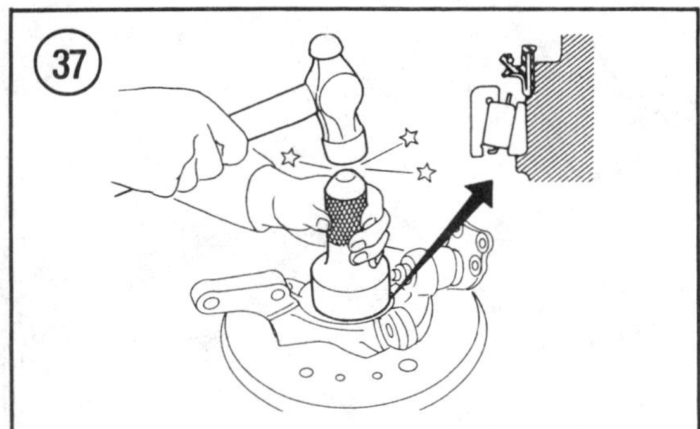

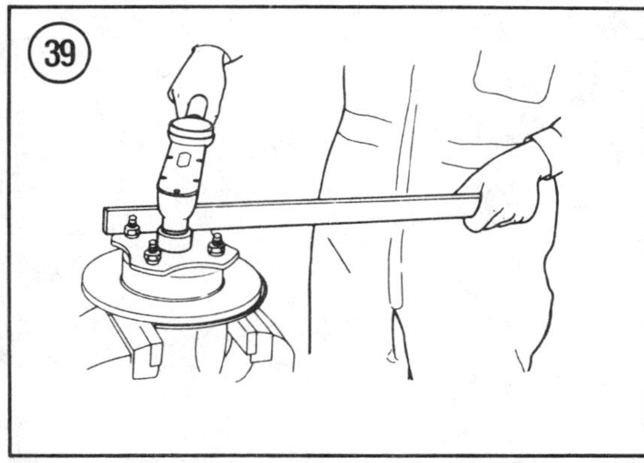

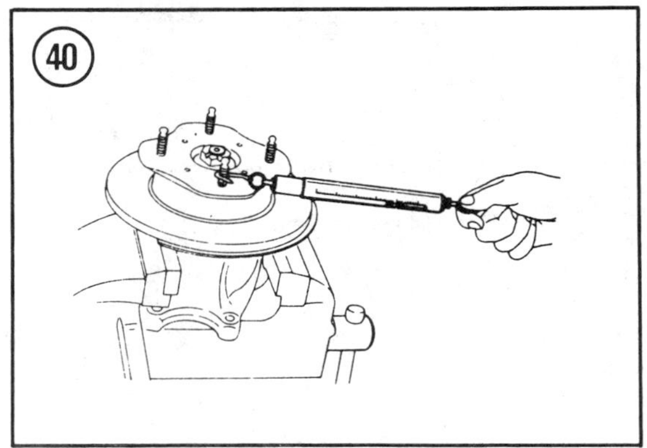

shown in **Figure 46**. Use a block of wood as shown to keep the cover from being scratched. Make sure the cover does not rattle, then bend it around its entire circumference.

13. Apply a coat of gasket sealer to the boot's contact surface on the axle shaft. Install a new small boot band and boot. Don't fasten the boot band yet.

> *CAUTION*
> *If you don't have the correct drift for the next step, have it done by a machine shop.*

14. Place the axle shaft in a soft-jawed vise, then position the spider assembly on the axle shaft. If the old spider assembly is being reinstalled, align the match marks made during disassembly. If a new spider assembly is being installed, use the old spider assembly and its match mark as a guide to position the new spider assembly.

15. Tap the spider assembly on as shown in **Figure 47**. The chamfer on the spider assembly faces the axle shaft.

16. Install a new snap ring with its rounded surface facing the spider assembly.

17. Pack the boot with approximately 180 grams (6 1/3 oz.) of the grease contained in the axle shaft repair kit.

> *NOTE*
> *Different types of grease are used for the inner and outer ends of the axle shaft. Make sure you use the right type.*

18. Install and fasten a new large boot band as shown in **Figure 48**.

19. Position the boot so its length (L, **Figure 49**) is as specified in **Table 1** at the end of the chapter. Make sure the boot is not distorted, then fasten the small boot band.

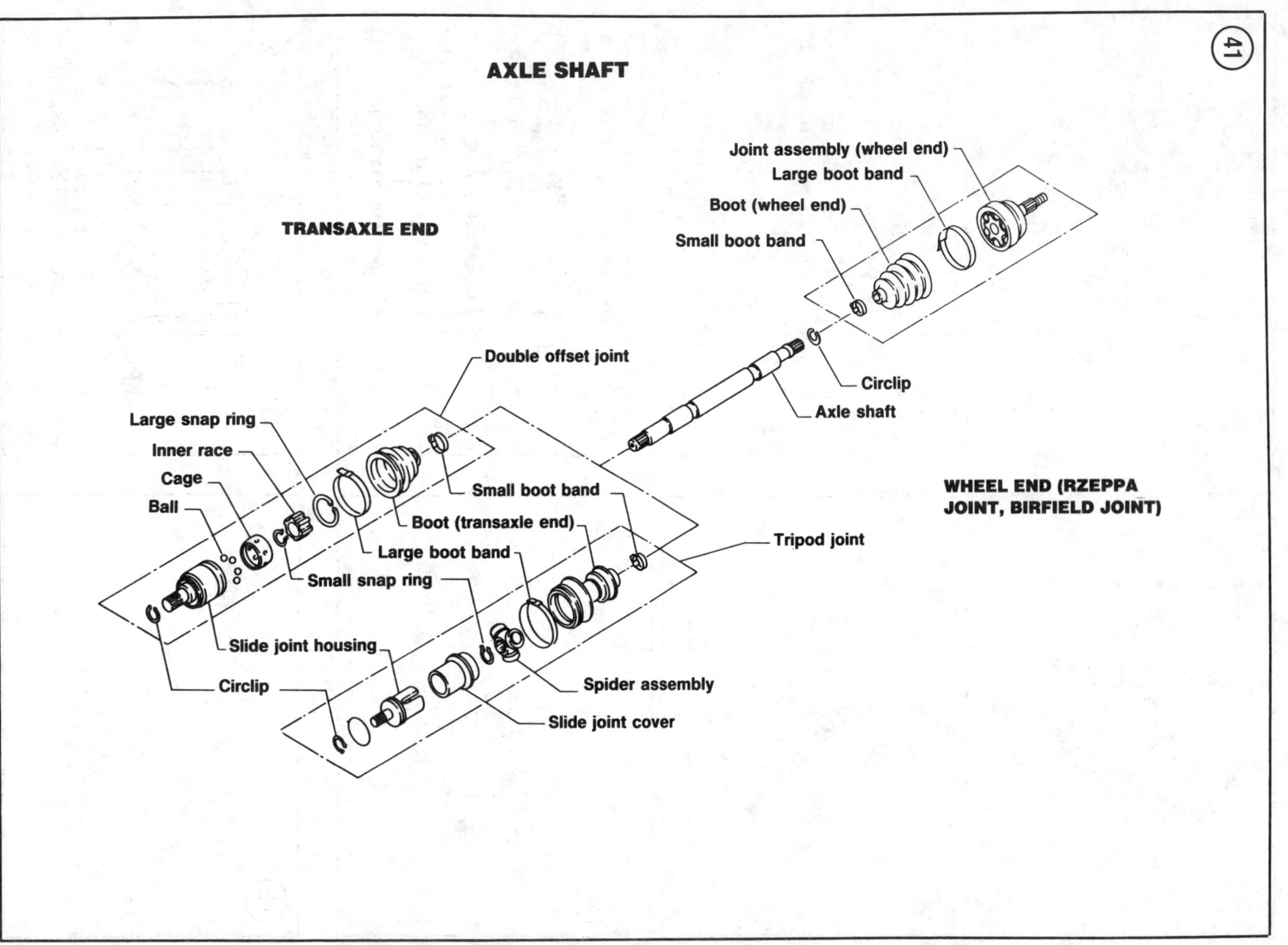
41
AXLE SHAFT
TRANSAXLE END
Joint assembly (wheel end)
Large boot band
Boot (wheel end)
Small boot band
Double offset joint
Circlip
Axle shaft
Large snap ring
Inner race
Cage
Ball
Small boot band
Boot (transaxle end)
Large boot band
Small snap ring
WHEEL END (RZEPPA JOINT, BIRFIELD JOINT)
Tripod joint
Slide joint housing
Circlip
Spider assembly
Slide joint cover

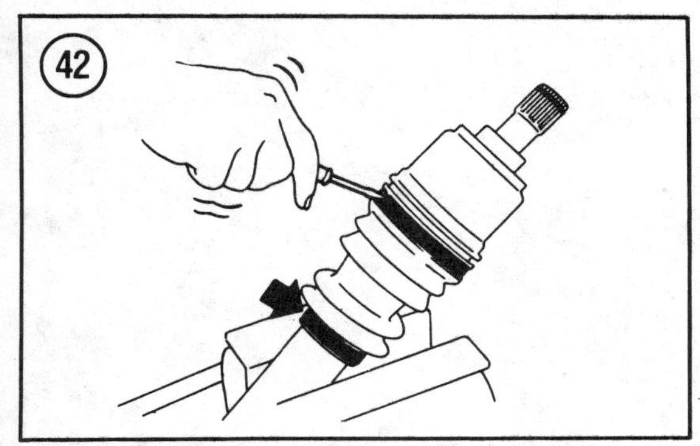

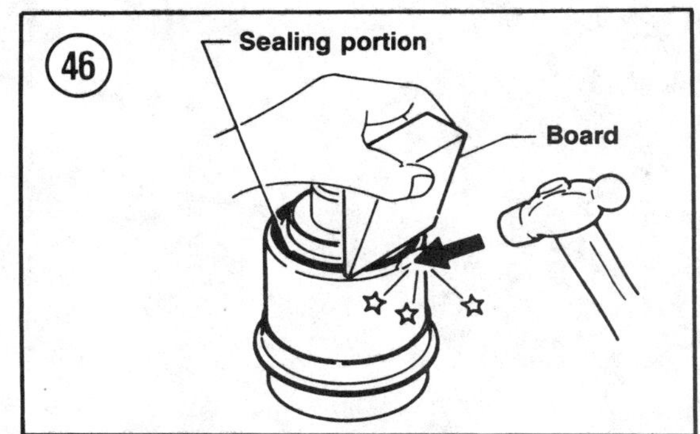
Sealing portion
Board

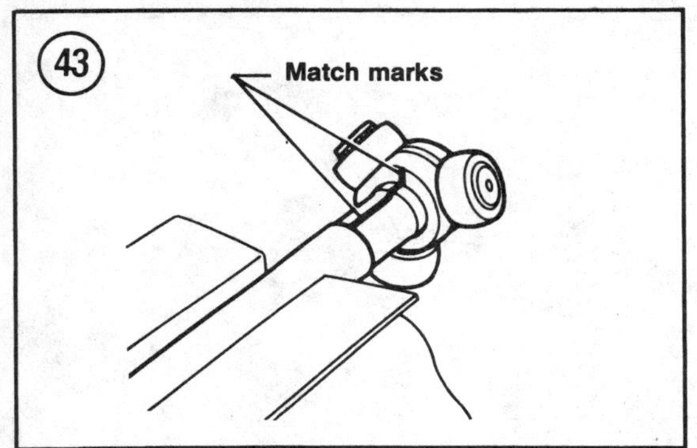
Match marks

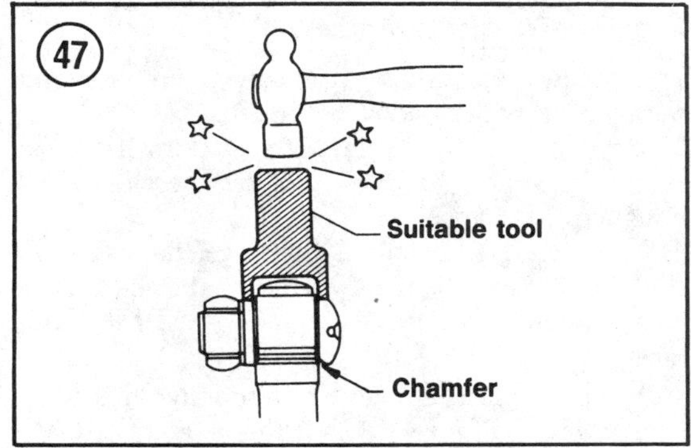
Suitable tool
Chamfer

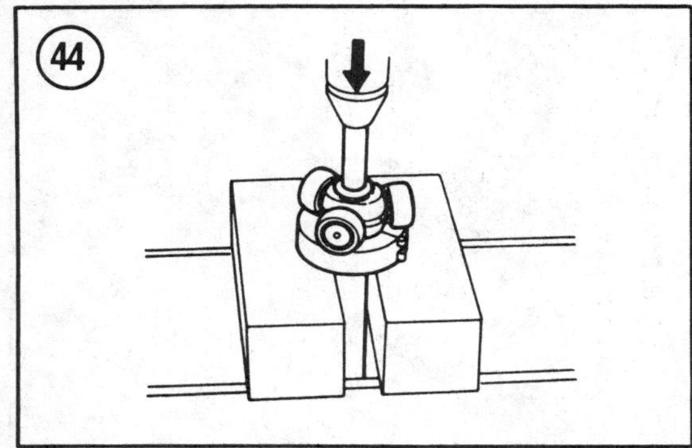

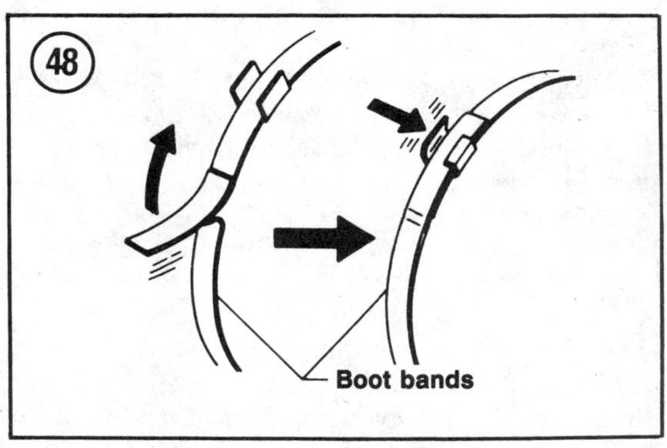
Boot bands

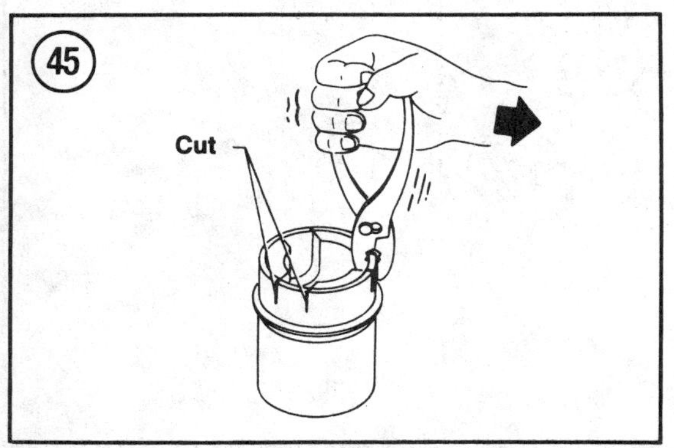
Cut

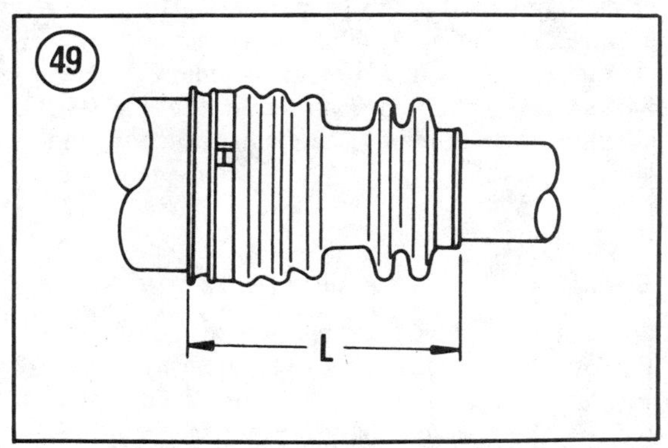
L

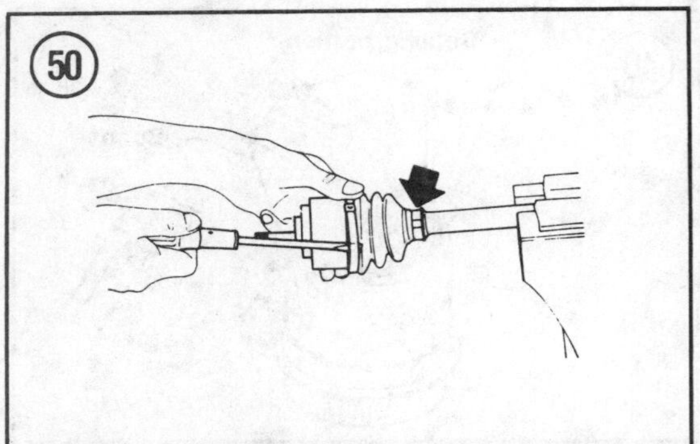

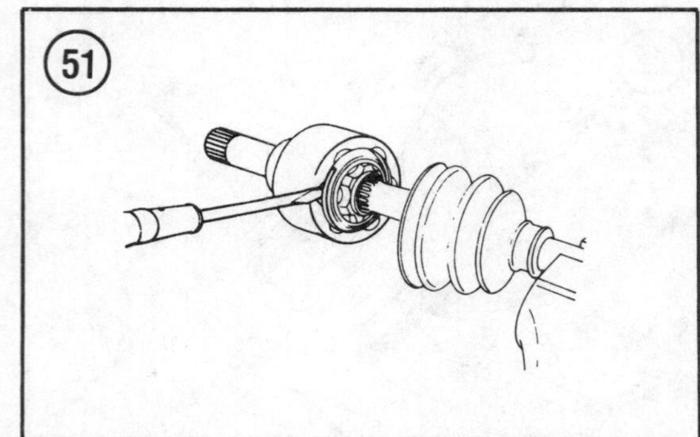

Double offset joint (inner end)

1. Place the axle shaft in a soft-jawed vise and remove the boot bands (**Figure 50**).

2. Pry off the snap ring with a screwdriver as shown in **Figure 51**, then pull off the slide joint housing.

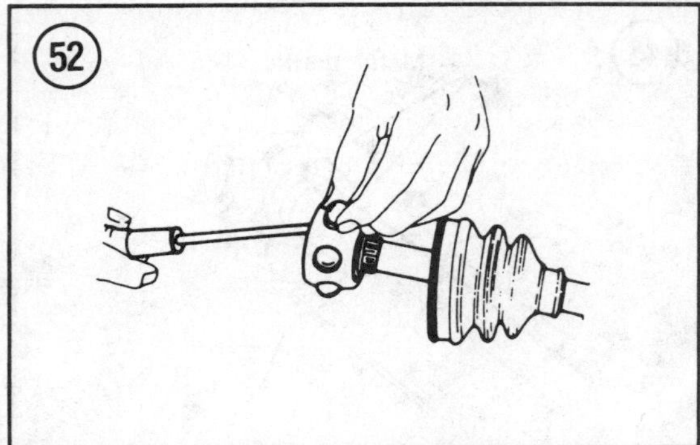

3. Wipe the grease off the ball cage, then tap out the balls. See **Figure 52**. Turn the ball cage approximately 1/2 turn and take it off the inner race.

4. Remove the inner race's snap ring with snap ring pliers (**Figure 53**). These are available inexpensively at auto parts stores.

5. Gently tap the inner race off the axle shaft with a soft-faced mallet.

6. Take the boot off the axle shaft.

7. Thoroughly clean all parts in solvent and blow dry. While cleaning, check for obvious wear or damage and replace parts that show these conditions.

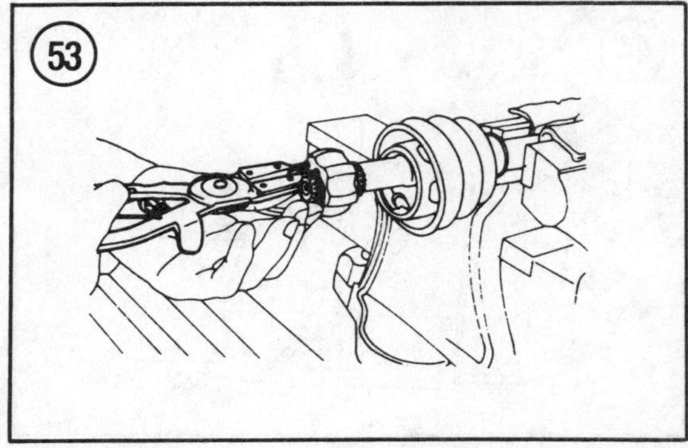

8. Check all parts for corrosion, burn marks or wear. Replace as needed.

9. Check the slide joint housing's grooves for wear, cracks or deterioration. Replace it if these conditions are found.

10. Assemble by reversing Steps 1-6. Use new snap rings and boot bands. Pack the boot with grease contained in the repair kit. The specified amount is listed in **Table 1** at the end of the chapter. Position the boot so its length (L, **Figure 54**) is as specified in **Table 1** at the end of the chapter. Fasten the boot bands as shown in **Figure 48**.

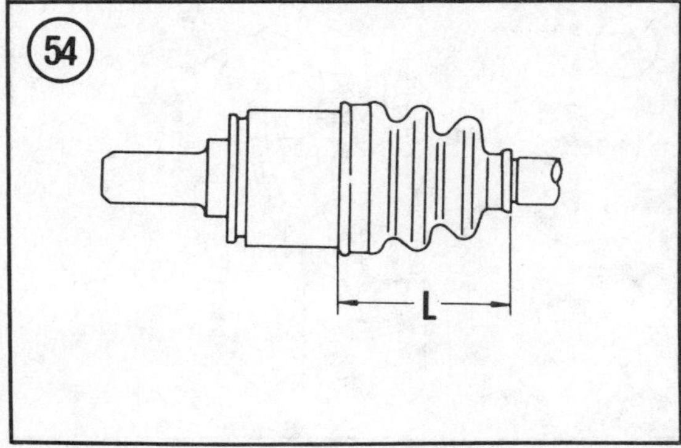

Birfield joint or Rzeppa joint (outer end)

The outer end's joint cannot be disassembled. Replace it as a unit if worn or damaged.

1. Place the axle shaft in a soft-jawed vise and remove the boot bands. See **Figure 55**.

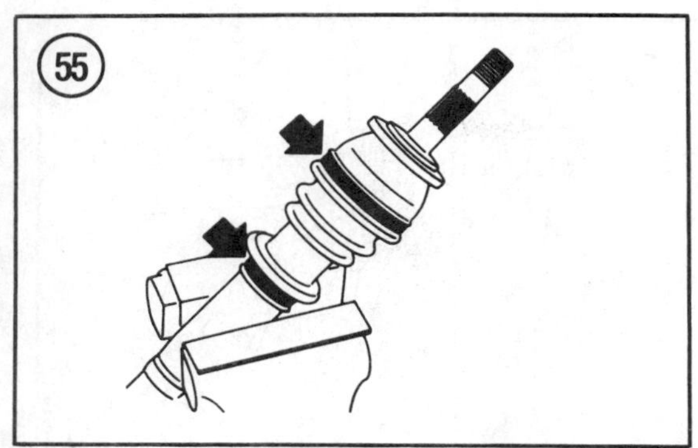

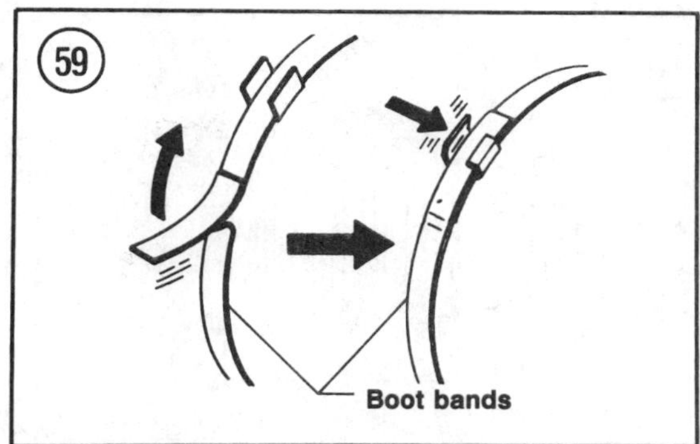

2. Make match marks on the joint and axle shaft, then tap the joint assembly and circlip off as shown in **Figure 56**.

> *NOTE*
> *The circlip must be replaced with a new one, even if the joint assembly is reused.*

3. Thoroughly clean the joint and axle shaft with solvent and blow dry. Check the joint and axle shaft for wear and damage and replace as needed.

4. Install the boot and a new small boot band on the axle shaft. Don't fasten the boot band yet.

5. Lightly tap the joint assembly and a new circlip onto the axle shaft.

6. If equipped with a Rzeppa joint at the outer end of the axle shaft, pack it with approximately 110 grams (3 3/4 oz.) of the grease contained in the repair kit. If equipped with a Birfield joint, pack the boot with approximately 100 grams (3 1/2 oz.).

7. Install a new large boot band. Wrap it twice around the boot, pull tight with pliers and a screwdriver as shown in **Figure 57**, then bend the end up approximately 90°.

8. Lock the end of the band with a punch as shown in **Figure 58**. Position the punch mark so the unsecured end of the band is the same length as the band is wide.

9. Bend the end of the band back over itself and secure it as shown in **Figure 59**.

10. Position the boot so its length (L, **Figure 60**) is as specified in **Table 1** at the end of the chapter. Make sure the boot is not distorted, then fasten the small boot band as shown in **Figure 59**.

Axle Shaft Installation

Installation is the reverse of removal, plus the following.

1. Install a new axle shaft oil seal in the transaxle. Refer to Chapter Nine for details.

2. Install a new circlip on the inner end of the axle shaft.

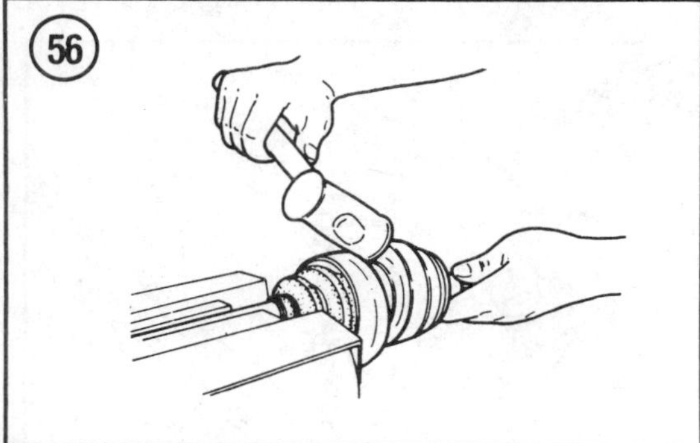

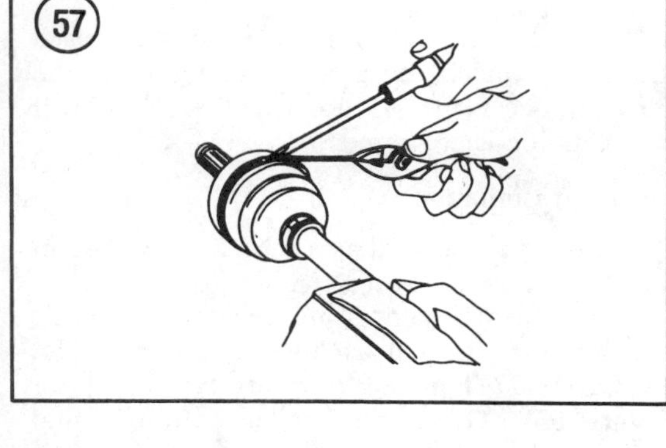

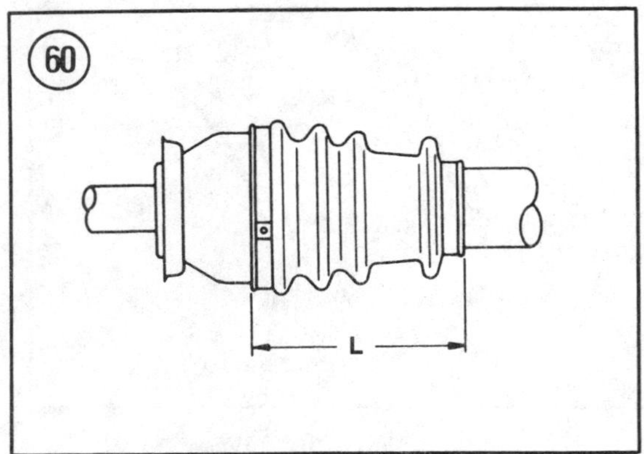

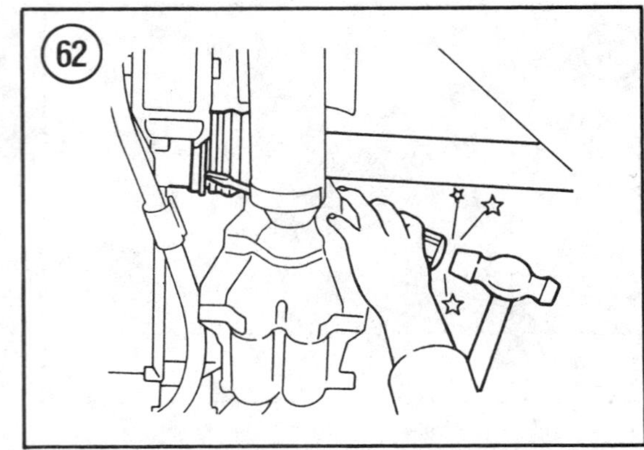

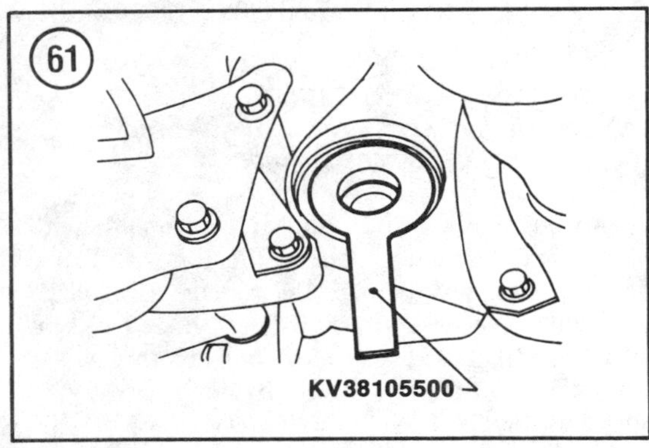

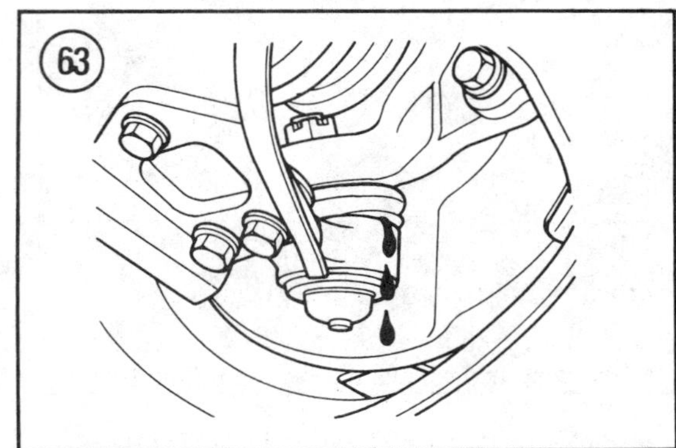

3. If available, use a tool such as Nissan tool part No. KV38105500 (**Figure 61**) to protect the oil seal during axle shaft installation. If the tool is not available, use extreme care to prevent the end of the axle shaft from damaging the seal.

4. Position the axle shaft inner end in the transaxle, then tap the axle shaft in with a hammer and screwdriver as shown in **Figure 62**. When the axle shaft is properly seated in the transaxle, it should not be possible to pull the axle shaft out by hand.

5. Use new cotter pins and ball-joint lower mounting nuts.

6. Tighten all fasteners to specifications (**Table 2**, end of chapter).

7. Fill the transaxle with oil as described in Chapter Three.

BALL-JOINTS

Inspection

1. Set the handbrake. Securely block both rear wheels so the car will not roll in either direction.

2. Loosen the front wheel nuts. Jack up the front end of the car, place it on jackstands and remove the front wheels.

3. Check the ball-joint for looseness or a damaged dust boot. Check for grease leaking from the ball-joint. See **Figure 63**. Replace the ball-joint if these conditions are found.

Removal/Installation

1. Remove the hub and axle shaft as described in this chapter.

2. Detach the ball-joint from the steering knuckle with a remover such as Nissan tool part No. HT72520000 (**Figure 64**) or a fork-type separator (**Figure 65**). These are available from rental dealers.

> *CAUTION*
> *Do not damage the ball-joint dust boot.*

3. Installation is the reverse of removal. Always use new ball-joints self-locking nuts. Tighten all bolts to specifications (**Table 2**).

STEERING

All models use rack and pinion steering. Power steering is optional. **Figure 66** shows the steering system.

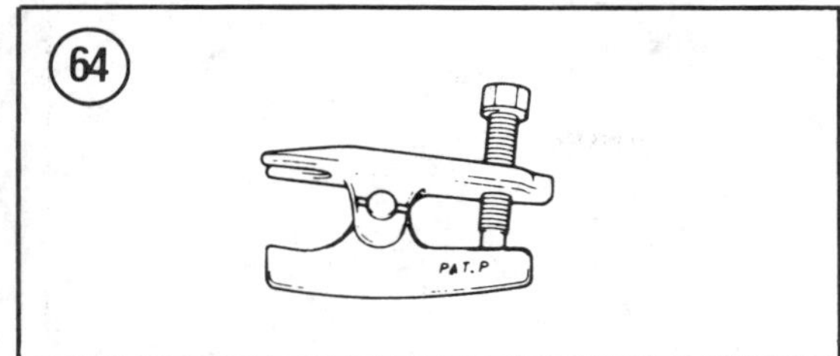

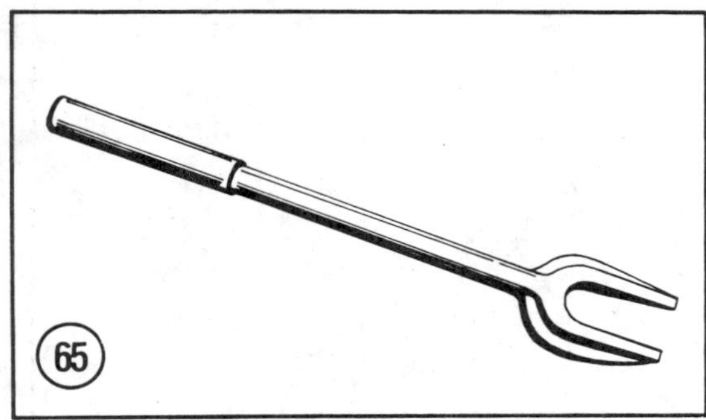

Steering Wheel Removal/Installation

1. Disconnect the negative cable from the battery.
2. Make sure the wheels are in the straight-ahead position.
3. Remove the horn pad as shown in **Figure 67**.
4. Remove the steering wheel nut.

> *CAUTION*
> *During the next step, do not use an impact puller or pound on the steering wheel. This can damage the steering column.*

5. Remove the steering wheel with a puller like the one shown in **Figure 68**. These are available at auto parts stores.
6. Installation is the reverse of removal. Apply multipurpose grease to the friction surface shown in **Figure 69**. Make sure the punch mark on the steering column (**Figure 70**) is straight up. Install the steering wheel in the straight-ahead position, then tighten the nut to specifications (**Table 2**). See **Figure 71**.

Steering Lock Removal/Installation

1. Remove the steering wheel as described in this chapter.
2. Remove the steering column shell (**Figure 72**).
3. Remove the Phillips screws and drill out the self-shearing screws that secure the steering lock. See **Figure 73**. Remove the drilled-out screws with a screw extractor. These are available from auto parts stores.

4. Installation is the reverse of removal. Align the steering lock protrusion with the hole in the steering column tube. Install new self-shearing screws and tighten them until their heads snap off. See **Figure 74**.

Steering Column Lower Joint Removal/Installation

1. Make sure the wheels are in the straight-ahead position.
2. Remove the lower joint clamp bolts (**Figure 75**).

> *NOTE*
> *The clamp bolts pass through cutouts in the steering gear and column, so they must be removed, not just loosened.*

3. Slide the joint up the steering column (1, **Figure 75**), swing it outward (2) and slide it off the steering column (3).

> *NOTE*
> *If necessary, remove the steering column hole cover (**Figure 76**) to ease removal.*

4. Installation is the reverse of removal. Apply multipurpose grease to the contact point of lower joint and steering column hole cover. Make sure the cutouts (**Figure 77**) align perfectly with the clamp bolt holes. Make sure the lower joint slit aligns with the cap or spacer mark on the steering gear (**Figure 78**). Tighten all fasteners to specifications (end of chapter).

Steering Column Removal/Installation

Refer to **Figure 79** for this procedure.
1. Remove the steering wheel and steering column lower joint as described in this chapter.
2. Remove the combination switch as described in Chapter Seven.
3. Remove the heater ducts as described in Chapter Six.
4. Remove the steering column bolts (**Figure 80**). Take the column out.

> *CAUTION*
> *Do not lose the sliding washers mounted between the column and dash.*

5. If necessary, remove the column hole cover (**Figure 76**).
6. Installation is the reverse of removal. Tighten all fasteners loosely, then tighten them to specifications (end of chapter). Make sure the steering wheel turns smoothly and that the number of turns from full left lock to full right lock is the same.

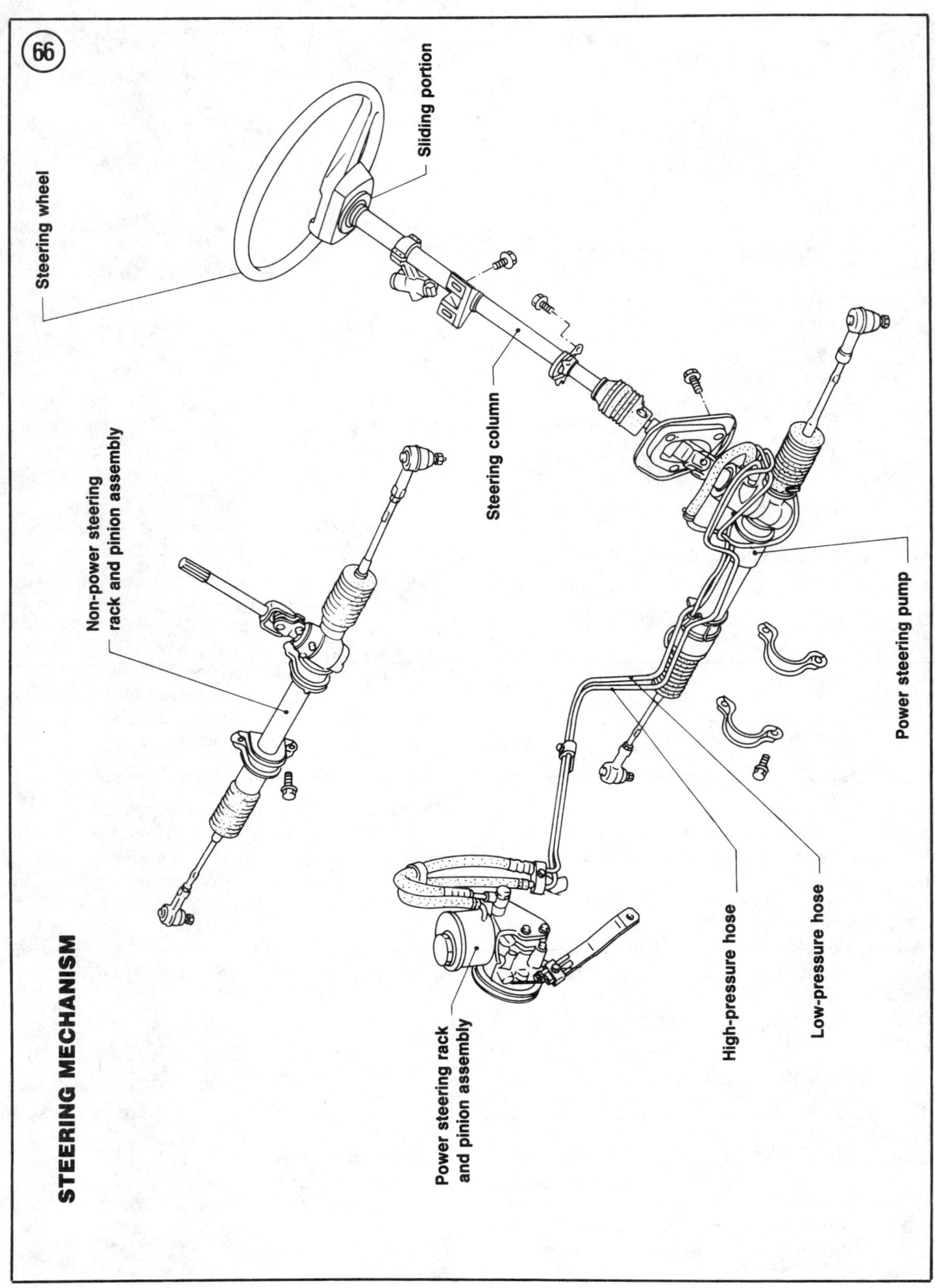
66
STEERING MECHANISM
Steering wheel
Sliding portion
Steering column
Non-power steering
rack and pinion assembly
Power steering rack
and pinion assembly
High-pressure hose
Low-pressure hose
Power steering pump

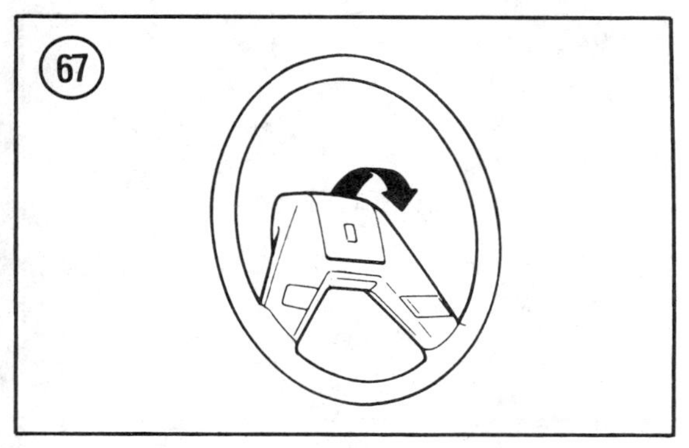

67

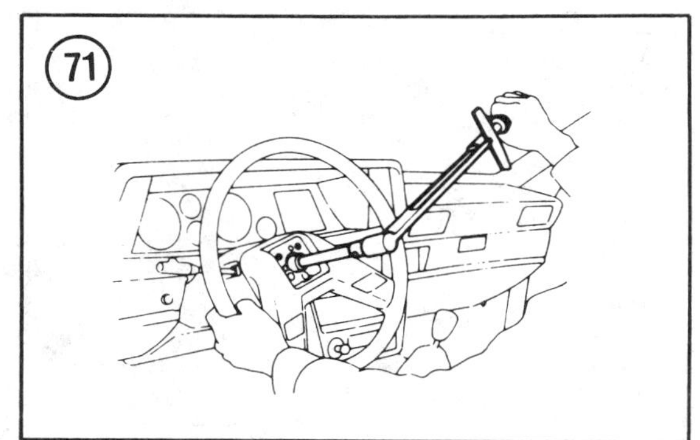

71

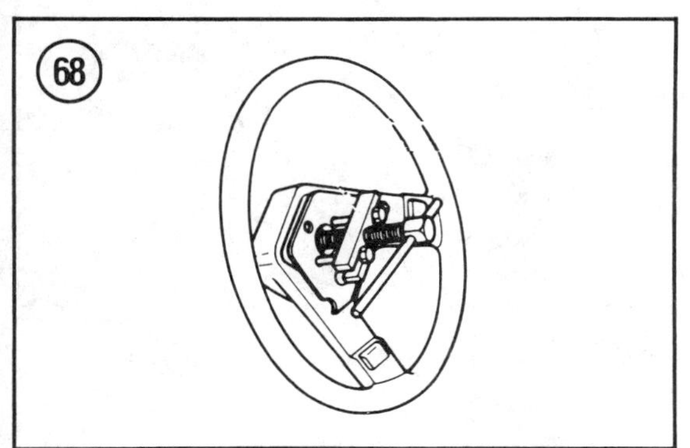

68

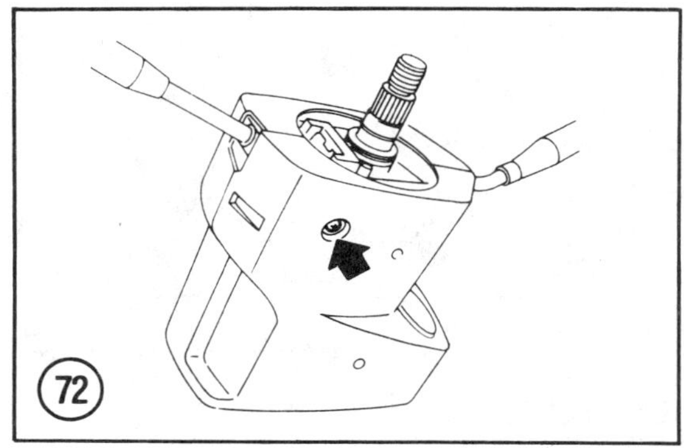

72

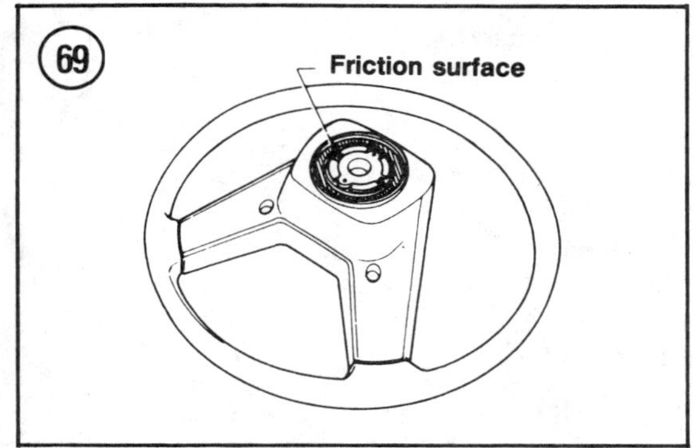

69

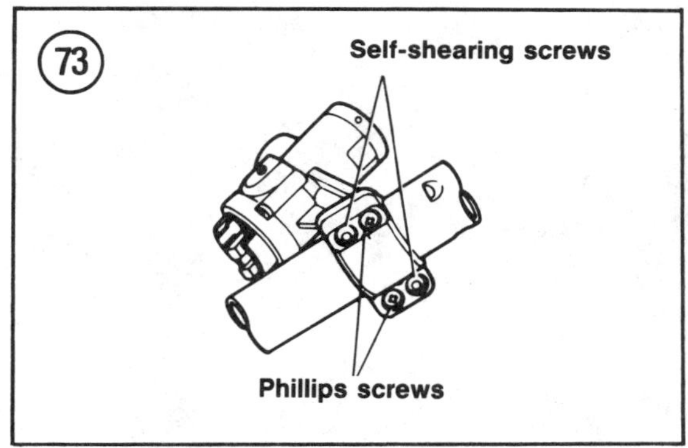

73

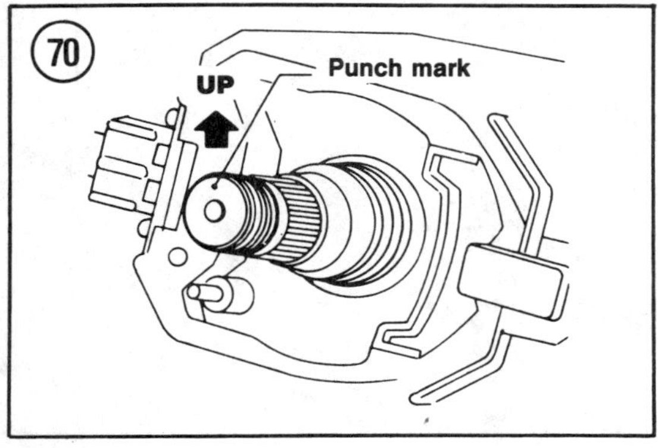

70

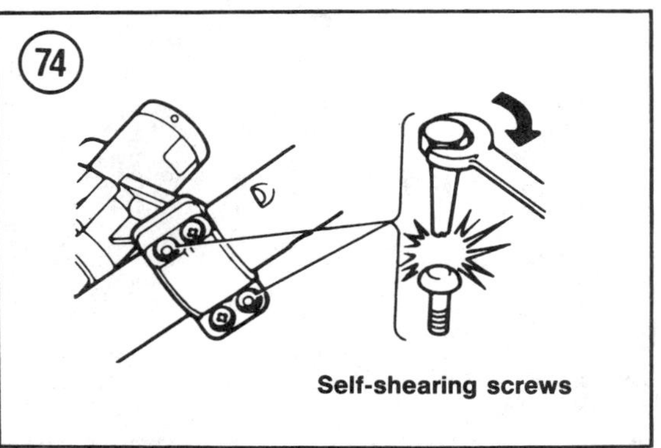

74

75
3
2
1
Remove

77
Cutout
Lower joint

76

78
Slit position
Mark

STEERING COLUMN
Spring washer
Washer
Steering wheel locknut
Wave washer
Sliding plate
Snap ring
Jacket tube assembly
Snap ring
Column shaft assembly
Lower joint
Boot band
Boot
79

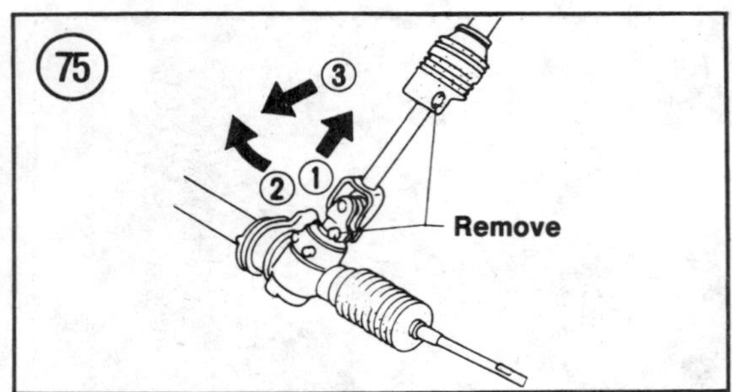

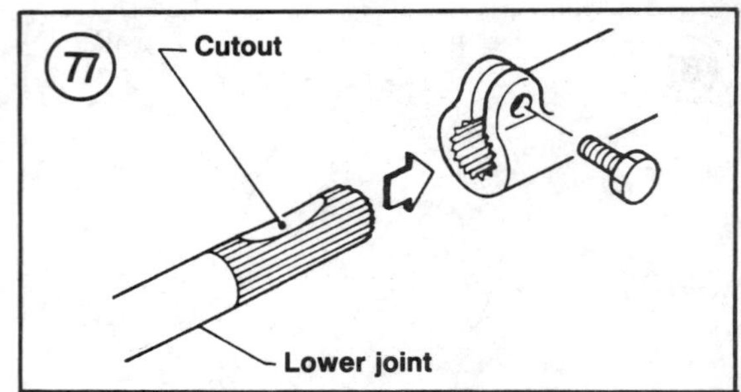

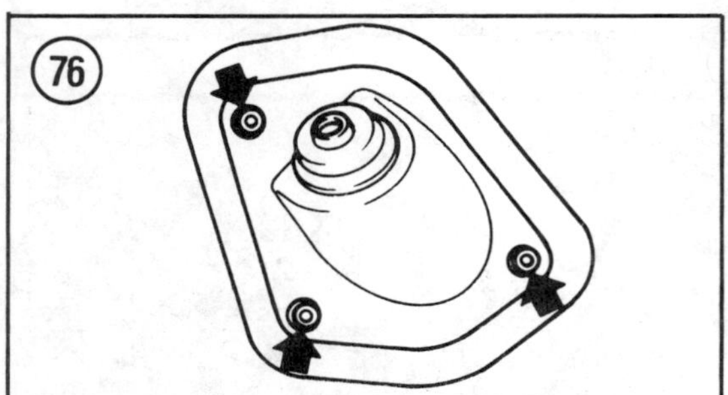

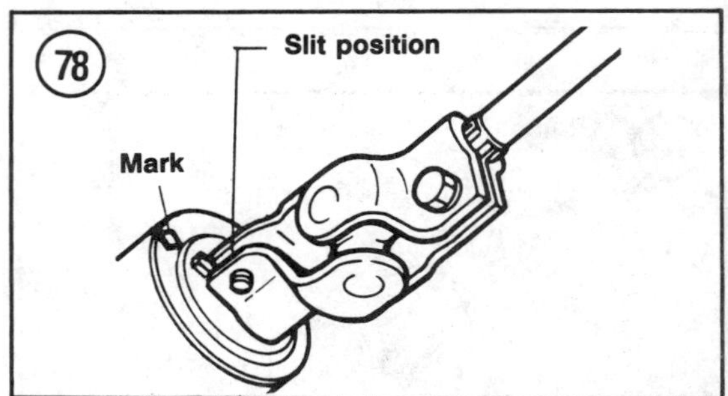

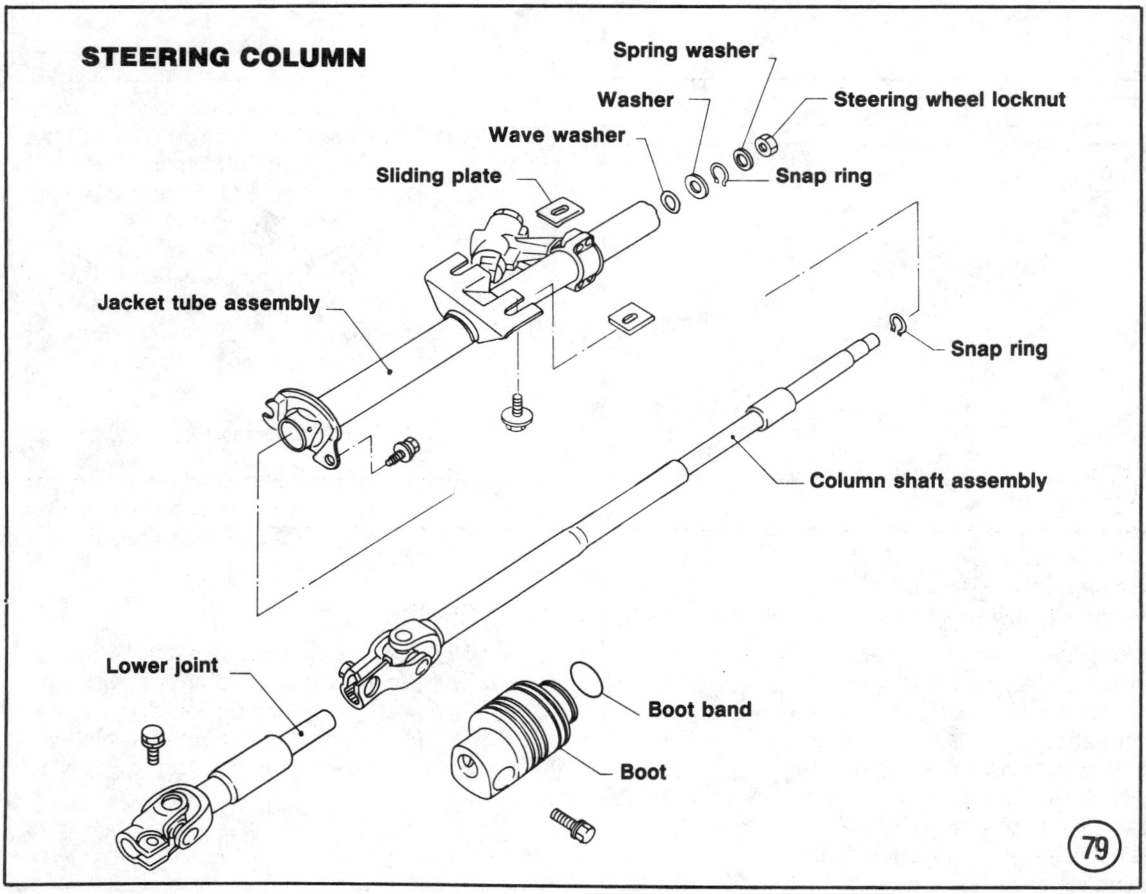

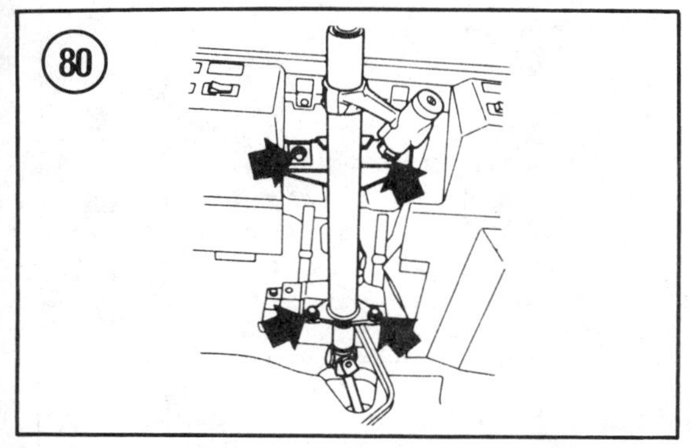

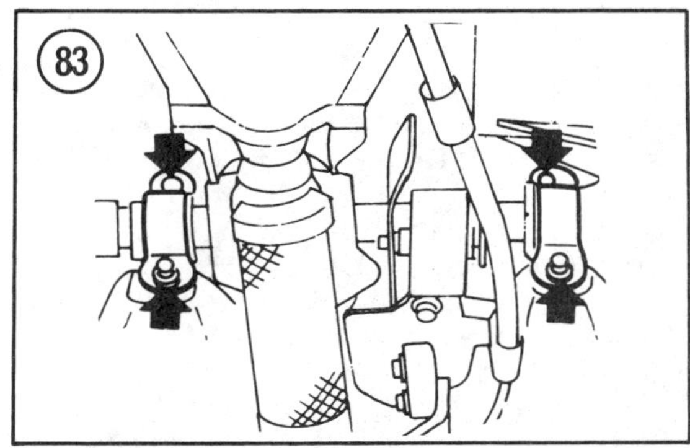

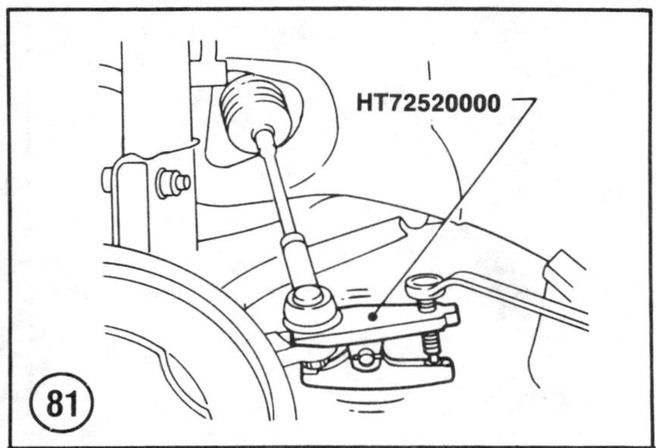

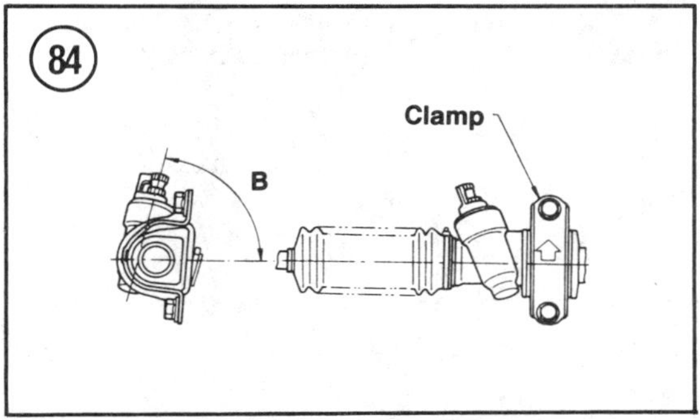

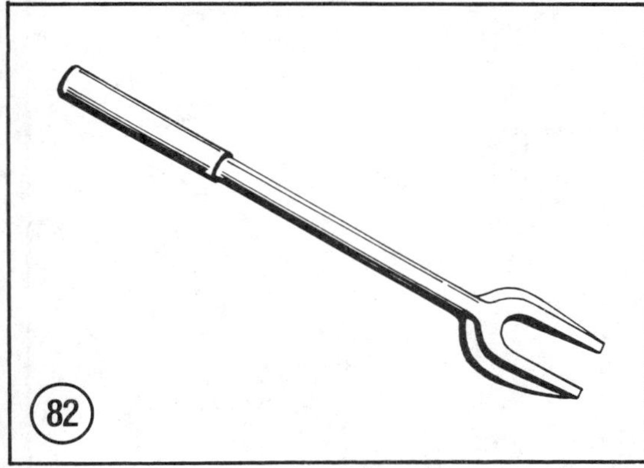

4. Loosen the rack and pinion assembly mounting bolts (**Figure 83**), then remove the steering column lower joint as described in this chapter.

5. Remove the mounting bolts (**Figure 83**), then take the rack and pinion assembly out.

6. Installation is the reverse of removal. The arrow marks on mounting bushings and clamps point upward. See **Figure 84**. Angle B, **Figure 84**, is 76.5°. Tighten all fasteners to specifications (end of chapter). Have wheel alignment checked by a dealer or front-end shop.

POWER STEERING

The following procedures apply only to the power steering system. Procedures not covered in this section are described under *Steering* in this chapter.

System Bleeding

Bleeding is necessary whenever air enters the system. Start the procedure with a cold engine.

1. Set the handbrake. Securely block both rear wheels so the car will not roll in either direction.

2. Jack up the front of the car and place it on jackstands.

3. With the engine off, quickly turn the steering wheel all the way to left and right 10 times. Turn the wheel far enough so the steering knuckles

Rack and Pinion Assembly
Removal/Installation (Non-power Steering)

1. Set the handbrake. Securely block both rear wheels so the car will not roll in either direction.

2. Jack up the front end of the car and place it on jackstands.

3. Remove the tie rod end cotter pins and nuts. Detach the tie rods from the knuckle arms with a tool such as Nissan part No. HT72520000 (**Figure 81**) or a fork-type separator (**Figure 82**). These are available from rental dealers.

lightly contact the stoppers at the end of each stroke.

4. Check fluid level on the dipstick (**Figure 85**). Top up if necessary with DEXRON type automatic transmission fluid. Do not use any other type of fluid.

5. Warm the engine until power steering fluid temperature reaches 60-80° C (140-176° F). Check this with a thermometer to ensure accuracy.

6. Turn off the engine and recheck fluid level. Top up if necessary.

7. Run the engine for 3-5 seconds, then shut it off.

8. Recheck fluid level and top up if necessary.

9. With the engine off, quickly turn the steering all the way to left and right 10 times. Turn the wheel far enough so the steering knuckles lightly contact the stoppers at the end of each stroke.

10. Recheck fluid level and top up if necessary.

11. Run the engine and let it idle. Check the power steering fluid for bubbles. If bubbles can still be seen, repeat Steps 3-11 until the bubbles disappear.

CAUTION
During the next step, do not hold the steering wheel at full lock for more than 15 seconds.

12. If the power steering fluid cannot be bled completely, hold the steering wheel at full left lock and full right lock for 5 seconds. Check for fluid leaks while the steering wheel is at full lock. Fix any leaks, then repeat this procedure.

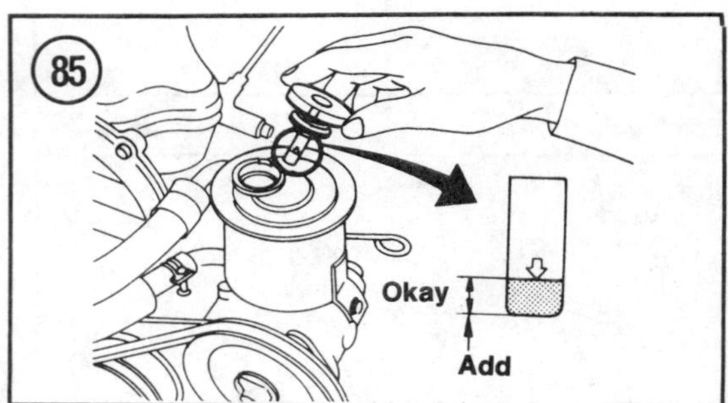

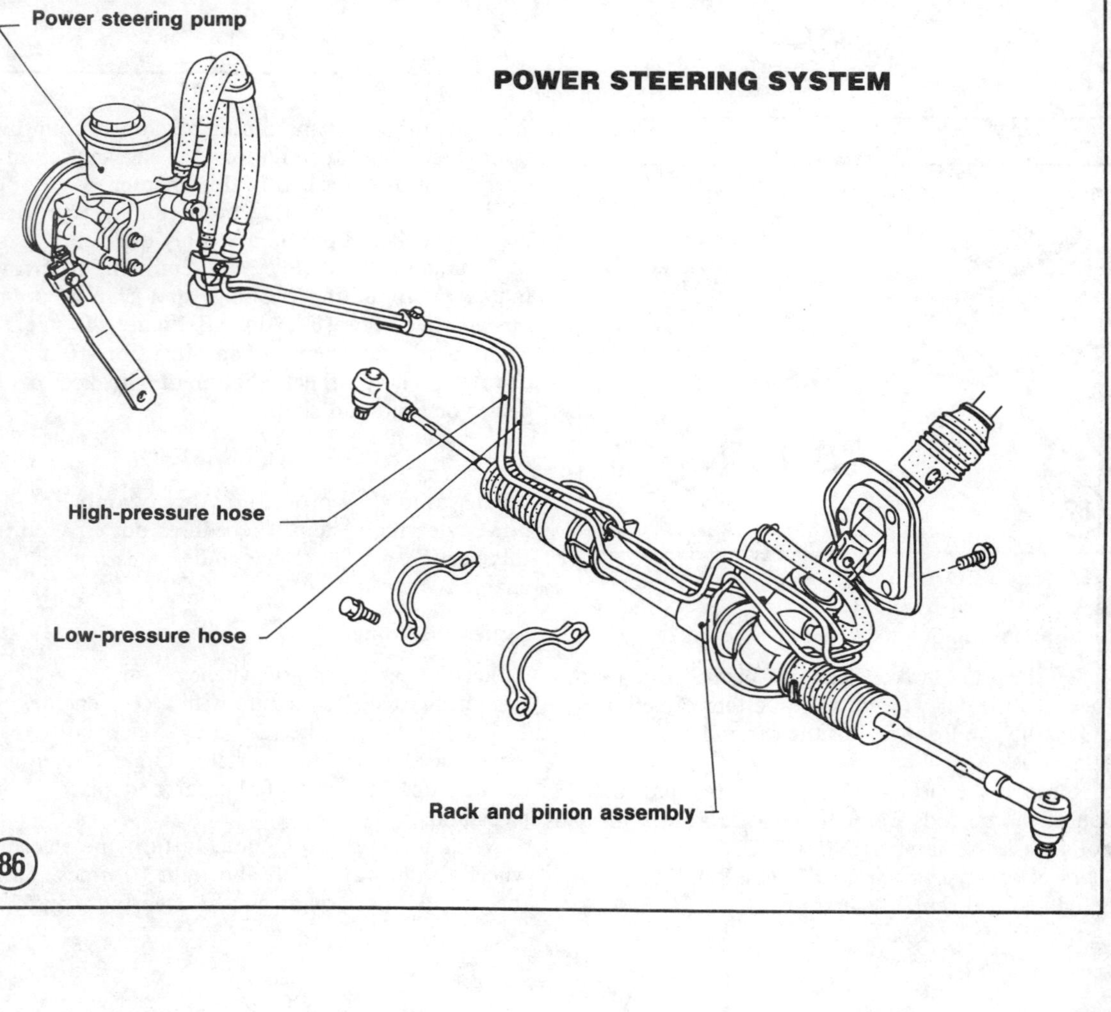

POWER STEERING SYSTEM

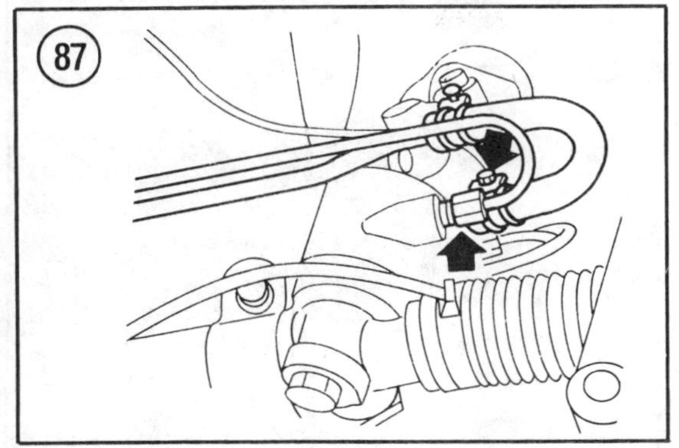

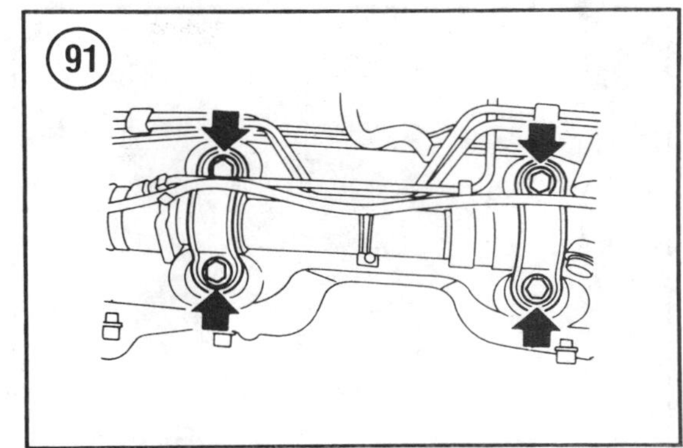

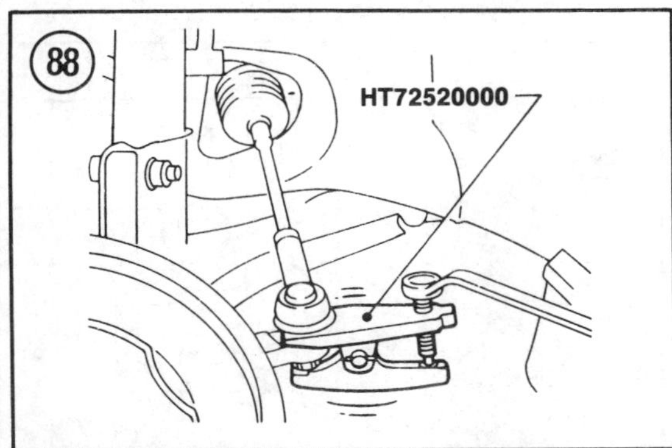

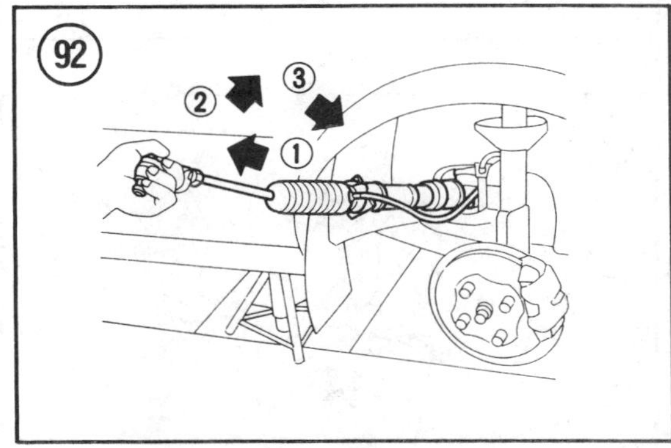

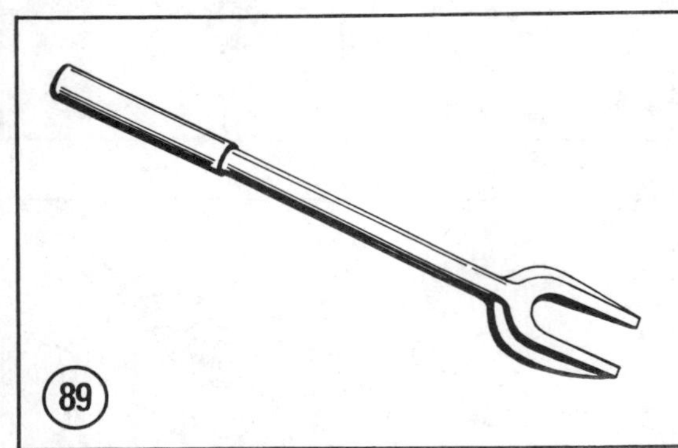

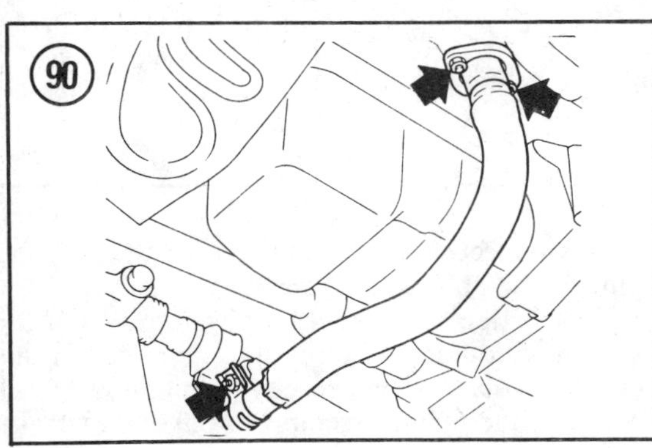

Rack and Pinion Assembly Removal/Installation

Refer to **Figure 86** for this procedure.

1. Set the handbrake. Securely block both rear wheels so the car will not roll in either direction.

2. Jack up the front of the car and place it on jackstands.

3. Disconnect the hose clamp at the gear. See **Figure 87**.

4. Undo the flare nut (**Figure 87**) with a flare nut wrench. These are available at auto parts stores.

5. Remove the cotter pins and nuts from the tie rod ends. Detach the tie rod ends from the knuckle arms with a separator such as Nissan tool No. HT72520000 (**Figure 88**) or a fork-type separator (**Figure 89**). These are available from tool rental dealers.

6. Place a jack beneath the transaxle to support it.

7. Remove the front exhaust tube (**Figure 90**).

8. Remove the rear motor mount. See *Engine Removal* in Chapter Four.

9. Remove the rack and pinion assembly mounting bolts (**Figure 91**).

10. Remove the steering column lower joint as described in this chapter.

11. Remove the rack and pinion assembly from the car as shown in **Figure 92**.

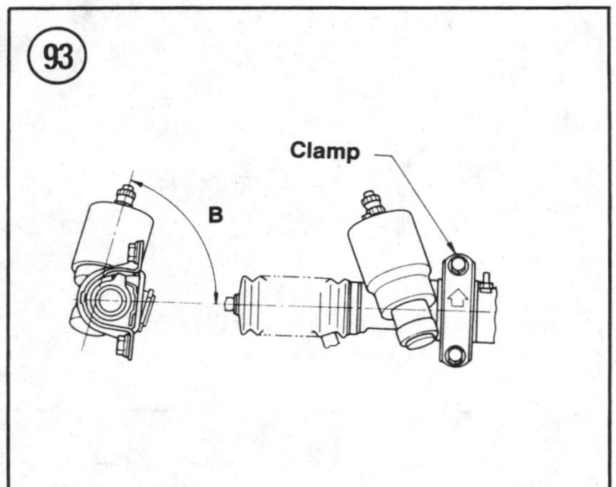

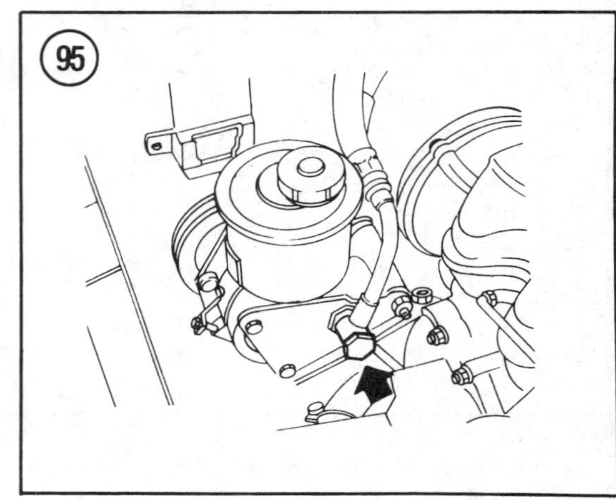

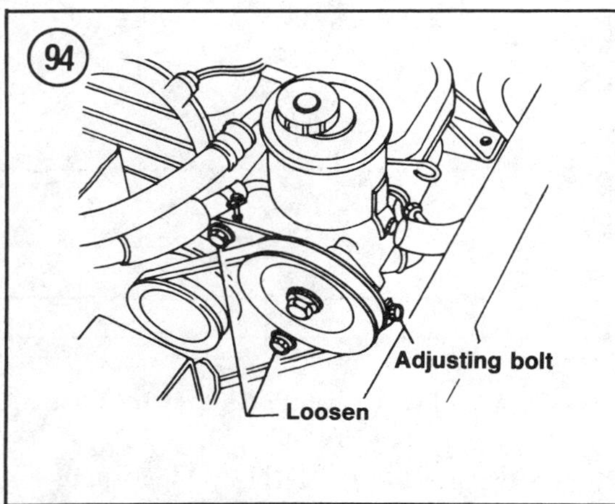

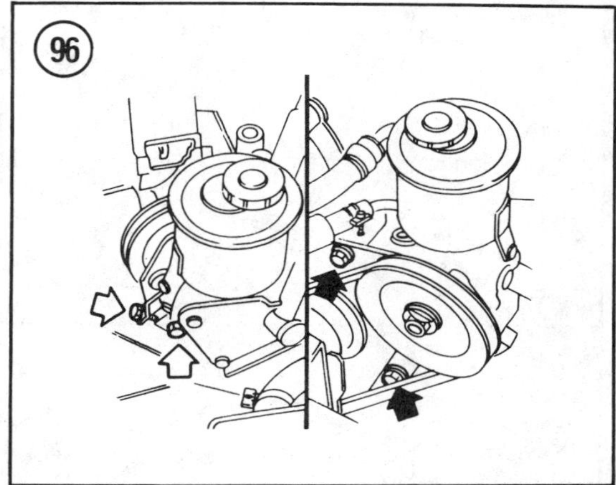

12. Installation is the reverse of removal. The arrow marks on mounting bushings and clamps point upward. See **Figure 93**. Angle B, **Figure 93**, is 70.7°. Tighten all fasteners to specifications (end of chapter). Fill the system with fluid and bleed it as described in this chapter. Total system capacity (pump, hoses, lines and rack and pinion assembly) is 0.9 liter (one qt.). Have wheel alignment checked and adjusted if necessary by a dealer or front-end shop.

Pump and Hose Removal/Installation

1. Loosen the lockbolts for the power steering pump adjusting bolt. See **Figure 94**. Loosen the adjusting bolt and take the pump drive belt off.
2. Place a pan beneath the pressure hose to catch dripping fluid, then disconnect the hose. See **Figure 95**.
3. Remove the return hose clamp.
4. Remove the pump mounting bolts and take it off the engine. See **Figure 96**.

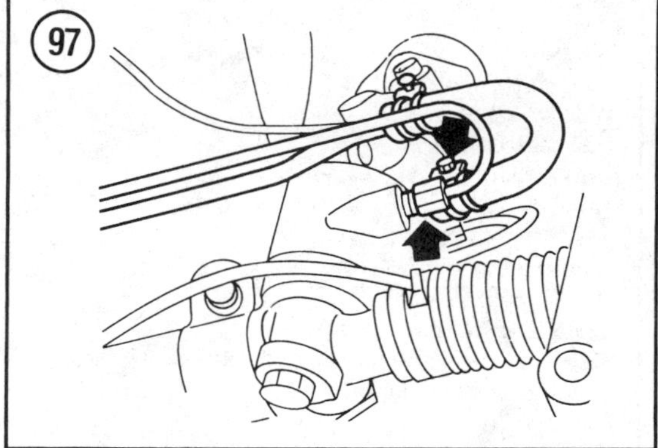

5. Disconnect the hose and line from the rack and pinion assembly. See **Figure 97**.
6. Installation is the reverse of removal. Fill the system with fluid and bleed it as described in this chapter. Total system capacity (pump, hoses, lines and rack and pinion assembly) is 0.9 liter (one qt.).

Table 1 FRONT SUSPENSION SPECIFICATIONS

Wheel bearing rotating force	1.4-1.9 kg (3.1 lb.)
Axle boot dimension "L"	
Transaxle end, tripod joint	112 mm (4.41 in.)
Transaxle end, double offset joint	84 mm (3.31 in.)
Inner end, Rzeppa joint	100 mm (3.94 in.)
Inner end, Birfield joint	90 mm (3.54 in.)
Wheel alignment	
Camber	-35' to 1° 05'
Caster	45' to 2° 15'
Toe-in	3-5 mm (0.12-0.20 in.)
Steering axis inclination	12° 10' to 13° 40'
Standard tie rod length	175.9 mm (6.93 in.)
Steering lock angles	
Gasoline	
Inner wheel	40-44°
Outer wheel	31-35°
Diesel (manual)	
Inner wheel	37-41°
Outer wheel	29-33°
Diesel (automatic)	
Inner wheel	33-37°
Outer wheel	27-31°

Table 2 TIGHTENING TORQUES

Fastener	N·m	ft.-lb.
Front suspension		
Strut to body	15-24	11-17
Strut to knuckle arm	69-88	51-65
Ball-joint to suspension arm	54-64	40-47
Ball-joint stud nut		
1982	42-54	31-40
1983	34-49	25-36
Suspension arm bracket bolts	79-98	58-72
Suspension arm bushing nuts	98-118	72-87
Suspension arm gusset to body	78-98	58-72
Axle shaft to hub	118-196	87-145
Hub to brake disc	25-33	18-25
Brake disc backing plate	3.2-4.3	2.4-3.2
Steering		
Steering wheel nut	29-39	22-29
Lower joint to column	29-39	22-29
Lower joint to gear	29-39	22-29
Column grommet to floor	4-6	3-4
Column lower bracket to pedal bracket	9-14	6.5-10.0
Column upper bracket to dash	9-14	6.5-10.0
Tie rod locknuts	37-46	27-34
Tie rod stud nuts	29-49	22-36
Rack and pinion clamp bolts	59-78	43-58
Power steering		
High-pressure hose to pump	29-49	22-36
High-pressure hose to gear	20-29	14-22
Pump to bracket	19-25	14-19
Bracket to engine	16-22	12-16
Idler pulley locknut	42-62	31-46

9

Table 3　SPACER THICKNESSES

Mark	mm	in.
05	7.381-7.440	0.2906-0.2929
06	7.441-7.500	0.2930-0.2953
07	7.501-7.560	0.2953-0.2976
08	7.561-7.620	0.2977-0.3000
09	7.621-7.680	0.3000-0.3024
10	7.681-7.740	0.3024-0.3047
11	7.741-7.800	0.3048-0.3071
12	7.801-7.860	0.3071-0.3094
13	7.861-7.920	0.3095-0.3118
14	7.921-7.980	0.3118-0.3142
15	7.981-8.040	0.3142-0.3165
16	8.041-8.100	0.3166-0.3189
17	8.101-8.160	0.3189-0.3213
18	8.161-8.220	0.3213-0.3236
19	8.221-8.280	0.3237-0.3260
20	8.281-8.340	0.3260-0.3283
21	8.341-8.400	0.3284-0.3307
22	8.401-8.460	0.3307-0.3331

REAR SUSPENSION AND WHEEL BEARINGS

The Sentra uses an independent rear suspension with coil springs and tube shock absorbers. The brake drums ride on spindles attached to the rear suspension arms.

This chapter provides service procedures for the rear spindles, wheel bearings and rear suspension. Tightening torques are listed in **Table 1** at the end of the chapter.

REAR SUSPENSION

Rear Shock Absorber Replacement

1. Securely block both front wheels so the car will not roll in either direction.
2. Jack up the rear end of the car and place it on jackstands.

3. Place a jack beneath the suspension arm to support it.
4. Hold the upper end of the shock absorber from turning with a screwdriver and remove the mounting nut. See **Figure 1**.
5. Remove the mounting bolt and nut from the lower end of the shock absorber. See **Figure 2**.
6. Slowly lower the jack and take the shock absorber out.
7. Check the shock absorber for leaks. Check all parts for wear or damage, especially rubber bushings. Replace as needed.
8. Installation is the reverse of removal. Arrange the upper end bushings and washers as shown in **Figure 3**. Tighten the mounting nuts and bolts to specifications (end of chapter).

Spring Removal/Installation

Refer to **Figure 4** for this procedure.
1. Securely block both front wheels so the car will not roll in either direction.
2. Jack up the rear end of the car and place it on jackstands.
3. Place a jack beneath the suspension arm to support it.
4. Remove the shock absorber lower mounting nut and bolt (**Figure 2**).
5. Slowly lower the jack beneath the suspension arm. Take the spring out.

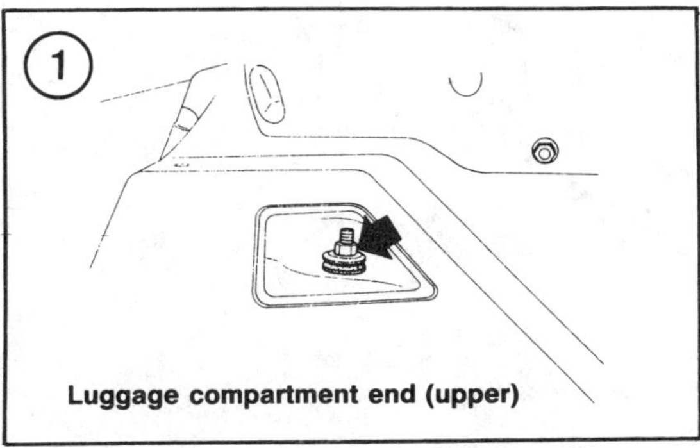

10

6. Check the spring for deformation or cracks. Check all parts for wear or damage, especially the rubber seat and rebound bumper. Replace as needed.

7. Installation is the reverse of removal. Be sure the flattened end of the spring is upward and correctly positioned on the spring seat. See **Figure 5**.

Suspension Arm Removal/Installation

Refer to **Figure 4** for this procedure.

1. Securely block both front wheels so the car will not roll in either direction.

2. Jack up the rear end of the car and place it on jackstands.

3. Place a jack beneath the suspension arm to support it.

4. Remove the spring as described in this chapter.

CAUTION
Do not use an adjustable wrench for the next step. It may round off the nut.

5. Disconnect and plug the brake line at the rear suspension arm. To do this, undo the flare nut with a flare nut wrench such as Datsun tool part No. GG94310000 (**Figure 6**). Pull out the clip with pliers and detach the brake hose from the bracket. Immediately plug the openings to keep dirt out of the brake system. Vacuum caps, available from auto parts stores, work well for this.

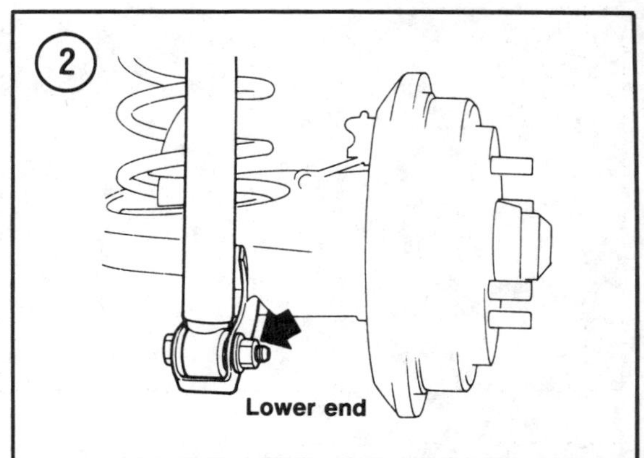

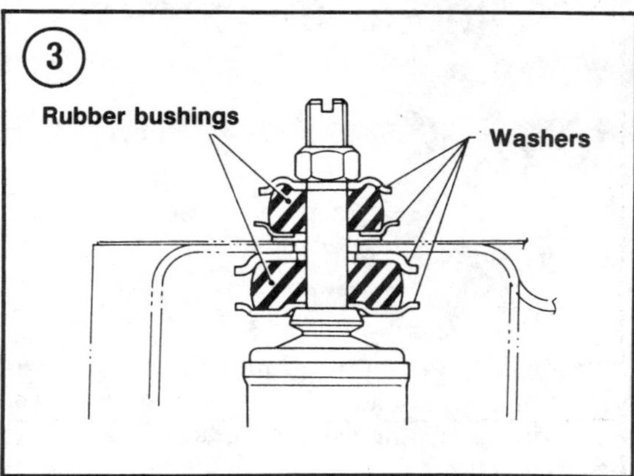

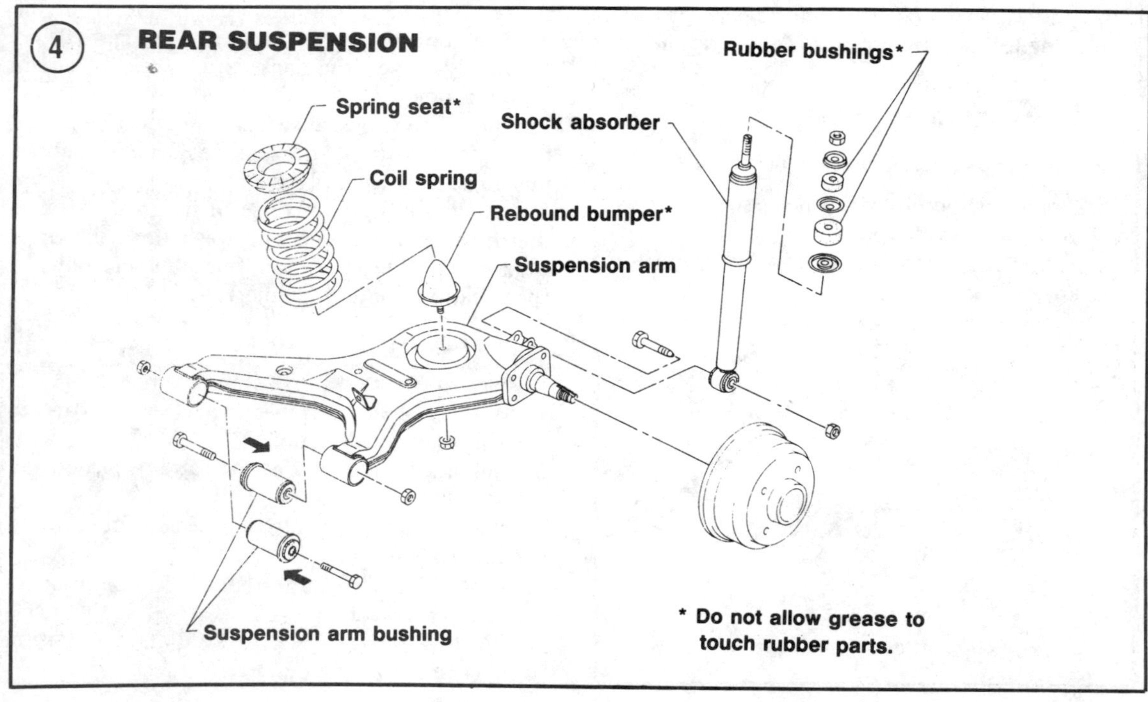

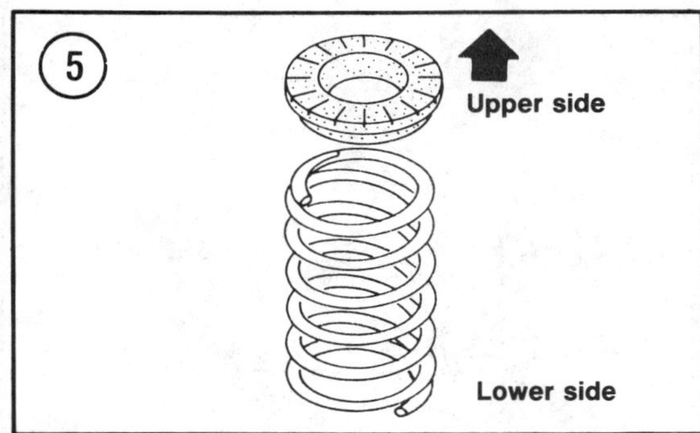

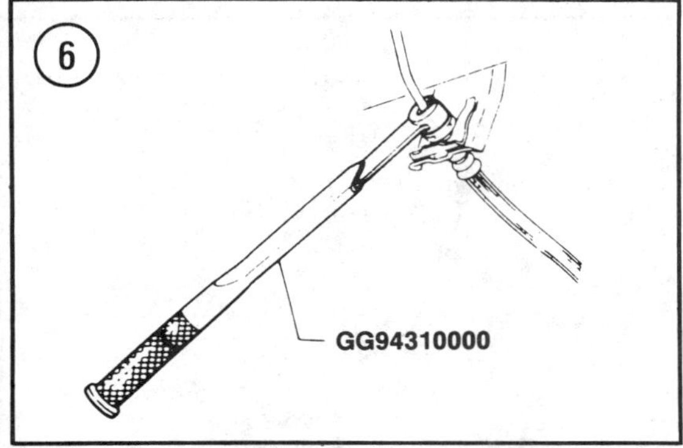

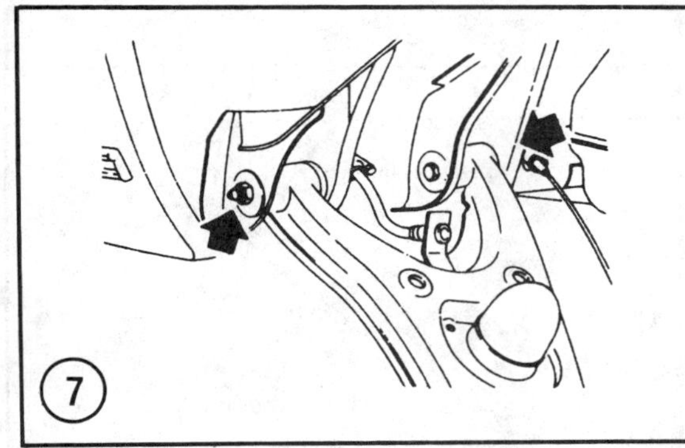

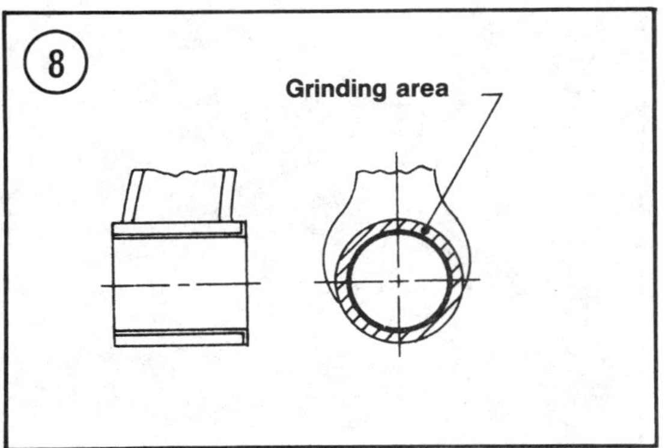

6. Remove the rear brake assembly as described in Chapter Eleven.

7. Remove the suspension arm pivot bolts and nuts (**Figure 7**). Take the suspension arm out.

8. Installation is the reverse of removal. Tighten the pivot nuts and bolts slightly while the car is on jackstands. Tighten all other fasteners to specifications (end of chapter). Install the wheels and lower the car. Roll it several feet in each direction and bounce it several times. Then tighten the pivot nuts and bolts to specifications with the car's weight resting on the wheels.

Suspension Arm Inspection

1. Check the suspension arm for cracks, bending or corrosion. Replace it if these conditions are found.

2. Check the rebound bumper for wear, cracks or deterioration. If these conditions are found, remove the bumper securing nut, take the bumper out and install a new one.

3. Check the pivot bushings for wear, cracks or deterioration. If these conditions are found, replace the bushings as described in this chapter.

Suspension Arm Bushing Replacement

This procedure requires a press and support tools. It can be done inexpensively by a machine shop if you don't have the proper equipment.

1. Grind away the bushing flange as shown in **Figure 8**.

2. Press the bushing out as shown in **Figure 9**.

3. Press the bushing in as shown in **Figure 10**. The bushing should be positioned as shown in **Figure 11** after installation.

REAR WHEEL BEARINGS

Refer to **Figure 12** for the following procedures.

Removal

1. Securely block both front wheels so the car will not roll in either direction.

10

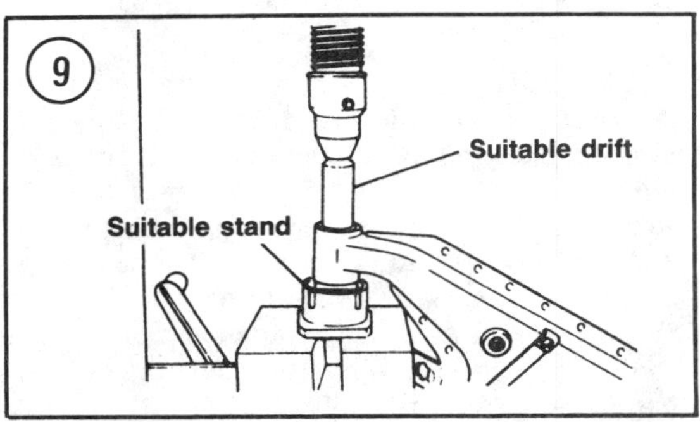

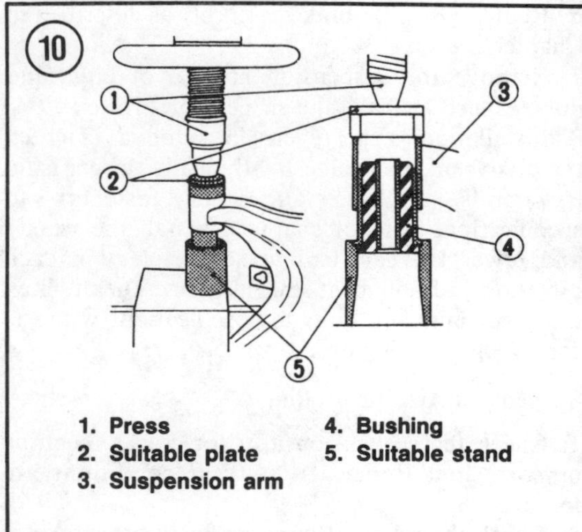

1. Press
2. Suitable plate
3. Suspension arm
4. Bushing
5. Suitable stand

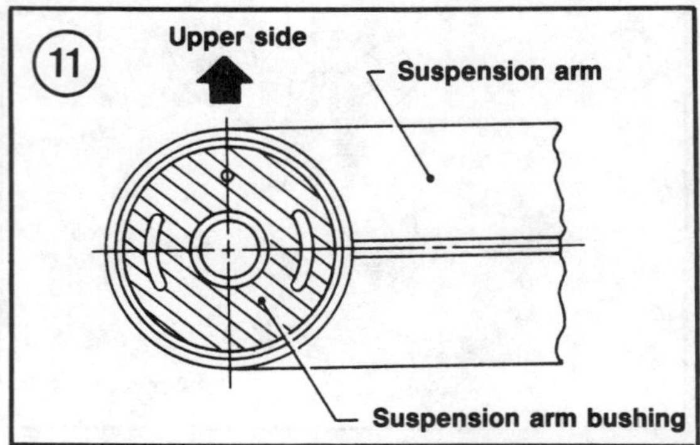

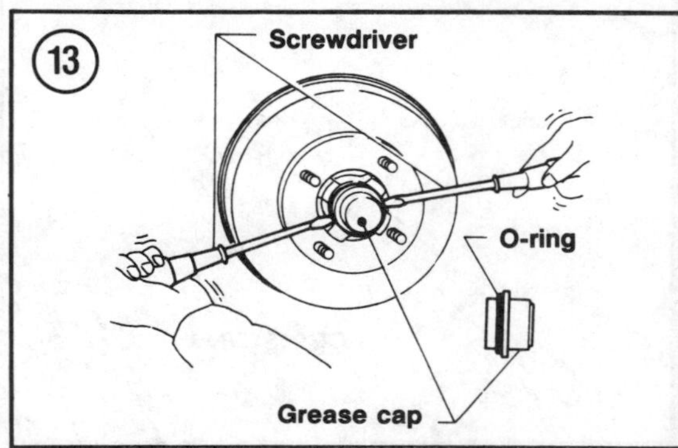

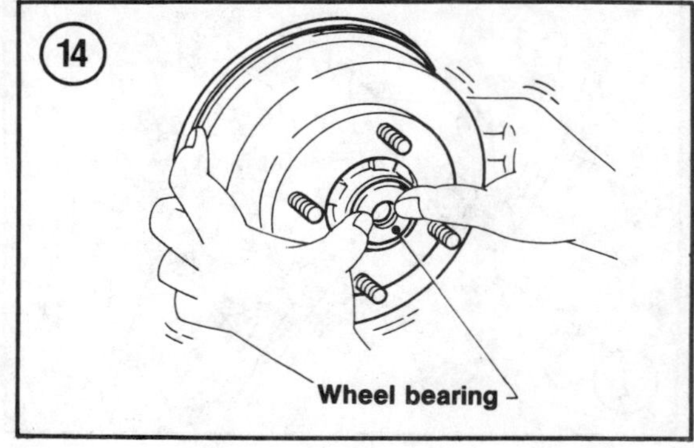

2. Loosen the rear wheel nuts. Jack up the rear end of the car, place it on jackstands and remove the rear wheels.

3. Place a jack beneath the suspension arm to support it.

4. Pry out the grease cap with 2 screwdrivers as shown in **Figure 13**.

5. Straighten the cotter pin and pull it out. Remove the adjusting cap and undo the wheel bearing nut.

6. Pull out the brake drum partway as shown in **Figure 14**. Push it back onto the spindle and take off the washer and outer wheel bearing. Then pull the brake drum off.

7. Pry the grease seal out of the hub. See **Figure 15**.

8. Take out the inner wheel bearing cone, referring to **Figure 12**.

Inspection

1. Thoroughly clean all parts in solvent and blow dry.

> *WARNING*
> *Do not spin ungreased bearings with compressed air. They may fly apart and cause injury.*

2. Check the bearings for wear, damage and the blue tint that indicates overheating. Compare the bearing cones and outer races (which are still in the hub) with the defective bearings in **Figure 16**. Replace any bearings that show these conditions.

3. Bearing cones and outer races must be replaced as a set. If the bearings need to be replaced, drive out the outer races with a hammer and brass bar as shown in **Figure 17**. Tap in new outer races with a hammer and drift as shown in **Figure 18**.

12
REAR WHEEL BEARINGS
AND HUB
Grease seal*
Inner wheel bearing
Brake drum and hub
Outer wheel bearing*
Bearing washer
Wheel bearing nut
Adjusting cap
O-ring*
Grease cap*
Cotter pin
* Lubricate with multipurpose grease

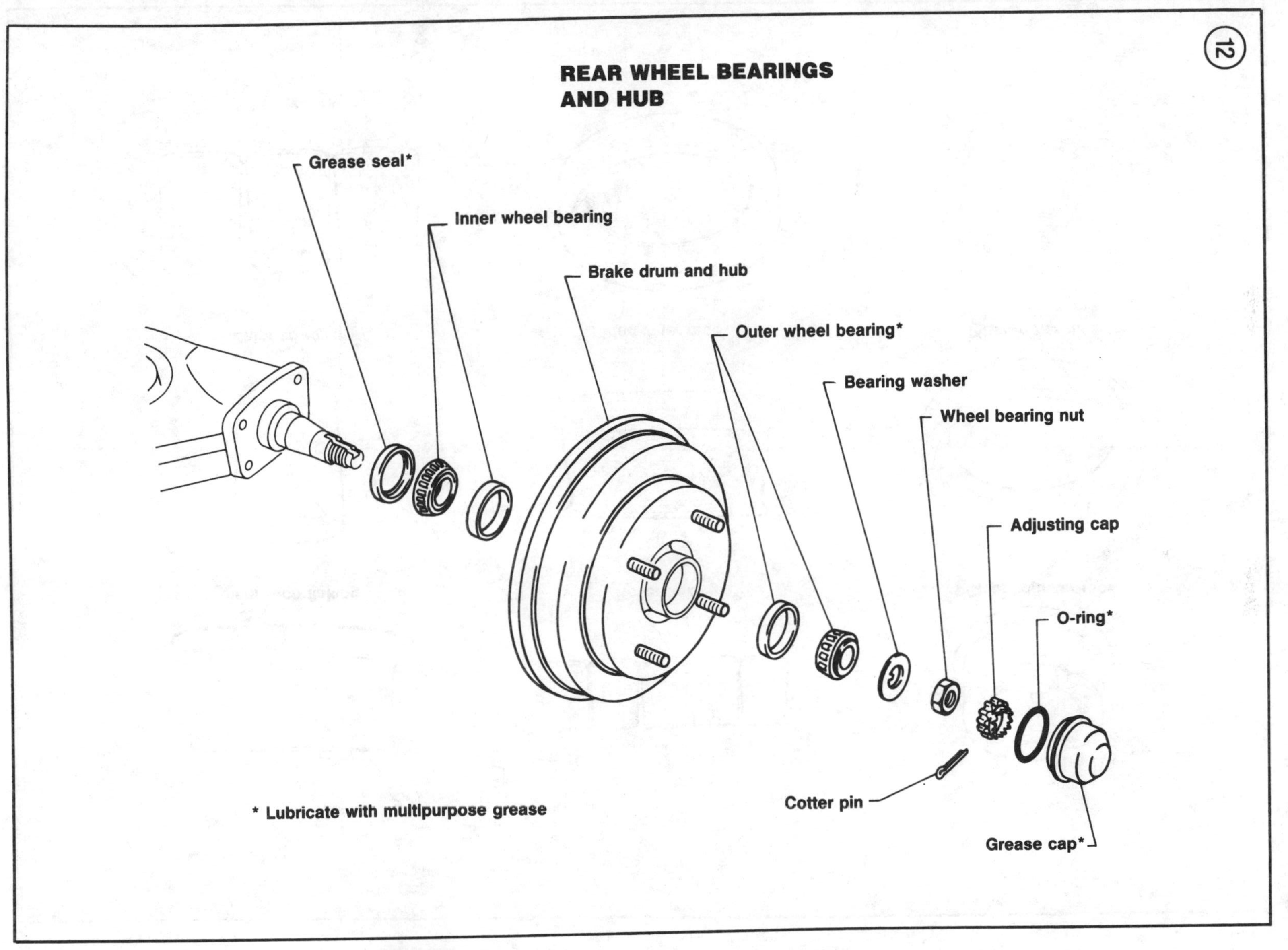

10

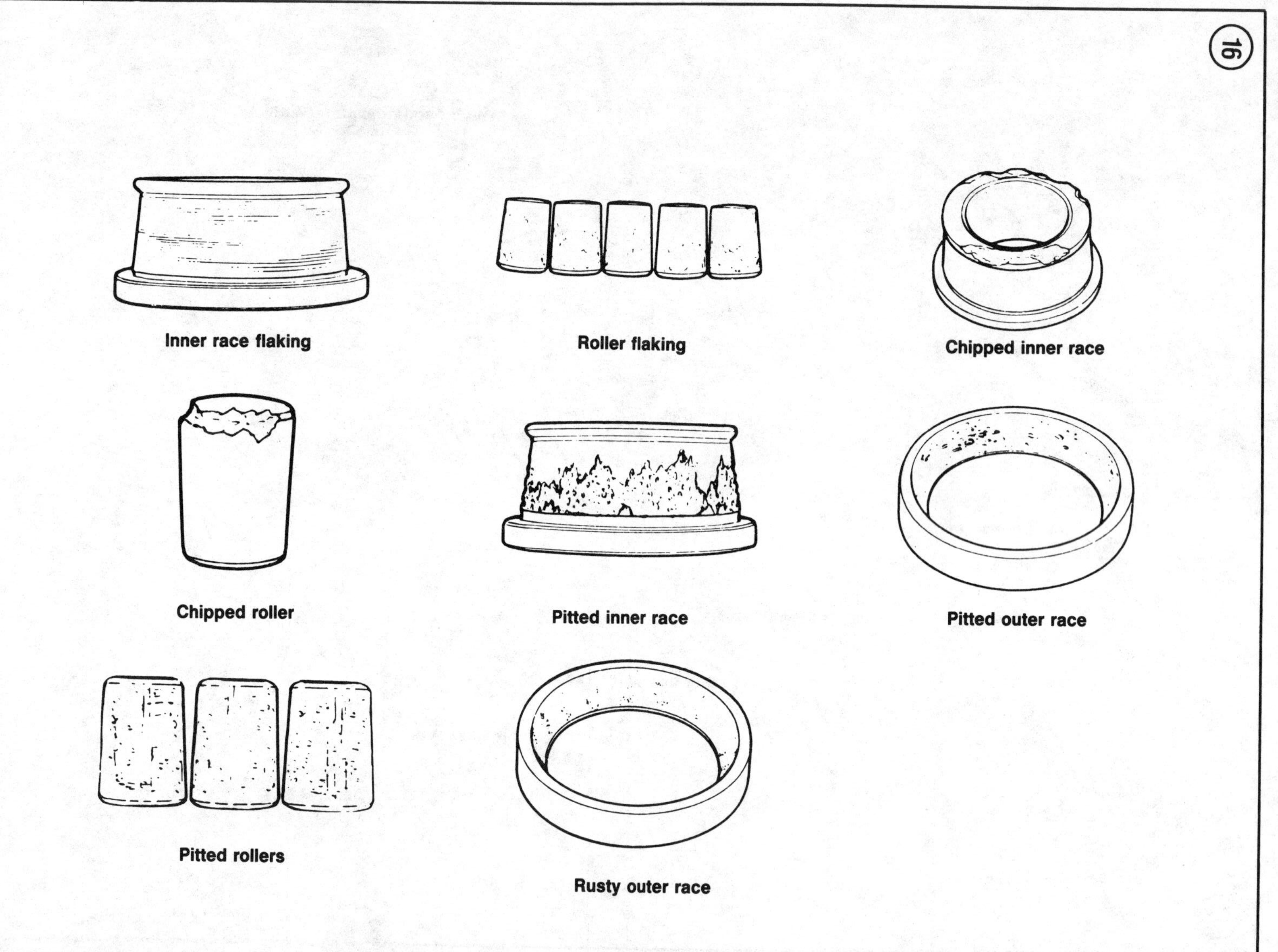
16
Inner race flaking
Roller flaking
Chipped inner race
Chipped roller
Pitted inner race
Pitted outer race
Pitted rollers
Rusty outer race

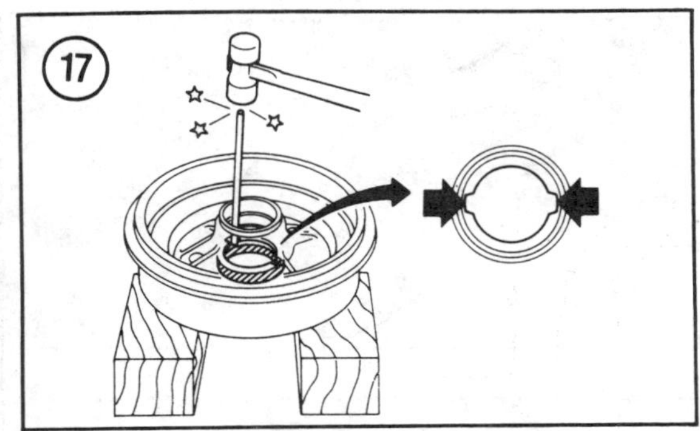

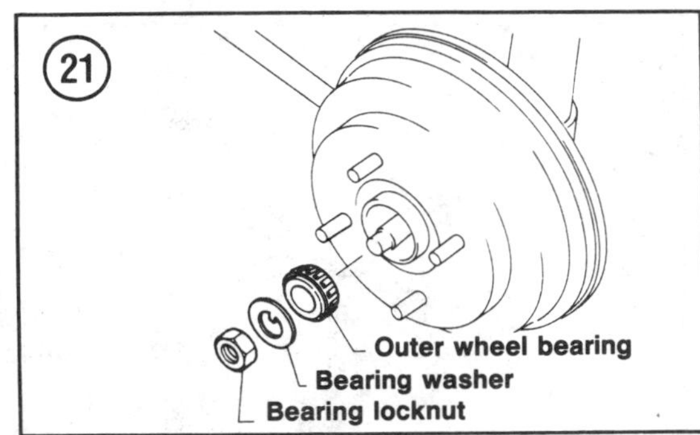

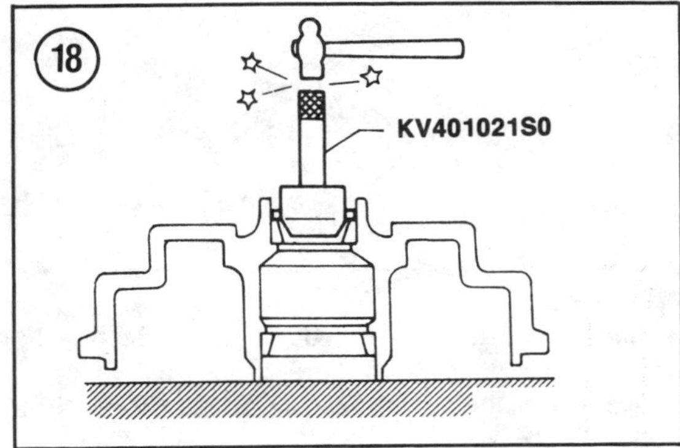

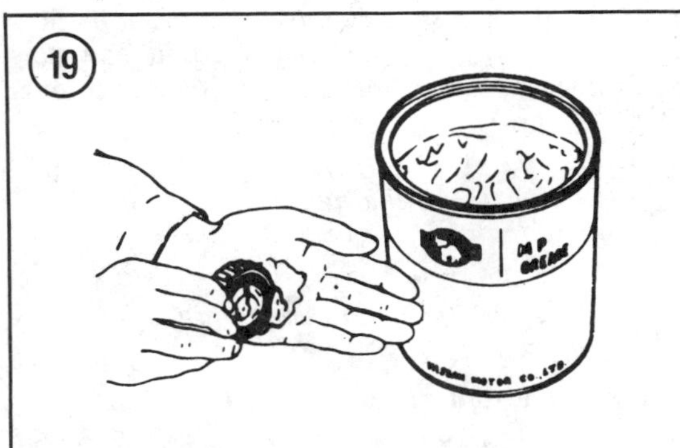

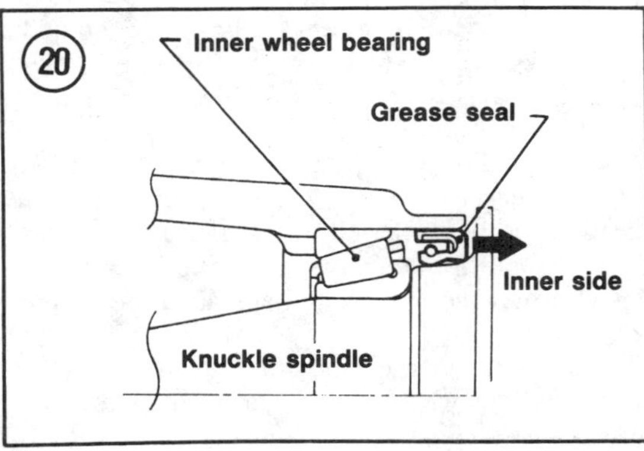

4. Check the bearing spindle on the suspension arm for cracks or other damage. Replace the suspension arm as described in this chapter if the spindle is worn or damaged.

5. Inspect the brake drum as described in Chapter Ten.

Installation

1. Lubricate the inner bearing with multipurpose lithium grease. Drag the bearing through the grease as shown in **Figure 19** and work as much grease as possible between the rollers.

2. Place the inner bearing in the hub. Tap in a new grease seal so it faces into the hub as shown in **Figure 20**. Use a block of wood to spread the hammer's force so the seal won't tilt sideways and jam.

3. Apply a light coat of multipurpose lithium grease to the following parts:
    a. Spindle threads.
    b. Inner surface of wheel bearing nut.
    c. Both surfaces of the wheel bearing washer.
    d. Grease seal lip.

4. Install the brake drum, then install the outer wheel bearing, washer and nut. See **Figure 21**.

5. Adjust preload as described in this chapter.

6. Install the wheels, lower the car and tighten the wheel nuts.

Adjustment

1. If you haven't already done so, apply a light coat of multipurpose lithium grease to the following surfaces:
    a. Spindle threads.
    b. Inner surface of wheel bearing nut.
    c. Both surfaces of wheel bearing washer.
    d. Grease seal lip.

2. Pack the grease cap with grease at the points shown in **Figure 22**.

3. Tighten the wheel bearing nut to 39-44 N•m (29-33 ft.-lb.). See **Figure 23**.

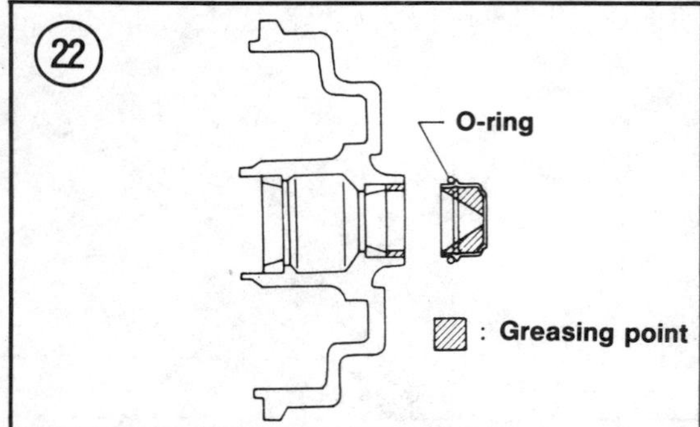

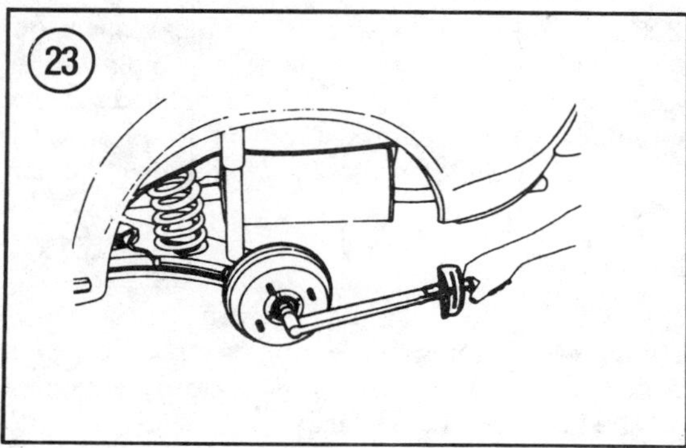

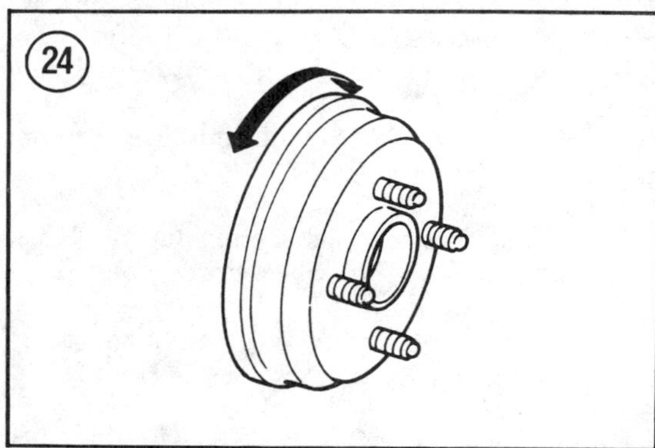

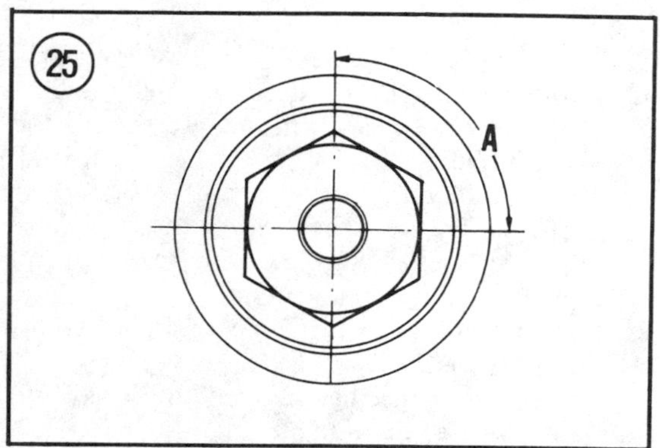

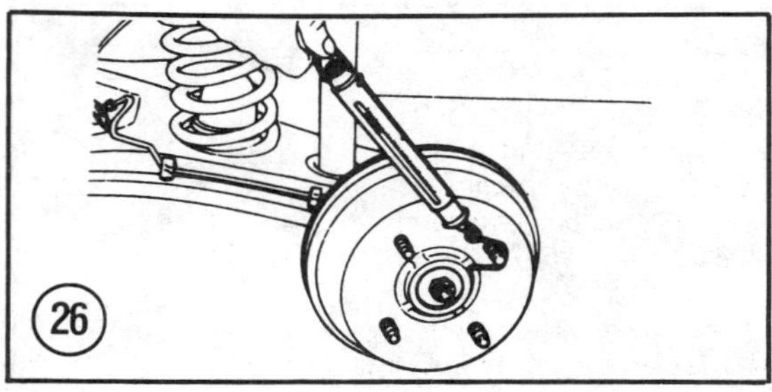

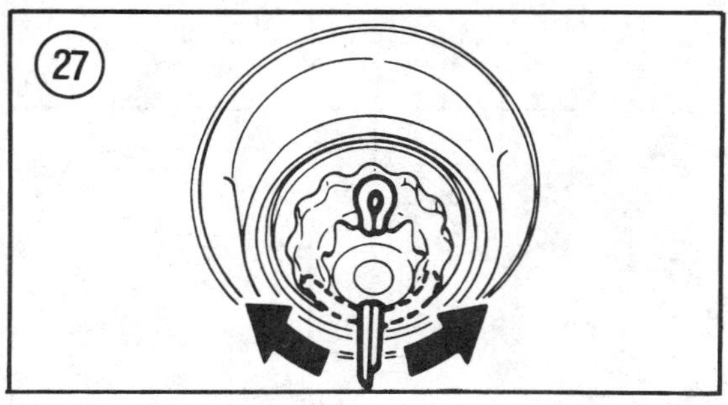

4. Turn the hub 2 or 3 turns in each direction to settle the bearings. See **Figure 24**.

5. Retighten the wheel bearing nut to 39-44 N•m (29-33 ft.-lb.).

6. Loosen the nut 90° (1/4 turn). See **Figure 25**.

7. Install the adjusting cap. Align any 2 of its slots with the hole in the spindle. If the hole and slots don't line up, tighten the nut up to an additional 15° (1/24 turn).

> *CAUTION*
> *Do not loosen the nut. Do not tighten more than the specified amount.*

> *NOTE*
> *Make sure the brakes don't drag before performing the next step.*

8. Connect a spring scale to one of the wheel studs as shown in **Figure 26**. Turn the brake drum 2 or 3 turns in both directions and measure the required pulling force:
   a. With a new grease seal, pulling force should be 1.4 kg (3.1 lb.) or less.
   b. With a used grease seal, pulling force should be 0.7 kg (1.5 lb.) or less.

If the pulling force is not within specifications, repeat Steps 3-7. There must not be any wheel bearing end play after adjusting preload.

9. Once pulling force is within specifications, install a new cotter pin and spread it. See **Figure 27**.

10. Install the grease cap with a new O-ring.

11. Install the wheels, lower the car and tighten the wheel nuts.

Table 1 TIGHTENING TORQUES

Fastener	N•m	ft.-lb.
Wheel bearing nut	See text	
Shock absorber upper nuts	9-12	7-9
Shock absorber lower bolt		
1982	35-47	26-35
1983	59-69	43-51
Suspension arm to body	59-69	43-51
Rebound bumper to suspension arm	9-12	7-9

Table 1 TIGHTENING TORQUES

Fastener	N•m	ft.-lb.
Wheel bearing nut	See text	
Shock absorber upper nuts	9-12	7-9
Shock absorber lower bolt		
1982	35-47	26-35
1983	59-69	43-51
Suspension arm to body	59-69	43-51
Rebound bumper to suspension arm	9-12	7-9

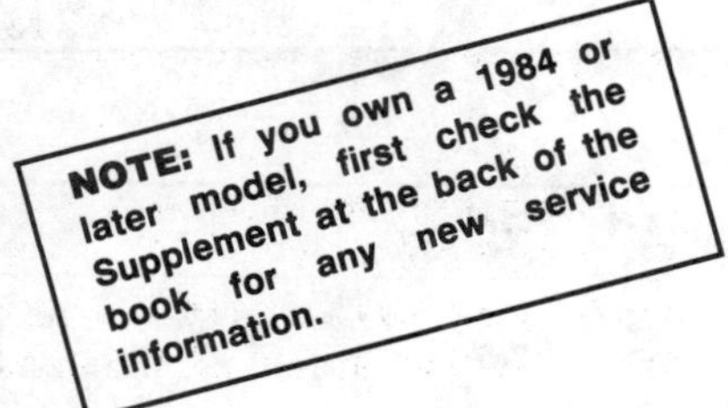

CHAPTER ELEVEN

BRAKES

The Sentra uses disc brakes at the front and drum brakes at the rear. The handbrake is a mechanical type which operates the rear brakes through a rod and cables. A Master-Vac vacuum booster (power brakes) reduces braking effort. A vacuum pump provides the necessary vacuum for diesel engine models. A dual proportioning valve controls hydraulic pressure to the rear brakes.

Table 1 and **Table 2** are at the end of the chapter.

FRONT BRAKES

The 1982 models are equipped with type CL18B disc brakes at the front. The 1983 models may be equipped with type CL18B or AD20V disc brakes at the front.

Pad Replacement (CL18B)

1. Set the handbrake. Securely block both rear wheels so the car will not roll in either direction.
2. Loosen the front wheel nuts. Jack up the front end of the car, place it on jackstands and remove the front wheels.
3. Inspect pads through the inspection hole in the back of the cylinder body (**Figure 1**). Pads must be replaced if the friction material is worn to less than specifications (**Table 1**).

> *CAUTION*
> *Always replace pads in sets of 4 (both front wheels).*

4. Remove the lockpin (**Figure 2**).
5. Pivot the caliper upward as shown in **Figure 3**, then remove the pad retainers, pads and shims. See **Figure 4**.

> *CAUTION*
> *Do not press the brake pedal after the next step or the pistons will be forced out and the calipers will have to be rebuilt.*

6. Carefully clean the space which holds the brake pads, as well as the outside of the cylinder body. While cleaning, check for brake fluid leaks (**Figure 5**). If brake fluid has been leaking, rebuild the calipers as described in this chapter.

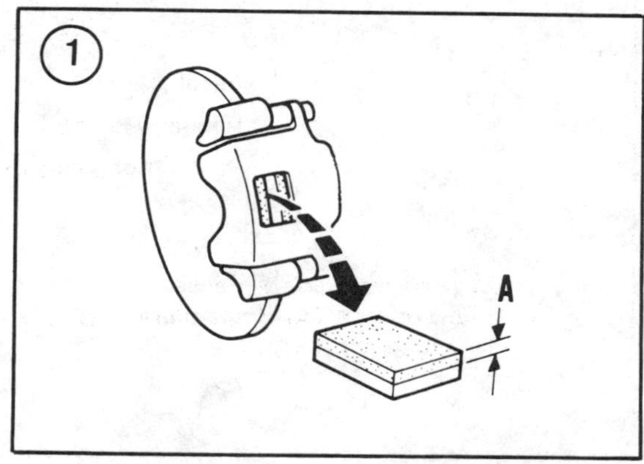

7. Inspect the pads. Light surface grease or oil stains may be sanded off. If oil or grease has penetrated the surface, replace the pads. Since brake fluid will ruin the friction material, brake pads must be replaced if any brake fluid has touched them. Pads must also be replaced if the friction material is worn to less than specifications (**Table 1**).

CAUTION
Keep the grease mentioned in the next step off the pads and disc.

8. Apply a light coat of high-temperature disc brake grease to the friction points of pads and torque member.

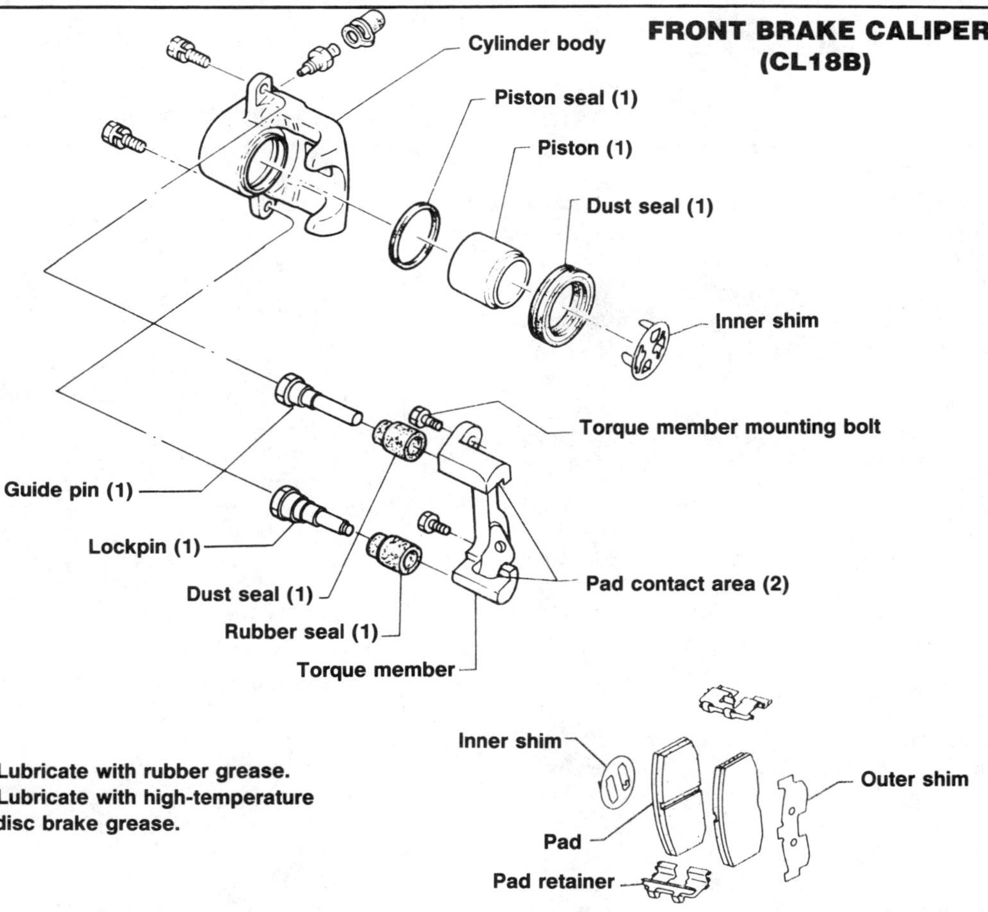

9. Install the inner pad and its shims, referring to **Figure 4**.

2

3

4

FRONT BRAKE CALIPER (CL18B)

1. Lubricate with rubber grease.
2. Lubricate with high-temperature disc brake grease.

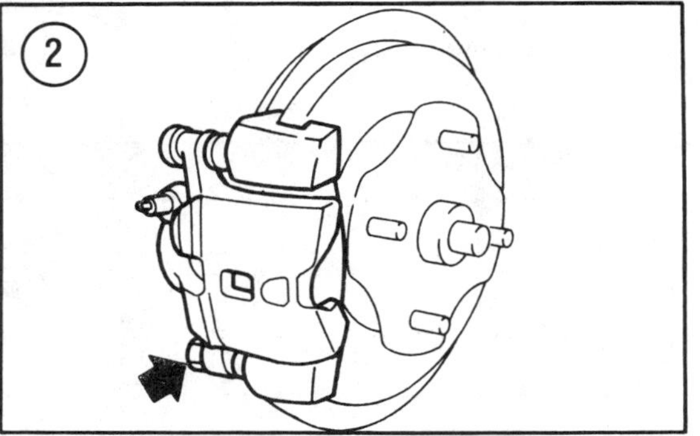

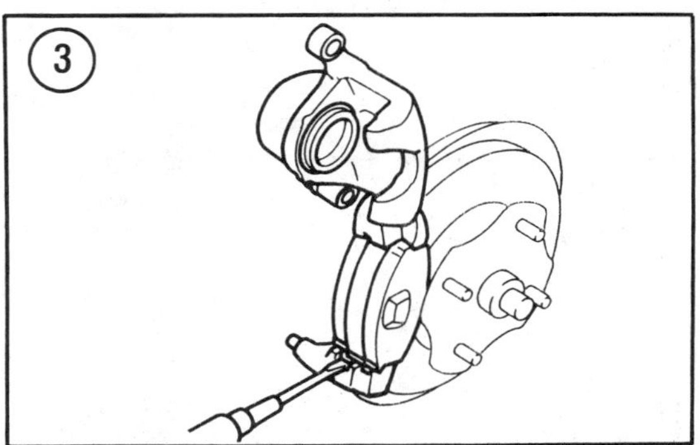

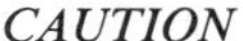

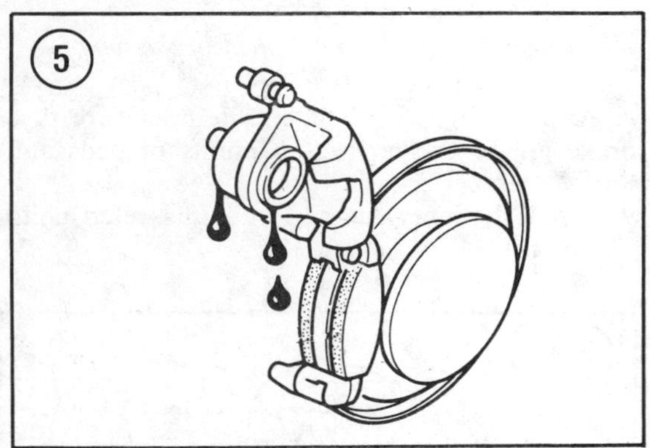

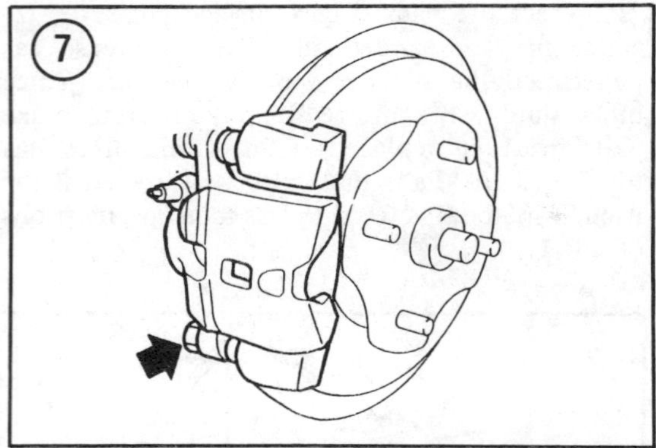

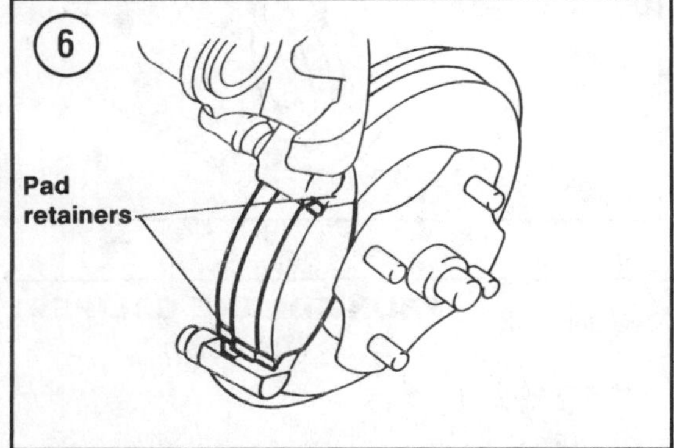

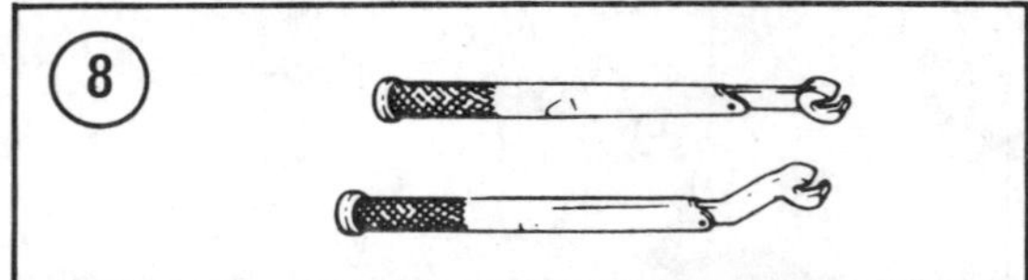

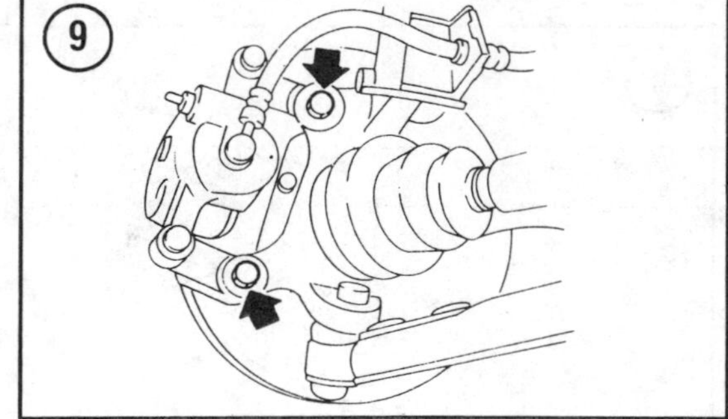

10. Pull the cylinder body outboard to provide installation clearance for the outer pad, then install the pad and its shim.

11. Install the pad retainers (**Figure 6**).

12. Pivot caliper downward and install the lockpin (**Figure 7**). Tighten to specifications (**Table 2**).

13. Install the wheels, lower the car and tighten the wheel nuts.

14. Press the brake pedal several times to seat the pads. Unblock the rear wheels and road test the brakes.

> *WARNING*
> *Make sure the brake pedal feels firm before driving the car. If it feels mushy, bleed the brakes as described in this chapter.*

Caliper Removal/Installation (CL18B)

1. Set the handbrake. Securely block both rear wheels so the car will not roll in either direction.

2. Loosen the front wheel nuts. Jack up the front end of the car, place it on jackstands and remove the front wheels.

3. Disconnect the caliper brake hose at its connection to the metal line. Use a flare nut wrench such as Nissan tool part No. GG94310000 (**Figure 8**). These are available from auto parts stores.

4. Remove the caliper mounting bolts (**Figure 9**). Take the caliper off.

5. Installation is the reverse of removal. Tighten all fasteners to specifications (**Table 2**). Bleed the brakes as described in this chapter.

Caliper Overhaul (CL18B)

Refer to **Figure 4** for this procedure.

1. Remove the caliper as described in this chapter.

2. Detach the cylinder body from the torque member. See **Figure 10**.

3. Push out the piston together with its dust seal and retainer ring as shown in **Figure 11**.

4. Remove the piston seal from the cylinder bore. See **Figure 12**.

5. Thoroughly clean all parts in new, clean brake fluid or aerosol brake cleaner. Do not clean with

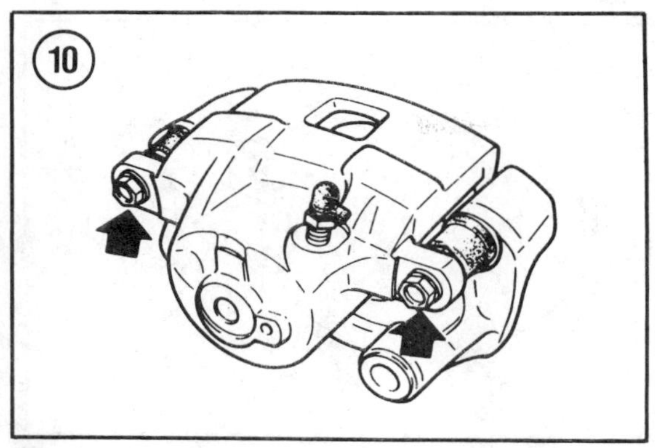

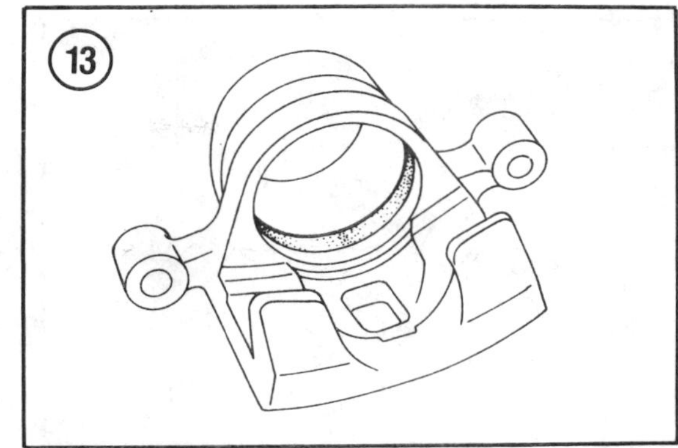

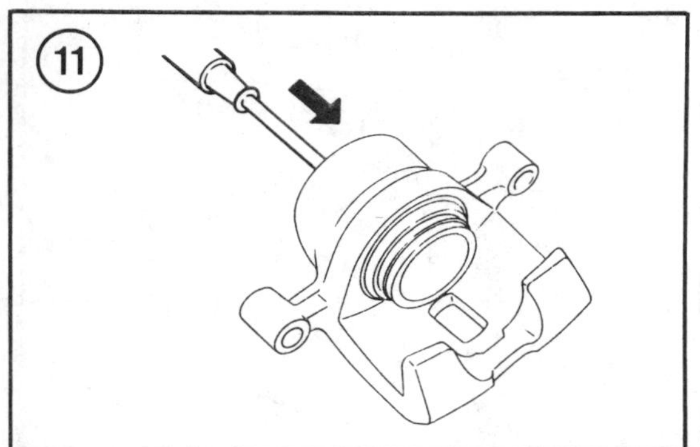

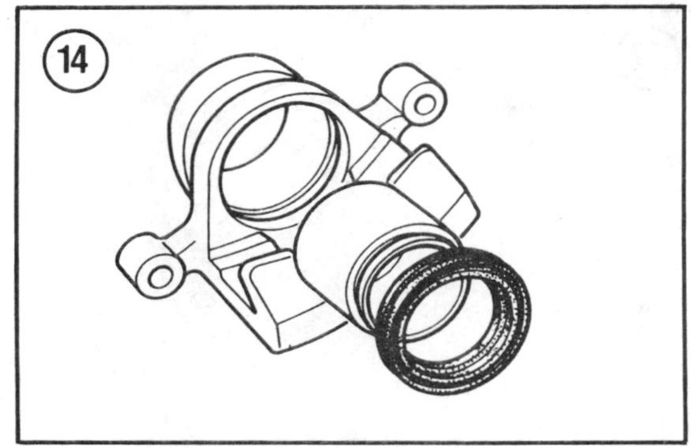

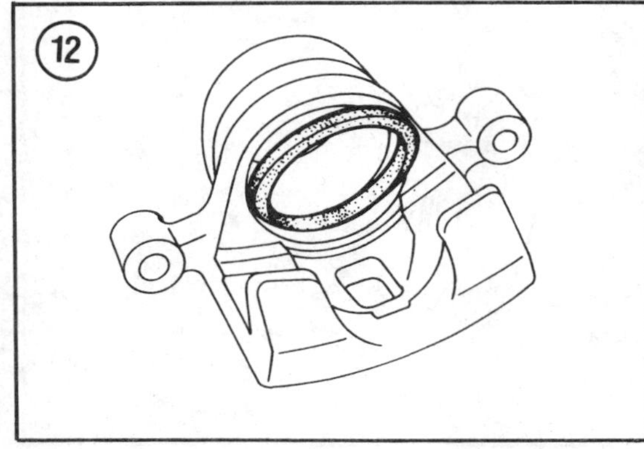

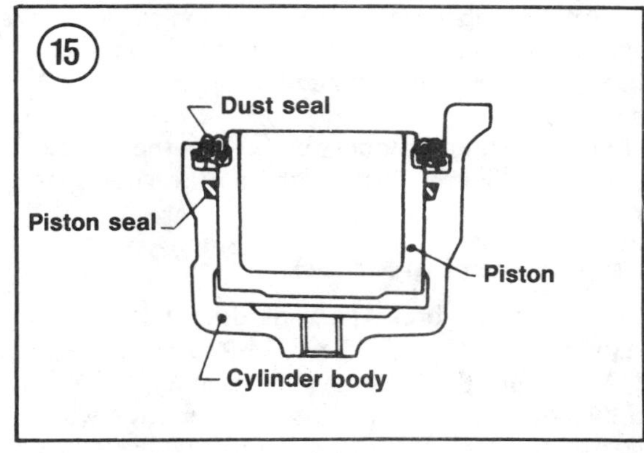

gasoline, kerosene or solvent. These leave residues which can cause rubber parts to soften and swell.

6. Check the torque member for wear, cracks or other visible defects. Replace if any of these can be seen.

7. Inspect the cylinder bore. Replace the cylinder body if wear or damage can be seen. Light rust or dirt may be removed with fine emery paper. Replace the cylinder body if dirt or rust is heavy.

8. Inspect the piston. Since it is chrome plated, the piston can't be sanded. If the piston can't be cleaned with a rag, replace it.

9. Check the guide pin, lockpin and boots for wear or damage. Replace worn or damaged parts.

10. Coat a new piston seal and its groove in the cylinder with rubber grease or new, clean brake fluid, then install it in the piston. See **Figure 13**.

11. Coat the piston and the inside of the dust seal with rubber grease or brake fluid. Install the piston and dust seal as shown in **Figure 14**.

12. Place the dust seal in the cylinder body groove, then secure it with the retaining ring. See **Figure 15**.

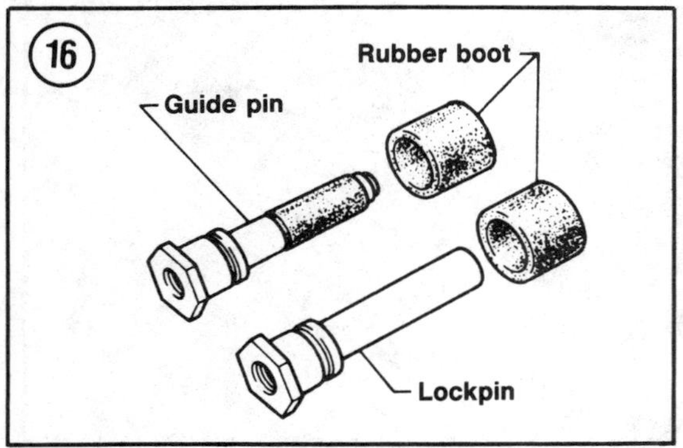

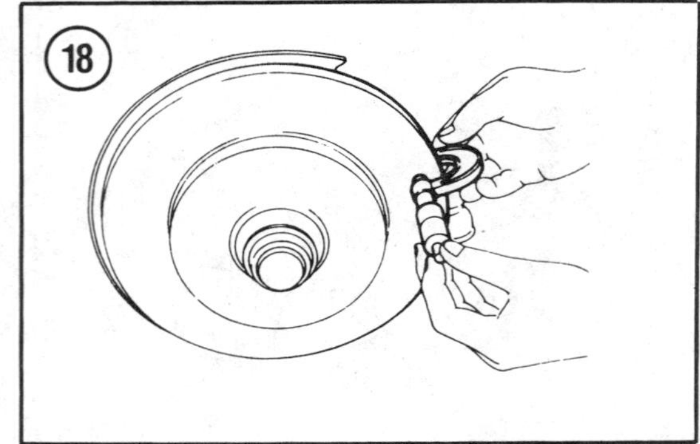

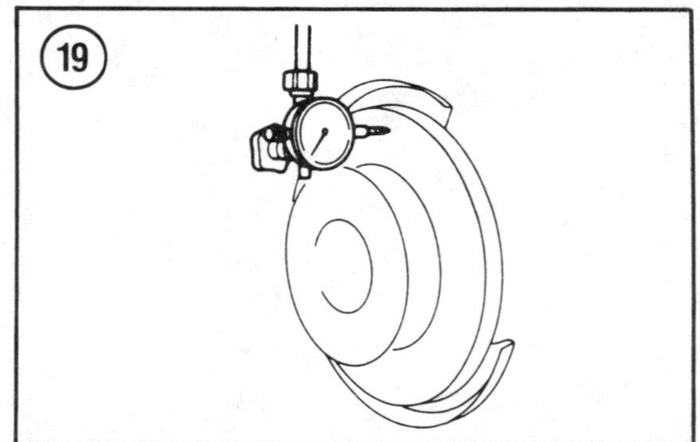

13. Apply rubber grease to the friction surfaces of guide pin and lockpin. Install the boots (**Figure 16**), then install the guide pin and lockpin in the torque member.

14. Install the cylinder body on the torque member (**Figure 17**). Tighten the bolts to specifications (**Table 2**).

Disc Inspection (All Models)

1. Remove the brake pads as described in this chapter.

2. Make sure the brake disc turns smoothly. Pull in and out on the brake disc to check for wheel bearing end play. If the disc turns roughly or there is end play in the wheel bearings, remove and inspect the wheel bearings as described in Chapter Three. Check the disc for rust, scratches or cracks. If cracks are visible, replace the disc. If rust is visible or if scratches are deep enough to snag a fingernail, have the disc turned by a machine shop.

4. Check thickness at several points around the disc with a micrometer. See **Figure 18**. Compare with **Table 1** (end of chapter). Replace the disc if thinner than the minimum.

5. Set up a dial indicator so its pointer contacts the center of the disc's swept area. See **Figure 19**. Rotate the disc one full turn and measure runout.

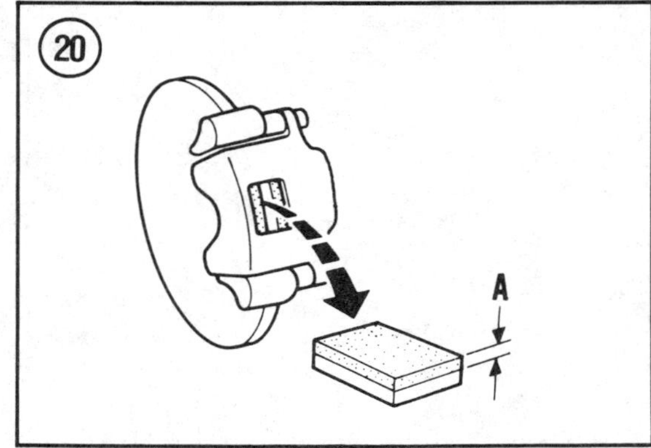

If it exceeds specifications (**Table 1**), the disc can be reconditioned by a machine shop. If the disc would have to be cut thinner than the specified minimum to eliminate runout, the disc must be replaced.

Disc Removal/Installation (All Models)

The disc is removed together with the front hub and axle shaft. See Chapter Nine for details.

Pad Replacement (AD20V)

1. Set the handbrake. Securely block both rear wheels so the car will not roll in either direction.

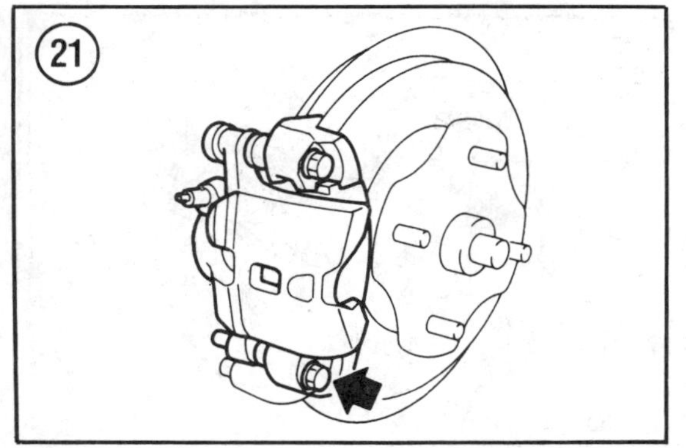

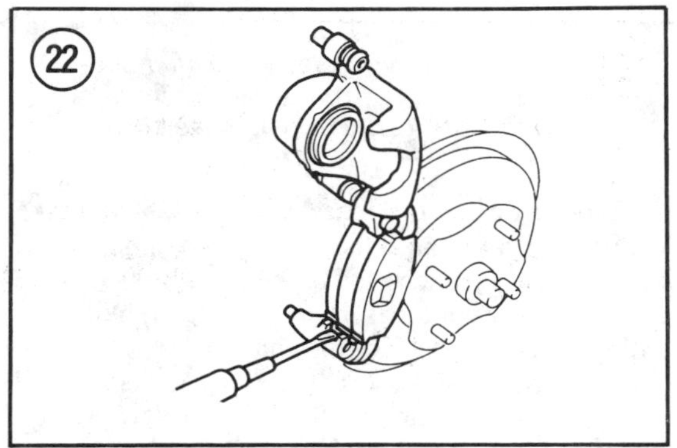

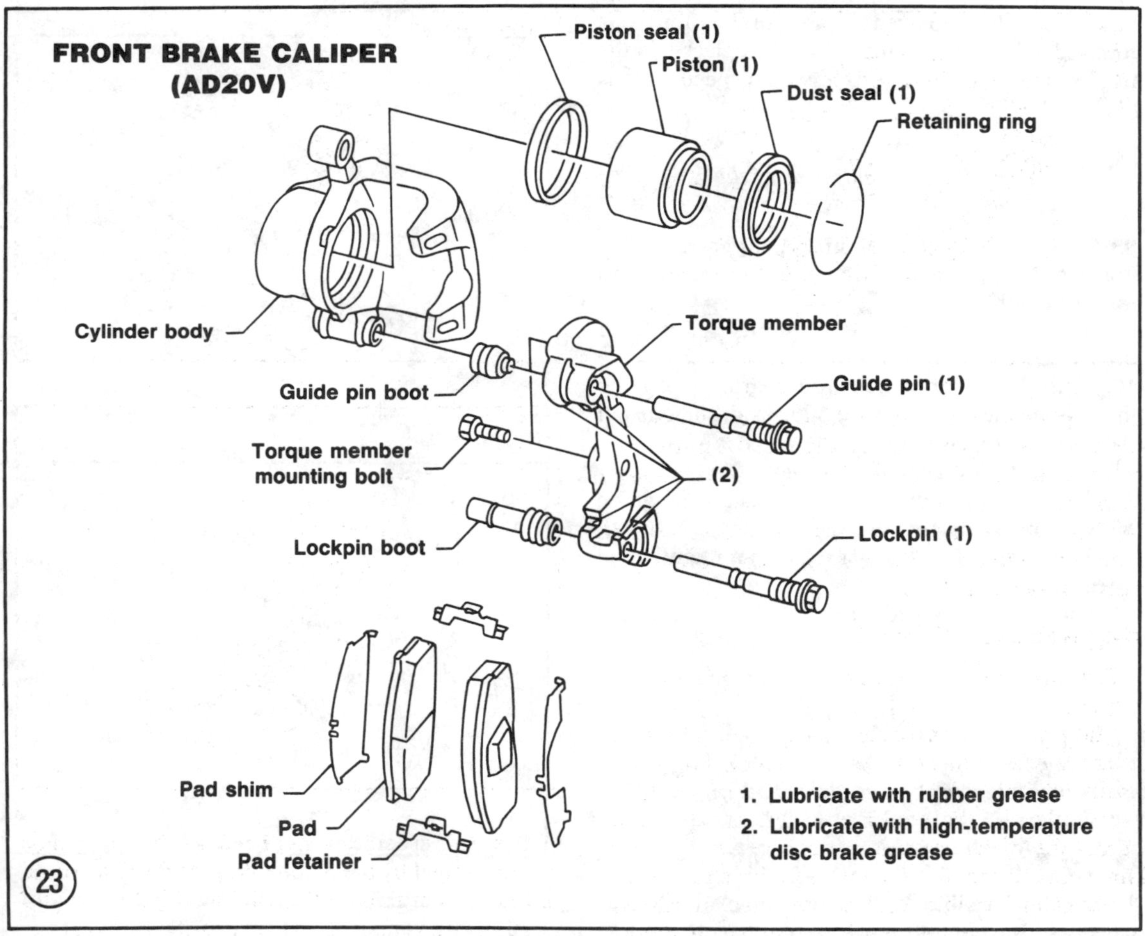

FRONT BRAKE CALIPER (AD20V)

2. Loosen the front wheel nuts. Jack up the front end of the car, place it on jackstands and remove the front wheels.

3. Inspect pads through the inspection hole in the back of the cylinder body (**Figure 20**). Pads must be replaced if the friction material is worn to less than specifications (**Table 1**).

CAUTION
Always replace pads in sets of 4 (both front wheels).

4. Remove the guide pin (**Figure 21**).

5. Pivot the caliper upward as shown in **Figure 22**, then remove the pad retainers, pads and shims. See **Figure 23**.

Do not press the brake pedal after the next step or the pistons will be forced out and the calipers will have to be rebuilt.

6. Carefully clean the space which holds the brake pads, as well as the outside of the cylinder body. While cleaning, check for brake fluid leaks (**Figure 24**). If brake fluid has been leaking, rebuild the calipers as described in this chapter.

7. Inspect the pads. Light surface grease or oil stains may be sanded off. If oil or grease has penetrated the surface, replace the pads. Since brake fluid will ruin the friction material, brake pads must be replaced if any brake fluid has touched them. Pads must also be replaced if the friction material is worn to less than specifications (**Table 1**).

CAUTION
Keep the grease mentioned in the next step off the pads and disc.

8. Apply a light coat of high-temperature disc brake grease to the friction points of pads and torque member.

9. Install the inner pad and its shims, referring to **Figure 23**.

10. Pull the cylinder body outboard to provide installation clearance for the outer pad, then install the pad and its shim.

11. Install the pad retainers (**Figure 25**).

12. Pivot caliper downward and install the guide pin (**Figure 26**). Tighten to specifications (**Table 2**).

13. Install the wheels, lower the car and tighten the wheel nuts.

14. Press the brake pedal several times to seat the pads. Unblock the rear wheels and road test the brakes.

WARNING
Make sure the brake pedal feels firm before driving the car. If it feels mushy, bleed the brakes as described in this chapter.

Caliper Removal/Installation (AD20V)

1. Set the handbrake. Securely block both rear wheels so the car will not roll in either direction.

2. Loosen the front wheel nuts. Jack up the front end of the car, place it on jackstands and remove the front wheels.

3. Disconnect the caliper brake hose at its connection to the metal line. Use a flare nut wrench such as Nissan tool part No. GG94310000 (**Figure 27**). These are available from auto parts stores.

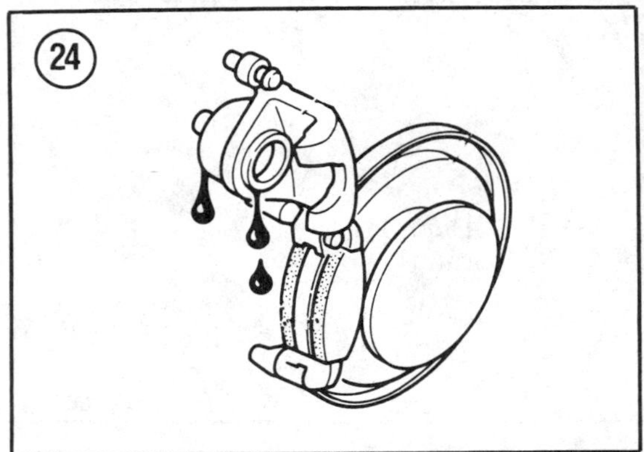

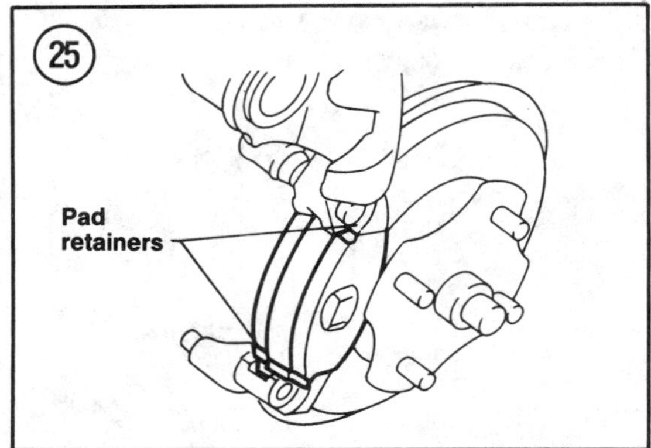

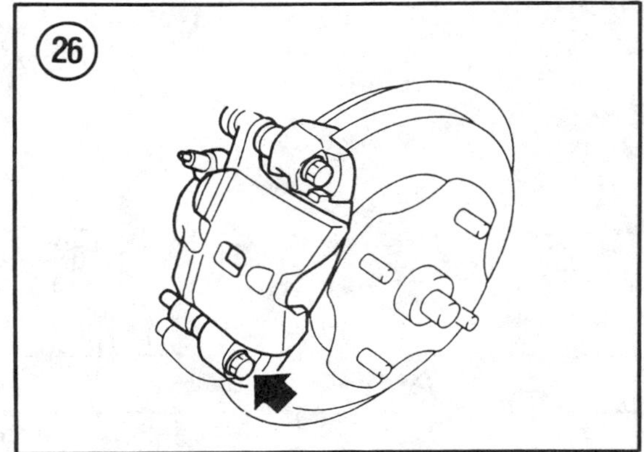

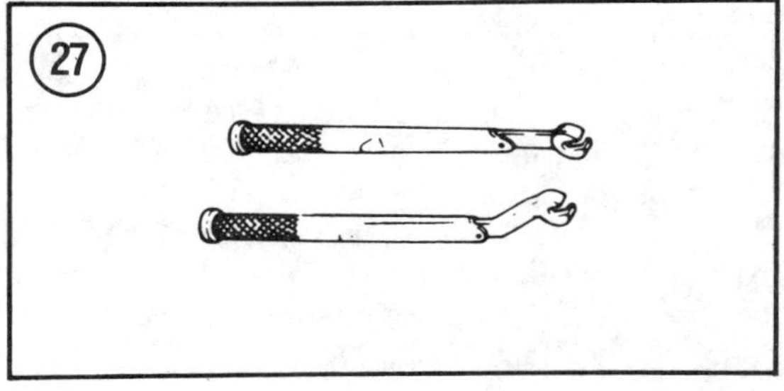

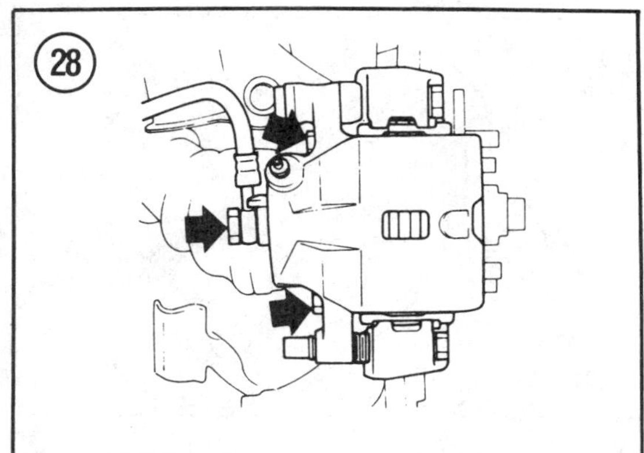

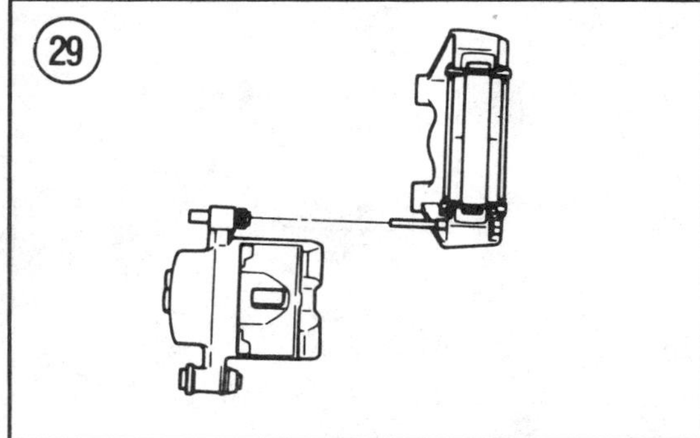

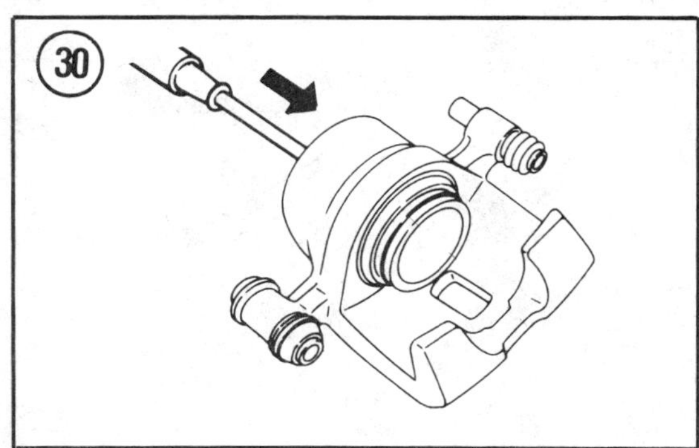

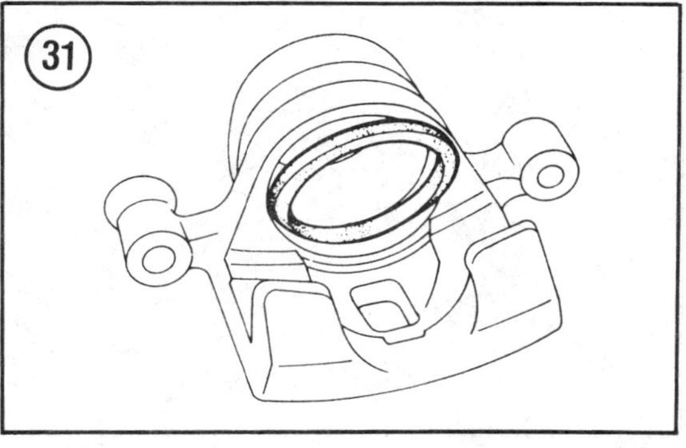

4. Detach the brake hose and remove the caliper mounting bolts (**Figure 28**). Take the caliper off.

5. Installation is the reverse of removal. Tighten all fasteners to specifications (**Table 2**). Bleed the brakes as described in this chapter.

Caliper Overhaul (AV20V)

Refer to **Figure 23** for this procedure.

1. Remove the caliper as described in this chapter.

2. Detach the cylinder body from the torque member. See **Figure 29**.

3. Push out the piston together with its dust seal and retainer ring as shown in **Figure 30**.

4. Remove the piston seal from the cylinder bore. See **Figure 31**.

5. Thoroughly clean all parts in new, clean brake fluid or aerosol brake cleaner. Do not clean with gasoline, kerosene or solvent. These leave residues which can cause rubber parts to soften and swell.

6. Check the torque member for wear, cracks or other visible defects. Replace if any of these can be seen.

7. Inspect the cylinder bore. Replace the cylinder body if wear or damage can be seen. Light rust or dirt may be removed with fine emery paper. Replace the cylinder body if dirt or rust is heavy.

8. Inspect the piston. Since it is chrome plated, the piston can't be sanded. If the piston can't be cleaned with a rag, replace it.

9. Check the guide pin, lockpin and boots for wear or damage. Replace worn or damaged parts.

10. Coat a new piston seal and its groove in the cylinder with rubber grease or new, clean brake fluid, then install it in the piston. See **Figure 32**.

11. Coat the piston and the inside of the dust seal with rubber grease or brake fluid. Install the piston and dust seal as shown in **Figure 33**.

12. Place the dust seal in the cylinder body groove, then secure it with the retaining ring. See **Figure 34**.

13. Apply rubber grease to the friction surfaces of guide pin and lockpin. Install the boots (**Figure 35**), then install the guide pin and lockpin in the torque member.

14. Install the cylinder body on the torque member (**Figure 36**). Tighten the lockpin and guide pin to specifications (**Table 2**).

REAR BRAKES

Figure 37 shows the LT18A and LT20A rear brakes. The LT18A brakes use a horseshoe-type return spring and the LT20A brakes use coil return springs. The LT20A drum and wheel cylinder are slightly larger than the equivalent LT18A parts. Except for these differences, service procedures are the same for both types of brakes.

Removal

1. Remove the brake drum as described under *Wheel Bearings* in Chapter Ten.

2. Disconnect the handbrake cable at the backing plate.

3. Grasp the anti-rattle pins with pliers. Twist them as shown in **Figure 38** so the pin head aligns with the slot in the retainer. Release the spring tension, then remove the retainer, spring and spring seat.

4. Remove the return spring(s), then take off the brake shoes. See **Figure 39**.

Inspection

> *WARNING*
> *Do not inhale brake dust. It contains asbestos, which can cause lung injury.*

1. Clean all parts with aerosol brake cleaner or new brake fluid. Do not clean with gasoline, kerosene or solvent. These leave residues which can cause rubber parts to soften and swell.

> *CAUTION*
> *If cleaning with brake fluid, keep it off the linings. Brake fluid will ruin the linings and they will have to be replaced.*

2. Check drums for visible scoring, excessive or uneven wear and rust. If you have precision measuring equipment, measure the drums for wear and out-of-roundness. If you don't have the equipment, this can be done by a machine shop. If the drum has surface damage or excessive runout, it can be turned by a machine shop. However, the inside diameter must not exceed specifications (**Table 1**, end of chapter). If the drum would have to be cut larger than this to correct it, it must be replaced.

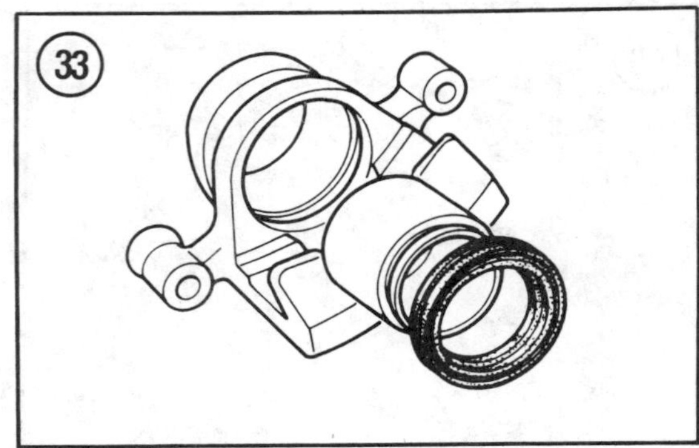

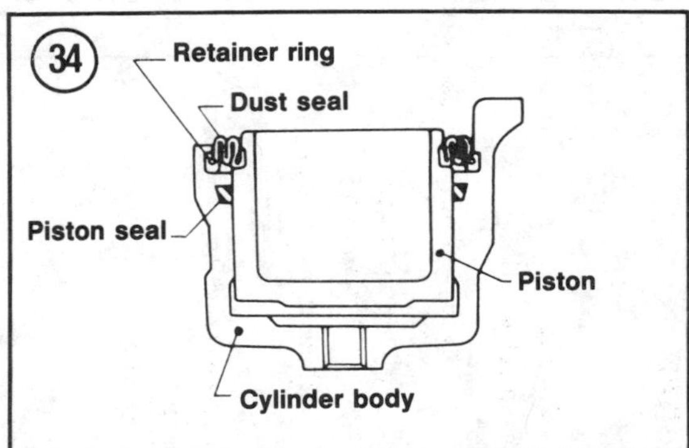

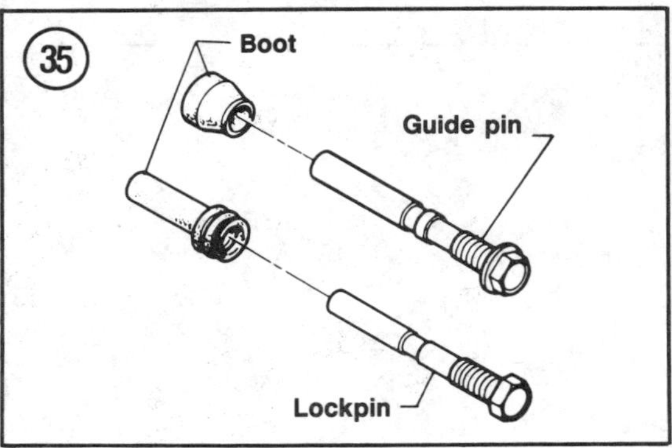

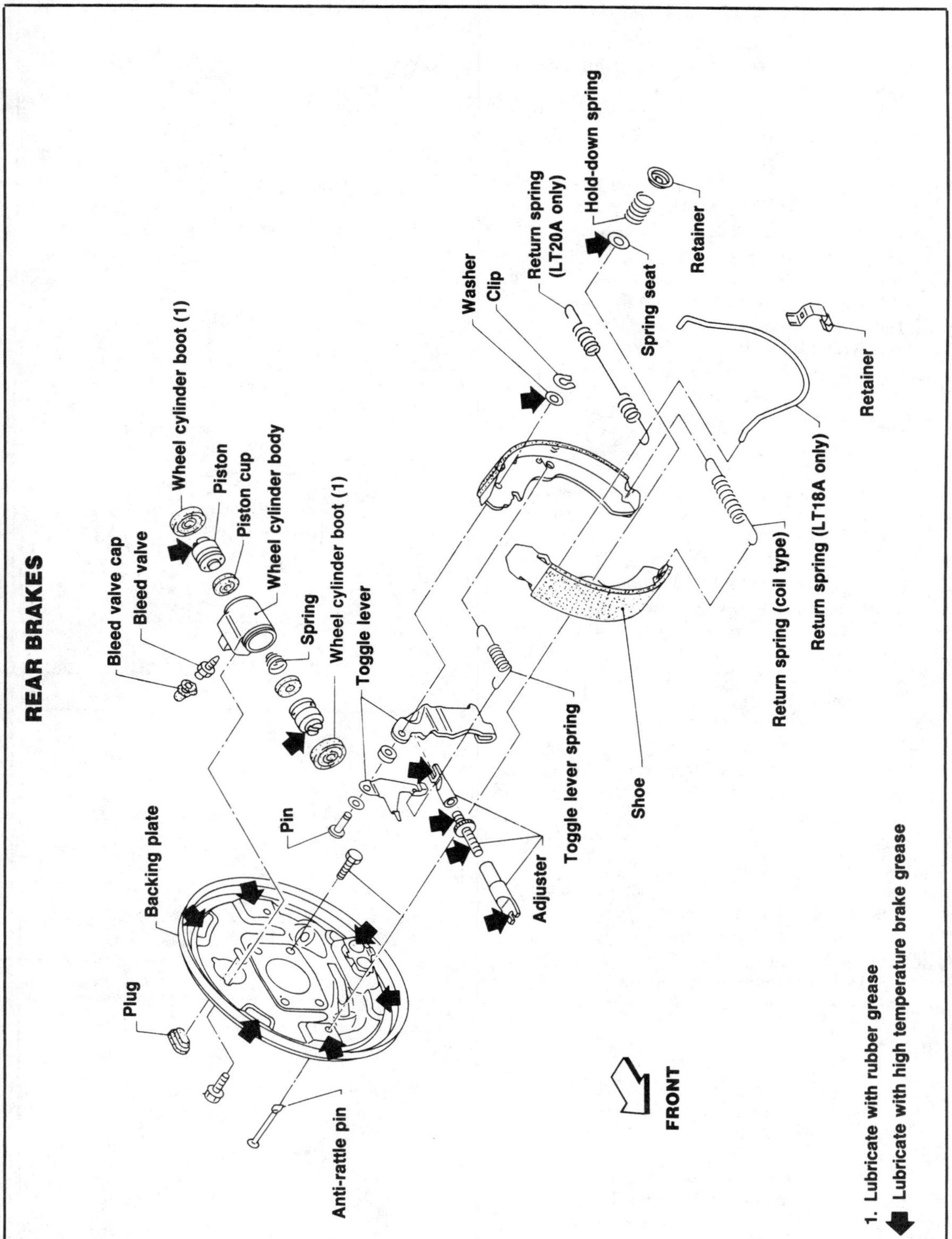

REAR BRAKES
37
Bleed valve cap
Bleed valve
Wheel cylinder boot (1)
Piston
Piston cup
Wheel cylinder body
Spring
Wheel cylinder boot (1)
Toggle lever
Washer
Clip
Return spring
(LT20A only)
Hold-down spring
Spring seat
Retainer
Retainer
Return spring (LT18A only)
Return spring (coil type)
Shoe
Toggle lever spring
Adjuster
Pin
Backing plate
Plug
Anti-rattle pin
FRONT
1. Lubricate with rubber grease
Lubricate with high temperature brake grease

3. Check brake shoes for the following:
   a. Excessive wear—If the friction material is worn to less than specifications, replace the shoes.
   b. Cracked, unevenly worn or separated friction material—Replace the shoes if these conditions are found.
   c. Oil or grease—Light surface stains may be sanded off. If oil or grease has penetrated the surface, replace the shoes.
   d. Brake fluid stains—Since brake fluid can cause the friction material to crumble, replace the shoes if brake fluid has touched the linings.

4. If the shoes are to be replaced, detach the adjuster assembly from the old rear shoe and install it on the new rear shoe. See **Figure 40**.

5. Check the springs, adjuster parts and anti-rattle pins for wear or damage. Replace as needed.

Wheel Cylinder Overhaul

1. Disconnect the brake line from the cylinder. Use a flare nut wrench such as Nissan tool part No. GG94310000 (**Figure 41**). Flare nut wrenches are available from auto parts stores.

2. Unbolt the wheel cylinder and take it off.

3. Unscrew the bleed valve (**Figure 42**).

4. Remove the dust covers (**Figure 42**). Take out the pistons, piston cups and spring.

5. Thoroughly clean all parts in clean brake fluid or brake cleaner. Do not use solvent, kerosene or gasoline. These leave residues which can cause rubber parts to soften and swell.

6. Check the cylinder bore and piston for wear, pits, scoring, cracks or rust. Replace the cylinder if these can be seen.

7. Check the bleed valve for wear or damage. Replace it if these can be seen.

8. Coat the cylinder bore with rubber grease or new brake fluid. Install the spring.

9. Install the cups with their lips (wide sides) facing into the cylinder, then install the pistons.

10. Pack the dust covers with rubber grease, then install them on the cylinder body.

> *CAUTION*
> *Do not use ordinary grease on the cylinder bore or dust covers. This will cause the piston cups and dust covers to deteriorate.*

11. Install the bleed valve and its cap.

12. Install the wheel cylinder on the backing plate.

Installation

Installation is the reverse of removal, plus the following.

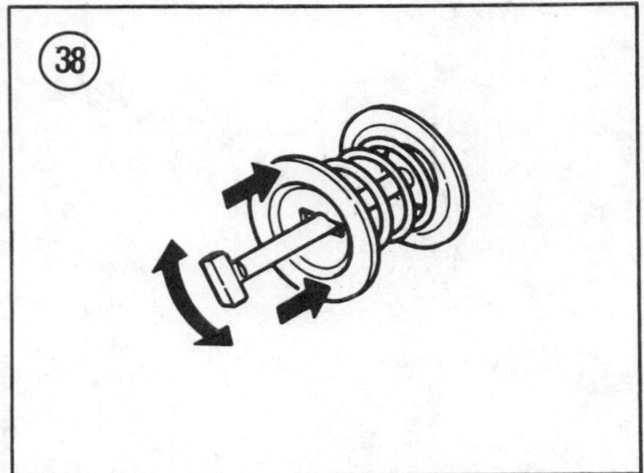

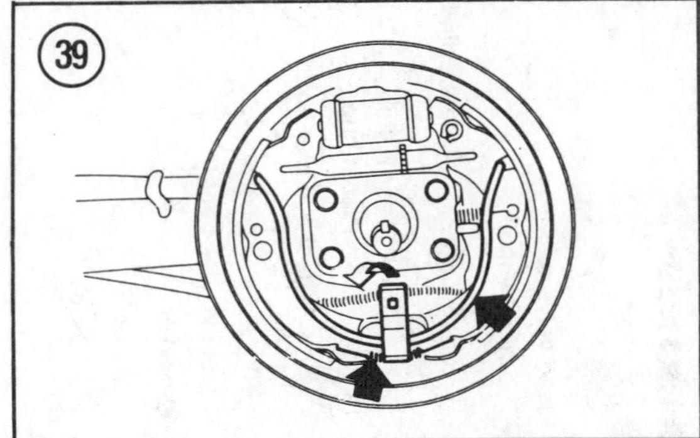

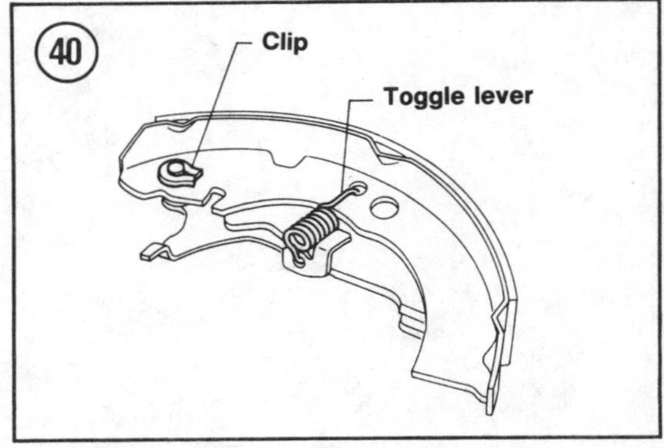

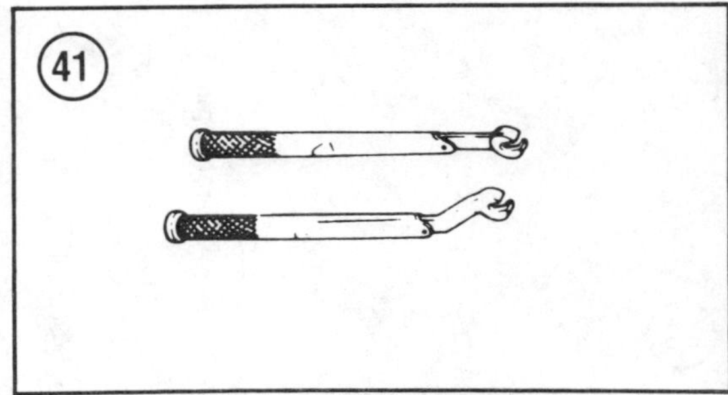

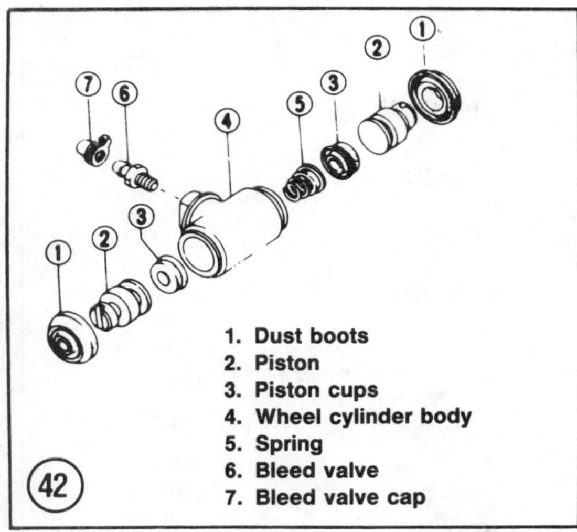

1. Dust boots
2. Piston
3. Piston cups
4. Wheel cylinder body
5. Spring
6. Bleed valve
7. Bleed valve cap

(42)

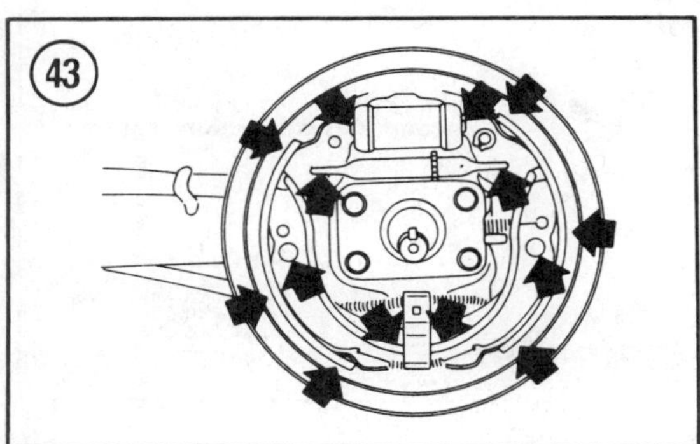

(43)

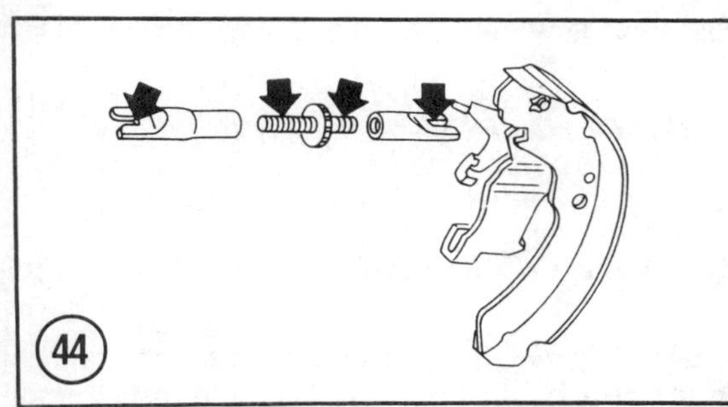

(44)

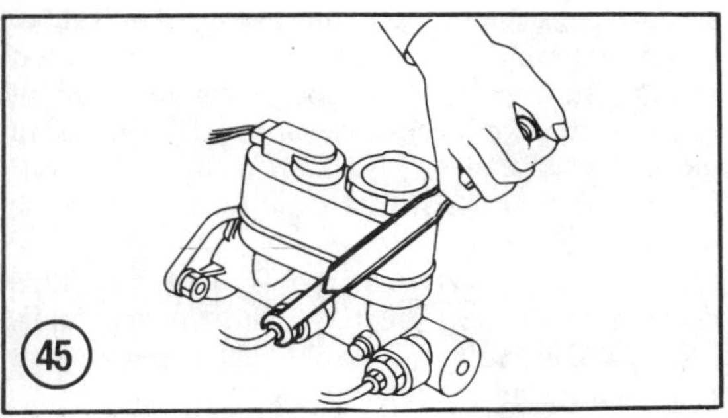

(45)

1. Apply high-temperature brake grease to the friction points shown in **Figure 43**.

> *CAUTION*
> *Do not use ordinary multipurpose grease or it may melt and contaminate the linings.*

2. Apply high-temperature grease to the adjuster bolt threads and ends. See **Figure 44**.

> *NOTE*
> *The right-hand adjuster has right-hand threads (turns clockwise to shorten). The left-hand adjuster has left-hand threads (turns counterclockwise to shorten).*

3. After installing the shoes, use the adjuster to set shoe-to-drum clearance so the drum just fits over the shoes.
4. After installing the drum, operate the handbrake several times to adjust the rear brakes.

MASTER CYLINDER

On-car Inspection

Testing a master cylinder on the car can be done simply by pressing the brake pedal to stop the car. If the pedal feels soft and sinks too low on the first push, bleed the brakes as described in this chapter and check the brake lines, calipers and wheel cylinders for fluid leaks. If bleeding doesn't help and there are no visible fluid leaks, the master cylinder is probably at fault. Disassemble and inspect it as described in this chapter.

Removal/Installation

1. Disconnect the brake fluid warning wires from the reservoir cap.
2. Place rags beneath the master cylinder to catch dripping brake fluid.

> *CAUTION*
> *Brake fluid can damage paint. Wipe up any spilled fluid immediately, then wash the area with soap and water.*

3. Disconnect the brake lines from the master cylinder. Use a flare nut wrench such as Nissan tool part No. GG94310000 (**Figure 45**). Flare nut wrenches are available from auto parts stores.
4. Remove the master cylinder mounting nuts and take the master cylinder off the brake booster.
5. Installation is the reverse of removal. Tighten the mounting nuts to specifications (**Table 2**). Bleed the brakes as described in this chapter.

11

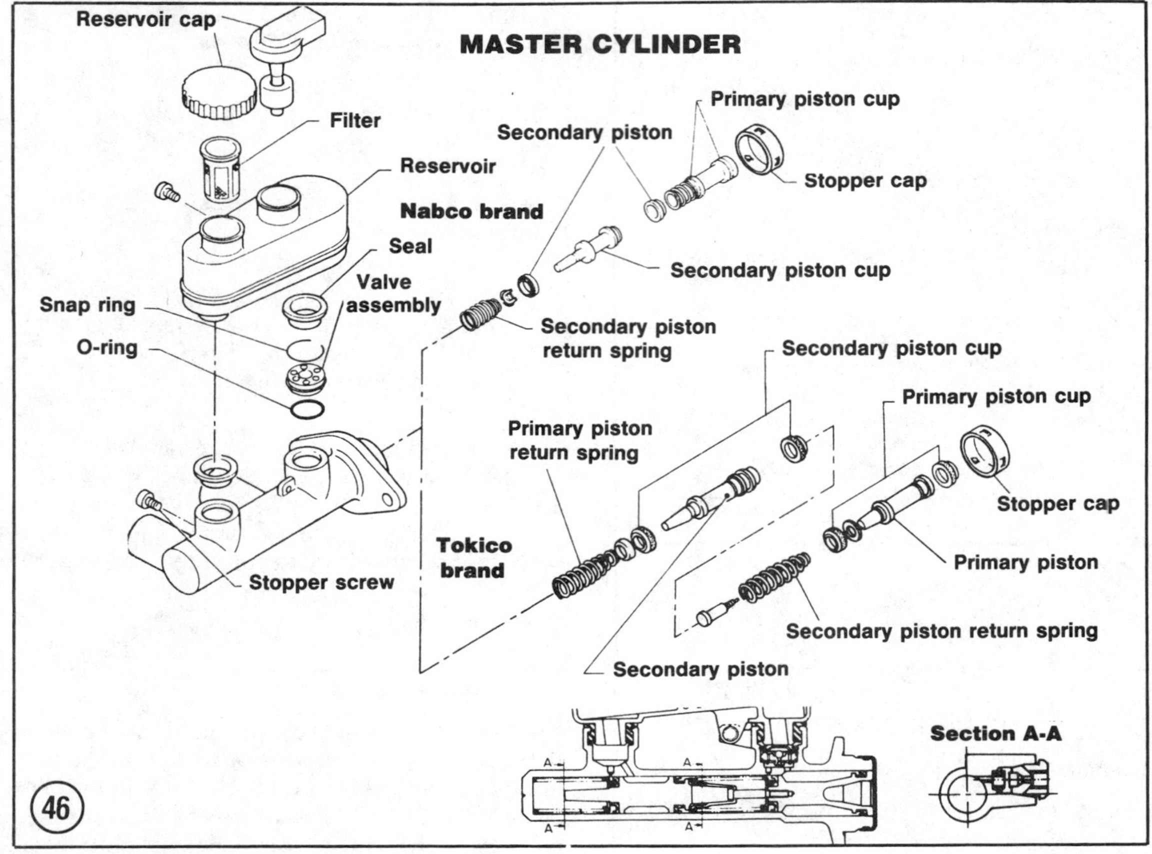

Overhaul

Refer to **Figure 46** for this procedure.

> *CAUTION*
> *Both Nabco and Tokico brand master cylinders are used in production. Although the internal parts are similar, they are not interchangeable. Be sure to get the right brand when buying a repair kit.*

1. Pry off the stopper cap and take out the primary piston assembly.
2. Remove the stopper screw (**Figure 47**) and take out the secondary piston assembly.
3. Remove the brake fluid reservoir.
4. Remove the valve assembly seal, then remove the snap ring, valve assembly and O-ring. Discard the O-ring. It must not be reused.
5. Thoroughly clean all parts in clean brake fluid or aerosol brake cleaner. Do not use solvent, gasoline or kerosene. These leave residues which can cause rubber parts to soften and swell.
6. Check the cylinder bore and pistons for wear, scratches, pitting, rust and cracks. Replace the master cylinder as an assembly if any of these conditions is found.

> *NOTE*
> *The next step does not apply to Nabco brand primary pistons. If the car has a Nabco master cylinder, replace the entire primary piston whenever the master cylinder is disassembled.*

7. Carefully note how the piston cups are installed on the pistons, then remove them and install new ones.
8. Coat the cylinder bore and pistons with rubber grease or brake fluid. Install the secondary piston and its return spring in the bore. Push the piston in with a screwdriver to compress the spring and install the stopper screw.
9. Install the primary piston and secure it with the stopper cap.
10. Install a new valve assembly O-ring. Install the valve assembly and secure it with the snap ring. Install a new valve assembly seal and reservoir seal, then install the reservoir.

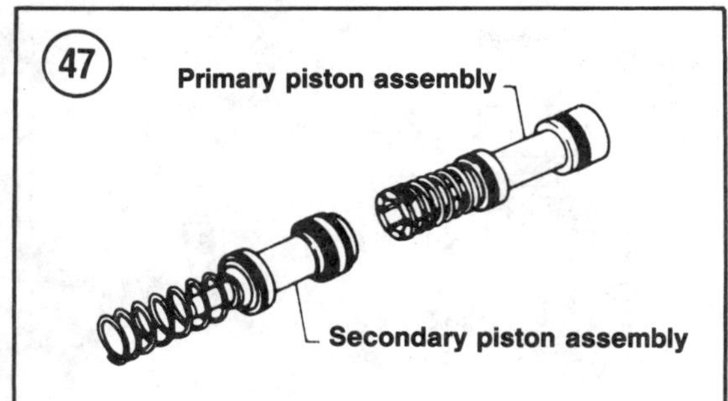

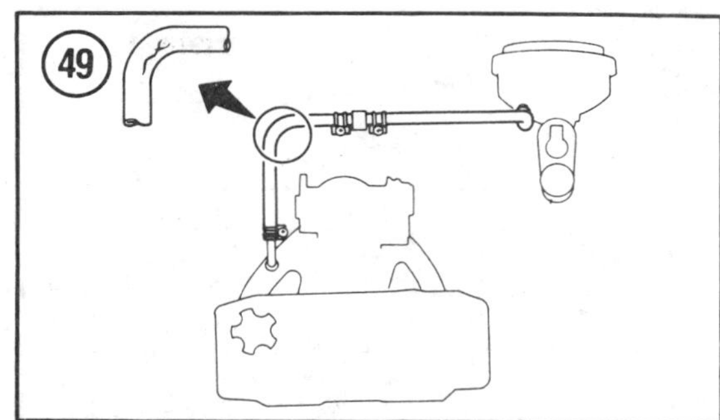

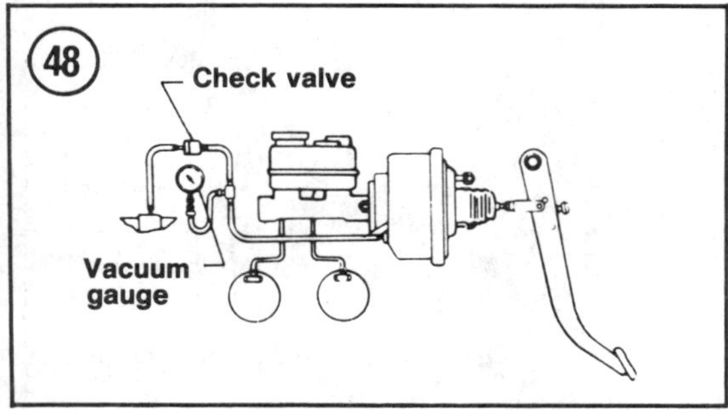

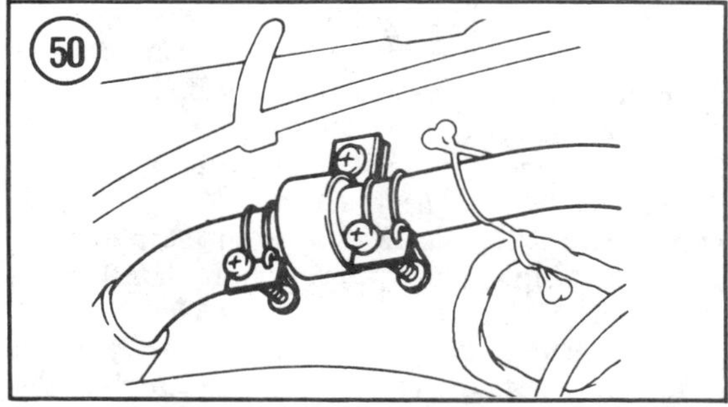

BRAKE BOOSTER

Function Test

1. Park the car on a level surface and set the handbrake.

2. Press the brake pedal several times to use up vacuum in the brake booster. After several pushes, pedal travel should stay the same.

3. Hold the brake pedal down and start the engine. The pedal should sink slightly when the engine starts.

4. Hold the pedal down and turn the engine off. Keep holding the pedal down for about 30 seconds and make sure brake pedal height does not change.

5. Release the brake pedal, start the engine and let it run for one minute.

6. Turn the engine off and press the brake pedal several times. Pedal travel should decrease slightly each time the pedal is pushed. After several pushes, travel should stay the same.

7. If the pedal has performed as specified so far, the brake booster is okay. If not, perform the following tests to isolate the problem.

Airtightness Test (No Load)

1. Connect a vacuum gauge between the check valve and brake booster as shown in **Figure 48**.

2. Start the engine. Raise engine speed until vacuum on the gauge reaches 500 mm Hg (20 in. Hg).

3. Turn off the engine and watch the vacuum gauge for 15 seconds. If the reading drops by more than 25 mm Hg (one in. Hg), the problem may be in the check valve hoses or connections, check valve or booster. Perform the following test to isolate the problem.

Airtightness Test (Under Load)

1. Connect a vacuum gauge between the check valve and brake booster as shown in **Figure 48**. Place the gauge where it can be seen from the driver's seat.

2. Start the engine. Hold the brake pedal down and raise engine speed until vacuum on the gauge reaches 500 mm Hg (20 in. Hg).

3. Hold the brake pedal down, turn off the engine and watch the vacuum gauge for 15 seconds. If the reading drops by more than 25 mm Hg (one in. Hg), the problem may be in the check valve or booster. Perform the following test to·isolate the problem.

Check Valve Inspection

1. Inspect the check valve hoses (**Figure 49**) for cracks or loose connections. Tighten or replace as needed.

2. Remove the check valve (**Figure 50**). Try to blow air into each side of the valve as shown in

11

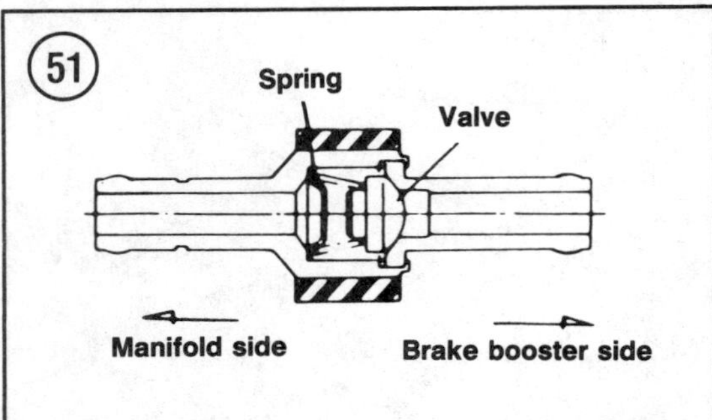

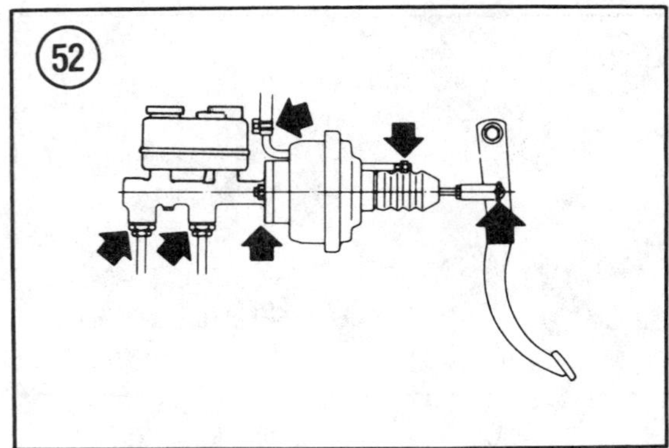

Figure 51. It should be possible to blow air into the brake booster side of the valve, but not into the manifold side. If air can be blown both ways or neither way, replace the check valve.

3. If a vacuum pump is available, apply 500 mm Hg (20 in. Hg) to the brake booster side of the valve. Watch the vacuum gauge on the pump for 15 seconds. If the reading drops more than 10 mm Hg (0.4 in. Hg), replace the check valve.

4. If the check valve performs as specified and the airtightness tests indicated a problem, replace the brake booster.

Booster Removal/Installation

1. Remove the master cylinder as described in this chapter.

2. Disconnect the booster vacuum hose. See **Figure 52**.

3. Working inside the car, remove the cotter pin and clevis pin that secure the booster input rod to the brake pedal, then remove the booster mounting nuts.

4. Remove the booster into the engine compartment.

5. Check output rod length (**Figure 53**) and input rod length (**Figure 54**). Compare with specifications in **Table 1**. Output rod length cannot be adjusted. Replace the booster if it is incorrect. To adjust input rod length, loosen the locknut, turn the clevis as needed and tighten the locknut.

6. Installation is the reverse of removal. Tighten all fasteners to specifications (end of chapter). Bleed the brakes as described in this chapter.

VACUUM PUMP

The vacuum pump supplies vacuum for the brakes on cars equipped with diesel engines.

Removal/Installation

1. Disconnect the hoses from the vacuum pump.

2. Drain oil from the pump. To do this, loosen the alternator belt as described in Chapter Three. Turn

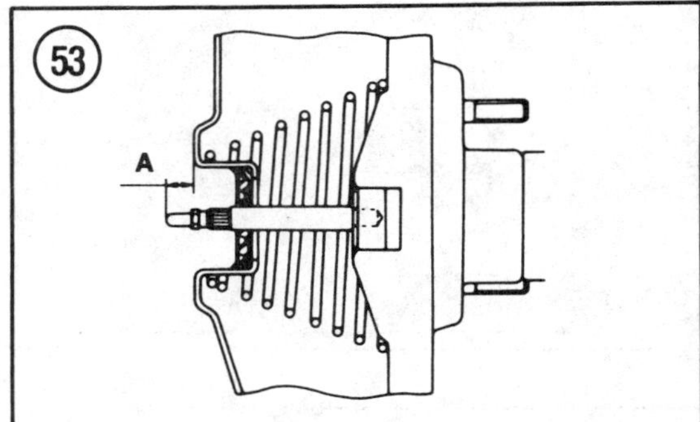

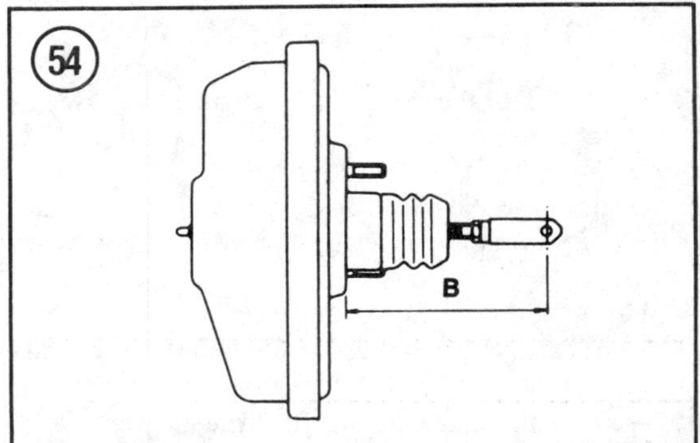

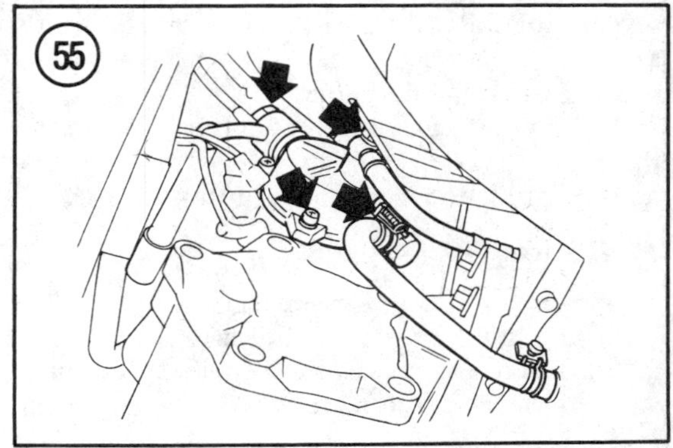

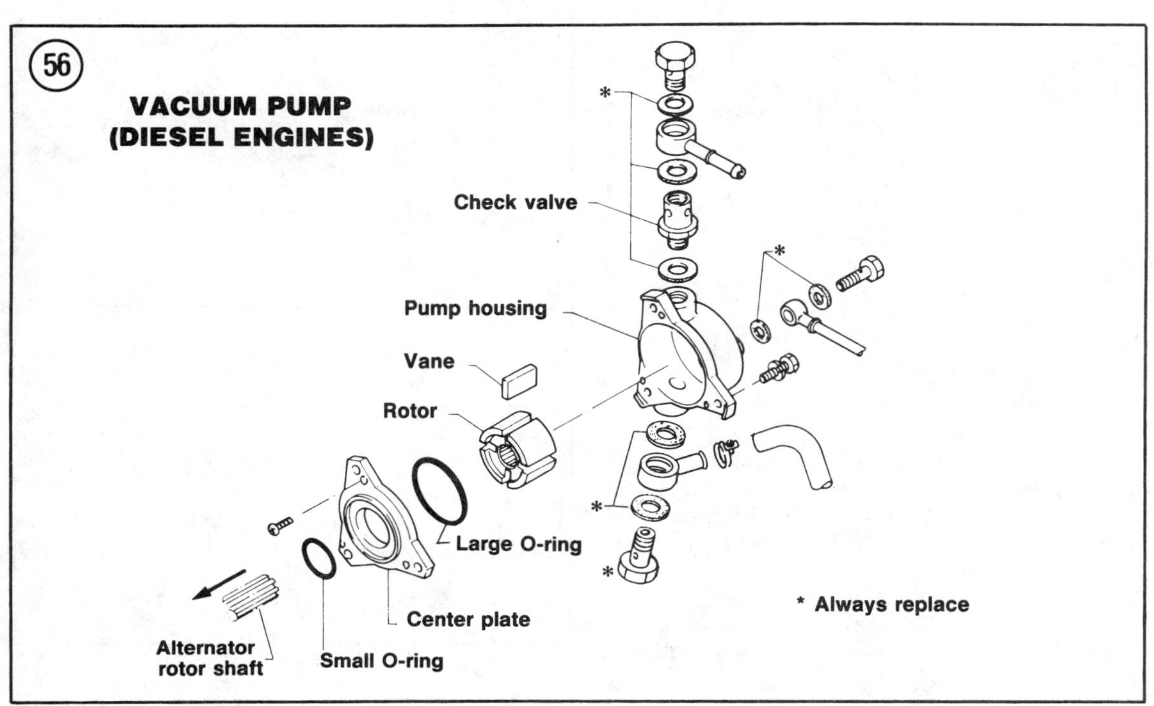

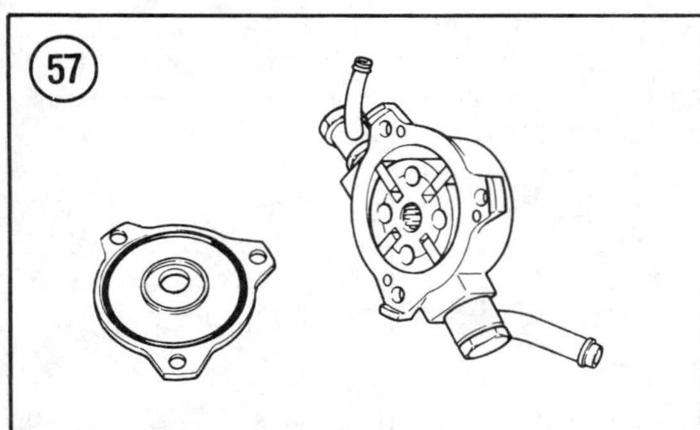

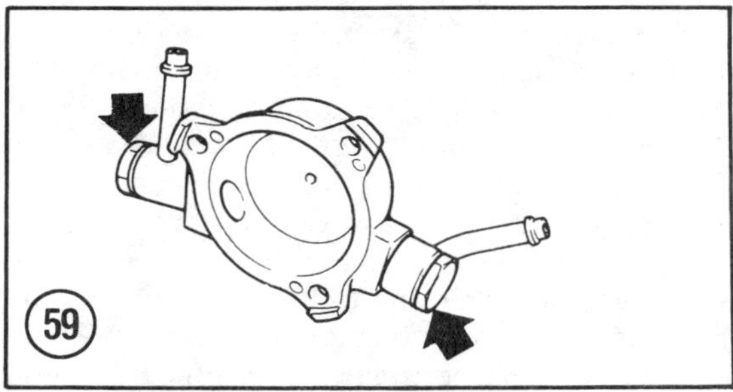

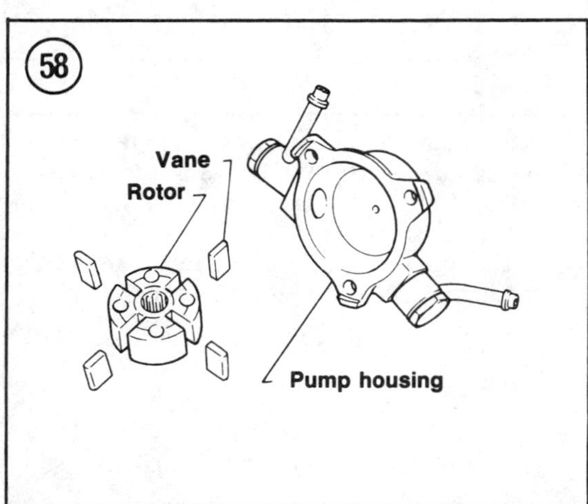

the alternator pulley by hand clockwise (viewed from the driver's side of the car) several turns to discharge any remaining oil.

3. Detach the vacuum pump from the alternator and take it off. See **Figure 55**.

4. Installation is the reverse of removal. Inject approximately 5 cc (0.2 oz.) of engine oil into the pump with an oil can. Turn the alternator pulley by hand and make sure the vacuum pump rotates smoothly.

Overhaul

Refer to **Figure 56** for this procedure.

1. Separate the center plate and housing (**Figure 57**).

2. Take the rotor and vanes out of the pump housing. See **Figure 58**.

3. Remove the valve assemblies (**Figure 59**).

11

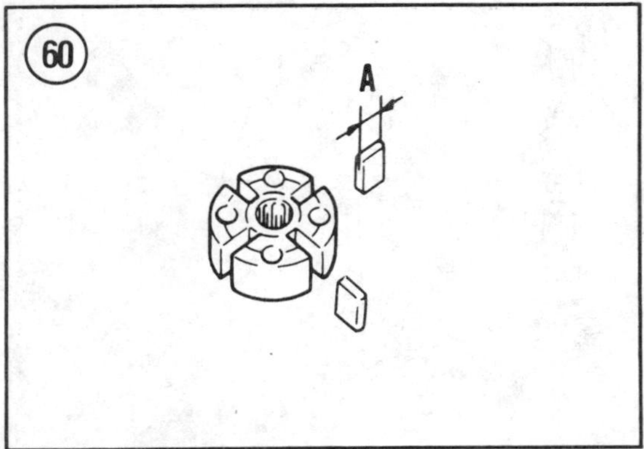

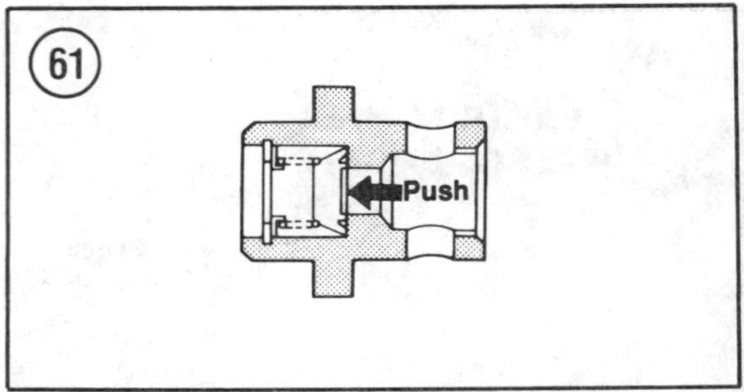

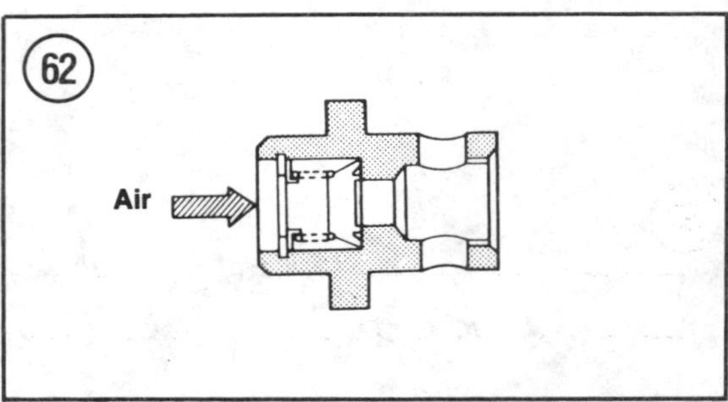

4. Thoroughly clean all parts in solvent and blow dry. While cleaning, check the mating surfaces on the rotor, center plate and pump housing for visible wear or scratches. Replace parts that show wear or scratches.

5. Check the vanes for wear or scatches and replace as needed. If vane condition is in doubt, have a machine shop measure length (A, **Figure 60**). Replace the vanes if their length is less than specifications (**Table 1**).

6. Check the pump housing inner wall for wear. If its condition is in doubt, have the housing inner diameter measured by a machine shop. Replace the housing if worn beyond specifications (**Table 1**).

7. Check the rotor shaft's hole in the center plate for wear or damage. Replace the center plate if worn or damaged.

8. Check the rotor shaft (on the back of the alternator) for wear or damage. Replace as needed.

9. Check the valve mounting points and hose fittings for wear or damage. Replace as needed.

10. Inspect the check valve. Insert a rod from the direction shown in **Figure 61** and push the valve away from its seat. It should return under spring pressure. If not, replace the check valve.

11. Try to blow air into the check valve as shown in **Figure 62**. This should not be possible. If it is, replace the check valve.

HANDBRAKE

Figure 63 shows the handbrake mechanism.

Lever and Front Cable Replacement

1. Detach the equalizer from the rear cable. See **Figure 64**.
2. Remove the center console.
3. Unplug the parking brake warning light wiring connector.
4. Remove the seat belt anchor bolts.

5. Remove the lever mounting bolts and front cable bracket screws (**Figure 65**). Remove the lever and front cable into the passenger compartment.

6. If necessary, drill out the pin (**Figure 66**) and separate the lever from the front cable. Replacement front cables with clevis pins and cotter pins are available from dealers.

7. Install by reversing Steps 1-5. Apply multipurpose grease to all friction points. Tighten all fasteners to specifications (**Table 2**). Adjust the handbrake as described in this chapter.

Rear Cable Replacement

1. Securely block both front wheels so the car will not roll in either direction.

2. Jack up the rear end of the car and place it on jackstands.

3. Disconnect the cables from the handbrake levers at the brake backing plates.

4. Separate the cables at the equalizer (**Figure 64**) and detach them from the front cable. Remove the rear cables from the clips and take them out from under the car.

5. Installation is the reverse of removal. Adjust the handbrake as described in this chapter.

ADJUSTMENTS

Front Brakes

Front disc brakes are adjusted automatically by the piston seals. No means of manual adjustment is necessary or provided.

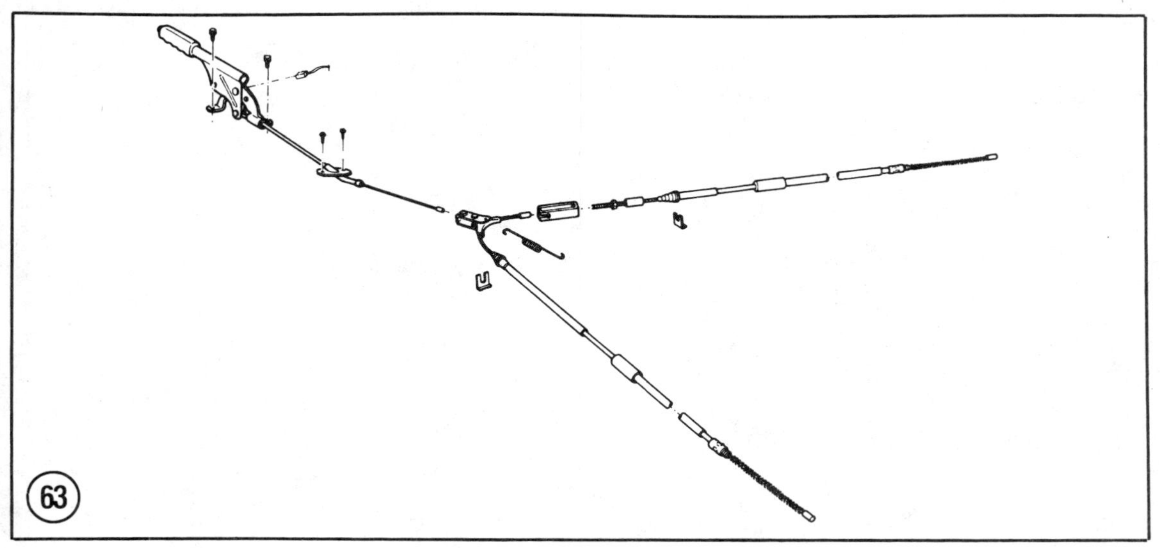

Figure 63

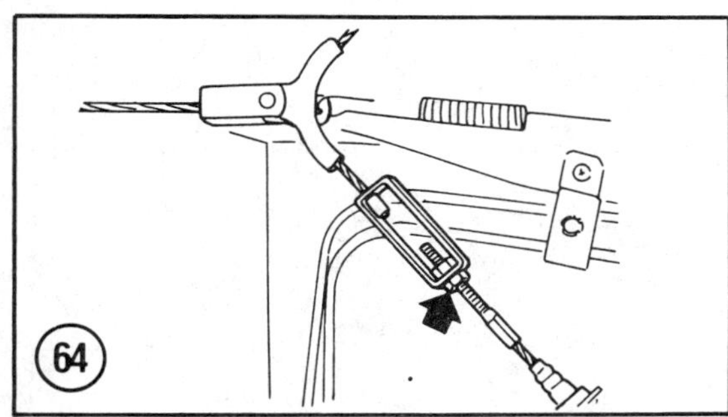

Figure 64

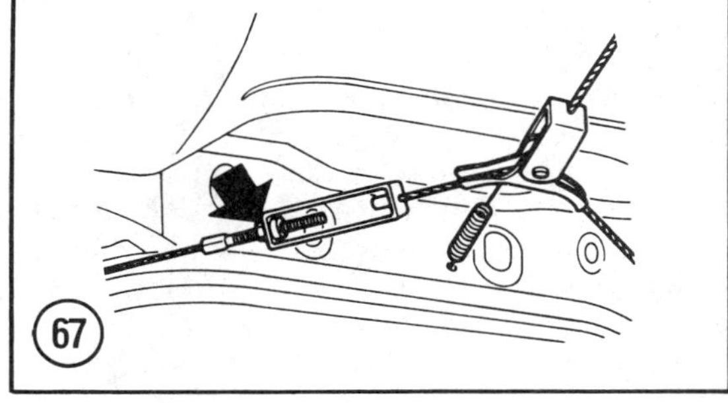

Figure 67

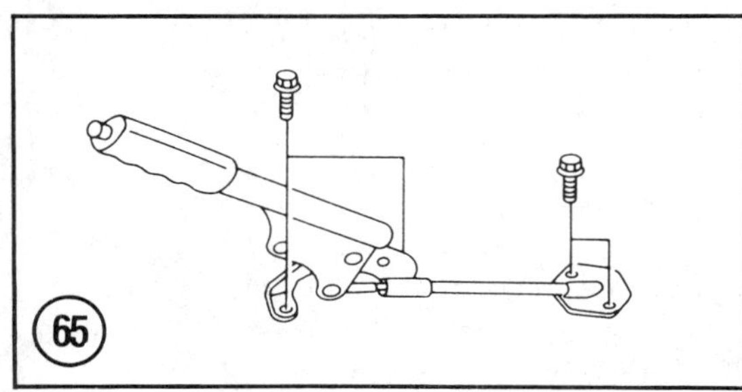

Figure 65

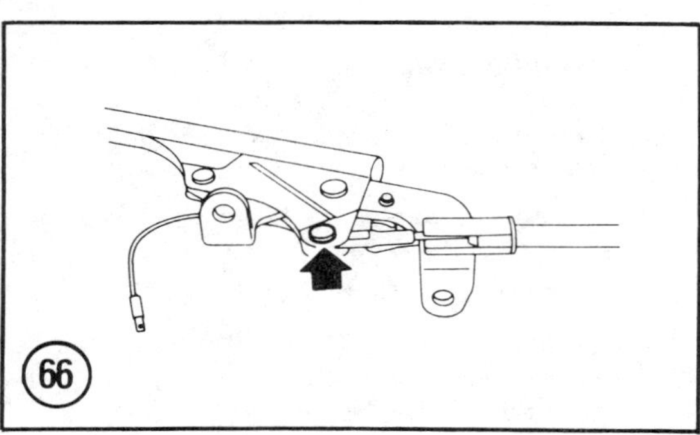

Figure 66

Rear Brakes

The brakes are adjusted automatically by the adjusters. The only manual adjustment required is to operate the handbrake lever several times after the brake shoes are replaced. If the rear brakes require adjustment at any other time, remove the adjusters and check them for wear or damage.

Handbrake

The handbrake should lock the rear wheels when the lever is raised 6-7 notches. Adjust as follows.
1. Securely block both front wheels so the car will not roll in either direction.
2. Jack up the rear end of the car and place it on jackstands.
3. Loosen the equalizer locknut (**Figure 67**). Turn the equalizer to adjust the cable, then tighten the locknut.
4. Make sure the handbrake locks the rear wheels when the lever is raised 6-7 notches. Make sure the rear wheels turn freely when the lever is lowered.
5. Remove the jackstands and lower the car.

11

Brake Pedal

1. Measure brake pedal height from the asphalt sheet on the car floor. See **Figure 68**. Compare with specifications at the end of the chapter. If pedal height is incorrect, loosen the locknut on the brake booster input rod. Rotate the input rod to adjust pedal height, then tighten the locknut.

2. Measure clearance between the threaded end of the brake light switch and the rubber stopper on the brake pedal. See **Figure 68**. If not within specifications (end of chapter), loosen the brake light switch locknut. Rotate the switch to adjust the clearance, then tighten the locknut.

BRAKE LINES

The brake lines are arranged in 2 hydraulic circuits. If one circuit develops a leak, one front brake and the opposite rear brake will still work. See **Figure 69**.

Dual Proportioning Valve

The dual proportioning valve (**Figure 70**) regulates pressure to the rear brakes. The valve cannot be disassembled. If the rear brakes lock prematurely or don't lock at all, check the front and rear brakes for wear or damage, referring to the appropriate section of this chapter. If the brakes are good, disconnect the lines and replace the valve with a new one. Then bleed the brakes as described in this chapter.

BRAKE BLEEDING

The hydraulic system should be bled whenever air enters it. This is because air in the brake lines will compress, rather than transmitting pedal pressure to the brake operating parts. If the pedal feels spongy or if pedal travel increases considerably, brake bleeding is usually called for. Bleeding is also necessary whenever a brake line is disconnected.

To replace the brake fluid, follow this procedure. Continue adding fresh fluid to the reservoir and bleeding fluid from the valves until the fluid leaving the valves is clean and free of air bubbles.

This procedure requires handling brake fluid. Be careful not to get any fluid on brake discs, pads, shoes or drums. Clean all dirt from bleed valves before beginning. Two people are needed; one to operate the brake pedal and the other to open and close the bleed valves.

Bleeding should be done in the order shown in **Figure 71**.

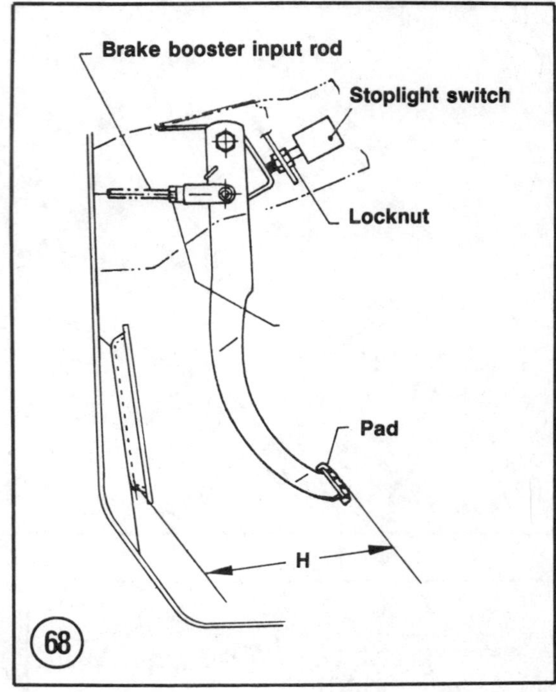

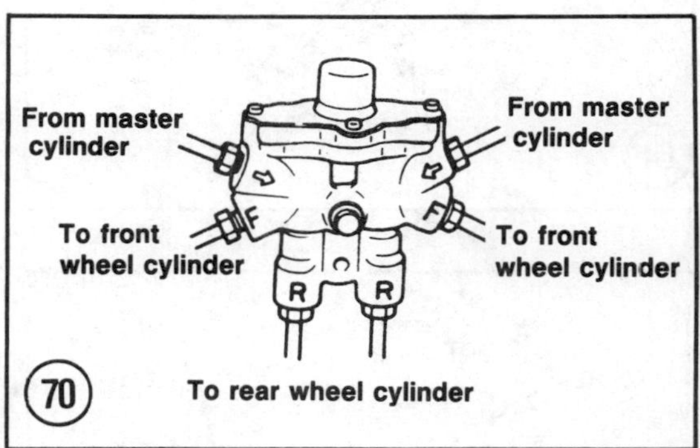

1. Clean away any dirt around the master cylinder reservoir. Top up the master cylinder with brake fluid marked DOT 3. See **Figure 72**.

> *NOTE*
> *DOT 3 means the brake fluid meets current Department of Transportation quality standards. If the fluid doesn't say DOT 3 somewhere on the label, buy a brand that does.*

2. Attach a plastic tube to the bleed valve (**Figure 73**). Immerse the other end of the tube in a jar containing several inches of clean brake fluid.

> *NOTE*
> *Do not allow the end of the tube to come out of the brake fluid during*

69
Rear brake 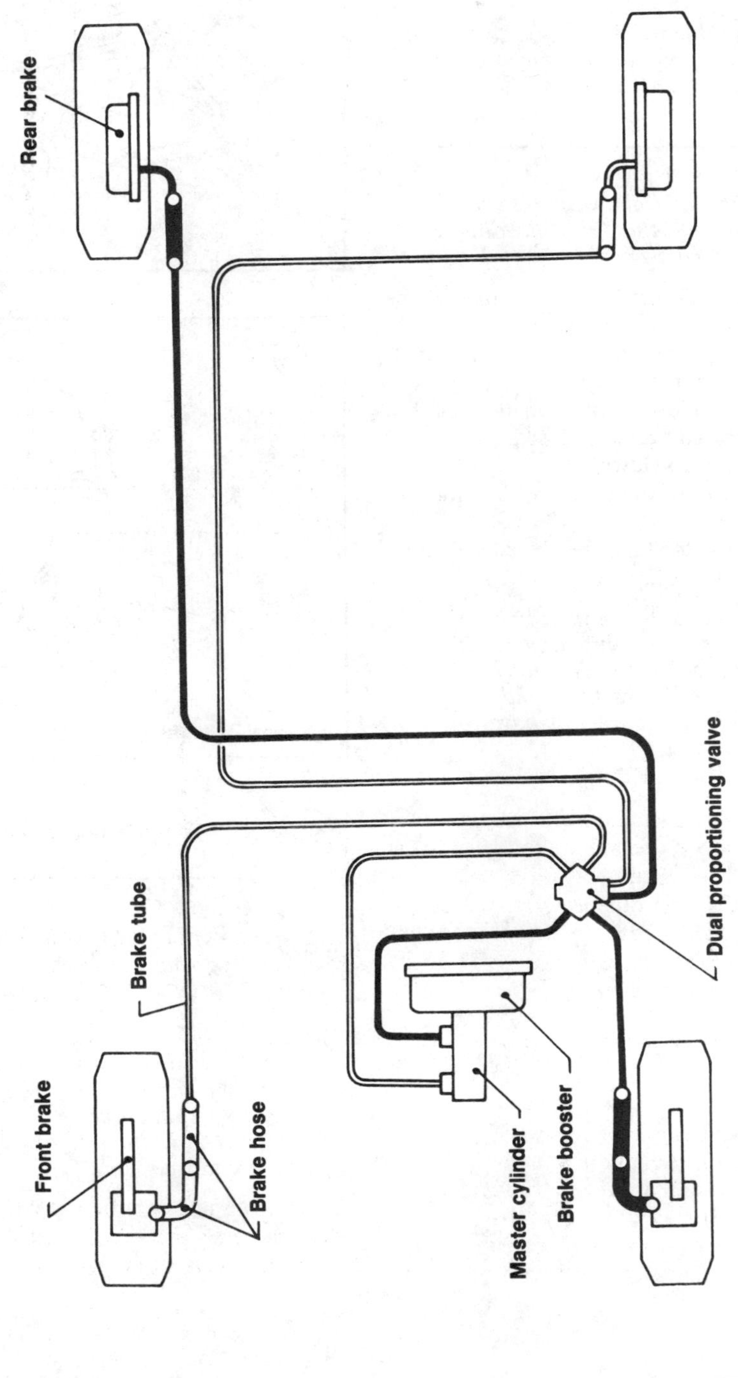
Brake tube
Front brake
Brake hose
Master cylinder
Brake booster
Dual proportioning valve
11

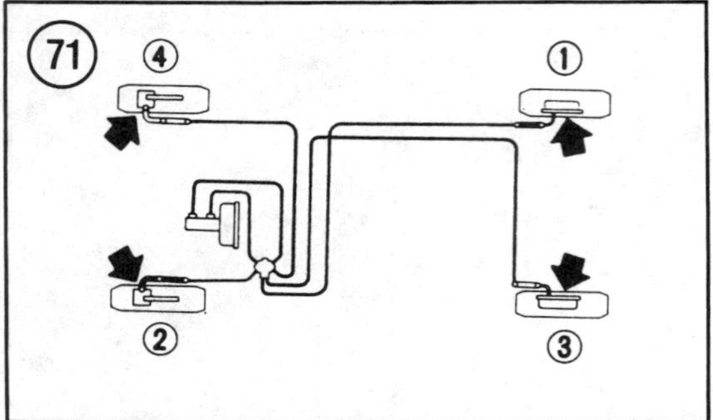

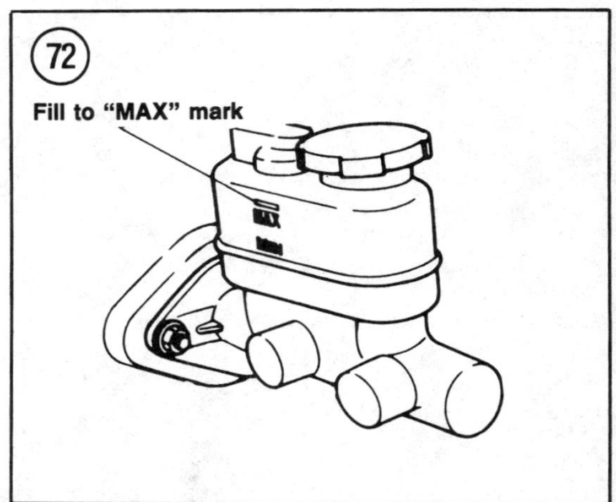

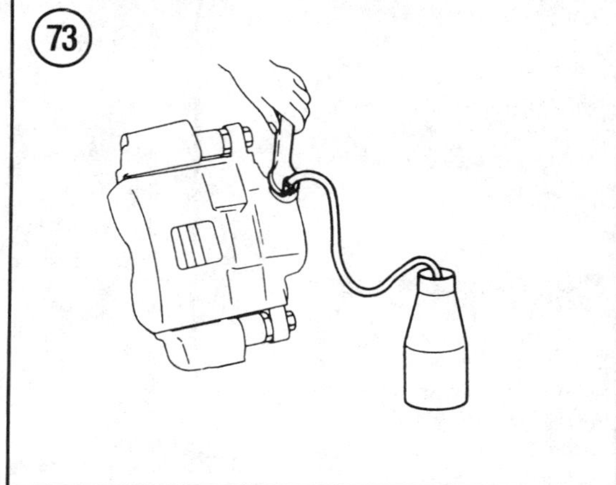

bleeding. This could allow air into the system, requiring that the bleeding procedure be done over.

3. Slowly press the brake pedal 2 or 3 times, then hold it down.

4. With the brake pedal down, open the bleed valve 1/3-1/2 turn. Let the brake pedal sink to the floor, then close the bleed valve. Do not let the pedal up until the bleed valve is closed.

5. Let the pedal back up slowly.

6. Repeat Steps 3-5 until the fluid entering the jar is free of air bubbles.

7. Repeat the process for the other bleed valves.

NOTE
Keep an eye on the brake fluid level in the master cylinder during bleeding. If the fluid level is allowed to drop too low, air will enter the brake lines and the entire bleeding procedure will have to be repeated.

Table 1 BRAKE SPECIFICATIONS

	mm	in.
Brake pad thickness, minimum	2.0	0.79
Brake disc runout, maximum	0.07	0.003
Brake disc thickness variation, maximum	0.03	0.0012
Brake disc thickness, minimum		
1982	11	0.433
1983 (CL18B)	10	0.394
1983 (AD20V)	16	0.63
Brake drum inner diameter, maximum		
LT18A	181.0	7.13
LT20A	204.5	8.05
Brake drum out-of-roundness, maximum		
1982	0.015 mm	0.0006 in.
1983	0.03 mm	0.0012 in.
Brake booster output rod length	10.275-10.525	0.4045-0.4144
Brake booster input rod length	150	5.91
Vacuum pump vane length (diesel only)	12.5-13.5	0.492-0.531
Vacuum pump inner diameter (diesel only)	57.0-57.1	2.244-2.248
Pedal height		
1982 manual transaxle	191-197	7 1/2-7 3/4
1982 automatic transaxle	193-199	7 5/8-7 7/8
1983 manual transaxle	194-204	7 5/8-8
1983 automatic transaxle	197-207	7 3/4-8 1/8

Table 2 TIGHTENING TORQUES

Fastener	N·m	ft.-lb.
Brake booster to body	8-11	6-8
Master cylinder to booster	8-11	6-8
Master cylinder piston stop bolt		
brand	1.5-2.9	1.1-2.2
brand	2.0-3.4	1.4-2.5
Bleed valves	7-9	5.1-6.5
Brake tube flare nuts	15-18	11-13
Brake hose connections	17-20	12-14
Disc brake baffle plate		
CL18B	3.2-4.3	2.4-3.2
AD20V	8-11	6-8
Torque member mounting bolts		
CL18B	54-64	40-47
AD20V	72-97	53-72
Cylinder body to torque member		
CL18B	22-31	16-23
AD20V	31-41	23-30
Disc-to-hub bolts	25-33	18-25
Drum brake backing plate bolts		
LT18A	25-33	18-25
LT20A	22-26	16-20
Wheel cylinder to backing plate	6-8	5-6

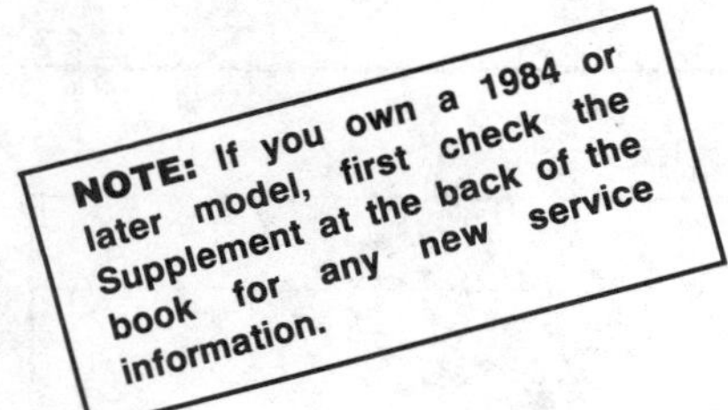

CHAPTER TWELVE

BODY

This chapter provides service procedures for the bumpers, grille, front fenders, doors, instrument panel and seats. Other procedures require special skills and tools and should be left to a dealer or body shop.

BUMPERS

Front Bumper Removal/Installation

To remove and install front bumpers, see **Figure 1** (1982) or **Figure 2** (1983). Remove the fasteners securing the back bar to the fascia with wire cutters as shown in **Figure 3**.

Rear Bumper Removal/Installation

To remove and install the rear bumper, see **Figure 4**. Detach the bumper from the body as shown in **Figure 5** (sedan and coupe) or **Figure 6** (wagon). If necessary, detach the bumper shock absorber from the frame, referring to **Figure 7**.

GRILLE AND FENDERS

Refer to **Figure 8** for these procedures.

Grille Removal/Installation

CAUTION
The grille is plastic. Do not force it off and do not let oil touch it.

1. Remove the Phillips screw securing the grille with a screwdriver.

2. Remove the plastic grille fasteners with pliers:
   a. To remove the fasteners shown in **Figure 9**, turn the fasteners 45° and pull them out.
   b. To remove the fasteners shown in **Figure 10**, squeeze the fasteners with pliers and pull them out.
3. Installation is the reverse of removal. Turn fasteners 45° as shown in **Figure 11** (if so equipped).

Fender Removal/Installation

1. Remove the front apron (**Figure 8**).
2. Remove the fender mounting bolts. Pull the fender out, unplug the side marker light's wiring connector and take the fender off.
3. Installation is the reverse of removal. Apply gasket sealer to mating surfaces of fender and front apron.

HOOD

Refer to **Figure 12** for these procedures.

Removal/Installation

1. Open the hood. Place a thick layer of rags beneath the trailing edge of the hood to protect the paint.
2. With a soft lead pencil, make alignment marks around the hood hinges directly onto the hood. The marks will ease installation.

① FRONT BUMPER (1982)

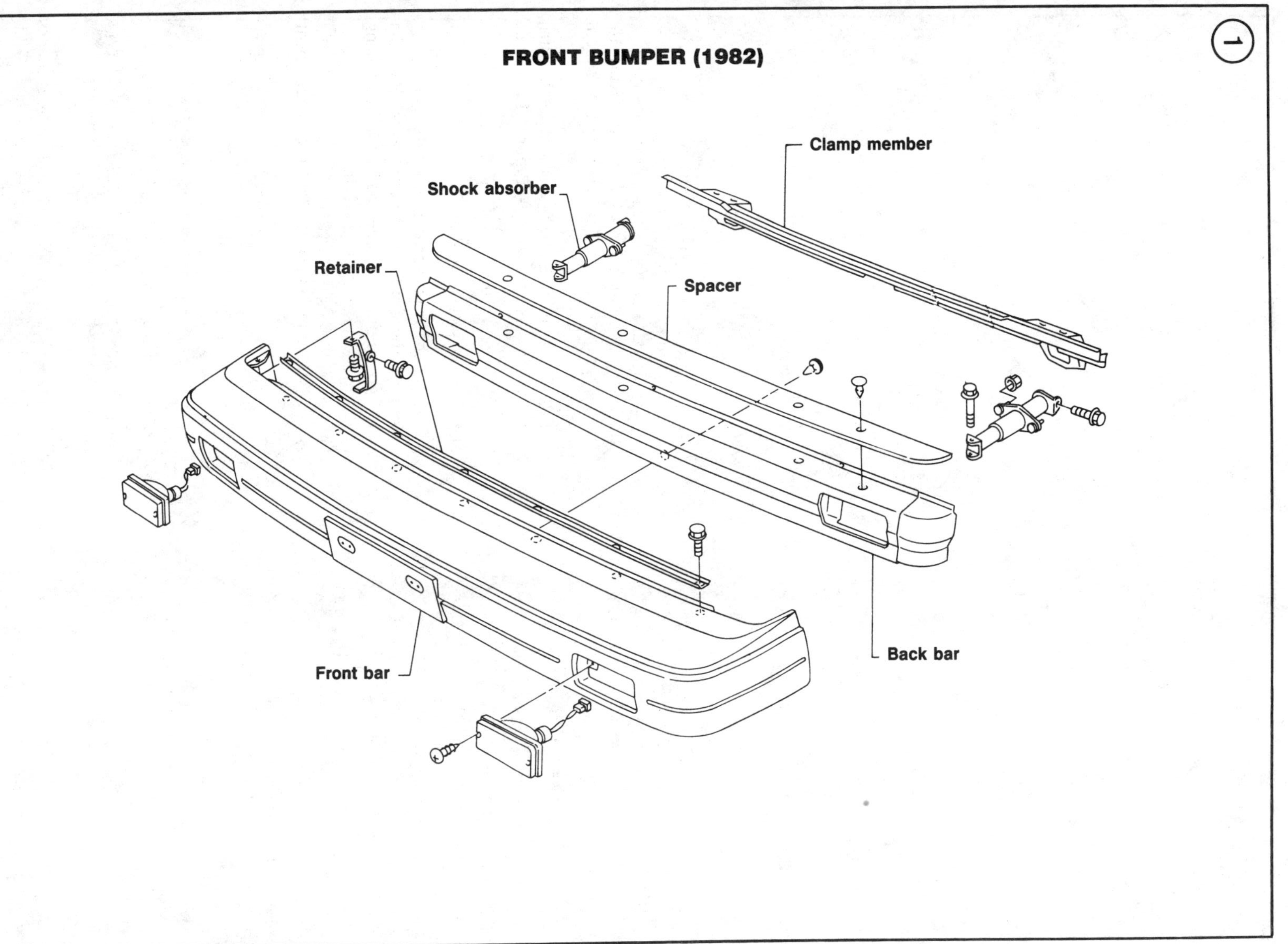

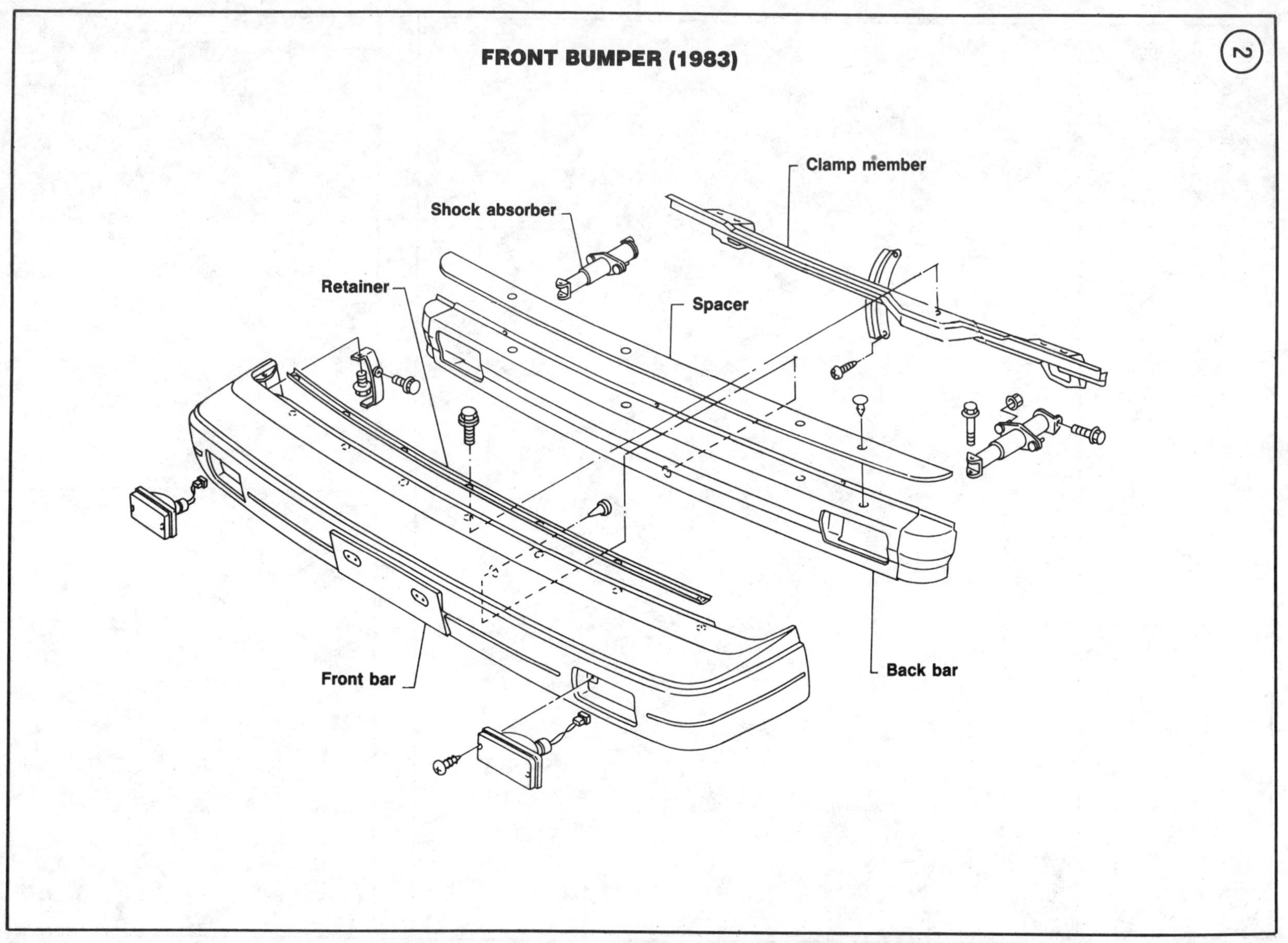

2
FRONT BUMPER (1983)
Clamp member
Shock absorber
Retainer
Spacer
Front bar
Back bar

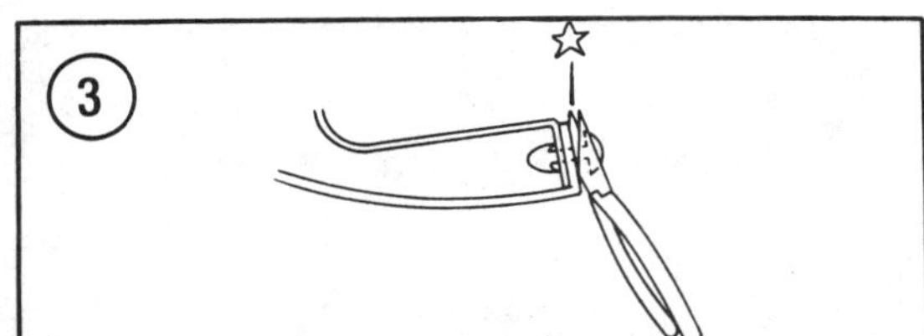

3. While an assistant supports one side of the hood, unbolt one hinge from the hood. Have the assistant unbolt the other side and lift the hood off.

4. To remove the insulator on diesel-engined cars, pry out the clips as shown in **Figure 12**.

5. Installation is the reverse of removal. Adjust the hood as described in this chapter.

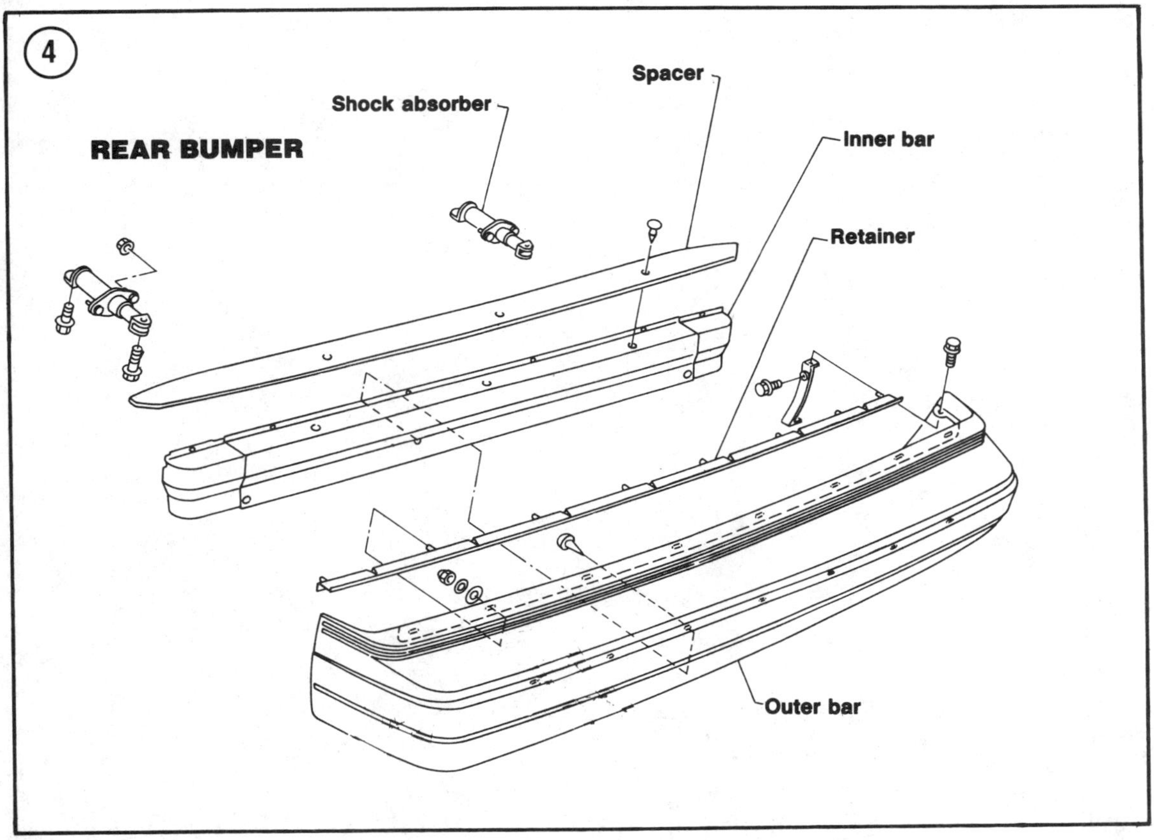

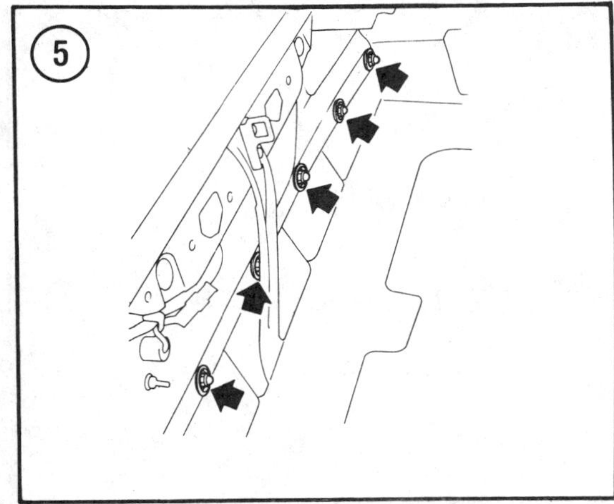

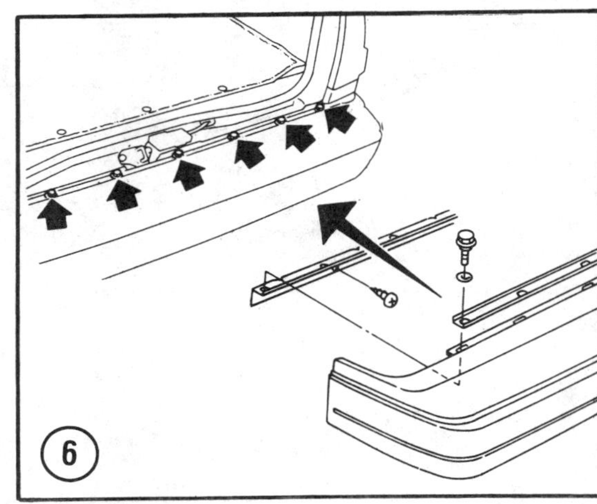

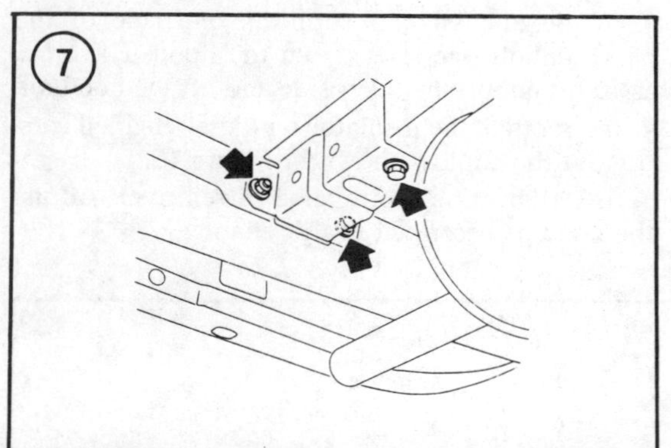
7

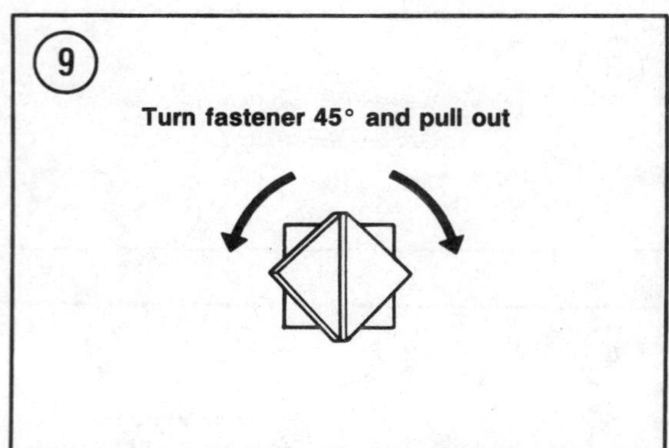
9
Turn fastener 45° and pull out

8
Cowl top cover 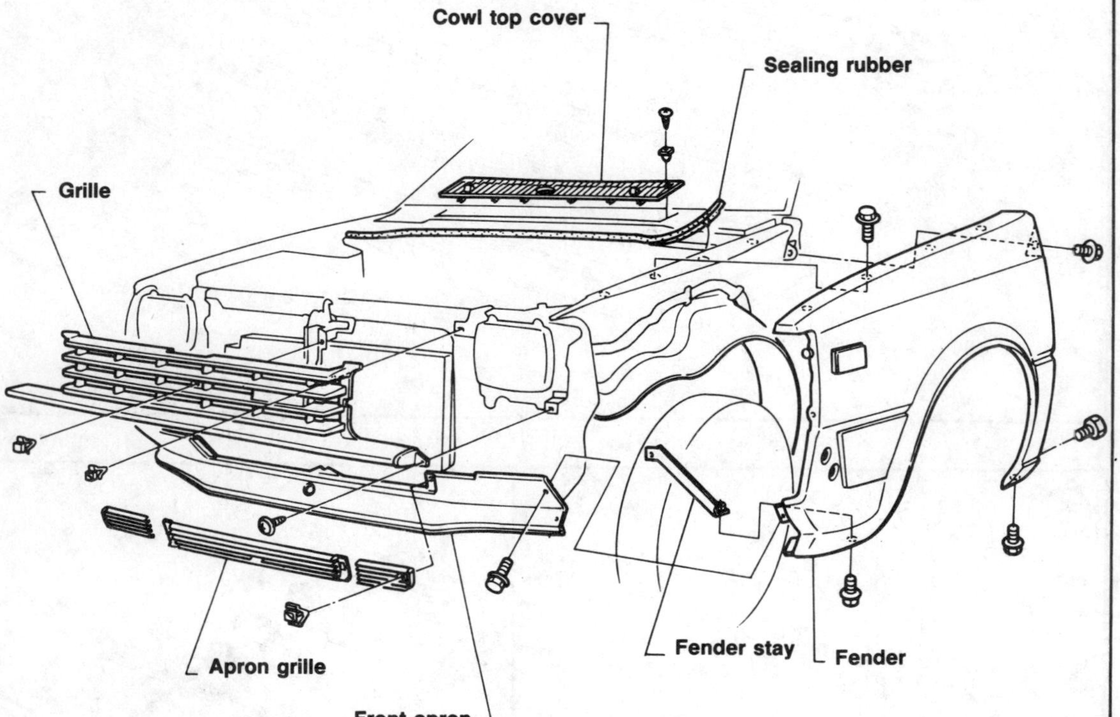
Sealing rubber
Grille
Apron grille
Front apron
Fender stay
Fender

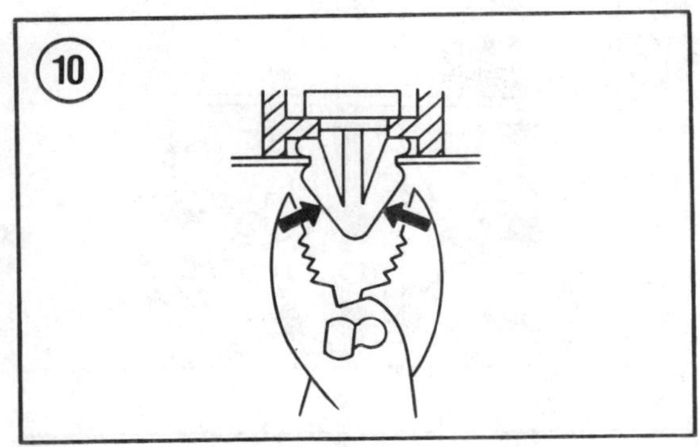

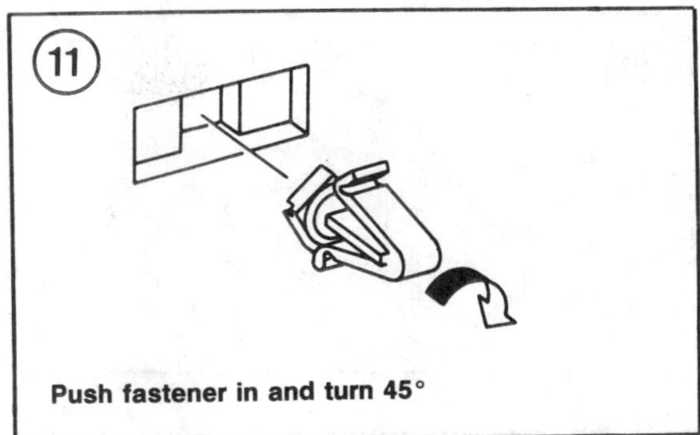

10

11
Push fastener in and turn 45°

12
Screwdriver
Clip
Insulator
Control cable

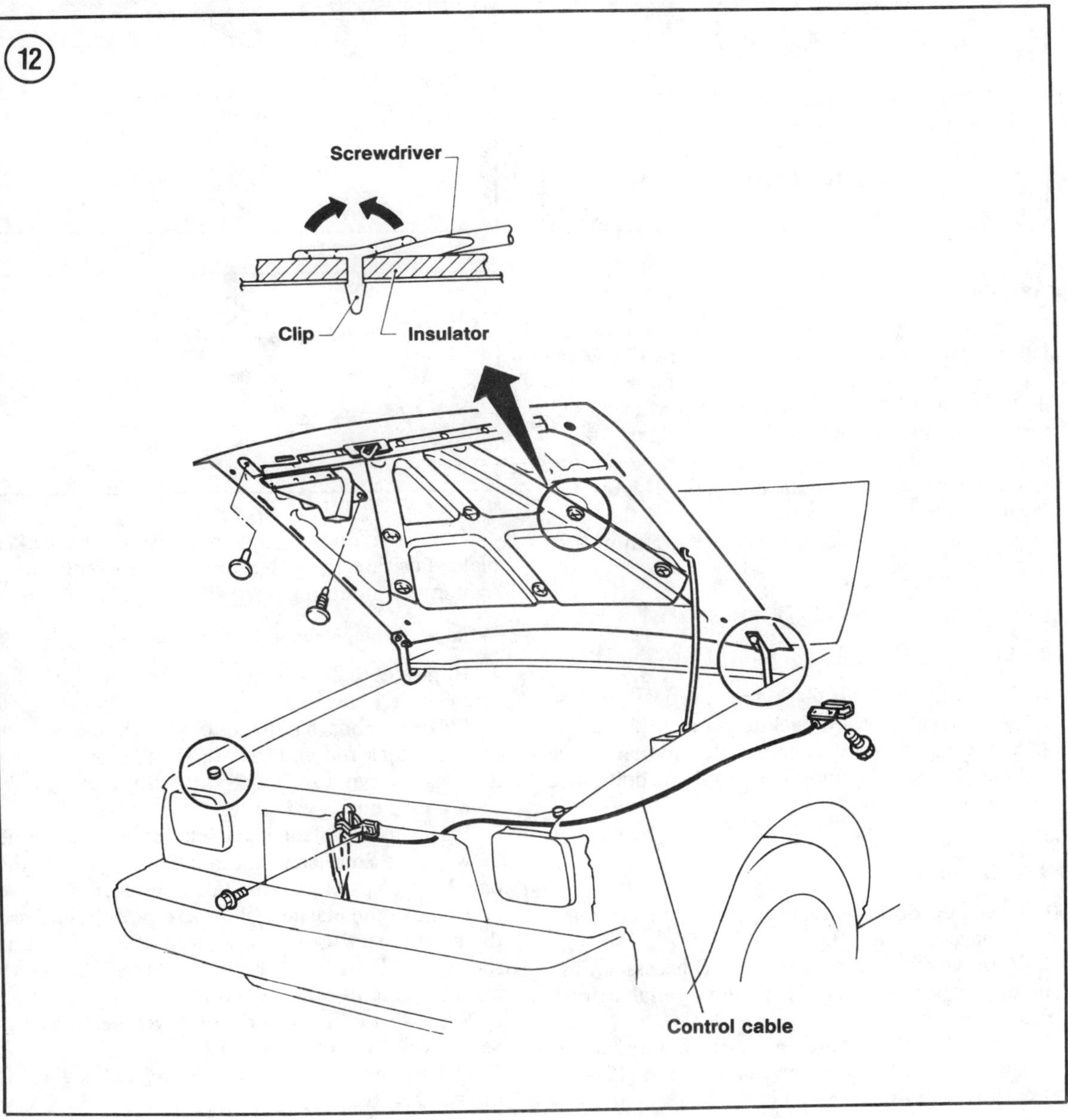

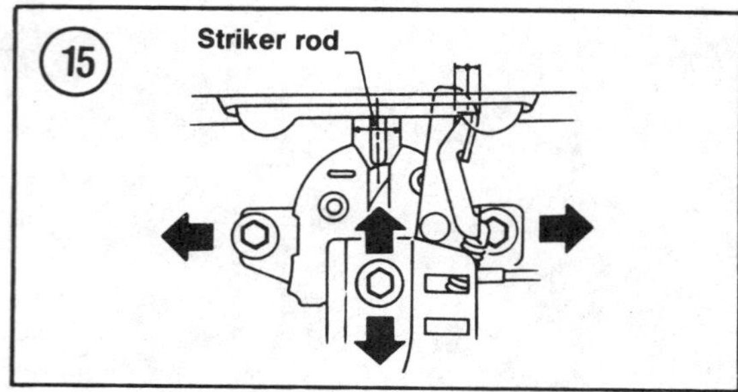

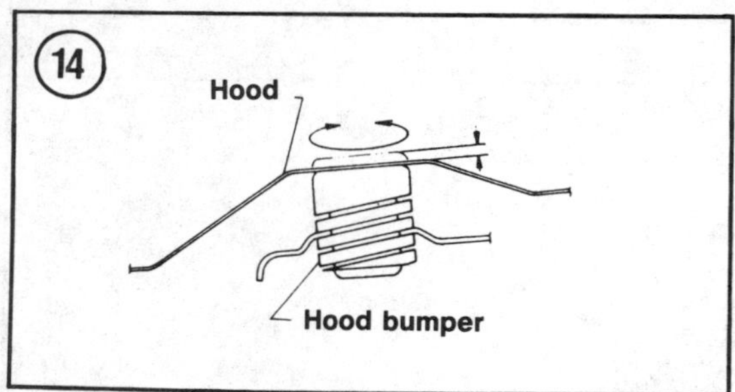

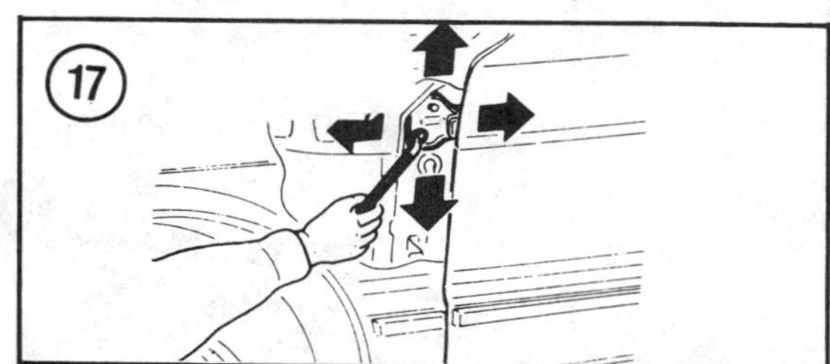

Adjustment

1. To move the hood forward, back or to one side, loosen the hinge-to-hood bolts (**Figure 13**). Move the hood as needed, then tighten the bolts.
2. If the hood is too loose or too tight when closed, turn the hood bumpers as shown in **Figure 14**.
3. If the hood is difficult to close or moves to one side when closed, loosen the latch bolts (**Figure 15**). Position the latch as needed, then tighten the bolts. Be sure the safety catch hooks at least 5 mm (0.20 in.) of the bracket on the hood.

FRONT DOORS

Removal

1. Open the door and place a jack beneath it. Use a rag between door and jack to protect the paint.
2. While an assistant supports the door, remove the check link pin and hinge-to-door bolts. See **Figure 16**.
3. Lift the door off.

Installation

1. Check the door weatherstripping. If deteriorated or damaged, replace it.
2. Remove the door striker plate. If necessary, use an impact screwdriver. These are available from auto parts stores.
3. Close the door and check its alignment. If necessary, loosen the hinge bolts (**Figure 17**) and reposition the door.

4. Once the door is aligned, install the striker plate. Position it so the door closes evenly, then tighten the mounting screws.

Window Replacement

1. Remove the armrest and door handle trim screws. See **Figure 18**.
2. Pull the door handle out. Detach the handle from the lock rod and take the handle off.
3. Snag the window crank clip with a wire hook, then pull it out. See **Figure 19**.
4. Insert a wide-bladed screwdriver or putty knife between the door panel and door. Carefully pry the panel out of its clips, then take the panel off.
5. Remove the plastic sealing screen. Pull gently so the plastic isn't torn. Use a piece of cardboard as shown in **Figure 20** to keep the screen's adhesive from sticking to other parts.
6. Remove the inner and outer weatherstripping. See **Figure 18** and **Figure 21**.
7. Detach the window from the regulator and lift the window out.

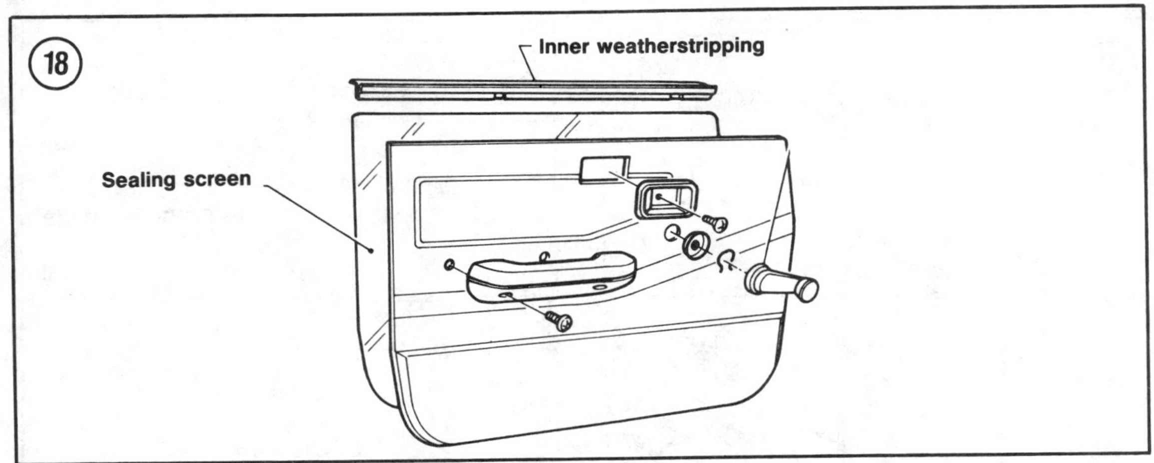

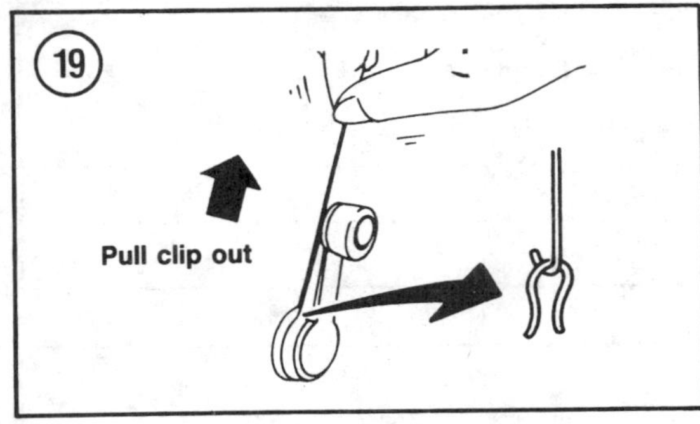

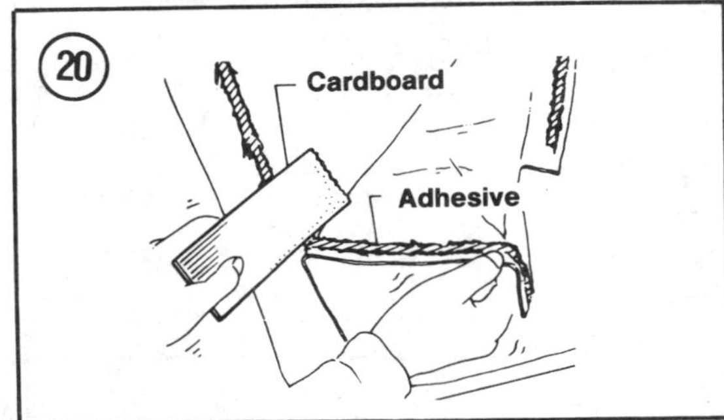

8. If necessary, detach the regulator assembly (**Figure 21**) and remove it through the access hole in the door.

9. Installation is the reverse of removal. When installing the window crank, place the clip on the crank, then push the crank onto the shaft. Position the crank as shown in **Figure 22** with the window closed.

10. To adjust the window, raise it all the way. Move the regulator guide up or down as needed. See **Figure 23**.

Lock Removal/Installation

1. Raise the window all the way.

2. Perform Steps 1-5 of *Window Replacement* in this chapter.

3. Detach the lock rods. See **Figure 21**. Remove the lock cylinder from the door.

4. If necessary, disconnect the outside handle link, remove the mounting nuts and take off the outside handle. See **Figure 21**.

5. If necessary, remove the lock mechanism mounting screws (**Figure 21**) and remove the lock mechanism through the access hole in the door.

6. Installation is the reverse of removal. If the outside handle was removed, turn the adjusting nut so the clearance shown in **Figure 24** is 0.5-1.5 mm (0.020-0.059 in.).

REAR DOORS

Figure 25 shows a rear door and related parts. Service procedures are basically the same as for front doors, with the following exceptions.

1. To remove the corner glass, remove its upper screw and pull it out as shown in **Figure 26**. Install in the reverse order.

2. To adjust the door position, loosen the hinge bolts (**Figure 27**). Position the door as needed and tighten the bolts.

3. To adjust the door window, loosen the glass-to-regulator bolts (**Figure 28**). Position the window as needed and tighten the bolts.

TRUNK LID (SEDAN)

Removal/Installation

1. Open the trunk. Place a thick layer of rags beneath the leading edge of the trunk lid to protect the paint.

12

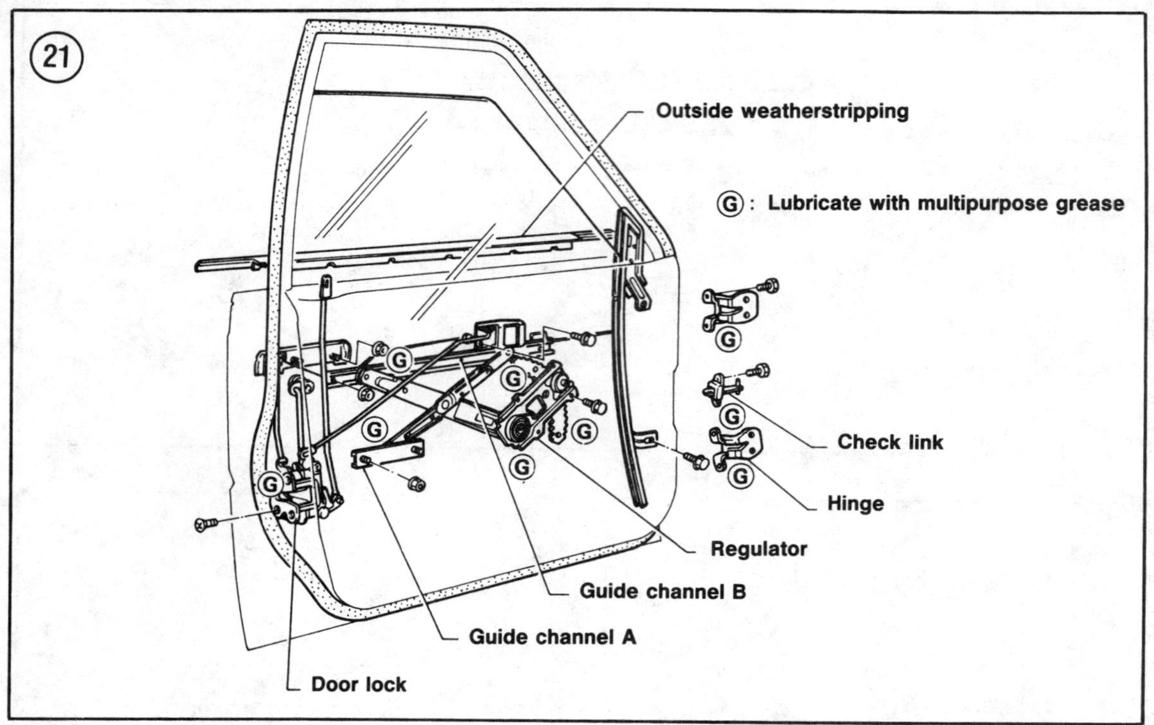

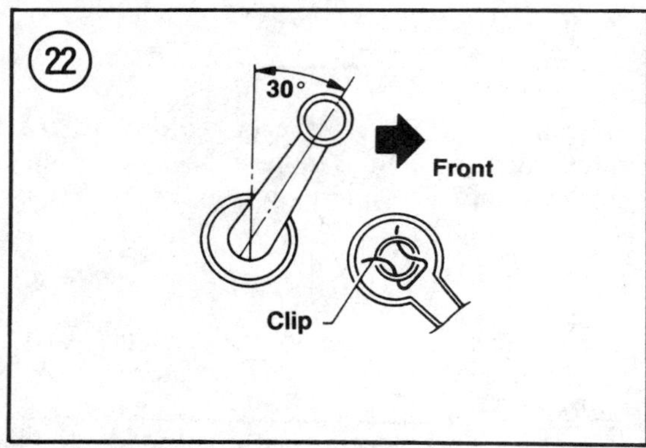

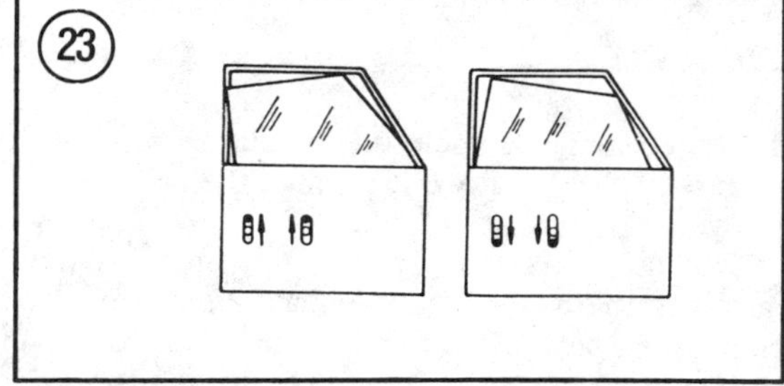

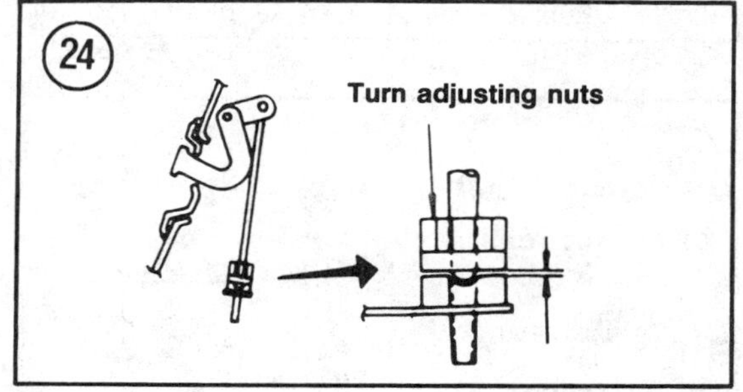

2. With a soft lead pencil, make alignment marks around the hinges onto the trunk lid. The marks will ease installation.

3. While an assistant supports one side of the trunk lid, remove the hinge-to-trunk lid bolts (**Figure 29**).

4. Have the assistant unbolt the other hinge, then lift the trunk lid off.

5. Inspect the trunk lid weatherstripping and replace it if worn or deteriorated. When installing the new weatherstripping, align the white paint mark with the center of the car. See **Figure 30**.

6. Installation is the reverse of removal. Adjust the trunk lid as described in this chapter.

Adjustment

1. To align the trunk lid with the body, loosen the hinge-to-trunk lid bolts (**Figure 29**) or hinge-to-body bolts (**Figure 31**). Reposition the trunk lid as needed, then tighten the bolts.

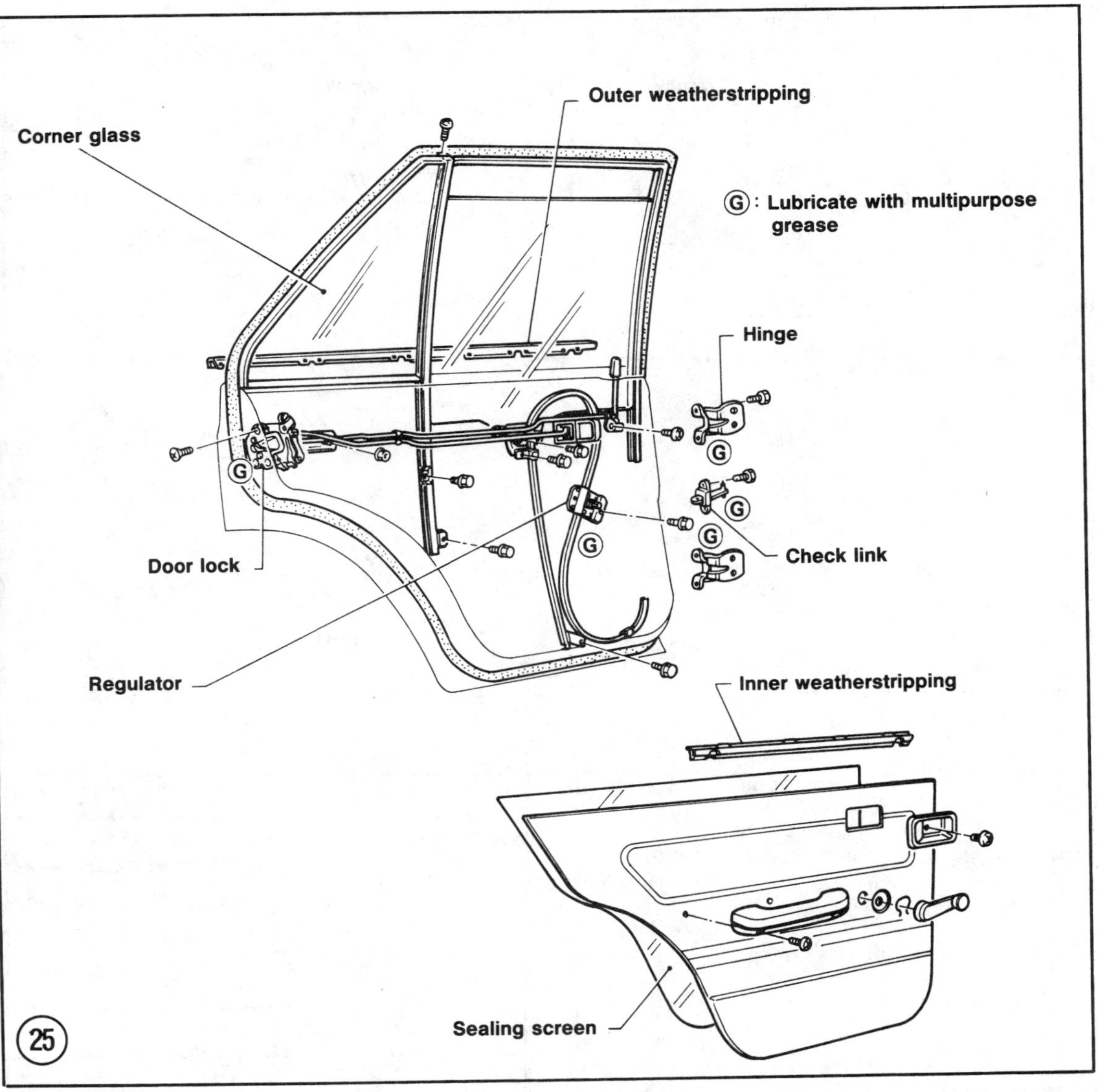

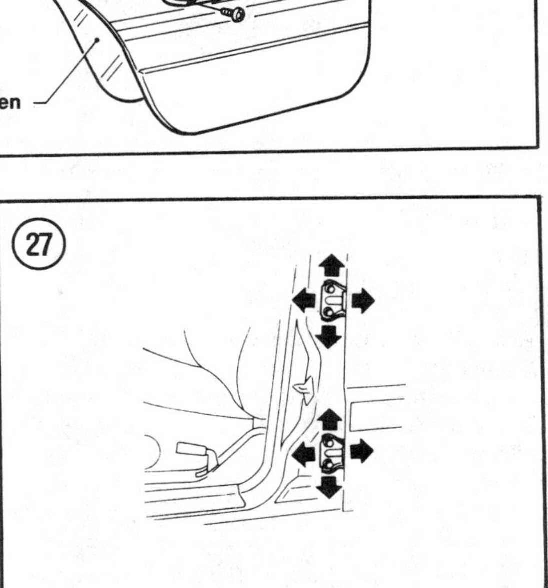

Corner glass
Outer weatherstripping
Ⓖ : Lubricate with multipurpose grease
Hinge
Ⓖ
Ⓖ
Ⓖ
Ⓖ
Check link
Door lock
Regulator
Inner weatherstripping
Sealing screen
25

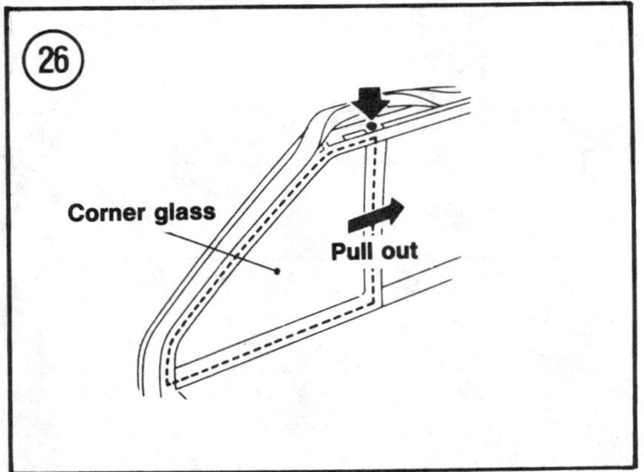

26
Corner glass
Pull out

27

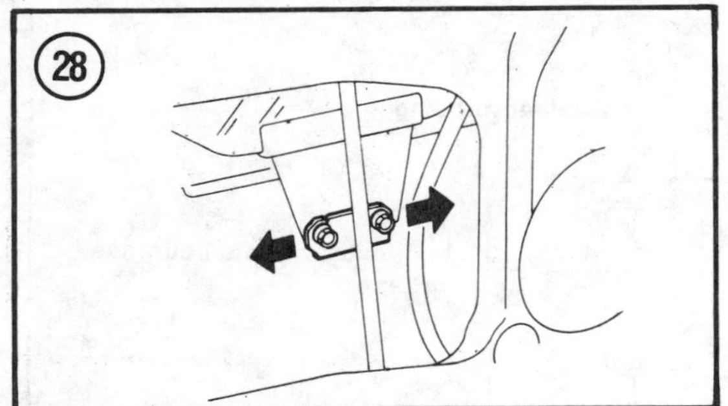

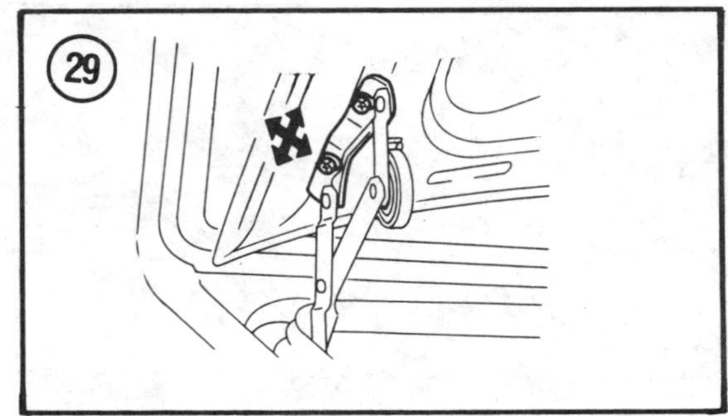

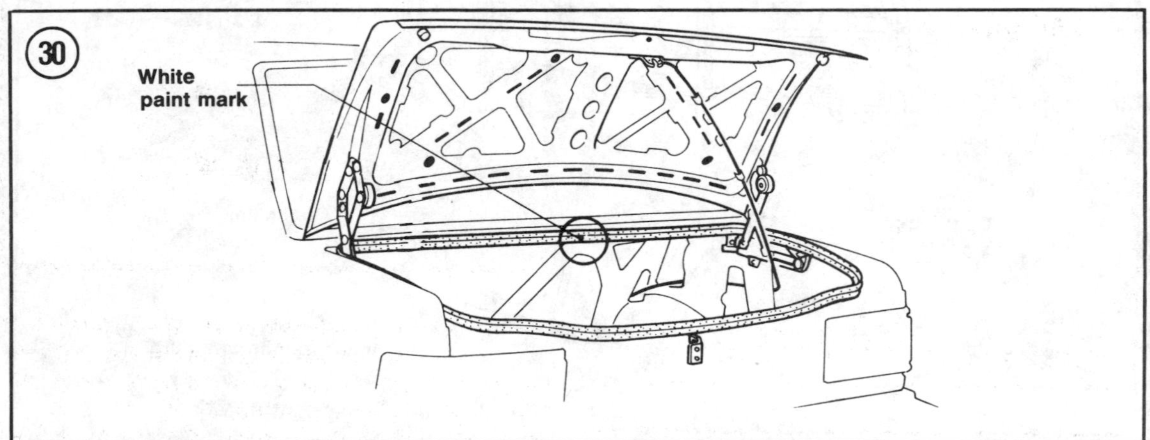

2. If the trunk lid is too loose, difficult to close or moves to one side when closed, loosen the striker mounting bolts (**Figure 32**). Reposition the striker as needed and tighten the bolts.

HATCHBACK (COUPE)

Removal/Installation

1. Place a thick layer of rags between the body and upper edge of the hatchback to protect the paint.
2. Unplug the wiring connectors (**Figure 33**).

> *CAUTION*
> *Do not scratch the stay rods. This will allow the gas inside the stay to leak out and the stay will have to be replaced.*

3. While an assistant supports one side of the hatchback, detach the stay (**Figure 34**) and remove the hinge-to-body bolts (**Figure 33**). Support the hatchback while the asistant detaches the other side, then lift it off.

> *WARNING*
> *Do not disassemble the stays, puncture them or expose them to heat. They contain gas under high pressure and may explode.*

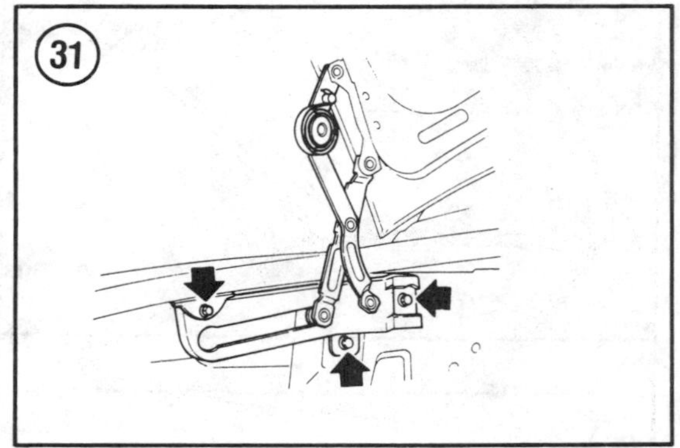

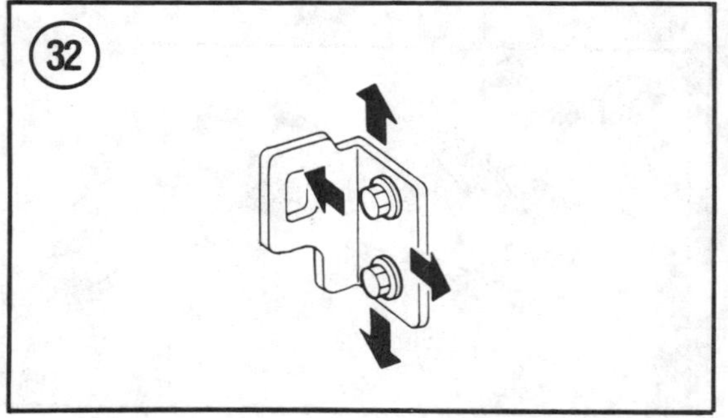

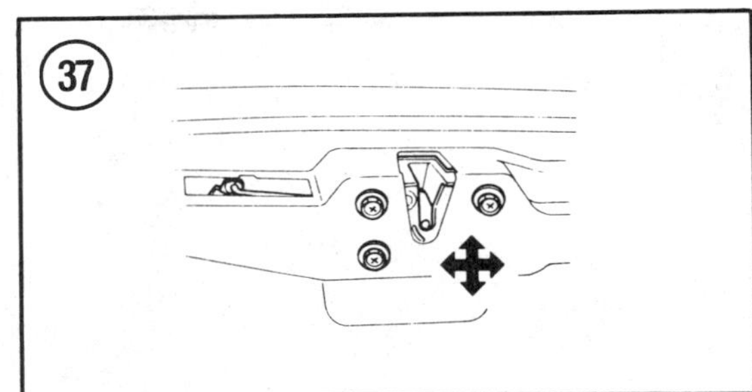

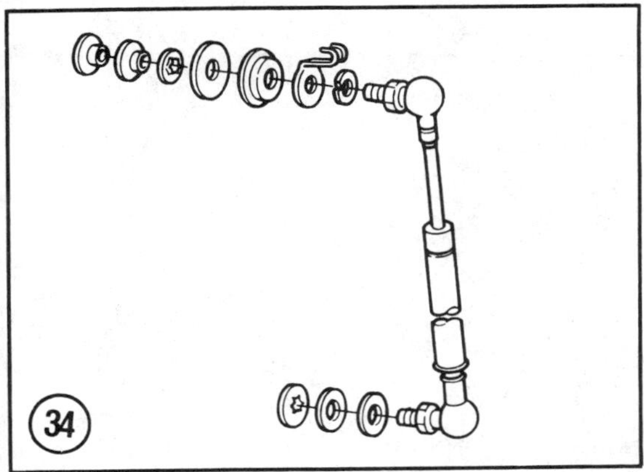

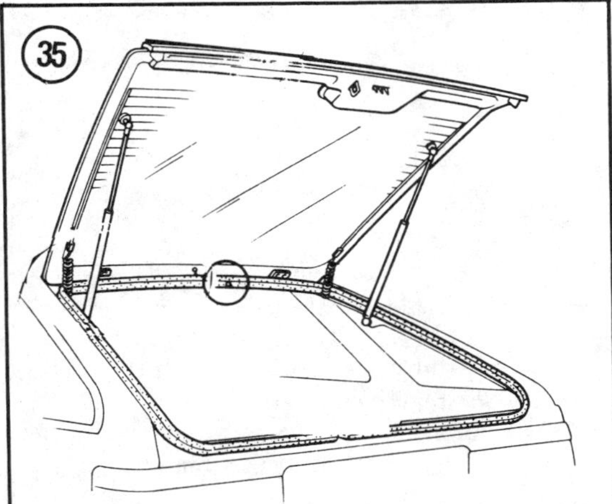

4. Inspect the weatherstripping and replace it if worn or deteriorated. When installing the new weatherstripping, align the white paint mark with the center of the car. See **Figure 35**.

5. Installation is the reverse of removal. Adjust the hatchback as described in this chapter.

Adjustment

1. To align the hatchback with the body, loosen the hinge-to-body bolts (**Figure 36**). Reposition the hatchback as needed, then tighten the bolts.

2. If the hatchback is too loose, difficult to close or moves to one side when closed, loosen the lock mounting screws (**Figure 37**). Position the lock as needed, then tighten the screws.

TAILGATE (STATION WAGON)

Removal/Installation

1. Open the tailgate. Place a thick layer of rags between the body and upper edge of the tailgate to protect the paint.

2. Unplug the wiring connectors (**Figure 38**). If the wiring harness must be removed from the tailgate, tie lengths of string to the disconnected ends of the harness. Pull the harness out of the tailgate, leaving the lengths of string exposed at both ends. This will ease installation of the harness, since the string can be used to pull the harness back into the tailgate.

3. With a soft lead pencil, make alignment marks around the hinges onto the tailgate. The marks will ease installation.

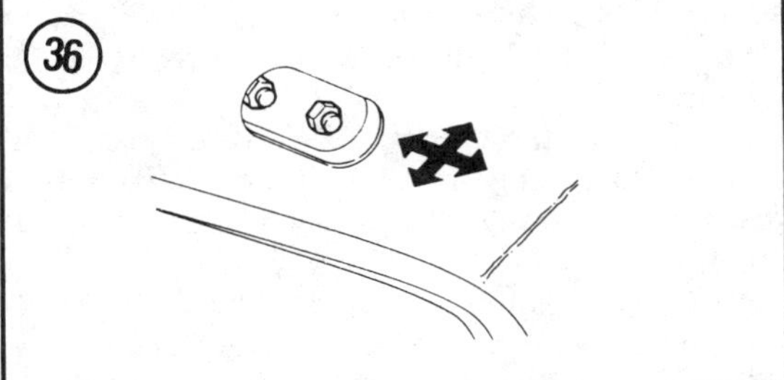

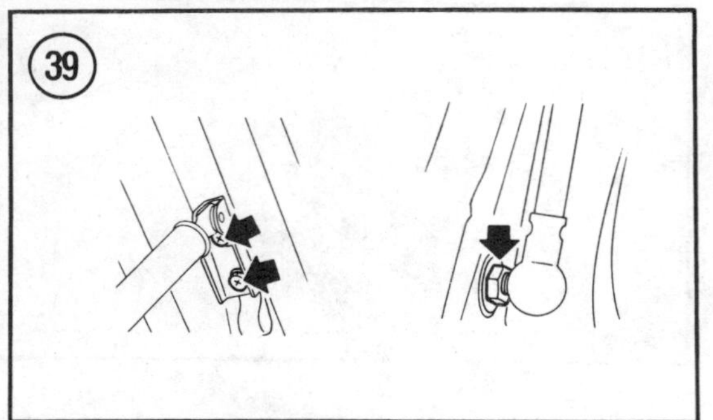

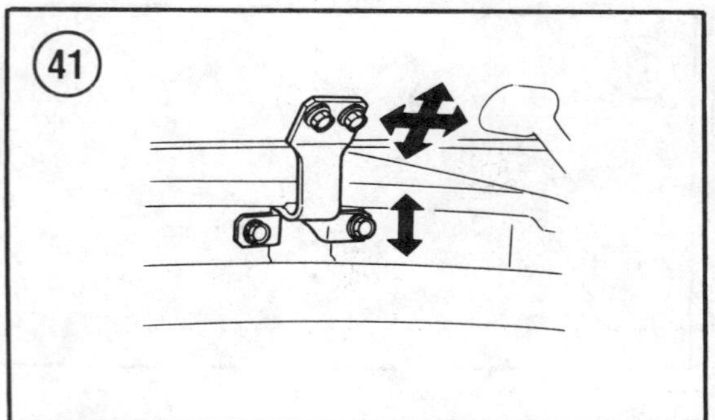

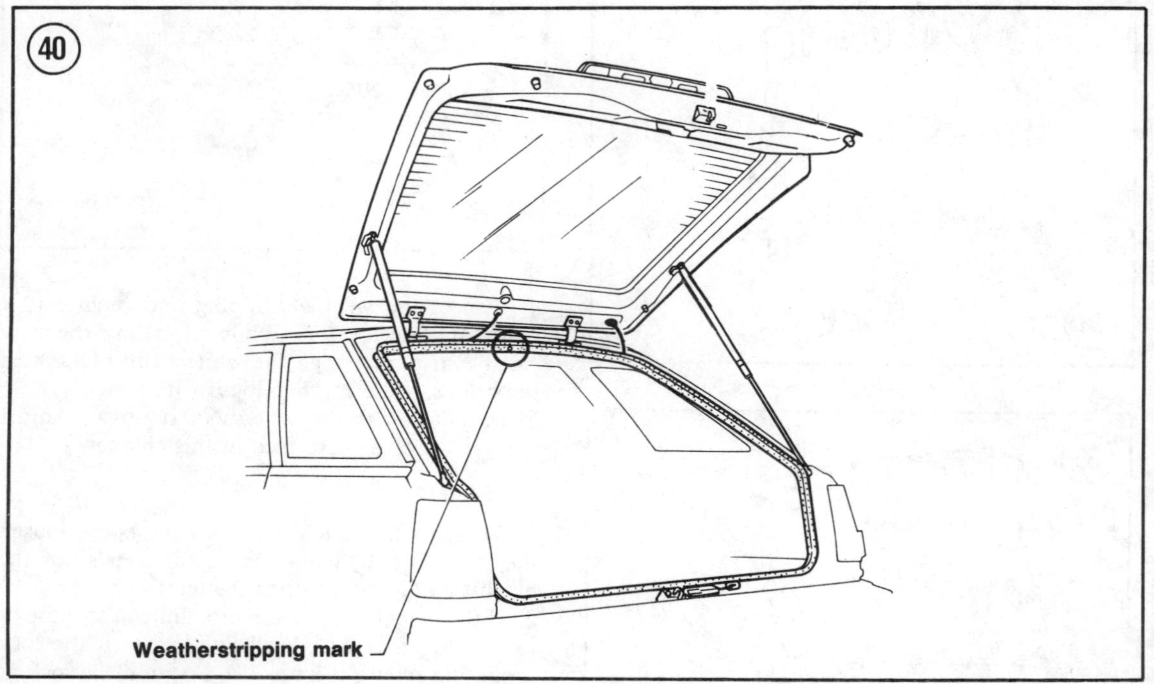

Weatherstripping mark

CAUTION
Do not scratch the stay rods. This will allow the gas inside the stay to leak out and the stay will have to be replaced.

4. While an assistant supports the tailgate, detach the stay (**Figure 39**) and remove the hinge-to-tailgate bolts (**Figure 38**). Have the assistant detach the other side, then lift the tailgate off.

WARNING
Do not disassemble the stays, puncture them or expose them to heat. They contain gas under high pressure and may explode.

5. Inspect the weatherstripping. Replace it if worn or deteriorated. Install the new weatherstripping so the white paint mark is aligned with the center of the car. See **Figure 40**.

6. Installation is the reverse of removal. Adjust the tailgate as described in this chapter.

Adjustment

1. To move the top edge of the tailgate forward or back, loosen the hinge-to-body bolts (**Figure 41**). Position the tailgate as needed, then tighten the bolts.

2. To move the tailgate up, down or to one side, loosen the hinge-to-tailgate bolts (**Figure 41**). Position the tailgate as needed, then tighten the bolts.

3. If the tailgate is too loose, difficult to close or moves to one side when closed, adjust the striker (**Figure 42**). To move the striker forward or back,

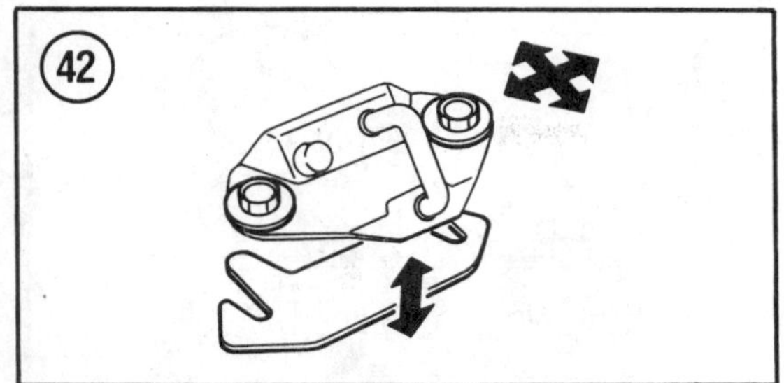

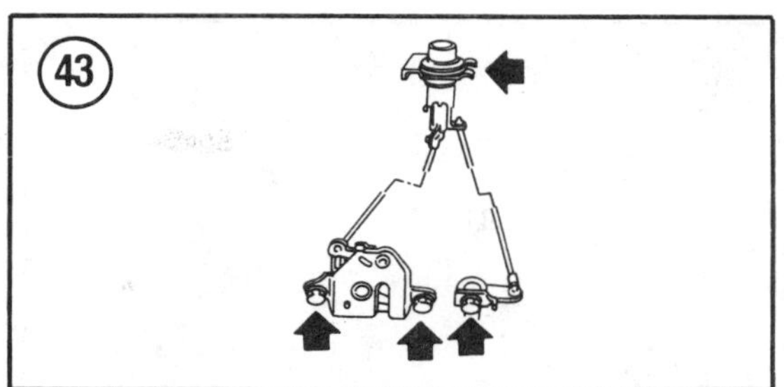

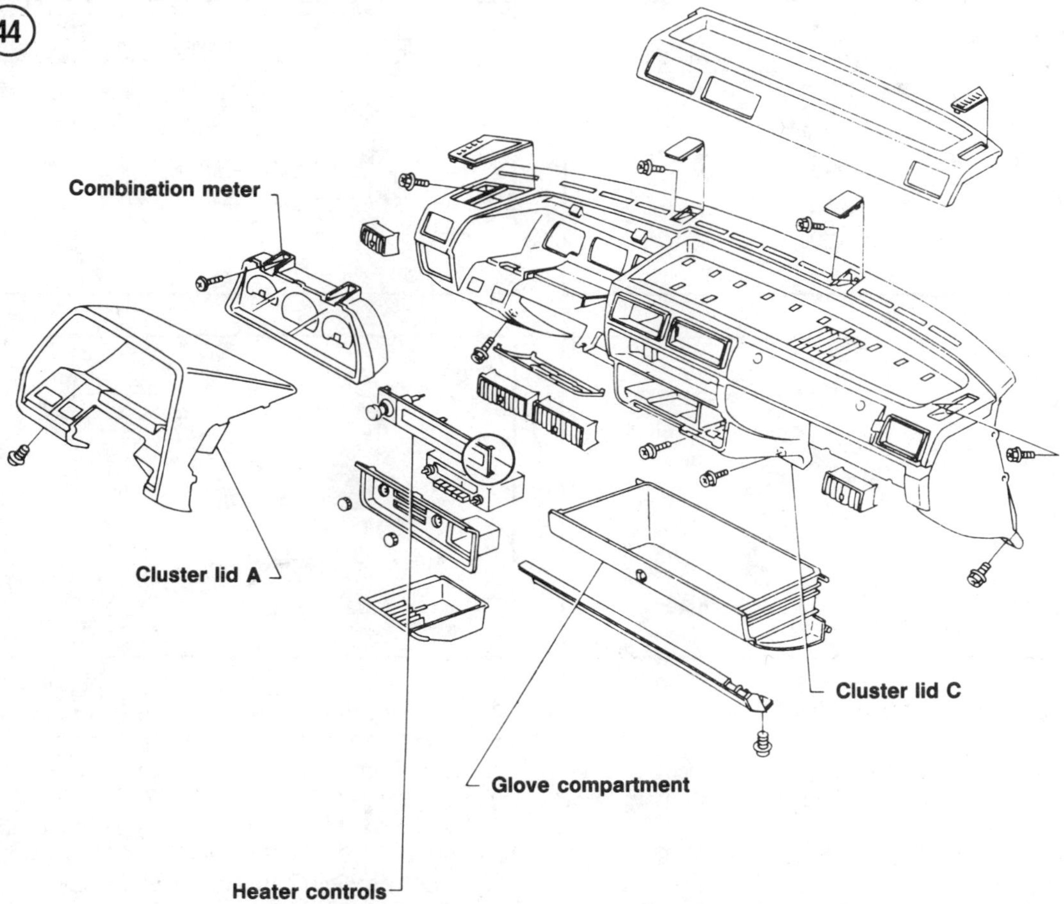

loosen the mounting screws, reposition the striker and tighten the screws. To raise or lower the striker, add or remove shims between the striker and body.

Lock Mechanism Removal/Installation

1. To remove the lock mechanism, disconnect the rods, remove the bolts and take it out. See **Figure 43**. Install in the reverse order. The lock mechanism is not adjustable.

2. To remove the lock cylinder, disconnect the rods, pull out the clip and take the cylinder out. See **Figure 43**. Install in the reverse order.

INSTRUMENT PANEL

Removal/Installation

1. Disconnect the negative cable from the battery.
2. Remove cluster lid A. See **Figure 44** and **Figure 45**.

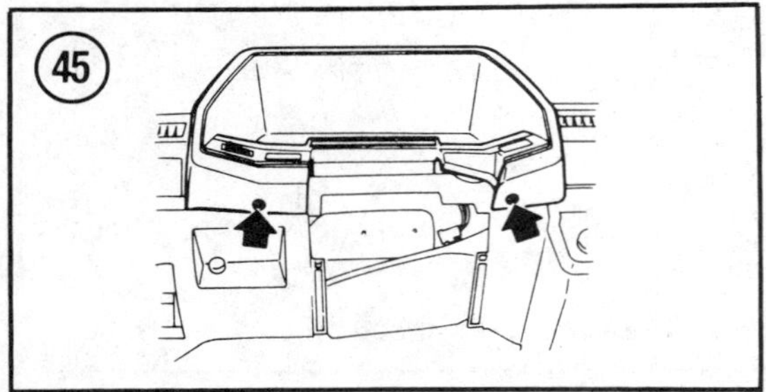

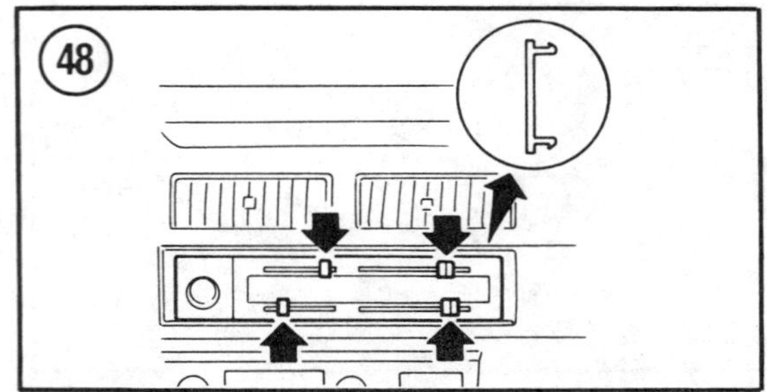

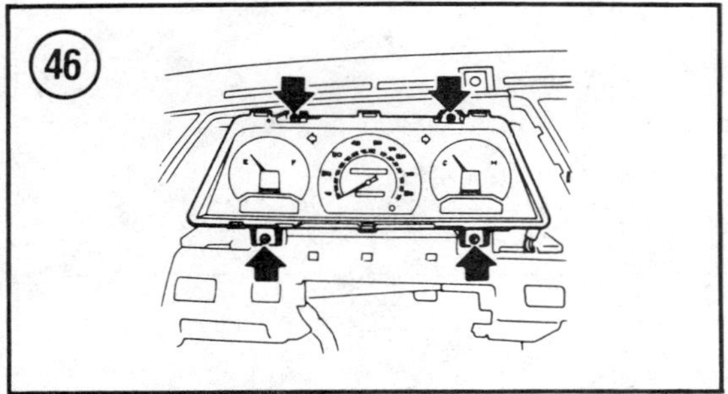

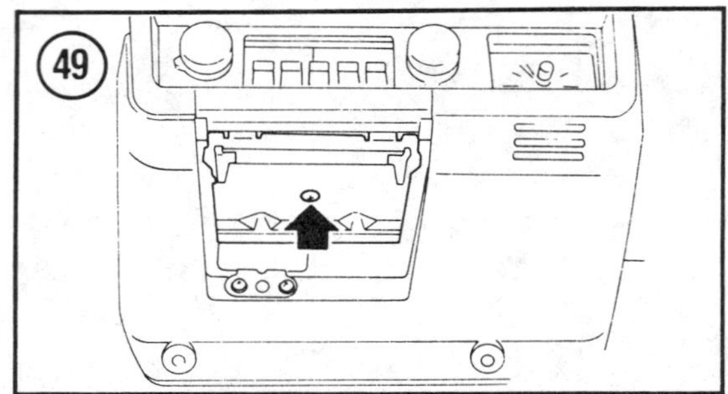

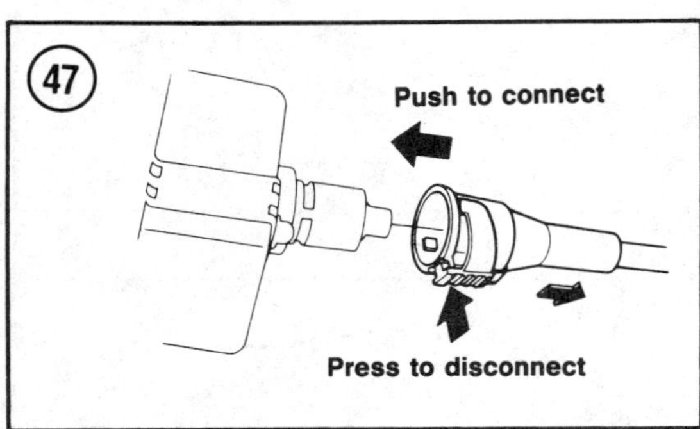

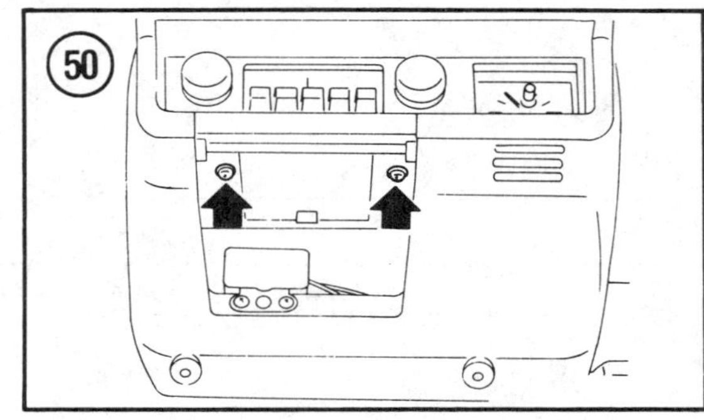

3. Remove the instrument cluster mounting screws (**Figure 46**).

4. Pull the instrument cluster out. Disconnect the speedometer cable (**Figure 47**) and instrument wiring. Take the instrument cluster out.

5. Pull off the heater knobs (**Figure 48**). Compress the trim panel prongs and take the panel out.

6. Remove the ashtray, then remove its bracket. See **Figure 49**.

7. Remove the radio mounting screws (**Figure 50**).

8. Pull off the radio knobs and remove the nuts from the knob shafts. Detach the radio faceplate from its clips and take it off. See **Figure 51**.

9. Disconnect the radio wires and take the radio out.

10. Remove the glove compartment. See **Figure 52** and **Figure 44**.

11. Detach the hood release cable from the instrument panel.

12. Remove cluster lid C. See **Figure 53** and **Figure 44**.

13. Remove the package tray from the top of the instrument panel.

14. Remove the instrument panel fasteners and take the panel off. See **Figure 44**.

15. Installation is the reverse of removal.

SEATS

Front Seat Removal/Installation

1. Slide the seat forward and remove the rear seat track bolts. See **Figure 54**.

2. Slide the seat rearward and remove the front seat track bolts.

3. Lift the seat out.

4. Installation is the reverse of removal.

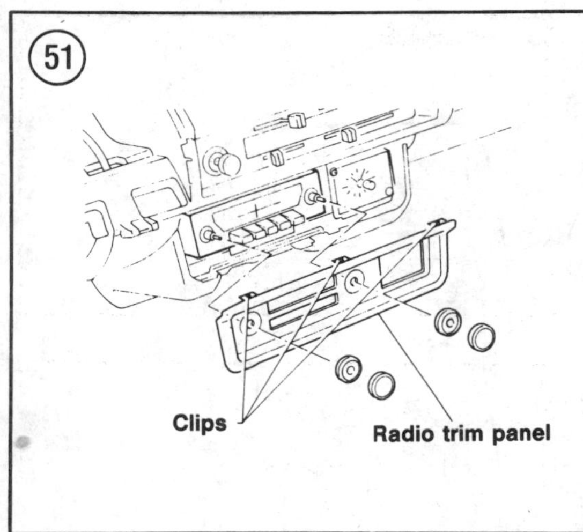

Rear Seat Removal/Installation (Sedan)

1. Lift up the leading edge of the seat cushion, then pull the cushion out. See **Figure 54**.
2. Remove the screws securing the lower edge of the seatback.
3. Lift the cushion up off its hooks and take it out.
4. Installation is the reverse of removal.

Rear Seat Removal/Installation (Coupe and Wagon)

1. Lift up the leading edge of the seat cushion, then pull the cushion out. See **Figure 55**.
2. Detach the luggage compartment carpet from the seatback.
3. Detach the hinges from the seatback, then lift the seatback out.
4. Installation is the reverse of removal.

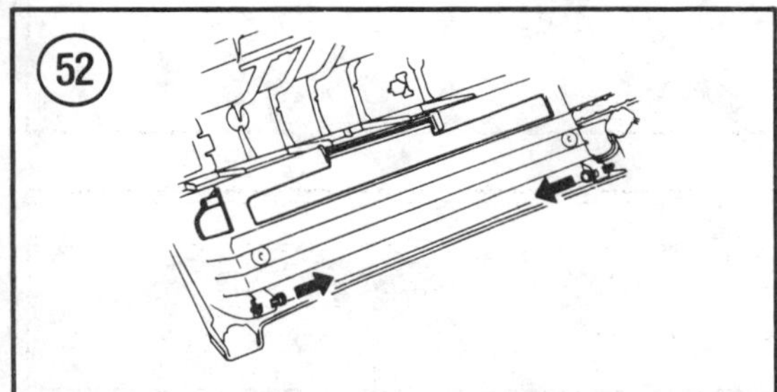

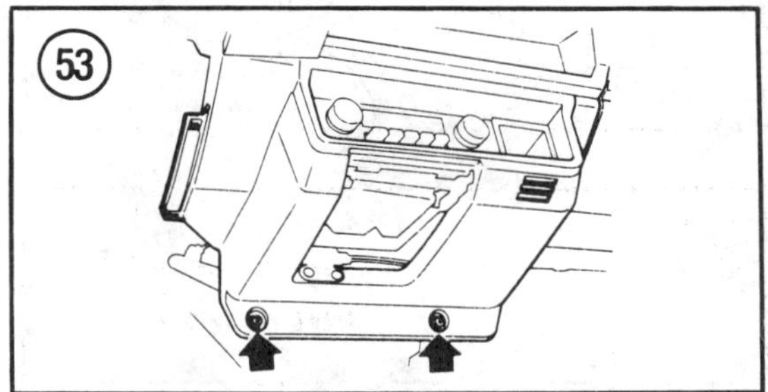

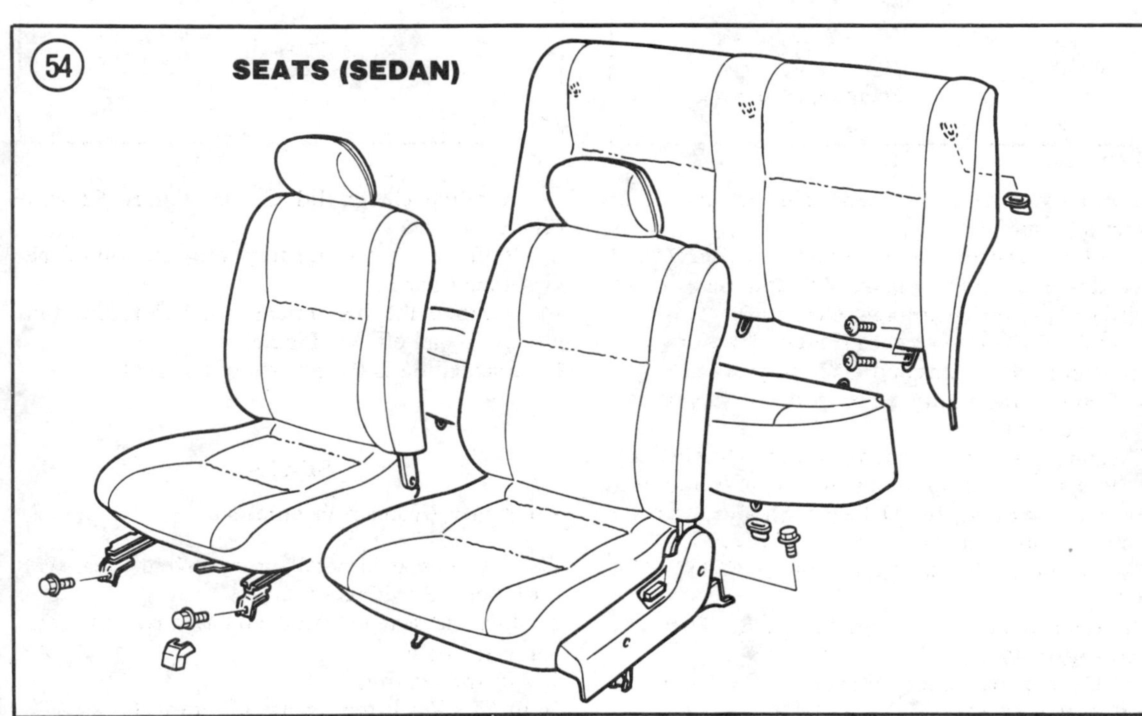

12

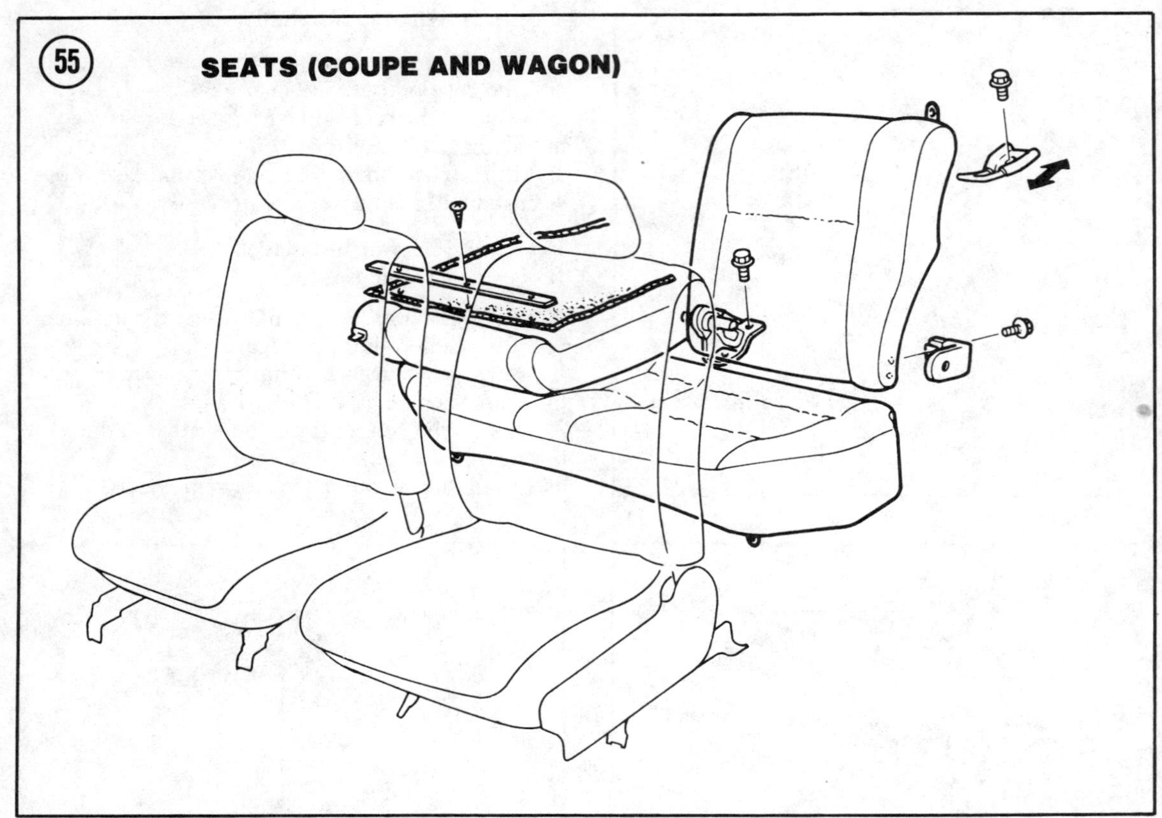
55
SEATS (COUPE AND WAGON)

1984 AND LATER SERVICE INFORMATION

This supplement contains service and maintenance information for the 1984 and later Nissan Sentra. The information supplements the procedures in the main body (Chapters One through Tweleve) of the book, referred to in this supplement as the "basic book."

The chapter headings and titles in this supplement correspond to those in the basic book. If a chapter is not included in the supplement, there are no changes affecting 1984 and later models.

If your vehicle is covered by this supplement, carefully read the supplement and then read the appropriate chapters in the basic book before beginning any work.

CHAPTER THREE

LUBRICATION, MAINTENANCE AND TUNE-UP

FUEL STOP CHECKS

Tire Pressures

Tire pressures for 1984 and later models are listed on a placard in the glove compartment.

SCHEDULED MAINTENANCE

Most maintenance procedures are the same as for 1983 models. These are described in Chapter Three of the basic book. Procedures which differ from 1983 are described in this supplement. Maintenance schedules are listed in **Table 1** (1984) and **Table 2** (1985). Diesel engine maintenance for 1984 and later models is listed in **Table 3**.

Some maintenance procedures must be done more often under severe driving conditions. These are listed in **Table 4**.

Some refill capacities on 1984 and later models differ from 1983. These are listed in **Table 5**.

Some tune-up specifications differ from 1983. These are listed in **Table 6**.

Idle Speed Control Actuator and Vacuum Modulator Valve Filters

These filters are used on 1984 and later models. They should be replaced at intervals specified in **Table 1**, **Table 2** or **Table 4**.

With the engine off, remove each filter from its bracket and install a new one. See **Figure 1**.

Exhaust Gas Sensor Inspection

This procedure is required on 1984 and later U.S. models. The procedure need be done only once in the life of the car. After the first inspection, the exhaust gas sensor warning light may be disconnected so it does not come on again.

California models

The procedure for 1984 and later California models is the same as for 1983 models, described in Chapter Three of the basic book.

49-state models

1. Warm up the engine until the temperature needle points to the middle of the gauge.
2. Run the engine at approximately 2,000 rpm for 5 minutes.
3. Locate the diagnosis start switch on the electronic control unit under the driver's seat. Turn the switch off. See **Figure 2**.
4. Make sure the inspection lamp on the instrument panel flashes off and on at least 5 times during a 10-second period.
5. If the system has performed as described so far, it is okay. If not, have it tested by a dealer or mechanic familiar with Nissan emission controls.

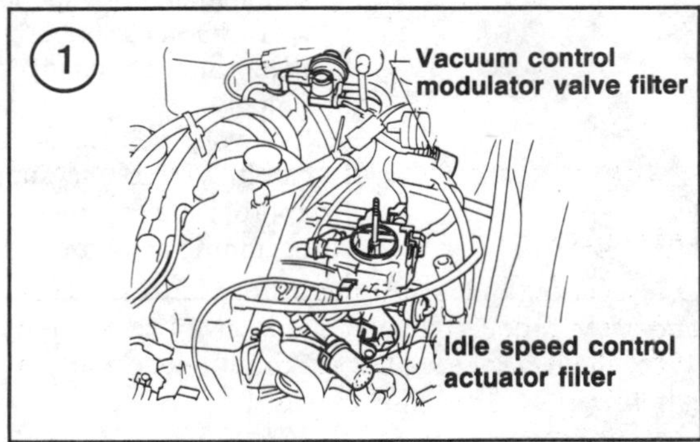

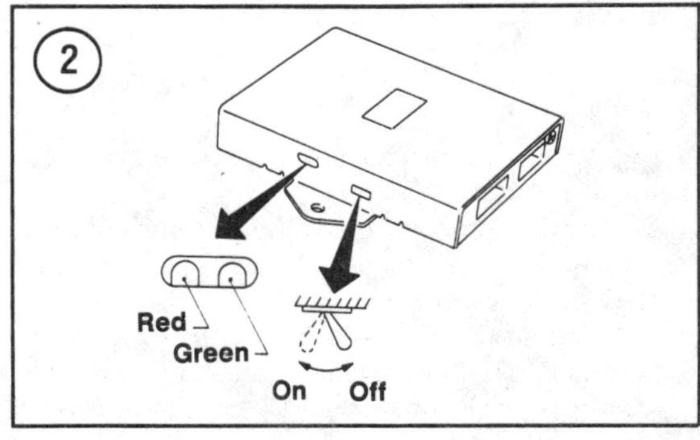

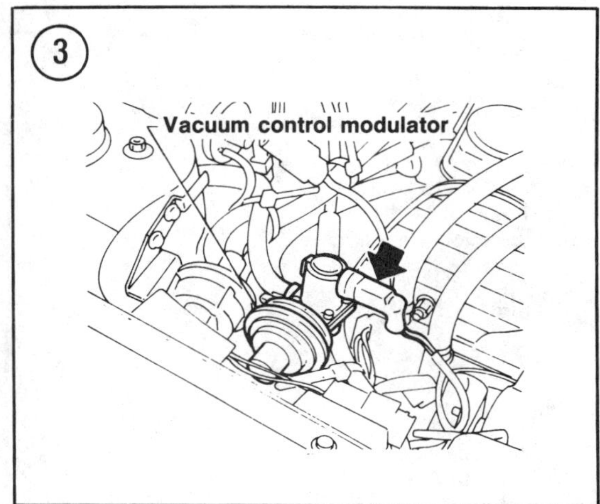

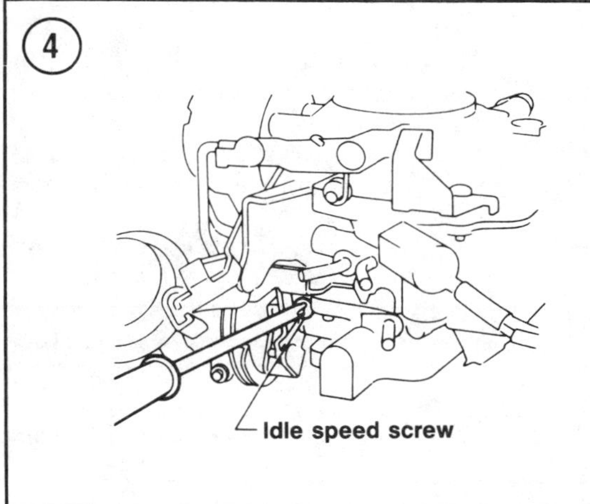

Drive Belts

Inspection and adjustment procedures for 1984 and later models are the same as for 1983. For 1985, the factory specifies maximum deflection for gasoline-engine belts as follows:

a. Alternator—19 mm (0.75 in.).
b. Air conditioner—12.5 mm (0.49 in.).
c. Power steering—10.5 mm (0.41 in.).

TUNE-UP

Some tune-up specifications differ from 1983. These are listed in **Table 6**.

As with 1983 models, not all procedures need to be done at each tune-up. Intervals for each procedure are as follows:

a. Valve adjustment—each tune-up.
b. Spark plugs—alternate tune-ups on U.S. models; each tune-up on Canadian models.
c. Distributor cap, rotor and ignition wires—alternate tune-ups on 1984 U.S. models; each tune-up on 1984 Canadian models; every 2 years on 1985 models.
d. Idle speed (U.S. models)—each tune-up.
e. Ignition timing, idle speed and mixture ratio (Canadian models)—each tune-up.

Idle Speed Adjustment

California models

This procedure is the same as for 1983 U.S. cars and Canadian MPG models, described in Chapter Three of the basic book.

Non-California models

1. Warm up the engine until the temperature needle points to the middle of the gauge. Block the front wheels securely.
2. Make sure engine speed is below 1,000 rpm.
3. Open the hood. Connect a tune-up tachometer to the engine, following manufacturer's instructions.
4. Let the engine idle for 2 minutes.
5. Turn off the engine.
6. Unplug the vacuum control modulator wiring connector (**Figure 3**).
7. Start the engine.
8. Rev the engine 2 or 3 times to 2,000-3,000 rpm in NEUTRAL, then let it idle.
9. Check idle speed on the tachometer:
   a. On manual transaxles, it should be 700 ±50 rpm in NEUTRAL.
   b. On automatic transaxles, it should be 550 ±50 rpm in PARK.

Adjust if necessary by turning the idle speed screw (**Figure 4**).

10. Turn off the engine.
11. Reconnect the wiring connector to the vacuum control modulator.
12. Start the engine.
13. Rev the engine 2 or 3 times to 2,000-3,000 rpm in NEUTRAL, then let it idle.
14. Recheck idle speed on the tachometer:
   a. On manual transaxles, it should be 800 ±100 rpm in NEUTRAL.
   b. On automatic transaxles, it should be 650 ±100 rpm in DRIVE.

Adjust if necessary by turning the idle speed screw.

13

Table 1 SCHEDULED MAINTENANCE (1984)

Every 7,500 miles (6 months)	• Engine oil and filter change[1]
Every 15,000 miles (12 months)	• Brake inspection • Manual transaxle oil level check • Automatic transaxle fluid level check • Power steering line and hose inspection • Steering linkage and suspension inspection • Hinges, latches, locks lubrication • Exhaust system inspection • Seat belt inspection • Choke inspection[2] • ATC air cleaner inspection[2] • Tune-up
Every 30,000 miles (24 months)	• Drive belt inspection • Air cleaner element replacement • Idle speed control actuator filter replacement[3] • Vacuum control modulator valve filter replacement[3] • Choke inspection[4] • Vapor line inspection • Fuel line inspection • Coolant change • ATC air cleaner inspection • Exhaust gas sensor inspection • Brake fluid change • Front wheel bearing inspection
As needed (see text)	• PCV filter replacement • Fuel filter replacement

1. On California and Canadian models, replace oil filter @ every oil change. On 49-state models, replace oil filter @ first oil change, then @ alternate oil changes.
2. Canadian models only.
3. 49-state models only.
4. California models only.

Table 2 SCHEDULED MAINTENANCE (1985)

Every 7,500 miles (6 months)	• Engine oil and filter change[1]
Every 15,000 miles	• Manual transaxle oil level check • Automatic transaxle fluid level check
Every 15,000 miles (12 months)	• Brake inspection • Power steering line and hose inspection • Steering linkage and suspension inspection • Hinges, latches, locks lubrication • Exhaust system inspection • Seat belt inspection • Choke inspection[2] • ATC air cleaner inspection[2] • Tune-up
Every 30,000 miles	• Air cleaner element replacement • ATC air cleaner inspection
Every 30,000 miles (24 months)	• Drive belt inspection • Idle speed control actuator filter replacement[3] • Vacuum control modulator valve filter replacement[3]

(continued)

Table 2 SCHEDULED MAINTENANCE (1985) (continued)

Every 30,000 miles (24 months) (cont.)	• Choke inspection[4] • Vapor line inspection • Fuel line inspection • Coolant change • Exhaust gas sensor inspection • Brake fluid change • Front wheel bearing inspection
As needed (see text)	• PCV filter replacement • Fuel filter replacement

1. On California and Canadian models, replace oil filter @ every oil change. On 49-state models, replace oil filter @ first oil change, then @ alternate oil changes.
2. Canadian models only.
3. 49-state models only.
4. California models only.

Table 3 DIESEL ENGINE MAINTENANCE (1984-ON)*

Every 5,000 miles (6 months)	• Engine oil (1984 California, 1985 U.S.)
Every 10,000 miles (12 months)	• Oil filter (1984 California, 1985 U.S.)
Every 7,500 miles (6 months)	• Engine oil (1984 non-California, 1985 Canada)
Every 15,000 miles (12 months)	• Oil filter (1984 non-California, 1985 U.S.) • Drive belt inspection • Injection nozzle inspection** • Valve clearance adjustment
Every 30,000 miles (24 months)	• Air cleaner element replacement • Fuel line inspection and rubber hose inspection • Fuel filter replacement • Coolant change • Idle speed adjustment • Injection timing adjustment
Every 60,000 miles As needed (see text)	• Timing belt replacement • Fuel system water removal • Fuel system bleeding

* On 1984 non-California diesels and 1985 U.S. diesels, change the oil filter @ every oil change during the first 15,000 miles, then @ alternate oil changes.
** 30,000 miles on California models.

Table 4 SEVERE SERVICE MAINTENANCE (1984-ON)

Procedure	Interval	Condition (See notes)
Air cleaner element replacement	As needed	3
Idle speed control actuator filter replacement	As needed	3
Engine oil Gasoline	3,000 miles (3 months)	1, 2, 3, 5
	(continued)	

13

Table 4 SEVERE SERVICE MAINTENANCE (1984-ON) (continued)

Procedure	Interval	Condition (See notes)
Engine oil (cont.)		
Diesel		
1984 non-California	3,750 miles (3 months)	1, 2, 3, 5
1984 California	2,500 miles (3 months)	1, 2, 3, 5
1985 U.S.	2,500 miles (3 months)	1, 2, 3, 5
1985 Canada	3,750 miles (3 months)	1, 2, 3, 5
Oil filter		
Gasoline		
1984 California	3,000 miles (3 months)	1, 2, 3, 5
1984 49-states	First oil change, then every second oil change	1, 2, 3, 5
1984 Canada	3,000 miles (3 months)	1, 2, 3, 5
1985 California	3,000 miles (3 months)	1, 2, 3, 5
1985 non-California	First oil change, then every second oil change	1, 2, 3, 5
Diesel		
1984 California	5,000 miles (3 months)	1, 2, 3, 5
1984 non-California	3,750 miles (3 months)[9]	1, 2, 3, 5
1985 U.S.	5,000 miles (3 months)	1, 2, 3, 5
1985 Canada	3,750 miles (3 months)[9]	1, 2, 3, 5
Brake inspection	7,500 miles (6 months)	1, 3, 5, 6, 7
Steering linkage and suspension inspection	7,500 miles (6 months)	7
Ball-joint inspection	7,500 miles (6 months)	
Axle shaft boots inspection	7,500 miles (6 months)	4, 6, 7
Hinges, latches, locks lubrication	7,500 miles (6 months)	6
Exhaust system inspection	7,500 miles (6 months)	1, 5, 6, 7
Brake fluid change[10]	15,000 miles (12 months)	8
Manual transaxle oil change	30,000 miles (24 months)	5, 7
Automatic transaxle fluid change	30,000 miles (24 months)	5, 7

1. Frequent short trips	6. Road salt or other corrosive materials
2. Extended idling	7. Rough or muddy roads
3. Dust	8. Humid areas or mountains
4. Extremely hot or cold weather	9. After the first 15,000 miles, change every 7,500 miles or 6 months.
5. Towing a trailer	10. 1984 only.

Table 5 APPROXIMATE REFILL CAPACITIES (1984-ON)

	Liters	Quarts
Cooling system (gasoline)		
Manual transmission	4.7	5
Automatic transmission	5.3	5 5/8
Cooling system (diesel)	7	7 3/8
Cooling system reservoir tank	0.7	3/4
Engine oil (gasoline)		
With filter change		
1984	3.7	3 7/8
1985	3.3	3 1/2
Without filter change		
1984	3.3	3 1/2
1985	2.9	3 1/8

(continued)

Table 5 APPROXIMATE REFILL CAPACITIES (1984-ON) (continued)

	Liters	Quarts
Engine oil (diesel)		
With filter change	4.1	4 3/8
Without filter change	3.5	3 3/4
Transaxle		
4-speed manual	2.3	4 7/8 pt.
5-speed manual	2.7	5 3/4 pt.
Automatic	6	6 3/8
Windshield washer tank	1.5	1 5/8
Power steering system		
1984	1	1 1/8
1985	0.9	1
Fuel tank		
All except MPG diesel	50	13 1/4 gal.
MPG diesel	40	10 5/8 gal.

Table 6 TUNE-UP SPECIFICATIONS (1984-ON)

Engine compression	
Standard	12.7 kg/cm² (181 psi)
Minimum	10 kg/cm² (142 psi)
Valve clearance (gasoline)	
Warm engine	0.28 mm (0.011 in.)
Cold engine	0.22 mm (0.009 in.)
Valve clearance (diesel)	
Intake	0.2-0.3 mm (0.008-0.012 in.)
Exhaust	0.4-0.5 mm (0.016-0.020 in.)
Spark plug type (NGK brand)*	
Standard type (U.S.)	BPR5ES-11
Hot type (U.S.)	BPR4ES-11
Cold type (U.S.)	BPR6ES-11
Standard type (Canada)	BPR5ES
Hot type (Canada)	BPR4ES
Cold type (Canada)	BPR6ES
Spark plug gap	
U.S. (except BP4ES)	1.0-1.1 mm (0.039-0.043 in.)
U.S. (BP4ES)	0.8-0.9 mm (0.031-0.035 in.)
Canada	0.8-0.9 mm (0.031-0.035 in.)
Firing order	1-3-4-2 counterclockwise
Ignition timing (at idle speed)**	
California	5 ±2° ATDC
49-state manual	15 ±2° BTDC
49-state automatic	8 ±2° BTDC
Canada	5 ±2° ATDC
Idle speed (rpm)	
California manual	750 ±50
California automatic	650 ±50 (in DRIVE)
49-state manual	800 ±100
49-state automatic	650 ±100 (in DRIVE)
Canada manual	750 ±50
Canada automatic	650 ±50 (in DRIVE)
Idle mixture (Canada only)	2 ±1 per cent

13

* Some 1984 models were equipped with BP4ES spark plugs after the car was initially sold. These are indicated by a sticker on the air cleaner. On these models, use only the plug specified on the sticker.
** On California and Canadian models, disconnect and plug the distributor vacuum line.

CHAPTER FOUR

ENGINE

Some engine tightening torques differ from 1983. These are listed in **Table 7**.

ENGINE REMOVAL/INSTALLATION

Procedures are the same as for 1983 models, described in Chapter Four of the basic book. Some engine mounting brackets differ from 1983 models. See **Figure 5**.

DISASSEMBLY CHECKLISTS

General Overhaul

Procedures are the same as for 1983 models. The 1985 models have a modified oil filter adapter (**Figure 6**). The jackshaft on 1984 and later models uses a triangular reinforcing plate in front of the shaft (**Figure 7**).

ROCKER ASSEMBLY

Service procedures are the same as for 1983 models, with one exception. The 1984 and later rocker assembly uses bolt stoppers to secure No. 1 and No. 5 mounting bolts. See **Figure 8**.

CYLINDER HEAD

Service procedures on 1984 and later models are the same as for 1983, except for the head bolt tightening procedure. During the following steps, always tighten in the order shown in **Figure 9** to prevent warping the head.
1. Tighten all bolts, in the order shown in **Figure 9**, to 29 N•m (22 ft.-lb.).
2. Tighten all bolts to 69 N•m (51 ft.-lb.).
3. Loosen all bolts completely.
4. Tighten all bolts to 29 N•m (22 ft.-lb.).
5. Tighten all bolts to 69-74 N•m (51-54 ft.-lb.).

VALVES AND VALVE SEATS

Service procedures are the same as for 1983 models. Install new valve stem seals with Nissan tools part No. KV10107501 and KV10109100 (**Figure 10**).

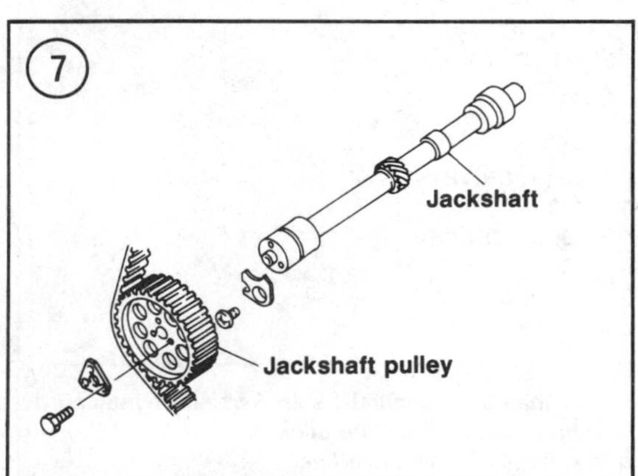

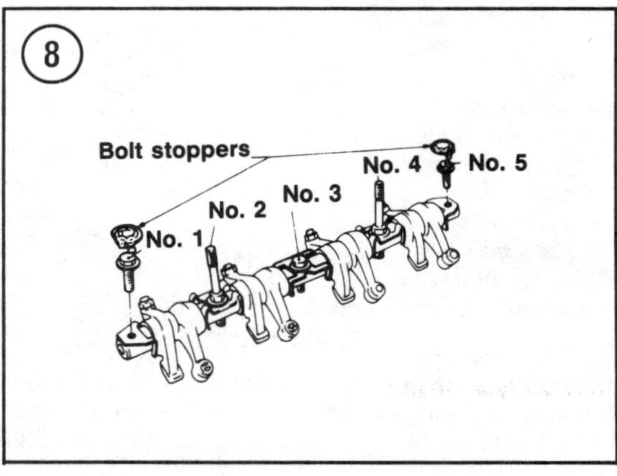

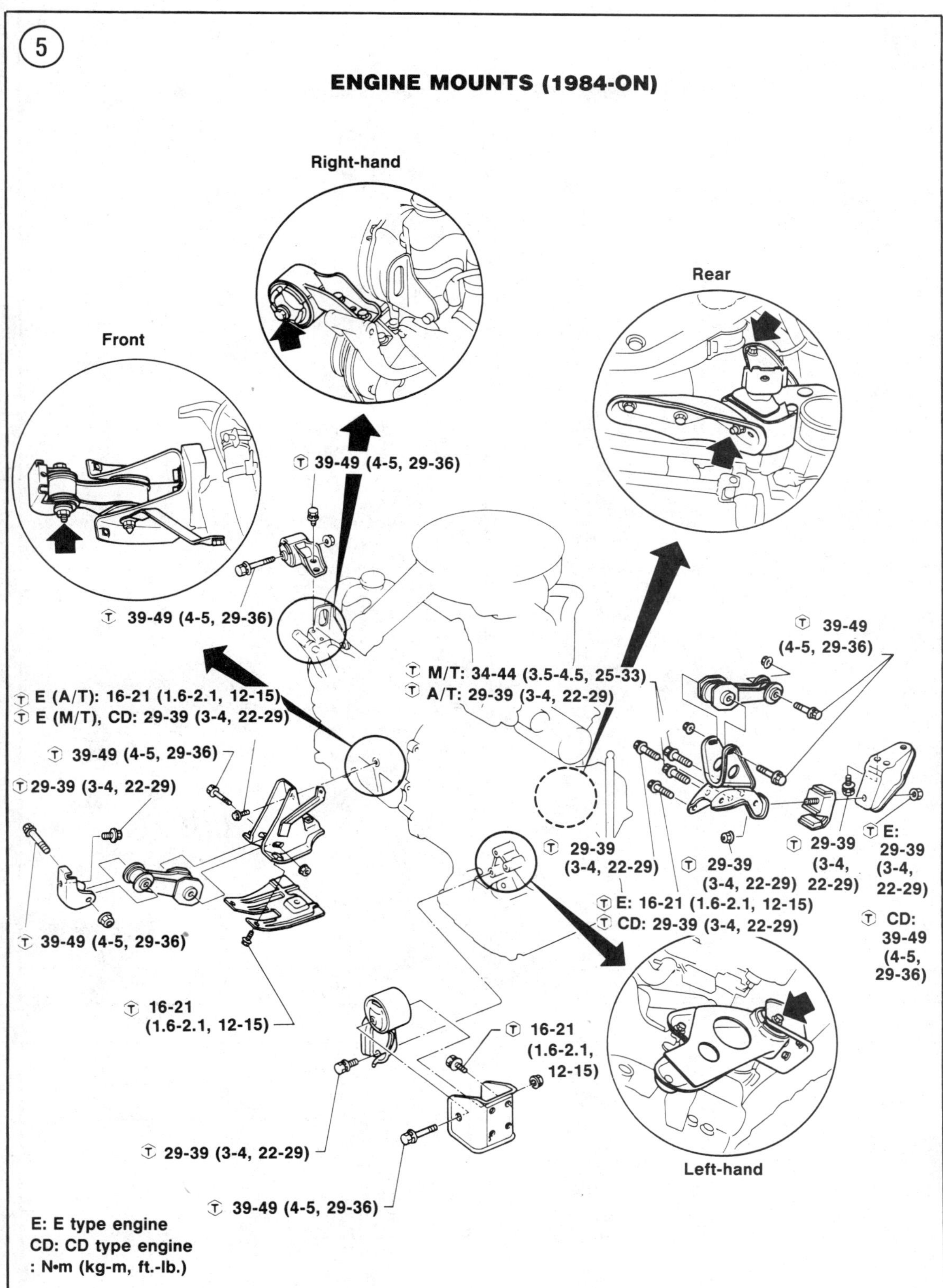
5
ENGINE MOUNTS (1984-ON)
Right-hand
Rear
Front
39-49 (4-5, 29-36)
39-49 (4-5, 29-36)
39-49 (4-5, 29-36)
E (A/T): 16-21 (1.6-2.1, 12-15)
E (M/T), CD: 29-39 (3-4, 22-29)
39-49 (4-5, 29-36)
29-39 (3-4, 22-29)
M/T: 34-44 (3.5-4.5, 25-33)
A/T: 29-39 (3-4, 22-29)
29-39 (3-4, 22-29)
29-39 (3-4, 22-29)
E: 16-21 (1.6-2.1, 12-15)
CD: 29-39 (3-4, 22-29)
E: 29-39 (3-4, 22-29)
CD: 39-49 (4-5, 29-36)
39-49 (4-5, 29-36)
16-21 (1.6-2.1, 12-15)
16-21 (1.6-2.1, 12-15)
29-39 (3-4, 22-29)
39-49 (4-5, 29-36)
Left-hand
E: E type engine
CD: CD type engine
: N•m (kg-m, ft.-lb.)

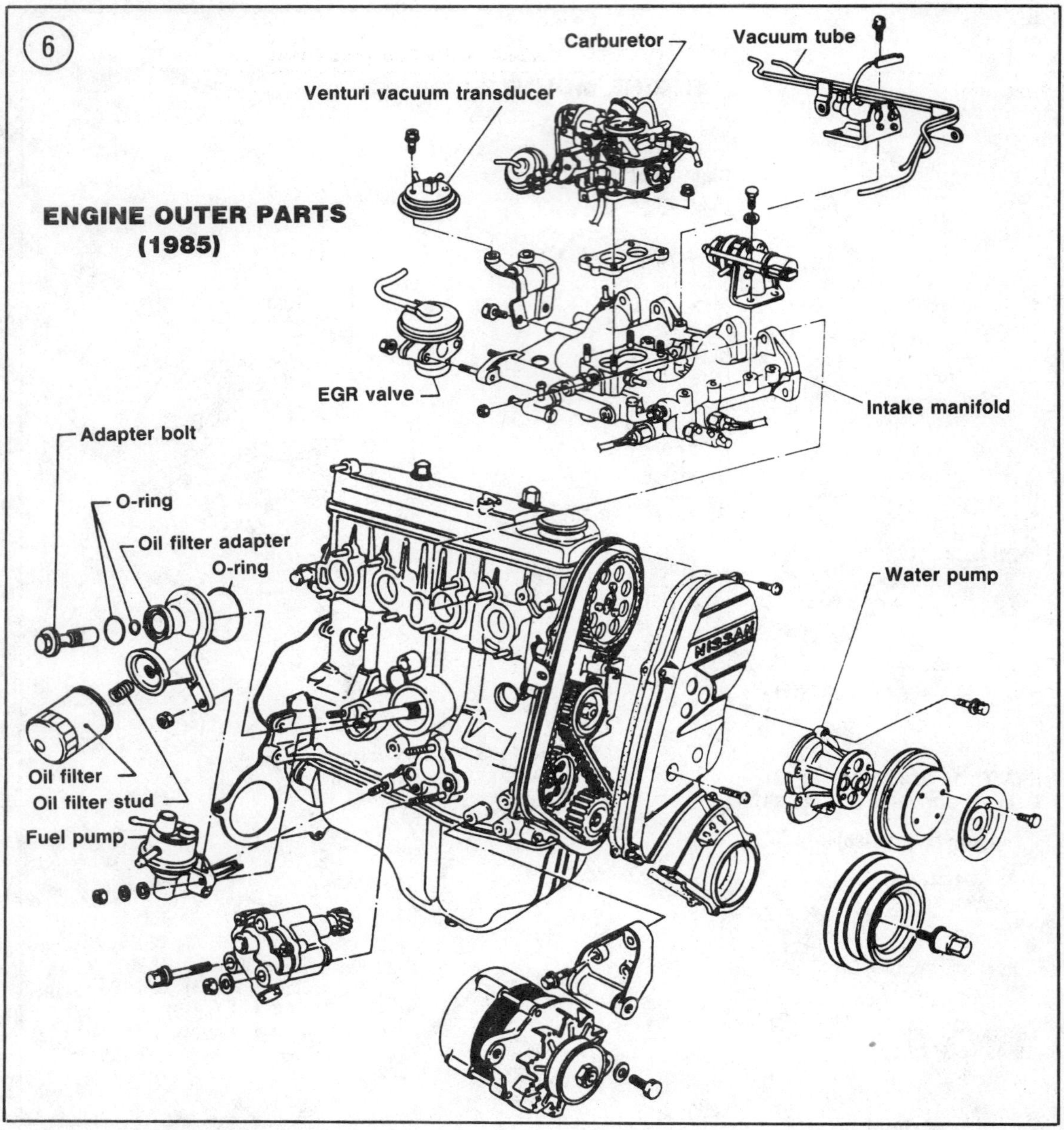

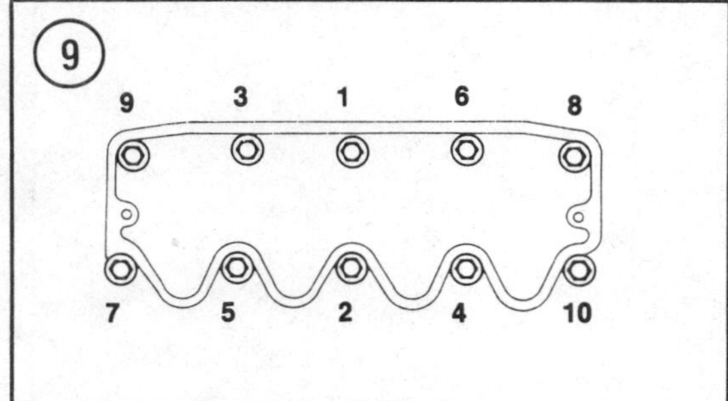
6

Venturi vacuum transducer
Carburetor
Vacuum tube

ENGINE OUTER PARTS
(1985)

EGR valve
Intake manifold

Adapter bolt
O-ring
Oil filter adapter
O-ring
Water pump
Oil filter
Oil filter stud
Fuel pump

NISSAN

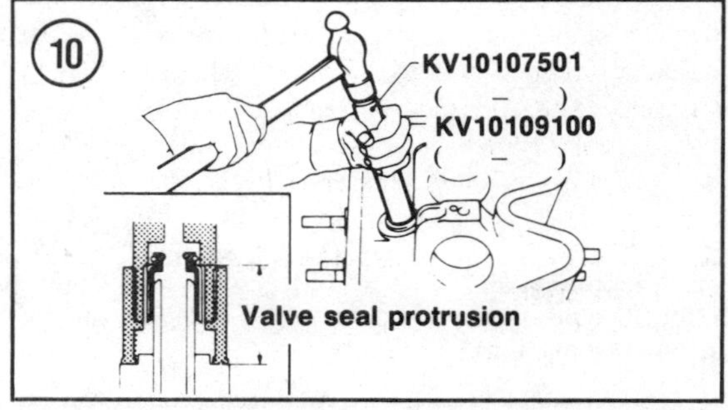
9

9   3   1   6   8

7   5   2   4   10

10

KV10107501
(—   )
KV10109100

Valve seal protrusion

Table 7 ENGINE TIGHTENING TORQUES (1984-ON)

Fastener	N·m	ft.-lb.
External parts		
Alternator bracket bolt		
1984	9-14	6.5-10
1985	8-10	6-7
Oil pump nuts		
1984	9-14	6.5-10
1985	8-10	6-7
Oil pump bolt		
1984	9-14	6.5-10
1985	8-10	6-7
Thermostat housing bolts	4-6	2.9-4.3
Internal parts		
Camshaft pulley bolts	9-12	6.5-8.7
Cylinder head bolts	See text	
Jackshaft pulley bolts	9-12	6.5-9.0
Oil pan bolts and nuts	4-6	2.9-4.3
Oil pan drain plug (1985)	30-40	22-30
Rocker shaft bolts	18-21	13-15

CHAPTER FIVE

FUEL, EXHAUST AND EMISSION CONTROL SYSTEMS

Some carburetor specifications differ from 1983 models. These are listed in **Table 8**.

CARBURETOR

The carburetor on 1984 and later California models is the same as the carburetor on 1983 California non-MPG models, shown in Chapter Five of the basic book.

The carburetor on 1984 and later Canadian models is the same as the carburetor on 1983 non-California non-MPG models, shown in Chapter Five of the basic book.

The carburetor on 1984 and later 49-state models has a cold enrichment system which replaces the automatic choke. See **Figure 11**. Service procedures are basically the same as for 1983 carburetors.

EXHAUST SYSTEM

The exhaust systems on 1984 and later Canadian and diesel cars are the same as for 1983 models. To remove and install exhaust system parts on 1984 and later U.S. models, refer to **Figure 12** (1984) or **Figure 13** (1985).

EMISSION CONTROLS

Vacuum Lines

Emission control vacuum lines for 1984 and later California models are the same as for 1983 California models. For 1984 and later non-California models, refer to the following illustrations:

   a. 1984 49-state—**Figure 14**.
   b. 1985 49-state—**Figure 15**.
   c. 1984 Canada—**Figure 16**.
   d. 1985 Canada—**Figure 17**.

ELECTRONICALLY CONTROLLED CARBURETOR

This system, used on 1984 and later U.S. models, is similar to the system used on 1983

13

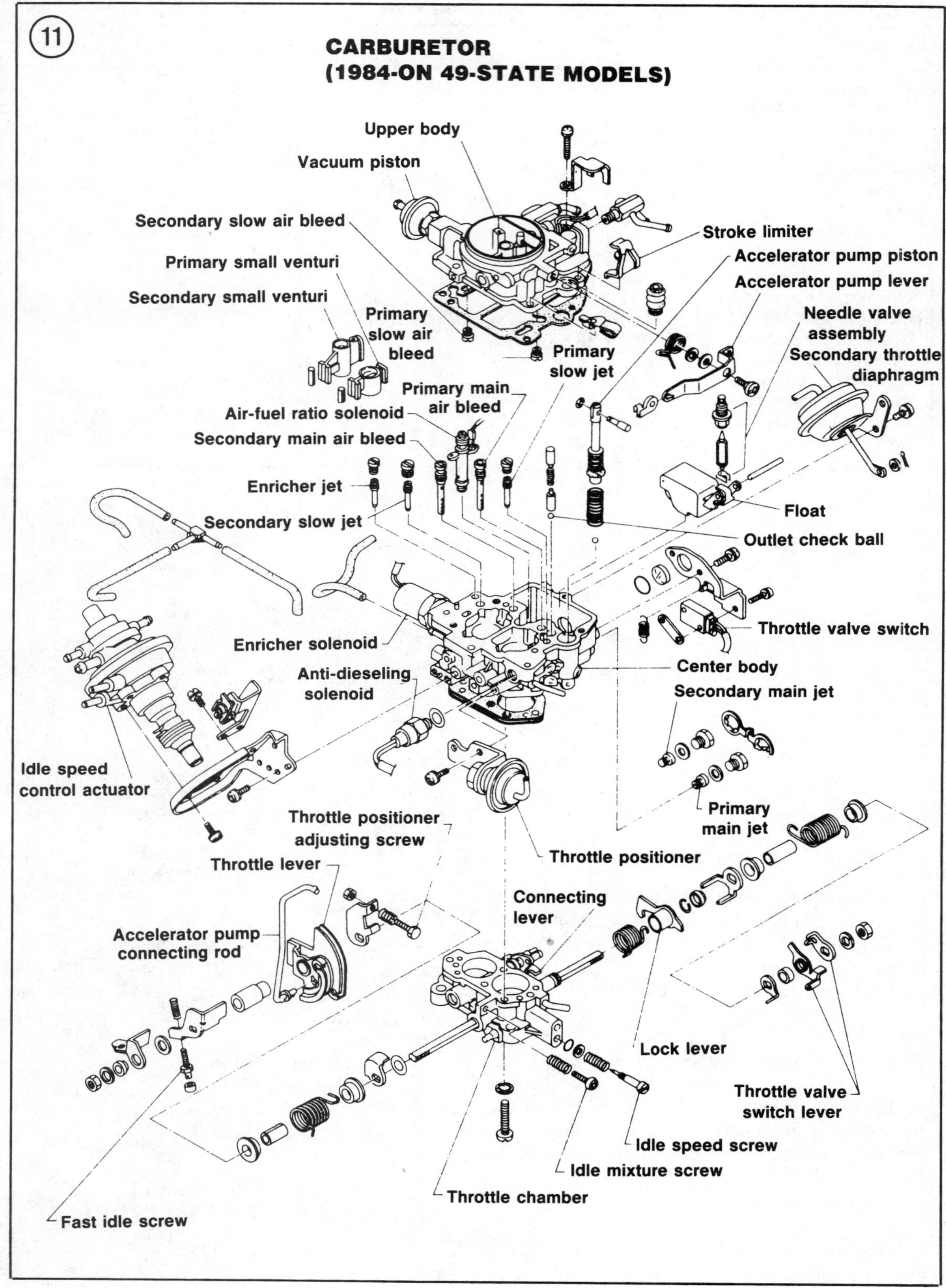
11
CARBURETOR
(1984-ON 49-STATE MODELS)
Upper body
Vacuum piston
Secondary slow air bleed
Primary small venturi
Secondary small venturi
Primary slow air bleed
Air-fuel ratio solenoid
Secondary main air bleed
Primary main air bleed
Primary slow jet
Stroke limiter
Accelerator pump piston
Accelerator pump lever
Needle valve assembly
Secondary throttle diaphragm
Enricher jet
Secondary slow jet
Float
Outlet check ball
Enricher solenoid
Anti-dieseling solenoid
Throttle valve switch
Center body
Secondary main jet
Idle speed control actuator
Primary main jet
Throttle positioner adjusting screw
Throttle positioner
Throttle lever
Connecting lever
Accelerator pump connecting rod
Lock lever
Throttle valve switch lever
Idle speed screw
Idle mixture screw
Throttle chamber
Fast idle screw

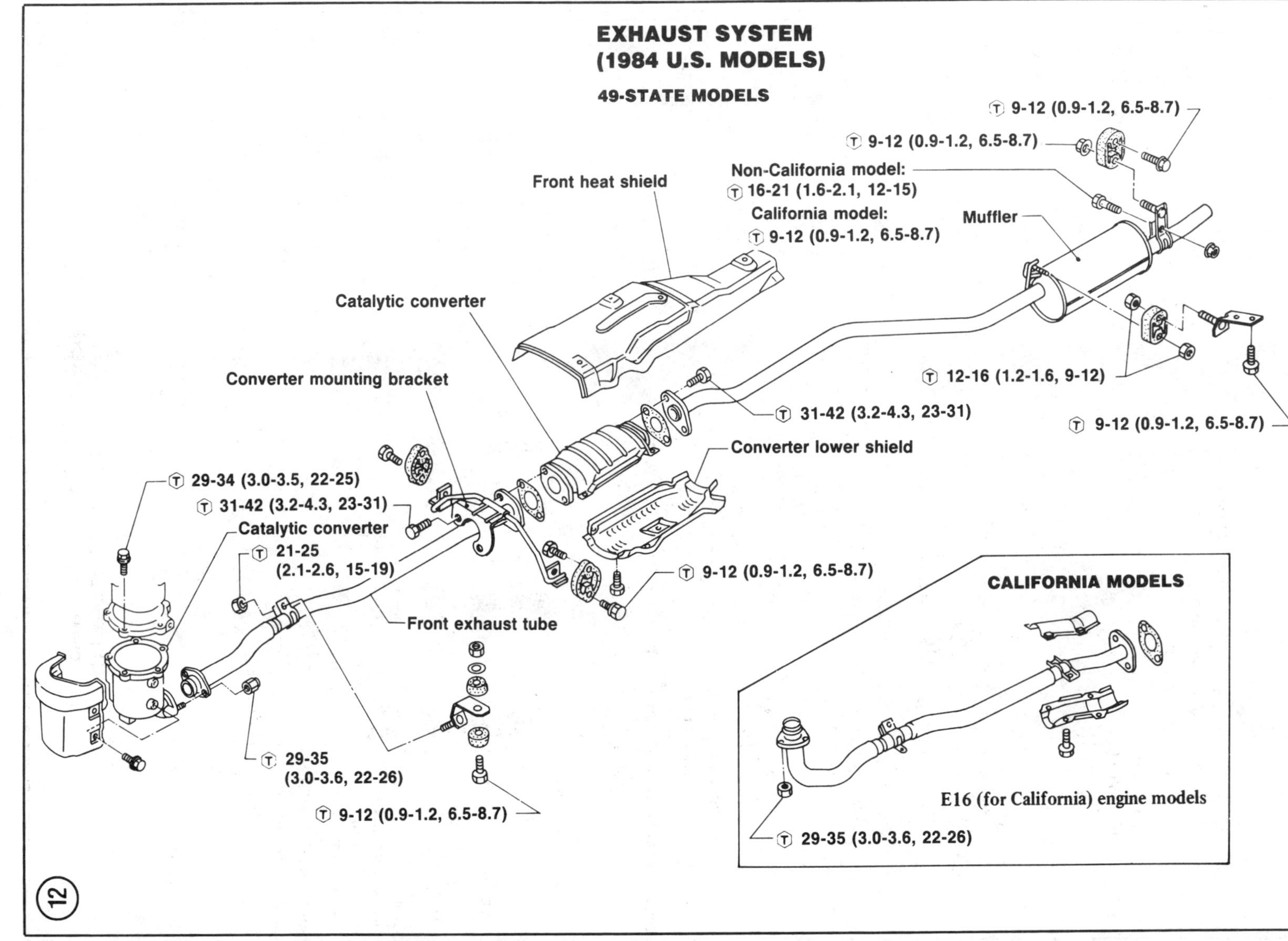
13
EXHAUST SYSTEM
(1984 U.S. MODELS)
49-STATE MODELS
T 9-12 (0.9-1.2, 6.5-8.7)
T 9-12 (0.9-1.2, 6.5-8.7)
Front heat shield
Non-California model:
T 16-21 (1.6-2.1, 12-15)
California model:
T 9-12 (0.9-1.2, 6.5-8.7)
Muffler
Catalytic converter
Converter mounting bracket
T 12-16 (1.2-1.6, 9-12)
T 31-42 (3.2-4.3, 23-31)
Converter lower shield
T 9-12 (0.9-1.2, 6.5-8.7)
T 29-34 (3.0-3.5, 22-25)
T 31-42 (3.2-4.3, 23-31)
Catalytic converter
T 21-25 (2.1-2.6, 15-19)
T 9-12 (0.9-1.2, 6.5-8.7)
Front exhaust tube
CALIFORNIA MODELS
T 29-35 (3.0-3.6, 22-26)
T 9-12 (0.9-1.2, 6.5-8.7)
E16 (for California) engine models
T 29-35 (3.0-3.6, 22-26)
12

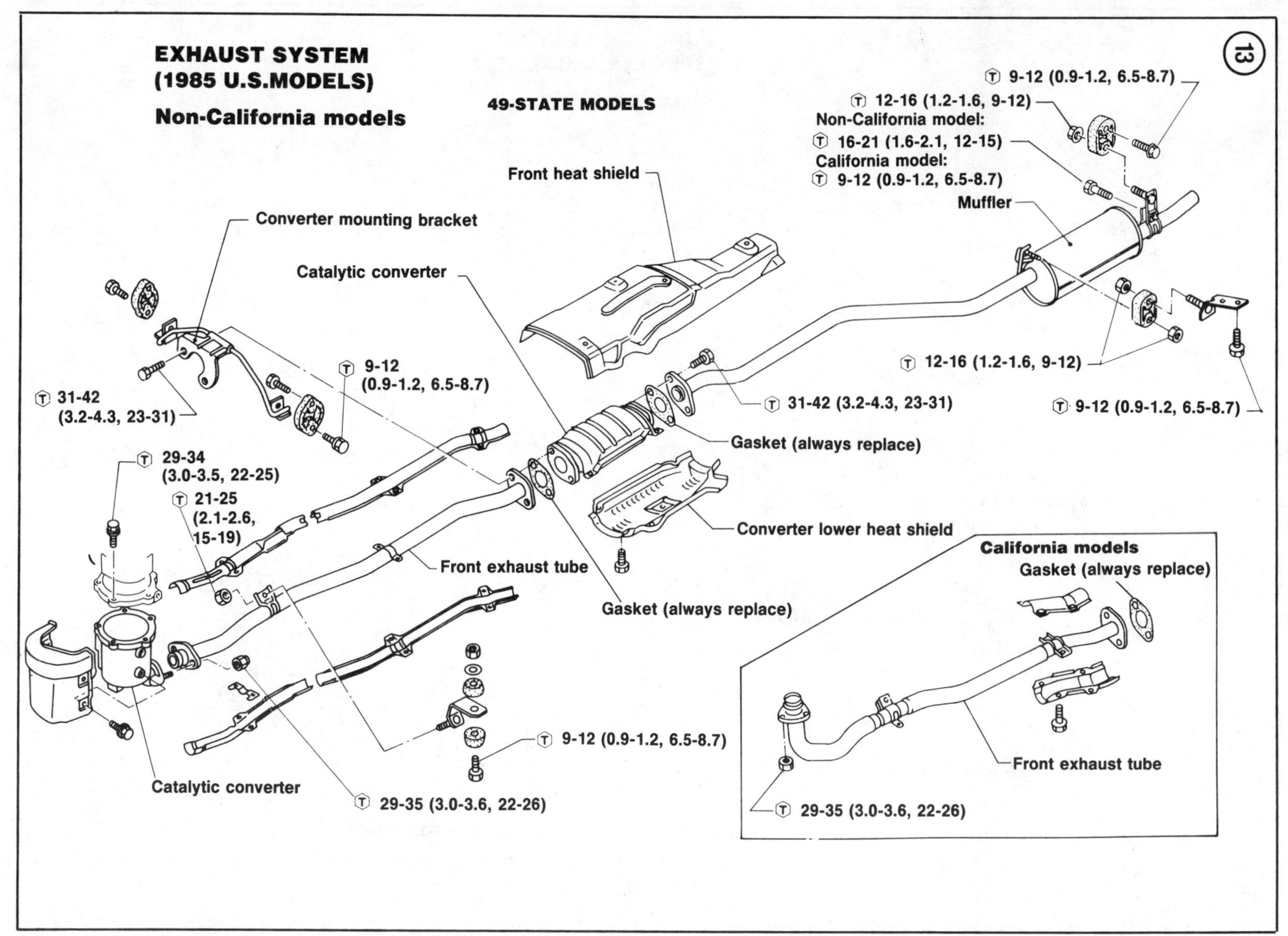
13
EXHAUST SYSTEM
(1985 U.S.MODELS)
Non-California models
49-STATE MODELS
Front heat shield
9-12 (0.9-1.2, 6.5-8.7)
12-16 (1.2-1.6, 9-12)
Non-California model:
16-21 (1.6-2.1, 12-15)
California model:
9-12 (0.9-1.2, 6.5-8.7)
Muffler
Converter mounting bracket
Catalytic converter
9-12 (0.9-1.2, 6.5-8.7)
31-42 (3.2-4.3, 23-31)
31-42 (3.2-4.3, 23-31)
12-16 (1.2-1.6, 9-12)
9-12 (0.9-1.2, 6.5-8.7)
Gasket (always replace)
29-34 (3.0-3.5, 22-25)
21-25 (2.1-2.6, 15-19)
Converter lower heat shield
Front exhaust tube
Gasket (always replace)
California models
Gasket (always replace)
9-12 (0.9-1.2, 6.5-8.7)
Front exhaust tube
Catalytic converter
29-35 (3.0-3.6, 22-26)
29-35 (3.0-3.6, 22-26)

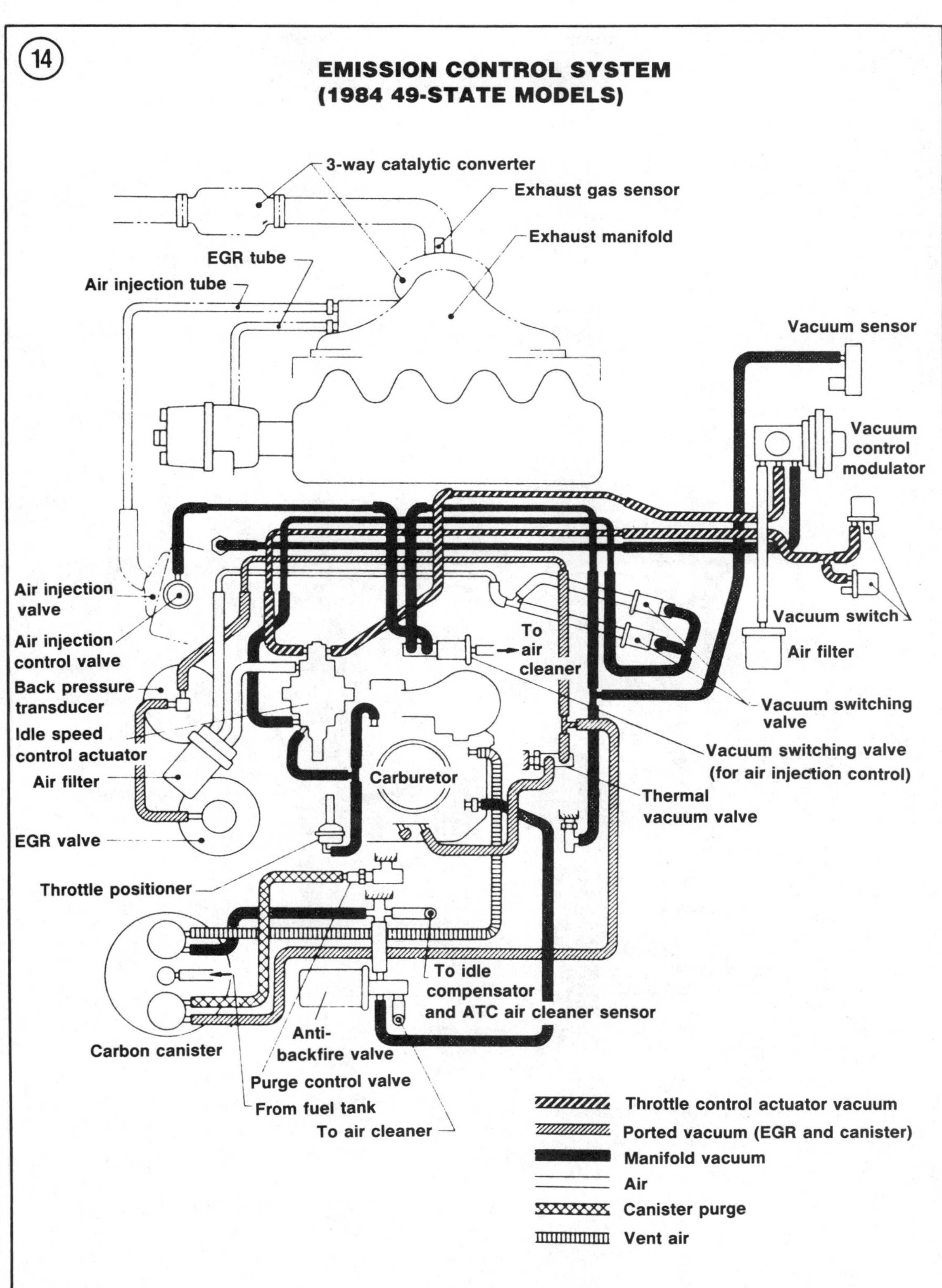
14
EMISSION CONTROL SYSTEM
(1984 49-STATE MODELS)
3-way catalytic converter
Exhaust gas sensor
Exhaust manifold
EGR tube
Air injection tube
Vacuum sensor
Vacuum control modulator
Air injection valve
Air injection control valve
Back pressure transducer
Idle speed control actuator
Air filter
EGR valve
Throttle positioner
To air cleaner
Carburetor
Vacuum switch
Air filter
Vacuum switching valve
Vacuum switching valve (for air injection control)
Thermal vacuum valve
To idle compensator and ATC air cleaner sensor
Carbon canister
Anti-backfire valve
Purge control valve
From fuel tank
To air cleaner
Throttle control actuator vacuum
Ported vacuum (EGR and canister)
Manifold vacuum
Air
Canister purge
Vent air

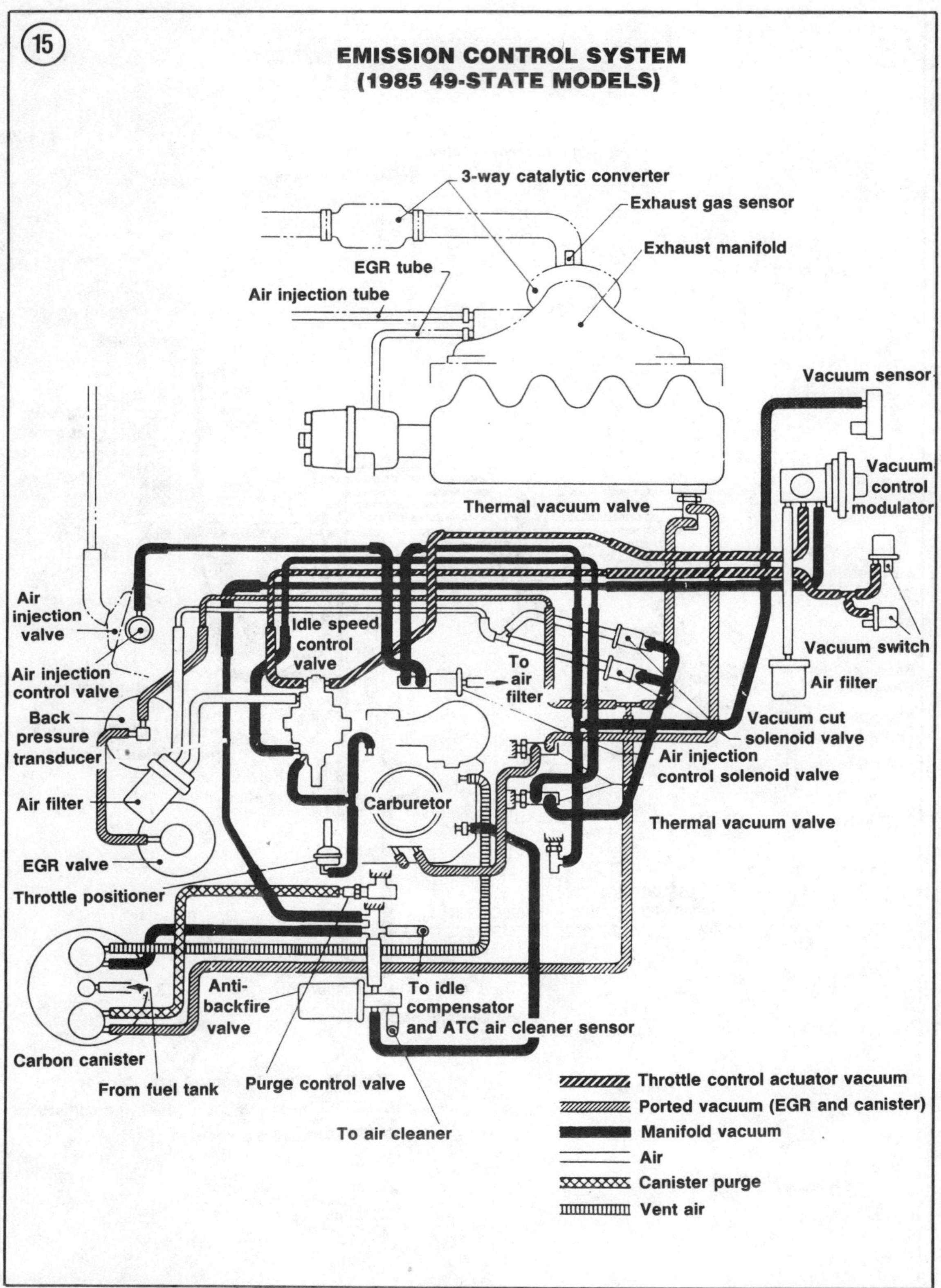
15
EMISSION CONTROL SYSTEM
(1985 49-STATE MODELS)
3-way catalytic converter
Exhaust gas sensor
Exhaust manifold
EGR tube
Air injection tube
Vacuum sensor
Vacuum control modulator
Thermal vacuum valve
Air injection valve
Idle speed control valve
To air filter
Vacuum switch
Air filter
Air injection control valve
Back pressure transducer
Vacuum cut solenoid valve
Air injection control solenoid valve
Air filter
Carburetor
Thermal vacuum valve
EGR valve
Throttle positioner
Anti-backfire valve
To idle compensator and ATC air cleaner sensor
Carbon canister
From fuel tank
Purge control valve
To air cleaner
Throttle control actuator vacuum
Ported vacuum (EGR and canister)
Manifold vacuum
Air
Canister purge
Vent air

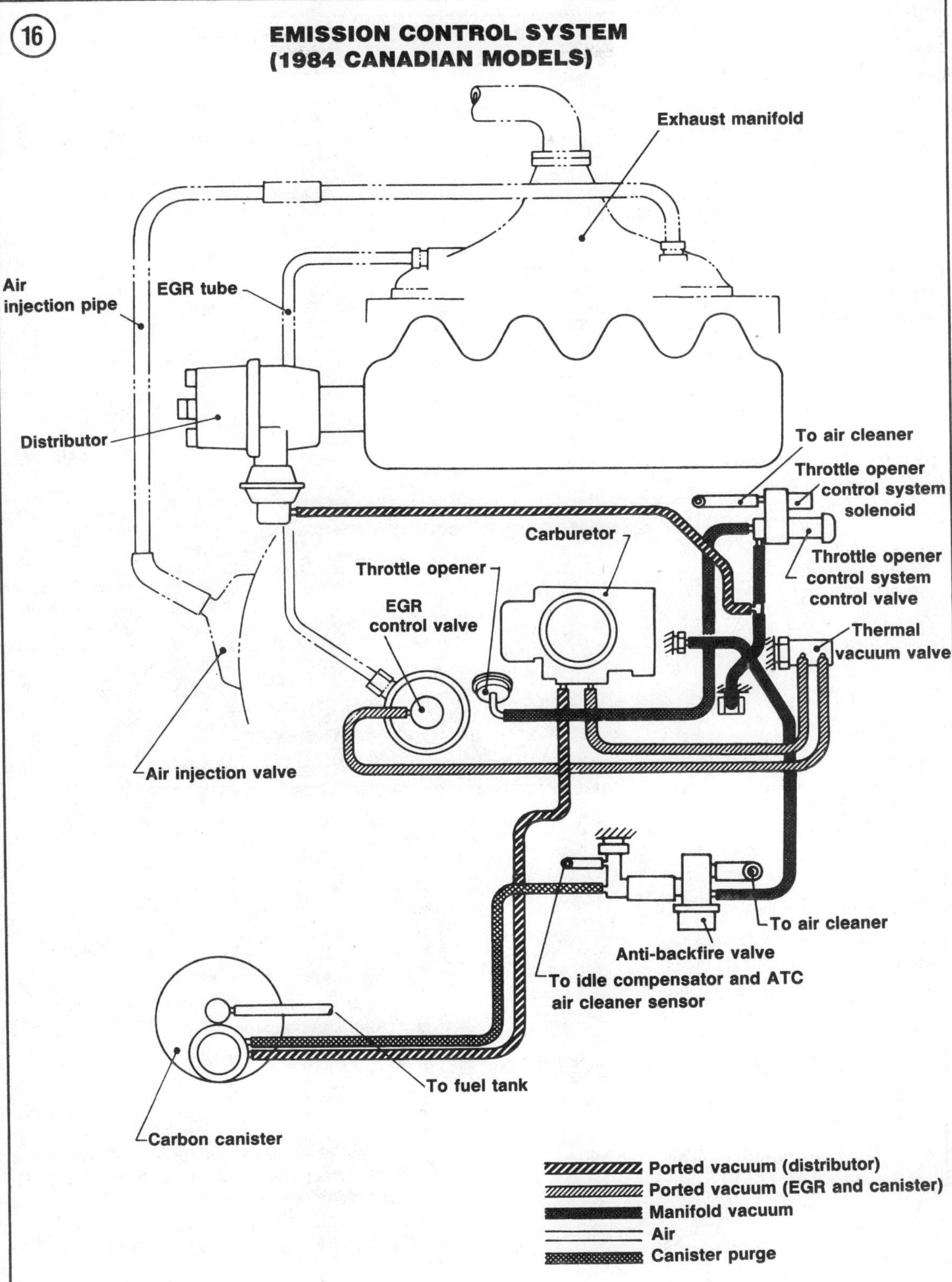
16
EMISSION CONTROL SYSTEM
(1984 CANADIAN MODELS)
Exhaust manifold
Air injection pipe
EGR tube
Distributor
To air cleaner
Throttle opener control system solenoid
Carburetor
Throttle opener
EGR control valve
Throttle opener control system control valve
Thermal vacuum valve
Air injection valve
To air cleaner
Anti-backfire valve
To idle compensator and ATC air cleaner sensor
To fuel tank
Carbon canister
Ported vacuum (distributor)
Ported vacuum (EGR and canister)
Manifold vacuum
Air
Canister purge
13

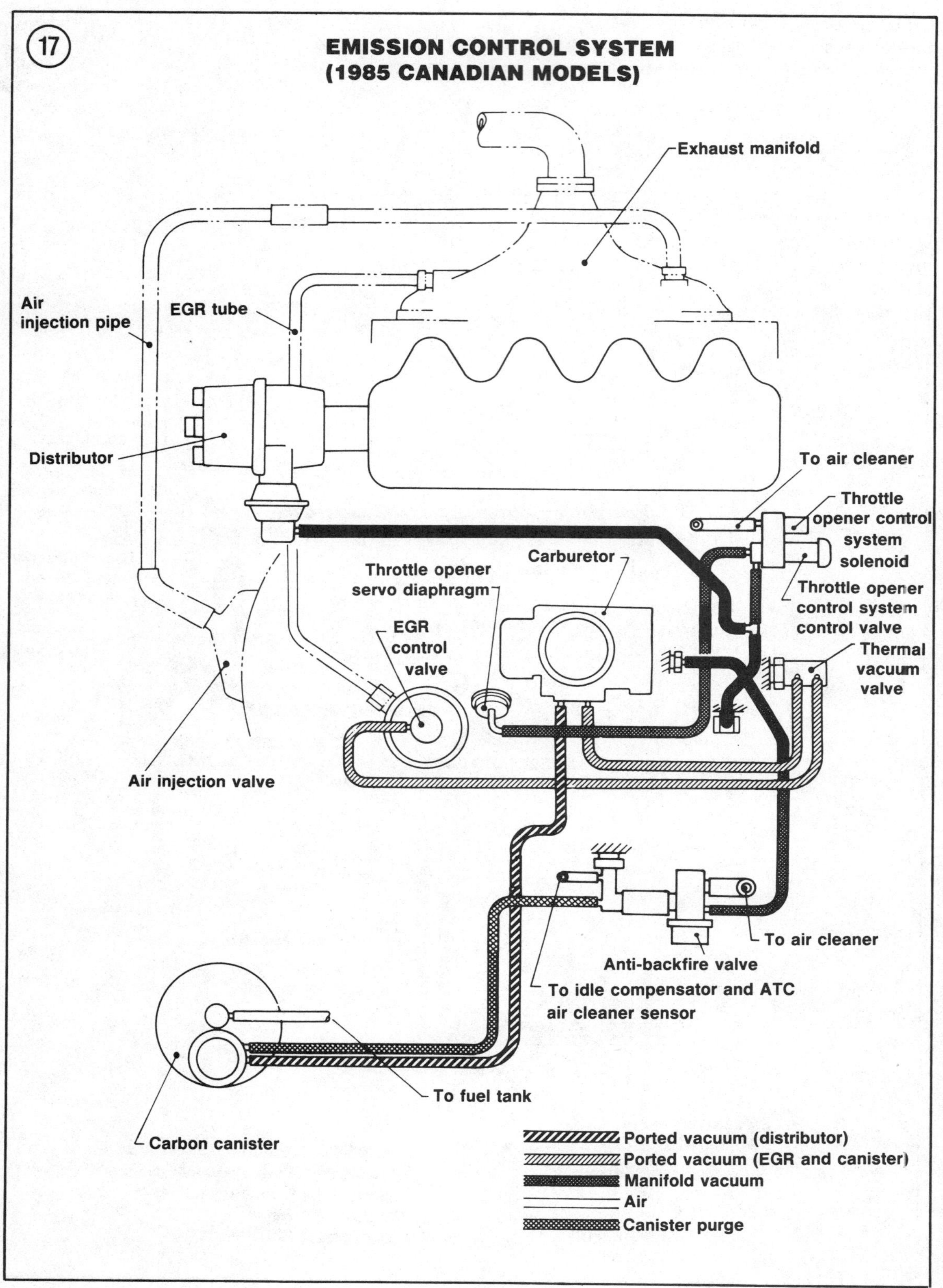

17
EMISSION CONTROL SYSTEM
(1985 CANADIAN MODELS)
Exhaust manifold
Air injection pipe
EGR tube
Distributor
To air cleaner
Throttle opener control system solenoid
Throttle opener control system control valve
Throttle opener servo diaphragm
Carburetor
Thermal vacuum valve
EGR control valve
Air injection valve
To air cleaner
Anti-backfire valve
To idle compensator and ATC air cleaner sensor
To fuel tank
Carbon canister
Ported vacuum (distributor)
Ported vacuum (EGR and canister)
Manifold vacuum
Air
Canister purge

California cars. As with the 1983 version, testing and diagnosis should be done by a dealer or mechanic familiar with Nissan emission controls.

AIR INJECTION SYSTEM

This system, used on 1984 and 1985 non-California models, is basically the same as the air induction system used on earlier models. The 49-state version is part of the electronically controlled carburetor system. Inspection on these models should be done by a dealer or mechanic familiar with Nissan emission controls. The Canadian version can be inspected using the procedure under *Air Induction System* Chapter Five of the basic book.

EXHAUST GAS RECIRCULATION SYSTEM

The EGR system on 1984 and later California models is the same as the 1983 California system, described in Chapter Five of the basic book. The 1984 and later Canadian EGR system is the same as the 1983 Canadian EGR system.

Construction details of the EGR systems used on 1984 and later 49-state models differ from 1983. See **Figure 18** and **Figure 19**. Test procedures for 1984 and later 49-state models are the same as for 1983.

EVAPORATIVE EMISSION CONTROL SYSTEM

The evaporative emission control system for 1984 and later California models is the same as the 1983 California system. The system on 1984 and later Canadian models is the same as for 1983 Canadian models. The 1984 and later 49-state systems differ in construction details, but inspection procedures are the same as for 1983 49-state systems. See **Figure 20** (1984) or **Figure 21** (1985).

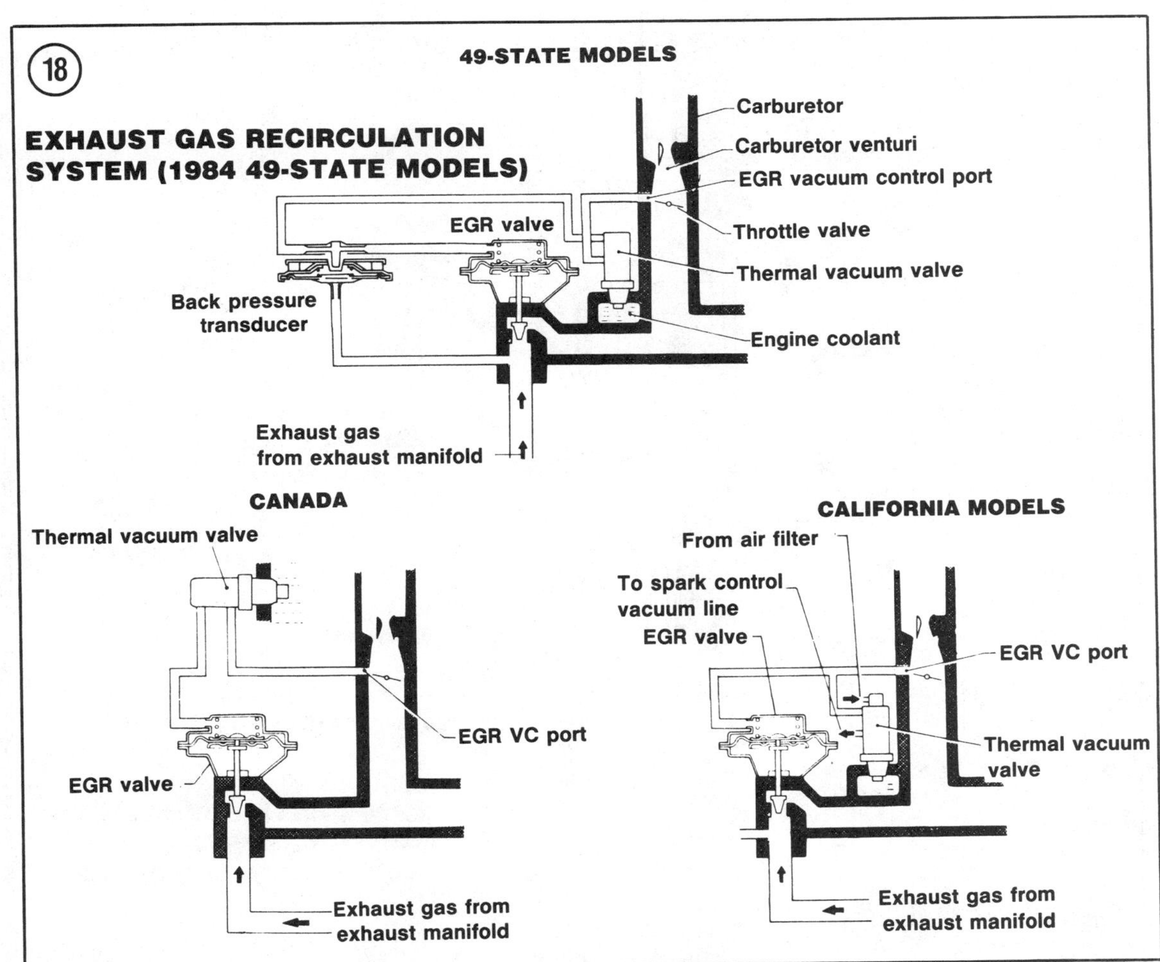

13

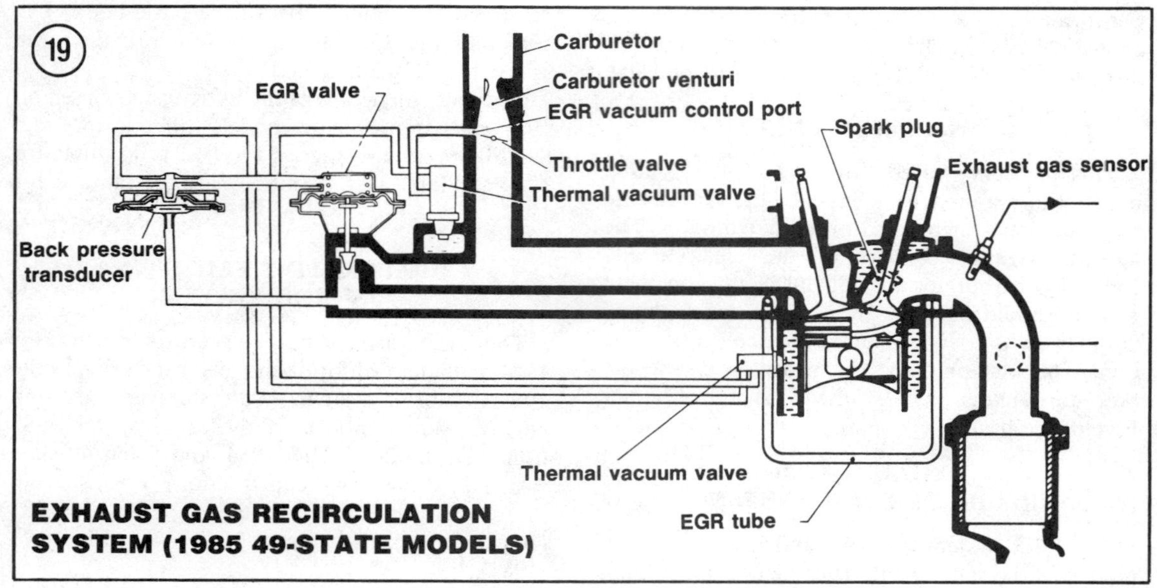
19
Carburetor
Carburetor venturi
EGR valve
EGR vacuum control port
Spark plug
Throttle valve
Exhaust gas sensor
Thermal vacuum valve
Back pressure transducer
Thermal vacuum valve
EGR tube
EXHAUST GAS RECIRCULATION SYSTEM (1985 49-STATE MODELS)

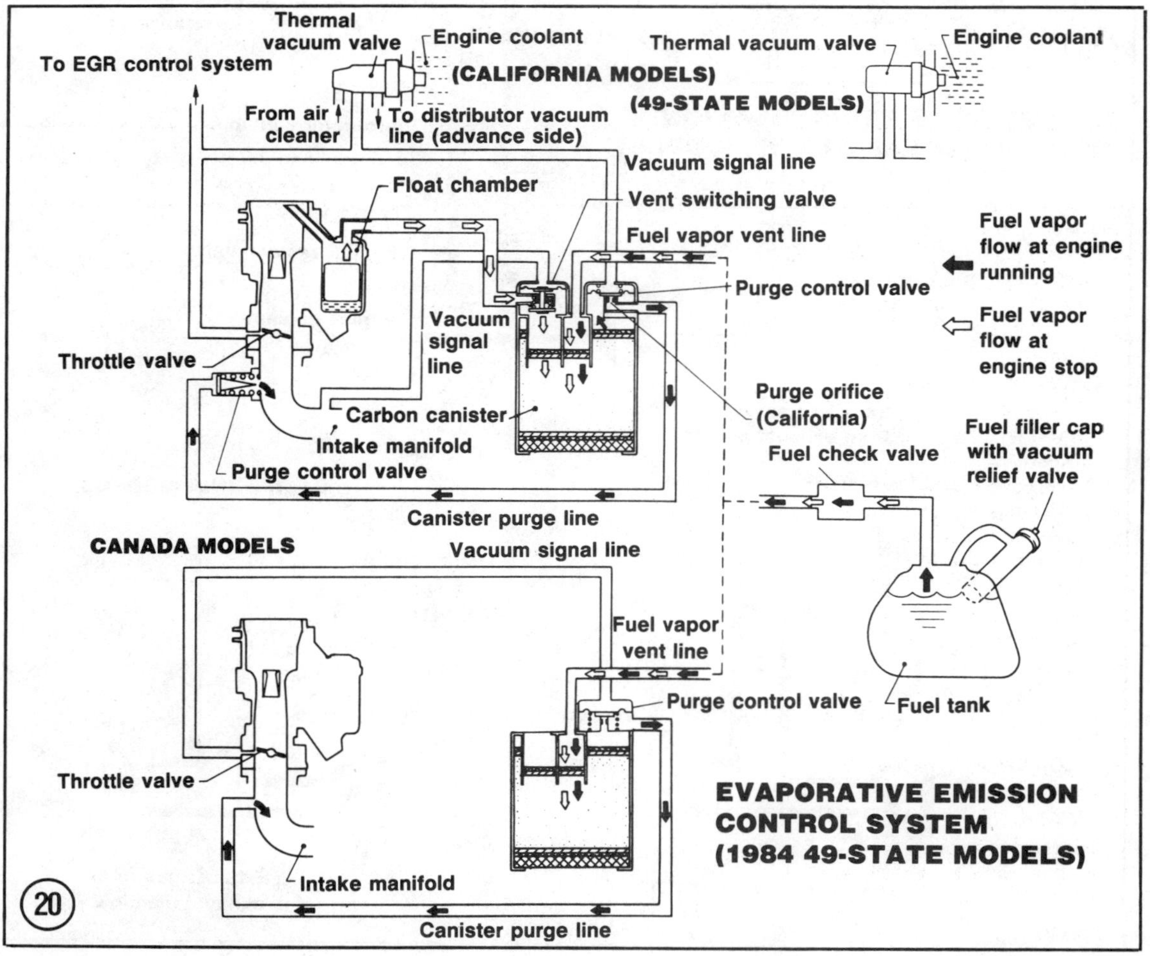

Thermal vacuum valve
Engine coolant
To EGR control system
(CALIFORNIA MODELS)
Thermal vacuum valve
Engine coolant
(49-STATE MODELS)
From air cleaner
To distributor vacuum line (advance side)
Vacuum signal line
Float chamber
Vent switching valve
Fuel vapor vent line
Fuel vapor flow at engine running
Purge control valve
Fuel vapor flow at engine stop
Vacuum signal line
Throttle valve
Purge orifice (California)
Carbon canister
Fuel filler cap with vacuum relief valve
Intake manifold
Fuel check valve
Purge control valve
Canister purge line
CANADA MODELS
Vacuum signal line
Fuel vapor vent line
Purge control valve
Fuel tank
Throttle valve
EVAPORATIVE EMISSION CONTROL SYSTEM (1984 49-STATE MODELS)
Intake manifold
20
Canister purge line

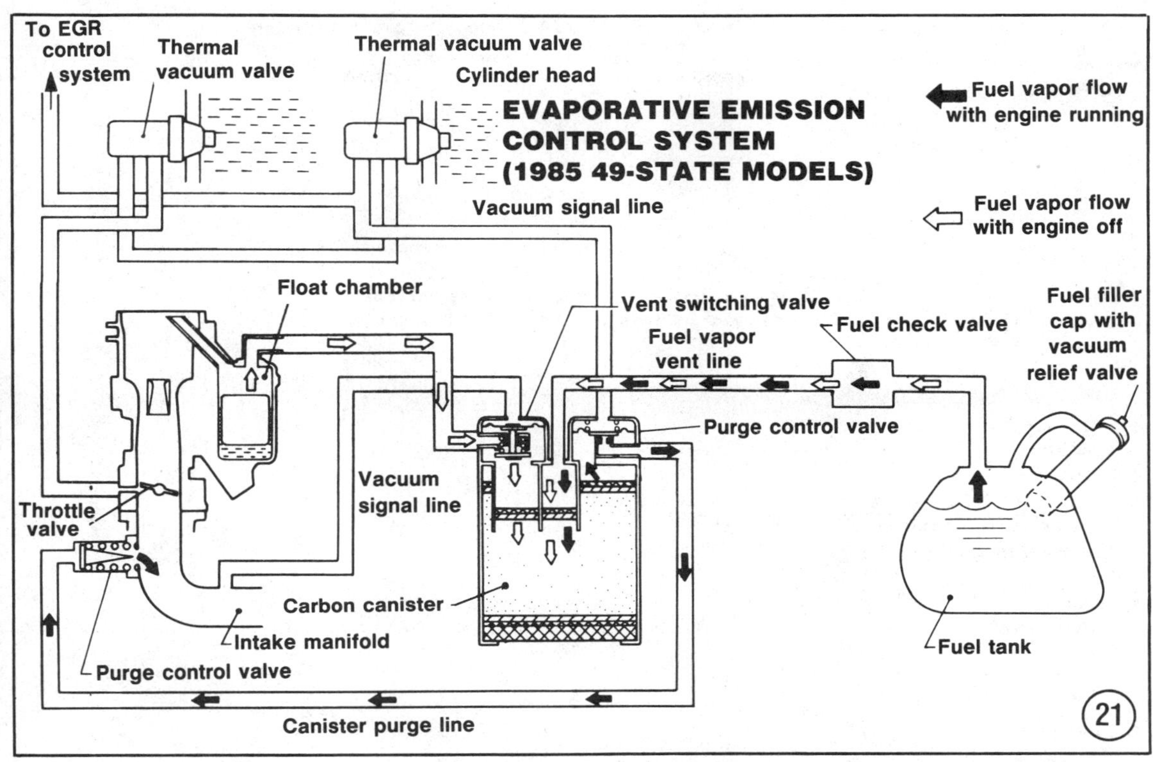

Table 8 FUEL SYSTEM SPECIFICATIONS (1984-ON)

Jets and air bleeds	
Primary main jet	
California	91
49-state manual	90
49-state automatic	82
Canada	100
Secondary main jet	
California	130
49-state	105
Canada	135
Primary main air bleed	
California	110
49-state manual	80
49-state automatic	110
Canada	110
Secondary main air bleed	
California	60
49-state	70
Canada	60
Primary slow jet	
California	43
49-state manual	43
49-state automatic	45
Canada	43
Secondary slow jet (all)	65
Primary slow air bleed	
California	170

(continued)

13

Table 8 CARBURETOR SPECIFICATIONS (1984-ON) (continued)

Primary slow air bleed (cont.)	
49-state manual	150
49-state automatic	160
Canada	180
Secondary slow air bleed	
California	80
49-states	90
Canada	100
Power jet (Canada only)	35
Solenoid controlled slow air bleed	
California	220
49-state	250
Canada	—
Solenoid controlled fuel orifice	
California	90
49-state	100
Canada	—
Carburetor CO percentage	
Measurement standard	1-5%
Adjustment standard	3.0 ±1%
Float adjustment	
Dimension "H"	12 mm (0.47 in.)
Dimension "h"	1.3-1.7 mm (0.051-0.067 in.)
Fast idle speed	
California manual	2,600-3,400
California automatic	2,900-3,700
Canada manual	1,900-2,700
Canada automatic	2,400-3,200
Fuel pump pressure	19.6-26.5 kPa (2.8-3.8 psi)
Fuel pump capacity (30 seconds)	650 cc (22 fl. oz.) or more
Dashpot adjusting speed	
California (automatic only)	1,900-2,100 rpm
Canada manual	2,250-2,450 rpm
Canada automatic	1,900-2,100 rpm

CHAPTER SIX

COOLING HEATING, AND AIR CONDITIONING SYSTEMS

RADIATOR AND FAN

Radiator Inspection

This procedure is the same as for 1983 models, described in Chapter Six of the basic book. The temperature switch on gasoline-engine radiators differs slightly. See **Figure 22**.

Fan Motor Test

The procedure on 1984 and later models is the same as for 1983. The fan motor circuit differs slightly. See **Figure 23**.

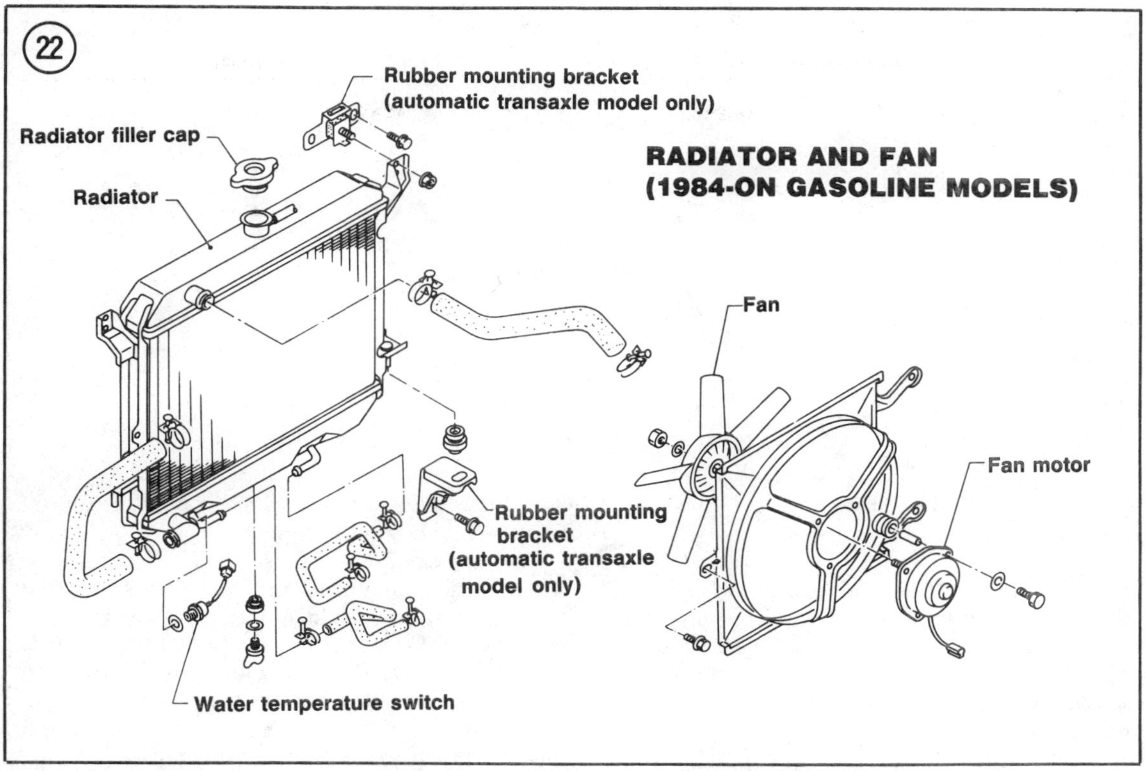
22
RADIATOR AND FAN
(1984-ON GASOLINE MODELS)
Rubber mounting bracket
(automatic transaxle model only)
Radiator filler cap
Radiator
Fan
Fan motor
Rubber mounting
bracket
(automatic transaxle
model only)
Water temperature switch

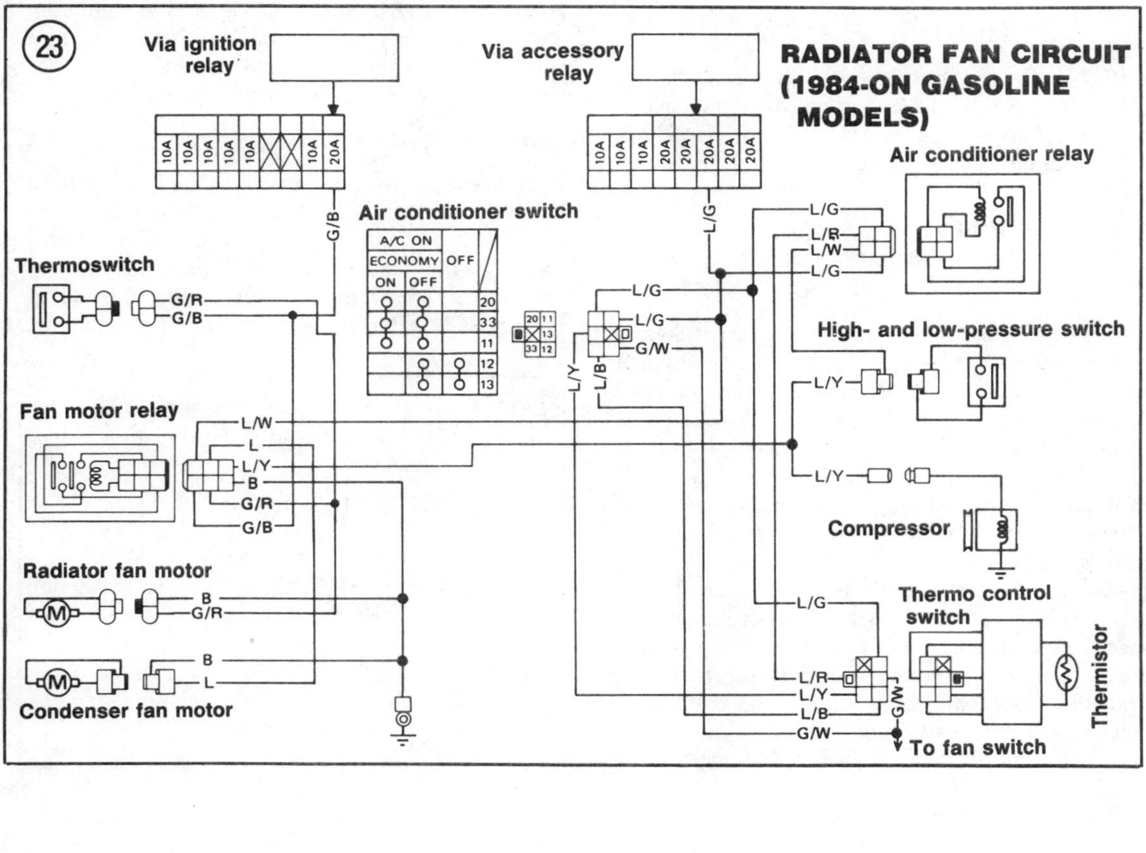
23
RADIATOR FAN CIRCUIT
(1984-ON GASOLINE
MODELS)
Via ignition
relay
Via accessory
relay
10A
20A
Air conditioner switch
A/C ON
ECONOMY
OFF
ON
OFF
Air conditioner relay
Thermoswitch
G/R
G/B
L/G
L/R
L/W
L/Y
L/B
G/W
High- and low-pressure switch
Fan motor relay
L
B
Compressor
Radiator fan motor
Thermo control
switch
Thermistor
Condenser fan motor
To fan switch

CHAPTER SEVEN

ELECTRICAL SYSTEM

BATTERY

Testing

Battery testing on 1984 and later models is done with a hydrometer in the same manner as unsealed batteries, described in Chapter Seven of the basic book. The hydrometer is inserted through the test plug hole (**Figure 24**).

> *CAUTION*
> *Never add water or electrolyte through the test plug hole.*

LIGHTING SYSTEM

1984 bulb specifications are the same as for 1983. For 1985, the following bulbs have changed:
  a. Headlamps (65/45 watts, trade number 9004).
  b. Clearance lamps (5 watts, no trade number).

IGNITION SYSTEM (CRANKSHAFT ANGLE SENSOR TYPE)

This type of ignition system is used on 1984 and later 49-state models. The crankshaft angle sensor serves 2 purposes; it detects engine rpm and determines the position of each piston. These signals are used by the engine control unit to control ignition timing and several fuel and emission system functions. The crankshaft angle sensor is built into the distributor. See **Figure 25** and **Figure 26**.

The signal rotor plate in the distributor has 360 slits, spaced 1 degree apart. It also has 4 slits spaced 90° apart. The 4 slits indicate piston position. (A piston comes to top dead center each time the crankshaft rotates 180°. The distributor turns at half the speed of the crankshaft, so the slits inside the distributor are spaced 90° apart.) The 360 slits provide a signal which is used to control idle speed and ignition timing.

The crankshaft angle sensor has 2 diodes and a wave-forming circuit. As each slit passes between the light emitting diode and photo diode, the slit cuts the light beam from the LED to the photo diode. See **Figure 27** and **Figure 28**. This produces alternating current, which is converted to on-off pulses by the wave-forming circuit. The on-off pulses are sent to the control unit (**Figure 25**).

This ignition system is extremely complicated. Except for distributor removal and installation, system service requires special equipment and skills. All testing and adjustment procedures should be done by a Nissan dealer.

Distributor Removal/Installation

This is basically the same as for the 1983 ignition system described in this Chapter Seven of the basic book. If the engine is turned with the distributor out, align the match marks on camshaft pulley and front cover. See **Figure 29**. This places No. 1 piston at top dead center on its compression stroke.

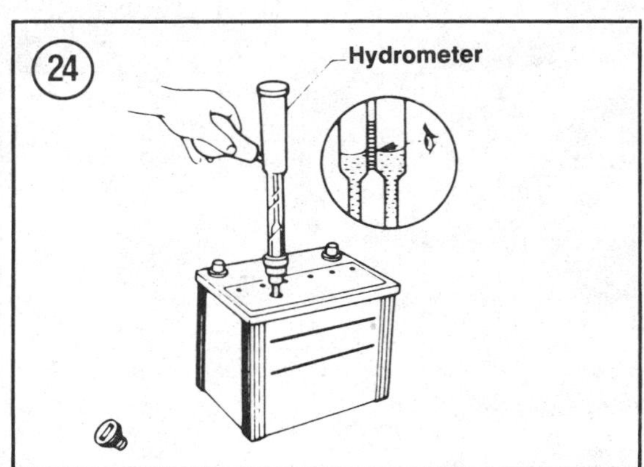

25
IGNITION SYSTEM
(1984-ON 49-STATE MODELS)
Ignition key
Battery
B S IG
To starter
Secondary winding
Ignition coil
Primary winding
Power transistor
Vacuum sensor
Cap
Check angle 1 degree signal
Rotor head
Crank angle 180 degree signal
Electronic control unit
Distributor (crank angle sensor built into distributor)
Water temperature sensor
1
3
4
2
Spark plug

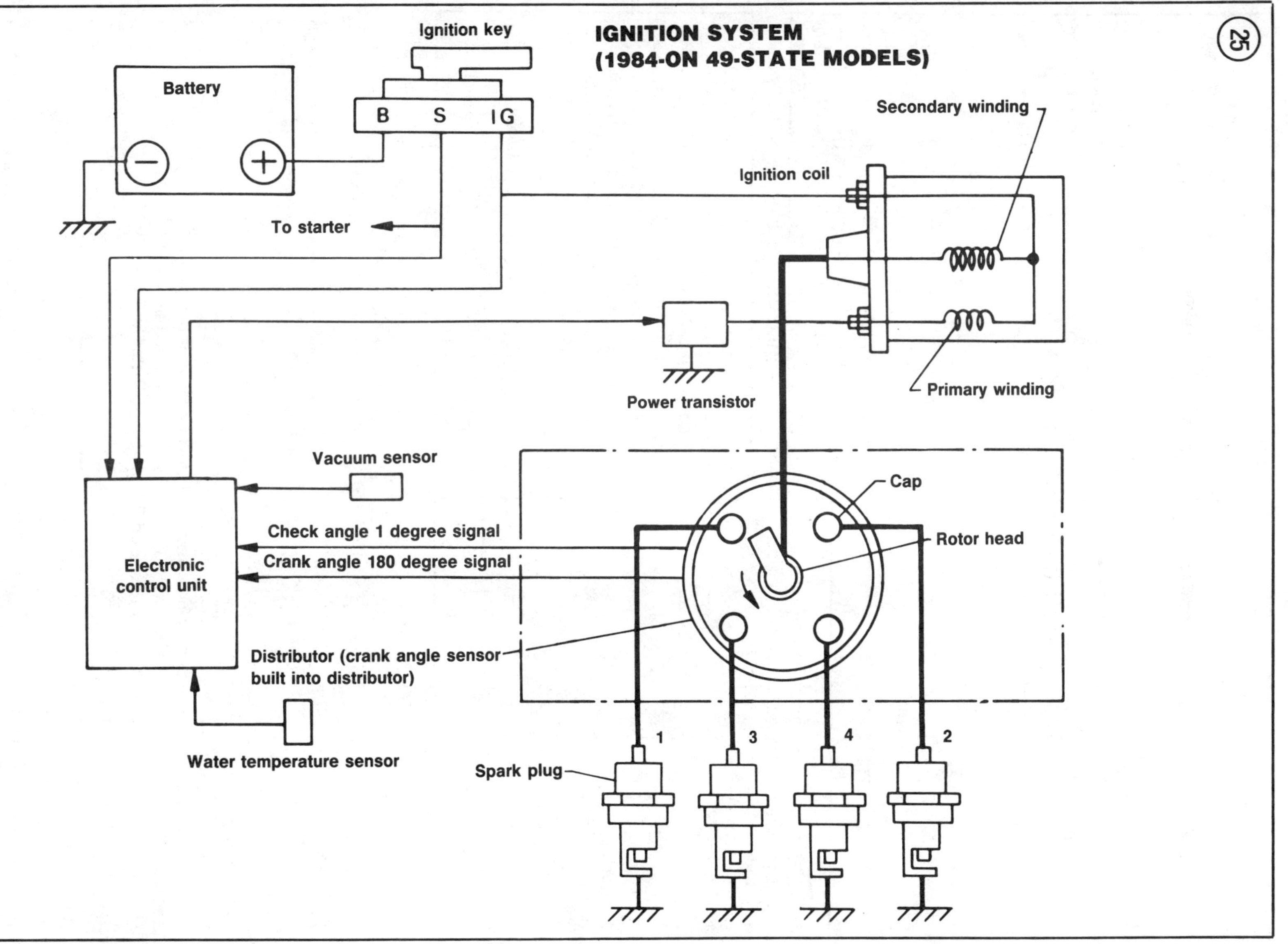

13

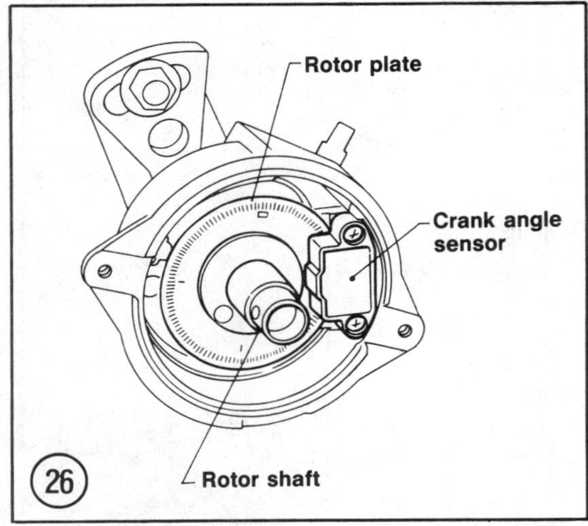

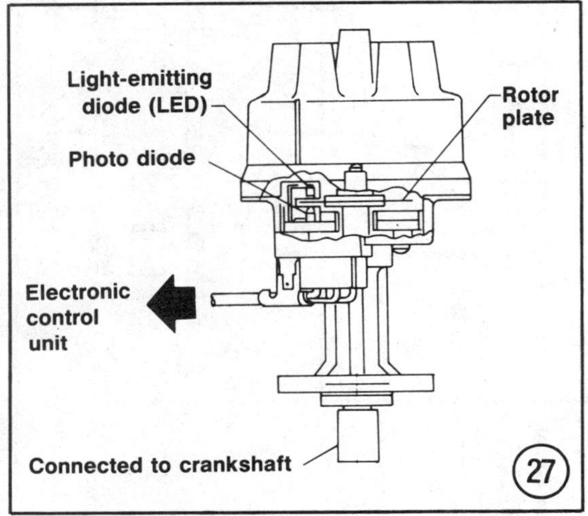

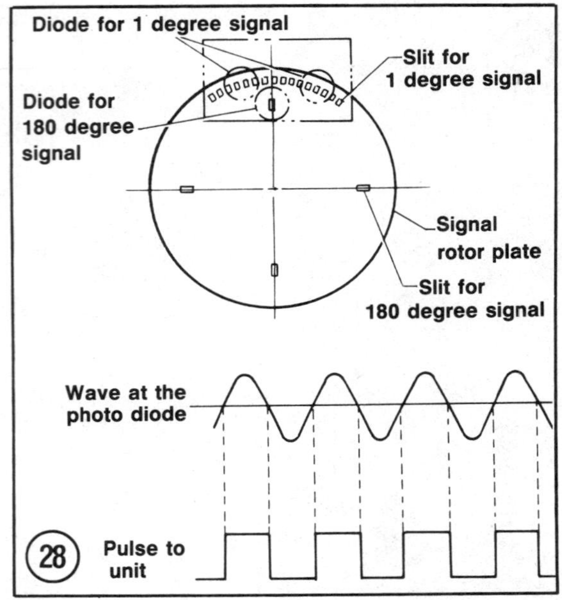

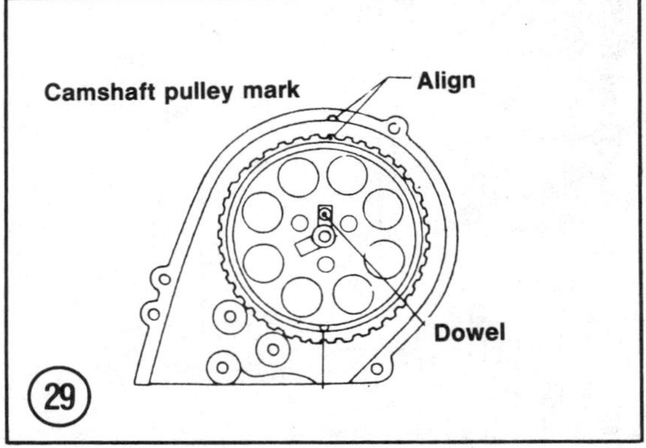

CHAPTER EIGHT

CLUTCH AND TRANSAXLE

Service procedures for 1984 and later models are the same as for 1983. Some specifications and tightening torques differ. These are listed in **Table 9** and **Table 10**.

Table 9 CLUTCH SPECIFICATIONS (1985)

	mm	in.
Pedal height	209-214 mm	(8 1/4-8 7/16 in.)
Pedal free travel	12.5-17.5 mm	(1/2-5/8 in.)

Table 10 CLUTCH AND TRANSAXLE TIGHTENING TORQUES (1985)

Fastener	N·m	ft.-lb.
Clutch		
Clutch switch locknut (U.S.)	12-15	9-11
Pedal stopper locknut (Canada)	16-22	12-16
Clutch cable locknut		
Gasoline	3-4	2-3
Diesel	9-125	7-9
Clutch cable bracket bolts	8-11	6-8
Pressure plate bolts	22-29	16-22
Manual transaxle		
Front buffer rod bracket		
To engine	29-39	22-29
To transaxle	16-21	12-15
Left motor mount to transaxle	29-39	22-29
Rear motor mount to body	29-39	22-29
Rear motor mount buffer rod	39-49	29-36
Speedometer pinion gear	3.7-5.0	3-4
Shift control rod to transaxle	6.3-8.3	4.6-6.1
Shift support rod to transaxle	9-12	7-9
Linkage select stopper bolt	3.1-5.0	2.3-3.7
Linkage rubber holder to body	9-12	7-9
Automatic transaxle		
Drive plate to torque converter	49-69	36-51
Converter housing to engine		
M8 bolts	16-22	12-16
M10 bolts	39-49	29-36

CHAPTER NINE

FRONT SUSPENSION, WHEEL BEARINGS AND STEERING

Some front suspension specifications and tightening torques differ from 1983 models. These are listed in **Table 11** and **Table 12**.

FRONT SUSPENSION

The front suspension on 1984 models is the same as for 1983. On 1985 models, the front suspension includes a stabilizer bar. See **Figure 30** and **Figure 31**.

Stabilizer Bar
Removal/Installation (1985)

WARNING
Make sure the exhaust system is cool before starting this procedure.

1. Set the handbrake. Securely block both rear wheels so the car will not roll in either direction.

2. Jack up the front end of the car and place it on jackstands.

3. Remove the front exhaust tube No. 1 and No. 2 mounts. See **Figure 32**.

4. Detach the stabilizer bar from the body, then from the transverse links. See **Figure 33**. Take the stabilizer bar out.

5. Check all parts for wear and damage, especially rubber bushings. Replace as needed.

6. Installation is the reverse of removal. Tighten all fasteners to specifications in **Table 12**.

13

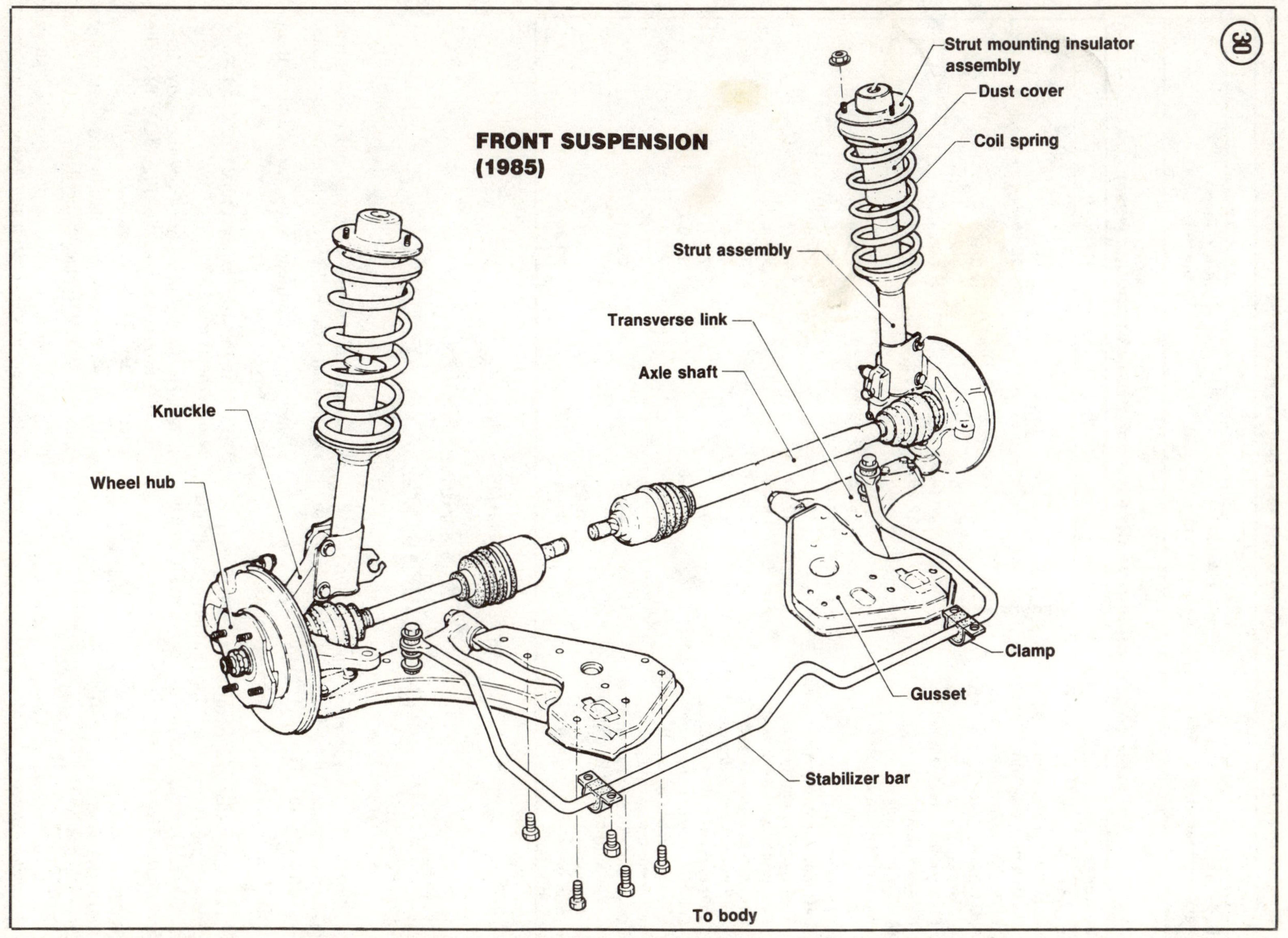
30
FRONT SUSPENSION
(1985)
Strut mounting insulator
assembly
Dust cover
Coil spring
Strut assembly
Transverse link
Axle shaft
Knuckle
Wheel hub
Clamp
Gusset
Stabilizer bar
To body

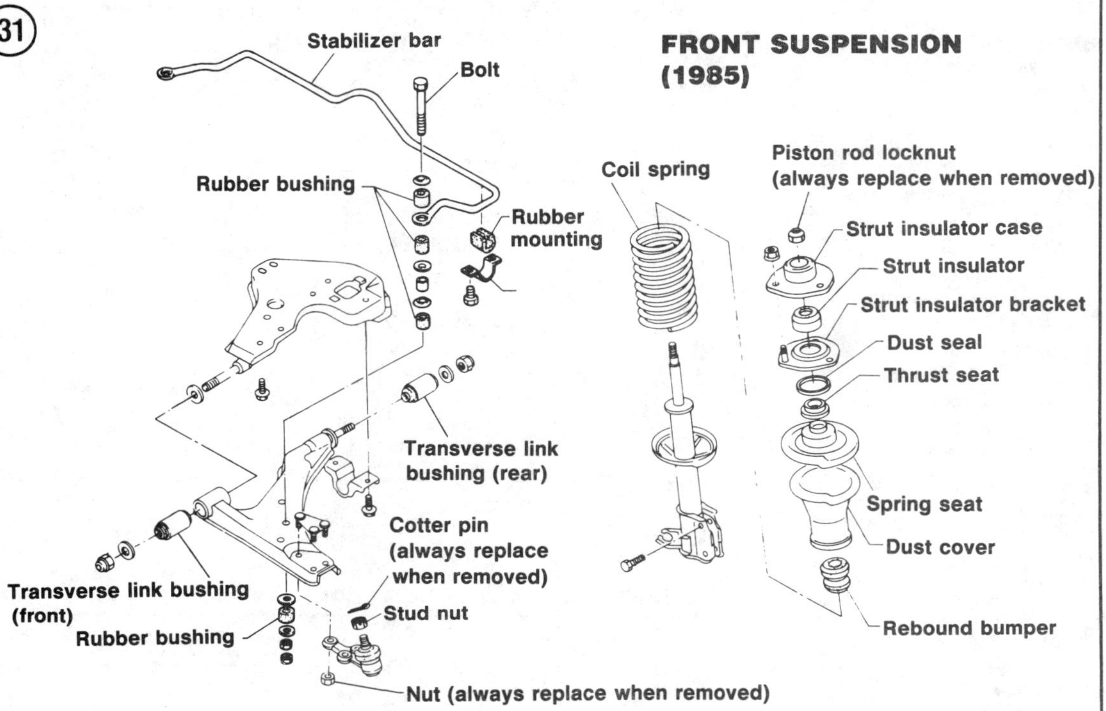

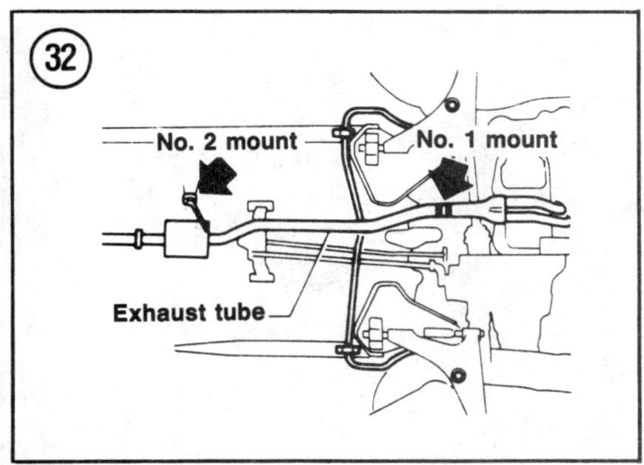

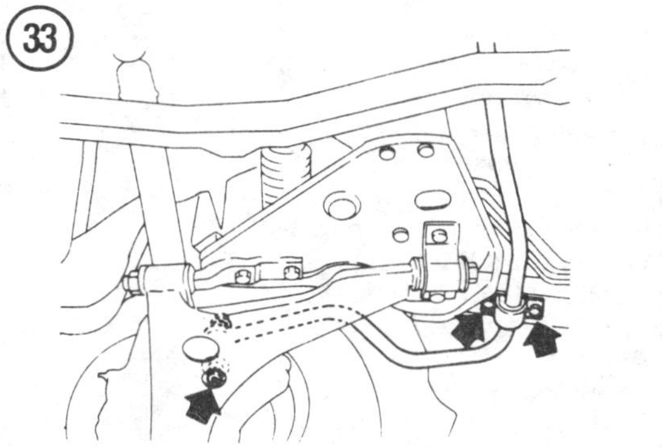

Table 11 FRONT SUSPENSION SPECIFICATIONS

Wheel bearing rotating force	1.4-4.9 kg (3.1-10.8 lb.)
Axle boot dimension "L"	
Transaxle end, left side	96.5 mm (3.799 in.)
Transaxle end, right side	110.4 mm (4.346 in.)
Inner end	100 mm (3.94 in.)
Wheel alignment	
Camber	-25' to 1° 05'
Caster	45' to 2° 15'
Toe-in	3-5 mm (0.12-0.20 in.)
(continued)	

13

Table 11 FRONT SUSPENSION SPECIFICATIONS (continued)

Steering axis inclination	12° 10' to 13° 40'
Standard tie rod length	175.9 mm (6.93 in.)
Steering lock angles	
1984	
Inner wheel	40° 30' to 43° 30'
Outer wheel	31° 30' to 34° 30'
1985 (manual transaxle)	
Inner wheel	43° 30' to 43° 30'
Outer wheel	31° 30' to 34° 30'
1985 (automatic transaxle, non-power steering)	
Inner wheel	40° 30' to 43° 30'
Outer wheel	29° 30' to 32° 30'
1985 (automatic transaxle, power steering)	
Inner wheel	40° 30' to 43° 30'
Outer wheel	31° 30' to 34° 30'

Table 12 FRONT SUSPENSION TIGHTENING TORQUES (1984-ON)

Fastener	N•m	ft.-lb.
Front suspension		
Strut to body	31-42	23-31
Strut to knuckle arm	98-118	72-87
Ball-joint to suspension arm	54-64	40-47
Ball-joint stud nut	29-49	22-36
Suspension arm bracket bolts	88-108	65-80
Suspension arm bushing nuts	98-118	72-87
Suspension arm gusset to body	88-108	65-80
Axle shaft to hub	118-196	87-145
Hub to brake disc		
CL18B brakes	33-43	25-32
AD20V brakes	50-60	37-44
Torque member mounting bolt		
1984 (CL18B brakes)	33-43	25-32
1984 (AD20V brakes)	50-60	37-44
1985	54-64	40-47
Steering		
Steering wheel nut	29-39	22-29
Lower joint to column	29-39	22-29
Lower joint to gear	29-39	22-29
Column grommet to floor	4-6	3-4
Column lower bracket to pedal bracket	9-14	6.5-10.0
Column upper bracket to dash	9-14	6.5-10.0
Tie rod locknuts	37-46	27-34
Tie rod stud nuts	29-49	22-36
Rack and pinion clamp bolts	59-78	43-58
Power steering		
High-pressure hose to pump	29-49	22-36
High-pressure hose to gear	15-25	11-18
Pump to bracket	19-25	14-19
Bracket to engine	16-22	12-16
Idler pulley locknut	42-62	31-46

CHAPTER TEN

REAR SUSPENSION AND WHEEL BEARINGS

Some tightening torques differ; these are listed in **Table 13**.

Table 13 REAR SUSPENSION TIGHTENING TORQUES (1984-ON)

Fastener	N·m	ft.-lb.
Wheel bearing nut	See text	
Shock absorber upper nuts	9-12	7-9
Shock absorber lower bolt	69-88	51-65
Suspension arm to body	69-78	51-58
Rebound bumper to suspension arm	9-25	7-18

CHAPTER ELEVEN

BRAKES

Some brake specifications and tightening torques differ from 1983 models. These are listed in **Table 14** and **Table 15**.

FRONT BRAKES

CL18B front brakes are the same as for 1983. AD20V front brakes are basically the same, but use redesigned shims. See **Figure 34**.

Service procedures for 1984 and 1984 front brakes are basically the same as for 1983 models, except for caliper piston removal.

WARNING
During this step, the piston may shoot out like a bullet. Use a block of wood as shown in Figure 35. Keep your fingers out of the way.

To remove the caliper pistons on 1984 and later models, blow compressed air into the caliper as shown in **Figure 35**. Use a service station air hose if you don't have a compressor.

MASTER CYLINDER

Service procedures for the 1984 and later master cylinder are basically the same as for the 1983 version. Construction details differ. See **Figure 36**.

CAUTION
Do not disassemble the primary piston during master cylinder overhaul.

ADJUSTMENTS

Brake system adjustments are the same as for 1983, with the exception of brake pedal adjustment on 1985 models.

13

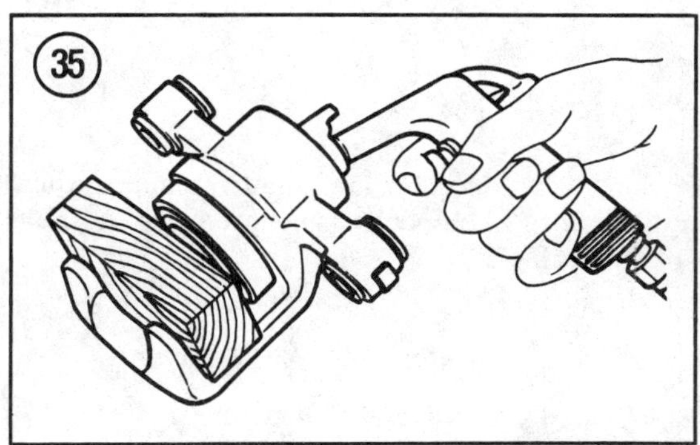

(34) FRONT BRAKES (1984-ON, TYPE AD20V)

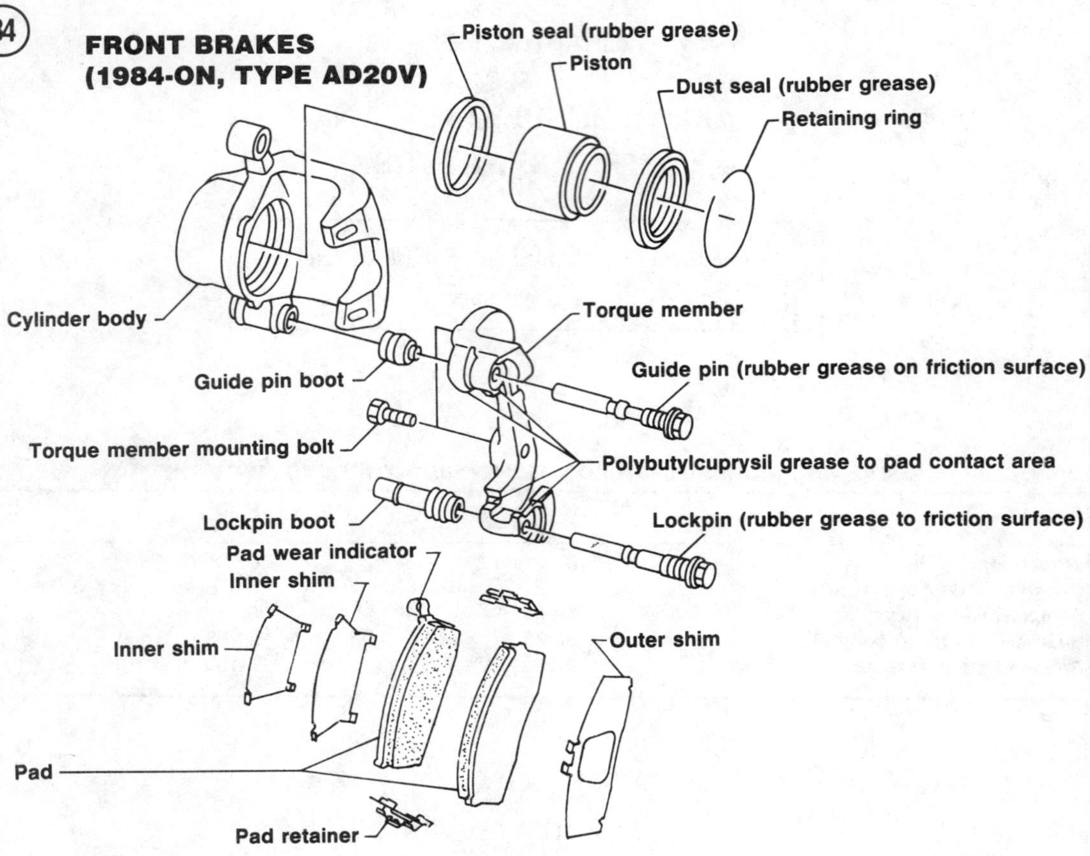

Brake Pedal (1985)

1. Measure pedal height from the floor as shown in **Figure 37**. Compare with **Table 14**.
2. If pedal height is incorrect, loosen the pedal stopper locknut. Turn the pedal stopper to change pedal height, then tighten the locknut.
3. Check pedal free travel and compare with **Table 14**. If it is incorrect, recheck pedal height. If pedal height is correct, check for a worn brake pedal, master cylinder or brake pads and shoes. If these are okay, bleed the brakes as described in this supplement.

BRAKE LINES

The brake lines on 1984 and later models differ slightly from 1983. See **Figure 38** (1984) or **Figure 39** (1985).

BRAKE BLEEDING

Brake bleeding on 1984 and later models includes the master cylinder. Bleed 1984 and later models as follows. Be sure to bleed *all three* sections of the brake system when any one of the sections has been opened.

NOTE
The following procedures require 2 people, one to operate the brake pedal and the other to open and close brake lines and bleed valves.

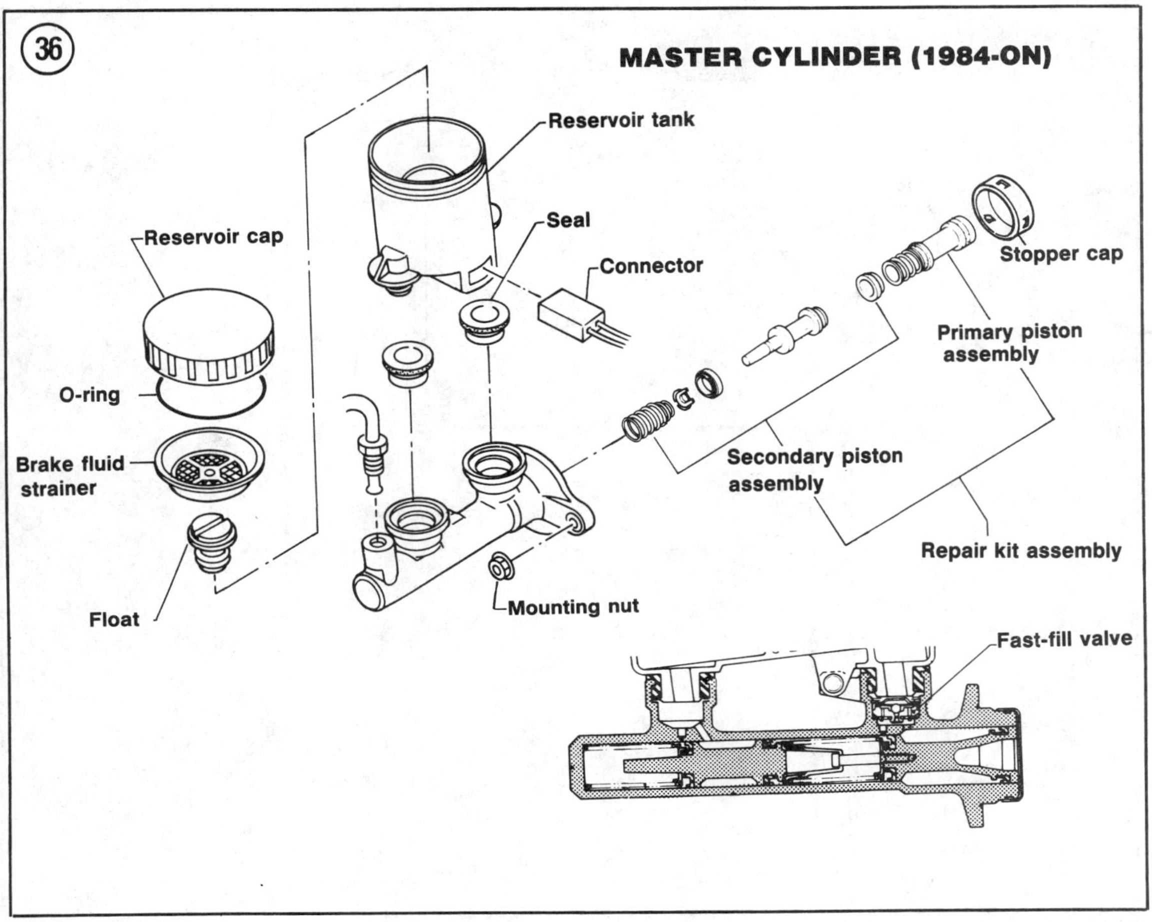

(36)

MASTER CYLINDER (1984-ON)

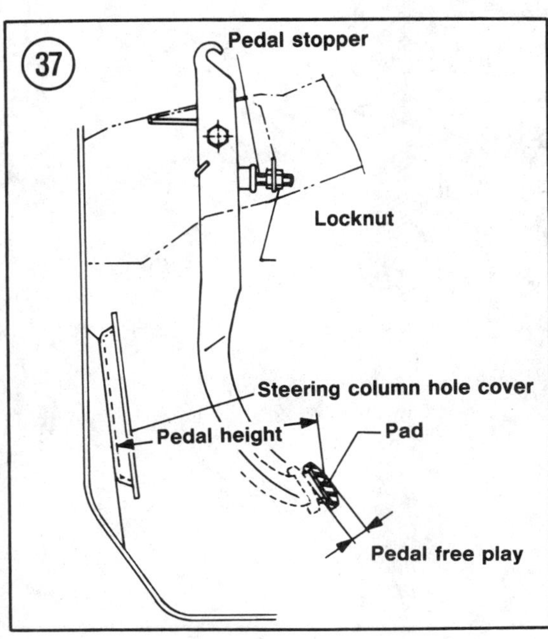

(37)

Master cylinder

1. Fill the reservoir (**Figure 40**) with DOT 3 brake fluid. Do not use any other type.

> *NOTE*
> *DOT 3 means the brake fluid means current Department of Transportation quality standards. If a can of fluid doesn't say DOT 3 somewhere on the label, buy a brand that does.*

> *CAUTION*
> *Place rags or a container beneath the master cylinder to catch dripping brake fluid. Brake fluid will damage paint. If any spills onto a painted surface, wipe it up immediately and clean the area with soap and water.*

2. Disconnect the primary line from the master cylinder. This is the line at the rear of the cylinder, nearest the brake booster.

3. Slowly press the brake pedal all the way to the floor, then slowly let it up.

13

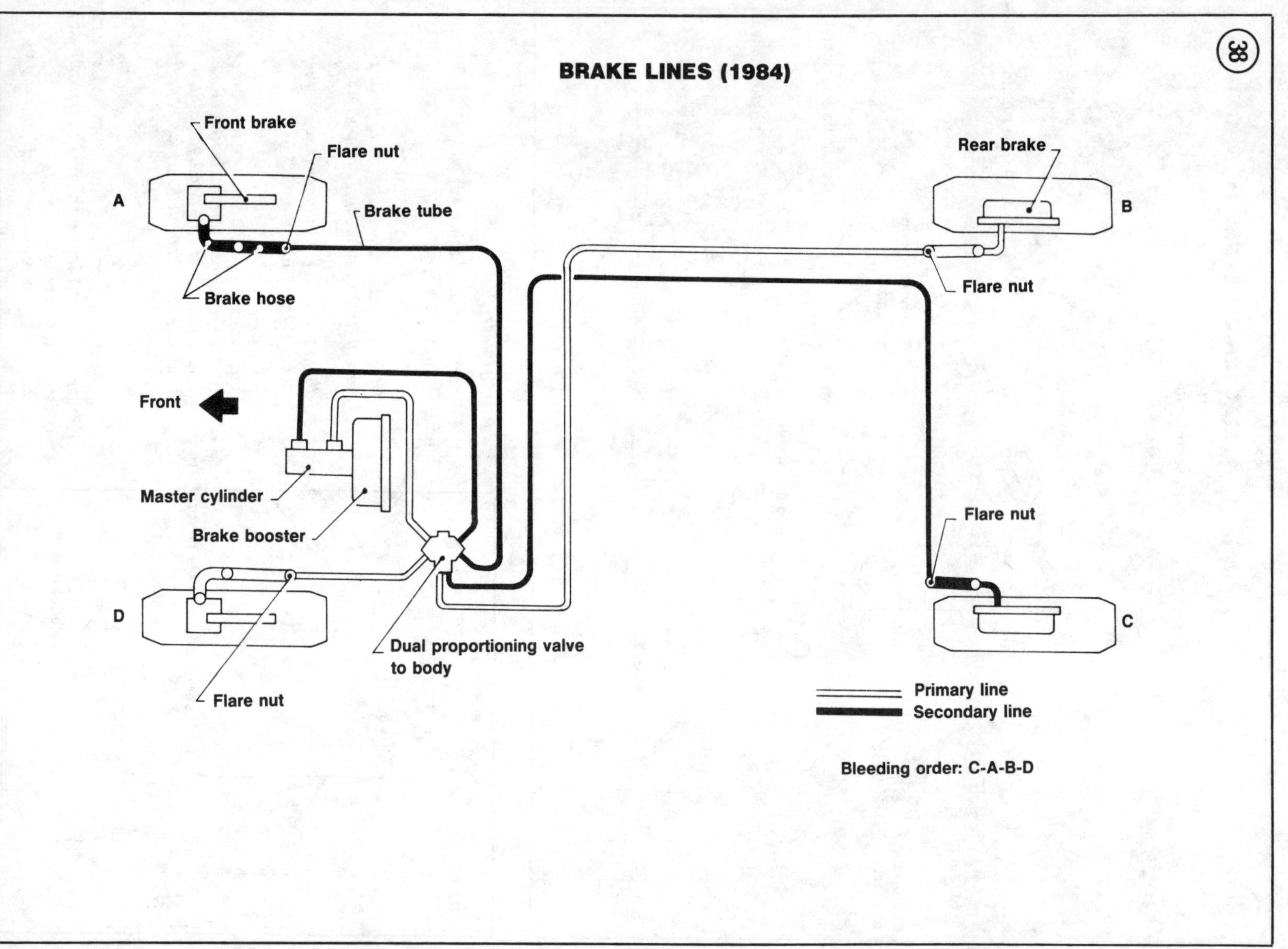
38
BRAKE LINES (1984)
Front brake
Flare nut
A
Brake tube
Brake hose
Rear brake
B
Flare nut
Front
Master cylinder
Brake booster
D
Dual proportioning valve
to body
Flare nut
Flare nut
C
Primary line
Secondary line
Bleeding order: C-A-B-D

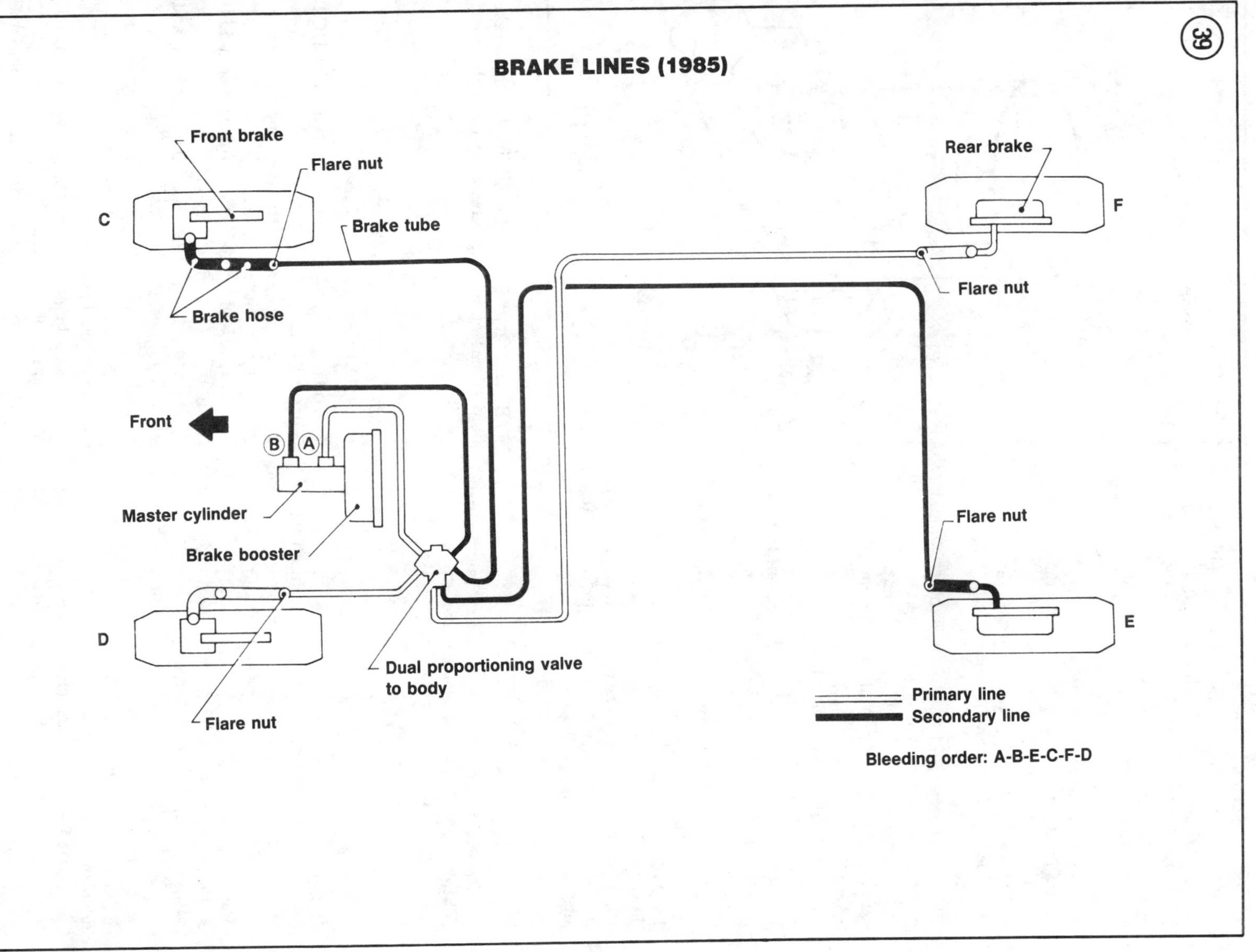
39
BRAKE LINES (1985)
Front brake
Flare nut
C
Brake tube
Brake hose
Rear brake
F
Flare nut
Front
B
A
Master cylinder
Brake booster
D
Flare nut
Dual proportioning valve to body
Flare nut
E
Primary line
Secondary line
Bleeding order: A-B-E-C-F-D
13

4. Wait 5 seconds.
5. Repeat Step 3 and Step 4 until clear, bubble-free brake fluid flows from the master cylinder.
6. Reconnect the primary line to the master cylinder and tighten securely.
7. Press the brake pedal to the floor and hold it down.
8. Loosen, but do not disconnect, the primary line at the master cylinder to bleed the remaining air out of the line fitting.
9. Tighten the primary line securely.
10. Slowly let the brake pedal back up.
11. Wait 5 seconds.
12. Repeat Steps 7-11 until clear, bubble-free fluid comes out of the primary line fitting.
13. Disconnect the secondary line from the master cylinder. This is the line at the front of the cylinder.
14. Slowly press the brake pedal all the way to the floor, then slowly let it up.
15. Wait 5 seconds.
16. Repeat Step 14 and Step 15 until clear, bubble-free brake fluid flows from the master cylinder.
17. Reconnect the secondary line to the master cylinder and tighten securely.
18. Press the brake pedal to the floor and hold it down.
19. Loosen, but do not disconnect, the secondary line at the master cylinder to bleed the remaining air out of the line fitting.
20. Tighten the secondary line securely.
21. Slowly let the brake pedal back up.
22. Wait 5 seconds.
23. Repeat Steps 18-22 until clear, bubble-free fluid comes out of the secondary line fitting.

Left rear wheel cylinder and right front caliper

1. Top up the master cylinder reservoir with DOT 3 brake fluid.
2. Connect a clear plastic tube to the bleed valve on the left rear wheel cylinder. Immerse the other end of the tube in a clear glass jar full of clean brake fluid.
3. Press the brake pedal to the floor and hold it down. Do not pump the pedal.
4. Open the bleed valve, let mixed air and brake fluid come out, then close the bleed valve.
5. Slowly let the brake pedal up.
6. Wait 20 seconds.
7. Repeat Steps 3-6 until clear, bubble-free brake fluid comes out of the tube. Then tighten the bleed valve.
8. Transfer the plastic tube and glass jar to the right front caliper bleed valve.

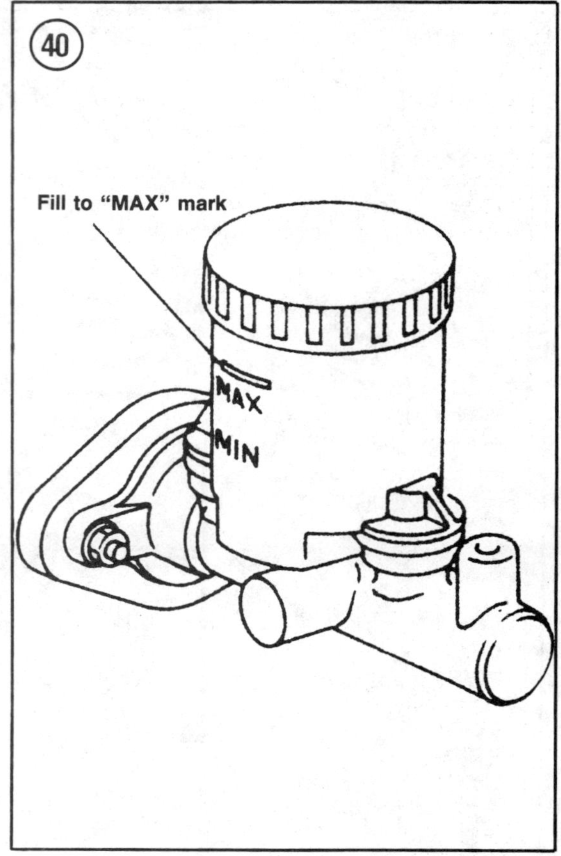

9. Repeat Steps 3-7 until clear, bubble-free brake fluid comes out of the tube, then close the bleed valve.

Right rear wheel cylinder and left front caliper

1. Top up the master cylinder reservoir with DOT 3 brake fluid.
2. Connect the clear plastic tube and glass jar to the right rear wheel cylinder.
3. Press the brake pedal several times, then hold it down.
4. Open the bleed valve. Let the mixed air and brake fluid escape, then close the bleed valve.
5. Repeat Step 3 and Step 4 until clear, bubble-free brake fluid emerges from the tube.
6. Tighten the bleed valve.
7. Transfer the plastic tube and glass jar to the left front caliper bleed valve.
8. Repeat Step 3 and Step 4 until clear, bubble-free brake fluid emerges from the tube, then close the bleed valve.

Table 14 BRAKE SPECIFICATIONS (1984-ON)

	mm	in.
Brake pad thickness, minimum	2.0	0.79
Brake disc runout, maximum	0.07	0.003
Brake disc thickness, minimum		
CL18B	10	0.394
AD20V	16	0.63
Brake drum inner diameter, maximum		
LT18A	181.0	7.13
LT20A	204.5	8.05
Brake drum out-of-roundness, maximum	0.03	0.0012
Vacuum pump vane length (diesel only)	12.5-13.5	0.492-0.531
Vacuum pump inner diameter (diesel only)	57.0-57.1	2.244-2.248
Pedal height		
Manual transaxle	194-204	7 5/8-8
Automatic transaxle	197-207	7 3/4-8 1/8

Table 15 BRAKE TIGHTENING TORQUES (1984-ON)

Fastener	N·m	ft.-lb.
Cylinder body to torque member		
CL18B	22-31	16-23
AD20V	50-60	37-44
Disc to hub		
CL18B	33-43	25-32
AD20V	50-60	37-44
Drum brake backing plate	25-33	18-25
Wheel cylinder mounting bolts	6-8	4.3-5.8
Master cylinder to brake booster	8-11	6-8
Secondary piston stopper bolt		
Tokico	2.0-3.4	1.4-2.5
Nabco	1.5-2.9	1.1-2.2
Brake booster to pedal bracket	8-11	6-8
Brake booster input rod locknut	16-22	12-16
Dual proportioning valve mounting bolt	4-5	3-4
Brake tube flare nuts	15-18	11-13
Brake hose connectors	17-20	12-14
Bleed valves	7-9	5.1-6.5
Brake light switch locknut	12-15	9-11

CHAPTER TWELVE

BODY

> ## BUMPERS
>
> The 1984 and later models may be equipped with shock absorber-type bumpers or stay-type bumpers. Shock absorber-type bumpers are the same as for 1983 models. Stay-type bumpers are shown in **Figure 41** (front) and **Figure 42** (rear).
>
> ## GRILLE
>
> The grille on 1984 and later models differs slightly from the 1983 grille. To remove and install the 1984 and later grille, see **Figure 43**.

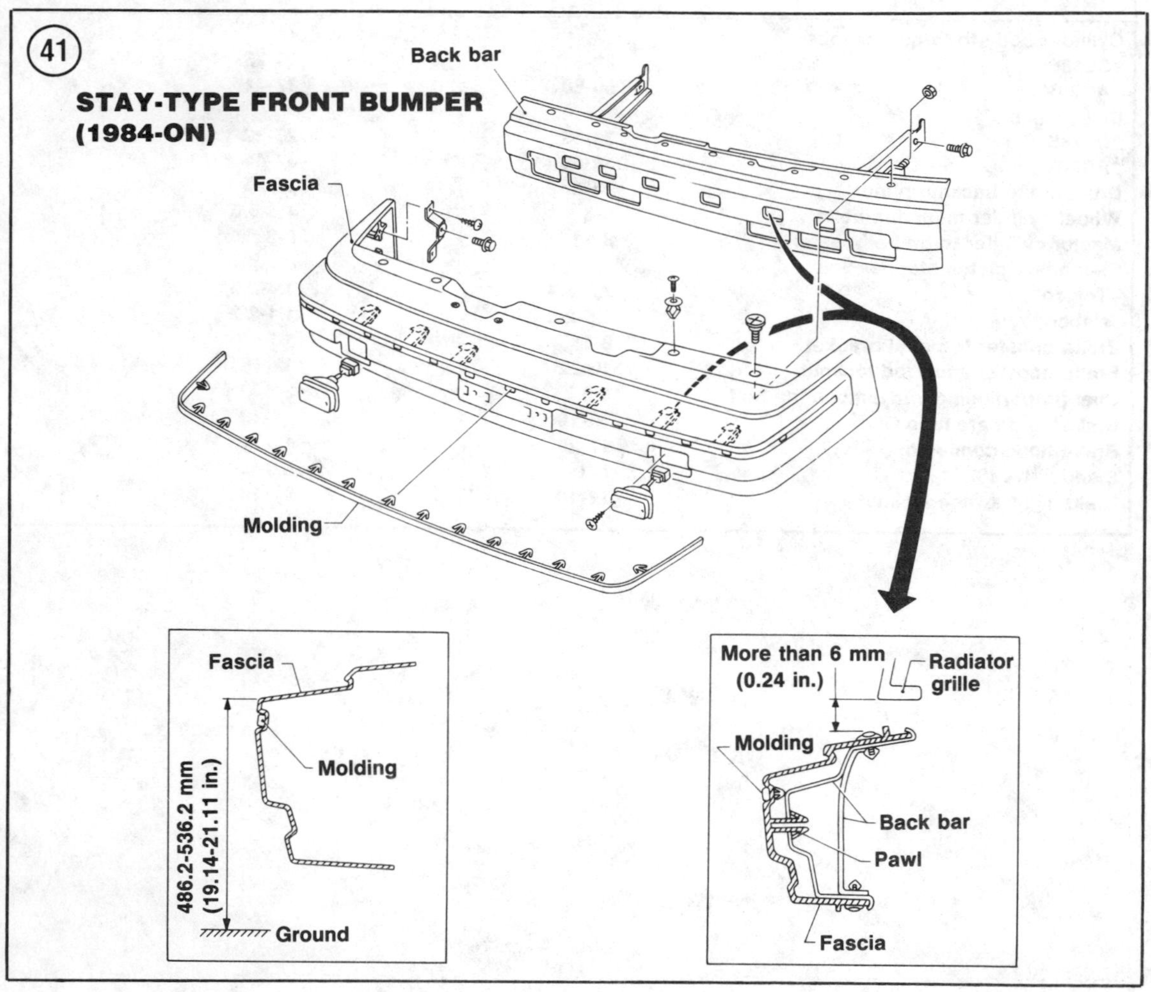

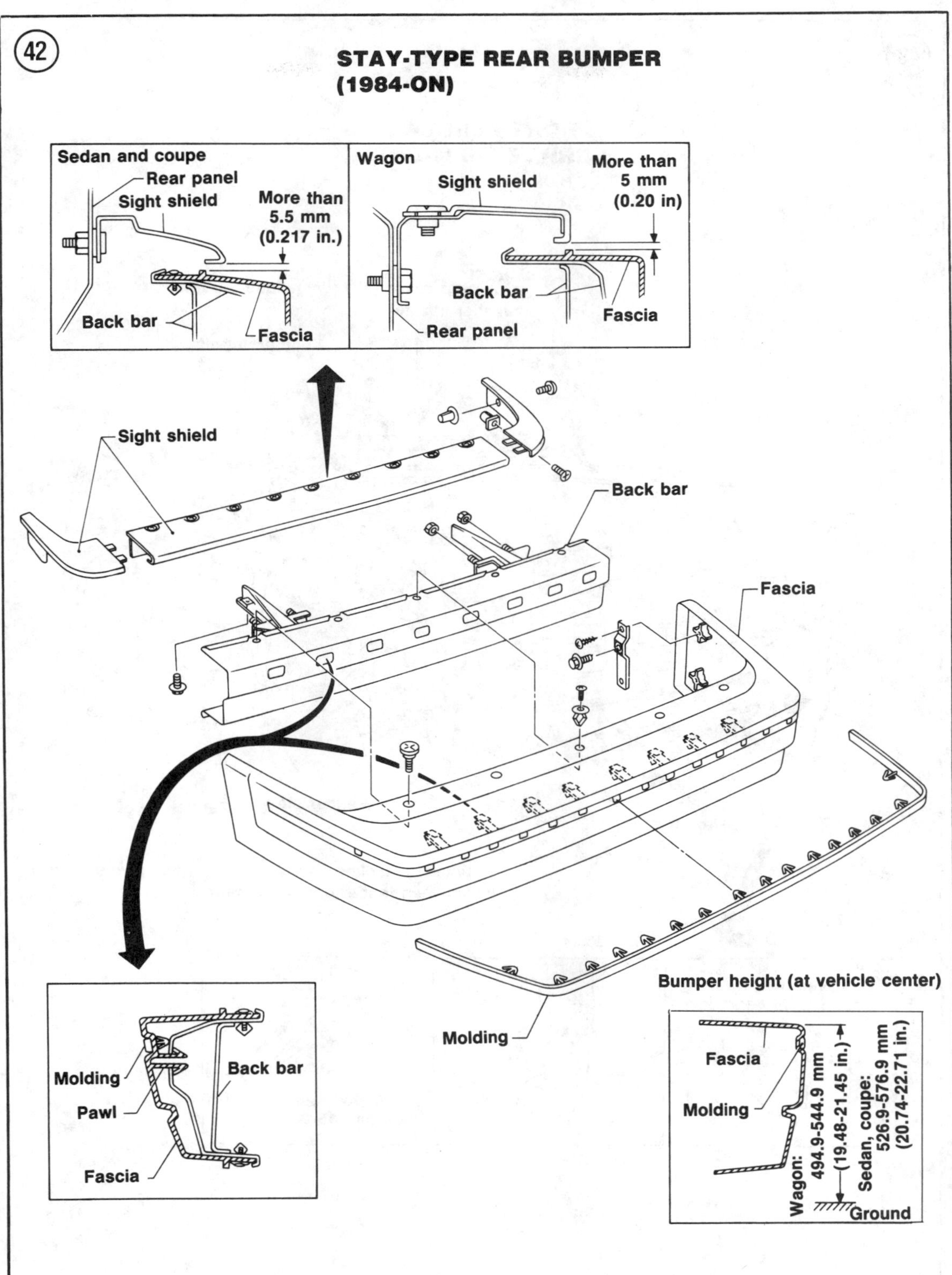
42
STAY-TYPE REAR BUMPER
(1984-ON)
Sedan and coupe
Rear panel
Sight shield
More than
5.5 mm
(0.217 in.)
Back bar
Fascia
Wagon
Sight shield
More than
5 mm
(0.20 in)
Back bar
Fascia
Rear panel
Sight shield
Back bar
Fascia
Molding
Molding
Back bar
Pawl
Fascia
Bumper height (at vehicle center)
Fascia
Molding
Wagon:
494.9-544.9 mm
(19.48-21.45 in.)
Sedan, coupe:
526.9-576.9 mm
(20.74-22.71 in.)
Ground

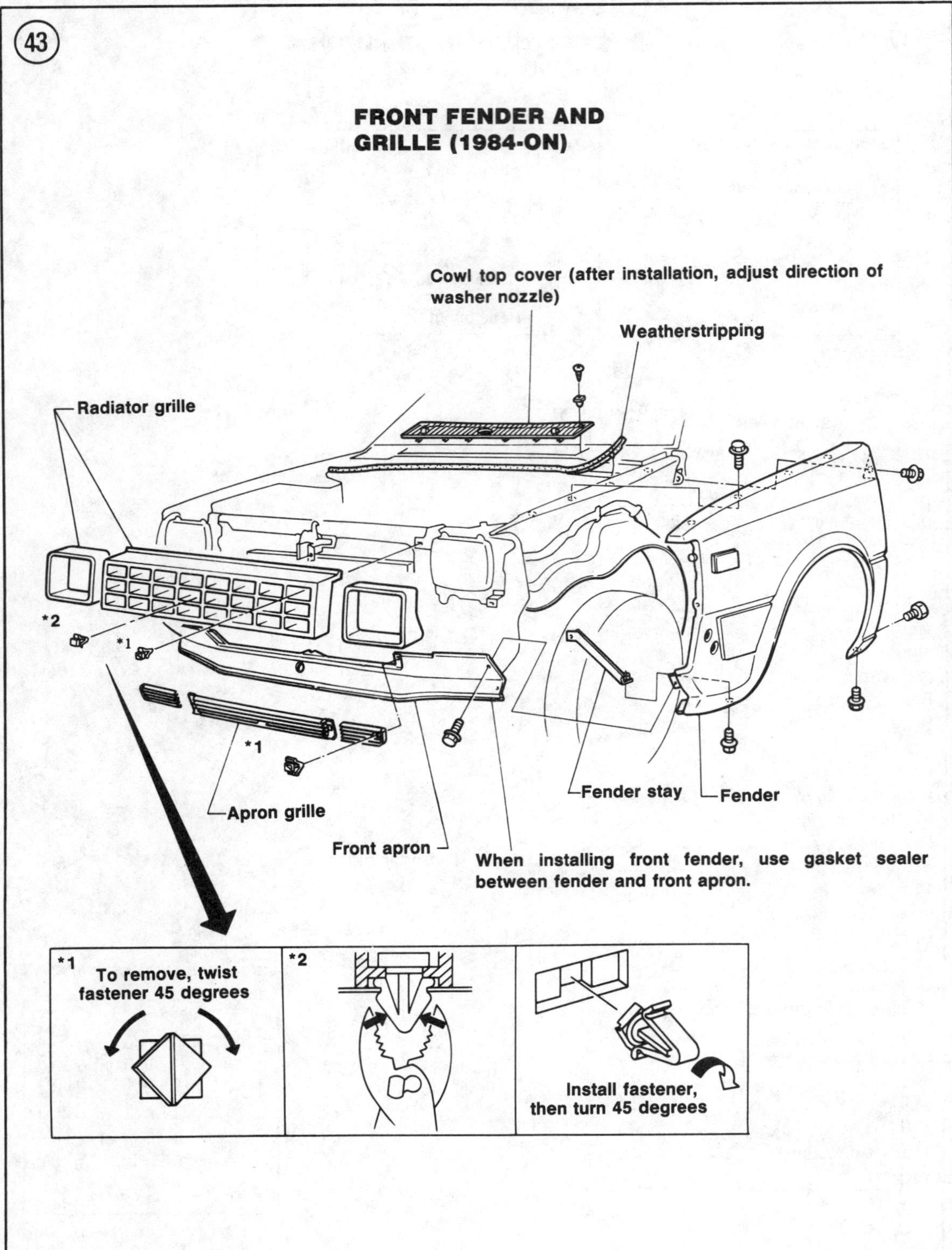

43

FRONT FENDER AND
GRILLE (1984-ON)

Cowl top cover (after installation, adjust direction of
washer nozzle)

Weatherstripping

Radiator grille

*2

*1

*1

Apron grille

Front apron

Fender stay

Fender

When installing front fender, use gasket sealer
between fender and front apron.

*1 To remove, twist
fastener 45 degrees

*2

Install fastener,
then turn 45 degrees

INDEX